Practical Entity Framework

Database Access for Enterprise Applications

Brian L. Gorman

Practical Entity Framework: Database Access for Enterprise Applications

Brian L. Gorman
Jesup, IA, USA

ISBN-13 (pbk): 978-1-4842-6043-2   ISBN-13 (electronic): 978-1-4842-6044-9
https://doi.org/10.1007/978-1-4842-6044-9

Managing Director, Apress Media LLC: Welmoed Spahr
Acquisitions Editor: Jonathan Gennick
Development Editor: Laura Berendson
Coordinating Editor: Jill Balzano

Cover image designed by Freepik (www.freepik.com)

Distributed to the book trade worldwide by Springer Science+Business Media New York, 233 Spring Street, 6th Floor, New York, NY 10013. Phone 1-800-SPRINGER, fax (201) 348-4505, e-mail orders-ny@springer-sbm.com, or visit www.springeronline.com. Apress Media, LLC is a California LLC and the sole member (owner) is Springer Science + Business Media Finance Inc (SSBM Finance Inc). SSBM Finance Inc is a **Delaware** corporation.

For information on translations, please e-mail booktranslations@springernature.com; for reprint, paperback, or audio rights, please e-mail bookpermissions@springernature.com.

Apress titles may be purchased in bulk for academic, corporate, or promotional use. eBook versions and licenses are also available for most titles. For more information, reference our Print and eBook Bulk Sales web page at http://www.apress.com/bulk-sales.

Any source code or other supplementary material referenced by the author in this book is available to readers on GitHub via the book's product page, located at www.apress.com/9781484260432. For more detailed information, please visit http://www.apress.com/source-code.

Printed on acid-free paper

*This book is dedicated to my wife Cassie and
my children Kiera, Karson, and Kreighton, who have all made
many sacrifices to give me space and time to write, as well as for
your daily, unceasing love, grace, patience, and encouragement.*

*This book is further dedicated to you, dear reader.
Thank you for allowing me to be part of your journey to greatness.*

Table of Contents

Chapter 6: Data Access (Create, Read, Update, Delete) 245

About the Author

 **Brian L. Gorman** is a developer, computer science instructor, and trainer and has been working in .NET technologies as long as they have existed. He was originally MCSD certified in .NET 1 and has recently recertified with MCSA: Web Apps, and MCSD: App Builder certifications. Additionally, he became an MCT as of April 2019 and is focusing on developing and training developers with full-stack web solutions with .NET Core and Azure.

In addition to working with .NET technologies, Brian also teaches computer science for Franklin University, where his courses taught have included data structures, algorithms, design patterns, and, more recently, full-stack enterprise solutions in the capstone practicum course. In July 2020, due to COVID-19, Brian decided to host an online virtual developer conference called SciFiDevCon.

Brian also has a passion for music and has been writing and releasing original Christian music for the last six years. His music can be found online at any of the major streaming venues such as Spotify or iTunes.

Brian currently lives in Eastern Iowa with his wife and three young children.

About the Technical Reviewer

 **André van Meulebrouck** has a keen interest in functional programming, especially Haskell and F#.

He also likes data technologies from markup languages to databases and F# type providers.

He lives in Southern California with his wife "Tweety", and is active in athletics: hiking, mountain biking, and gravity/balance sports like freestyle skating (inline and ice), skateboarding, surfing, and sandboarding.

To keep his mind sharp, he does compositional origami, plays classical guitar, and enjoys music notation software.

Acknowledgments

I would not have been able to write this book if it were not for a number of people who have both influenced and helped me throughout my career, as well as the multitudes of grace and support that I have received from my family throughout this process.

I'd like to begin by thanking the partners and team members at Far Reach. Thank you, Kate Washut, Jason Nissen, Lana Wrage, Chris Rouw, and Chad Feldmann for allowing me to flex and reduce hours to continue to work on projects like this one and to all the team at Far Reach for helping me to learn and grow in both tech and soft skills and for generally having as much fun as possible at work for the last four years.

A special thanks as well to Andre van Meulebrouck for his excellent work as a technical reviewer and editor. Andre's thoughts and comments throughout the process have greatly helped to shape this book. Also, his incredible patience with working through a couple of bugs with the solution files has been an invaluable resource to help ensure the resources work and the directions are easy to follow. An extra special thanks to Andre as well for consistently putting up with my misuse of setup vs. set up.

I'd also like to thank the many friends and acquaintances I've made at various tech conferences in the past few years. I've learned so much from all of you. There are a few that I must mention, however. First, Mike Cole, my peer and friend, thank you for introducing me to AutoMapper projections, and thanks for all your candid conversations around EF with me as I wrote this book. Thanks to Mitchel Sellers for your talk on Entity Framework that I got to see at Iowa Code Camp and again at our CVINETA meeting addressing the performance pitfalls that arise from misusing Language Integrated Query (LINQ). Thanks, Jonathan "J" Tower, for your awesome talk on ORMLite and Dapper at Codemash, which solidified my thoughts on including a chapter on the topic in this book.

Thank you to Apress and the team who have believed in me and have helped to make this book possible. Thanks to Jonathan Gennick and Jill Balzano for running the project, editing, and overseeing the entire schedule and process.

ACKNOWLEDGMENTS

I would be remiss if I didn't also thank Dustin Behn, the leader of the Inspired Nation, and his life coaching and his Emergence program. Thank you for coaching me these past few years and for helping me get out of my own way to do things like this book.

Last, and most importantly, to my wife Cassie and our kids, to whom the book is also dedicated. Thank you for giving me time and space to make this book happen and for continually checking on my progress by asking how many chapters I have done and how many I have left.

Introduction

Entity Framework is the ORM of choice for .Net development for a majority of enterprise application development teams. Through the years, EF has gone through a number of changes, and the move into the .Net Core world has seen EF become more performant and more user-friendly.

As this book begins, we'll take a look at the state of things as they are, and the state of things to come. In the first couple of chapters, we'll even look at differences in approaches to working with EF, whether you are working with EF6 or EFCore. We'll touch on the two different approaches to working with the database: database first and code first. After the first three chapters, we settle in on the code-first approach with EFCore.

The great news is that no matter what approach to the database or version of EF you are using, with just a few minor exceptions, things will generally work in a similar fashion, so all of the information in this book is relevant to anyone working with Entity Framework.

Who this book is for

Practical Entity Framework is written for anyone that is new to Entity Framework or is still learning and wants to become much better with Entity Framework.

If you are already an expert or a well-established developer with a few years of EF under your belt, this book will likely not have a lot of new information for you.

Overall, the book is designed to work through the moving pieces that are necessary to understand and work with EF, as well as how to approach architecting SOLID solutions around EF. The practical nature of each activity will give you many examples and cover a lot of the basic and advanced topics you will likely encounter in real-world applications.

How this book is structured and what is covered in the chapters

This book has been developed into four parts. Part 1 contains the first three chapters and covers many of the introductory topics and contrasts in approaches to using the database in EF. Part 2, which includes Chapters 4–10, is about building out the database solution and covers core operations for the code-first approach to working with EF. Part 3 includes Chapters 11–13 and covers critical ways to enhance your solutions. Part 4 includes Chapters 14 and 15 and discusses more recipes for success and a look into the future of EF.

Part 1 – Getting Started

Chapter 1, "Introduction to Entity Framework," begins by discussing the current state of enterprise applications with Entity Framework. In the chapter, we take a look at how to get set up and start building out a solution with Entity Framework.

Chapter 2, "Working with an Existing Database," discusses the approach developers might need to take if there is already an established database and the solution needs to use EF. The chapter uses a copy of the AdventureWorks database and covers how to work with the EFCore tools to reverse engineer a database, as well as how to use the database-first approach in EF6.

Chapter 3, "Entity Framework: Code First," starts with a discussion of what it means to be code first and when it may not make sense to use the approach, and then quickly moves into the benefits of using a code-first approach. The activities walk through implementing a code-first approach in EFCore and EF6.

Part 2 – Building the Data Solution

Chapter 4, "Models and the Data Context," covers working with our entities to build out the objects that represent the tables in the database and then execute the migrations to make sure the tables exist as defined in code. The activities in this chapter reinforce that learning.

Chapter 5, "Constraints, Keys, and Relationships," takes a look at how to set the primary keys, multiple column keys, and database relationships that you will likely encounter. The activities cover setting up constraints, index, and relationships in EFCore.

Chapter 6, "Data Access (Create, Read, Update, Delete)," is a critical chapter to learn how to do the CRUD operations against your database. In the activity for this chapter, we spin up a website and see how quickly we can build out CRUD operations.

Chapter 7, "Stored Procedures, Views, and Functions," continues our learning of practical applications of EF with a good luck at what it takes to incorporate database objects into the code-first solution. The activities cover setting up and working with stored procedures, functions, views, and seeding data.

Chapter 8, "Sorting, Filtering, and Paging," takes a deeper dive into working with LINQ to get data and ensuring that our operations are as efficient as possible with EF. The activity for the chapter walks through sorting, filtering, and paging the data, as well as looking at working with a disconnected dataset.

Chapter 9, "LINQ for Queries and Projections," introduces the valuable use of projections in our queries and also covers using AutoMapper in our solution. The activities get us started with projections and then implement AutoMapper into our solution.

Chapter 10, "Encryption of Data," takes a look at the two main ways to encrypt our data – either through the AlwaysEncrypted built-in approach or through a customized approach using certificates and keys to encrypt or decrypt our data.

Part 3 – Enhancing the Data Solution

Chapter 11, "Repository and Unit of Work Patterns," takes a look at two of the more critical patterns around working with data and ORMs. Although EF has built-in repository (repo) and unit of work (UoW) patterns, sometimes we need to have a bit more flexibility. The activities for this chapter involve refactoring our code into layers and then implementing our own UoW.

Chapter 12, "Unit Testing, Integration Testing, and Mocking," discusses the importance of unit testing and integration testing, as well as what it means to mock data. The activities enhance our learning around mock data, as well as implement unit tests and integration tests.

Chapter 13, "Alternatives to Entity Framework: Dapper," provides information on how we can wire up a lightweight ORM to enhance our query performance. The activities for the chapter build out the ability to see the selection of data from Dapper.

Part 4 – Recipes for Success

Chapter 14, "Asynchronous Data Operations and Multiple Database Contexts," begins by refactoring everything to use the async/await pattern for leveraging the threading operations in our solutions. The chapter concludes with a look at what it takes to work with multiple databases, including the mandatory use of the fully qualified context name in order to generate or run database migrations.

Chapter 15, ".Net 5 and Entity Framework," concludes our book with a forward-looking chapter, in that here we take a first look into what is coming in the vNext (EFCore5) version of Entity Framework.

Code samples and exercises

This book is designed to be a training manual for information and the practical use of Entity Framework. Therefore, each chapter has from one to three workable activities. To get the most out of this book, you are encouraged to work through each example. To aid you in this process, I have provided a starter and a final pack for each activity. You can download the code resources from the book's catalog page on Apress.com to find downloads. The code is available at github.com/Apress/practical-entity-framework.

Connect with the author

I would love to hear from you and/or connect with you. I am especially interested in any thoughts you have around the book, ways I could have improved it, and/or any errors you find through your learning journey. Please don't hesitate to connect with me on LinkedIn or Twitter. I reserve Facebook connections to people that I know, so please don't try to connect with me there. I can also be reached via email.

LinkedIn: `www.linkedin.com/in/brianlgorman/`
Twitter: `https://twitter.com/blgorman`
Email: `brian@majorguidancesolutions.com`

PART I

Getting Started

CHAPTER 1

Introduction to Entity Framework

In this chapter, we are going to cover the history and origins of Entity Framework and then continue into discussions of where Entity Framework is headed. We'll conclude what it takes to get Entity Framework into any .Net project.

One, two, three versions? Oh my!

Before we begin doing anything, it's important to note that at the time that I'm writing this book, there are currently two active versions of Entity Framework in play, and by the time you are reading it, there may still be two, possibly one, or maybe there will be yet a third live version of the Entity Framework. In the next few pages, we'll examine where we came from; how we got to this situation of having multiple, active versions; and where we're going from here. Let's start at the very beginning.

When it all began

Microsoft SQL databases have been around for quite some time. In fact, they existed long before .Net was ever around.

OLEDb and Spaghetti Database access

Prior to the .Net Framework, often a database connection was handled through code in an Object Linking and Embedding Database Object (OLEDb). Developers would often write SQL queries inline and then connect to the database and perform actions using these tools. Furthermore, queries often lacked any kind of security and organization. Similar or identical calls might be written from multiple pages. As if this

© Brian L. Gorman 2020
B. L. Gorman, *Practical Entity Framework*, https://doi.org/10.1007/978-1-4842-6044-9_1

approach didn't have enough problems to begin with, SQL queries might have even existed within the html, which is easily viewable from a simple "right-click and view-source" operation. In the most egregious situations, database credentials might have even been easily viewable in this same source. Finally, and yes it gets even worse, often the user credentials that were used in these pages had full access to everything in the database, perhaps even multiple databases.

In addition to the problems of having a spaghetti code approach to database operations, exposing queries and credentials to the world leads to extremely dangerous security breaches. One of the most common security risks when working with data, even to this day, is an attack known as a SQL Injection query.

Imagine your update statement was fully exposed in source on your web page. All it would take at that point is a savvy hacker to come along and "inject" a few statements along with your query, and they could accomplish anything from dropping tables to exporting your customer list. Even if your query wasn't directly exposed, if you had given them a form text field to work with, then they could easily place SQL code right in that form text and hijack or corrupt your database. Obviously, some better approaches were needed.

ADO.Net – A better tool for application database interaction

For .Net developers, the next step in working with a database relied on a technology known as *ADO.Net*. Believe it or not, ADO.Net is actually still in use, and it's quite possible to use it in your projects, even today (and some developers might even die on the hill of the efficiency of this approach).

ADO.Net was developed to help prevent a few of the problems we've previously discussed. One of the most important aspects of the ADO.Net library was the ability to easily parameterize queries. This approach means that we no longer were creating our SQL queries directly inline with our application code. Rather, we create a base connection object with credentials obscured and the connection string stored in one common, secure location. The connection object was directly referenced through a SQL command object. The SQL command object had settings allowing us to toggle the command to work as a regular query or to execute a database object such as a stored procedure. Most importantly, the query allows the parameters to be defined and constrained by type, as well as automatically replacing bad characters often used in SQL Injection attacks.

Once the queries were executed from the command, they could be used to hydrate a result set, such as a `DataReader` or a `DataSet`. These objects were then used to get the relevant data and render it back to the end user. This approach was the best tool we had as developers before Entity Framework (or other ORMs such as *NHibernate*).

A brief note about ADO.Net

Even today, it is still possible to program database operations with ADO.Net; however, ADO.Net is rarely used directly in current enterprise applications. We almost always want to wrap our database operations with a unit of work and also potentially provide access through repositories (e.g., the unit of work and repository patterns). Entity Framework takes ADO.Net to the next level by providing that wrapper for us.

Entity Framework makes its debut

In 2008, when EF was created, the only version of the .Net Framework in play was just that – the .Net Framework. The framework actually had been released in version 2.0 and then 3.0, and finally, some additional tools came in the framework version 3.5 release. The next obvious iteration was 4.0, and where we landed is a final release of version 4.8 in late September of 2019.

With each iteration of the .Net Framework, Microsoft revolutionized the way we program in relation to the database with the introduction of Entity Framework and the query syntax known as *LINQ* (Language INtegrated Query).

Entity Framework and LINQ

In tandem, *EF* and *LINQ* made it possible to not only work against our database objects using C# or VB.Net code but also gave us the ability to define database structures directly in code. Being able to define and work with objects in memory that modeled the database object while also directly tracking changes against the database was quite powerful. Directly tracking the changes in memory also leads to a new level of understanding of concurrency issues for those of us who were used to working with disconnected data. This was a very good thing, even if it was a slightly painful transition.

While EF and LINQ were some of the more important database tools that were made available to us with each iteration of the .Net Framework, there was more going on than just these language and paradigm changes. The introduction of a new CEO would start to take Microsoft down an entirely different path.

A new direction and a new visionary leader

In early 2014, Microsoft got a new CEO in Satya Nadella. Mr. Nadella started Microsoft on a new course that would shock the developer community. Almost immediately after starting, he simply announced that Linux (which could be seen as a direct competitor to Microsoft Windows) would be embraced. Following that, Microsoft quickly started releasing tools that would be able to be run not just on Windows but also on other platforms like Macs and Linux computers. While these initial steps were a revolutionary change in Microsoft's standard operating procedure, what came next was completely unexpected.

Microsoft goes all in for all developers

In late 2016, Microsoft announced that .Net was going to be open sourced. This meant that going forward, all of the tools and code that developers work with on a daily basis could be directly extended and were made open for suggested extensions to the entire world. Any developer with an idea could create a pull request and ask for their changes to be directly implemented into some of the base libraries of the .Net Framework.

From this point on, Microsoft, and the .Net Framework, was no longer going to be a black-box operation. Microsoft was now fully and intentionally engaging with the entire community of developers, not just its core of .Net developers.

A new vision requires a new path

Making .Net open source was a very strategic and arguably a very wildly successful decision. However, with great changes often come great needs for new tools and processes. Moving to be an open source language wasn't going to be enough. It was also apparent that the code itself, like some of the recent tools Microsoft was releasing, must also run on any platform. Perhaps it is even as a result of these changes that you are reading this book.

In order for the code that is written to be able to live on any server on any operating system, or even in a container like Docker and Kubernetes, the framework had to be independent of any windows-specific API calls. While it might have been possible to run compiled .Net code on a platform like Mono or Xamarin on a Linux or Mac,

developing, compiling, and executing code directly were simply not possible with the
.Net Framework. Therefore, along with the release of the information that Microsoft
was going open source came the release of what we now refer to as the "Core" platform
with the release of .Net Core 1.0 and a new class library type called the .Net Standard
Library. The initial release of .Net Core was really built for web developers, specifically
those using the .Net MVC web development framework. Because of the limitations of
what could be done with the framework, as well as with the overall change not being
extremely lucrative, initial adoption of the Core platform by .Net developers and
organizations was fairly slow.

Adoption definitely started to increase with a major release in the Core platform 2.0.
However, the final release of .Net Core, version 3.0, has opened the doors for more than
just web development and has accelerated the move to .Net Core across the board.

Another side effect of this new path was the effect that it had on the path for Entity
Framework. With the rewrite of the .Net Framework into .Net Core along came a new
EF, also called *Entity Framework Core*. Therefore, at the time of this writing, and into the
direct future for the next few foreseeable years, there will be a minimum of two active
versions of EF in play, *EF6* and *EFCore*.

The state of the union

Although EF6 has reached end of life on new features, the support for EF6 will go on,
likely through the beginning of 2029. Additionally, .Net Core 3.1 will also have a life cycle
that will continue until likely around 2030. With the majority of applications in the real
world at the time of this writing that use Entity Framework being non-core applications,
and the majority of applications in the real world being written in the future in the .Net
Core stack, it will be very important to understand and know both of these frameworks
(EF6 and EFCore) for the next five to ten years.

The good news is that for the most part, both frameworks are doing the same thing
and accomplishing the same goals, with the same architectural concepts. The bad news
is that they are not the same when it comes to working with commands, how they deal
with code-first migrations, working with legacy objects like EDMX Files (only in older
versions of EF), and there are many variances in levels of efficiency when it comes to the
two versions, with EFCore often outperforming EF 6.

The future

Having two versions of a framework is likely not the most efficient use of time and resources. At the time of this writing, there is a planned path to bring all the horses back into the same barn, which will likely be in play by the time this book is in print and in your hands. In September of 2020, a new version of .Net will be available. This new version is likely going to be called .Net 5. For the remainder of this book, we'll call it *vNext* and will refer to EF for .Net 5 as *EFvNext or EFCore5*.

I will do my best to keep this book and the appropriate resources up to date so that the entirety of this book will remain relevant, even after that date. Additionally, the longer life cycles of support for .Net Framework 4.8 and .Net Core 3.0/3.1 will mean that you and me, as developers, will likely encounter legacy code that is actively used in production in one or both of these frameworks in the next few years. As we encounter this code, it is also likely we will be responsible for maintaining and performing feature updates with the full understanding of how each of these versions of EF works.

Activity 0101: Getting started with Entity Framework

In this section of the chapter, we're going to go through the steps it takes for us to implement Entity Framework into any solution. As with most things in development, there are multiple approaches that can be taken to get started, so we're going to look at each of these.

Note   It is entirely likely you won't need to do a lot of the things you'll see in the remainder of this chapter as many .Net projects already contain EF as part of the working solution.

In any project, we can easily set up Entity Framework. Before we do this, however, a great question to ask yourself as the developer/architect is if the database operations might need to be used across multiple solutions or projects. To use EF across multiple solutions or projects, the best approach is to create a reusable code library that stores your database code, including your context, configuration, and migrations.

Regardless of using a separate library or just including in a single package, the initial setup will be exactly the same to bring the libraries into your solution or project. Since using a separate library is a more robust and reusable approach, we'll walk through how to do this in our next activity. We'll begin by taking a look at a greenfield project and importing the Entity Framework libraries.

Create a new project and add the EF packages

To get started creating a new project, make sure you have previously installed the Visual Studio IDE latest edition. Visual Studio Community is available for free academic use and can easily be installed on any machine; however, there may be some limitations if installed on Max or Linux. Downloads can be found here: `https://visualstudio.microsoft.com/downloads/`. If the link is no longer working, simply run a google search for `Visual Studio Community Download`.

Step 1: Create a new .Net Core project

Open the Visual Studio IDE and select `Create a new project` as shown in Figure 1-1.

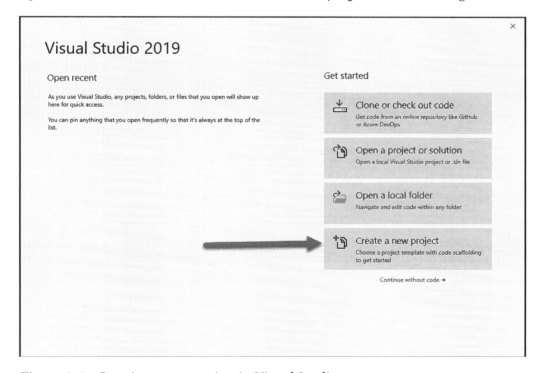

Figure 1-1. *Creating a new project in Visual Studio*

Step 2: Search and select Class Library (.Net Core)

For this step, it will be important to select the correct project type. In this activity, we are creating a new C#.Net Core Class Library. Search for Class Library and then select the .Net Core version of your choice (C# or Visual Basic). Once you have found the correct library of choice, select Next. Review Figure 1-2 for important details on what to look for when creating your new project.

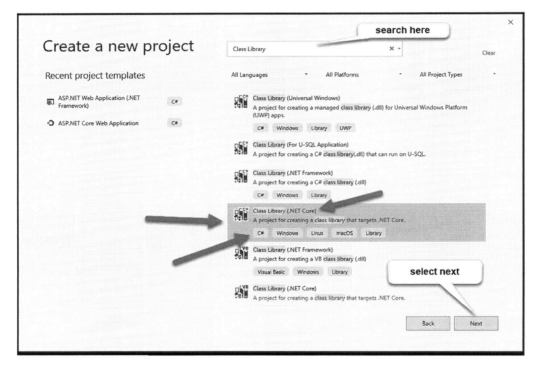

Figure 1-2.   *Selecting a C#.Net Core Class Library*

Step 3: Name your project and select the storage location

Once we've selected the type of project, we need to name it and select the correct place to store it. Name your project EF_Activity001 and select a good location on your computer where you store your projects. For example, I like to store projects under C:/<Client>/Projects or C:/<Client>/Code. Here, I'll place the project in a folder C:/ApressEntityFramework/Code/. Figure 1-3 highlights what my creation page looked like.

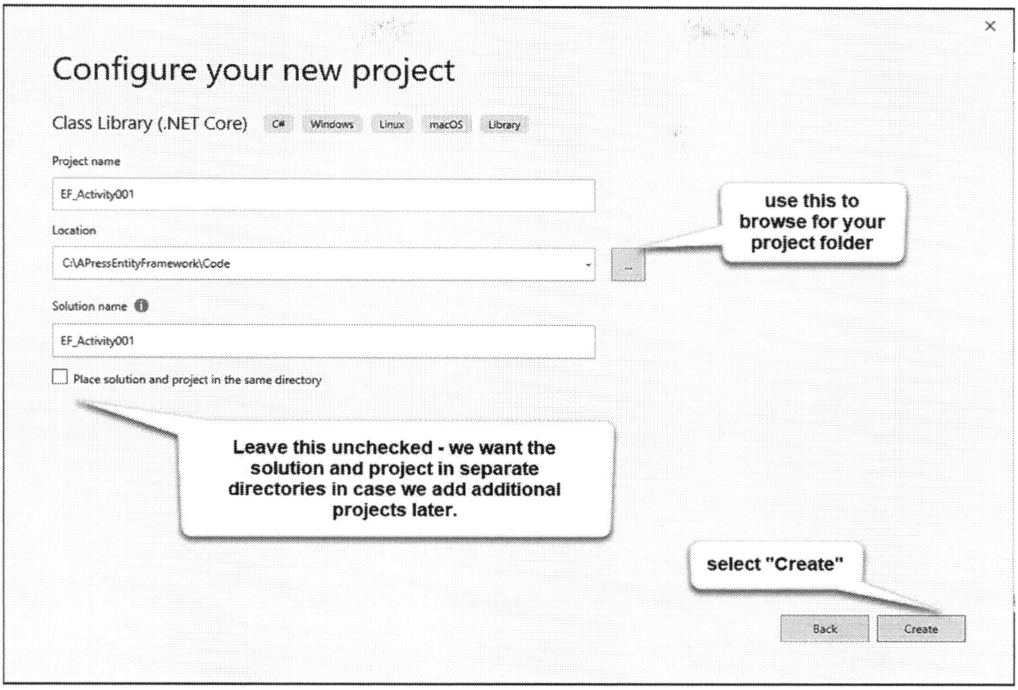

Figure 1-3. *Configuring your new project*

After you have selected Create, a new project will be generated with your default
Class1.cs file as your class library. This should open automatically and should look
similar to what is shown here in Figure 1-4.

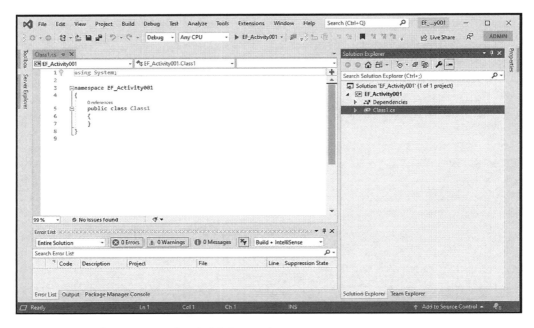

Figure 1-4. *The project after initial creation*

Step 4: Determine the latest version of Entity Framework

In this activity, we're using Entity Framework Core, so I want to install the latest version. To find the latest version, I will just do a quick search for `Entity Framework Core NuGet Package` which should point me to this page: `www.nuget.org/packages/Microsoft.EntityFrameworkCore/`.

Once there, I can easily see the latest version and the command to install it, as shown here in Figure 1-5.

Microsoft.EntityFrameworkCore 3.0.0 ✅

Entity Framework Core is a lightweight and extensible version of the popular Entity Framework data access technology.

Commonly Used Types:
Microsoft.EntityFrameworkCore.DbContext
Microsoft.EntityFrameworkCore.DbSet

ⓘ There is a newer prerelease version of this package available.
See the version list below for details.

Requires NuGet 3.6 or higher.

Package Manager	.NET CLI	PackageReference	Paket CLI

```
PM> Install-Package Microsoft.EntityFrameworkCore -Version 3.0.0
```

this is the installation command to run

> Dependencies

> GitHub Usage

preview versions are not yet stable

n History

this is the latest stable version of the EF Core Libraries

Version	Downloads	
3.1.0-preview2.19525.5	5,257	
3.1.0-preview1.19506.2	13,647	a month ago
3.0.0	603,967	2 months ago

Figure 1-5. *Finding the latest version of Entity Framework Core*

Important notes as shown in the diagram are

- The command to run is located in the main portion of the page. In this case, it is Install-Package Microsoft.EntityFrameworkCore -Version 3.0.0.

- There are preview versions available. While they are easily installed, they may not yet be stable. When working on application code, I would recommend using the latest stable version.

- Although the version is specified, if you run the command for install without the version, then the latest stable version would automatically be installed for you (in this case Entity Framework Core 3.0.0).

While you can use version 3.0.0 even after further versions are released, you should just use the latest version 3 release, for example, version 3.1.3 which was released at the end of March 2020.

Step 5: Add the Entity Framework libraries to your project

Now that our class library is set up, we can add the Entity Framework libraries using the Package Manager Console (PMC). Using the Tools menu at the top of the Visual Studio IDE, select Tools ➤ NuGet Package Manager ➤ Package Manager Console as shown in Figure 1-6.

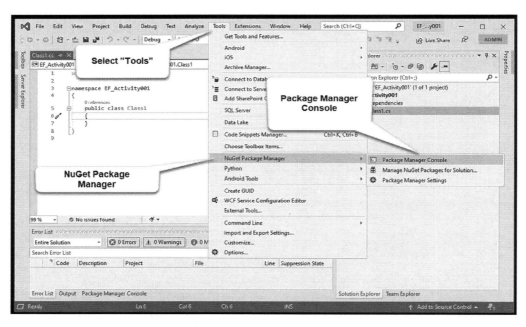

Figure 1-6. *Opening the NuGet Package Manager Console*

This will bring the Package Manager Console (PMC) open in the bottom portion of the Visual Studio IDE.

Once the PMC is open, run the command as found in step 4. The command and the PMC are illustrated in Figure 1-7 below:

Figure 1-7. *Inputting the command to bring the EFCore libraries into our project in the Package Manager Console*

Once we press Enter, the packages will install, and our project will be set up for using the Entity Framework in this code library.

Your installation should be similar to the output as shown here in Figure 1-8.

```
PM> Install-Package Microsoft.EntityFrameworkCore -Version 3.0.0
Restoring packages for C:\APressEntityFramework\Code\EF_Activity001\EF_Activity001\EF_Activity001.csproj...
Installing NuGet package Microsoft.EntityFrameworkCore 3.0.0.
Committing restore...
Writing assets file to disk. Path: C:\APressEntityFramework\Code\EF_Activity001\EF_Activity001\obj\project.assets.json
Restore completed in 772.39 ms for C:\APressEntityFramework\Code\EF_Activity001\EF_Activity001\EF_Activity001.csproj.
Successfully installed 'Microsoft.EntityFrameworkCore 3.0.0' to EF_Activity001
Successfully installed 'Microsoft.EntityFrameworkCore.Abstractions 3.0.0' to EF_Activity001
Successfully installed 'Microsoft.EntityFrameworkCore.Analyzers 3.0.0' to EF_Activity001
Successfully installed 'Microsoft.Extensions.Caching.Abstractions 3.0.0' to EF_Activity001
Successfully installed 'Microsoft.Extensions.Caching.Memory 3.0.0' to EF_Activity001
Successfully installed 'Microsoft.Extensions.Configuration 3.0.0' to EF_Activity001
Successfully installed 'Microsoft.Extensions.Configuration.Abstractions 3.0.0' to EF_Activity001
Successfully installed 'Microsoft.Extensions.Configuration.Binder 3.0.0' to EF_Activity001
Successfully installed 'Microsoft.Extensions.DependencyInjection 3.0.0' to EF_Activity001
Successfully installed 'Microsoft.Extensions.DependencyInjection.Abstractions 3.0.0' to EF_Activity001
Successfully installed 'Microsoft.Extensions.Logging 3.0.0' to EF_Activity001
Successfully installed 'Microsoft.Extensions.Logging.Abstractions 3.0.0' to EF_Activity001
Successfully installed 'Microsoft.Extensions.Options 3.0.0' to EF_Activity001
Successfully installed 'Microsoft.Extensions.Primitives 3.0.0' to EF_Activity001
Successfully installed 'System.Collections.Immutable 1.6.0' to EF_Activity001
Successfully installed 'System.ComponentModel.Annotations 4.6.0' to EF_Activity001
Successfully installed 'System.Diagnostics.DiagnosticSource 4.6.0' to EF_Activity001
Successfully installed 'System.Threading.Tasks.Extensions 4.5.2' to EF_Activity001
Executing nuget actions took 1.65 sec
Time Elapsed: 00:00:02.6197589
PM> |
99 %    ▾
```

Figure 1-8. *Running the installation of the EFCore libraries into our project using the Package Manager Console*

We have now successfully created a class library that references Entity Framework, but we still have some work to do to get it set up to run against a database.

Step 6: Create a DBContext

In order to work against the database, we need a DBContext object. The DBContext (context) object is responsible to act as the interpreter between your code and the actual database. The context is where we'll define all of our entity sets and can also override some of the database schema using the Fluent API.

To make our context, we're going to convert our Class1.cs file. First, we need to rename it to something useful. Here, we will just name it ApplicationDbContext, but you could name yours after your actual application if you would like, such as MoviesDbContext or AccountingDbContext. The name of your context is entirely up to you. If using multiple contexts, then I would recommend distinctly naming them in a way that is easy to discern their intended purpose.

To rename the file, simply right-click the file in the Solution Explorer in Visual Studio and select "Rename" as shown in Figure 1-9.

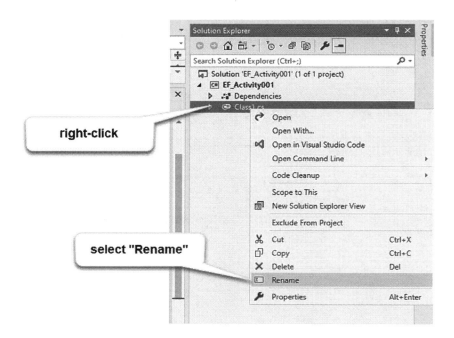

Figure 1-9. *Selecting the class file to rename*

Alternatively, selecting the file in the Solution Explorer and hitting F2 will automatically select the file for renaming.

Once the rename textbox appears with the original name in it, enter your new context name, such as ApplicationDbContext as shown in Figure 1-10.

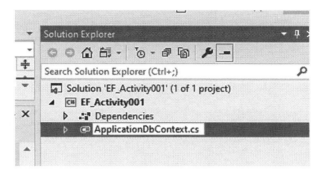

Figure 1-10.   *Renaming the Class1.cs file*

Hitting Enter will prompt you to perform a rename in all code elements for the file. We want to do this, so we will select Yes as shown in the dialog in Figure 1-11.

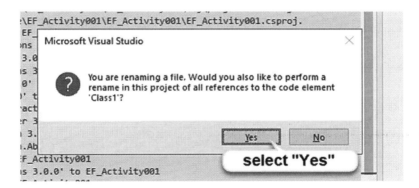

Figure 1-11.   *Selecting "Yes" to allow auto-rename of the class in all code elements*

After rename and selecting Yes, Class1.cs should also be renamed to whatever you named your context (i.e., ApplicationDbContext) with the constructor named to match as shown in Figure 1-12.

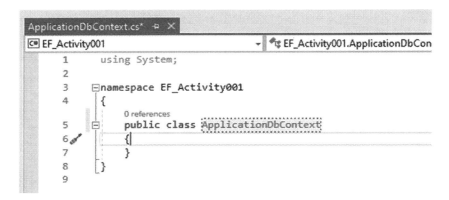

Figure 1-12. *The Class1.cs file has been renamed and the constructor is now named appropriately*

Step 7: Alter your context to implement DbContext correctly

Now that our name is changed to be our context, we need to alter the context so that it is implemented correctly. To do this, we must accomplish two things:

1. We must inherit and extend DbContext.

2. We must have a constructor that allows for injecting the context options.

First, let's make our ApplicationDbContext and actual DBContext by becoming a subclass of DbContext. Extend DBContext and make sure to add the using statement for *Microsoft.EntityFrameworkCore* as shown in Figure 1-13.

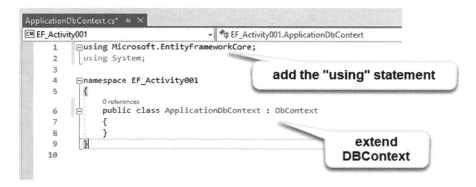

Figure 1-13. *Extending the DBContext class*

Next, we need to set the constructor to take in the DBOptions on injection as shown in Figure 1-14.

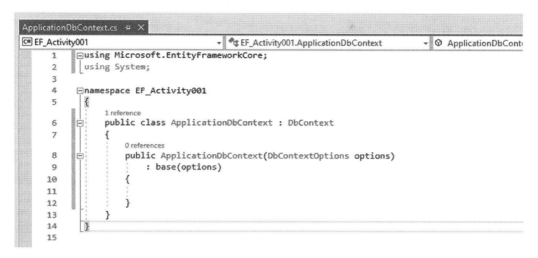

```
ApplicationDbContext.cs  ⇄ ✕

C# EF_Activity001                                ⚙ EF_Activity001.ApplicationDbContext           ⊙ ApplicationDbConte

    1    using Microsoft.EntityFrameworkCore;
    2    using System;
    3
    4    namespace EF_Activity001
    5    {
             1 reference
    6        public class ApplicationDbContext : DbContext
    7        {
                 0 references
    8            public ApplicationDbContext(DbContextOptions options)
    9                : base(options)
   10            {
   11
   12            }
   13        }
   14    }
   15
```

Figure 1-14. *Adding the DBOptions as an injectable object to the constructor*

Note that in order to accomplish this task, we make a public function with no return type since it's a constructor. The name is the exact same as the name of the class, and the constructor has one injectable parameter of type DbContextOptions. This parameter will include critical information, such as the connection string to our database. Making these options injectable will ensure that the context can be used from any application pointing to any correctly configured database.

Activity summary

In the previous activity, we created a class library and then imported the Entity Framework Core library. After completing that import, we renamed the class file and we set up our DBContext to be ready to be used in any project.

As of right now, we can't necessarily prove that our setup is ready, but we can trust that it is either ready or will be very easy to modify once we get an actual application to use the project.

You might ask the question as to why we stopped here and not just make sure that everything is working as expected. To answer that, we need to first decide how we are going to work against our database. Will we use a "code-first" approach for our database, or are we going to run against an existing database using a "reverse-engineering" approach? We'll take a look at each of these in the next couple of chapters.

Activity supplemental information

In the previous activity, as we created the application, we had worked with Entity Framework Core as our library. In many instances, you may need to work with the .Net Framework version of the Entity Framework. As with the earlier activity, this is easily accomplished. Following the preceding steps, make these changes to work against the Entity Framework 6 libraries:

1. In step 2, create a .Net Framework Class Library as shown in Figure 1-15.

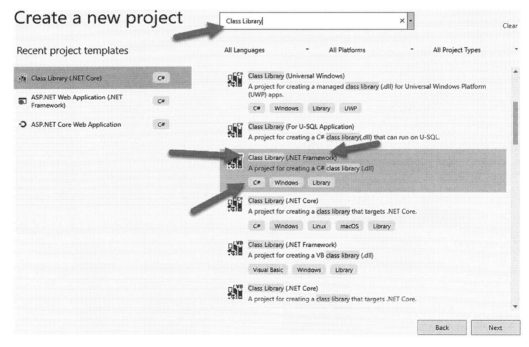

Figure 1-15.   *Create a .Net Framework Class Library*

When the create dialog comes up, you'll have the opportunity to select the latest version of the .Net Framework that is installed on your machine.

---

2. In step 4, find the .Net Entity Framework 6 NuGet Library as
    shown in Figure 1-16.

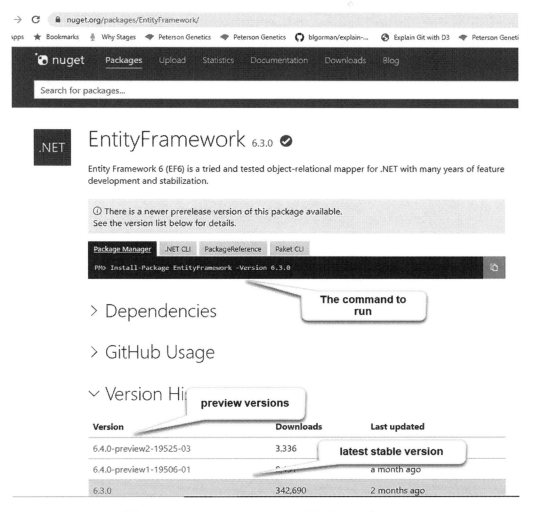

Figure 1-16. *Find the .Net Entity Framework 6 NuGet Packages*

3. In step 7, create the DbContext by implementing DBContext
    and importing the library System.Data.Entity. Create the
    public constructor with a string input for the connection string.
    Reference Figure 1-17 for more information.

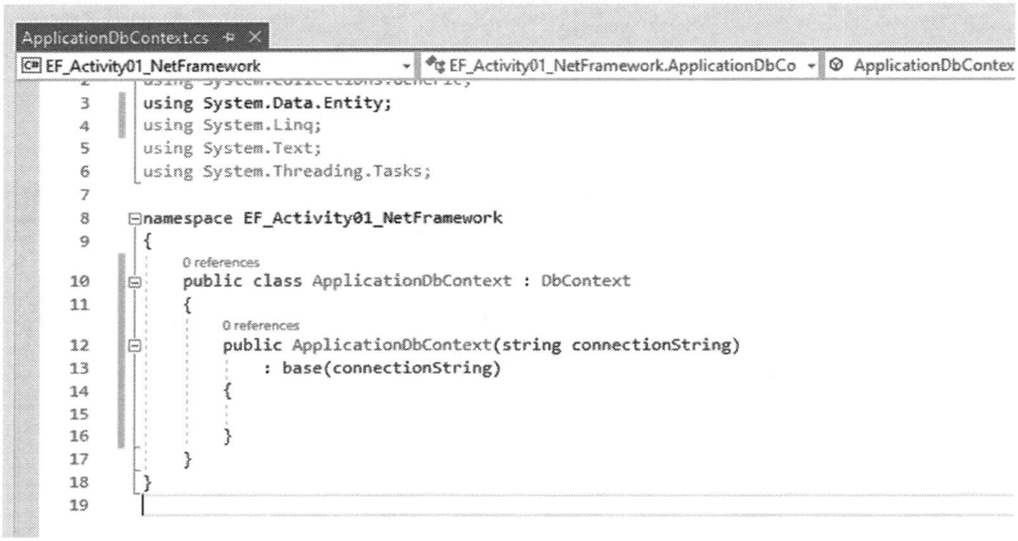

Figure 1-17. *Create the DbContext for a .Net Framework project*

As with the EFCore activity, the EF6 library is not yet working. The paths to create a "code-first" application with EF6 and EFCore are very similar; however, the "database-first" vs. "reverse-engineered" approaches in Core and .Net are quite a bit different. We will cross these bridges together as we reach them.

Chapter summary

In this first chapter, we have taken a good look at the history of coding against data and how and why that history has led us to the Entity Framework. We then moved into creating a project in a class library that would be ready to work as a shareable database code library.

Although our activity didn't create a fully functional library, we were able to get a good start and an overview of what it takes at the foundational level to work with Entity Framework. We've also gained an entry-level understanding of the DBContext object and are now familiar with how we set up the application to leverage the Entity Framework.

Important takeaways

After working through this chapter, the things we should be in command of are as follows:

- The history of coding against data and the problems that have existed before Entity Framework wrapped the ADO.Net libraries

- How Entity Framework can be implemented into a class library for use in any project (still not useable, but the setup is in place)

- A few differences between EF6 and EFCore in their setup and implementations

Closing thoughts

In the next chapter, we will examine how to create a project against an existing database using the "database-first" EF6 or "reverse-engineered" approach (EFCore).

CHAPTER 2

Working with an Existing Database

In this chapter, we are going to look at what it takes to get up and running with Entity Framework when our project already has an existing database. We'll conclude with a couple of activities to reverse engineer a database in *EFCore* and use the database-first approach in *EF6* to generate an *EDMX* model.

Reverse engineering or database first

When working with an existing database, we have many options, and how we accomplish this task depends on what technology we are using. If we are working in .Net Core Entity Framework (*EFCore*) or *EFvNext*, we'll need to perform a reverse-engineering operation. If we are working in the .Net Framework and using *EF6*, we'll need to approach this with a database-first operation.

Before we dive into the how of these operations, we should discuss the why, as well as what some of the good and bad things are about this approach.

Why would we approach Entity Framework in this manner?

There are going to be times when an application is needed for a database that already exists. In these cases, the database may have many years of history and may be quite involved. Starting from scratch is usually not possible in these cases, because the overall amount of work it would take would overwhelm even the best development teams. However, in these cases, it is also desirable to begin new projects, perhaps to break a monolith into a serverless approach, or to create a new access layer for a specific application.

© Brian L. Gorman 2020
B. L. Gorman, *Practical Entity Framework*, https://doi.org/10.1007/978-1-4842-6044-9_2

Rather than spend time trying to work new code into an old system, it is often desirable for both efficiency and security reasons to build new solutions. In these cases, when the database is mature, and the desired application is new, a database-first or reverse-engineering approach makes sense.

Database-first or reverse-engineered solutions

The really good news about this approach is that there are tools in place that allow for us to very quickly generate the code we need to work against the database. The bad news is that this code is not very flexible, as we'll see throughout this chapter. To sum it up, essentially a database-first or reverse-engineered approach requires regenerating code any time the database is changed where the application needs to interact with the database objects. Need to add a column? You'll need to add it in the database through your official channels, and then you'll need to regenerate your database context.

An additional drawback to using the database-first or reverse-engineered approach is that your database code is often not stored in the repository. While you will have generated models for the objects you include, the code that actually created them in the database is often not present. Additionally, there is not a good history of objects and their state in the database. This can make it tricky when trying to restore to a previous patch but needing to have the database also in the state it was at the time of that patch.

Keeping everything in sync

A couple of final thoughts about this approach. In the older version of *EF6*, we often had an *EDMX* file that is a conceptual model of the database. This *EDMX* file is a gigantic *XML* file. If you've ever had to do a code merge in *GIT* or *TFS* when a large *XML* file is involved for multiple developers, you don't need me to tell you why that isn't a desirable situation to be in.

As such, creating the database changes in this approach requires a great deal of coordination from team members. Additionally, you'll likely need some tool or some other way to make sure you keep track of your database history, changes, scripts, and other important details.

Interacting with the existing database

Now that we have a decent understanding of why we might want to take a database-first or reverse-engineered approach to the application, let's take some time to work through a couple of activities on how to make this happen.

Working with a preexisting database activities

In this section of the chapter, we're going to work through setting up Entity Framework to work against a preexisting database. We'll begin by getting a copy of *AdventureWorks* and getting that installed and then walk through the steps to use Entity Framework against the *AdventureWorks* database. To complete this activity, you'll need to have a version of Visual Studio, a working local copy of *SQL Express* or SQL Developer edition, and *Microsoft SQL Server Management Studio (SSMS)* installed.

Download the backup file for the latest version of AdventureWorks

Microsoft has made a free database available for use when learning or training on SQL products. The database is called *AdventureWorks* and is available here: `https://docs. microsoft.com/en-us/sql/samples/adventureworks-install-configure?view=sql- server-ver15`. Regardless of which version of Entity Framework you want to use for this activity, the first two steps to get the database restored will be the same. After completing the database restoration, skip to the activity that is appropriate for the version of *EF* that you are using.

Step 1: Download the latest version of AdventureWorks DB

Begin by downloading the latest *AdventureWorksXXXX.bak* file to your local machine (e.g., AdventureWorks2017.bak). Figure 2-1 shows the download page on Microsoft's website.

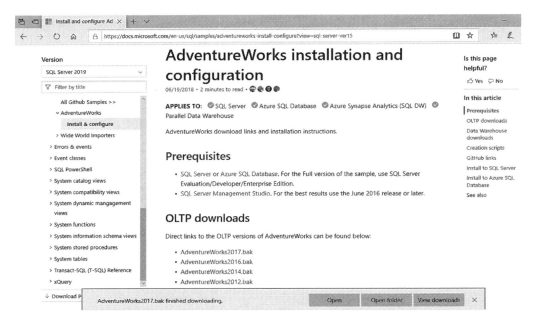

Figure 2-1. *Downloading the latest version of AdventureWorks*

Step 2: Restore the AdventureWorks database to your local SQL instance

After downloading the backup file, we need to restore it to our local *SQL Express* or *SQL Developer* instance (if you don't have one of these installed, you'll need to do this first).

Connect to your database in SSMS as shown in Figure 2-2. Then right-click the *Databases* folder under your local server name and then select *Restore Database.*

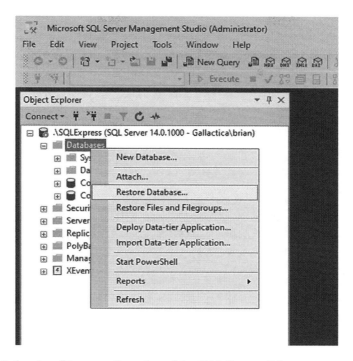

Figure 2-2. *Selecting "Restore Database" in SQL Server Management Studio*

Selecting *Restore Database* brings up the restoration dialog shown in Figure 2-3.

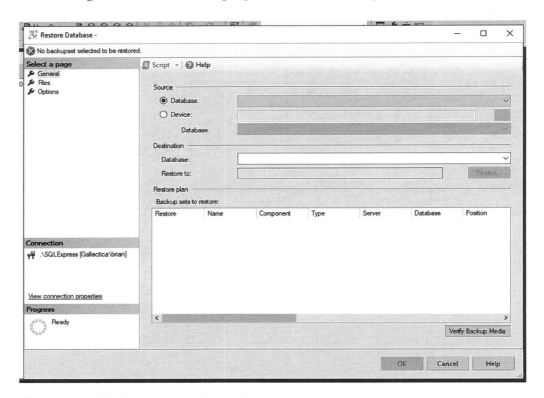

Figure 2-3. *The Restore Database dialog*

With the restore database dialog open, select *Device* and then select the button with three periods, which will bring up a dialog *Select Backup Devices*. In this dialog, select *Add* and then note the default location for backup files as in Figure 2-4.

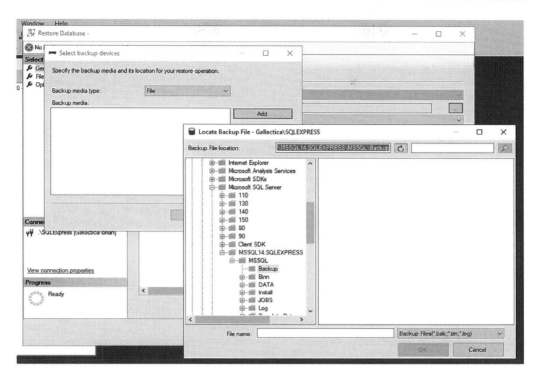

Figure 2-4. *Finding the backup location in the Select Backup Devices - Add dialog*

Move the backup file from your downloads into the backup location found in the *Locate Backup File* dialog shown in Figure 2-4.

You can copy the location from the dialog directly and open a new file explorer to that path, or you can make note of the directory location in the directory tree on the left-half of the *Locate Backup File* dialog.

Cancel the *Locate Backup File* dialog and then select *Add* again. You should see a result like in Figure 2-5. Now that your backup file is in the default location, it should show in the window for selection.

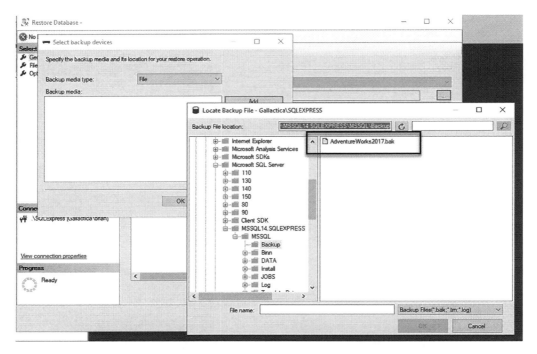

Figure 2-5. *The backup file shows in the dialog once placed in the default backups folder*

Now that the file is there, select the file and then *OK*, and then select *OK* again on the *Select Backup Devices* dialog. This will fill information for the backup dialog to the point that we can restore the database.

Before we restore, let's take a quick look and see if there is anything we want to change. Start by looking at Figure 2-6.

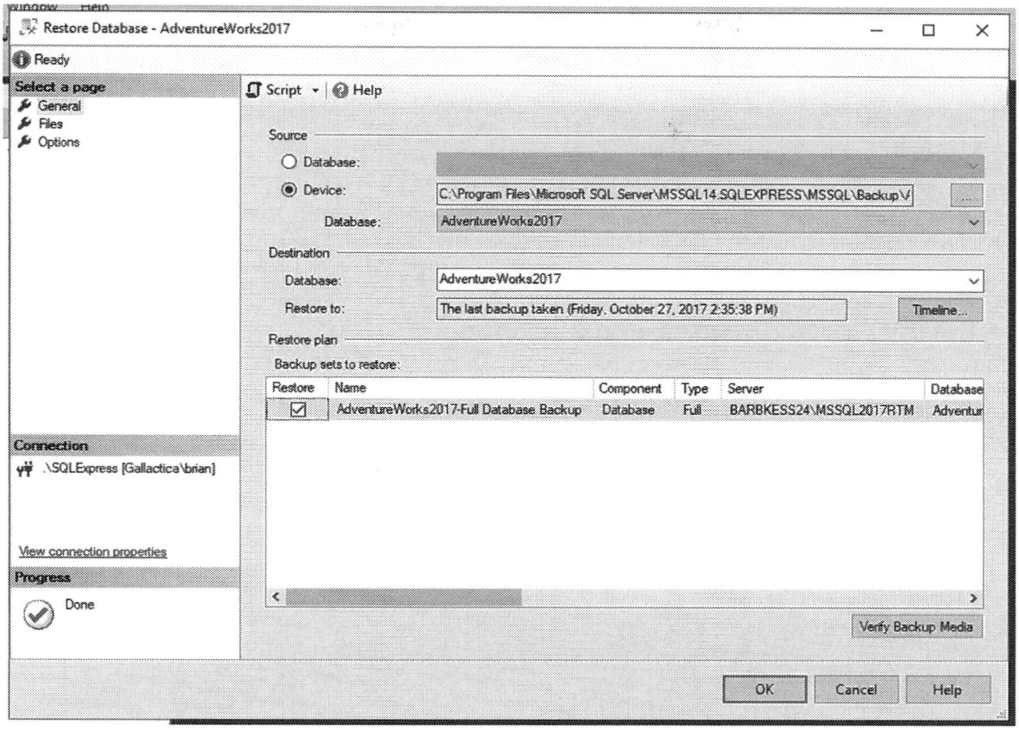

Figure 2-6. *AdventureWorks backup file loaded for potential restore operation*

Most importantly, take note that you can change the database name in the Database dialog (see Figure 2-7). For example, here I am going to remove the year *2017* from the database name. Additionally, you can change the default file location and other options using the *Files* and *Options* tabs on the upper left *Select a page* dialog. I am going to leave both tabs with all the default options as set automatically.

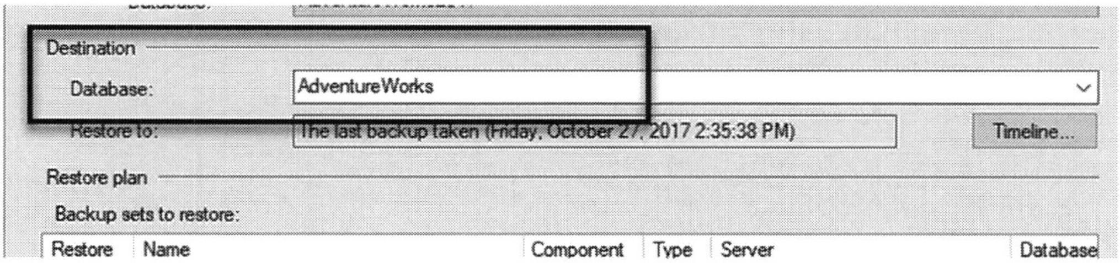

Figure 2-7. *Changing the database name before restoration*

Once all the options you want are selected and the database name is as you want it to be, select *OK* to restore the database. Figure 2-8 shows the resulting progress bar.

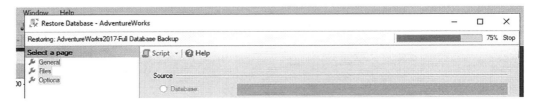

Figure 2-8. *Restore database operation in progress*

Once the restoration is completed, a confirmation dialog (Figure 2-9) will appear.

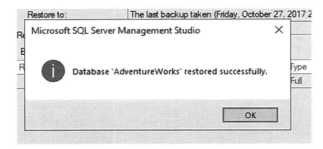

Figure 2-9. *Restore database operation completed*

You can then easily browse in *SSMS* to see the database and its existing tables and other structures. Your database should look similar to what is shown in Figure 2-10.

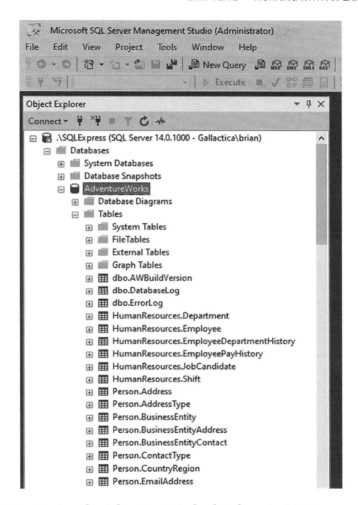

Figure 2-10. *Reviewing the AdventureWorks database in SSMS*

Activity 0201: Creating a reverse-engineered database in Entity Framework Core

In this activity, we'll use the existing database *AdventureWorks* database, which we have previously restored to our local machine. Our main task is to create a working Entity Framework database context to work against the existing database.

For this activity and the activities that follow throughout the book, you will be able to find two versions of the code. The versions are labeled as ActivityXXXX-Name_Starter or ActivityXXXX-Name_Final. The starter pack gives you the ability to quickly get going at the start of the activity. You can always use the final version to compare my completed project to what you have done to help debug any issues you encounter. You may also look at the example download for this book, which you can find on the book's catalog page on Apress.com.

Step 1: Create the project and solution

Begin the activity by creating a simple C# console application which will be our startup project. Name the project something simple, such as *Activity0201_ExistingDbCore*, or just use the starter pack.

The `Create a new project` dialog is shown in Figure 2-11.

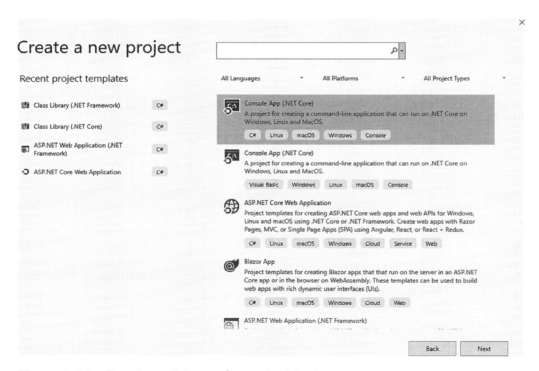

Figure 2-11. *Creating a C# console app in .Net Core*

Step 2: Reference the code for the EFCore Library created in Chapter 1, Activity 0101

Next, reference the project from Chapter 1 where we created our Entity Framework Core library.

If you are not using a repository at this point, I recommend making a copy of the activity one files for ease of reuse and recovery.

Copy the project from Chapter 1 to the folder with your recently created solution. Your folder structure should look like what is shown in Figure 2-12.

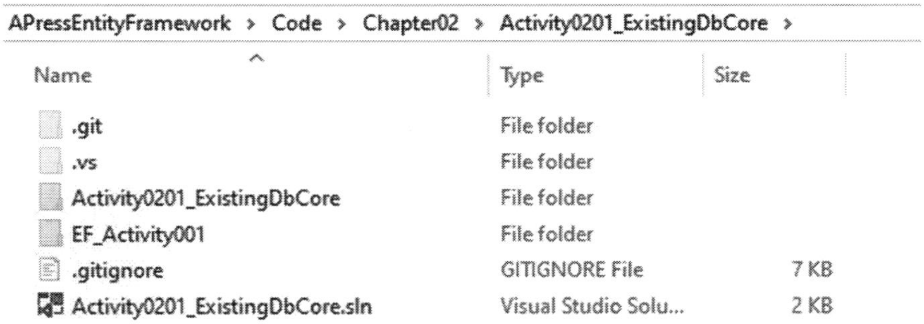

APressEntityFramework › Code › Chapter02 › Activity0201_ExistingDbCore ›

Name	Type	Size
.git	File folder	
.vs	File folder	
Activity0201_ExistingDbCore	File folder	
EF_Activity001	File folder	
.gitignore	GITIGNORE File	7 KB
Activity0201_ExistingDbCore.sln	Visual Studio Solu...	2 KB

Figure 2-12.   A potential folder structure for your projects and the activity 02 core solution

After setting the folders and code structure, add a reference to the project within the solution. First, right-click the Solution and select Add ➤ Existing Project as is shown in Figure 2-13.

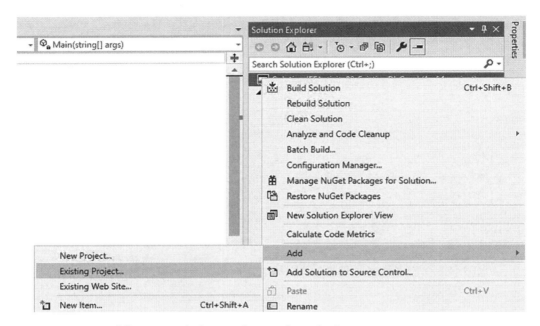

Figure 2-13. *Adding an existing project to the solution*

Next, right-click the new project for activity two, and select Add Reference. Browse and reference the code library from activity 01 in the console project (see Figure 2-14).

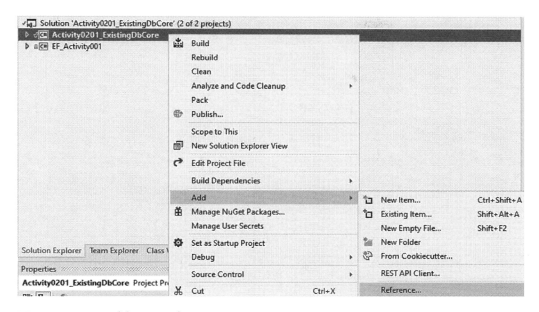

Figure 2-14. *Adding a reference to an existing project*

Select the activity one project from your current solution to reference in the activity two project as in Figure 2-15.

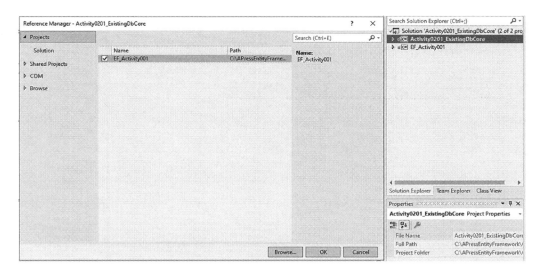

Figure 2-15. *Selecting a project to reference*

After setting your projects correctly, rebuild the solution. Your project structure should look similar to what is shown in Figure 2-16.

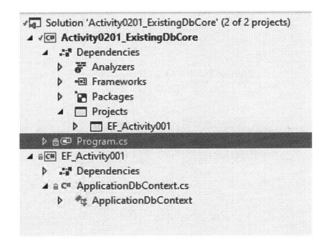

Figure 2-16.   *Overall project structure*

Step 3: Install Entity Framework tools

In order to reverse engineer the database, we'll need the Entity Framework tools. These are easily installed via NuGet.

First, open the Package Manager Console, and then select the Default project where Entity Framework is installed in your current solution as shown in Figure 2-17.

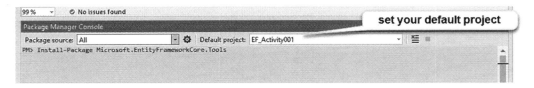

Figure 2-17.   *Setting default project and installing Entity Framework Core tools*

Next, type the command Install-Package Microsoft.EntityFrameworkCore.Tools.

If for some reason you are not on the latest version of Entity Framework, make sure to set the version number in the tools installation to match your current version of Entity Framework Core by simply adding -version X.Y.Z to your command.

To validate that the tools are in place, or to see the commands available at any time, simply type the command Get-Help EntityFrameworkCore in the Package Manager Console (will require updating local help if you have not done this before).

Step 4: Install Entity Framework for SQL Server

One of the steps we could have done prior to this activity would be to set the provider. In this book, we're using *SQL Server* as our main database, so we need to install the *EF* provider for *SQL* Server so that we can connect to a *SQL* database. To do this, run the command Install-Package Microsoft.EntityFrameworkCore.SqlServer from the Package Manager Console while pointed at your default Entity Framework library project as shown in Figure 2-18.

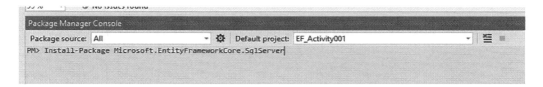

Figure 2-18. *Install Package for Microsoft Entity Framework Core using SQL Server*

Step 5: Reference all of the EF packages in the startup project

In order for the project to work, both the library and the startup project need to reference the EFCore packages. To get the packages installed, open Tools ➤ Manage NuGet Packages for Solution and browse to the Installed tab. Another way to get there is to simply right-click the Solution and select Manage NuGet Packages for Solution. Managing NuGet Packages can be accessed as shown in Figure 2-19.

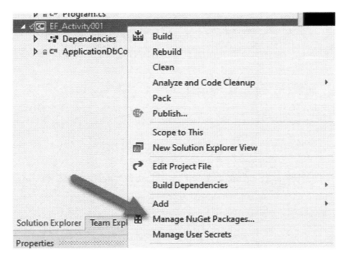

Figure 2-19. *Use the right-click context menu to get to the Manage NuGet Packages for Solution dialog*

Select all *EF* packages that are installed and install them on the startup project. At this point, there should be three. Make sure to match currently installed versions. Review Figure 2-20 to see all of the places to match versions and select projects.

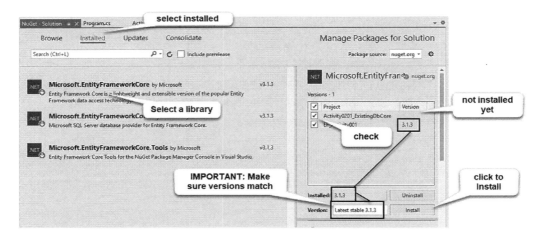

Figure 2-20. *Installing Entity Framework packages to startup project*

Make sure to match your versions of the Entity Framework. In general, just use the latest stable release across all projects.

Step 6: Scaffold a new context using the Scaffold-Context command

Before we scaffold, let's address the options associated with scaffolding a context. Most importantly, note that the context will require a database connection string to be passed in as an option in the options parameters. This is a good thing. That being said, when we scaffold, we'll connect directly to the database.

In order to perform the scaffold operation, we're going to need to add another NuGet Package. In the PMC, select the main program project (e.g., *EFActivity02_ ExistingDbCore)* and then run the command Install-Package Microsoft. EntityFrameworkCore.Design to get the design tools on the main program (review Figure 2-21 for more information).

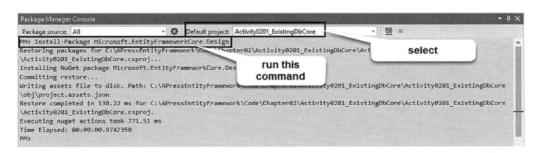

Figure 2-21. *Getting the EntityFrameworkCore.Design package*

It's important to note that by default all tables and schemas are going to be scaffolded unless otherwise specified. In order to make this happen, you simply run the command with the connection string and the provider specified.

Make sure to once again select the EF_Activity001 project in the Package Manager Console. We'll be running the scaffold command against the database project. With the EF_Activity001 project selected, run the command Scaffold-DbContext <connection_string.> [optional params].

For example, when using *SQLExpress*, the command Scaffold-DbContext 'Data
Source=.\SQLExpress;Initial Catalog=AdventureWorks;Trusted_Connection=True'
Microsoft.EntityFrameworkCore.SqlServer will generate a full version of the
database. Figure 2-22 shows the command in context, in the Package Manager Console.

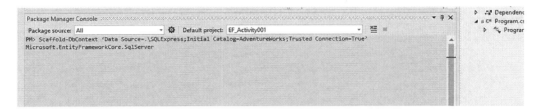

Figure 2-22. *Using PMC to scaffold a database context*

Please note that your database connection string's server may vary based on
your installed version of SQL. For example, *SQL Developer* edition often uses
localhost. Some installations use (local) or (local)\ServerName.
Sometimes you can get away with just a ".". The easiest way to determine your
installation is to try to connect via *SSMS* with each of the different versions of the
server [(local), localhost, .\SQLExpress, just a "."]. Once connected,
you'll need to leverage the correct server in all connection strings going forward.

When this command runs, we get a full DBContext generated and available for use.
Also note, there were a number of warnings given with this database generation, due to the
complexity of the database. The output of the scaffold operation is shown in Figure 2-23.

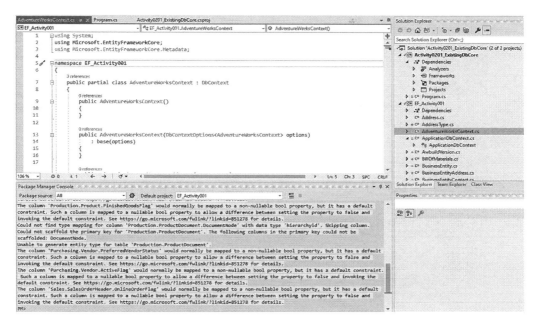

Figure 2-23. *Scaffolding completed*

At this point, we could start working against the database in our console application, and in fact, this is what we will use later in this activity, with a slight tweak that has no effect on the overall project for this activity.

Step 7: Repeat the scaffold operation but change parameters

As an optional learning experiment, let's wipe out what we just did (just delete all models and the new context) or create a new solution and then run the scaffold operation again. To delete all of the models and the new context, find the newly created files in the EF_Activity001 project and simply delete them (make sure to keep the ApplicationDbContext.cs file). Review Figure 2-24 to validate the files to keep.

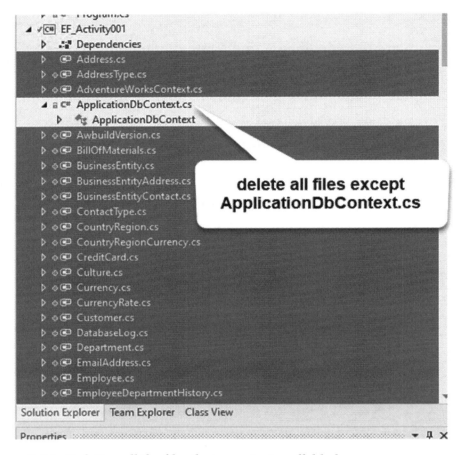

Figure 2-24. *Deleting all the files that were just scaffolded*

For this run, let's specify only one schema to scaffold (you can go further on your own to specify specific tables if you would like). Additionally, instead of using the *Fluent API*, let's specify that we want to use *data annotations*. We'll cover the *Fluent API* and *data annotations* later in this book, but for now just know the difference is in how the models and context work to implement things like required fields, length or size of fields, and overall relationships between the entities. For the scaffold command, this time specify the flag -Schema and then implement only the Person schema. Additionally, use the -DataAnnotations flag to generate data annotations on the models instead of fully relying on the Fluent API.

On the default project without anything scaffolded, run this command:

```
Scaffold-DbContext 'Data Source=.\SQLExpress;Initial
Catalog=AdventureWorks;Trusted_Connection=True' Microsoft.
EntityFrameworkCore.SqlServer -Schema 'Person' -DataAnnotations
```

As before, type the command into the Package Manager Console as shown in Figure 2-25.

Figure 2-25. *Scaffolding a limited context by schema and data annotations*

Once this command is completed, the difference will be easy to see when looking at any of the models that are generated, as the models will have data annotations on fields as shown in Figure 2-26.

```
namespace EF_Activity001
{
    [Table("Password", Schema = "Person")]
    4 references
    public partial class Password
    {
        [Key]
        [Column("BusinessEntityID")]
        4 references
        public int BusinessEntityId { get; set; }
        [Required]
        [StringLength(128)]
        1 reference
        public string PasswordHash { get; set; }
        [Required]
        [StringLength(10)]
        1 reference
        public string PasswordSalt { get; set; }
        [Column("rowguid")]
        1 reference
        public Guid Rowguid { get; set; }
        [Column(TypeName = "datetime")]
        1 reference
        public DateTime ModifiedDate { get; set; }

        [ForeignKey(nameof(BusinessEntityId))]
        [InverseProperty(nameof(Person.Password))]
        1 reference
        public virtual Person BusinessEntity { get; set; }
    }
}
```

Figure 2-26. *Reviewing a generated model class to see data annotations*

Step 8: Creating the final context and configuration files for connection

In order to connect to the database, we're going to need to do some configuration. As the project exists right now, there are no settings files, so we need to get those added in. In the settings files, we'll establish our database connection string, which we will then pass into the context in order to connect to the database.

Before doing that, I'm going to reset and use the full context with data annotations. This will give me the best amount of available data for further learning. The command I want to run to scaffold this out is `Scaffold-DbContext 'Data Source=.\SQLExpress;Initial Catalog=AdventureWorks;Trusted_Connection=True' Microsoft.EntityFrameworkCore.SqlServer -DataAnnotations`

The command is exactly the same as the last command, with the exception that the `-Schema` flag has been removed. Figure 2-27 shows the full results.

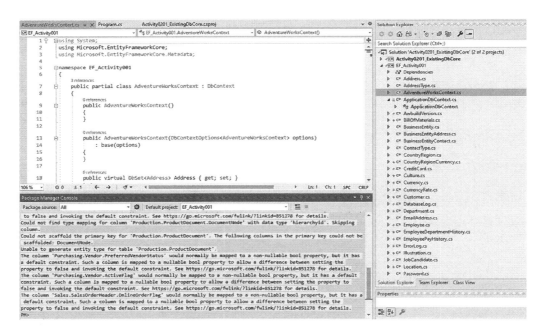

Figure 2-27. *Regenerating the entire database with data annotations*

Now that the context is ready, I'll add a file named *appsettings.json* to the current activity, as well as the same file in the console application startup project. Additionally, I want to set the file as *Content* and *Copy if newer* for future deployments of the project. After creating and setting the files as needed, your project structure should look similar to what is shown in Figure 2-28.

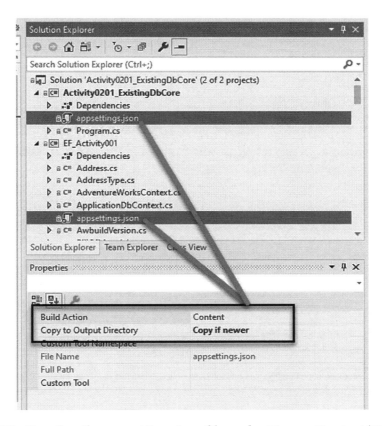

Figure 2-28.   *Creating the appsettings.json file and setting as Content/Copy if newer in each of the projects*

It is very important to remember to set the file as *Content* and *Copy if newer*. Failure to do this will prevent the connection string from being read when the code executed. Next, we need to add three more NuGet Packages. Hopefully this is becoming second

nature by now. Use the Package Manager Console (*PMC*) to add the following three
packages to the console project (don't forget to select the console project in the drop-
down):

1. Microsoft.Extensions.Configuration

   ```
   Install-Package Microsoft.Extensions.Configuration
   ```

2. Microsoft.Extensions.Configuration.FileExtensions

   ```
   Install-Package Microsoft.Extensions.Configuration.
   FileExtensions
   ```

3. Microsoft.Extensions.Configuration.Json

   ```
   Install-Package Microsoft.Extensions.Configuration.Json
   ```

After installing the three packages, review the installed packages in the NuGet
Package Manager as shown in Figure 2-29.

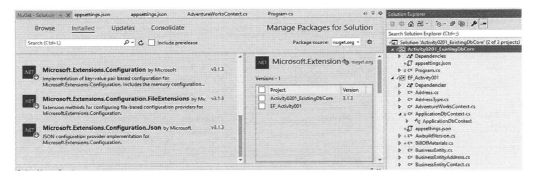

Figure 2-29. *A quick review of NuGet packages to make sure they are installed*

Create the connection string in the `appsettings.json` file. While you likely only
need it in the console application, it's not a bad thing to put it in both files to keep the
connection string with the library (all startup projects will need their own `appsettings.`
`json` in any situation to reference the connection string).

Add the following lines of code to your *appsettings.json* file:

```
"ConnectionStrings": {
    "AdventureWorks": "Data Source=.\\SQLExpress;Initial
    Catalog=AdventureWorks;Trusted_Connection=True"
}
```

Note that you will need to make sure to set your connection string correctly, and be aware that the use of a double slash (\\) is **critical** in the connection string path. This connection string should be identical to the connection string used to generate the context earlier in the activity, with the exception of the double slash.

If your appsettings.json file already contains a node, such as Exclude and you want to add the connection string, place a comma at the end of the current existing node and add the ConnectionStrings entry following the comma, just as you would do with any JSON-formatted text.

In the Program.cs file in the console application, we need to add the connection string to the builder so that we can leverage it in the future. To do this, add a static variable and a function to the Program.cs file.

The variable should be declared above the Main method as follows: static IConfigurationRoot _configuration;

After adding the code, make sure to hover over the red-squiggly line for IConfigurationRoot and select Show Potential Fixes. When the statements come up, select the statement to add the using statement for Microsoft.Extensions. Configuration.

Continue by adding a call to a new method: BuildConfiguration in the Main method.

Next, add the method code as follows:

```
static void BuildConfiguration()
{
    var builder = new ConfigurationBuilder()
                    .SetBasePath(Directory.GetCurrentDirectory())
                        .AddJsonFile("appsettings.json", optional: true,
                        reloadOnChange: true);

    _configuration = builder.Build();
}
```

Figure 2-30 shows where in the class definition to insert this code. You may also look at the example download for this book, which you can find on the book's catalog page on Apress.com.

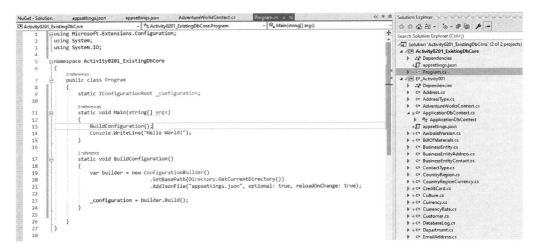

Figure 2-30. *Add configuration code to the Program.cs file*

Remember that any time the Visual Studio IDE shows a red-squiggly line, there are errors in your code. For each red-squiggly line, attempt to use the suggested fixes. Most of the time you'll just need to add missing using statements. A quick shortcut is to hit the key-chord combination ctrl + "." – which will bring up the suggestions for you.

Step 9: Connecting to the database and showing results

In this final step, we'll write the code to connect and show results from our existing database. It is imperative that step 8 has been completed prior to this step.

Add another static variable to store the options builder information. This is a DbContextOptionsBuilder object, which is a generic, with a type argument that contains the type of your generated DbContext. In my case, this was AdventureWorksContext. Therefore, my static variable is declared as static DbContextOptionsBuilder<Adventu reWorksContext> _optionsBuilder;

Add the variable into the Program class as shown in Figure 2-31.

```
0 references
class Program
{
    static IConfigurationRoot _configuration;
    static DbContextOptionsBuilder<AdventureWorksContext> _optionsBuilder;

    0 references
    static void Main(string[] args)
    {
```

Figure 2-31. *A look at the static variables in the Program.cs file*

Next, add a new method to build the database context options:

```
static void BuildOptions()
{
    _optionsBuilder = new DbContextOptionsBuilder<AdventureWorksContext>();
    _optionsBuilder.UseSqlServer(_configuration.GetConnectionString("Advent
    ureWorks"));
}
```

This method sets the options builder to a new instance of the options builder on the DBContext and then tells the builder to use *SQL* Server with the configuration settings for the connection string as defined in the appsettings.json file. Place the code for the BuildOptions method in the Program class following the BuildConfiguration method.

In order to get the data, we'll need a query and output method. Create a method called ListPeople as follows:

```
static void ListPeople()
{
    using (var db = new AdventureWorksContext(_optionsBuilder.Options))
    {
        var people = db.Person.OrderByDescending(x => x.LastName).Take(20).
        ToList();

        foreach (var person in people)
        {
            Console.WriteLine($"{person.FirstName} {person.LastName}");
        }
    }
}
```

The ListPeople method should be added in the Program class following the BuildOptions method. Also remember that any time you are concerned about placement or are having any issues with the code, feel free to review the final version of the files to see how and where I implemented the solution.

Please note that depending on your generation settings, you may need to use Persons or People in the name of the entity set (the entity set is directly defined in the context, if you want to search for it). Review the following image if you are having trouble finding the Person DbSet property - DbSet<Person>. Also note that if you don't see Person, you can use another DbSet, or you may have set the options incorrectly and need to regenerate the database context in its entirety. The generated AdventureWorksContext with the DbSet<Person> entry is shown in Figure 2-32.

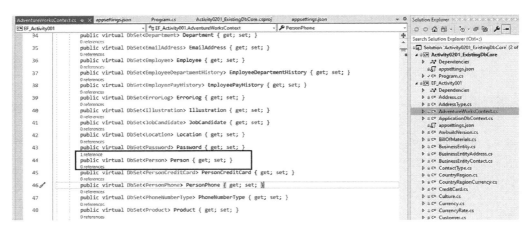

Figure 2-32. *Finding the Person DbSet in the AdventureWorksContext*

Finally, if you haven't already done this, set the Main method to call the BuildConfiguration method, then the BuildOptions method, and then the ListPeople method in order and conclude the program execution by adding a simple statement to make sure the console doesn't close automatically at the end of execution. After modification, the Main method should appear as follows:

```
static void Main(string[] args)
{
    BuildConfiguration();
    BuildOptions();
    ListPeople();
```

```
    Console.WriteLine("Press any key to exit");
    Console.ReadKey();
}
```

Running the program should generate a list of 20 names in reverse alphabetical order by last name similar to the output shown in Figure 2-33.

```
C:\APressEntityFramework\Code\Chapter02\EFActivity02_ExistingDbCore\EFActivity02_ExistingDbCore\
Michael Zwilling
Michael Zwilling
Jake Zukowski
Judy Zugelder
Patricia Zubaty
Carla Zubaty
Karin Zimprich
Karin Zimprich
Tiffany Zimmerman
Marc Zimmerman
Krystal Zimmerman
Kimberly Zimmerman
Juanita Zimmerman
Jo Zimmerman
Jenny Zimmerman
Jack Zimmerman
Henry Zimmerman
Curtis Zimmerman
Christy Zimmerman
Candice Zimmerman
Press any key to exit
```

Figure 2-33. *The output from executing the program as connected to the database and listing the last 20 names by last name descending*

Final thoughts

In this past activity, we were able to create the code for working against an existing database in *EFCore* using the reverse-engineering option. We then saw what it would take to set up a connection configuration and inject the options into the context for direct use in code. While we only did a simple query, we can be confident that our database connection code is working as expected, and we are ready to move on to learning some more advanced concepts using Entity Framework.

A final thought to remember before moving on is that with *EFCore*, and likely in *EF vNext*, there will not be any *EDMX* file or any type of visual conceptualization of the database. While this lack of a visual file may be scary to some of us, we need to think about the reasoning behind this approach. Having all of the Entity Framework interaction with the database defined strictly as code is much more robust and maintainable. Additionally, the ability to keep conflicts to a minimum is much more possible with this code-only implementation. The conflicts that happen in source control on a giant *XML* file (such as the *EDMX* file) creates more problems than it ultimately solves. Having the ability to avoid those painful merge operations in the future is a real win for everyone on the team.

Activity 0202: Creating a database-first project in Entity Framework 6

As with creating Entity Framework code libraries, there are a couple of small differences in how *EF6* works against an existing database. In this activity, we'll look at how a project can utilize Entity Framework against an existing database in the *EF6*/.Net Framework space. I just want to stress that it is my personal belief that these types of projects will remain critical to understand for quite a few more years, which is why I want to give you this resource. If you don't want to work on a .Net Framework, *EF6* project, please feel free to move on to the next chapter. If you want to work on the project but don't want to go through the setup, get a copy of the files `Activity0202_ExistingDbNetFrameworkEF6_Starter`. With that solution, get the project up and running and then skip to step 3.

Step 1: Create the project and solution

To begin, we need to create a new .Net Framework C# Console application. Using the filters, select the language C# and the Type Console to easily filter for the correct project. Make sure to select the .Net Framework template as shown in Figure 2-34.

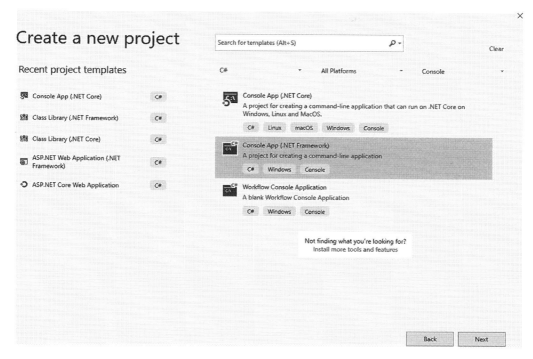

Figure 2-34. *Create a new C# .Net Framework Console application*

Name the project *Activity0202_ExistingDbNetFrameworkEF6*. Make sure to place the project in a location that makes it easy for you to find in the future (see Figure 2-35).

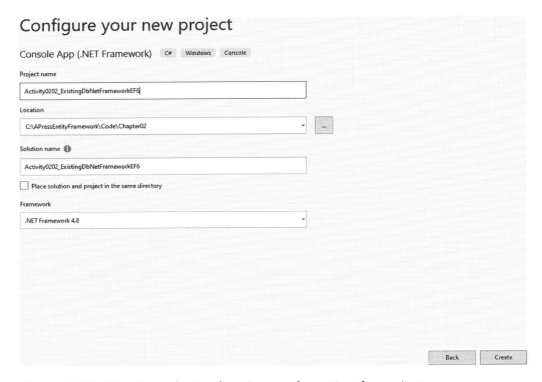

Figure 2-35. *Naming, selecting location, and creating the project*

Step 2: Reference the code for the .Net Framework with EF6 Library created in Chapter 1, Activity Supplemental Information

After creating the console application, reference the project from Chapter 1 where we created our .Net Framework Entity Framework *EF6* library.

If you are not using a repository at this point, I recommend making a copy of the activity one files for ease of reuse and recovery.

Copy the project from Chapter 1 to the folder with your recently created solution. Figure 2-36 shows what your folder structure should look like.

APressEntityFramework › Code › Chapter02 › Activity0202_ExistingDbNetFrameworkEF6		
Name ^	Type	Size
.git	File folder	
.vs	File folder	
Activity0202_ExistingDbNetFrameworkEF6	File folder	
EF_Activity01_NetFramework	File folder	
.gitignore	GITIGNORE File	7 KB
Activity0202_ExistingDbNetFrameworkEF...	Visual Studio Solu...	2 KB

Figure 2-36. *A potential folder structure for your two projects and the new solution*

After setting the folders and code structure, add a reference to the project within the solution. First, right-click the Solution and select Add ➤ Existing Project as shown in Figure 2-37.

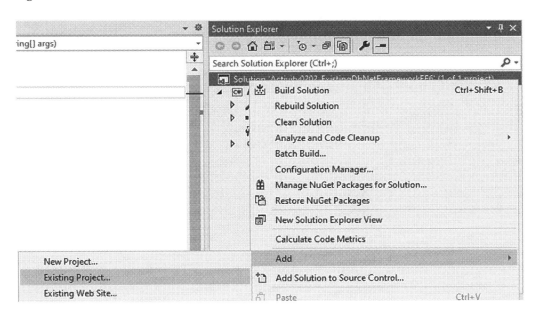

Figure 2-37. *Add an existing project to the solution*

Browse to the location on your drive where the copy of the *EF_Activity_01_
NetFramework* code project is located and add that to your solution. When completed,
your project structure should look like what is shown in Figure 2-38.

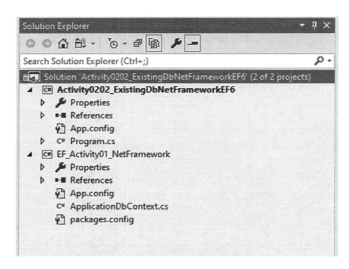

Figure 2-38. *A view of the Solution Explorer after adding the existing project*

After adding the new project, add the existing project as a reference
to the main console project. To do this, right-click the main *Activity0202_
ExistingDbNetFrameworkEF6* project and select Add Reference (note, although you
cannot see the project name in Figure 2-39, I right-clicked the *Activity0202_Existing...*
project as shown in Figure 2-38).

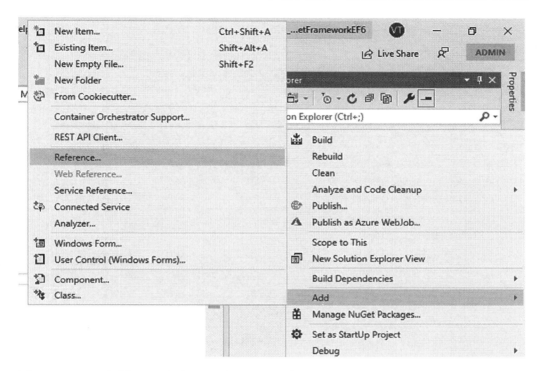

Figure 2-39. *Add an existing project as a reference*

Selecting Add Reference brings up the dialog to choose an existing project from the solution. Choose the EF_Activity01_NetFramework project and complete the operation to add it as a reference as shown in Figure 2-40.

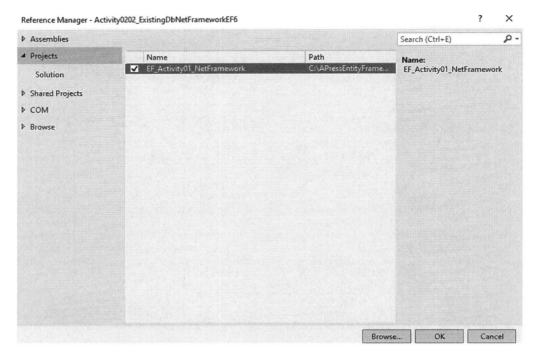

Figure 2-40. *Selecting the existing project to add as a reference*

After correctly adding the project and referencing it, build the project. If there are any errors, resolve them. After the successful build, the project should look similar to what is shown in Figure 2-41.

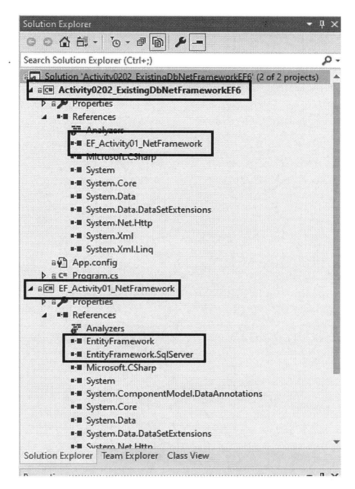

Figure 2-41. *A view of the Solution Explorer after correctly referencing the existing project*

Step 3: Use the ADO.Net Entity Data Model to create a DBContext

There are a couple of approaches we can take in an *EF6* project to do the database-first approach. In this part, we'll examine what it takes to do this with the context generator.

Begin by right-clicking the *EF_Activity01_NetFramework* project and selecting Add ➤ New Item as shown in Figure 2-42.

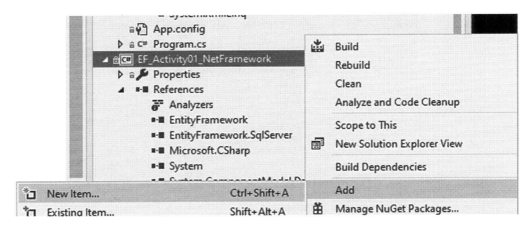

Figure 2-42. *Adding a new item to the existing database project*

From the menu *Visual C# Items* on the left, select Data and then select the ADO.
NET Entity Data Model (note the many different options available). Name your model
AdventureWorks to match the restored database name from earlier in the chapter (see
Figure 2-43 for clarity).

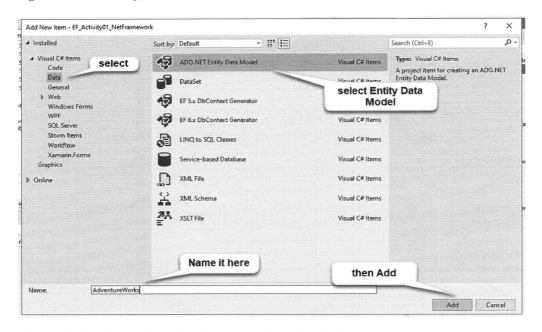

Figure 2-43. *Using the ADO.Net Entity Data Model to create a new
AdventureWorks data model*

In the next step, we can create the designer or set it up as a code first from database. Here, we'll select the EF Designer from database option. Review Figure 2-44 to see the selection.

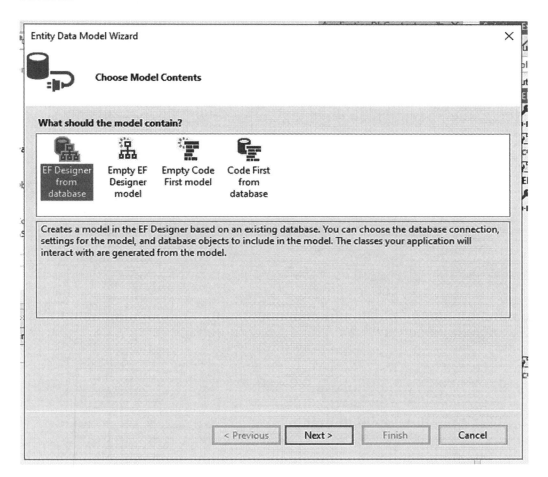

Figure 2-44. *Selecting the EF Designer from database*

After selecting the EF Designer from database and hitting Next to move through the wizard, the next step we need to do is create a new connection. Use the New Connection button to start setting up a new database connection to your installation of *AdventureWorks*.

Select the option for using a `Microsoft SQL Server Data source`, use the default data provider in the data provider drop-down, and, optionally, uncheck `Always use this selection` and then select `Continue` as shown in Figure 2-45.

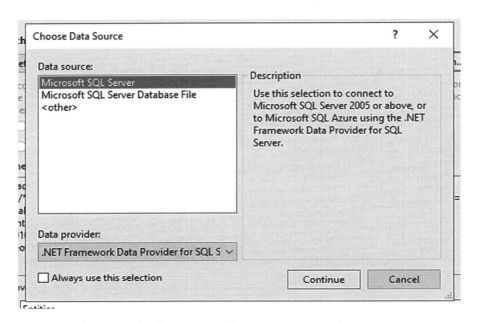

Figure 2-45. *Choosing the data source for a new connection*

Select your database server from the drop-down if it shows up. If it does not, you'll need to type the name of your server. This is likely going to be *(local)* or the name of your machine, followed by *\SQLExpress* based on how you installed *SQL Express* (or if you are running *SQL Developer edition*, you may use *localhost*). You will know you have the server name correct when you can see the database in the list of the database to select from, as shown in Figure 2-46.

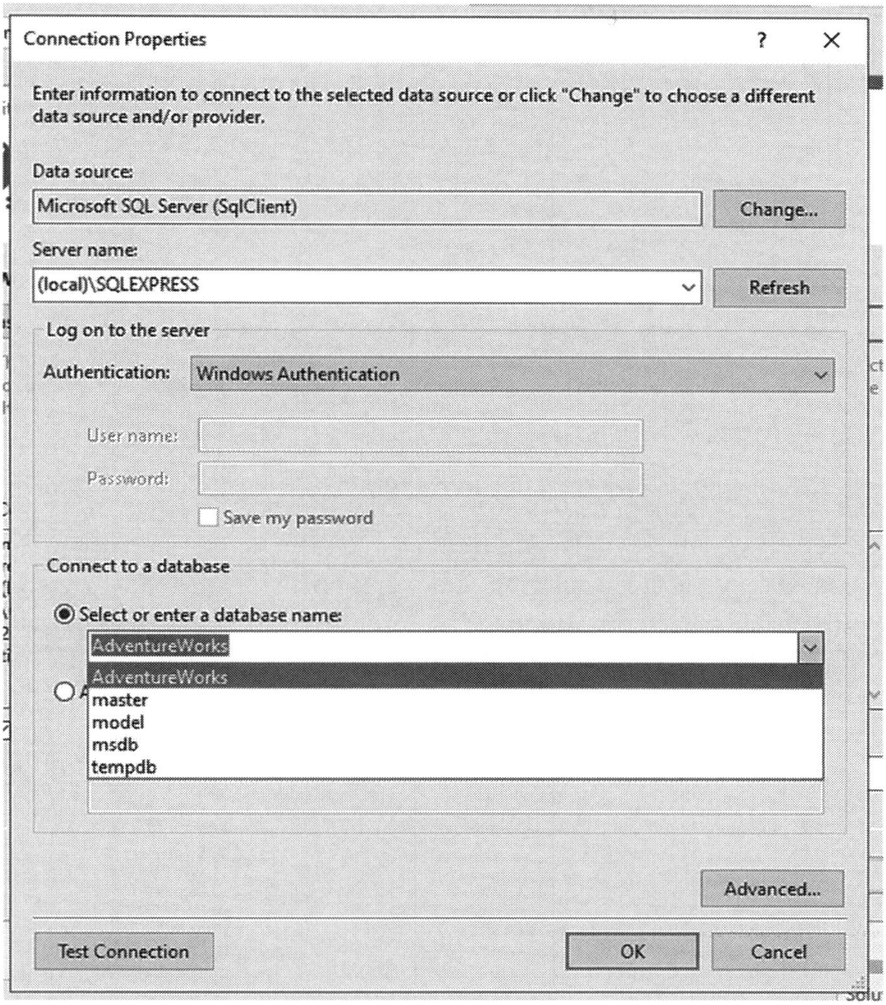

Figure 2-46. *Setting the connection properties*

Make sure to always hit the Test Connection button to ensure your database connection is set as expected (see Figure 2-47).

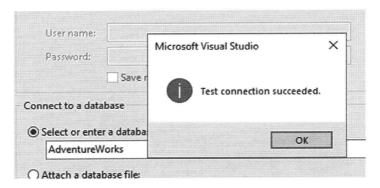

Figure 2-47. *Testing the connection success message*

Continue through the wizard to the next step, where the connection string information is set. Make sure to note the name of the entities for the connection string. We'll use the default *AdventureWorksEntities* in order to easily identify the connection later. Review Figure 2-48 for more information.

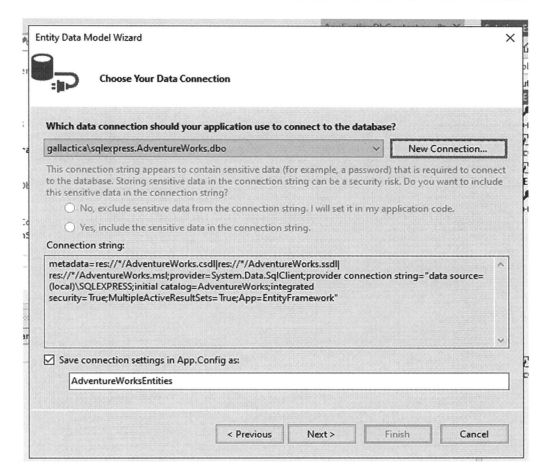

Figure 2-48. *Setting the connection string name and continuing through the wizard*

In the next step, we get to choose what to include in the database entity sets. Here you can select specific tables, procedures, and other objects you want access to in your code via Entity Framework. An important thing to remember is that you can always update the model later if you want to make changes or your database structure/schema changes.

For the purposes of brevity, I'll select all of the existing database objects and will keep all the selections checked (see Figure 2-49). Additionally, the default name *AdventureWorksModel* will be my named model.

If you wanted to separate the lines of business, you could create multiple models, selecting only by schema and naming each model appropriately.

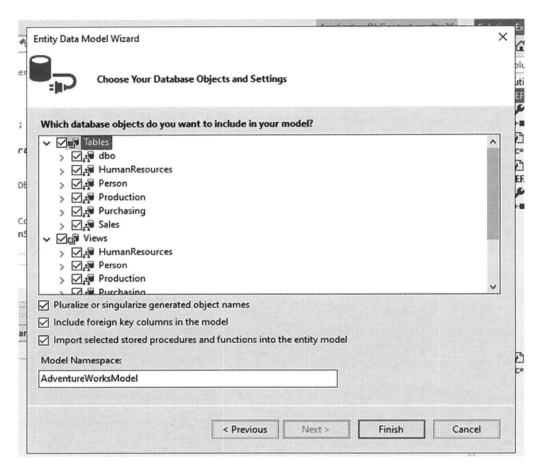

Figure 2-49. *Selecting the database objects to generate and naming the model*

On completion, the model will be generated and is easily able to be reviewed. This would be the EF Context you would reference going forward to work against your existing database. Figure 2-50 shows the *EDMX* diagram and files as generated.

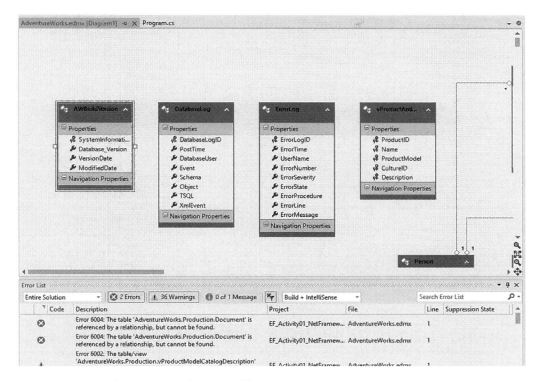

Figure 2-50. *The generated EDMX file*

You might note that there were a couple of errors during generation. The overall complexity of the *AdventureWorks* database and a couple of bad relationships have been found referencing a table that doesn't exist. In the real world, I'd need to fix this in my *DB* Schema or determine why these relationships are bad and potentially remove them and regenerate the *EDMX* file. At any point, the *EDMX* file can be updated by right-clicking the designer window and selecting *Update Model from Database* (shown in Figure 2-51).

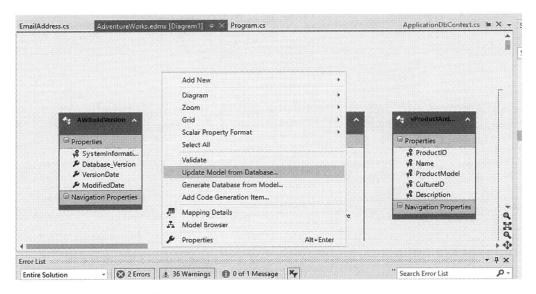

Figure 2-51. *Update from Database*

Also note the reverse is possible – Generate Database from Model.

Another note is to remember that each model is under the *t4* templates section of the overall *EDMX* document. In the future, if your database needs to change, you would update the *EDMX* document from database after applying database changes, which would regenerate all of the database model code. You should therefore **never** rely on changes that you make directly in the models here in this code, as those changes will get blown away the next time the model is regenerated. This information is noted in the generated model files directly, as shown in Figure 2-52.

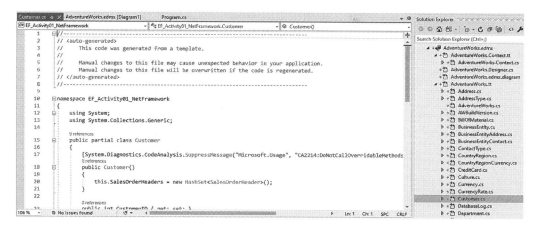

Figure 2-52. *Models are generated from the t4 templates when the EDMX file is updated*

Step 4: Connect and display data

In this step, we'll connect from our console application to display the data from the database very quickly. We will not go past a basic operation here, but this will give us enough context to take it further should we need to. In the future, we'll only be focusing on the concepts and interactions with Entity Framework, so once you have your connection established, the rest of the concepts can be applied at your convenience.

In the console application, we'll need to add the connection string to the `App.config` file. This connection string is important because the startup project must reference the connection and we don't want to hard-code that information. Copy the connection string from the *EF_Activity01_NetFramework* project to your *Activity0202_ExistingDbNetFrameworkEF6* `App.config` file.

As a note, the connection string should be something similar to this:

```
<connectionStrings>

    <add name="AdventureWorksEntities" connectionString="metadata=r
    es://*/AdventureWorks.csdl|res://*/AdventureWorks.ssdl|res://*/
    AdventureWorks.msl;provider=System.Data.SqlClient;provider connection
    string=&quot;data source=(local)\SQLEXPRESS;initial catalog=Adventure
    Works;integrated security=True;MultipleActiveResultSets=True;App=Entity
    Framework&quot;" providerName="System.Data.EntityClient" />
  </connectionStrings>
```

Place the connection string entry in the file below the `<startup>..</startup>` xml node and before the closing `</configuration>` tag.

Next, open the NuGet Package Manager by selecting `Tools ➤ NuGet Package Manager ➤ Manage NuGet Packages for Solution`, or by right-clicking the *ExistingDBNetFramework* project and selecting Manage NuGet Packages.

Make sure to include the correct version of *Entity Framework* by selecting the `Installed` tab, and then on the Entity Framework package, check to include in the console project and then select `Install`. Review Figure 2-53 for clarity.

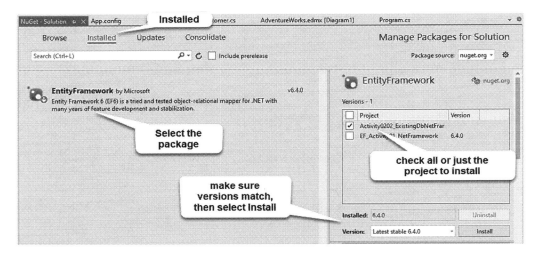

Figure 2-53. *Install Entity Framework on the console application*

Select `OK` and accept any changes you are prompted to select.

Now that the package is installed and the connection string is in `App.config`, let's add some code to the `Main` method in `Program.cs` to connect to the person table in the database, retrieve, and display some data:

```
using (var db = new AdventureWorksEntities())
{
    var people = db.People.OrderByDescending(x => x.LastName).Take(20);

    foreach (var person in people)
    {
        Console.WriteLine($"{person.FirstName} {person.LastName}");
    }
```

```
    Console.WriteLine("Press any key to exit");
    Console.ReadKey();
}
```

Please note that you'll need to add a using statement to your
ExistingDbNetFrameworkEF6 project for the reference to the AdventureWorksEntities
to make sure your code can find the context. My using statement was as follows: using
EF_Activity01_NetFramework;

And the output should look something like what you see here in Figure 2-54.

Figure 2-54. *Output from a simple query against an existing database, listing 20
people ordered by last name descending*

EF6 from an existing database: Final thoughts

In this activity, we were able to create a context from an existing database and connect
to it in the console application. Going forward, we would be able to interact against the
database context with other using statements and valid queries just like what we have done
here. While we only queried (read from the database) and did not actually do any create,
update, or delete operations at this point, using *Entity Framework* to modify the data is
something that would be entirely possible with the context as generated in this activity.

Final thoughts for this chapter

In this chapter, we've seen how to generate an *EF* database context against an existing database in either the *EFCore* (and likely the *EFvNext*) approach or the *EF6* approach. To this point in the book, we haven't done a lot against the database; however, at this point, we should have no trouble integrating our learning into these projects going forward, and we are positioned well to start learning some more advanced concepts.

Overall things we learned

- Use the Entity Framework tools in *EFCore* (and likely *vNext*) to generate a context against an existing database.

- *EFCore* and likely *EFvNext* do not have a database model. Instead, all contexts are generated in code. Updates to the database require a new context generation.

- Traditional .Net Framework *EF6* can exist with a database model *EDMX* that provides a visual diagram of all included database objects.

- Updates to the database in EF6 require regenerating the model from the database in the *EDMX* designer.

- Both of these approaches shown here do not employ migrations and therefore rely on other manual database operations to create the physical objects in the database.

- Because there are no migrations, database objects are not automatically included in the repository along with your codebase.

Moving forward

Now that we've seen how to create an *EF* library that interacts with the database for an existing database, it's time to examine how to create an *EF* library that works against the database when the database is greenfield. We'll cover this concept in the next chapter where we'll discuss the *code-first* approach to the database.

CHAPTER 3

Entity Framework: Code First

In this chapter, we are going to look at what it takes to get up and running with Entity Framework using the code-first approach. As we move through this chapter, we'll learn about the code-first approach to Entity Framework, and we'll take note of some of the advantages that working with a code-first approach brings to our development process. We'll conclude this chapter by working through some activities to create a couple of code-first Entity Framework projects in *EFCore* and *EF6*.

Code first doesn't always mean code first

Even though the name *code first* implies that the database doesn't exist until code is written, it is entirely possible to employ a code-first approach with an existing database, as well as in a new greenfield project. As with any development scenario, there are multiple things to consider when attempting to determine if the code-first approach is correct for your project.

When not to use the code-first approach

Sometimes when trying to determine when something is the right answer, the way to start is to determine when it is not the right answer. That being said, in most production applications that you'll encounter in today's world, there are very few reasons that code first doesn't make a lot of sense.

The primary reason to avoid using the code-first approach would relate to having a legacy system that is not capable of supporting the required tools, for example, a project that was written in any .Net Framework prior to .Net 3.5. In those projects, Entity Framework didn't exist, so using the code-first approach is simply not possible.

© Brian L. Gorman 2020
B. L. Gorman, *Practical Entity Framework*, https://doi.org/10.1007/978-1-4842-6044-9_3

Another reason that you may be forced to avoid the code-first approach could be organizational restrictions. Perhaps there are greater security concerns at play, making it against the law or highly dangerous for your company to expose so much power over the data structure to any developer through code. Perhaps your company will not allow anyone but that one mysterious *DBA* to touch the database for any reason. In both of the previous cases, there may be some training or education that can overcome the issues, or it may truly just be impossible to work with code first in your development efforts.

Yet another reason to avoid using the code-first approach with EF could be due to personal preference. Perhaps you don't like the normalization structure required to use an ORM. You might also have another solution that you prefer for database interaction, such as F# type providers. Maybe you've been using NHibernate and you don't want to change something that you know already works, although you could also do code first with NHibernate.

A final reason to avoid using code first could simply be that there is a high risk of losing data in a mature database. While it is entirely possible to overcome this issue, there will always be a chance that forgetting to plan for database migrations that affect data can (and perhaps will) happen. Before leaning on this argument as the reason not to choose code first in your solution, please remember that you would have to overcome the same data loss issues in traditional database development and that the solution is usually exactly the same. For example, it is entirely possible to create a migration that runs a script that backs up data from a table and then run a migration to modify the table, truncating or causing data loss, and then another final migration to restore the original data massaged to fit the new table structure, just as you would traditionally have to do with scripts to modify the database structure. As we'll soon see, the advantages of a code-first approach could even make it a better choice in this situation.

When to use the code-first approach

If you're wondering when you should use the code-first approach going forward, simply put, the answer is likely going to be every time you can. While there may still be situations as discussed in the previous section that exist where you cannot use the code-first approach, anytime you can use code first, you should use code first.

With *EFCore* and *EFvNext*, there is no longer an ability to create a model file like the *EDMX* file we saw in the previous chapter. While we can always generate a reverse-engineered database, the fact remains that we will likely have a model-based approach to all development going forward. This is a very good thing for several reasons.

Code first in an existing project

Now that you've bought in and are ready to build out a code-first approach with Entity Framework, what do you do when you have an existing and mature project, with an existing database? Since the database already exists, we could begin by scaffolding the data models such as we've seen in the reverse-engineering approach to get the models auto-generated in our solution, as well as have the *DBContext* generated and populated for us (as we've seen in Chapter 2). To make the project operate in a code-first manner, we would then just need to enable migrations and start working with the migrations against the data structures.

From then on, the project would be able to continue to build out new models and database objects and apply further migrations as needed. A great level of care would still be needed in this approach, however, as the database that is already mature needs to be protected from accidental changes that might truncate data from tables or break critical performance enhancements (such as a change dropping a view or an index might do), especially if other line-of-business applications are relying on these data structures for normal operation.

Code first in a new project against a mature database

Another approach that might be taken when working with Entity Framework in a code-first manner might be to develop a new application, but still need to use an existing database.

In a situation such as this, the development team will need to again use a great deal of caution to avoid breaking legacy functionality that might exist in other applications. Additionally, any changes made in the code-first project would need to be propagated into any legacy applications to avoid potentially causing outages or even more disastrous consequences for other business units in the organization.

Code first in a new project with a new database

This greenfield scenario is an obvious choice for working with a code-first approach. Even when we don't want to use migrations, at some point we still need data models that define how to work with the various database objects in order to use Entity Framework.

Since the project is new and has a new database to accompany it, using code first will provide the best flexibility and ease of use from our codebase. In this case, it only makes sense to use the code-first approach.

The benefits of a well-executed code-first development effort

In case there is still any doubt about the level of success your team can achieve by using the code-first approach, I'd like to take a moment to highlight some of the greatest benefits of using the code-first approach.

Ability to get up and running quickly

Since the entire database structure is defined in code via migrations, any developer can open the project, validate the connection string works, and run a simple command to get the database in the exact state that it is in any environment where it is deployed. Obviously, there would still be work with some data, as while some data would likely be created by seeding the database, there would be a number of data tables that need human interaction. This is no different than the issues any project using a database would encounter.

A complete record of database changes in source control

As mentioned previously, using the code-first approach allows for every piece of the database to be imperatively defined in code. As the structure and needs of the database were changed, these changes were implemented in code files and a new migration was created and executed to affect the changes on the database.

In the past, you might have tried migrations and found them to be tricky. In fact, migrations before EFCore might have even caused you pain when multiple developers created conflicting migrations. Even if the migrations didn't conflict, you still were forced to re-scaffold your migration if another developer pushed theirs first since the overall model hash code saved in the database would be different. With EFCore, most of these pain points have been eliminated, and, although migration conflicts can still happen, they are mainly the result of conflicting changes to the same database objects.

Since our code is defined directly within the project in this approach, the files and changes are all tracked in source control. There is no longer any need to create a database project with a bunch of generated and non-generated scripts, or worse, manually put your scripts into source control and hope developers keep them up to date.

Having the changes in source control is a very important advantage and should not be taken lightly. If drives and backups fail, there is always a potential of losing your database entirely. Even if you don't lose your database, when a database failure happens, you would likely still lose all the transactions that had been run since the previous backup. Although both database and backup failure combined is rare and may never happen, if it did, and you still have your project code, migrations could be run to restore the structure and seed data from the database. Really this feature is more useful for developer machines. As soon as one developer's changes make it into your developer source branch, other developers can update their own local database with a few quick commands. This is highly advantageous when it comes to avoiding conflicts and bugs.

Agility when needing to revert to a previous state

With the code being in source control, EF migrations also have the added benefit that, when written correctly, can easily roll back a change against the database. Rolling back a change can be a destructive event that loses data, but this is also something that is rarely, if ever, done in production. In fact, there is a camp where some users don't rely on rollbacks at all. The theory there being that just adding another migration to move the database back in a forward direction is a better approach. Either way, you're still going to need to plan for how the data is affected.

With the ability to revert, however, it is extremely easy to set a local developer database to match the exact state a database was in at any point of development. For example, it is easy to roll back the database to the state in time when a bug was introduced to your codebase or a patch was released. This allows for effectively coding against the database as it was at that time, making it easier and safer to release a common modification across all official releases of your project or to patch a bug fix.

Another advantage of the migrations is the fact that changes can be reverted at will. For example, if a feature is released and then eventually eliminated, migrations allow the feature to continue to exist at a patch level but to be removed from future development.

Having this history and ability to easily reset the database to the state it needs to be is all managed by the code in the migrations. Therefore, as a developer, you don't have to spend your time trying to remember which scripts to run and testing to make sure your tables and other object structures are correct for the patch, fix, or feature on which you are working.

Shifting from declarative to imperative database programming

Another important concept with the use of code-first database development is that we are making a conscious transition to *imperative* database programming and saying goodbye to *declarative* programming around our database.

Imperative programming is the concept that as a developer, we are directly defining what should happen, thereby locking in the details of the implementation, leaving little to interpretation or fluctuation of implementation.

Declarative programming is just getting to an end result, regardless of how you get there. In this paradigm, often the details of the implementation can be murky or fluent, as long as the result is achieved.

For example, a declarative approach to development around the database might look something like you know there is a table that holds some data that was defined somewhere. You could query that data and perhaps connect to another table or maybe a view to build out a result set, but as long as the data shows up, it is not important how you got it to render. Also, you can sort of count on some fields being in the table for the important information like name, age, date of birth, email, or maybe even a phone number, but it may have changed, so you better double-check before counting on that data. If the data isn't there, or has changed, maybe I can ask to store that important information somewhere and someone can build out the database scripts so that I can get it eventually.

An imperative approach is more defined, and code first is most definitely imperative by nature. Every database structure is exactly modeled in code. This means you know exactly what tables exist and what fields exist on those tables. In fact, you can easily create an instance of a model that holds exactly the correct data, with exactly the correct limitations that exist in the database, including type and any other constraints like length or range. Furthermore, relationships are directly defined, so you can be certain that a foreign key exists in each related table and you can easily query and populate related data.

For the most part, Entity Framework has always been somewhat imperative, with well-defined structures in place. However, the code-first approach has solidified the imperative approach with the ability to force the database to conform to specific requirements, rather than relying on things to potentially be implemented correctly in the database.

It's time to see code-first database programming in action

Now that we've seen some of the advantages and reasons behind using a code-first approach, it's time to dive in with a couple of activities. These activities will help us learn more about how the code-first approach works and also see the power that it gives us to work with this approach.

One thing we will not see here is what it would take to put code first into an existing project that is mature. The overall approach would be the same as if using against an existing database. Code would then need to be updated to start working against the EF library for new and maintenance development, and the original connections and code (such as *ADO.Net* implementation) could remain in place.

In the next three activities, we'll look at using code-first approach in a new greenfield project in both *EFCore* and *EF6*. We'll also use *EFCore* to create a new implementation against a mature database.

I want to take a final moment before diving into some coding activities to make sure a couple of other things are clear. We're about to learn how to implement the Entity Framework against an existing and a new database in *EFCore* and also an existing *EF6* project (this would be a scenario such as upgrading an older application to use *EF6* in the .Net Framework).

Please note that in order to keep the focus on the actual implementation and use of Entity Framework, I've chosen to make the startup projects work as console applications. We all know this is not likely to be how your project will work in the real world. However, learning to do things like making web controllers and displaying data on views or rendering information to Xamarin forms, or other similar practical activities, is outside of the scope of this book. It is my belief that if you are a web developer or a Xamarin developer or a UWP or WPF developer, you already have the skills you need in those arenas (or you will likely have resources available to learn them). Therefore, the choice to restrict the GUI portion of these activities to a minimal implementation is a conscious choice.

With that choice comes a small price, however, which I feel is important to address. If you are building out solutions in WPF, UWP, Xamarin, and/or ASP.Net MVC, it is highly likely that those project templates scaffold out an implementation directly to Entity Framework for you, so going through the setup and working in a new manner may not be necessary in many of these cases. Even so, learning how to build out a solution from the ground up will position you to rearchitect your solutions to make a more robust implementation. By the end of these activities, you'll likely have everything you need to understand how to build out an Entity Framework code-first solution into any existing or new project.

Activity 0301: Creating a new code-first implementation against an existing database project in EFCore

In this first activity, we're going to go through building out an *EFCore* code-first implementation against an existing database. This will give us the opportunity to see what it might be like to spin up a new project in a mature business environment, against a mature database that likely has other line-of-business applications working against it.

Use the starter files, or your project from Chapter 2

To begin, we're going to pick up where we left off at the end of Chapter 2, where we had built out a reverse-engineered database project against the *AdventureWorks* database, using Entity Framework Core.

If for some reason you do not have these files or you simply want a fresh start, the code resources for this book include a starter zip file package for this activity called `Activity0301_EFCore_Starter`.

I did modify the implementation a bit to use a singleton configuration builder and of course named my project for this chapter; other than that, everything else is the same as where we landed at the end of Chapter 2. At any point, you can use the starter files or leverage the finished files `Activity0301_EFCore_Final` as a reference during this activity. At this point, I'm assuming you are well versed in getting started with Visual Studio and getting a project open or up and running, so we're going to dive right in. Moving the builder code to a singleton is not necessary; I've simply done this to get the code out of the way of our learning. If you want to see how to implement, you can review the implementation in the starter files for `activity 0301`.

Step 1: Setup and getting started

To begin, either open the starter files entitled `Activity0301_EFCore_Starter.zip` or your previous files from Chapter 2. Once the project is opened, validate that you have the correct database connection in the appsettings.json file(s). Once that is correct, validate that your project structure is similar to what is shown in Figure 3-1.

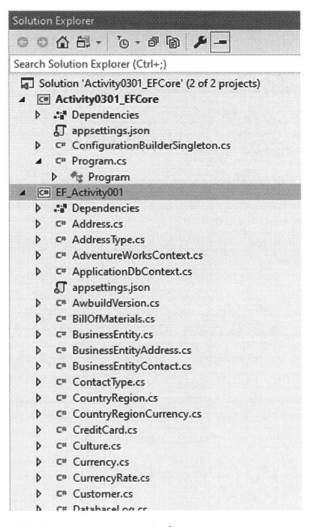

Figure 3-1. *The initial project structure is shown*

Once you've validated the project setup, run the project to verify that it is working correctly as per the EFCore activity from Chapter 2.

If we run the project as is, we get a console output of the list of the last 20 non-distinct users in the person table as shown in Figure 3-2.

```
C:\APressEntityFramework\Code\Chapter03\Activity0301_EFCore
Michael Zwilling
Michael Zwilling
Jake Zukowski
Judy Zugelder
Patricia Zubaty
Carla Zubaty
Karin Zimprich
Karin Zimprich
Tiffany Zimmerman
Marc Zimmerman
Krystal Zimmerman
Kimberly Zimmerman
Juanita Zimmerman
Jo Zimmerman
Jenny Zimmerman
Jack Zimmerman
Henry Zimmerman
Curtis Zimmerman
Christy Zimmerman
Candice Zimmerman
Press any key to exit
```

Figure 3-2. *Simple console output at the start of the project*

This is essentially where we had left off using the existing database at the end of Chapter 2.

Step 2: Make sure EF is ready to scaffold migrations

Ensure that you have installed the `Microsoft.EntityFrameworkCore.Design` package on the starter project. To do this, right-click the Solution and select `Manage NuGet Packages for Solution`. Once the window opens, select the Installed tab and then make sure that `Microsoft.EntityFrameworkCore.Design` is installed with the latest version of *EFCore*.

If the design package is not installed, switch to browse and then find the package and install it to the starter project. The EF_Activity001 project will not need this library. You can see what this looks like as shown in Figure 3-3.

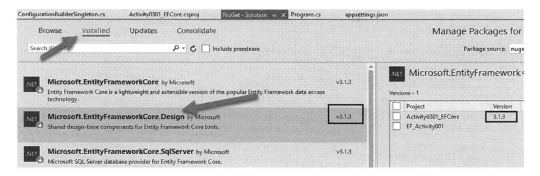

Figure 3-3. *Use the Manage NuGet Packages for Solution dialog to ensure that the Microsoft.EntityFrameworkCore.Design package is installed*

Step 3: Create the initial migration

Now let's create our *initial migration* in order to begin working with the code-first approach in our application.

To begin, let's try running a command in the *PMC*. The command to run is add-migration "Initial Migration." Before running the command, make sure that you have selected the Entity Framework library project that contains the actual database context. If you fail to select the correct project, you will get an error. Figure 3-4 shows the incorrect project selected.

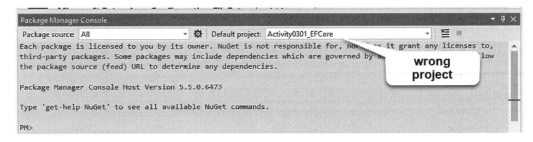

Figure 3-4. *Running a command with an incorrect default project selected*

Running this command generates the following error as shown in Figure 3-5.

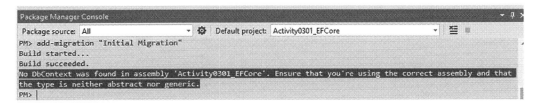

Figure 3-5. *The error received when trying to run migrations against an incorrect default project*

Change the Default project drop-down to point to the project with the actual *AdventureWorks DBContext* in it, and then run the command again. Do you think it will work? Figure 3-6 shows the outcome.

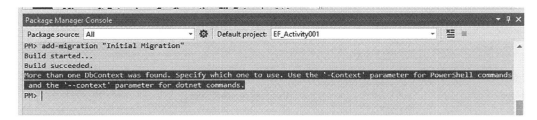

Figure 3-6. *Failure to create database migration when multiple contexts are present*

In this case, it didn't work, because we have two database contexts in our project. If you remember back to Chapter 1, we created a context by default for our use. Then in Chapter 2 we generated a new context. Up to this point, we haven't used migrations, so we directly instantiated the correct context when we needed it. Now, with two contexts, Visual Studio doesn't know which one to use to scaffold the migration. Later in the book, we'll cover how to work with multiple contexts. For now, let's just delete the unused context from this project. Find the file *ApplicationDbContext.cs* that we created in the *EF_Activity001* project, *right-click it*, and select *Delete*. This is shown in more detail in Figure 3-7.

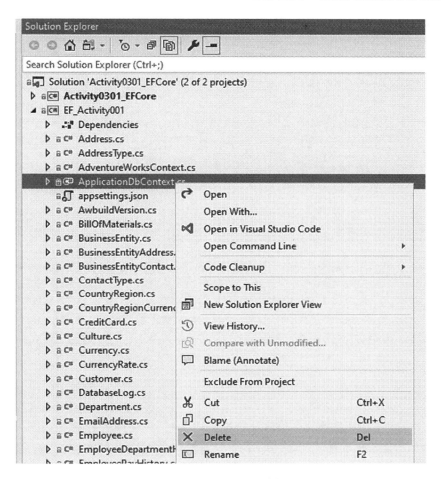

Figure 3-7. *Delete the unused database context file*

When the warning pops up about permanent deletion, just select *OK* and allow the file to be destroyed.

It is important to remember that changes to the structure of the project require a rebuild before attempting to add the migration. After deleting the second database context, remember to rebuild the solution before moving on.

If we fail to rebuild and try to apply the migration, we will get the exact same error as before, letting us know that more than one *DbContext* was found.

With the file now deleted and the project rebuilt, once again, let's attempt to make our first migration. Do you think it will work this time? Review Figure 3-8 to see what happens when we run the command again.

```
 4    namespace EF_Activity001.Migrations
 5    {
          1 reference
 6        public partial class InitialMigration : Migration
 7        {
              0 references
 8            protected override void Up(MigrationBuilder migrationBuilder)
 9            {
10                migrationBuilder.EnsureSchema(
11                    name: "Person");
12
13                migrationBuilder.EnsureSchema(
14                    name: "Production");
15
16                migrationBuilder.EnsureSchema(
17                    name: "Sales");
18
19                migrationBuilder.EnsureSchema(
20                    name: "HumanResources");
21
22                migrationBuilder.EnsureSchema(
23                    name: "Purchasing");
```

106 % ⊘ No issues found   Ln:

```
Package Manager Console
Package source: All        ▼  ⚙  Default project: EF_Activity001        ▼
PM> add-migration "Initial Migration"
Build started...
Build succeeded.
To undo this action, use Remove-Migration.
PM>
```

Figure 3-8. *The initial migration has been created*

Step 4: Review the migration

Now that we have a migration ready to go, we might be tempted to jump right in and run the migration. This would be a very big mistake, as the initial migration scaffolded has a lot of tables that it is planning to create which already exist in our database.

Remember our earlier discussion of the pros and cons of using the code-first approach? This is one of the cons. Right now, we have no migrations applied in the database, so the migration builder thinks we need to create all the tables. However, our database already has all the tables, so we need to make sure that they don't get created for us. Review Figure 3-9 to see the table creation statements as generated in the migration.

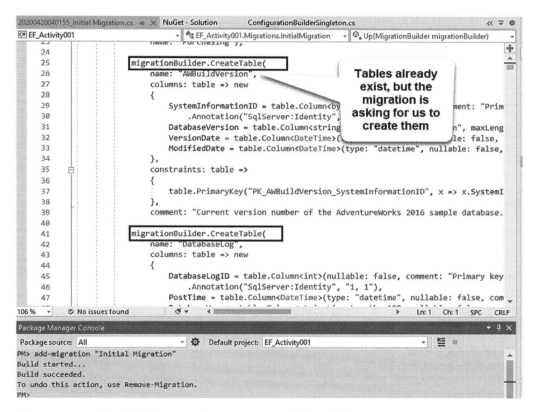

Figure 3-9. *The initial migration contains all the table create statements, even though tables already exist in the database*

So, what should we do next? There are actually a couple of approaches we can take. One approach would be to comment out everything in the "Up" method and apply the migration with the update-database command.

This approach should work, but it begs the question about what the next developer would do, and the developer after that, if they have a fresh start on an existing database on their machine. A potential solution to that problem could be to run the migration with the code commented out and then propagate the changes and run on other machines or simply modify other developer databases so that the first migration would appear to have already been applied. However, no matter what we do here, care would need to be exercised when running for the first time in production to avoid any potential problems.

Since our database is existing, there should not be a reason that we need to generate the tables as is. Therefore, let's go ahead and comment out the code in the *Up* method. You could also remove it if you wanted, assuming everyone would have access to an existing sample of the database. Additionally, we will likely never want to delete these existing tables, so let's also entirely delete the code in the *Down* method.

Step 5: Comment out the code in the "Up" method and delete Down method code

Comment out the code in the Up method, and delete the code in the Down method in this initial migration. Since the Up method is very large, collapse the method and then select it; then just hit the key chord ctrl+k and then ctrl+c to apply the block comment. Once that is complete, uncomment the method declaration and closing brace. Figure 3-10 shows how we can comment the code in the migration to avoid execution when the update-database command is run.

```
20200420040155_Initial Migration.cs  ₊ ✕  NuGet - Solution        ConfigurationBuilderSingleton.cs        Activity0301_EFCo

C# EF_Activity001                                            ▼  ⁂ EF_Activity001.Migrations.InitialMigration

2768          //    migrationBuilder.CreateIndex(
2769          //        name: "PXML_Store_Demographics",
2770          //        schema: "Sales",
2771          //        table: "Store",
2772          //        column: "Demographics");
2773
2774          //    migrationBuilder.CreateIndex(
2775          //        name: "AK_Store_rowguid",
2776          //        schema: "Sales",
2777          //        table: "Store",
2778          //        column: "rowguid",
2779          //        unique: true);
2780
2781          //    migrationBuilder.CreateIndex(
2782          //        name: "IX_Store_SalesPersonID",
2783          //        schema: "Sales",
2784          //        table: "Store",
2785 💡       //        column: "SalesPersonID");
2786          }
2787
              0 references
2788          protected override void Down(MigrationBuilder migrationBuilder)
2789          {
2790              //we will NEVER roll back the db since it was already existing.
2791          }
2792      }
2793  }
2794
```

Figure 3-10. *The Up method code is commented out and the Down method code is revmoved for the initial migration*

With the migration prepared to run with no effect on our data, let's feel free to run the update-database command in the *PMC* and see what happens.

There is no need to fear this command right now. If this operation goes sideways, we can restore from backup. Please do not do this against a production database until you are certain the results you want will be achieved.

In the PMC, run the command update-database as shown in Figure 3-11.

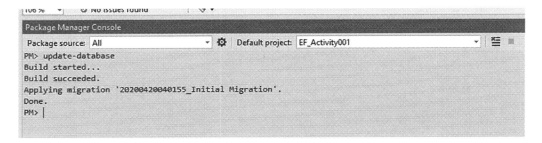

Figure 3-11. *Running the update-database command in the PMC*

Step 6: Examine the database

Looking directly at the database, we can now see that a table was added, and we have an entry in it. Notice the command I ran earlier performed an insert into the database table __EFMigrationsHistory. Let's look at this table in our database. Figure 3-12 shows the database structure after the migration is executed.

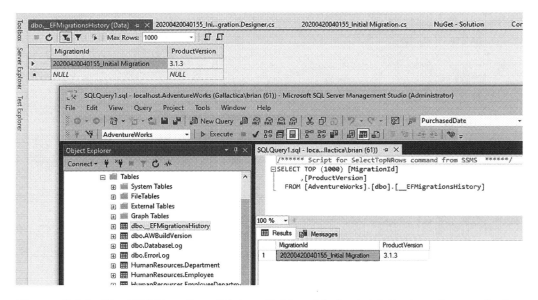

Figure 3-12. *The EF Migrations History Table with the initial migration tracked as having been run. Note that the table can be viewed from SSMS or from within Visual Studio using the Server Explorer*

Now that we have the data reviewed, we can see how EF knows what migrations to apply in our database. If the migration exists by name in the table (MigrationId column), then the update-database command will not run that migration.

Having the name of a migration in the table prevents execution. For other developers and production databases, we could simply script out and then add the __EFMigrations table to developer or production databases and then insert the first entry by Id so that the initial migration will never be executed on another database.

Here we see the name of the database migration as generated, which is nothing more than a datetime stamp with the name of the migration as named by us. It would be very easy to script the __EFMigrations table, insert it into any database that is going to work with this project, and insert the first record into the table to prevent the migration from ever being run.

Step 7: Add another migration to see what happens

What happens if we leave the code commented out? Let's leave the migration as is and then add another migration to find out. Run the command add-migration "testing migrations" to see what is generated. Figure 3-13 shows the expected output when no changes exist, which is what we should see now.

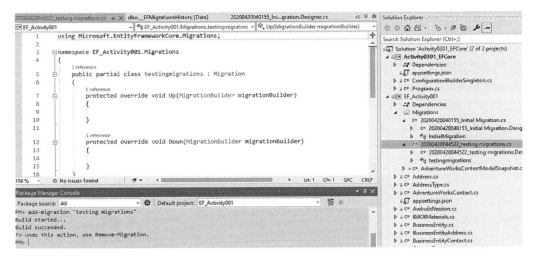

Figure 3-13. *Adding a second migration*

As we can see, this migration is blank. Therefore, we do not need to uncomment our code (in fact, we could remove it) from the first initial migration. With that in mind, we should be ok to push to another machine with the existing database or even our production machine without fear of causing any problems in the future. That being said, it's always wise to make a quick backup before doing something like this, just in case. If you can't get a backup due to regulations, space, or other mitigating factors, then you could consider scheduling your initial deployment to run immediately following your next automated backup.

Step 8: Remove the blank migration

In the last step, we added a migration that has nothing in it. Therefore, we should just remove it from our migrations as it is not accomplishing anything. If you noticed, the last statement in the *PMC* when we ran `update-database` was "*To undo this action, use Remove-Migration.*" Let's go ahead and run that `remove-migration` command now. The command is shown in Figure 3-14.

Figure 3-14. *Removing a migration*

In this case, we had not applied the migration. If for some reason you had run the migration that was blank, you would first need to roll back your migration history to the previous migration and then run the `remove-migration` command. Although we are not covering this in our activity, the command to roll back a migration would be as follows: `update-database -migration [name-of-your-migration]` command; in this case, it is something like `update-database -migration InitialMigration`. Please also note the command is different in *EF6*, where we would specify `-target` instead of `-migration` in the command to roll back a migration [`update-database -target [name-of-your-migration]`].

Final thoughts

In this activity, we saw what it takes to get our database set up to work with code-first migrations when the database already exists. We did not cover how to start modifying the database, but we are position to do so.

The most important takeaways from this activity are as follows:

- It is very easy in *EFCore* to get up and running with code-first against an existing database.

- Make sure to avoid using destructive code in your initial migration. The system should be smart enough from that time on to not try to re-create the database.

- Use the commands add-migration [migration name] and update-database to create and execute migrations.

- Use the command remove-migration to remove a migration that has not been applied to the database. If the migration is applied, use the update-database command with the -migration [migration name] flag to first roll back to the previous migration and then run the remove-migration command.

In the next activity, we'll start fresh with a new project and a new database, and then we'll see what it takes to start modifying data in our new database using code-first migrations. Do not fear, the ability to modify data as shown in the next activity would work in exactly the same manner in our existing database project from this point on.

Activity 0302: Creating a new code-first project in EFCore

In this second activity, we're going to create a new code-first project in *EFCore*. To begin this activity, we're going to start a new project, with a new purpose and setup. We'll set our connection strings as before within the configuration files, and then we'll start working with the code-first approach with a new database. Although you likely have similar code in place, it may be confusing where I'm starting with this activity. For this reason, I recommend that you simply start with the files from the project Activity0302_ EFCoreNewDb_Starter which has been pre-configured with a code library and startup

97

console project. Feel free to update the versions of *EFCore* as to the latest version at the time you are starting this project.

What are we building?

In this activity, we're going to build a simple database to manage inventory. Inventory items could be any object you have around your house, such as a bunch of movies or books or board games, and can also include items like computers, cameras, and even clothes. We will be building this from the ground up, and this will be the start of what we'll be building with for the remainder of the book.

If you are using the starter files, skip to step 2. Step 1 is going to show how to build this project from the ground up.

Step 1: Set up and use a new project

To begin from scratch, create a new .Net Core Console project and name the project `Activity0302_EFCoreNewDb`. Start by opening Visual Studio and selecting `Create a new project`. Creating a new project is shown in Figure 3-15.

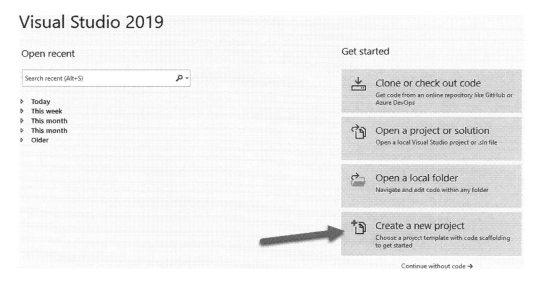

Figure 3-15. *Create a new project*

Create a new Console App (.Net Core) project. Selecting a console app is shown in Figure 3-16.

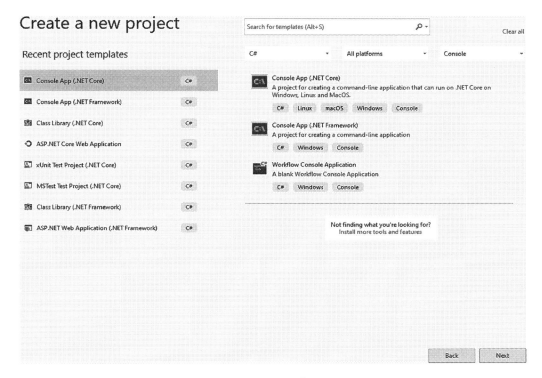

Figure 3-16. *Creating a new .Net Core Console project*

Configure your project to save to a location on your drive that is easy to find; name the project as stated above Activity0302_EFCoreNewDb. Figure 3-17 shows how we can name the project and select the storage location for our code.

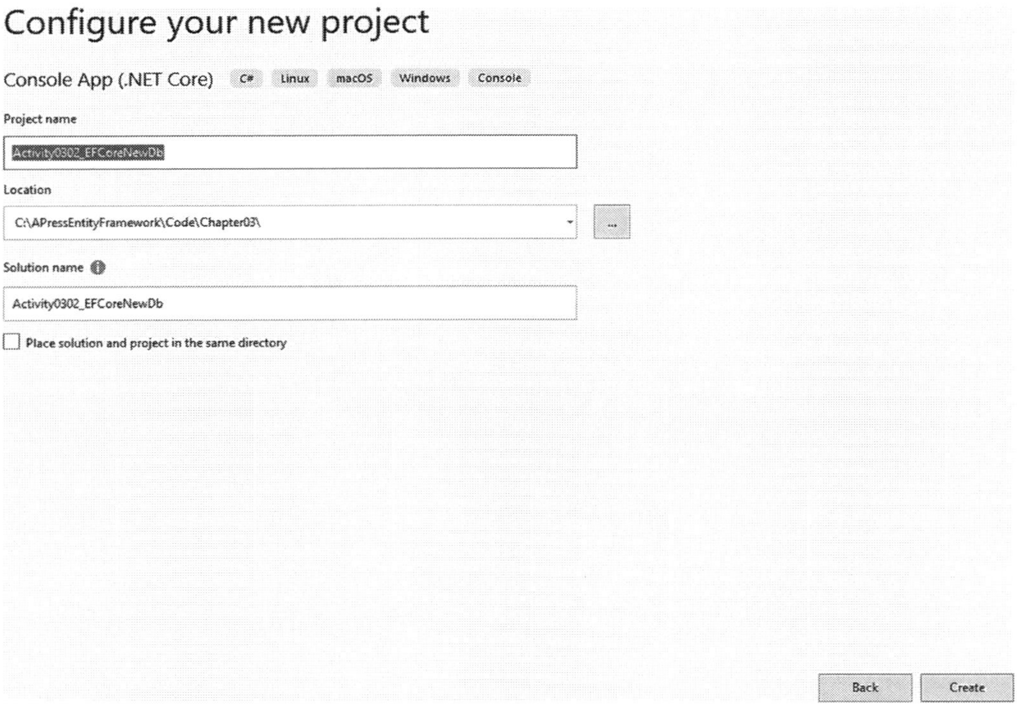

Configure your new project

Console App (.NET Core)   C#   Linux   macOS   Windows   Console

Project name

Activity0302_EFCoreNewDb

Location

C:\APressEntityFramework\Code\Chapter03\   ▾   ...

Solution name ⓘ

Activity0302_EFCoreNewDb

☐ Place solution and project in the same directory

                                                            Back   Create

Figure 3-17. *Configuring the new project*

The project should be created as expected. Once created, it should look similar to what is shown in Figure 3-18.

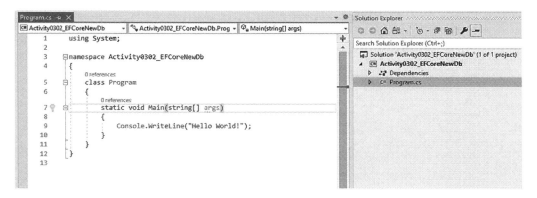

Figure 3-18. *The current project as generated during creation*

Next, we need to add a project to house our database operations. Right-click the
Solution and select Add ➤ New Project (see Figure 3-19).

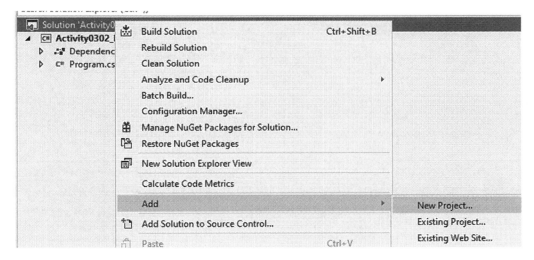

Figure 3-19. *Adding a new project to the solution*

For this project, select `Class Library (.Net Core)`, shown in Figure 3-20.

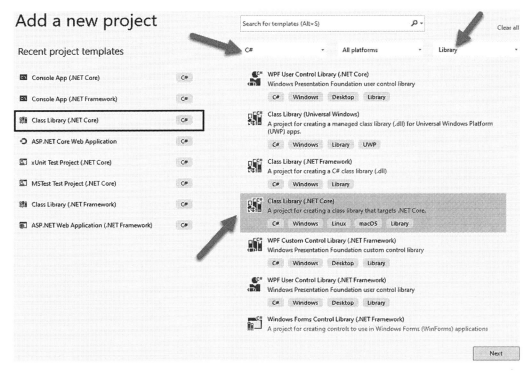

Figure 3-20. *Use the .Net Core Class Library template*

Name the new project `InventoryDatabaseCore` and set it to save in the same folder as your other project. Review Figure 3-21 for more information on configuring the project.

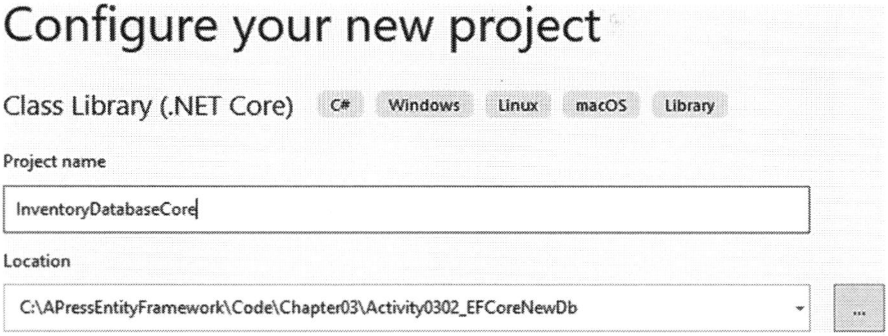

Configure your new project

Class Library (.NET Core)   C#   Windows   Linux   macOS   Library

Project name

InventoryDatabaseCore

Location

C:\APressEntityFramework\Code\Chapter03\Activity0302_EFCoreNewDb

Figure 3-21. *Configure the DB Project name and folder location*

Add a reference to the new project in the Activity0302_EFCoreNewDb project by right-clicking the project and selecting Add ➤ Reference (as shown in Figure 3-22).

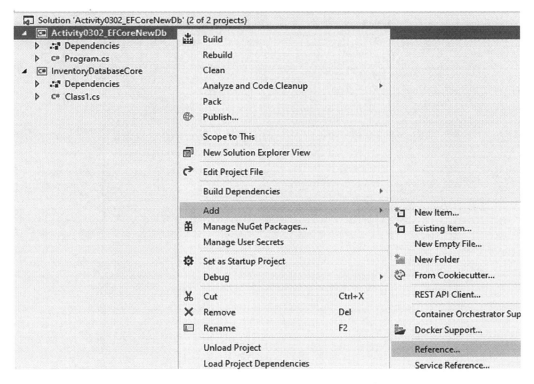

Figure 3-22. *Adding a reference to the new DB project in the starter project*

Select the DB project to reference it in the starter project (see Figure 3-23).

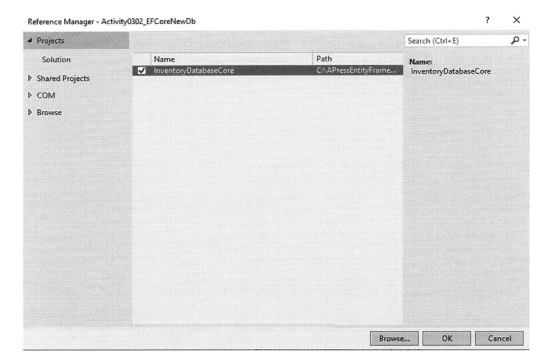

Figure 3-23. *Selectin the DB project as a project reference*

Right-click the Solution and select Manage NuGet Packages for Solution, as shown in Figure 3-24.

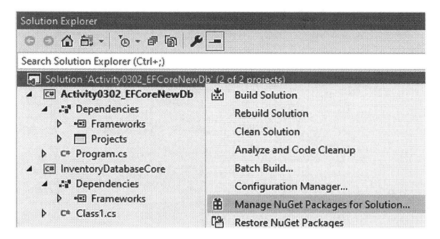

Figure 3-24. *Bring up the Manage NuGet Packages for Solution dialog*

Install the following packages to both projects:

```
Microsoft.EntityFrameworkCore
Microsoft.EntityFrameworkCore.SqlServer
Microsoft.Extensions.Configuration.FileExtensions
Microsoft.Extensions.Configuration.Json
```

Install the following packages to the starter project [Activity0302_EFCoreNewDb]:

```
Microsoft.EntityFrameworkCore.Design
Microsoft.Extensions.Configuration
```

Install the following packages to the DB project [InventoryDatabaseCore]:

```
Microsoft.EntityFrameworkCore.Tools
```

Installing NuGet packages is shown in Figure 3-25.

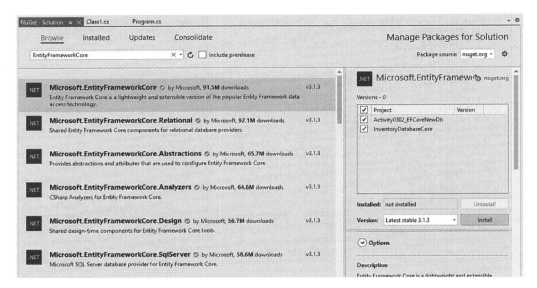

Figure 3-25. *Installing NuGet packages to the projects*

In the end, you should have the following entries as shown in Figure 3-26 in the starter project file.

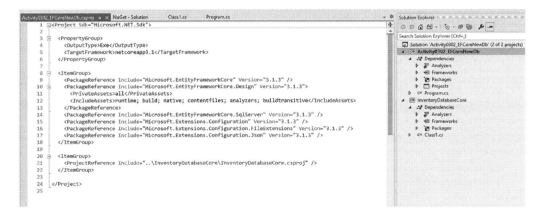

Figure 3-26. *The package and project references are shown in the .csproj file*

And the DB project should have the entries as shown in Figure 3-27.

```
InventoryDatabaseCore.csproj* ☰ ✕   NuGet - Solution
  1 ⊟<Project Sdk="Microsoft.NET.Sdk">
  2
  3 ⊟   <PropertyGroup>
  4         <TargetFramework>netcoreapp3.1</TargetFramework>
  5     </PropertyGroup>
  6
  7 ⊟   <ItemGroup>
  8         <PackageReference Include="Microsoft.EntityFrameworkCore" Version="3.1.3" />
  9         <PackageReference Include="Microsoft.EntityFrameworkCore.SqlServer" Version="3.1.3" />
 10 ⊟       <PackageReference Include="Microsoft.EntityFrameworkCore.Tools" Version="3.1.3">
 11           <PrivateAssets>all</PrivateAssets>
 12           <IncludeAssets>runtime; build; native; contentfiles; analyzers; buildtransitive</IncludeAssets>
 13         </PackageReference>
 14         <PackageReference Include="Microsoft.Extensions.Configuration.FileExtensions" Version="3.1.3" />
 15         <PackageReference Include="Microsoft.Extensions.Configuration.Json" Version="3.1.3" />
 16     </ItemGroup>
 17
 18 </Project>
 19
```

Figure 3-27. *The DB project package references*

Next, rename the class in the InventoryDatabaseCore project from Class1.cs to InventoryDbContext.cs. When prompted, select Yes to allow renaming (as seen in Figure 3-28).

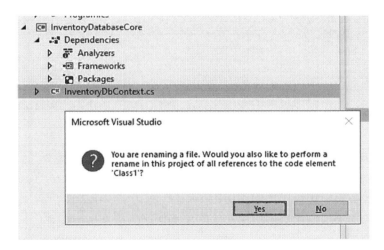

Figure 3-28. *Renaming the Class1.cs file to be our new InventoryDbContext*

Change the class code in the InventoryDbContext to be a DB Context type and implement a constructor to allow injection of DBContextOptions:

```
public class InventoryDbContext : DbContext
{
    public InventoryDbContext(DbContextOptions options)
        : base()
    {

    }
}
```

Add an `appsettings.json` file to each project. In the file, add the connection string to connect to your database. Use `.\\SQLExpress` if you are using *SQLExpress* or `localhost` if you are using *SQLDeveloper* edition.

```
{
  "ConnectionStrings": {
    "InventoryManager": "Data Source=.\\SQLExpress;Initial Catalog=Inventory
    Manager;Trusted_Connection=True"
  }
}
```

Figure 3-29 shows what an appsettings.json file should look like with an active connection string and also highlights the two locations to add the new file.

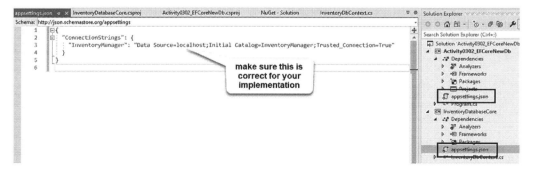

Figure 3-29. *Setting the connection string in appsettings.json*

Make sure to set the appsettings.json files as Copy to Output Directory ➤ Copy if newer for the starter project EFCoreNewDb (as shown in Figure 3-30).

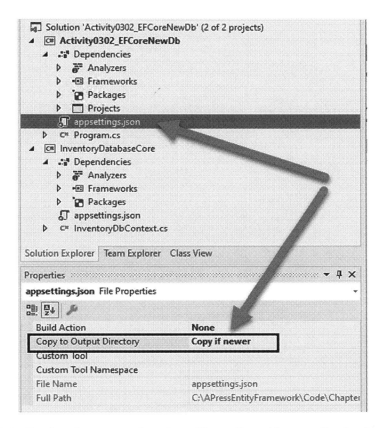

Figure 3-30. *Setting the appsettings.json file as Copy if newer for deploy*

In the starter project, add a new file: ConfigurationBuilderSingleton.cs. In the new file, place the code as follows:

```
public sealed class ConfigurationBuilderSingleton
{
    private static ConfigurationBuilderSingleton _instance = null;
    private static readonly object instanceLock = new object();

    private static IConfigurationRoot _configuration;
```

```
    private ConfigurationBuilderSingleton()
    {
        var builder = new ConfigurationBuilder()
                            .SetBasePath(Directory.GetCurrentDirectory())
                            .AddJsonFile("appsettings.json", optional:
                            true, reloadOnChange: true);

        _configuration = builder.Build();
    }

    public static ConfigurationBuilderSingleton Instance
    {
        get {
            lock (instanceLock)
            {
                if (_instance == null)
                {
                    _instance = new ConfigurationBuilderSingleton();
                }
                return _instance;
            }
        }
    }

    public static IConfigurationRoot ConfigurationRoot
    {
        get
        {
            if (_configuration == null) { var x =
            ConfigurationBuilderSingleton.Instance;  }
            return _configuration;
        }
    }
}
```

After adding the singleton class, change the program.cs file to contain the following code:

```
class Program
{
    static IConfigurationRoot configuration;
    static DbContextOptionsBuilder<InventoryDbContext> _optionsBuilder;

    static void Main(string[] args)
    {
        BuildOptions();
        Console.WriteLine(_configuration.GetConnectionString("Inventory
        Manager"));
        ListInventory();
    }

    static void BuildOptions()
    {
        _configuration = ConfigurationBuilderSingleton.ConfigurationRoot;
        _optionsBuilder = new DbContextOptionsBuilder<InventoryDbContext>();
        _optionsBuilder.UseSqlServer(_configuration.GetConnectionString
        ("InventoryManager"));
    }

    static void ListInventory()
    {

    }
}
```

Run the program to validate that everything is set up and that your connection string is printed out as expected. Figure 3-31 shows the expected output of the connection string (your output may vary if your connection string is different than mine).

As a final reminder, when adding a lot of code such as we've done in this activity in the last two steps, if something goes wrong and you are getting a lot of errors, don't forget to compare your code to the final version of the files.

■ Microsoft Visual Studio Debug Console

```
Data Source=localhost;Initial Catalog=InventoryManager;Trusted_Connection=True

C:\APressEntityFramework\Code\Chapter03\Activity0302_EFCoreNewDb\Activity0302_EFCoreNewDb\bi
ty0302_EFCoreNewDb.exe (process 11396) exited with code 0.
To automatically close the console when debugging stops, enable Tools->Options->Debugging->/
le when debugging stops.
Press any key to close this window . . .
■
```

Figure 3-31. *The program is set up and working as expected*

As you are already sure your project is working as expected, skip to step 3.

Step 2: Make sure your project is set up correctly

As mentioned previously, the easiest approach for starting this activity is to get the starter files for the activity. Once you have the files, open the project, then make sure the connection string is set to match your local environment database, and finally run the program to make sure it works as expected.

When the program is working as expected, the output should be similar to what is shown in Figure 3-31 at the end of step 2.

Step 3: Add a reusable library for our database models – the "code" of code first

While it is entirely possible to put your code in the same location as the context, it is much more flexible for future use if we separate the models to their own class. Right-click the Solution, and then select Add ➤ New Project. Use the Class Library (.NET Core) project template. Name the new project InventoryModels and save the project in the same directory as your other projects in the solution.

After creation, the project should look as follows in Figure 3-32.

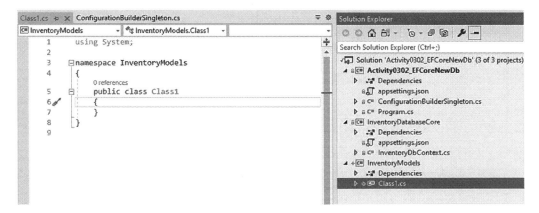

Figure 3-32. *Creating the class library for the inventory system models*

Rename Class1 to Item.cs. When prompted, select Yes to rename. In the Item.cs file, add a public property for Id as int and Name as string. We will modify this class in more detail later in the book, but we'll keep it simple here.

```
public class Item
{
    public int Id { get; set; }
    public string Name { get; set; }

}
```

Next, reference the InventoryModels project in the InventoryDatabaseCore Library project. Right-click the InventoryDatabaseCore project, select Add ➤ Reference, and then select the InventoryModels project as a project reference as shown in Figure 3-33.

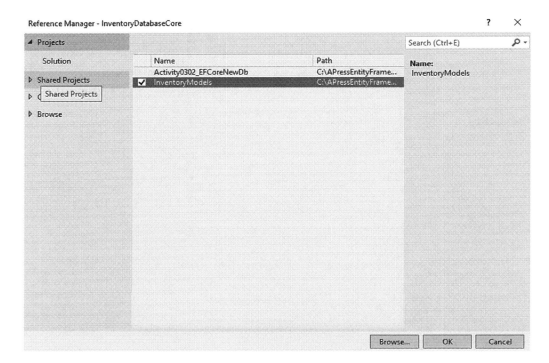

Figure 3-33. *Referencing the InventoryModels library in the InventoryDatabaseCore library*

Step 4: Reference the library in an entity DbSet

This next step is one of the most critical steps in the process. If we forget to do this, our migration will scaffold successfully with nothing to update in the database, creating a blank migration. Therefore, if you run the add-migration command after creating a model, and the migration is blank, consider checking your DbContext to make sure you included a reference to the DBSet.

In the file InventoryDbContext in the InventoryDatabaseCore library, add the following line of code:

```
public DbSet<Item> Items { get; set; }
```

Adding this line of code will require a using statement to reference the Models project using InventoryModels. See Figure 3-34 for more clarity.

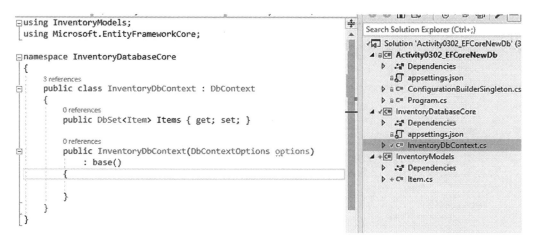

Figure 3-34. *Adding the DbSet<Item> to the Inventory DB Context*

Step 5: Add a new migration

We are now ready to begin creating migrations for our new database. To do this, after ensuring that we have set everything up to this point as covered, we can run the command add-migration "Initial Migration" in the *PMC*.

Make certain the Default project drop-down is pointing to the *InventoryDatabaseCore* project. Once this is in place, run the command as shown earlier for the initial migration. Review Figure 3-35 for more clarity.

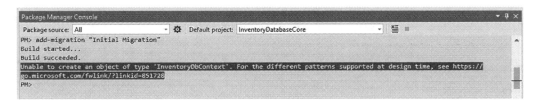

Figure 3-35. *Adding the initial migration for our new database creates an error*

Note that this generated an error. The error is *"Unable to create an object of type 'yourdbcontext'..."*. *The error is not very helpful as to what went wrong.*

This error is happening because we do not have a default constructor in the context file. Let's add a default constructor and try again.

Use the following code to add a new default constructor:

```
public InventoryDbContext() : base() { }.
```
Additionally, make sure to add the options in as a parameter to the base method in the explicit constructor:
```
public InventoryDbContext(DbContextOptions options)
    : base(options)
{

}
```

Review Figure 3-36 to see the code as placed into the file.

Figure 3-36. *Fixing the class with a default constructor*

Now that this is fixed, try to add the migration again. Do you think it will work this time?

If you guessed "no," you get a prize. The prize is yet another error (see Figure 3-37).

Figure 3-37. *Another error. No database provider has been configured for this DbContext*

The text of this error is actually *"No database provider has been configured for this DbContext. A provider can be configured by overriding the DbContext.OnConfiguring method or by using AddDbContext on the application service provider. If AddDbContext is used, then also ensure that your DbContext type accepts a DbContextOptions<TContext> object in its constructor and passes it to the base constructor for DbContext."*

So how do we fix this issue?

As it turns out, we need to do what it says in the error. The easiest solution is simply to override the OnConfiguring method. In fact, if we go back to activity one from this chapter and look at the context that was generated, we'll see exactly the code that we need. Review Figure 3-38 to see the code from the OnConfiguring method in activity 0301.

```
0 references
protected override void OnConfiguring(DbContextOptionsBuilder optionsBuilder)
{
    if (!optionsBuilder.IsConfigured)
    {
g  To protect potentially sensitive information in your connection string, you should move it out of source code. See http://go.microsoft.com
        optionsBuilder.UseSqlServer("Data Source=localhost;Initial Catalog=AdventureWorks;Integrated Security=True");
    }
}
```

Figure 3-38. Activity 0301 had placed an override for OnConfiguring in the DbContext

A couple of important notes. This code from activity 0301 is exactly the same as the options builder that we are using in our startup project. In this case, however, the startup project was not run, so the context did not get an options builder injected (remember, we added a default constructor that takes no parameters in order to run migrations). Therefore, the context itself needs to know how to connect to the database.

Another important note is the fact that the context is literally begging us to change out the code so that we don't use a hard-coded connection string. While we could get away with that for now, we really should update it to prevent having our connection string information in code (eventually we'll need to connect to a production database with something other than the trusted windows login).

Let's add the code for the OnConfiguring method to our *DbContext*:

```
protected override void OnConfiguring(DbContextOptionsBuilder
optionsBuilder)
{
    if (!optionsBuilder.IsConfigured)
    {
```

```
    optionsBuilder.UseSqlServer("Data Source=localhost;Initial Catalog=
    AdventureWorks;Integrated Security=True");
  }
}
```

Next, let's remove the direct reference to the connection string. The good news is that we already have an *appsettings.json* file in place. Now we just need to leverage that from our database context.

Just as we did in the startup, we'll need to build out the connection string from the builder. If we were using an Asp.Net core application, we could leverage the services and just work through that, but from this console project, it's a bit trickier.

Also, we can't reference the startup project static builder that we built, because that would create a circular dependency. So, let's just rehash the builder code directly.

In the InventoryDatabaseContext, add the following code directly into the OnConfiguring override method:

```
protected override void OnConfiguring(DbContextOptionsBuilder
optionsBuilder)
{
    if (!optionsBuilder.IsConfigured)
    {
        var builder = new ConfigurationBuilder()
                    .SetBasePath(Directory.GetCurrentDirectory())
                    .AddJsonFile("appsettings.json", optional: true,
                    reloadOnChange: true);

        _configuration = builder.Build();
        var cnstr = _configuration.GetConnectionString("InventoryManager");
        optionsBuilder.UseSqlServer(cnstr);
    }
}
```

You'll also need to reference any missing using statements such as using Microsoft.Extensions.Configuration; and using System.IO; at the top of the file.

Additionally, you'll need to add a class-level variable before the Main method:
static IConfigurationRoot _configuration;

Let's try that add-migration command one more time (see Figure 3-39).

Figure 3-39. *Adding the migration succeeds now that we have access to the configuration and have correctly set up the database context to run with a code-first approach*

Step 6: Updating the database

Now that we have an initial migration in place, we are ready to update our local database. Let's see what happens if we just run the update-database command in the *PMC*. The successful command execution is shown in Figure 3-40.

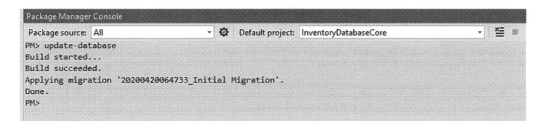

Figure 3-40. *Updating the database was successful*

There is a chance this will not work for you out of the box. Depending on your local instance and how things are configured, you may need to make sure that you can connect with local windows accounts and/or set to *mixed mode* if you want to use a *SQL Server* user id and password.

119

In some rare instances, you may need to create the database yourself and then run the update-database command. In the end, you should be able to get the update-database command to work as expected.

Examining the database using *SQL Server Management Studio (SSMS)* proves the database exists as we would expect (see Figure 3-41).

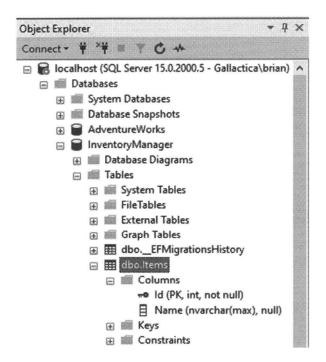

Figure 3-41. *Examining the newly created database*

Step 7: Insert and retrieve a set of items

As a final part to this activity, let's insert and retrieve some items from the Items table in our database. This part of the activity is optional, as we'll be covering how to work with the database in more detail later in the book. However, I'm a big believer in taking things one step at a time, and this simple insert and retrieve is a good way to get our feet wet.

If you consider yourself to be well versed in *EF* and *LINQ*, perhaps step away from the activity and attempt to write the insert and read/write of about five items to and from the Items table.

To begin, in the console startup, let's add a method to populate the database. This method should be called `InsertItems`. Add any using statements for `System. Collections.Generic` and the `InventoryModels` project as needed. In the method, we'll get an instance of the context and then insert a prefabricated list of items. The `InsertItems` method should be added anywhere in the `Program` class. I generally just add to the end when adding new methods.

```
static void InsertItems()
{
    var items = new List<Item>() {
        new Item() { Name = "Top Gun" },
        new Item() { Name = "Batman Begins"},
        new Item() { Name = "Inception" },
        new Item() { Name = "Star Wars: The Empire Strikes Back"},
        new Item() { Name = "Remember the Titans"}
    };

    using (var db = new InventoryDbContext(_optionsBuilder.Options))
    {
        db.AddRange(items);
        db.SaveChanges();
    }
}
```

Additionally, let's remove the printout of the connection string and replace with a call to the `InsertItems` method within the `Main` method:

```
static void Main(string[] args)
{
    BuildOptions();
    InsertItems();
    ListInventory();
}
```

By doing this, we'll quickly discover how poor our initial DB design is, as there will be many things we want to enhance about the `Items` table.

Also note, we are not going to prevent duplicates for now. As stated, we'll learn more in the future about how to do things correctly against the database.

Finally, let's query the database and output each returned item, taking just the top five for now since we know that if we run this method multiple times, there will be duplicates inserted on every run. Add a new method called `ListInventory` within the `Program` class, following the `InsertItems` method.

```
static void ListInventory()
{
    using (var db = new InventoryDbContext(_optionsBuilder.Options))
    {
        var items = db.Items.Take(5).OrderBy(x => x.Name).ToList();
        items.ForEach(x => Console.WriteLine($"New Item: {x.Name}"));
    }
}
```

Run the application. The results should be similar to what you see in Figure 3-42.

```
Microsoft Visual Studio Debug Console
New Item: Batman Begins
New Item: Inception
New Item: Remember the Titans
New Item: Star Wars: The Empire Strikes Back
New Item: Top Gun

C:\APressEntityFramework\Code\Chapter03\Activity0302_EFCoreNewDb\Activity0302_E
ty0302_EFCoreNewDb.exe (process 13760) exited with code 0.
To automatically close the console when debugging stops, enable Tools->Options-
le when debugging stops.
Press any key to close this window . . .
```

Figure 3-42. *The output of our first code-first application*

Final thoughts

In this activity, we have worked through the steps that it takes to get a new project up and running with the *EFCore* code-first approach. By now, you should be very familiar with the idea of how code-first database interaction works. However, it's always a great idea to highlight and review our takeaways from this learning activity.

- The *DbContext* is the controller for interaction with the database. All the information we need is handled by the context, including *DbSets*, and *configuration* to connect.

- The *Model* classes dictate how the table will be structured. Adding *public properties* will generate columns in the tables.

- Add the *model* to the *context* as a *DbSet* in order to make sure the *migration* includes that model in the scaffolding.

- For the migrations to work, we need the `Microsoft.EntityFrameworkCore.Tools` package and we need to override the `OnConfiguring` method in the *DbContext* to make sure the database connection is set as expected. Additionally, the startup project needs the package `Microsoft.EntityFrameworkCore.Design`.

- We create the migration with the command `add-migration [migration name]` and then run `update-database` to execute the migration against the database

- Migrations are tracked in the database in the table __ *EFMigrationsHistory*

One final note is that we will be leveraging this project for much of the remainder of the book. If you are fluent with source control, now would be a good time to add your project to a repository so that you can easily work with it in the future.

Activity 0303: Creating a code-first project in EF6

In the final activity for this chapter, we're going to implement an *EF6* code-first implementation against an existing project that uses classic *ADO.Net* as its data access layer. In the real world, your existing project may have another version of Entity Framework already in place (*EF2, EF3, EF4, EF5*) and may just need a few tweaks to update to use *EF6*. Additionally, another path with a project that has an existing older EF implementation could just build a data access library for new functionality in *EF6*. However, it is likely that if you need to do this sort of upgrade, it is to bring some older application up to the last LTS version of the *.Net Framework* and *EF6* to extend its life with the best security and architecture possible, in a manner that is much less expensive than a full rewrite.

Why not a new project?

You could create a new project with a new *.Net 4.8* and *EF6* architecture implementation. However, if a new project is going to be built, I encourage you to build it in the latest version of Core or in *.Net 5 (vNext)*, depending on when you are reading this book.

Using an existing project to implement an EF6 code-first approach

Before we begin, it's important to note that there will be a few major differences in how this works from what we've learned in the *EFCore* activities, as working with *EF6* and the database context with migrations has a couple of minor differences. Additionally, while the overall idea remains the same, a couple of the commands are different in the *PMC* for *EF6* vs. *Core*.

Pre-activity setup

To get started with this activity, it will be easiest to just grab a copy of the starter files `Activity0303_EF6_UpdateFromExisting_Starter`. Extract the files and work along with me as we build out the solution using *EF6* code first.

Step 1: Configure the connection if necessary and run the project

As with other projects, this code is pointed at our restored version of *AdventureWorks* and should use a similar connection string. Make sure the connection string is set up correctly and run the project. You should see output similar to what is shown in Figure 3-43.

```
C:\APressEntityFramework\Code\Chapter03\Activity0303_EF6_UpdateFromExisting\Activity0303_
Found Person: Jossef Goldberg
Found Person: Diane Margheim
Found Person: Janice Galvin
Found Person: Sariya Harnpadoungsataya
Found Person: Mary Gibson
Completed.  Press any key to exit
```

Figure 3-43. *Initial output from a pseudo-legacy application against the AdventureWorks database*

Step 2: Create a new library and add the Entity Framework libraries

As with other projects, we're going to create a new library and then add the Entity Framework libraries to this project. We'll also need to add the Entity Framework libraries to the startup project. Begin by adding the new library project and naming it something like AWEFDataAccessLayer (see Figure 3-44).

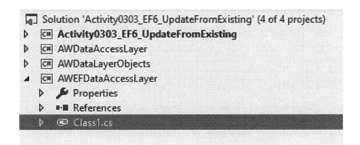

Figure 3-44. *The new data access layer library for our existing project*

Next, add the EntityFramework NuGet Package to both the new DAL project and the original startup project as shown in Figure 3-45.

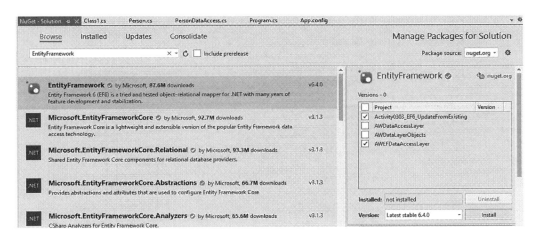

Figure 3-45. *Installing Entity Framework to the library and the startup project*

Step 3: Delete the EFMigrations History table from the AdventureWorks database

If you completed the previous activities in this chapter, you should already have an *EFMigrations* table in the *AdventureWorks* database. You'll want to make sure to delete this table before running the wizard in step 4. You can easily delete the table by right-clicking and selecting `Delete` in the *SSMS*. Another solution would be to script the table as delete and then execute the script. A third solution would be to restore the backup to a new instance of the AW database and then just point to that new instance in this activity. A final solution would be to just leave it but remove it from the generated context and code after running the wizard in the next step. Figure 3-46 shows how to delete the migrations table.

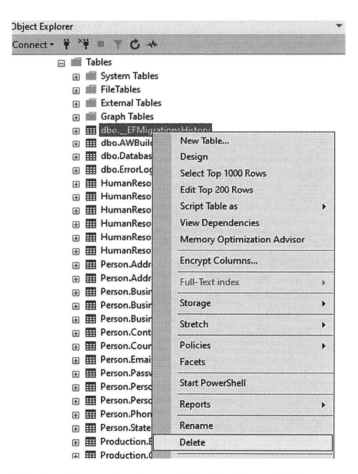

Figure 3-46. *Deleting the previously created migrations table*

Step 4: Create the code-first implementation

Thinking back to our *EF6* implementation against the existing database from Chapter 2, we had an auto-generated context that was built out for us. With this project, we will not end up with an *EDMX* file that will generate code for us. Instead, we're going to have regular model files and a context which we'll be able to leverage going forward.

To begin, right-click the project and select Add ➤ New Item (see Figure 3-47).

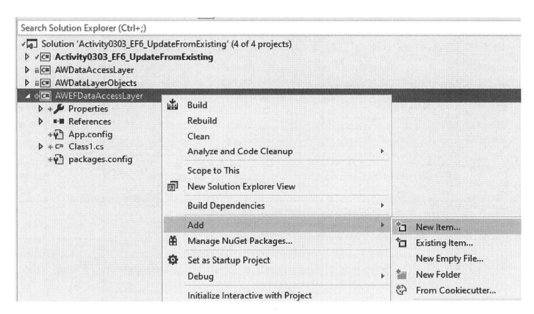

Figure 3-47. *Add a new item to your data access layer library project*

In the Add New Item dialog, on the left navigation pane, select Data. Then select ADO. Net Entity Data Model. Name the model AdventureWorks and select Add. Figure 3-48 shows the Add New Item dialog.

Figure 3-48. *Creating the new code-first data model*

In the `Entity Data Model Wizard`, select `Code First from database` (see Figure 3-49).

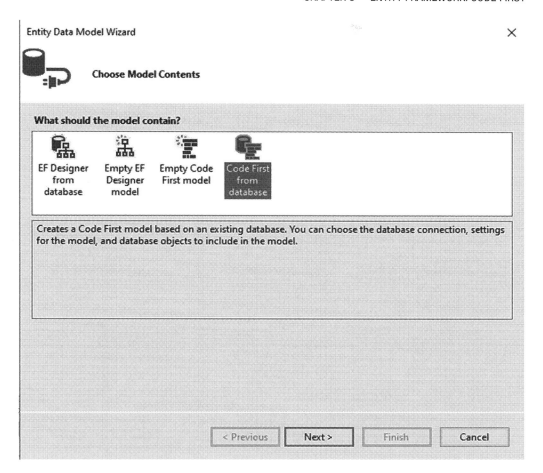

Figure 3-49. *Selecting the Code First from database option*

If you've worked through other activities, you likely already have a connection to choose from. If not, you'll need to create a new connection. If creating the new connection, review the *EF6* activity against an existing database from Chapter 2 for more information. Once you have the connection, select it. Name your connection in the App.Config as the default, which is the name of your model. In my case, this is AdventureWorks. There are some slight differences that we'll want in this connection string, so you can name this connection string anything but AdventureWorksDb, which is the configuration string name for the classic database instance in these activity files. Setting up the configuration string is shown in Figure 3-50.

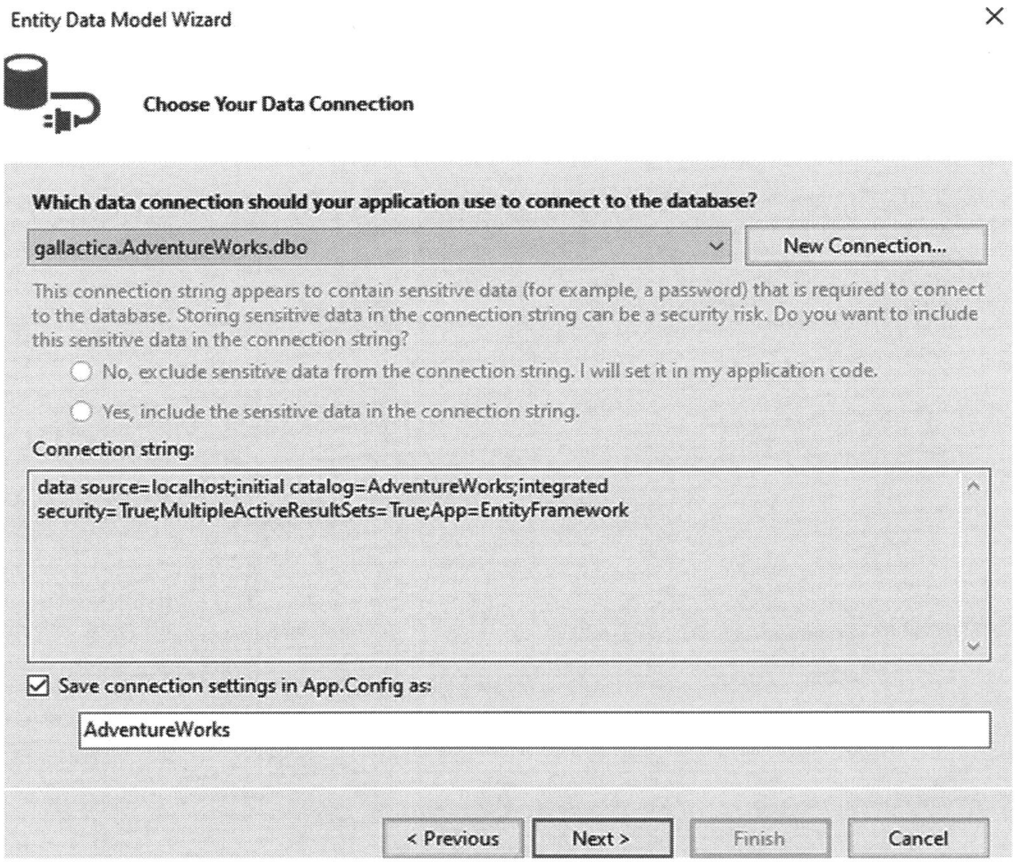

Figure 3-50. *Setting the connection and connection string properties*

Once the database connection is set, you'll get the options for what tables and views to include. Since we'll be doing an initial migration and we want to ultimately squelch all of this from being re-created, make sure to just select all of the tables and views (see Figure 3-51).

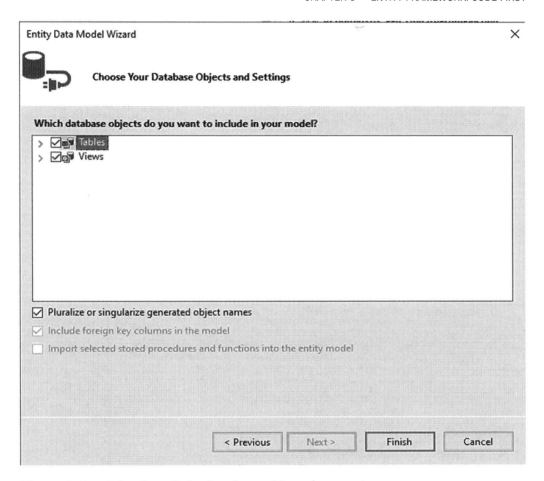

Figure 3-51. *Selecting all the database objects for creation*

Leave the box to Pluralize or singularize checked, and then select Finish. In the end, you'll have a DBContext file and a bunch of model files.

Figure 3-52 shows the AdventureWorks DBContext. Make note of the way the connection string is directly passed to this context by name (as opposed to builder options as in *EFCore*).

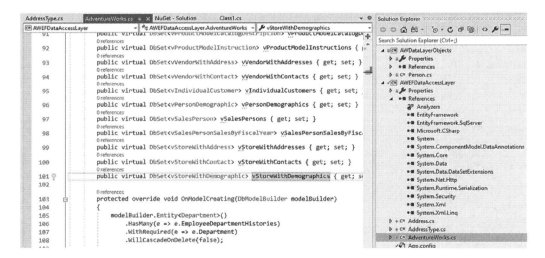

```
1 reference
public partial class AdventureWorks : DbContext
{
    0 references
    public AdventureWorks()
        : base("name=AdventureWorks")
    {
    }

    0 references
    public virtual DbSet<AWBuildVersion> AWBuildVersions { get; set; }
    0 references
    public virtual DbSet<DatabaseLog> DatabaseLogs { get; set; }
    0 references
    public virtual DbSet<ErrorLog> ErrorLogs { get; set; }
    0 references
    public virtual DbSet<Department> Departments { get; set; }
    0 references
    public virtual DbSet<Employee> Employees { get; set; }
    0 references
    public virtual DbSet<EmployeeDepartmentHistory> EmployeeDepartmentHistories
    0 references
    public virtual DbSet<EmployeePayHistory> EmployeePayHistories { get; set; }
    0 references
    public virtual DbSet<JobCandidate> JobCandidates { get; set; }
```

Figure 3-52. *A quick look at the generated DBContext*

Also make note of how the views are referenced in the generated context (see Figure 3-53).

Figure 3-53. *A look at how the views are defined in the generated DBContext*

You should also note all of the other models that are defined as expected and the lack of an *EDMX* file.

Step 5: Enable migrations

Now that we have the database structure defined with models and the DBContext, it's time to generate the initial migration.

Remember that any time our database models or context have changed, it's important to rebuild the project and make sure there are no errors. You should have no errors at this point. However, make sure to build now, and then fix any errors if any exist. We cannot generate migrations if the project will not build.

Next, open the *PMC*, then point to the EFDataAccessLayer project as the default, and run the command add-migration "Initial Migration" to see what happens (review Figure 3-54).

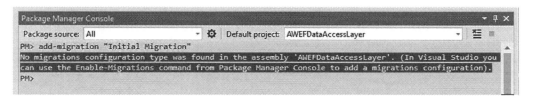

Figure 3-54. *Attempting to add the initial migration in our EF data access layer library*

Here, we see there is an error, telling us that no configuration type is found. To fix this, we need to run the command enable-migrations. However, before we do that, we need to consider what we are going to enable. Enabling migrations can be configured to run automatically (on project startup) or can be left as a manual operation (requires intervention). On a new instance, automatic migrations are what we likely want. In this case, however, we need to be extremely careful as automatic migrations may remove or delete objects or data from our existing database. Therefore, we'll want to make sure automatic migrations are not enabled. We can check and easily change this setting later in the DBContext file.

Run the command enable-migrations in the PMC to see what happens. The output with an error is shown in Figure 3-55.

```
No migrations configuration type was found in the assembly 'AWEFDataAccessLayer'. (In Visual Studio you
can use the Enable-Migrations command from Package Manager Console to add a migrations configuration).
PM> enable-migrations
Checking if the context targets an existing database...
System.InvalidOperationException: No connection string named 'AdventureWorks' could be found in the
application config file.
   at System.Data.Entity.Internal.LazyInternalConnection.Initialize()
   at System.Data.Entity.Internal.LazyInternalConnection.get_Connection()
   at System.Data.Entity.Infrastructure.DbContextInfo..ctor(Type contextType, DbProviderInfo
modelProviderInfo, AppConfig config, DbConnectionInfo connectionInfo, Func`1 resolver)
   at System.Data.Entity.Migrations.DbMigrator..ctor(DbMigrationsConfiguration configuration, DbContext
usersContext, DatabaseExistenceState existenceState, Boolean calledByCreateDatabase)
   at System.Data.Entity.Migrations.DbMigrator..ctor(DbMigrationsConfiguration configuration)
   at System.Data.Entity.Migrations.Design.MigrationScaffolder..ctor(DbMigrationsConfiguration
migrationsConfiguration)
   at System.Data.Entity.Infrastructure.Design.Executor.CreateMigrationScaffolder
(DbMigrationsConfiguration configuration)
   at System.Data.Entity.Infrastructure.Design.Executor.ScaffoldInitialCreateInternal(DbConnectionInfo
connectionInfo, String contextTypeName, String contextAssemblyName, String migrationsNamespace, Boolean
auto, String migrationsDir)
   at
System.Data.Entity.Infrastructure.Design.Executor.ScaffoldInitialCreate.<>c__DisplayClass0_0.<.ctor>b__0
()
   at
System.Data.Entity.Infrastructure.Design.Executor.OperationBase.<>c__DisplayClass4_0`1.<Execute>b__0()
   at System.Data.Entity.Infrastructure.Design.Executor.OperationBase.Execute(Action action)
No connection string named 'AdventureWorks' could be found in the application config file.
PM>
```

Figure 3-55. *Error for no connection string in the application config file*

This error might be particularly confusing. If we look at the *app.config* file in our library, the connection string is definitely there. However, the config for the console startup project does not have this connection string.

Copy the connection string from the configuration file in the library to the startup project. For convenience, the code is shown first here, and then the placement is shown in Figure 3-56.

```
<connectionStrings>
  <add name="AdventureWorks"
      connectionString="data source=localhost;initial catalog=AdventureWor
      ks;integrated security=True;MultipleActiveResultSets=True;App=Entity
      Framework"
      providerName="System.Data.SqlClient" />
</connectionStrings>
```

Figure 3-56. *Copying the connection string to the startup project app.config file*

One more important note is that there is an additional section added to the config file in both projects when we referenced the Entity Framework packages. If this section is missing, EF will likely not work. Make sure both config files have the following config sections:

```
<configSections>
  <section name="entityFramework"
          type="System.Data.Entity.Internal.ConfigFile.
          EntityFrameworkSection, EntityFramework, Version=6.0.0.0,
          Culture=neutral, PublicKeyToken=b77a5c561934e089"
          requirePermission="false" />
</configSections>
<entityFramework>
  <providers>
    <provider invariantName="System.Data.SqlClient" type="System.Data.
    Entity.SqlServer.SqlProviderServices, EntityFramework.SqlServer" />
  </providers>
</entityFramework>
```

The placement of the code is shown in Figure 3-57.

```
1    <?xml version="1.0" encoding="utf-8"?>
2    <configuration>
3      <configSections>
4        <section name="entityFramework"
5                type="System.Data.Entity.Internal.ConfigFile.EntityFrameworkSection, EntityFramework, Version=6.0.0.0, Culture=neutral, PublicKeyToken=b77a5c561!
6                requirePermission="false" />
7      </configSections>
8      <entityFramework>
9        <providers>
10         <provider invariantName="System.Data.SqlClient" type="System.Data.Entity.SqlServer.SqlProviderServices, EntityFramework.SqlServer" />
11       </providers>
12     </entityFramework>
13     <connectionStrings>
14       <add name="AdventureWorks"
15               connectionString="data source=localhost;initial catalog=AdventureWorks;integrated security=True;MultipleActiveResultSets=True;App=EntityFramework"
16               providerName="System.Data.SqlClient" />
17     </connectionStrings>
18   </configuration>
```

Figure 3-57. *Validate the config sections and Entity Framework entries in each project's config file*

If for some reason this section of the config is messed up, try to remove and then reinstall the Entity Framework libraries to the project. That should clear up the config file. Also note that you'll have two connection strings in the App.config file for the main project as the legacy code connection already existed.

Once again, run the command `enable-migrations` to see what happens (see Figure 3-58).

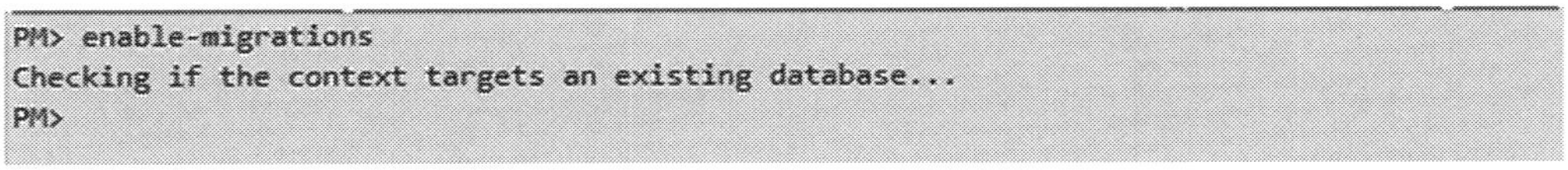

```
PM> enable-migrations
Checking if the context targets an existing database...
PM>
```

Figure 3-58. *Migrations are now enabled*

With the migrations enabled, we can see that there is a folder "Migrations" in the AWEFDataAccessLayer project. If we look at the configuration file, we can see the line for enabling the migrations right in the constructor (review Figure 3-59).

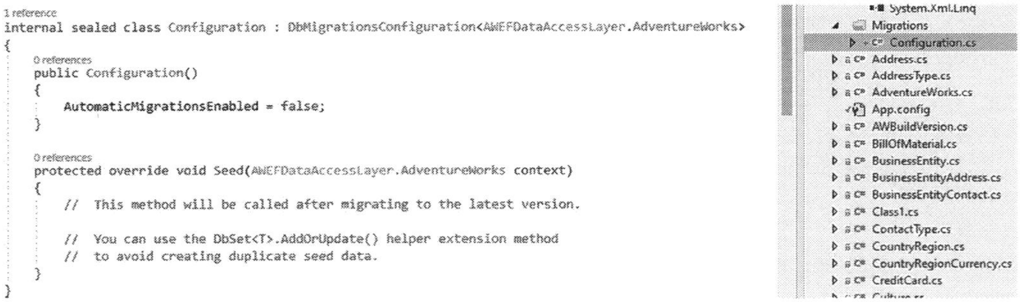

Figure 3-59. *The configuration file for our migrations is now in place*

Note the line for `AutomaticMigrationsEnabled = false`. If we want to turn automatic migrations on, we can set this option to `true`. We could have also used that as a flag in the `enable-migrations` command with the command `Enable-Migrations -EnableAutomaticMigrations`.

Step 6: Create the initial migration

In some cases, the initial migration may already have been created for you. In our case, it is likely we need to generate it.

Continue to make sure your project builds and that you are in the *PMC* pointing to the default project of your AWEFDataAccessLayer.

The next part of this activity is only going to happen if you are working against all the data in *AdventureWorks* or in any other database which includes geography data. I opted to keep this spatial data in for this example, even though referencing geography data will create a number of additional problems for us to solve.

Run the command add-migration "Initial Migration" to see what happens.

If you don't get an error for spatial types, skip to step 8.

Here, if you do get a geography error, as shown in Figure 3-60, we'll need to fix it.

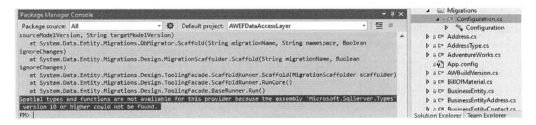

Figure 3-60. *Spatial types geography error*

This error might happen if you are using an older version of EF6, such as a version less than or equal to version 6.3. This error should not happen on version 6.4+ of *EF6*.

To fix this error, install the NuGet package Microsoft.SqlServer.Types on the AWEFDataAccessLayer project and the startup console project (see Figure 3-61).

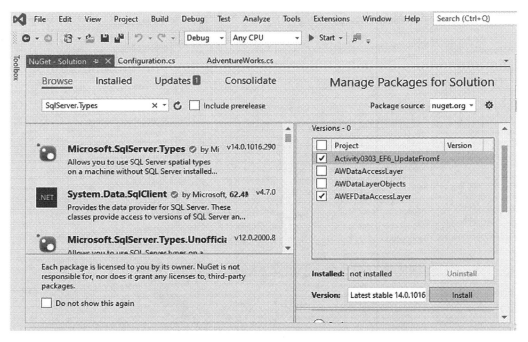

Figure 3-61. *Installing the Microsoft SqlServer Types library*

Make sure to rebuild the solution after adding NuGet packages. Failure to rebuild the solution will not allow the PMC to recognize new NuGet packages. Once the solution is rebuilt, the package(s) will be recognized in the PMC.

In order for our migrations to work, we need to tell Entity Framework to use this spatial types provider. We might be able to map it in the providers section of the *app. config* file. However, a guaranteed way to make this work is to add the following two lines of code to the constructor of the *AdventureWorks* context:

```
SqlProviderServices.SqlServerTypesAssemblyName =
    "Microsoft.SqlServer.Types, Version=14.0.0.0, Culture=neutral,
PublicKeyToken=89845dcd8080cc91";    SqlServerTypes.Utilities.
LoadNativeAssemblies(AppDomain.CurrentDomain.BaseDirectory);
```

Upon completion, this would look similar to what is shown in Figure 3-62.

```
AdventureWorks.cs  ⊡ ✕
AWEFDataAccessLayer                                          AWEFDataAccessLayer.AdventureWorks              Database
    1    ⊟namespace AWEFDataAccessLayer
    2      {
    3    ⊟    using System;
    4           using System.Data.Entity;
    5           using System.Data.Entity.SqlServer;
    6
           3 references
    7    ⊟    public partial class AdventureWorks : DbContext
    8         {
               0 references
    9    ⊟        public AdventureWorks()
   10                : base("name=AdventureWorks")
   11              {
   12                  SqlProviderServices.SqlServerTypesAssemblyName =
   13                    "Microsoft.SqlServer.Types, Version=14.0.0.0, Culture=neutral, PublicKeyToken=89845dcd8080cc91";
   14                  SqlServerTypes.Utilities.LoadNativeAssemblies(AppDomain.CurrentDomain.BaseDirectory);
   15              }
   16
               0 references
   17              public virtual DbSet<AWBuildVersion> AWBuildVersions { get; set; }
```

Figure 3-62. *Setting the provider in the constructor of the context*

Once again, run the command add-migration "Initial Migration" to see what happens. When successful, the new migration should be generated.

Step 8: Comment all "Up" code, delete all "Down" code, update the database

As in the previous activity (activity 0302), we don't want to re-create all the tables (running would likely error and let us know that the objects already exist). Therefore, we need to clean up our initial migration.

Start by commenting the code for the initial migration's *Up()* method. Likely, we will never need or want this code. However, in case the code needs to be restored for some reason, we will still have it (see Figure 3-63).

```
2 references
public partial class InitialMigration : DbMigration
{
    0 references
    public override void Up()
    {
    //        CreateTable(
    //            "Person.Address",
    //            c => new
    //                {
    //                    AddressID = c.Int(nullable: false, identity: true),
    //                    AddressLine1 = c.String(nullable: false, maxLength: 60),
    //                    AddressLine2 = c.String(maxLength: 60),
    //                    City = c.String(nullable: false, maxLength: 30),
    //                    StateProvinceID = c.Int(nullable: false),
    //                    PostalCode = c.String(nullable: false, maxLength: 15),
    //                    SpatialLocation = c.Geography(),
    //                    rowguid = c.Guid(nullable: false),
    //                    ModifiedDate = c.DateTime(nullable: false),
    //                })
    //            .PrimaryKey(t => t.AddressID)
    //            .ForeignKey("Person.StateProvince", t => t.StateProvinceID)
    //            .Index(t => t.StateProvinceID);
```

Figure 3-63. *Comment out (or remove) all code in the "Up" method for the initial migration*

There should not be a situation where we ever want to run the down code on this migration, as it would be highly destructive, so just remove any code and replace with a comment to note the intentional removal of code (see Figure 3-64).

```
    0 references
    public override void Down()
    {
        //we never want to destroy the existing data, so all code has been purposefully removed.
    }
}
```

Figure 3-64. *Remove the "Down" method code for the initial migration*

After cleaning up the initial migration, build the project. Then run the update-database command in the *PMC*. Figure 3-65 shows the successful update of the database with the new migration.

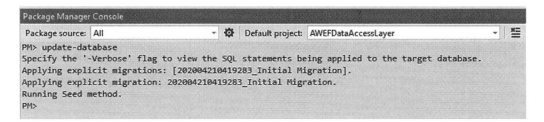

Figure 3-65. *Updating the database*

Validate that the next migration does not require the models again by adding another migration with the command add-migration "test scaffolding" to see what happens (as shown in Figure 3-66).

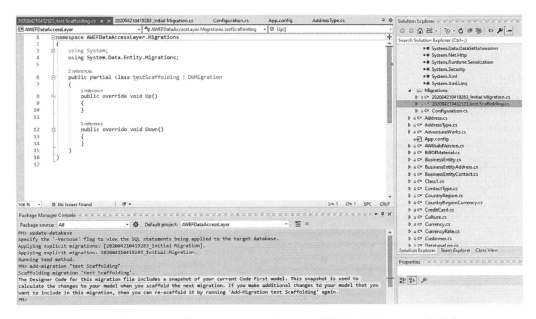

Figure 3-66. *Making sure the next migration scaffolds with no model changes*

Since this new migration is blank, we know we are not going to cause any issues, and we can just delete the test migration. *Right-click* the file and select *Delete*. If for some reason you had applied this migration, just revert with the command update-database -targetmigration InitialMigration and then delete the test migration.

Step 9: Leverage the new context from the startup app

Now that our context is wired up, we can leverage it from the regular code in our startup application.

Reference the new library project in the console startup application (shown in Figure 3-67).

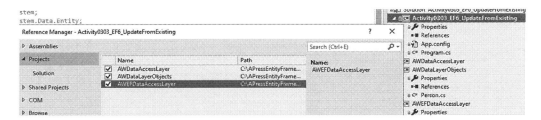

Figure 3-67. *Referencing the new EF library in the startup project*

Add a new method called GetPeopleEF to the Program class, which returns a list of Person, and is coded as follows:

```
private static List<Person> GetPeopleEF()
{
    var people = new List<Person>();
    using (var context = new AdventureWorks())
    {
        var result = context.People
                        .Where(x => x.LastName.StartsWith("G"))
                        .Take(5)
                        .OrderBy(x => x.LastName).ToList();

        foreach (var p in result)
        {
            var person = new Person()
            {
                BusinessEntityID = p.BusinessEntityID,
                FirstName = p.FirstName,
                LastName = p.LastName,
                PersonType = p.PersonType,
                Suffix = p.Suffix,
```

```
            Title = p.Title
        };
        people.Add(person);
    }
  }
  return people;
}
```

Note that we'll need to set a using statement to map Person now, since there is a conflict between our original *DAL* and the new *EF DAL*. Assuming all functional UI will rely on the original mappings, we'll have to map our EF objects back to DAL objects to ensure we don't break legacy applications. The using statement for Person is as follows:

```
using Person = AWDataLayerObjects.Person;
```

In case you've never seen a using statement assigned to a variable before, review Figure 3-68 to see what the code should look like.

```
using System.Collections.Generic;
using AWEFDataAccessLayer;
using Person = AWDataLayerObjects.Person;
using System.Linq;

namespace Activity0303_EF6_UpdateFromExisting
{
```

Figure 3-68. *The using statement to eliminate ambiguity for the Person object*

Finally, to complete the program, add two lines of code to the *program.cs* Main method:

```
var efPeople = GetPeopleEF();
efPeople.ForEach(p => Console.WriteLine($"Next Person: {p.GetFullName()}"));
```

This code should come right before the completion of the program.

Run the program to see it in action. Your output should be similar to the output in Figure 3-69.

```
▓ C:\APressEntityFramework\Code\Chapter03\Activity0303_EF6_Up
Found Person: Jossef Goldberg
Found Person: Diane Margheim
Found Person: Janice Galvin
Found Person: Sariya Harnpadoungsataya
Found Person: Mary Gibson
Next Person: Lawrie Gaffney
Next Person: Bob Gage
Next Person: Aldeen Gallagher
Next Person: Michael Galos
Next Person: Janice Galvin
Completed.  Press any key to exit
▀
```

Figure 3-69. *The final output of the program*

Final thoughts

In this final activity, we have worked through creating a new code-first *EF6* library against an existing database. Creating against a new database would be a similar process, although creating new EF6 projects is likely something you will not be doing very much of in the future. If a new database and project are being built, you should consider moving to *EFCore* or *.Net vNext (.Net 5+)*.

As a reminder, there are some major differences when using *EF6* in a code-first manner. We saw a few of them in play in this activity.

- Code-first migrations require a configuration file.

- The configuration file must have migrations enabled.

- Migrations can be automatic or manual, based on a flag in the configuration file.

- Use the command add-migration [migration name] to scaffold a new migration.

- Use the command update-database to apply the next migration.

- Use the command update-database -targetmigration [migration name] to roll back the database to a previous migration.

- EF6 implementations have a much more verbose config file.

- EF6 implementations generally require the connection string to specify that multiple active result sets are allowed.

Final thoughts for this chapter

In this chapter, we have taken an in-depth look at how we can get different projects set up to work with the code-first approach to database development.

We have also gained a basic understanding of what it takes to make changes via migrations when working with the code-first approach.

We also saw that getting things to work manually can sometimes be excessively painful, while somehow beautiful. There is a certain reassurance that happens when you know for sure that your code and your database are completely in sync with each other. We also saw that while there were errors during setup, they were easily overcome, and we are prepared to set up projects of all types in the future.

Our key takeaways for this chapter are

- Code-first migrations can be applied to any project, at any stage of maturity.

- Models are the key to generating database objects and working with the data in code.

- The DBContext acts as a definition for all database objects available.

- A DbSet<T> is essentially a table of the object defined in its generic type T.

- Migrations need to be scaffolded.

- Migrations can be applied in a forward or backward direction.

- Migrations are tracked in the database.

- Code-first development allows any developer to quickly build out a copy of the database by structure on any machine.

- Code-first development could be considered as an imperative approach to database programming.

Final thoughts on section 1

In these first three chapters, we've seen what it takes to work with Entity Framework in both the classic manner (*.Net Framework <= 4.8* and *EF6*) and in the new manner (`.Net Core 3.0`/`EFCore 3.0`). This was a necessary thing to cover because as developers we will likely encounter both versions for many years to come in legacy apps and new development.

For the remainder of the book, we'll be focused on *EFCore* and *vNext* Entity Framework concepts and database programming. Even so, almost every concept we learn will still be relevant, even to the *EF6* implementations, even if the older versions have a small difference in implementation or syntax.

Now that we have a very good understanding of how to get projects up and running with Entity Framework, in the next section, we'll start diving deeper into building out the data solution, beginning with a deeper look at models, contexts, and migrations.

PART II

Building the Data Solution

CHAPTER 4

Models and the Data Context

In this chapter, we are going to examine the data context and the creation of models, as well as look in a bit more detail about how these objects work in concert for code-first database programming with Entity Framework.

By the end of the chapter, we'll have reviewed and become even more familiar with some of the inner workings of the database context. Through practical examples, we'll also become very familiar with using models to build out our database tables.

What is the database context, and why do we need it?

Taking a quick step back, if you are reading this and you are used to working with an older version of EF (pre-EF4.1) or a non-code-first approach, you've perhaps never used the `DBContext` before. Instead, you might be familiar with an object called the `ObjectContext`. The `ObjectContext` contains all of the methods necessary to work against the database, such as `CreateDatabase`, `SaveChanges`, and more (see `https://docs.microsoft.com/en-us/dotnet/api/system.data.entity.core.objects.objectcontext?view=entity-framework-6.2.0` for more information).

© Brian L. Gorman 2020
B. L. Gorman, *Practical Entity Framework*, https://doi.org/10.1007/978-1-4842-6044-9_4

DBContext vs. ObjectContext

In the previous versions of EF, DbContext could, in some instances, act like a decorator on the ObjectContext, as it is possible for the DBContext to be created by wrapping an ObjectContext. It was also possible to gain access to the underlying ObjectContext from the DBContext when necessary.

In *EF6*, both DBContext and ObjectContext are implementations of the same interface, the IObjectContextAdapter. By having this common definition, and the ability for a DBContext to work like a decorator, it was possible to make the transition from the older-style *EF* with the **.edmx* files from existing databases to the code-first approach with no **.edmx* files, while still being able to support the original **.edmx* implementations.

In both *EF6* and *EFCore*, and likely also in *EFvNext*, the DbContext object is a critical component for code-first implementations. The DBContext contains all of the critical methods necessary to work against the database. With *EF* using a DBContext, a lot of the underlying patterns are implemented by default and don't require manual intervention.

We will focus on working with the DBContext for the remainder of this book. Additionally, we will be homing in on *EFCore* and *vNext* for our examination of the DBContext, as the future of the DBContext is likely more relevant to you. Along the way, however, we will still make a few notes about how things were different in *EF6*, just in case you're working with *EF6* in legacy code, or in the case where you are upgrading and need to know about the differences between the two implementations.

What is the DBContext?

To begin looking at the DBContext, let's get the official statement from the Microsoft documents about what the DbContext class is. The official documentation from https://docs.microsoft.com/en-us/dotnet/api/microsoft.entityframeworkcore. dbcontext?view=efcore-3.0 states the following about the DbContext Class:

> *A DbContext instance represents a session with the database and can be used to query and save instances of your entities. DbContext is a combination of the Unit Of Work and Repository patterns.*

Using the DbContext, therefore, we get orchestration around two significant patterns in database development, the *unit of work (UoW)* pattern and the *repository* design pattern. This means that by using the DBContext, we don't have to explicitly manage simple transactions when working with the DBContext, as they will be handled by the context implementing the *UoW* pattern. In other words, when working with the code to apply changes, until calling the SaveChanges method, everything that has been set to be modified is managed in the same implicit transaction. If something fails during that call to SaveChanges, the entire modified set is rolled back, which can be both a blessing and a curse.

To be more prepared and to gain a better understanding of this, we will take a deeper look at the *UoW* and *repository* patterns in more detail later in the book, as well as discuss working with explicit transactions and when to use them. Until then, we'll just leverage the built-in *UoW* and *repository* patterns.

Although most of the interaction we will have with the DBContext in many applications will be limited to adding DBSets and a few other small code modifications, it is a good use of our time to learn more about how the DBContext works, is constructed, and some of the options available to us through it. We can examine this in more detail by diving into the inner workings of the DBContext.

Constructing a new DBContext

In *EFCore* and likely *vNext*, there are only two constructors for the DBContext. We've already seen both constructors in use in our example Activity0302_EFCoreNewDb_Final. If you have not worked through that activity, you may want to take a moment to do so at this time.

In most cases, when creating the DBContext, we'll use the complex constructor, which takes a DBContextOptions object, but there are specific instances when the default constructor with no parameters will be used. Primarily, the default constructor is used when running migrations, as we saw in the previous chapter. The default constructor could also be used in a system without dependency injection anytime a DBContext is instantiated.

The DBContext class gives us the ability to inject options for use during normal operation of the database interactions with EF via the DBContextOptions class. When working with the DBContextOptions class, we generally will use a DBContextOptionsBuilder object, as the DBContextOptions class is usually composed and/or injected, not directly created.

The DBContextOptionsBuilder gives us a couple of critical operations that we'll leverage. In the last chapter, we set the type of database we wanted to use and injected the connection string for the DBContext through the DBContextOptionsBuilder and the DBContextOptions as follows:

```
protected override void OnConfiguring(DbContextOptionsBuilder
optionsBuilder)
```

```
    {
        if (!optionsBuilder.IsConfigured)
        {
            var builder = new ConfigurationBuilder()
                        .SetBasePath(Directory.
                        GetCurrentDirectory())
                        .AddJsonFile("appsettings.json", optional:
                        true, reloadOnChange: true);

            _configuration = builder.Build();
            var cnstr = _configuration.GetConnectionString
                        ("InventoryManager");
            optionsBuilder.UseSqlServer(cnstr);
        }
    }
```

Most importantly, in this implementation, we did not have a startup class or method in place that set up dependency injection via services at runtime. Therefore, no DBContextOptions were injected into the DBContext. To remedy this, we configured the options by overriding the OnConfiguring method as shown previously. As a result of overriding the OnConfiguring method and building the options builder as we did in this example, we could also further configure the DBOptionsBuilder if we needed to implement any other custom functionality, such as adding interceptors or enabling logging.

We should also note through this examination that any creation of the DBContext will use the OnConfiguring method, so we can continue to modify the options for our DBContext, even if the system is leveraging dependency injection.

As an alternative to overriding the OnConfiguring method, we can build the options inline and inject them into the constructor of the DBContextOptions directly as is shown in the following code block (which is easily generated by creating a new *ASP.Net MVC* Project):

```
public void ConfigureServices(IServiceCollection services)
    {
        services.AddDbContext<ApplicationDbContext>(options =>
            options.UseSqlServer(
                Configuration.GetConnectionString
                ("DefaultConnection")));
```

What's important to note here is the fact that in the *ASP.Net MVC* project, the project template sets the DBContextOptions to use *SQL Server* and leverages a configuration entry by name to get the connection string.

In both the earlier cases, we've set the database to use *SQL Server*. There are many other database options available, if your organization or project cannot leverage *SQL Server*.

Critical properties and methods available when working with the DBContext

In the next couple of sections, we'll take a look at a couple of properties and methods that exist for our use when building up and working with a DBContext. This reference is not an exhaustive list of all properties and methods available but should cover many of the common properties and methods that we're likely to use. The full list of detailed specifications for each object is available in the documentation at Microsoft, which can be found here: https://docs.microsoft.com/en-us/dotnet/api/microsoft.entityfr ameworkcore?view=efcore-3.1.

Important properties on the DbContextOptions Builder object

Each of our objects used in the composition of the DBContext for normal operations contains a couple of noteworthy properties. At the time of this writing, there are two properties of the DbContextOptionsBuilder class, which are shown in Table 4-1.

Table 4-1. *Properties of the DbContextOptionsBuilder class*

Property	Purpose
IsConfigured	Allows us to determine if the options are configured and respond accordingly
Options	Gives direct access to the DBContextOptions object

We've already seen these properties in action in the last chapter, although the call for Options to get the connection string was implicit in the DBContext, whereas we directly coded against the IsConfigured property.

Important properties on the DBContextOptions object

Even though we don't directly create a DBContextOptions object, we may still wish to code against a couple of the properties. There are three properties available to us in the DBContextOptions class, as shown in Table 4-2.

Table 4-2. *Properties of the DbContextOptions class*

Property	Purpose
ContextType	Gets the type for the context, if no type is defined, then DBContext will be returned
Extensions	Gets a list of Extensions as configured, such as the type of database being leveraged
IsFrozen	Used to determine if the Context is open for further configuration. If true, the system cannot further override the context options in the OnConfiguring method

In most cases, we won't have a need to leverage these properties directly, but it's good to know they are available should we need to provide an implementation that is more defined than a default implementation would be. I can definitely see a use case where locking the options from further configuring could be a nice security feature, potentially preventing logging or even injecting a new database connection string.

Important properties on the DBContext object

The DbContext itself also has a couple of properties. As with the other objects, we don't have to do anything with these properties if we don't need to, but there are some cases where it might make sense to work with the properties. The four properties of the DBContext are listed in Table 4-3.

Table 4-3. *Properties of the DbContext class*

Property	Purpose
ChangeTracker	Allows us to get direct information about the interactions with entities in our context. Can be used to determine if LazyLoading is enabled and if the context entities have changes, and it is leveraged for major operations like accepting changes and cascading deletes
ContextId	Every context has a unique id. This can be useful information for logging what context was being leveraged to perform an operation when there are multiple contexts or multiple instances of a context
Database	This property implements a façade on the database and is primarily used for determining and working with critical database operations like connections, commands, and transactions
Model	Gets the metadata for the underlying entities and relationships as mapped in the database

Although it is not always necessary to work with these properties, there will be times when you'll want to get direct access to the underlying database to perform operations. A particularly common use of this would be to execute a command that runs a stored procedure, which we'll see in more detail later in the book.

In addition to the properties on each of these objects, there are some methods that we'll be leveraging for the remainder of our work in this book. Let's start with the DBContext, which contains the majority of the methods we'll be using.

Methods available on the DBContext

When working with the DBContext, we'll first note that most methods have both a traditional synchronous method and also have an asynchronous implementation. The main reason for using an asynchronous method is to try to avoid blocking your main threads when making calls to the database. In general, you should try to do this whenever possible for a better user experience. That being said, it's important to note that the DBContext is not a thread safe object, so you may run into concurrency issues and other painful situations if you are building out a multithreaded application.

As mentioned previously, the methods shown in Table 4-4 are not an exhaustive list of the methods available. To get the full list, you can always reference the full documentation at Microsoft. Table 4-4 shows some of the more common methods we'll use to give us a general idea of what the DBContext can do.

Table 4-4. *Methods of the DbContext class*

Method	Purpose
Add/AddAsync	Allows insertion of the entity into the database
Find/FindAsync	Find a specific entity by Id
OnConfiguring	Allows for us to override the options
OnModelCreating	Allows us to use the FluentAPI to further define our entities and their relationships
Remove	Delete an entity from the database
SaveChanges/ SaveChangesAsync	Apply the tracked changes in a single transaction
Update	Used to perform an update to the tracked entity

What we can see is that the DBContext itself has all the methods necessary for performing *CRUD* operations, as well as the critical method for saving changes. Even though these methods exist, as we'll see in upcoming examples, we'll actually leverage methods and extensions on the DBSet<T> objects to do the majority of our *CRUD* operations.

Methods and extensions on the DBSet<T> object

The DBSet<T> object has a couple of critical methods and extensions that we will leverage in code, specifically for *CRUD* operations. Table 4-5 shows some of the more important methods and extensions we will rely on when working with DBSet<T> objects.

Table 4-5. *Methods and extensions of the DBSet<T> object*

Name	Method or Extension	Purpose
Add	Method	Add the entity to the context for insert
AsNoTracking	Method	Gets an entity that is not tracked so that any modifications do not cause concurrency issues
Create	Method	Creates a new entity for the type T
Find/FindAsync	Method	Locates an entity by Id and attaches the entity
Include	Method	Used to fetch related entities
Remove	Method	Sets the entity as deleted in the context
SqlQuery	Method	Allows execution of a raw *SQL Query*
AddOrUpdate	Extension	Inserts the entity if it does not exist or updates the entity if it does exist

While the majority of the methods we work with will be from the DBSet<T> or DBContext objects, there may be a few instances where methods from the DBContextOptions and/or DBContextOptionsBuilder could be leveraged. For the DBContextOptions, the most common method that would likely be leveraged would be the Freeze method, which prevents the builder options from being further configured in the OnConfiguring method.

Methods and extensions for the DBContextOptions Builder object

The DBContextOptionsBuilder has the ability to set the specific database type using extensions and can also be leveraged to perform some configuration around logging and interceptors. Table 4-6 shows some of the methods and extensions available on the DBContextOptionsBuilder.

Note that the method names listed in Table 4-6 sometimes contain a space in the name. This is purely to allow the preceding table to wrap the text. In actual code, there are no spaces in the method names.

Table 4-6. *Methods and extensions of the DBContextOptionsBuilder*

Name	Method or Extension	Purpose
AddInterceptors	Method	Allows adding a list of interceptors to monitor or modify operations
Configure Warnings	Method	Used to change runtime behavior of warnings, can impact performance
EnableDetailed Errors	Method	Used to include detailed error messages generated by exceptions, can impact performance
EnableSensitive DataLogging	Method	Allows information to be logged that would ordinarily be suppressed, can be a security risk
UseInMemory Database	Extension	Allows the context to work against an in-memory database
UseLazyLoading Proxies	Extension	Enables the creation of proxies for lazy loading
UseSqlLite	Extension	Sets the context to use *SQL Lite* for the underlying storage.
UseSqlServer	Extension	Sets the context to use *SQL Server* for the underlying storage

Now that we have an overview of the objects, methods, and extensions we'll be using to interact with the database, let's just quickly review what it looks like to work with an entity that is modeled in code.

Working with models

Assuming you've worked through the previous chapters in this book, you've already had a chance to create a class called Item. You then were able to use the Item class as a model to define the structure of a table in the database by adding a property for DbSet<Item> in the InventoryDbContext and then creating and applying a code-first migration (for more information, review Activity0302_EFCoreNewDb_Final). In that activity, however, we just touched the surface.

Two immediate benefits of code-first models

The real power of writing the database objects as code is twofold. The first benefit is that we have an immediate object which we can directly use in code throughout our system.

The second benefit is that we get to define every critical piece of the database in a common language every developer understands, while also having that code tracked in our source control repository.

Building a database entity model

In a closer examination, a model is nothing more than another coded *C# .Net* class. This means we can implement models with all of the same tools and techniques we would expect for any object-oriented system.

For example, we can define properties, which then become fields in the database. We can also set constraints on the models, as well as track relationships. Since everything is defined in code, building the models correctly will be critical.

A final thought about models

To this point in the book, we have not done a lot with models. Don't worry, we'll be getting into working with models more substantially as we progress through the remainder of the text. In a future chapter, we'll cover what it takes to add constraints and build out relationships in the database.

For now, we simply need to be aware of the fact that we can model a table directly in a code-first implementation. This is accomplished by taking the following steps:

1. Create the model as a *C# .Net* class to generate a table.

2. Add public properties to the model with a data type and a name for fields.

3. Add the entity to the DBContext (if not already there) as DBSet<T> where T is the type of your model. If the model is already in the DBContext, proceed to step 4.

4. Generate a new code-first migration to apply any and all of the modeled changes using the add-migration command.

5. Update the database using the update-database command.

In general, these five steps directly translate to an EF6 code-first implementation of the database.

Activity 0401: Modifying the Item

In this activity, we will modify the Item class we created in the last chapter by adding a couple of additional properties. We will then add a new database migration and update the database to get the new fields into the database table.

After we have completed that operation for the critical fields on the Item class, we'll build out an auditing hierarchy to finish up the activity.

Practical application for your daily routine

Going forward, as you build out your systems, you will be using a similar flow in most of your daily work. This activity is an exercise to give us another chance to practice building model properties and using them to generate a database migration and then perform the update.

While everything we do in this activity could have been done in one set of operations, if you would like even more practice, take the time to add only one property at a time and create a new migration each time, and then update the database each time. Either way, this activity will give you more practice with generating migrations and updating the database, such as you would do in your day-to-day development routine.

Building out the solution

From this point on, you'll use the same project, so you can simply build out this project for the remainder of the text. However, starter and finished files will always be available for each activity. It may be more convenient and easier to follow along by just grabbing the starter files at the beginning of each activity.

Step 1: Getting started

To get started, grab the starter files `Activity0401_ModifyingTheItem_Starter.zip`, and get them open in your local development environment. Alternatively, you could work with the project files you created from `Activity0302_EFCoreNewDb`.

When grabbing starter files, make sure to set or validate the connection string to map to your database in the `appsettings.json` files, and then run an initial update-database command to get the database up to speed at the start of the project.

There is a small change in the starter files from the final version of Activity0302_ EFCoreNewDb. In the starter files for Activity0401_ModifyingTheItem, I've added a new project called InventoryHelpers, and I've moved the ConfigurationBuilderSingelton. cs file into that project and then referenced the project as needed.

After making sure the database is updated to the latest version by running an update-database command, run the project, and you should see output similar to what is shown in Figure 4-1 (note that your list may vary depending on how many times you have run the program).

```
Microsoft Visual Studio Debug Console
New Item: Batman Begins
New Item: Batman Begins
New Item: Batman Begins
New Item: Inception
New Item: Inception

C:\APressEntityFramework\Code\Chapter04\Activity0401_ModifyingTheItem\
3.1\Activity0401_ModifyingTheItem.exe (process 9940) exited with code
To automatically close the console when debugging stops, enable Tools-
le when debugging stops.
Press any key to close this window . . .
```

Figure 4-1. *Running the starter project and validating that it is working as expected*

Step 2: Adding fields to the Item class

Now that our project is up and running as expected, we can easily modify the Item model to make changes to the database.

For this example, we'll add an integer to track *Quantity*, strings for *Description* and *Notes*, and a boolean object for tracking if the item is on sale. Additionally, we'll use *nullable objects* to optionally track two DateTime fields and two decimal fields. These fields will be named PurchasedDate, SoldDate, PurchasePrice, and CurrentOrFinal price.

As we build this out, we're placing properties with non-nullable fields at the top and nullable properties at the bottom. Make a note that this is not a requirement. The properties could be in any order that you desire. For example, if you wanted, you could enforce that properties are listed alphabetically. We'll eventually see that the generated migration doesn't care how we order the properties.

One last thought before we modify some code. If you are experienced with database development, you might already be thinking about auditing the rows with things like *CreatedDate, CreatedBy, ModifedDate, ModifiedBy, IsActive, IsDeleted*, and any other auditing information you might find useful. We'll get to that before the end of the activity, so please be patient and do not add these fields until prompted to do so.

Begin by adding the `integer` for quantity with a property named *Quantity*:

```
public int Quantity { get; set; }
```

Follow that by adding `string` fields for *Notes* and *Description*:

```
public string Description { get; set; }
public string Notes { get; set; }
```

Continue by adding a `boolean` property for tracking if the item is listed for sale:

```
public bool IsOnSale { get; set; }
```

Next, add the `DateTime` fields with properties for *PurchasedDate* and *SoldDate*, using the *"?"* to make sure both fields are nullable in case we haven't yet sold the item or in case we simply don't remember or want to track the date of purchase:

```
public DateTime? PurchasedDate { get; set; }
public DateTime? SoldDate { get; set; }
```

Complete the initial `Item` object rework by adding the nullable `decimal` fields for purchased price and current or final value:

```
public decimal? PurchasePrice { get; set; }
public decimal? CurrentOrFinalPrice { get; set; }
```

The final Item class at this point should look similar to what is shown in Figure 4-2.

```
Item.cs  ⊕  ✕

InventoryModels                                              ▼   ⚙ InventoryModels.Item

   1        using System;
   2
   3        ⊟namespace InventoryModels
   4         {
                  7 references
   5         ⊟     public class Item
   6               {
                      0 references
   7                     public int Id { get; set; }
                      7 references
   8                     public string Name { get; set; }
                      0 references
   9                     public int Quantity { get; set; }
                      0 references
  10                     public string Description { get; set; }
                      0 references
  11                     public string Notes { get; set; }
                      0 references
  12                     public bool IsOnSale { get; set; }
                      0 references
  13                     public DateTime? PurchasedDate { get; set; }
                      0 references
  14                     public DateTime? SoldDate { get; set; }
                      0 references
  15                     public decimal? PurchasePrice { get; set; }
                      0 references
  16                     public decimal? CurrentOrFinalPrice { get; set; }
  17               }
  18         }
  19
```

Figure 4-2. *The additional properties have been added to the Item class*

Step 3: Add a new migration to get the fields into the database

With our model changed, we need to add a new migration to make the changes propagate into the database.

Begin by making sure to save all your changes, and then run a build. Generally, you'd hit the chord *ctrl+s* and then *ctrl+shift+b* to save and then build. That being said, building the solution should save changes, so the step to save may be extraneous.

163

To be clear, it is also not necessary to build the project. Building the project will happen before the add-migration command is applied. However, by building the project first, we ensure that we can clean up any errors before trying to create the migration. If we simply run the add-migration command and the project won't build, we'll get an error notification and the migration will not be generated.

Review the output window to make sure the build completes (see Figure 4-3).

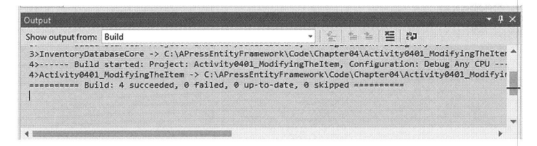

Figure 4-3. *Ensuring the build is completed without errors in the output window*

If you are using your files from the previous chapter, and you did not move the ConfigurationBuilderSingleton to its own project, your solution will likely state that you only have three projects where the build succeeded.

Next, open the *Package Manager Console (PMC)* and run the command to add the migration. Make sure to select the correct project which contains your DBContext. Failure to do so will result in an error (review Figure 4-4).

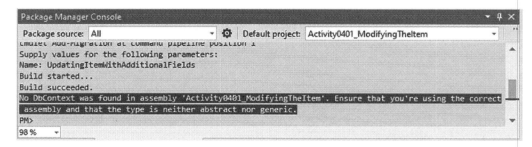

Figure 4-4. *Failing to set the correct project results in an error when trying to add a migration*

To create a new migration, use the command `add-migration "UpdateItem_AddCriticalFields"` as shown in Figure 4-5.

Package Manager Console
Package source: All
Default project: InventoryDatabaseCore
PM> add-migration "UpdateItem_AddCriticalFields"

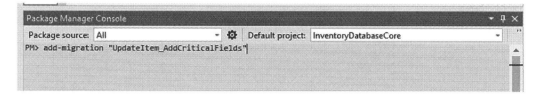

Figure 4-5. *Adding the migration to update the Items table*

After adding the migration completes, update the database using the command `update-database` as shown in Figure 4-6.

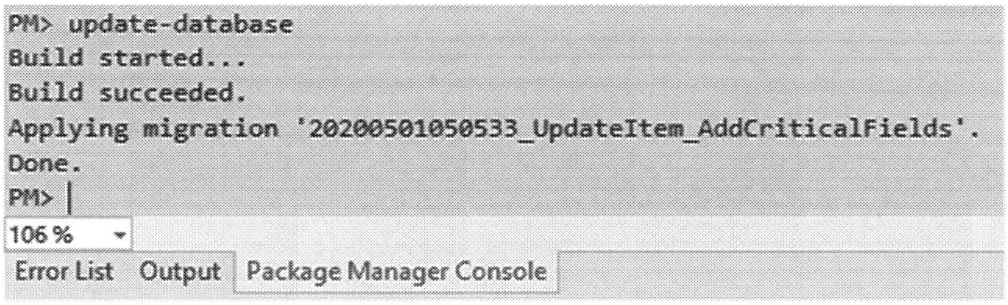

PM> update-database
Build started...
Build succeeded.
Applying migration '20200501050533_UpdateItem_AddCriticalFields'.
Done.
PM>
106 %
Error List
Output
Package Manager Console

Figure 4-6. *Updating the database with the modified Item columns*

Step 4: Review the database directly

After running an update, it is always a good idea to make sure the database was updated as expected. Take a moment now to look at the table directly using *SQL Server Management Studio (SSMS)* in your local database to make sure the fields are tracking with your `Item` class as defined in the code and migration. Figure 4-7 shows what the Items table should look like after adding the new fields and updating the database.

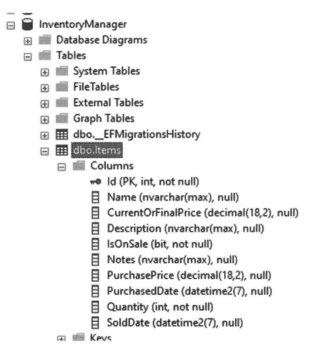

Figure 4-7. *The Items table after updating the database*

In Figure 4-7, after reviewing our database table, we see a couple of important notes. First, the fields that were just applied were applied in alphabetical order regardless of how we coded them in the model. If we had examined the migration, we would have seen them also laid out in this manner. Additionally, we see that the original fields are still at the top of the column list. This tells us that fields are generally created in alphabetical order, but their positions are kept in sequence with the migrations.

Step 5: Add the auditing class for easily creating auditing fields

As mentioned earlier, seasoned database programmers likely recognize that there are a couple of things that are generally very nice to track. As a caveat to this, however, I will say that with newer versions of *SQL Server*, it is possible to use timestamps to see what the database looked like at a specific time. Even so, it is generally a good idea to track who created, who modified, or deleted and when these things happened. Additionally, tracking if an entry is active or using a soft delete is often an approach that is favorable to help recover from problems created by users and can also be used to filter items without losing a lot of history.

166

To make the auditing for our system happen in a *SOLID* development approach, we will create a couple of small interfaces and then implement them in an auditing base class. We'll then extend the auditing base class for the *Item* class, create the resulting migration, and update the database.

Depending on how robust you want to build out your solution, you could choose to create a new project for shared objects to keep your interfaces separate from your implementations. To keep this example more contained, we'll just put the interfaces in the Models project.

Begin by creating a new interface file in the `InventoryModels` project called `IIdentityModel.cs` and add the following code to the file:

```
public interface IIdentityModel
{
    public int Id { get; set; }
}
```

Remember that if any part of the activity becomes confusing or you are encountering strange errors, you may always refer to my final solution for the activity to see how I intended for you to implement the code.

Depending on how you are tracking your users by Id, we'll need to respond accordingly with the type for user id. When working with built-in *ASP.Net MVC* users, likely this will be a string to map to a `guid`. For other systems, you might be using an `int` or `long` type. We don't have users in this system, so for now we'll use `integers`, and we could update this later as the need arises.

Create another file for `IAuditedModel.cs`, then write the code to create an interface called `IAuditedModel`, and add properties for tracking who created or modified the data row. We'll only require the created date for now. This will allow a system process to insert without tracking a user, and the default modification will not be set since the initial insert is a create operation, not a modification. All fields other than `CreatedDate` should be set as nullable.

```
public interface IAuditedModel
```

```
{
    public int? CreatedByUserId { get; set; }
    public DateTime CreatedDate { get; set; }
    public int? LastModifiedUserId { get; set; }
    public DateTime? LastModifiedDate { get; set; }
}
```

Next, let's create one final interface to track if an entity is active in the system. Create a file IActivatableModel.cs and add interface code as follows:

```
public interface IActivatableModel
{
    public bool IsActive { get; set; }
}
```

Now that all the interfaces are in place, we could create multiple base classes to make various entity implementations. Since we don't do multiple inheritance in *C# .Net*, we'll just create one base class to rule them all.

Create a new file called FullAuditModel.cs, then make the class abstract, and implement all three of our new interfaces. Also remember, we will never want to add this class to our DBContext as a DBSet. Keeping the base class as an abstract class should also prevent future confusion on this point.

```
public class FullAuditModel : IIdentityModel, IAuditedModel,
IActivatableModel
{
    public int Id { get; set; }
    public int? CreatedByUserId { get; set; }
    public DateTime CreatedDate { get; set; }
    public int? LastModifiedUserId { get; set; }
    public DateTime? LastModifiedDate { get; set; }
    public bool IsActive { get; set; }
}
```

Step 6: Extend the FullAuditModel base class on Item, add the migration, and update the database

Using the newly created FullAuditModel class, we'll implement auditing on the Items table by extending the audit class. After setting up the inheritance hierarchy, we'll need to add another migration and then update the database to complete this activity.

First, extend the FullAuditModel base class on Item. Additionally, don't forget to remove the local field for Id on the Item class to avoid creating a second Id column.

```
public class Item : FullAuditModel
{
    //removed Id Field
    public string Name { get; set; }
    public int Quantity { get; set; }
    //... additional fields here
```

After reworking the code, the Item class should look like what is shown in Figure 4-8.

```
namespace InventoryModels
{
    7 references
    public class Item : FullAuditModel
    {
        7 references
        public string Name { get; set; }
        0 references
        public int Quantity { get; set; }
        0 references
        public string Description { get; set; }
        0 references
        public string Notes { get; set; }
        0 references
        public bool IsOnSale { get; set; }
        0 references
        public DateTime? PurchasedDate { get; set; }
        0 references
        public DateTime? SoldDate { get; set; }
        0 references
        public decimal? PurchasePrice { get; set; }
        0 references
        public decimal? CurrentOrFinalPrice { get; set; }
    }
}
```

Figure 4-8. *Extending the FullAuditModel abstract class on Items*

Alternatively, we could have just implemented all the interfaces directly on the Item class, or we could have left the IsActive (IActivatableModel) boolean out of auditing, then implemented the base auditing, and then added the IActivatableModel interface directly to the Item class.

The way you implement any solution needs to make sense for your system. Here, we're taking the shortest route to success, but that may not always be the best way to write the code. It will always be up to you to make the best decisions for your system as the developer.

Always remember to save your changes and build the project. Then use the *PMC* to add a new migration with the command add-migration "UpdatedItem_AddedAuditing". The resulting migration should look similar to what is shown in Figure 4-9.

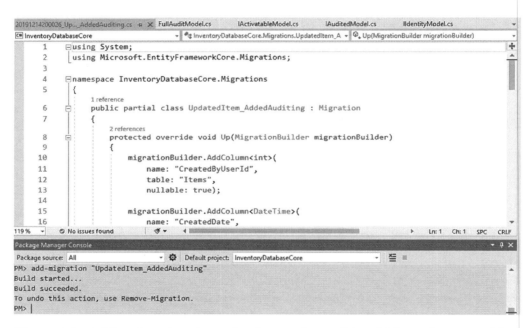

Figure 4-9. *Adding the migration to implement the auditing fields on the Items table*

Review the generated migration and make sure it looks to be adding the correct fields to your database as expected in the Up method.

Next, update the database using the update-database command in the *PMC (see Figure 4-10).*

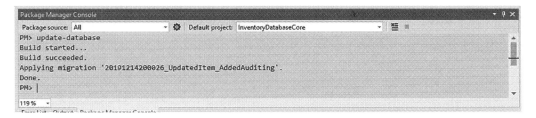

Figure 4-10. *Applying the database update*

Then review the table one last time to make sure your migration was applied as expected. In SSMS, find the Items table and right-click to refresh and then review the columns. The Items table should look like what is shown in Figure 4-11.

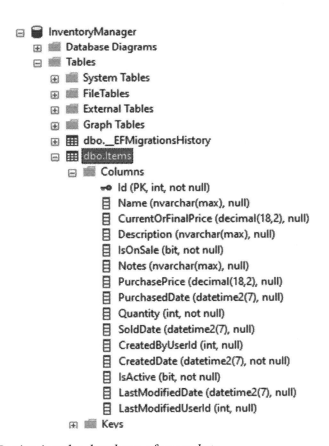

Figure 4-11. *Reviewing the database after update*

Final thoughts about modifying the models in our solution

At this point, we have completed the activity and are prepared to move on to the next activity. If you are tracking your code in source control, now would be a good time to commit your changes as an excellent restore point.

Please also note that if we tried to run the code from the console, it will not work since we are not handling the additional required fields (i.e., `CreatedDate`). We will be looking at this in more detail in the next activity.

Another point of note is that everything we have done in this activity could have easily been done in exactly the same manner in an *EF6* code-first approach.

Some of the key takeaways from this activity are

- We can create one migration with many changes, or we can make small changes and create a migration for each small change along the way.

- It is possible and desirable to use SOLID code patterns when building the models for our databases.

- The way that you implement your database is up to you, so you must make the best decisions around architecture.

- Adding the "?" operator to any public property will allow any normally non-nullable type to be nullable in the database.

- Strings and other nullable types are defaulted to nullable in the database.

- Using the add-migration and update-database commands will be a common operation for any developer in a code-first approach.

- It does not matter what order we create properties in the model class. Each migration will alphabetize the properties for creation.

- Additional properties in a consecutive migration are applied after original columns – the entire table is not restructured to alphabetize the order of columns.

- *EFCore* and *EF6* work nearly the same on basic operations for creating models, generating migrations, and updating the database from pending migrations.

Activity 0402: Using the ChangeTracker to inject some automated auditing

In this activity, we are going to set up our database to automate some of the audit trail for us. As with all things, what we do here could be further modified to suit our needs. Before we dive into the activity, let's take a moment to quickly review a few things about the DBContext object.

Setting up the context

We've already seen a few examples in this book and discussed scenarios where we've covered setting up the context to work against existing or new databases. The main takeaways from what we've already learned include

- The DBContext needs to be able to connect to the database via a connection string. This is accomplished in the pre-configured DbContextOptions in *EFCore* and was passed directly as a string to the constructor in *EF6*.

- *EFCore* gives us a method that allows us to check if the context options are configured. When they are not, we can perform custom code to ensure the configuration is built as needed.

- *EF6* allowed passing in a prebuilt ObjectContext to the constructor.

Common critical underlying objects

In addition to the things we've already seen, a couple of critical notes about the DBContext include the fact that in both *EF6* and *EFCore*, the underlying database is able to be exposed and used as an object. Additionally, both versions of the DBContext rely heavily on an object to track changes, which can be leveraged through the property ChangeTracker.

We'll take a deeper look at accessing the underlying database later in the book when we cover database objects like stored procedures. For this activity, we're going to concentrate on the ChangeTracker.

The ChangeTracker is the lifeblood of our interaction with the Entity Framework

In a typical workflow, some items are fetched and displayed to the user. After the user has time to review the objects, they may perform updates on one or more of the objects, may insert new objects, or may delete objects.

As the user performs actions, *EF* is working behind the scenes to orchestrate the changes, while having the ability to undo the changes if something goes wrong. The changes are generally only in memory, until a point when an explicit call is made to update the database via the DBContext - SaveChanges method.

At the time that the SaveChanges method is called, the changes that are stored in the ChangeTracker are applied to the database through the underlying connection to the database from *EF*.

Implementing automated auditing on our entities

By utilizing the ChangeTracker and the knowledge of SaveChanges, we can quickly write some code to intercept and inject auditing information.

Step 1: Getting started

The first thing we need to do is make sure we have a working version of the project ready to go. For simplicity, you could just get the starter files for the project Activity0402_ ImplementingAutomatedAuditing_Starter.

Alternatively, if you've completed the activities to this point in the book, you could just continue with your existing project. The name of the project is ultimately irrelevant, so don't spend time renaming your existing project if you are using your own version of the code.

As with prior activities, if you get the starter files, make sure to configure the database connection string correctly and perform an update-database command to ensure your version of the project is ready to proceed.

Step 2: Check out the current situation

Before we proceed, let's check out what the table is currently doing in the fields we've added in this chapter.

Open *SSMS* and right-click your Items table, and then select the option ➤ Select top 1000 rows. Depending on how many times you've run the program, you should have some multiple of 5 number of entries. I'm currently at 20 as shown in Figure 4-12.

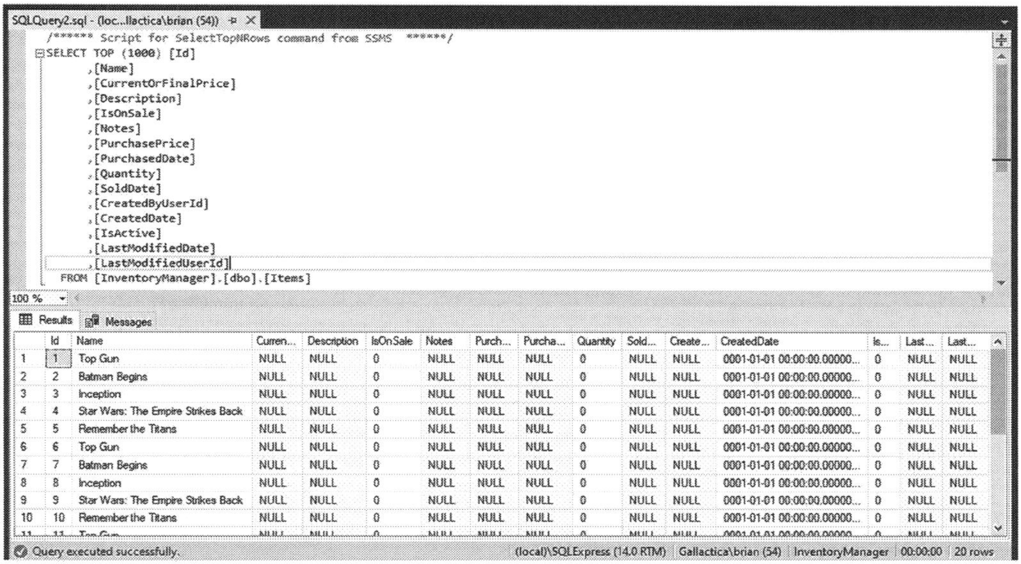

Figure 4-12. *The state of the database with duplicated entries and bad CreatedTime column data*

A careful review of the data in the table reveals that all the data in the fields is set to the default state. If the field is nullable, the value is null. If the field is an integer or bit (boolean), the value is 0 or false. The non-nullable CreatedDate field is set to a default date of 1/1/0001. Likely we didn't enter that data when Jesus was a baby, so this is certainly not a valid date for our inventory items.

To get our project back up to speed, we need to do a couple of cleanup items. In the process, we will look at the power of working with the ChangeTracker object.

Step 3: Clean up the data

The first thing that we should do is just delete all our stubbed in data. The easiest way to do this is to just write a script, and we could do that. However, we should examine what it looks like to remove entities using *EF* instead of writing scripts.

As a caveat, this solution is not ideal for an existing database with production data. In cases such as that, you would need to leave the data intact and then determine if you want to update the fields like CreatedDate or just leave them to a default date of some sort. Alternatively, you could do a migration scheme to back up your data, perform the updates, and then restore critical application data.

In the main program of the project, after the BuildOptions method and before the InsertItems method, let's just add a method for DeleteAllItems:

```
static void Main(string[] args)
{
    BuildOptions();
    DeleteAllItems();
    InsertItems();
    ListInventory();
}
```

Then implement the following DeleteAllItems method in the Program class following the BuildOptions method:

```
static void DeleteAllItems()
{
    using (var db = new InventoryDbContext(_optionsBuilder.Options))
    {
        var items = db.Items.ToList();
        db.Items.RemoveRange(items);
        db.SaveChanges();
    }
}
```

After this code is implemented, the *Program.cs* file should look something like what is shown in Figure 4-13.

```
0 references
static void Main(string[] args)
{
    BuildOptions();
    DeleteAllItems();
    InsertItems();
    ListInventory();
}

1 reference
static void BuildOptions()
{
    _configuration = ConfigurationBuilderSingleton.ConfigurationRoot;
    _optionsBuilder = new DbContextOptionsBuilder<InventoryDbContext>();
    _optionsBuilder.UseSqlServer(_configuration.GetConnectionString("InventoryManager"));
}

1 reference
static void DeleteAllItems()
{
    using (var db = new InventoryDbContext(_optionsBuilder.Options))
    {
        var items = db.Items.ToList();
        db.Items.RemoveRange(items);
        db.SaveChanges();
    }
}
```

Figure 4-13. *Implementing a method to delete all items*

Run the program and review your database table to validate that all items are deleted and then only the first five are added back (see Figure 4-14).

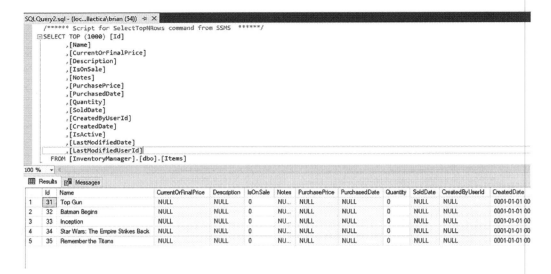

Figure 4-14. *The database is cleaned up with the new code*

Step 4: Intercept save changes to see the change tracker in action

In every instance where we are making changes to the database, the final step that we take is to call to the SaveChanges method. As of right now, we are letting the default operation take place. Let's change that.

In the InventoryDBContext file in the InventoryDatabaseCore project, add a method to override SaveChanges as follows:

```
public override int SaveChanges()
{
    var tracker = ChangeTracker;

    foreach (var entry in tracker.Entries())
    {
        System.Diagnostics.Debug.WriteLine($"{entry.Entity} has state
        {entry.State}");
    }

    return base.SaveChanges();
}
```

In my implementation, I placed the method at the bottom of the DBContext, below the OnConfiguring method, as shown here in Figure 4-15 (OnConfiguring method is collapsed in this view to save space).

```
24              public DbSet<Item> Items { get; set; }
25

                0 references
26      ⊞       protected override void OnConfiguring(DbContextOptionsBuilder optionsBuilder)⌐...⌐
39

                2 references
40      ⊟       public override int SaveChanges()
41              {
42                  var tracker = ChangeTracker;
43
44      ⊟           foreach (var entry in tracker.Entries())
45                  {
46                      System.Diagnostics.Debug.WriteLine($"{entry.Entity} has state {entry.State}");
47                  }
48
49                  return base.SaveChanges();
50              }
51          }
52      }
53
```

Figure 4-15. *Overriding the SaveChanges() method in the DBContext*

Place a breakpoint on the diagnostics debug line, and then run the program to validate this is working as expected. Once you have seen enough iterations to get a grasp on the ChangeTracker, feel free to remove the breakpoint and run to completion. Figure 4-16 shows the execution of this code, with the expected output values in the Output window.

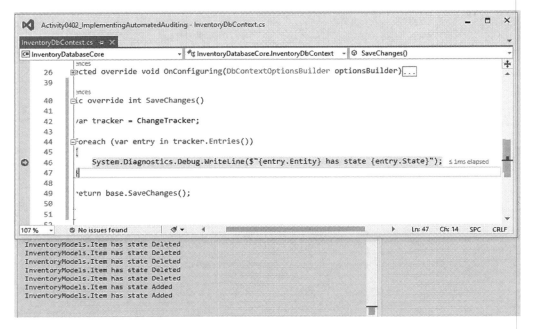

Figure 4-16. *The change tracker has a reference to every object that has been added or deleted in our example*

Taking a closer look at the valid states of an entity in the ChangeTracker, we can leverage any of these states in code. Additionally, our "logging" was fairly vanilla in this case, as we could also have grabbed the entity Id and other properties from the entry. Entity if we would have needed to do so.

Diving into the documentation at https://docs.microsoft.com/en-us/dotnet/api/ microsoft.entityframeworkcore.entitystate?view=efcore-3.1, we can see the valid entity states which we can code against. They are Added, Deleted, Detached, Modified, and Unchanged.

In our code, with the CreatedDate, we'll care about the Added state, and with the LastModifiedDate, we'll care about Deleted and Modified.

Step 5: Respond to the entity state in the change tracker

Before we build our automated logging, we need to address an elephant in the room. As of right now, our system is not tracking users. Therefore, at this time, we don't have a way to correctly set the valid user id. If we were working in *ASP.Net MVC* with default identities, we could grab the logged in user id from session and just pass it in with the model.

Additionally, if we want to ensure a user id, we'd likely need to block the default method from executing and create an *overload* that contains the user id as a parameter and then proceed to set the values accordingly and call to the base.SaveChanges method from the *overload*.

For this example, let's start by going back to the program and setting the user id on the Item model directly. This will simulate what we could do in our code provided we had some way to get the user id of the logged in user.

Add the following code in the DeleteAllItems method right after getting all of the items into the items list:

```
foreach (var item in items)
{
    item.LastModifiedUserId = 1;
}
```

And add the following code in the InsertItems method as the first statement in the using block:

```
foreach (var item in items)
{
    item.LastModifiedUserId = 1;
}
```

Next, we'll go back into the DBContext to set our automated auditing. One important thing we need to do is modify the entity's CreatedDate or LastModifiedDate property. This is a bit tricky, because we'll need to do some type checking first, to make sure the type has the correct field, and then set the value when it does. Even though we've set a pretty solid example, as of right now, there could still be a rogue entity that someone created without the auditing fields.

After validating that this is an entity type that has auditing, we can then create a switch to handle the various entity states and update our entry with a local reference accordingly.

Implement the following code to check entry entity type and use a switch when we are set to modify the entry:

```
public override int SaveChanges()
{
    var tracker = ChangeTracker;
```

```
    foreach (var entry in tracker.Entries())
    {
        if (entry.Entity is FullAuditModel)
        {
            var referenceEntity = entry.Entity as FullAuditModel;
            switch (entry.State)
            {
                case EntityState.Added:
                    referenceEntity.CreatedDate = System.DateTime.Now;
                    break;
                case EntityState.Deleted:
                case EntityState.Modified:
                    referenceEntity.LastModifiedDate = System.DateTime.Now;
                    break;
                default:
                    break;
            }
        }
    }

    return base.SaveChanges();
}
```

When implemented correctly, the code should look as follows in Figure 4-17.

```
40          2 references
41          public override int SaveChanges()
42          {
43              var tracker = ChangeTracker;
44
45              foreach (var entry in tracker.Entries())
46              {
47                  if (entry.Entity is FullAuditModel)
48                  {
49                      var referenceEntity = entry.Entity as FullAuditModel;
50                      switch (entry.State)
51                      {
52                          case EntityState.Added:
53                              referenceEntity.CreatedDate = System.DateTime.Now;
54                              break;
55                          case EntityState.Deleted:
56                          case EntityState.Modified:
57                              referenceEntity.LastModifiedDate = System.DateTime.Now;
58                              break;
59                          default:
60                              break;
61                      }
62                  }
63              }
64
65              return base.SaveChanges();
66          }
67      }
68  }
```

Figure 4-17. *Checking the type, then the state, and responding as needed for automating the auditing on our entities*

Run the application again, and then check the table for results. At this point, we should be back to only five records and they should all have a valid created date and user id. Figure 4-18 shows a sample of what the data should look like after a new run with the latest version of the code.

	Id	Name	Current...	Des...	IsOnSale	Not...	Purchase...	Purchas...	Qua...	Sol...	CreatedByUserId	CreatedDate	IsActive	LastModifiedDate	LastModifiedUserId
1	61	Top Gun	NULL	NU...	0	N...	NULL	NULL	0	NU...	1	2019-12-15 05:42:36.44355...	0	NULL	NULL
2	62	Batman Begins	NULL	NU...	0	N...	NULL	NULL	0	NU...	1	2019-12-15 05:42:36.44370...	0	NULL	NULL
3	63	Inception	NULL	NU...	0	N...	NULL	NULL	0	NU...	1	2019-12-15 05:42:36.44370...	0	NULL	NULL
4	64	Star Wars: T...	NULL	NU...	0	N...	NULL	NULL	0	NU...	1	2019-12-15 05:42:36.44370...	0	NULL	NULL
5	65	Remember th...	NULL	NU...	0	N...	NULL	NULL	0	NU...	1	2019-12-15 05:42:36.44370...	0	NULL	NULL

Figure 4-18. *The results are working as expected with a valid CreatedDate and CreatdByUserId*

Although the automated auditing is working, we really don't have a good validation on any updated items, and we don't have the `IsActive` flag set to true for the inserted items.

Step 6: Create an update method to prove out our auditing

Return to the *Program.cs* file, and add a method call to a new method named `UpdateItems` in the Main method, and in the Program.cs class, add a new method, `UpdateItems`, and then set the current price for all items as well as the last modified user id:

```
static void UpdateItems()
    {
        using (var db = new InventoryDbContext(_optionsBuilder.
        Options))
        {
            var items = db.Items.ToList();
            foreach (var item in items)
            {
                item.LastModifiedUserId = 1;
                item.CurrentOrFinalPrice = 9.99M;
            }
            db.Items.UpdateRange(items);
            db.SaveChanges();
        }
    }
```

And when implemented, the *Program.cs* code should look something like what is shown in Figure 4-19.

```
static void Main(string[] args)
{
    BuildOptions();
    DeleteAllItems();
    InsertItems();
    UpdateItems();
    ListInventory();
}

1 reference
static void BuildOptions()...

1 reference
static void DeleteAllItems()...

1 reference
static void InsertItems()...

1 reference
static void UpdateItems()
{
    using (var db = new InventoryDbContext(_optionsBuilder.Options))
    {
        var items = db.Items.ToList();
        foreach (var item in items)
        {
            item.LastModifiedUserId = 1;
            item.CurrentOrFinalPrice = 9.99M;
        }
        db.Items.UpdateRange(items);
        db.SaveChanges();
    }
}
```

Figure 4-19. Implemented UpdateItems method

With this code in place, run the program again, and then view the results in the database. If everything is working correctly, all entries should have a price and should also have a created and modified date (see Figure 4-20).

	Id	Name	CurrentOrFinalPrice	D...	Is...	N...	Purc...	Pu...	Quantity	S...	CreatedByUserId	CreatedDate	IsActive	LastModifiedDate	LastModifiedUserId
1	66	Top Gun	9.99	N...	0	N...	NULL	N...	0	N...	1	2019-12-15 05:50:17.87843...	0	2019-12-15 05:50:17.95794...	1
2	67	Batman Begins	9.99	N...	0	N...	NULL	N...	0	N...	1	2019-12-15 05:50:17.87862...	0	2019-12-15 05:50:17.95794...	1
3	68	Inception	9.99	N...	0	N...	NULL	N...	0	N...	1	2019-12-15 05:50:17.87862...	0	2019-12-15 05:50:17.95794...	1
4	69	Star Wars: The Empi...	9.99	N...	0	N...	NULL	N...	0	N...	1	2019-12-15 05:50:17.87862...	0	2019-12-15 05:50:17.95794...	1
5	70	Remember the Titans	9.99	N...	0	N...	NULL	N...	0	N...	1	2019-12-15 05:50:17.87862...	0	2019-12-15 05:50:17.95794...	1

Figure 4-20. *The results with auditing in place*

Step 7: Update the Insert to set all items as active, add Notes and Description

To complete the program and simulate a useable experience, let's set the active flag and description field. Back in the `InsertItems` method in the *Program.cs* file, update the creation of the items to include the active flag and description.

```
static void InsertItems()
{
    var items = new List<Item>() {
        new Item() { Name = "Top Gun", IsActive = true, Description="I feel
        the need, the need for speed" },
        new Item() { Name = "Batman Begins", IsActive = true
                    , Description="You either die the hero or live long
                    enough to see yourself become the villain"},
        new Item() { Name = "Inception", IsActive = true, Description="You
        mustn't be afraid to dream a little bigger" },
        new Item() { Name = "Star Wars: The Empire Strikes Back",
        IsActive = true
                    , Description="He will join us or die, master"},
        new Item() { Name = "Remember the Titans", IsActive = true,
        Description = "Attitude reflects leadership"}
    };
}
```

Figure 4-21 shows the reworked `InsertItems` method.

```
1 reference
static void InsertItems()
{
    var items = new List<Item>() {
        new Item() { Name = "Top Gun", IsActive = true, Description="I feel the need, the need for speed" },
        new Item() { Name = "Batman Begins", IsActive = true, Description="You either die the hero or live long enough to see yourself beco
        new Item() { Name = "Inception", IsActive = true, Description="You mustn't be afraid to dream a little bigger" },
        new Item() { Name = "Star Wars: The Empire Strikes Back", IsActive = true, Description="He will join us or die, master"},
        new Item() { Name = "Remember the Titans", IsActive = true, Description = "Attitude reflects leadership"}
    };

    using (var db = new InventoryDbContext(_optionsBuilder.Options))
    {
        foreach (var item in items)
        {
            item.CreatedByUserId = 1;
        }
        db.AddRange(items);
        db.SaveChanges();
    }
}
```

***Figure 4-21.** The code from the updated InsertItems method*

Run the program and then review the database to validate that all items are active and have a description, price, and a created and modified date and user id. Figure 4-22 shows the expected output.

Results | Messages

	Id	Name	CurrentOr...	Description	IsOnSale	Notes	Purc...	Purch...	Quantity	So...	CreatedByUserId	CreatedDate	IsActive	LastModifiedDate
1	71	Top Gun	9.99	I feel the need, the need fo...	0	NU...	NULL	NULL	0	N...	1	2019-12-15 06:01:08.60504...	1	2019-12-15 06:01:08.68232
2	72	Batman Begins	9.99	You either die the hero or li...	0	NU...	NULL	NULL	0	N...	1	2019-12-15 06:01:08.60515...	1	2019-12-15 06:01:08.68232
3	73	Inception	9.99	You mustn't be afraid to dr...	0	NU...	NULL	NULL	0	N...	1	2019-12-15 06:01:08.60515...	1	2019-12-15 06:01:08.68232
4	74	Star Wars: The ...	9.99	He will join us or die, master	0	NU...	NULL	NULL	0	N...	1	2019-12-15 06:01:08.60515...	1	2019-12-15 06:01:08.68233
5	75	Remember the Ti...	9.99	Attitude reflects leadership	0	NU...	NULL	NULL	0	N...	1	2019-12-15 06:01:08.60515...	1	2019-12-15 06:01:08.68233

***Figure 4-22.** The final results of the fully audited database context*

Final thoughts about working with the DBContext

We have now completed the automated auditing activity. Here are the key takeaways from our study of this practical implementation:

- The `ChangeTracker` object is the lifeblood of the changes against the database.
- Using the `ChangeTracker`, we can determine all of the entities that are tracked and check their state and then respond accordingly.
- There are other methods and properties from the `DBContext` that we have not yet explored.

We'll continue to work with the `DBContext` and our inventory system for the remainder of the book. If you are tracking your changes in source control, now would be a great time to check in your changes.

Final thoughts for this chapter

In this chapter, we've taken a deeper look at models and the DbContext. We reviewed the overall hierarchy for EFCore with the DBContext, DBContextOptions, and DbContextOptionsBuilder classes. We've leveraged all of these to create our connection string from the appsettings.json file.

We also made note of all of the major properties and methods available to us through the DBContext and DBContextOptions. While we will not have the need to use a lot of them in regular work, knowing they are out there and what they are for positions us to be better at providing the correct solution for each problem in the future.

We've also taken an in-depth look at a practical implementation that is positioning us to write a very good application, as we built out the solution over two new activities.

In our first activity, we started by looking at the Item model and discussing what it takes to create some new fields in the database. We then had the opportunity to practice creating a couple of database migrations and applying them.

We then finished up the chapter by looking at overriding the SaveChanges method so that we could implement automated auditing in our second activity.

There are many other properties and methods available to us that we didn't work through in the activities. Some of these we will leverage in the future.

There are a couple of issues with our system as it stands right now that we have noticed along the way. The first issue is that we are not preventing duplicates from being entered. Another issue that we have is that we didn't put any constraints on our database, which means our string fields are generated at max length. We need to fix this.

In the next chapter, we'll look at forming a more robust database structure with keys, constraints, and relationships.

CHAPTER 5

Constraints, Keys, and Relationships

In this chapter, we are going to learn about how we can use data annotations to further constrain our database structures from code. In addition, we'll look at how we can easily build out some relationships in our models that translate directly into relationships in the database.

When we've finished with this chapter, we'll have the ability to correctly create entities that not only specify type but have further constraints like primary and secondary keys and limit the length on strings. Additionally, we'll learn to enforce required fields and default values and how we can build one-to-many and one-to-one relationships modeled in code and enforced in *EF*.

As another reminder, our book from this point is focused on the *EFCore* and *EFvNext* versions of the Entity Framework; however, everything we do at this level can also be done in the same or a very similar manner in *EF6* if you are supporting a legacy *EF6* codebase.

Constraining our data to enhance our solutions

To this point in our book, we've simply created properties on our only model – the Item. We were able to work with this without any problem; however, as you might expect, working with everything in the default mode is usually not going to be considered the preferred mode. As such, we need to learn more about structuring our models so that we can build solutions in a preferred manner.

© Brian L. Gorman 2020
B. L. Gorman, *Practical Entity Framework*, https://doi.org/10.1007/978-1-4842-6044-9_5

One issue with leaving the properties of Item in a default state is that nothing is constrained. When working with databases, constraining the data means that we need to lock it down so that only the appropriate operations can take place. Some examples of constraints we'll examine in more detail are as follows:

- Size limitations – for example, minimum and maximum string length

- Value constraints – that is, min, max, and range of acceptable values on numeric fields

- Default values – such as making sure a bit is always true or false by default

As we approach each of these constraints, we'll need to evaluate our systems to make sure that what we are applying to the database constraints makes sense. It is also highly likely that as we maintain an existing project, we'll need to rely on a few of these constraints to keep from having to do further manipulation to protect existing data.

Size limitations

In our activity at the end of the chapter, we'll look at putting a size limitation on string properties. This is incredibly important, even though we've not applied the constraint in our earlier activities.

One thing you might have noted to this point is that in our original database, all our string fields have NVARCHAR(MAX) values. While this is definitely a functional solution, having an unlimited size is both unnecessary and is considered bad practice.

In most cases, your string field will not need to exceed 250, 500, or 1000 characters. In other instances, you might want 4000 or 8000 characters in a field for a longer input like a Notes or a Comments field. However, there are very few, if any, reasons to have a 2GB available allocation on the size of a single column.

Doing the math on this, we know there are one billion bytes in a GB, so this is *two billion available bytes*. Using NVARCHAR allows for unicode characters, which is useful if you need to store complex characters such as diacritical marks, Cyrillic, Arabic, Mandarin, or other similar characters. As an aside, the data type VARCHAR only stores non-unicode characters. No matter what you are storing, it is highly unlikely you need enough room to store the text of an entire novel in a single field, let alone also requiring multiple fields of unlimited length on the same table.

Going even one step deeper, we know that unicode characters require two bytes per character, and non-unicode characters would require only one byte of storage. Assuming we use NVARCHAR, this means we can store one billion characters in that single field when allocated as NVARCHAR(MAX). Fortunately, most instances of the database will grow to match size needs and not just use the full allocation of 2GB from the initial creation of the column. Even so, do we really want every row to have one or more fields that can expand to use up to 2GB of storage space? The entire size allotment of the *SQLExpress* database is only 2GB, so it would be really unfortunate to use that on one string column.

Imagine we have the most powerful supercomputer available to mankind, and it comes with unlimited storage, which therefore takes size constraints off the table as a reasonable reason to constrain a text field. Would it really be a problem to use NVARCHAR(MAX) in this case? The answer, of course, is a resounding "yes."

As database developers, we must consider what happens not just when we store data but also when we fetch or parse the data in queries. Assuming we have just a few of these unlimited length columns, and also assuming many of them have grown to very large lengths (i.e., each one is storing the entire text of a novel for some reason), what happens when we run a query that is looking for a partial match such as "WHERE field like '%contains_text%'"?

We can reasonably assume that queries such as those mentioned earlier will quickly become useless. With potentially unlimited text to search over multiple rows, the execution time would quickly balloon out of a reasonable response time (imagine how long it would take and the number of results you would get when searching for the word "jedi" in a database that stores the entire text of each of the Star Wars books ever written in plain-text fields).

To limit the length of a string field, we simply add a data annotation called StringLength, which is applied as an attribute by placing the following code above any string property in our model:

```
[StringLength(<size, int>)]
```

In addition, most annotations provide the ability to add an error message that is the default error message sent to the UI client when the validation fails. For example:

```
[StringLength(50, ErrorMessage = "The value of this field is limited to 50 characters")]
```

Value constraints

In addition to size constraints, another important type of constraint is a limitation on the expected value of a column. This value could be anything from a limitation on the numeric value to be in a range, such as minimum and maximum values. This could also be as simple as making sure that a field is not able to be set to *null* as its value.

Required fields are created with a simple attribute [Required] to reference the required *data annotation*, placed on top of any existing property. This attribute should be used anytime the database field needs to store a value other than *null* in the table, for example, a *primary* or *foreign* key.

The data annotation for setting minimum and maximum constraints on the properties in code is the *Range* attribute. For example, a range of 0 to max int could be [Range(0, int.MaxValue)]. In any range annotation, the first number is the minimum value and the second number is the max value.

Default values

A final consideration in constraining our data is the default value of an unset column. This is an extremely important aspect in a mature system, because null values on a row or loss of data could cause a lot of problems for your existing codebase and users.

As we add a field to any new or existing table, we can set a constraint on the field to enforce a default value. There are many situations where this approach can save a lot of trouble.

One critical use of this functionality would be adding a new field with a required value to an existing table with data. The field could be an easily managed field such as an IsActive boolean flag, or it could be more complex, such as a number to store the id of a user preference from a pre-defined list of options that references the available options stored in another table. In the first case, we can just set everything to active. The second case will never be as black and white as there are ramifications of every choice. What if we default to some simple value? What if we add an "unset" element to the options? How will this work in our current system?

Adding a default value is also accomplished with a data annotation, and looks as follows:

```
[DefaultValue(<the_value>)]
```

Other data annotations

In addition to those we've already discussed, there are a couple of other data annotations to be aware of. In every case, these annotations exist to apply further constraints on what can be used to store in the database. The main difference with a few of these is that while the constraint still applies, in some cases the constraint is accomplished at the code level, rather than the database level.

The StringLength, Range, and DefaultValue attributes each contributed a specific result to the underlying database structure. But what if you want to only allow an email address, zip code, phone number, or other special types of data into the field? In these cases, you can use another annotation, but just remember that these don't apply at the database level. For example, limiting to an email address is easily accomplished with the attribute:

```
[EmailAddress(ErrorMessage = "Invalid Email Address")]
```

In this case, our code will prevent inserting and updating if the input does not conform to a pre-defined email address format. However, the database is still just storing an NVARCHAR or VARCHAR and does not have any other information about the format of the string.

Other annotations to be aware of are as follows:

- ZipCode – though I've had better luck just using a regular expression.

- Regular Expression – format must match your expression for the model state to be valid.

- Display Name – sets the text to replace the name of the field in the UI. This is useful if you have a field like FirstName and you want to display "First Name."

- Table – it is possible to name the table differently than the name of the model if so desired (affects database structure).

- Index – applies an index to the column (affects database structure) (shown in the next section).

- NotMapped – allows a field to exist that is not tracked in the database.

- Compare – allows making sure one field is the same as another (i.e., password creation for a user taking a second input to validate) (does not affect database structure).

Further annotations can be found by looking at the DataType enumeration: `https://docs.microsoft.com/en-us/dotnet/api/system.componentmodel.dataannotations.datatype?view=netcore-3.1`.

Using keys in database tables for unique and relational results

We've already seen how using an Id field has generated a primary key on our Items table. However, there will be times when we need to do more than just define the primary key.

By default, the field `Id` is going to implicitly be the primary key. In addition to the implicit generation, we can explicitly define keys. This is accomplished with the `[Key]` annotation as an attribute.

Suppose, however, that we have a join table and we want to create a composite key on the two ids. In *EF6*, this could be accomplished a couple of ways using data annotations. The first way was to use the `[Key]` attribute with a column order `[Column(Order=n)]` (the order groups the keys). The problem with this is you cannot use the approach if you already have a primary key defined. The second approach was to use an index annotation as an attribute. This is a great way to do it in *EF6* but, unfortunately, at the time of this writing, is not possible in *EFCore*. To accomplish this in our final activity later in this chapter, we'll have to use the *FluentAPI*.

Indexes allow us to tell the database what fields are most important on the table, so that the database can precompile some statistics using those fields. This allows, among other things, more efficient queries where those fields are critical in searching for results. Additionally, indexes can be used to make sure column combinations are unique.

Applying an index for any field by itself is as simple as adding the `[Index]` annotation attribute to the field. When creating a *composite key* or *non-clustered* index, we can use the `[Index]` annotation with the order, just like the key with column order above, and we can also set a third property to make the combination unique with a unique constraint. For example, consider that we have items that have a group of unique objects (like movies with actors), and we create a table called "ItemObjects" that stores various actor/actress names and other common properties we care about across various objects. We need a many-to-many relationship to put objects and items together, but we don't want to create duplicates of the same relationship. In that case, we could use the following setup in a join table called `ItemObjects`:

194

```
[Index("IX_ItemObjectUnique", 1, IsClustered = false, IsUnique = true)]
public int ItemId {get;set;}
[Index("IX_ItemObjectUnique", 2, IsClustered = false, IsUnique = true)]
public int ActorId {get;set;}
```

Now that we have a good understanding of constraints and keys, we can examine what it takes to set up relationships between tables in the database.

Working with relational data

Most of the systems we build for line-of-business applications require some sort of relational data. Orders need Items and quantity. Addresses require States and/or Regions and Countries. User preferences require selections. SaaS systems often have editions and multi-tenancy. While it is possible to implement without an RDBMS (think NoSQL here), if we're using Entity Framework, we're also going to need to work with related data.

First-, second-, and third-normal form

A quick dive into relational database theory would help you to understand normalization and the difference between first-normal form (1NF), second-normal form (2NF), and third-normal form (3NF). There are also other normalization schemas in fourth-normal form (4NF) and Boyce-Codd-normal form (BCNF). In most business applications, the deepest level of normalization that is practical and performant would be 3NF. We will not touch on 4NF and BCNF in this text, but you may want to study them further if normalization is important and/or interesting to you. It is important to note that ORMs violate BCNF and 4NF by default to allow for efficiency gains and practical usage scenarios.

First-normal form (1NF)

1NF is the simplest form of normalization. For a database to be considered 1NF, the table rows must each have a unique key and the rest of the fields in any combination must not be the same as any other row.

Looking at the AdventureWorks database, there is a table Person.Contact which has a few fields. The fields include Title, FirstName, MiddleName, LastName, Suffix, EmailAddress, and a few others. The ContactID field is a unique key, and it can be assumed that although there may be multiple people who have the same title, first name, middle name, and last name, they likely have different email addresses. Therefore, this table is a great example of 1NF. Make note, however, that fields like Title and Suffix may have the same value across many rows (i.e., Mr., Mrs., Dr., Jr., Sr., III, etc.). Figure 5-1 shows the Contact table below:

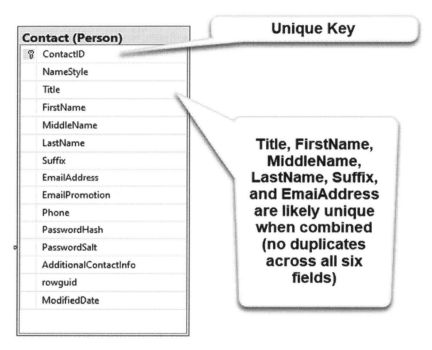

Figure 5-1. *The Person.Contact table from AdventureWorks as an example of first-normal form (1NF)*

Second-normal form (2NF)

2NF requires first that the table is in 1NF, but also prevents having duplicated data that can be directly related to another column in the table. For example, in AdventureWorks we have the table HumanResources.Employee, which has a field ManagerId. Suppose we also had tracked the name of the manager as a field, in addition to tracking the

ManagerId. If the ManagerId ever changed, then the ManagerName would also have
to change. Another example would be a field FullName in that table that is just a
combination of the FirstName and LastName Fields. In that case, if either the first or last
name changes, FullName would also have to change. The following query shows what
the table might look like in violation of 2NF:

```
select hre.EmployeeId, Contact.FirstName, Contact.LastName, Contact.
FirstName + ' ' + Contact.LastName as FullName
        , hre.ManagerId, manager.FirstName + ' ' + manager.LastName
        ManagerName
from HumanResources.Employee hre
inner join Person.Contact Contact on hre.ContactID = Contact.ContactID
inner join HumanResources.Employee empManager on hre.ManagerID =
empManager.EmployeeID
inner join Person.Contact manager on manager.ContactID = empManager.
ContactID
where hre.ManagerID = 21
```

Figure 5-2 shows the results of executing the query.

	EmployeeId	FirstName	LastName	FullName	ManagerId	ManagerName
1	7	JoLynn	Dobney	JoLynn Dobney	21	Peter Krebs
2	14	Taylor	Maxwell	Taylor Maxwell	21	Peter Krebs
3	16	Jo	Brown	Jo Brown	21	Peter Krebs
4	18	John	Campbell	John Campbell	21	Peter Krebs
5	25	Zheng	Mu	Zheng Mu	21	Peter Krebs
6	38	Jinghao	Liu	Jinghao Liu	21	Peter Krebs
7	51	Reuben	D'sa	Reuben D'sa	21	Peter Krebs
8	64	Cristian	Petculescu	Cristian Petculescu	21	Peter Krebs
9	74	Kok-Ho	Loh	Kok-Ho Loh	21	Peter Krebs
10	85	Pilar	Ackerman	Pilar Ackerman	21	Peter Krebs
11	87	David	Hamilton	David Hamilton	21	Peter Krebs
12	108	Eric	Gubbels	Eric Gubbels	21	Peter Krebs
13	123	Jeff	Hay	Jeff Hay	21	Peter Krebs
14	135	Cynthia	Randall	Cynthia Randall	21	Peter Krebs
15	143	Yuhong	Li	Yuhong Li	21	Peter Krebs

Both FullName and ManagerName violate 2NF in this simulated table

Figure 5-2. *What the Employee table could look like if it violated second-normal
form (2NF)*

There is another example in AdventureWorks where violation of 2NF is prevented. This is more common in our day-to-day work and very much like what we'll build in our examples.

The table Person.StateProvince is set up well to be in 2NF. For example, the table has the primary key of StateProvinceID, and then, instead of repeating data like the name of the Country or the name of the Territory, those pieces of information are brought in through foreign-key relationships to the tables Person.CountryRegion and Sales.SalesTerritory, respectively.

By following this normalization, the Names of the Country and Territory can be derived, but they are not going to require extra fields being changed in the StateProvince table if for some reason the country name changes or the territory name changes. Figure 5-3 highlights an example of 2NF.

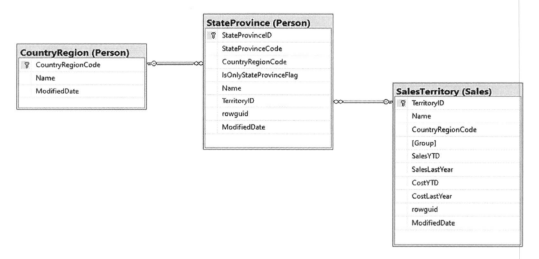

Figure 5-3. *The Person.StateProvince table follows 2NF*

Third-normal form (3NF)

3NF attempts to further break down 2NF into a unique group of columns (i.e., there are no transitive dependencies in the database) so that there is not any issue with compositional data becoming corrupted or incomputable due to changes in related data. For me, this can be a bit confusing, so it might help if you think in terms of auditing the database.

For example, in AdventureWorks, the Sales.SalesOrderHeader table has a column SubTotal and a column TaxAmt and then Freight and then TotalDue. Knowing that TotalDue is calculated from SubTotal, TaxAmt, and Freight, we have a couple of potential normalization problems, where either this table is in violation of 2NF (TotalDue changes if SubTotal, Tax, and/or Freight change for some reason) or we are in violation of 3NF. Since the TotalDue field is computed, the 2NF issues are mostly eliminated as the value automatically updates.

However, since that TaxAmt field is likely equal to the SubTotal multiplied by the TaxRate of the shipping address of the StateProvince where the customer lives and is likely calculated at the time of the order processing, then the problem becomes an auditing issue without 3NF.

Looking at the Sales.SalesTaxRate table, there is a column TaxRate and a foreign key to StateProvinceId. What happens if legislation changes in the StateProvince that raises the TaxRate for that region? In that case, the new TaxRate would be used on future orders, but the old one would have been used during the original calculation to create the TaxAmt. Because of this, the original TotalDue amount would appear as a different amount during an audit due to the change of the TaxRate. A violation of 3NF is shown in Figure 5-4.

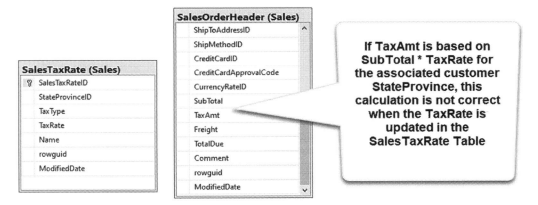

Figure 5-4. *A violation of 3NF happens when a field in one table is dependent on the value of another table, and that other table has a dependency on a third table. When that third table changes and results in changes to the related table, then the resulting dependency is also affected*

If the `Sales.SalesOrderHeader` table was in proper 3NF, the tax rate would have been stored at the time of the placement of the order so that the total due column could be correctly calculated using the subtotal multiplied by the tax rate at the time of the order.

While understanding the differences between 1NF, 2NF, and 3NF goes well beyond our text, it is important to be aware of them when creating our entities. With this awareness, we can now start to create proper, normalized relationships.

Types of relationships

When working with relational data, we have three types of relationships that we can use. They are

- One to one

- One to many

- Many to many

All three of the relationships have distinct purposes and are easily built out in code-first implementations. The way they are built is directly related to how the code is referenced from one model to another. What's more, in the many-to-many relationship, we can either define the join table explicitly, or we can rely on the implicit creation of the table. In most cases, we'll use a one-to-many or a many-to-many relationship, even if we have a one-to-one correlation as the result. However, we should know how a one-to-one relationship would work in case we ever need to set one up.

One-to-one relationships

One-to-one relationships are useful when there are two tables that are directly linked to each other but there is only one row in each table that is joined. The relationship is built with a primary key in one table and the foreign key in the other table and to be truly one-to-one should go in both directions (both tables are modified with a foreign key to relate to the only matching row in the other table).

One-to-one relationships generally provide additional attributes that are created to further define an object, which, when coupled, create a more detailed implementation of the object.

An example of a one-to-one relationship from AdventureWorks happens between the tables Sales.Customer and Sales.Individual, where each customer is given an ID and that ID is used to relate directly to an individual. This allows for a customer to have an account number as well as some demographics and be related indirectly to a contact in the system through the individual table. Figure 5-5 shows how the customer and individual tables form a one-to-one relationship.

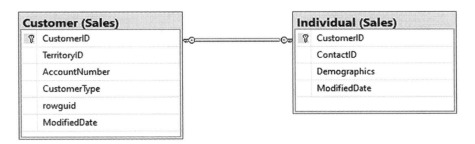

Figure 5-5. *The Sales.Customer and Sales.Individual tables are related in a one-to-one relationship*

One-to-many relationships

A one-to-many relationship is likely the most common relationship we'll encounter. Generally, one-to-many relationships rely on a key object that is then configured or further defined with options. One-to-many relationships are easily set up as drop-down lists or option lists when building out objects for making selections in the UI. For example, in AdventureWorks, Sales.SalesOrderHeader has a one-to-many relationship to Sales.SalesOrderDetail. For every Sales Order Header, we can have as many related details as we need to fulfill the order. A simpler example was already shown in Figure 5-3, where we had the Person.CountryRegion table having a one-to-many relationship with Person.StateProvinces and the Sales.SalesTerritory table also had a one-to-many relationship with StatesProvinces. Figure 5-6 illustrates how SalesOrderHeader to SalesOrderDetail is a one-to-many relationship.

Figure 5-6. *An example of a one-to-many relationship in the AdventureWorks database*

Many-to-many relationships

Many-to-many relationships are a bit more complex than the other two relationship types. In any many-to-many relationship, we are required to use a join table in order to relate entities to each other. This join table allows for a two-way relationship between the two entities. The first table can join and get all elements from the second table that match via the grouping in the join table, and the second table can do the same thing in reverse.

In a straightforward example, we might use many-to-many relationships for things like user preferences. We could look for any users that have set a single preference value, or we can look for all the preferences of a single user. This is very useful for correctly mapping data.

An example from AdventureWorks exists where the Person.Contact table is in a many-to-many relationship with the Sales.CreditCard table. This means that a single credit card could be used by multiple contacts, such as a couple of family members sharing a card, or a single contact could have multiple credit cards associated to them, such as would be the case for most individuals. We can perform queries in either direction and we can expect to get valid results. Figure 5-7 displays the many-to-many relationship between Contact and CreditCard via the ContactCreditCard join table.

Figure 5-7. *The Contact to CreditCard relationship in AdventureWorks has the join table ContactCreditCard to form a many-to-many relationship*

Some final thoughts about relationships and normalization

When working with any *RDBMS*, forming the correct relationships will be critical in order to effectively work with the data. By knowing the different types of normalization and relationships available to us, we can make sure to build out the best solutions as needed.

With the many different forms of normalization, we need to find the balance between what works and what works with efficiency. As the database developer, it will be our job to understand the trade-offs that will happen if we want to design a database to BCNF or 4NF, vs. the problems that might happen if we only use a 1NF strategy.

Activities for this chapter

The rest of the chapter is devoted to activities. For each of the activities, there will be a starter file set available. The activities will be designed in a way that you could easily work all or part of each of the activities. When opening a new starter pack, don't forget that you will need to configure the database connection string and run the update-database command to get the database updated to the state it needs to be at the start of the activity.

Alternatively, if you have been working along with the text to this point, you could simply use your files as is, with the only real difference again being the name of the project.

Finally, as with the previous chapter, these activities are focused on the *EFCore/EFvNext*. Everything we'll do in these activities could be done with an *EF6* implementation, with the potential of a couple of minor syntax differences.

Activity 0501: Add length, range, and other constraints to the Item model

In this activity, we will again dive into the Item class to build out a better database structure. This will give us the chance to see how to apply some of the common data annotations in our models to constrain our database.

By the end of the activity, we'll be able to set the minimum and maximum length of a string field, understand what it takes to make a field required, be able to set range limits, and apply default values for columns in our tables.

Step 1: Get started

To begin, open your solution, or get the files for `Activity0501_ConstrainingTheDatabase_Starter.zip`. Once open, make sure your database connection string is correct and update the database to make sure any pending migrations are applied.

Affecting the length of columns

In the next part of this activity, we will limit the length on all the columns currently sized to `NVARCHAR(MAX)`.

Step 2: Add length constraints to the strings on the Item class

Before beginning step 2, let's take a look at the table as it stands in the database. Right now, the fields `Name`, `Description`, and `Notes` are all `NVARCHAR(MAX)` length. Figure 5-8 shows the current database table with highlighted fields to illustrate the string length.

Figure 5-8. *All string fields are currently NVARCHAR(MAX) length*

In the real world, if we already have data in the tables, changing the length is likely to be a problem, because this could cause a loss of data if you decrease the length of the field. One way to prevent issues could be to quickly select the data from the table into a backup table using a query; then once the operation is completed, restore by selecting the data back into the table from the backup table. A great way to ensure you don't have mistakes in such a scenario would be to script this process and ensure it works as expected.

In our case, we are not concerned with lost data, so we will proceed as such.

Before we add the constraints, let's set some static constants in place, so we don't have to use magic numbers in our code. In the InventoryModels project, create a file called InventoryModelConstants.cs and add the following code to the file:

```
public const int MAX_DESCRIPTION_LENGTH = 250;
public const int MAX_NAME_LENGTH = 100;
public const int MAX_NOTES_LENGTH = 2000;
```

Figure 5-9 shows where the file is placed and what it should look like.

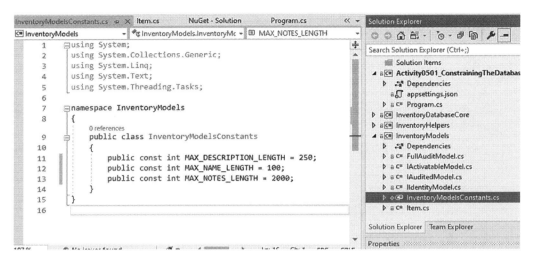

Figure 5-9. *The Length Constants in the Inventory Models Constants file*

With the constants in place, open the Item.cs file for the Item model and add the
following code above the Name property:

```
[StringLength(InventoryModelsConstants.MAX_NAME_LENGTH)]
```

Adding the StringLength annotation attribute will require adding the using
statement using System.ComponentModel.DataAnnotations to the top of the file.

Repeat the operation to add the following line of code above Description:

```
[StringLength(InventoryModelsConstants.MAX_DESCRIPTION_LENGTH)]
```

And add this line of code above Notes:

```
[StringLength(InventoryModelsConstants.MAX_NOTES_LENGTH, MinimumLength = 10)]
```

In this example, the minimum length is set to show that it can be done and how it
works. In the real world, the minimum length would likely be left blank. Make a note
that while the maximum length is enforced at the database level in schema, a minimum
length will be enforceable only by the model state. Even after creating this, someone
could come along and do a manual insert to the table with a Notes entry having a
length less than 10. Because I would ultimately remove this limitation, I did not create a
constant to map the minimum length of 10.

Figure 5-10 shows the reworked Item model with constraints applied.

```
7 references
public class Item : FullAuditModel
{
    [StringLength(InventoryModelsConstants.MAX_NAME_LENGTH)]
    7 references
    public string Name { get; set; }
    0 references
    public int Quantity { get; set; }
    [StringLength(InventoryModelsConstants.MAX_DESCRIPTION_LENGTH)]
    5 references
    public string Description { get; set; }
    [StringLength(InventoryModelsConstants.MAX_NOTES_LENGTH, MinimumLength = 10)]
    0 references
    public string Notes { get; set; }
    0 references
    public bool IsOnSale { get; set; }
```

Figure 5-10. *Enforcing maximum length on the string properties*

Step 3: Create the migration

With the length fields set, open the PMC and make sure to select the InventoryDatabaseCore project in the default project drop-down; then create a new migration with the add-migration "updateItem_enforceStringMaxLength" command. Upon completion, you should see output similar to what is shown in Figure 5-11.

```
PM> add-migration "updateItem_enforceStringMaxLength"
Build started...
Build succeeded.
An operation was scaffolded that may result in the loss of data. Please review the migration for accuracy.
To undo this action, use Remove-Migration.
PM> |
```

Figure 5-11. *Adding the migration to enforce maximum string length*

As we can see, this operation "may result in the loss of data." Even so, we can still apply the migration. This warning is to be expected, since we could be truncating strings if the current table has notes longer than 2000 characters, a Name longer than 100 characters, or a Description longer than 250 characters.

Take a look at the generated migration as shown in Figure 5-12.

```
3 references
protected override void Up(MigrationBuilder migrationBuilder)
{
    migrationBuilder.AlterColumn<string>(
        name: "Notes",
        table: "Items",
        maxLength: 2000,
        nullable: true,
        oldClrType: typeof(string),
        oldType: "nvarchar(max)",
        oldNullable: true);

    migrationBuilder.AlterColumn<string>(
        name: "Name",
        table: "Items",
        maxLength: 100,
        nullable: true,
        oldClrType: typeof(string),
        oldType: "nvarchar(max)",
        oldNullable: true);

    migrationBuilder.AlterColumn<string>(
        name: "Description",
        table: "Items",
        maxLength: 250,
        nullable: true,
        oldClrType: typeof(string),
        oldType: "nvarchar(max)",
        oldNullable: true);
}
```

Figure 5-12. *The migration as generated to enforce string maximum lengths*

Here we can see the columns will be altered to have a maxLength, but none of them have any limit on something like a minLength, even though we had specified that limitation in our annotation.

Step 4: Update the database

After reviewing the database migration, go ahead and run the update-database command to set the lengths as expected. After the command executes, check the Items table in the database to ensure that the correct lengths are now enforced. Reviewing the database should look similar to what is shown in Figure 5-13.

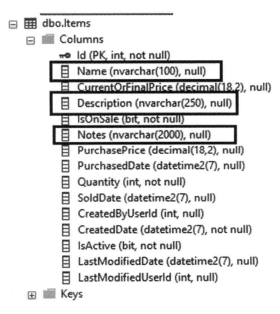

Figure 5-13. *The database table with maximum length in place for the string properties*

Creating a range on numeric fields

When working with the database, we'll often have fields that should be further constrained to limit what values make sense. For example, we should never have a negative quantity, and we likely want to lock down the price on an item so that it is also not negative.

Step 5: Add range values to the quantity and price fields

Once again, we don't want to use magic numbers, so let's start with some constants in the InventoryModelsContants file. Add a constant for minimum and maximum quantity and price.

```
public const int MINIMUM_QUANTITY = 0;
public const int MAXIMUM_QUANTITY = 1000;
public const double MINIMUM_PRICE = 0.0;
public const double MAXIMUM_PRICE = 25000.0;
```

Next, add the constraints in the Item class.

Above the Quantity Field, add the constraint as follows:

```
[Range(InventoryModelsConstants.MINIMUM_QUANTITY, InventoryModelsConstants.
MAXIMUM_QUANTITY)]
```

Above the PurchasePrice and CurrentOrFinalPrice, add the following code:

```
[Range(InventoryModelsConstants.MINIMUM_PRICE, InventoryModelsConstants.
MAXIMUM_PRICE)]
```

Once again, we'll see that these range values are not going to generate constraints on the table, but only constraints that our code would have to respect in the model state.

Step 6: Add the migration

Make sure to save and build, and then add the migration with the command
add-migration "updateItem_setMinMaxValuesOnQuantityAndPrice".

Generating the migration backs up what we expected – that the constraint from these data annotations is only on the model state and not enforced in the database. Perhaps to our surprise, the migration generates with no code in it as shown in Figure 5-14.

```
namespace InventoryDatabaseCore.Migrations
{
    1 reference
    public partial class updateItem_setMinMaxValuesOnQuantityAndPrice : Migration
    {
        4 references
        protected override void Up(MigrationBuilder migrationBuilder)
        {

        }

        4 references
        protected override void Down(MigrationBuilder migrationBuilder)
        {

        }
    }
}
```

Figure 5-14. *Adding a range constraint generates a blank migration*

Before we go rolling the migration back, however, there is something else we can do. We can apply a check constraint directly in the migration to set our ranges. To do this, simply add a couple of lines to the Up method to add the constraint using *TSQL*.

```
migrationBuilder.Sql(@"IF NOT EXISTS(SELECT *
    FROM INFORMATION_SCHEMA.TABLE_CONSTRAINTS
    WHERE CONSTRAINT_NAME='CK_Items_Quantity_Minimum')
    BEGIN
        ALTER TABLE [dbo].[Items] ADD CONSTRAINT CK_Items_Quantity_Minimum
        CHECK (Quantity >= 0)
    END

    IF NOT EXISTS(SELECT *
        FROM INFORMATION_SCHEMA.TABLE_CONSTRAINTS
        WHERE CONSTRAINT_NAME='CK_Items_Quantity_Maximum')
    BEGIN
        ALTER TABLE [dbo].[Items] ADD CONSTRAINT CK_Items_Quantity_Maximum
        CHECK (Quantity <= 1000)
    END");
```

Remember to also include a "rollback" statement to drop the constraint if it exists. Additionally, note that it is a good practice to ensure that your Down statements and Up statements are idempotent. In this manner, the migration can be run even if the objects do or don't exist, without error.

```
migrationBuilder.Sql(@"IF EXISTS(SELECT *
    FROM INFORMATION_SCHEMA.TABLE_CONSTRAINTS
    WHERE CONSTRAINT_NAME='CK_Items_Quantity_Minimum')
BEGIN
    ALTER TABLE [dbo].[Items] DROP CONSTRAINT CK_Items_Quantity_Minimum
END");

migrationBuilder.Sql(@"IF NOT EXISTS(SELECT *
    FROM INFORMATION_SCHEMA.TABLE_CONSTRAINTS
    WHERE CONSTRAINT_NAME='CK_Items_Quantity_Maximum')
BEGIN
    ALTER TABLE [dbo].[Items] DROP CONSTRAINT CK_Items_Quantity_Maximum
END");
```

Although it is not shown here, we could repeat these statements for the price columns to add the check constraints on price values.

Another note is that you can have more than one builder statement in a migration Up or Down method. For this reason, I split the Down method into two builder statements to show that this is possible. In effect, this is like using the "GO" statement between statements in a normal *TSQL* script, in that the first statement will complete before the second and consecutive statements start when split in this manner. With only one builder statement in the Up method, we could not use the GO statement and the entire statement is run in one transaction. For clarity, the reworked migration with constraint statements in the Up and Down method is shown in Figure 5-15.

```
4 references
protected override void Up(MigrationBuilder migrationBuilder)
{
    migrationBuilder.Sql(@"IF NOT EXISTS(SELECT *
        FROM INFORMATION_SCHEMA.TABLE_CONSTRAINTS
        WHERE CONSTRAINT_NAME='CK_Items_Quantity_Minimum')
        BEGIN
            ALTER TABLE [dbo].[Items] ADD CONSTRAINT CK_Items_Quantity_Minimum CHECK (Quantity >= 0)
        END

        IF NOT EXISTS(SELECT *
            FROM INFORMATION_SCHEMA.TABLE_CONSTRAINTS
            WHERE CONSTRAINT_NAME='CK_Items_Quantity_Maximum')
        BEGIN
            ALTER TABLE [dbo].[Items] ADD CONSTRAINT CK_Items_Quantity_Maximum CHECK (Quantity <= 1000)
        END");
}

4 references
protected override void Down(MigrationBuilder migrationBuilder)
{
    migrationBuilder.Sql(@"IF EXISTS(SELECT *
        FROM INFORMATION_SCHEMA.TABLE_CONSTRAINTS
        WHERE CONSTRAINT_NAME='CK_Items_Quantity_Minimum')
    BEGIN
        ALTER TABLE [dbo].[Items] DROP CONSTRAINT CK_Items_Quantity_Minimum
    END");

    migrationBuilder.Sql(@"IF NOT EXISTS(SELECT *
        FROM INFORMATION_SCHEMA.TABLE_CONSTRAINTS
        WHERE CONSTRAINT_NAME='CK_Items_Quantity_Maximum')
    BEGIN
        ALTER TABLE [dbo].[Items] DROP CONSTRAINT CK_Items_Quantity_Maximum
    END");
}
```

Figure 5-15. *Multiple or single migration builder statements allow scripts to be executed against the database using a migration*

Step 7: Run the migration to add the check constraints to match the range limitations in our data annotations

After saving and building the project, run the command update-database. Once the command has completed, right-click and script the Items table for create in *SSMS* to view the constraints and field information. The result of scripting the table for create is shown in Figure 5-16.

```
    [PurchasedDate] [datetime2](7) NULL,
    [Quantity] [int] NOT NULL,
    [SoldDate] [datetime2](7) NULL,
    [CreatedByUserId] [int] NULL,
    [CreatedDate] [datetime2](7) NOT NULL,
    [IsActive] [bit] NOT NULL,
    [LastModifiedDate] [datetime2](7) NULL,
    [LastModifiedUserId] [int] NULL,
 CONSTRAINT [PK_Items] PRIMARY KEY CLUSTERED
(
    [Id] ASC
)WITH (PAD_INDEX = OFF, STATISTICS_NORECOMPUTE = OFF, IGNORE_DUP_KEY = OFF, ALLOW_ROW_LOCKS = ON, ALLOW_PAGE_LOCKS = ON) ON [PRIMARY]
) ON [PRIMARY]
GO

ALTER TABLE [dbo].[Items] ADD  DEFAULT (CONVERT([bit],(0))) FOR [IsOnSale]
GO

ALTER TABLE [dbo].[Items] ADD  DEFAULT ((0)) FOR [Quantity]
GO

ALTER TABLE [dbo].[Items] ADD  DEFAULT ('0001-01-01T00:00:00.0000000') FOR [CreatedDate]
GO

ALTER TABLE [dbo].[Items] ADD  DEFAULT (CONVERT([bit],(0))) FOR [IsActive]
GO

ALTER TABLE [dbo].[Items]  WITH CHECK ADD  CONSTRAINT [CK_Items_Quantity_Maximum] CHECK  (([Quantity]<=(1000)))
GO

ALTER TABLE [dbo].[Items] CHECK CONSTRAINT [CK_Items_Quantity_Maximum]
GO

ALTER TABLE [dbo].[Items]  WITH CHECK ADD  CONSTRAINT [CK_Items_Quantity_Minimum] CHECK  (([Quantity]>=(0)))
GO

ALTER TABLE [dbo].[Items] CHECK CONSTRAINT [CK_Items_Quantity_Minimum]
GO
```

Figure 5-16.   *The check constraints are now in place on the database table schema*

Ensuring a field is a Key, making fields required, and setting default values on a column

As we've seen, a property called Id on the model acts implicitly as the primary key on the table. It is possible, however, to explicitly name a database field as a key. In fact, it is possible to have multiple fields as keys.

Step 8: Add the [Key] annotation to the Id field

In our code, we'll keep the Id field as the key, but we'll explicitly define it. In the FullAuditedModel.cs class, add the data annotation [Key] above the Id field (bring in the using statement once the Key annotation is added). Figure 5-17 shows what this should look like.

```
3 references
public abstract class FullAuditModel : IIdentityModel, IAuditedModel, IActivatableModel
{
    [Key]
    1 reference
    public int Id { get; set; }
```

Figure 5-17. *Setting a field as a Key is easily done with the [Key] annotation*

Step 9: Making some fields required

In most cases, the ability to make a field required in the database is determined by the data type. If we want the field to be non-nullable, we use a non-nullable type. If we want it to be nullable, we use the question mark to indicate a nullable type.

However, some fields could be ambiguous, like strings. To ensure that a field always has a value when we are working with our data, even if it is a nullable type, we can use the [Required] data annotation. The required annotation will enforce the field to be required in the database as well as invalidate the model state if the field is left null (note: null and empty string are not the same thing!).

Since every item should have a name, let's add the [Required] annotation attribute to the Name field in the Item.cs file as shown in Figure 5-18.

```
public class Item : FullAuditModel
{
    [StringLength(InventoryModelsConstants.MAX_NAME_LENGTH)]
    [Required]
    7 references
    public string Name { get; set; }
```

Figure 5-18. *Making the Name field required*

Feel free to make other fields required as you see fit.

Step 10: Adding a default value to a field

We've mentioned previously that there is a way to do a soft delete by adding an IsDeleted boolean value to the table. Once our table has data in it, however, we can only add fields as nullable, unless we enforce a default value.

Assuming that we want to make items able to be deleted without losing data, we can do this in our hierarchy. First, we create another interface in the InventoryModels project called ISoftDeletable, adding the property IsDeleted as a boolean:

```
public interface ISoftDeletable
{
    bool IsDeleted { get; set; }
}
```

We would then want to set the value to false and make the field required to avoid any confusion (is null deleted or not?).

Implement the interface on the FullAuditModel, and add the following data annotations:

```
[Required]
[DefaultValue(false)]
```

The DefaultValue requires bringing in the using statement: using System. ComponentModel;

All of this is shown in Figure 5-19.

```
3 references
public abstract class FullAuditModel : IIdentityModel, IAuditedModel, IActivatableModel, ISoftDeletable
{
    [Key]
    1 reference
    public int Id { get; set; }
    2 references
    public int? CreatedByUserId { get; set; }
    2 references
    public DateTime CreatedDate { get; set; }
    3 references
    public int? LastModifiedUserId { get; set; }
    2 references
    public DateTime? LastModifiedDate { get; set; }
    6 references
    public bool IsActive { get; set; }

    [Required]
    [DefaultValue(false)]
    1 reference
    public bool IsDeleted { get; set; }
}
```

Figure 5-19. *The FullAuditModel with the required annotation and default value set to false on the IsDeleted field*

Step 11: Create the migration

With all of the data formatting in place, let's create one last migration to lock down our database and create the changes we've requested. Run the command `add-migration "updateItem_addSoftDeleteKeyAndRequiredName"`. The migration generated should look similar to what is shown in Figure 5-20.

```
5 references
protected override void Up(MigrationBuilder migrationBuilder)
{
    migrationBuilder.AlterColumn<string>(
        name: "Name",
        table: "Items",
        maxLength: 100,
        nullable: false,
        oldClrType: typeof(string),
        oldType: "nvarchar(100)",
        oldMaxLength: 100,
        oldNullable: true);

    migrationBuilder.AddColumn<bool>(
        name: "IsDeleted",
        table: "Items",
        nullable: false,
        defaultValue: false);
}
```

Figure 5-20. *The migration generated by the additional constraints for required fields and default values*

In our generated migration, we note that the migration will in fact make Name non-nullable and will also add the `IsDeleted` attribute as non-nullable with a default value of false, as we would expect.

Step 12: Update the database and review

Save everything and build, and then run the `update-database` command. After running, open the table for review in *SSMS*. The table structure with fields, keys, and constraints is shown in Figure 5-21.

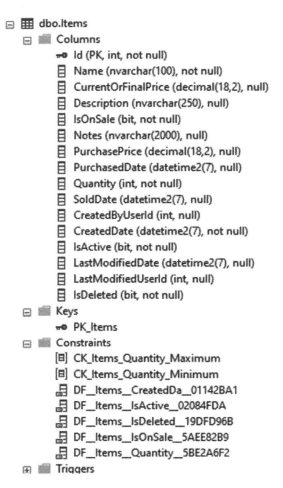

Figure 5-21. *The Items table after applying constraints from activity 0501*

We can now easily see how our constraints have been applied.

Key takeaways from activity 0501

This activity gave us a good look at how we can use annotations and migrations to modify our database. Some of the things we learned were

- Can set the key for the table with the [Key] annotation.

- Making fields required is possible with the [Required] annotation.

- Use [StringLength] to set the maximum length of a string.

- Use [DefaultValue(<value>)] to set the default value of a field.

- Some of the annotations only apply to the model state. In these cases, we can create a script to run *TSQL* statements.

- Use [Range] to set the minimum and maximum values of a field in the model state.

This concludes activity 0501.

Activity 0502: Setting up relationships

In this activity, we will create a one-to-one relationship and a one-to-many relationship. We'll build out the relationships and the data structures in code, but we will not yet be implementing them in the UI (we will finish the implementations in the coming chapter on *CRUD* operations).

By the end of the activity, we'll be able to define a one-to-one and a one-to-many relationship in code. We'll also understand the difference between the two types of relationships and when it will be appropriate to use either.

Creating a one-to-many relationship

One of the most common relationships we'll encounter is the one-to-many relationship. In this system, we'll create a table to store *Categories*, and then we'll create a one-to-many relationship so that we can create a few categories and then have many items in each category.

Step 1: Get set up

To get set up for this activity, grab the Activity0502_CreatingRelationships_Starter. zip file, extract and open the project, or feel free to continue working along in your current project. Once you have the files, make sure to build, set your connection string, and run the update-database command to ensure the table structure of your database is set up correctly. As always, please remember that if you get lost, don't understand a concept, or need more clarity on what code is being introduced, you can find my solution in the *_final.zip files.

Step 2: Create the Categories table entity

In the InventoryModels project, add a new entity entitled Category in a file Category.cs. For the Category, we'll use a FullAudited Entity and set an additional field for the Name of the category.

```
public class Category : FullAuditModel
{
    [StringLength(InventoryModelsConstants.MAX_NAME_LENGTH)]
    public string Name { get; set; }
}
```

Having this category entity in place, add the DBSet<Category> to the InventoryDbContext in the InventoryDatabaseCore file:

```
public DbSet<Category> Categories { get; set; }
```

This code should be placed directly below the DbSet<Item> Items { get; set; }.

With the context reference in place and the entity setup, we could create the migration; however, we have yet to create the one-to-many relation, so we should do that before adding the migration.

Step 3: Create the one-to-many relationship

To create a relationship in our code-first implementation, we need to reference the types that are related in the models involved in the relationship.

For this example, each of our Item objects should have one Category. Each of our categories can have many items. By saying this out loud, we can determine which types to place in each entity.

Since the Item only has one Category, we create a virtual reference to the single category. In the Item.cs file, add the lines:

```
        public virtual Category Category {get; set;}
        public int? CategoryId { get; set; }
```

We need to make the CategoryId nullable because the database may already have data at this point. With that data, we won't be able to set the category id to map until we have some categories to map to. Therefore, we'll allow null here to prevent the migration from failing. If you must make it required, you'll need to back up your data, delete from the table, and then re-insert with valid category ids after running the migration. Again, the best way to do backup operations such as this would be to use a script that you write to ensure you don't lose any data.

Note that it is also imperative that your Id field name matches exactly to the name of the virtual item. If these names are not the same, by convention an extra Id field would automatically be added to line up to your virtual Category field.

If for some reason your Category table has an Id field, but it's named something like CategoryId instead of Id, you can explicitly set the name of the Id field by using the data annotation [ForeignKey("CategoryId")].

Additionally, we want to use the virtual keyword on any of our relationships so that *EF* can override and/or extend the properties to support lazy loading of the relational data.

Next, on the Category object, we need to create a list of items. Remember, any category can have many items – which indicates an ICollection<Item> should be available, preferably IQueryable and IEnumerable. For that reason, it is very common to just use a List object. By default, a List is an IEnumerable object. If the List needs to be queried, you'll need to do a cast or use the LINQ expression .AsQueryable();. Add the following to your Category entity:

```
public virtual List<Item> Items { get; set; } = new List<Item>();
```

Make sure to set the List to a new list by default to avoid null reference exceptions on the list in the cases where the related items are not loaded into scope.

For clarity, the current code of the Category class is shown in Figure 5-22.

```
2 references
public class Category : FullAuditModel
{
    [StringLength(InventoryModelsConstants.MAX_NAME_LENGTH)]
    0 references
    public string Name { get; set; }

    0 references
    public virtual List<Item> Items { get; set; } = new List<Item>();
}
```

Figure 5-22. *The Category with the list of related items to finish out the one-to-many relationship*

Step 4: Create the migration

Make sure to save and build the solution. Since we have set the entities to relate to one another and have added Categories to the DBContext, let's add the migration using the command add-migration "createCategoriesTableForItemCategories". After running the command, the output should be similar to what is shown in Figure 5-23.

```
protected override void Up(MigrationBuilder migrationBuilder)
{
    migrationBuilder.AddColumn<int>(
        name: "CategoryId",
        table: "Items",
        nullable: true);

    migrationBuilder.CreateTable(
        name: "Categories",
        columns: table => new
        {
            Id = table.Column<int>(nullable: false)
                .Annotation("SqlServer:Identity", "1, 1"),
            CreatedByUserId = table.Column<int>(nullable: true),
            CreatedDate = table.Column<DateTime>(nullable: false),
            LastModifiedUserId = table.Column<int>(nullable: true),
            LastModifiedDate = table.Column<DateTime>(nullable: true),
            IsActive = table.Column<bool>(nullable: false),
            IsDeleted = table.Column<bool>(nullable: false),
            Name = table.Column<string>(maxLength: 100, nullable: true)
        },
        constraints: table =>
        {
            table.PrimaryKey("PK_Categories", x => x.Id);
        });

    migrationBuilder.CreateIndex(
        name: "IX_Items_CategoryId",
        table: "Items",
        column: "CategoryId");

    migrationBuilder.AddForeignKey(
        name: "FK_Items_Categories_CategoryId",
        table: "Items",
        column: "CategoryId",
        principalTable: "Categories",
        principalColumn: "Id",
        onDelete: ReferentialAction.Restrict);
}
```

Figure 5-23. *The generated migration for creating Categories with relation to items*

As you can see, there is a lot to unpack in this migration. First of all, we get the column for `CategoryId` added to the `Items` table and it is nullable, as we indicated. We can update these later and/or make it required for insert as we build out our solution.

The next part of the migration sets the table for the `Categories`. Note that there is nothing in this second part to indicate a relationship to the Items table. This is to be expected. `Categories` are independent of the Items.

The next statement is the index on the `CategoryId` field in the `Items` table. This is a common index we'll want since we'll likely sort or group by the `CategoryId`.

The final statement is the meat of the relationship. Note that the foreign key is added to `Items` related to `Categories` on `Category.Id`. Also notice the `onDelete:` `ReferentialAction.Restrict`. This action means that if we delete an item, it will not affect the categories table. However, a category will not be able to be deleted if any items exist that reference that category by id.

Step 5: Update the database

Now that we have the migration in place, we are ready to update the database. Run the command `update-database`, and then open *SSMS* and review the tables. The tables should have a relationship like the one shown in the diagram in Figure 5-24.

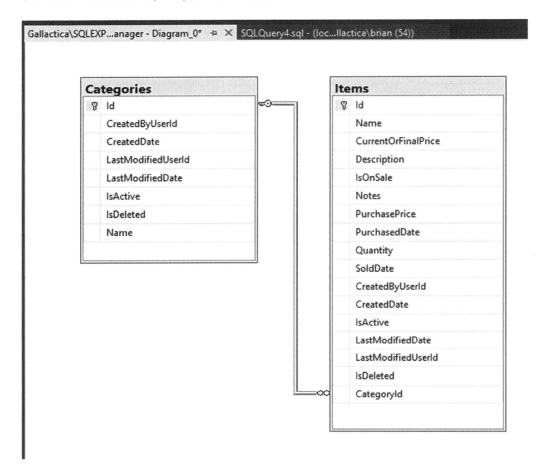

Figure 5-24. *The database now has Categories and the relationship is one-to-many with Items*

Creating a one-to-one relationship

In some instances, we will want to have a one-to-one relationship. For now, we'll just use a contrived example to show how to do this. Assume that we want to assign a hexadecimal web color to each Category and that we want the color to be unique to the category. We'll create a simple table to store the Color value and relate it directly to the Category in a one-to-one relationship.

Step 6: Create the Color entity

Create another entity in the Inventory Models project entitled CategoryColor by creating a new file called CategoryColor.cs in the project. This is going to be a simple entity with the default int Id and ColorValue as a string. Additionally, add a constant for the StringLength on the ColorValue field to be length 7.

Also, add the maximum color value length to the InventoryModelsContstants file: public const int MAX_COLORVALUE_LENGTH = 7;

Create the CategoryColor entity and implement IIdentityModel.cs. Add the ColorValue string property with the max length from the constants file, as well as the default Id property to implement the IIdentityModel interface.

```
public class CategoryColor : IIdentityModel
{
    [Key]
    [Required]
    public int Id { get; set; }

    [StringLength(InventoryModelsConstants.MAX_COLORVALUE_LENGTH)]
    public string ColorValue { get; set; }
}
```

To complete the creation of the entity, add the CategoryColor DBSet in the InventoryDBContext file: public DbSet<CategoryColor> CategoryColors { get; set; }, following the DBSet<Category> Categories property. Make sure to add any using statements as needed so the code will compile as expected.

Step 7: Create the one-to-one relationship

As with the one-to-many relationship, we still need to create the relationship in code before creating the migration.Here, we'll just add the direct one-to-one relationship by giving the color object one category and the category object one color.

In the CategoryColors entity, add the following code: public virtual Category Category { get; set; }

Then set the Key field to also be a foreign key to the Category (setting this makes it so that the table is related but does not store the CategoryId in the table):

```
[Key, ForeignKey("Category")]
[Required]
public int Id { get; set; }
```

For clarity, review Figure 5-25 to see what the CategoryColor entity model should look like.

```
1 reference
public class CategoryColor : IIdentityModel
{
    [Key, ForeignKey("Category")]
    [Required]
    2 references
    public int Id { get; set; }

    [StringLength(InventoryModelsConstants.MAX_COLORVALUE_LENGTH)]
    0 references
    public string ColorValue { get; set; }

    0 references
    public virtual Category Category { get; set; }
}
```

Figure 5-25. *The CategoryColor entity with reference to Category for one-to-one relationship*

Do not miss the ForeignKey constraint on the Id field. If you miss adding this, then the one-to-one relationship will not map and work as expected.

Once that is in place, add the relationship to the Category class as expected:

```
public virtual CategoryColor CategoryColor { get; set; }
public int? CategoryColorId { get; set; }
```

For further clarity, review Figure 5-26.

```
3 references
public class Category : FullAuditModel
{
    [StringLength(InventoryModelsConstants.MAX_NAME_LENGTH)]
    0 references
    public string Name { get; set; }

    0 references
    public virtual List<Item> Items { get; set; } = new List<Item>();

    0 references
    public virtual CategoryColor CategoryColor { get; set; }
    0 references
    public int? CategoryColorId { get; set; }
}
```

Figure 5-26. *The Category entity with reference to the color for one-to-one relationship*

Step 8: Create the migration

Now that the entities are in the context and the relationships are modeled to build a one-to-one relationship, add the migration with the command add-migration "createCategoryColorAndRelateToCategory".

Once the migration is completed, it should look as follows in Figure 5-27.

```
protected override void Up(MigrationBuilder migrationBuilder)
{
    migrationBuilder.AddColumn<int>(
        name: "CategoryColorId",
        table: "Categories",
        nullable: true);

    migrationBuilder.CreateTable(
        name: "CategoryColors",
        columns: table => new
        {
            Id = table.Column<int>(nullable: false),
            ColorValue = table.Column<string>(maxLength: 7, nullable: true)
        },
        constraints: table =>
        {
            table.PrimaryKey("PK_CategoryColors", x => x.Id);
            table.ForeignKey(
                name: "FK_CategoryColors_Categories_Id",
                column: x => x.Id,
                principalTable: "Categories",
                principalColumn: "Id",
                onDelete: ReferentialAction.Cascade);
        });
}
```

Figure 5-27. *The generated migration for building the Category to CategoryColor one-to-one relationship*

Note that the table is created and the entities are related as expected. The main difference is the onDelete action is set to ReferentialAction.Cascade. This means that if one is deleted, so is the other. If you think about it, this makes sense as we said every color needs a category and every category needs a color, so deleting one should delete the other.

Step 9: Update the database

With the migration reviewed, save and build, and then run the update-database command to execute the changes. Once the database migration has completed, open the tables in *SSMS* to review. See Figure 5-28, which shows the one-to-one relationship between Categories and CategoryColors.

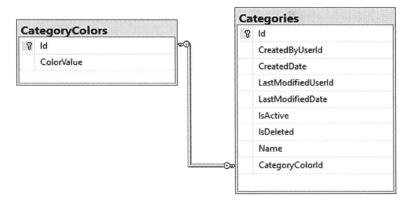

Figure 5-28. *The Categories and CategoryColors one-to-one relationship after database migrations are applied*

Key takeaways from activity 0502

In this activity, we learned how to build out a one-to-many relationship and also a one-to-one relationship. Important things to remember are

- Build out the entities, and then build the relations in the entities using virtual objects.

- If using a one-to-many, create a List of the related objects in the "one" table and a direct reference to the "one" object in the "many" object entity.

- Set both key and foreign key on the Id of a table in a one-to-one relationship.

- Cascading Delete can prevent delete if the entity has a related dependency with data.

- Cascading Delete can wipe out an entry if the other part of the relationship is deleted.

- Naming is done by convention, so use simple Id fields and then name the related field EntityId to easily map directly to the correct relational fields.

Activity 0503: Using a non-clustered unique index

This final activity for this chapter will be dual purposed in nature. First, we will examine what it takes to build out a many-to-many relationship. After setting up that relationship, we'll also see what it takes to create a non-clustered index that is unique on the many-to-many relationship. The unique constraint is critical to make sure that we don't have duplicate records in the database.

Soft delete or hard delete, either way, just make sure it works

A good thing to remember about this setup is that if we are using a soft-delete approach, we'll need to make sure that any relationships are still intact if we delete and then restore an object. This could be accomplished by soft deleting the join entry or just leaving it alone but making sure the data is handled correctly in both directions.

If we use a hard-delete approach, then deleting one of the sides of the relationship should also delete the entry in the join table via a cascading-delete operation.

By the end of the activity, we'll be able to define a many-to-many relationship in code, either implicitly or explicitly. We'll also understand what it means to set up a unique constraint as a non-clustered index on our database using the code-first approach.

Step 1: Set up and getting started

As with other activities, please find the files `Activity0503_ManyToManyWithUniqueNonClusteredIndex_Starter.zip` or use your solution that you continue to build out as we go. Once you have the solution open, make sure to set any connection strings, build the project, and run the update-database command to make sure your database is up to date with no pending migrations.

Step 2: Add the Genre entity

As we're tracking items, we likely have some inventory categories like movies and books, games, or other types of media. One common grouping that might exist across categories would be Genre. For example, we can have books and movies that are considered to be "Western" or "Sci-Fi."

To set this up, create a new entity in the InventoryModels project for Genre as a FullAuditModel. Add a string Name property to describe the Genre, and constrain the Name field using constraints that already exist. Make sure to add any missing using statements so the code will compile. We'll keep the Genre model pretty simple for purposes of demonstration and brevity.

```
public class Genre : FullAuditModel
{
    [Required]
    [StringLength(InventoryModelsConstants.MAX_NAME_LENGTH)]
    public string Name { get; set; }
}
```

Step 3: Add the migration and update the database

While we can likely create the Genre table, do the relationship mappings, and create the many-to-many relationship in one migration, I'm going to go ahead and create the table in a single migration first. The main reason I want to do this is just to keep my migration simple. The migration with the many-to-many relationship and join table will be a bit more complex, so I'd like to keep that migration separate from this table creation.

Make sure to add the public DbSet<Genre> Genres { get; set; } statement to the InventoryDbContext. The entry should follow the DbSet<CategoryColor> CategoryColors property.

Make sure to save and build the project, and then run the command add-migration "addGenreTable". Review the generated migration, which should look similar to the migration as shown in Figure 5-29.

```
protected override void Up(MigrationBuilder migrationBuilder)
{
    migrationBuilder.CreateTable(
        name: "Genres",
        columns: table => new
        {
            Id = table.Column<int>(nullable: false)
                .Annotation("SqlServer:Identity", "1, 1"),
            CreatedByUserId = table.Column<int>(nullable: true),
            CreatedDate = table.Column<DateTime>(nullable: false),
            LastModifiedUserId = table.Column<int>(nullable: true),
            LastModifiedDate = table.Column<DateTime>(nullable: true),
            IsActive = table.Column<bool>(nullable: false),
            IsDeleted = table.Column<bool>(nullable: false),
            Name = table.Column<string>(maxLength: 100, nullable: false)
        },
        constraints: table =>
        {
            table.PrimaryKey("PK_Genres", x => x.Id);
        });
}
```

Figure 5-29. *The migration generated to add the Genre table*

After reviewing the migration and making sure it is as expected, run the update-database command to add the table to the database. Review your database in *SSMS* to make sure the Genre table is in place as expected (see Figure 5-30).

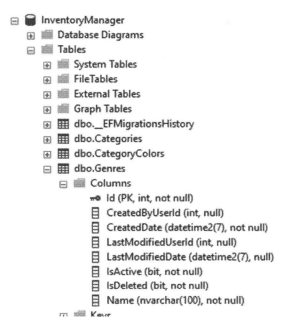

Figure 5-30. *The Genre table after creation*

Step 4: Add the ItemGenre entity

To make a many-to-many relationship, we'll use a join table called `ItemGenres`. This will track the `Item.Id` and `Genre.Id` fields to create a mapping of Items to Genres.

In *EF6*, if we did not want to explicitly create this table, adding the relationships directly as lists in each of the respective entities would implicitly create the table. In *EFCore*, it has so far been a requirement to directly define this object.

For the ability to both audit the join table and use the joins in code (rather than fully loading the entities to get join information), along with the fact that the migration likely won't work as expected in *EFCore* or *EFvNext* without the join object, I recommend just building out this entity explicitly. In the end, the table will get created either way, so you may as well take control of it.

Create the `ItemGenre` entity in the Inventory Models project as a `FullAuditModel`. Add two fields for each side of the relationship, an `ObjectTypeId` and the `List<ObjectType> ObjectTypes`, to map (just as we have done previously in a one-to-many relationship).

By building this out, it becomes clear that the join table is nothing more than a one-to-many relationship from the join to each side of the many-to-many relationship:

```
public class ItemGenre : FullAuditModel
{
    [Required]
    public int ItemId { get; set; }
    public virtual Item Item { get; set; }
    [Required]
    public int GenreId { get; set; }
    public virtual Genre Genre { get; set; }
}
```

Step 5: Make sure to reference the join table in the Item and Genre entities

If we create the migration right now, we won't get the join table as expected, because we did not yet set the list of entities to map in each of Item and Genre.

Starting with the Item class, create a `public virtual List<ItemGenre> ItemGenres { get; set; } = new List<ItemGenre>();` property. Make sure to add the missing using statement for `System.Collections.Generic` so the code will compile.

Do the same thing in the Genre class, but name the property as GenreItems. Again, don't forget to add any missing using statements.

For clarity, the Genre class is shown in Figure 5-31.

```
2 references
public class Genre : FullAuditModel
{
    [Required]
    [StringLength(InventoryModelsConstants.MAX_NAME_LENGTH)]
    0 references
    public string Name { get; set; }

    0 references
    public virtual List<ItemGenre> GenreItems { get; set; } = new List<ItemGenre>();
}
```

Figure 5-31. *The Genre model with the navigation property for GenreItems*

Step 6: Create the migration

Even though we have not added the ItemGenre directly to the DBContext, with the references in place on the left and right side (Item and Genre), the table should be created now as expected. Additionally, in case you missed it previously, make sure that you have added the DbSet<Genre> to the DBContext and have already generated the table for Genre prior to attempting to create this relationship.

After saving and building the solution, run the command add-migration "createdGenreAndItemGenreRelationship", then review the results. In your migration, you should see the table ItemGenre being created with the fields as expected, including an ItemId and GenreId. There should be constraints for the primary key, as well as two foreign keys set with ReferentialAction.Cascade onDelete. Finally, you should see two indexes, one for the ItemId field and one for the GenreId field.

After reviewing the migration, run the update-database command to set the table and relationships, and then review in *SSMS*. When created correctly, the table should look as shown in Figure 5-32.

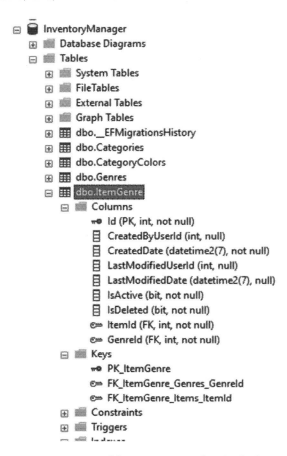

Figure 5-32. *The ItemGenre join table is generated to link the Genres and Items in a many-to-many relationship*

And to see it more clearly, a database diagram of the three tables shows the relationships (see Figure 5-33).

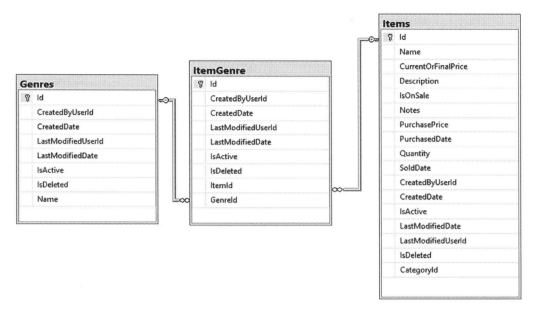

Figure 5-33. *The relationship as shown in a database diagram*

Adding a unique, non-clustered index to the ItemGenre table to make sure that the joins are unique

To keep from having multiple rows in the database that map the same two Item and Genre entities into a relationship, we'll create a new index that makes that combination unique. This is important so that we can make sure that when we perform a soft delete or restore from delete, we don't just create duplicate rows.

As mentioned earlier in the chapter, in *EF6* the first thing we could do is add the composite key in the join table. To do this, we could have added the [Key] attribute to the columns and set an order on the column to group them. This would create a composite key on the two columns. The problem with this approach is that it requires the composite key to be a primary key on the table. Already having the Id as the primary key would eliminate this approach. Just to show what it would have looked like in *EF6*, review Figure 5-34.

```csharp
using System.ComponentModel.DataAnnotations;
using System.ComponentModel.DataAnnotations.Schema;

namespace InventoryModels
{
    4 references
    public class ItemGenre : FullAuditModel
    {
        [Required]
        [Key]
        [Column(Order = 1)]
        0 references
        public int ItemId { get; set; }
        0 references
        public virtual Item Item { get; set; }
        [Required]
        [Key]
        [Column(Order = 2)]
        0 references
        public int GenreId { get; set; }
        0 references
        public virtual Genre Genre { get; set; }
    }
}
```

Figure 5-34. *In EF6, creating a composite key only works if the created key can be the table's primary key*

Another way to do this in *EF6* was to use the [Index] annotation.

Using the Index annotation would have looked something like what is shown in Figure 5-35.

```
4 references
public class ItemGenre : FullAuditModel
{
    [Required]
    [Index("IX_indexName", 1, IsUnique = true)]
    0 references
    public int ItemId { get; set; }
    0 references
    public virtual Item Item { get; set; }
    [Required]
    [Index("IX_indexName", 2, IsUnique = true)]
    0 references
    public int GenreId { get; set; }
    0 references
    public virtual Genre Genre { get; set; }
}
```

Figure 5-35. *Using the Index annotation is only available in EF6, not in EFCore*

Using the Fluent API

Up to this point, we've not used the FluentAPI, so we don't know a lot about it. That's ok. For now, I'll ask you to trust me and know that we will study the FluentAPI in more detail later in this book.

Step 7: Adding the unique index in the Fluent API

Before we add any code, let's first look at the file InventoryDbContextModelSnapshot. cs. Make note of the first line: this is a generated file. Looking further into the file, we see a bunch of FluentAPI-like syntax. However, we know that with this being generated, adding code here is a terrible idea. We need to do something like what we see for the relationships that are defined, but we need to do it in a place where we can guarantee it will always be applied correctly. Some of the code that exists in the generated InventoryDbContextModelSnapshot file is shown in Figure 5-36. What's very interesting about this generated code is this is the place where the code portion of the project lines up with the migrations. For example, you can easily see that the ItemGenre relationships are clearly defined in this file.

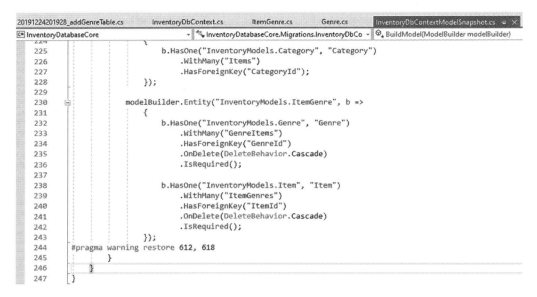

Figure 5-36. *A simple look at the generated model snapshot shows how some relationships can be formed in a Fluent-API like syntax*

Open the InventoryDbContext file and add the following code anywhere in the file. I chose to put the code after the constructors. This code allows us to override the OnModelCreating method.

```
protected override void OnModelCreating(ModelBuilder modelBuilder)
{
    ///code here...
}
```

Next, update the inner text for the method to add the non-clustered index for ItemGenre relationships with the following code:

```
//unique, non-clustered index for ItemGenre relationships
modelBuilder.Entity<ItemGenre>()
            .HasIndex(ig => new { ig.ItemId, ig.GenreId })
            .IsUnique()
            .IsClustered(false);
```

For clarity, the new code is shown in its entirety in Figure 5-37.

```
0 references
protected override void OnModelCreating(ModelBuilder modelBuilder)
{
    //unique, non-clustered index for ItemGenre relationships
    modelBuilder.Entity<ItemGenre>()
                .HasIndex(ig => new { ig.ItemId, ig.GenreId })
                .IsUnique()
                .IsClustered(false);
}
```

Figure 5-37. *The OnModelCreating method is used to implement custom FluentAPI declarations for further defining database schema*

Step 8: Add the migration

Make sure to save and build the solution, and then run the command add-migration "createUniqueNonClusteredIndexForItemGenre". Review the migration as shown in Figure 5-38 to see what is being applied.

```
public partial class createUniqueNonClusteredIndexForItemGenre : Migration
{
    10 references
    protected override void Up(MigrationBuilder migrationBuilder)
    {
        migrationBuilder.DropIndex(
            name: "IX_ItemGenre_ItemId",
            table: "ItemGenre");

        migrationBuilder.CreateIndex(
            name: "IX_ItemGenre_ItemId_GenreId",
            table: "ItemGenre",
            columns: new[] { "ItemId", "GenreId" },
            unique: true)
            .Annotation("SqlServer:Clustered", false);
    }
```

Figure 5-38. *Adding the unique, non-clustered index*

Step 9: Update the database and review the table

Now that we've seen the migration and can see how the index is added, we can run the command update-database. Once this is completed, let's review our table definition in *SSMS*. As shown in Figure 5-39, during the review of our table indexes, we can easily see the index is now created as expected.

Figure 5-39. *Reviewing the table reveals the created index is in place*

Final thoughts on activity 0503

In this activity, we saw what it takes to create a many-to-many relationship using code-first migrations, and then we took our first look at using the FluentAPI to generate a unique, non-clustered index. Some of the key takeaways were

- The many-to-many relationship uses a join table that consists of two one-to-many relationships.

- We don't want to add our join tables to the DBContext. Instead, we should force developers to work from one of the main data entities.

- EF6 had a nice data annotation for creating an index. EFCore requires using the FluentAPI.

- Creating a composite key is possible (two or more fields to create a unique identifier); however, the composite key must be the table's primary key in order to be created.

Final thoughts for this chapter

In this chapter, we've learned how to build out a better database schema in a code-first database approach. Specifically, we've learned about

- Limiting the length of fields

- Setting constraints on the values of the fields

- Setting default values on fields

- Creating one-to-one, one-to-many, and many-to-many relationships

- Adding unique indexes using the FluentAPI

At this point, we are in a really good place to start generating some solid database architectures and implementations. As the developer, it will be our job to know about these options that exist and how to work with them correctly to achieve the best overall results with our databases.

In the next chapter, we'll take a deeper dive into working with real data in this system we're building, so that we'll not only have the tools to architect a solid solution but the skills to develop against the data using common Create, Read, Update, and Delete (CRUD) actions.

CHAPTER 6

Data Access (Create, Read, Update, Delete)

In this chapter, we are going to learn about the basic tenets of data access using Entity Framework. By the end of the chapter, we'll have a good understanding of how to interact successfully with the data in our database.

CRUD

The common actions that most applications need are lovingly referred to as CRUD, which stands for Create, Read, Update, and Delete. Working with *EF* to perform CRUD operations is generally easy and efficient, but also requires at least a basic understanding of the Language Integrated Query (LINQ) syntax.

LINQ

You may already have some understanding of LINQ. You may even be an expert with LINQ. Perhaps you consider yourself fairly new to LINQ, or you have always felt that it is confusing. Luckily for all of us, there are tools we can use to generate some of the basic LINQ we would need when just getting started. Additionally, we will cover LINQ in a bit more detail later in this book.

Basic Interactions

In order to work against the database, we need to understand a few of the common commands that we'll rely upon when working against the database.

245

© Brian L. Gorman 2020
B. L. Gorman, *Practical Entity Framework*, https://doi.org/10.1007/978-1-4842-6044-9_6

Leverage the DbSet<T> objects

As we've built out our database library, we added properties on a few of our entities to the `InventoryDbContext` (context) using code such as `public DbSet<Item> Items { get; set; }`. By adding these properties, we can now leverage the power of *EF* and work against these entity sets directly.

For example, if we want to add a new Item, we can build a new Item object in code and then use the inventory context to add the item with code such as

```
using (var db = new InventoryDbContext(_optionsBuilder.Options))
        {
            db.Items.Add(item);
            db.SaveChanges();
        }
```

Here we've leveraged the context, specified the Items property, and used the extension `Add` to add a new item. We could leverage the commands `Remove` or `Update` as well.

Common commands

When getting started with *EF*, you will want to have a few commands in your toolbox. As you continue to learn and as we build on our skills through this text, we'll cover more than just some of these commands. For now, there are a few common commands we need to know.

A comprehensive list of commands will always be available on the official documentation site, which can be found here: `https://docs.microsoft.com/en-us/dotnet/api/microsoft.entityframeworkcore.dbset-1?view=efcore-3.1`.

An additional consideration is that there are some *asynchronous* methods available. When working with the methods that change the datastore, we should leverage the *synchronous* versions, such as `Add`, `Update`, and `Remove`. We then can use the *asynchronous* version of the save method – `SaveChangesAsync`. For queries where we are retrieving data, the async methods are readily available.

For our immediate understanding, Table 6-1 examines a few of the common commands. When looking at the code in Table 6-1 that follows, all commands would be run as shown previously, with the variable reference to the `DbContext`, and then the specific property to leverage the entity, followed by the command text. Examples from the work we've done so far include entities such as `Item`, `Genre`, and `Category`.

Table 6-1. *Common commands for CRUD operations against our datastore*

Command Text	Example	Use
Add	db.Items.Add(item)	Add a new `Item` (or other entity) to the database table
Find	db.Genres.Find(2)	Find a `Genre` (or other entity) by the Id (when the Id is a key)
Remove	db.Categories. Remove(aCategory)	Remove a `Category` (or other entity) by passing a tracked entity
Update	db.Items. Update(item)	Update a tracked `Item` (or other entity) by passing a tracked entity with modified values

As previously mentioned, there are other methods available to us, as well as more preferred ways to work with LINQ to get query results. We will see this in action in our practical activities that follow.

Activity 0601: Quick CRUD with scaffolded controllers

To this point in the text, we've stayed away from picking a *UI* implementation and have only worked with console applications.

However, to get started with our practical *CRUD* activities, I want to let the system do the work for us. For this reason, we're going to leverage a very simple *ASP.Net MVC* implementation with scaffolded views and controllers.

Our main point here will be the code that is generated in the controllers, but we'll also see how quickly we can spin up a basic web application in *.Net MVC Core*.

Step 1: Set up

For this activity, we are going to start from scratch and import the code we've already written. This will be a bit painful, so if you want to skip to step 2, get the starter pack `Activity0601_QuickCrud_Web_Starter.zip` files, extract the files, build, update the database, and run the project (will spin up a website locally). If you run into an issue with the database, change the connection string to point to your local database implementation, but use a different database than you've been using in previous chapters. If you want to see how this works for yourself, then complete the rest of step 1 that follows.

Open Visual Studio and create a new project. Select the `C# ASP.Net Core Web Application` template (see Figure 6-1).

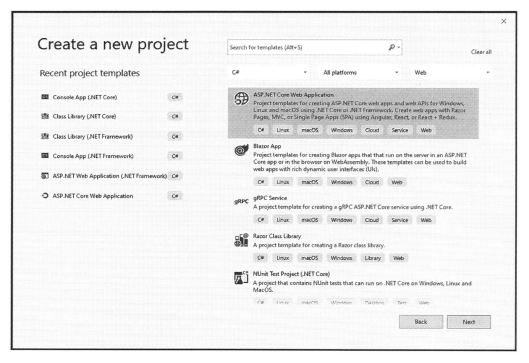

Figure 6-1. *Creating a new Core Web Application*

Name the application something like `Activity0601_QuickCrud_Web` and save it in a place that logically makes sense to you.

When prompted, select Web Application (Model-View-Controller). Keep Configure for HTTPS selected, and, most importantly, change the authentication using the very small *Change* link on the top right under authentication. Review Figure 6-2 for more information.

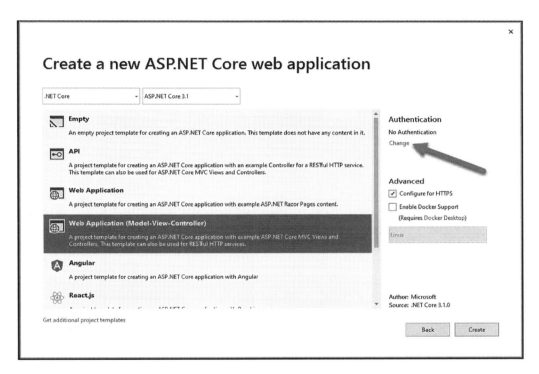

Figure 6-2. *Creating the project, select the Change Authentication link*

Select the option to use Individual User Accounts, and track them in-app. This will insert an ApplicationDBContext and user account management using the *ASP. Net Identity* schemas. If you forget to do this step, your project will build, but it won't have any default database setup. You can add the database later or you can build the project without user accounts later as well if you forget, but it will likely be easier to just generate a new project for our learning purposes. Review Figure 6-3 to see the Change Authentication dialog with the Individual User Accounts option selected.

Create a new ASP.NET Core web application

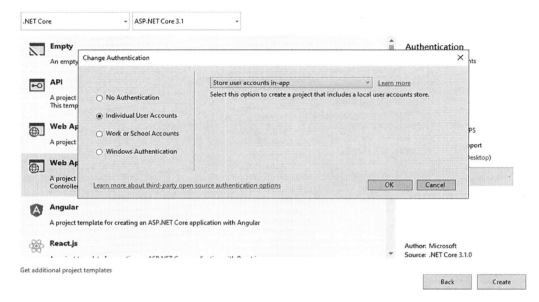

Figure 6-3. *Selecting the Individual User Accounts with the in-app storage option*

After selecting the authentication and hitting OK and then Create, your project will
be created. Note that there is a folder for Models and a folder for Data already in the
project.

In the Data folder, we get the ApplicationDbContext and the migrations for the
project, which include the initial migration to build out the user accounts (see Figure 6-4).

```
6 references
public class ApplicationDbContext : IdentityDbContext
{
    0 references
    public ApplicationDbContext(DbContextOptions<ApplicationDbContext> options)
        : base(options)
    {
    }
}
```

Figure 6-4. *The generated ApplicationDbContext*

Note that the ApplicationDbContext is implementing the IdentityDbContext (this
is where all the *Asp.Net Identity* models and tables come from). Without any work of our
own, we'll have full authentication capability baked into the application.

If you take time to examine the initial migration, you'll see all the tables for the AspNet users and roles are being built in that migration. Also note that the DBContextOptions are injected into the ApplicationDbContext.

Looking at the first migration, we see the tables for the *ASP.Net Identity* schema setup, as shown in Figure 6-5.

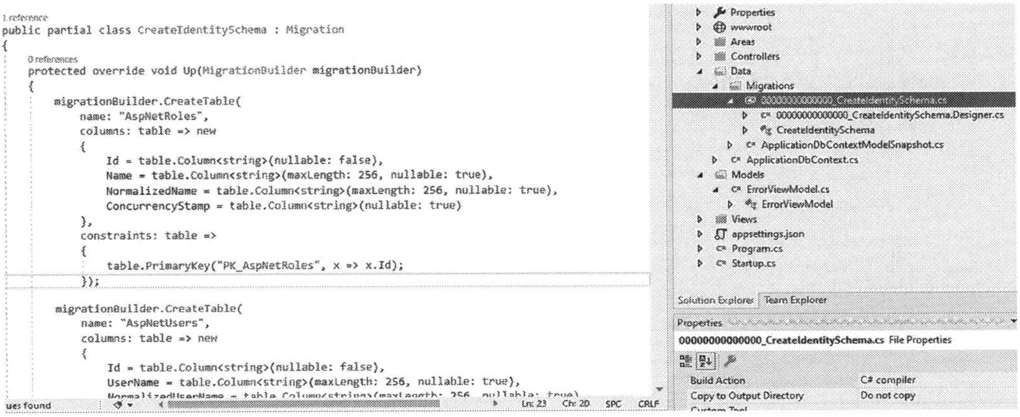

Figure 6-5. *The initial migration as generated by the Asp.Net identity schemas*

In *.Net Core*, the settings for an *ASP.Net Website* are stored in the appsettings. json file. If we look closely at the settings file, we see the database connection string is configured here. By default, it's set up to use the local database and just points to a filename. For our purposes, we can just leave this as is. If for some reason you don't have a local database (localdb) installed, you could set your connection string to map to *SQLExpress* or *SQLDeveloper* edition. The database connection in the appsettings.json file is shown in Figure 6-6.

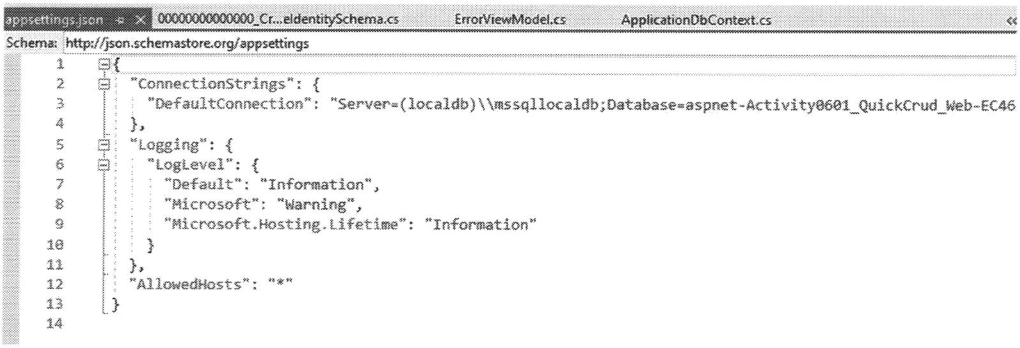

```json
{
    "ConnectionStrings": {
        "DefaultConnection": "Server=(localdb)\\mssqllocaldb;Database=aspnet-Activity0601_QuickCrud_Web-EC46
    },
    "Logging": {
        "LogLevel": {
            "Default": "Information",
            "Microsoft": "Warning",
            "Microsoft.Hosting.Lifetime": "Information"
        }
    },
    "AllowedHosts": "*"
}
```

Figure 6-6. *The database connection string is in the appsettings.json file*

Next, take a quick look at the Startup.cs file. A critical piece of the action happens in this file. In the ConfigureServices method, the services add the DBContext into scope. This is ultimately how the *ASP.Net Core Web Application* uses dependency injection for the DBContext object (see Figure 6-7).

Figure 6-7. *The startup.cs file in the web application uses dependency injection to register the ApplicationDbContext for use in the web application controllers*

There is much more going on here with this application, and it is by no means production-ready. However, these are the critical moving parts we need to know about for working with this code for the rest of this activity.

I also considered covering an approach of not using the context or, instead, bringing in our context, moving the models out to their own project, and making the application more professional, but decided to just keep this activity as a stand-alone activity for the most part with a basic web implementation. This will allow us to proceed quickly to the meat of the activity.

At the end of the book in Chapter 14, there is a section on using multiple database contexts in the same application. If you're interested in bringing in the InventoryDbContext and its associated models, then you should look into that section.

We are now ready to work with this web application to see some quick CRUD operations in action.

Step 2: Build the application, update the database, run the web application

Before we can do anything else, we need to make sure the application is working and that our connection string is going to work as generated. Build the application, and then update the database using the command update-database in the PMC (review Figure 6-8 for clarity).

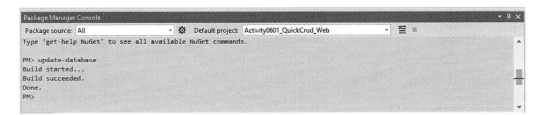

Figure 6-8. *Updating the database to implement the identity schema initial migration*

Once the migration has been applied, run the web application. If everything is working as expected, you should have no problem signing up for a new account and registering with the application (see Figure 6-9).

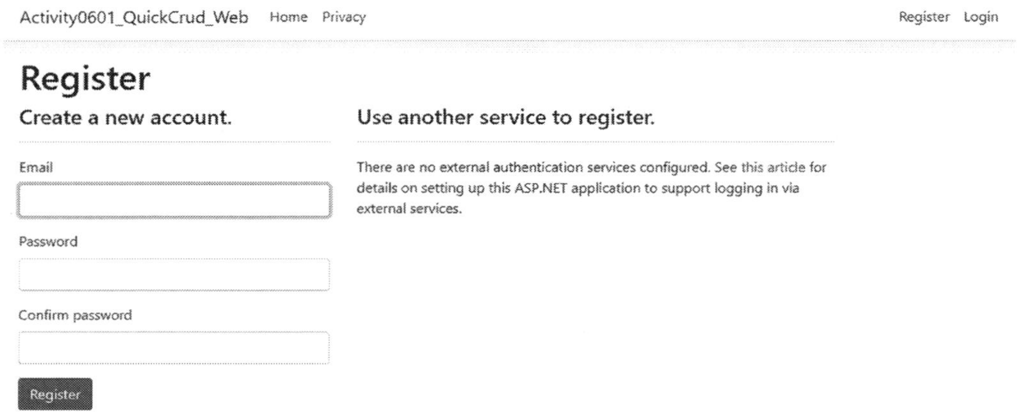

Activity0601_QuickCrud_Web
Home
Privacy
Register
Login
Register
Create a new account.
Email
Password
Confirm password
Register
Use another service to register.
There are no external authentication services configured. See this article for details on setting up this ASP.NET application to support logging in via external services.

Figure 6-9. *Registering with the local application*

After registering, **make sure to confirm** your account. If you don't do this, you'll need to go to the database and review the users table, find your user id, and update the value of `EmailConfirmed` to 1. Figure 6-10 highlights the link to click to avoid having to update the `EmailConfirmed` field manually.

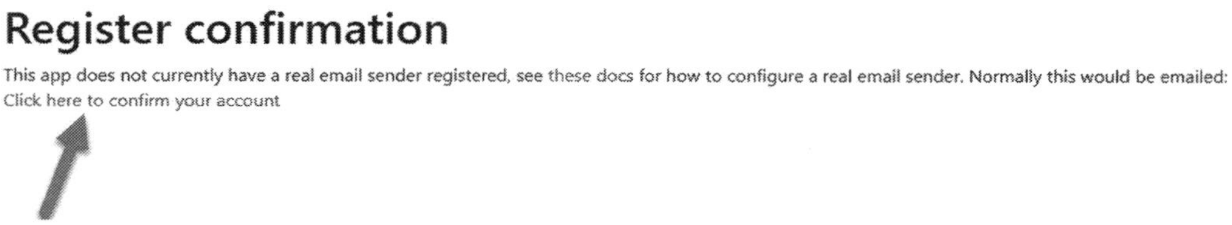

Register confirmation
This app does not currently have a real email sender registered, see these docs for how to configure a real email sender. Normally this would be emailed:
Click here to confirm your account

Figure 6-10. *It is imperative to confirm your account to avoid having to manually update the database to be able to log into your account*

After confirming, log in and your email should be shown at the top right of the application. Figure 6-11 shows the view for a logged in user.

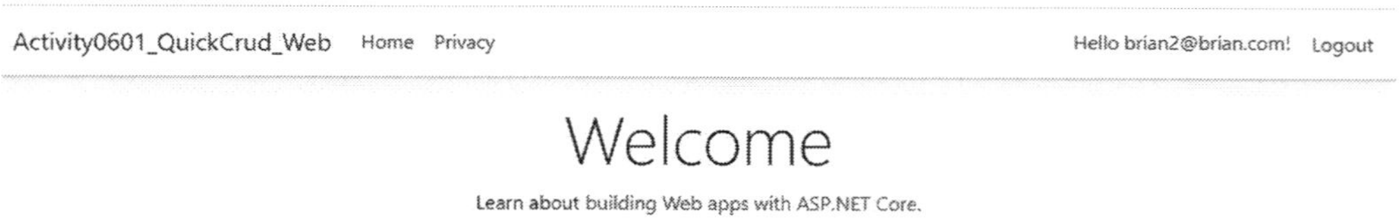

Activity0601_QuickCrud_Web
Home
Privacy
Hello brian2@brian.com!
Logout
Welcome
Learn about building Web apps with ASP.NET Core.

Figure 6-11. *Registration is confirmed and user is logged in*

Step 3: Review the database

Optionally, we can check out our database to ensure that it has the tables and users as we would expect. To do this, just open the Server Explorer in Visual Studio, which is located under the View menu. The server explorer can also be opened using the key-chord combination of *Ctrl+Alt+S* (see Figure 6-12).

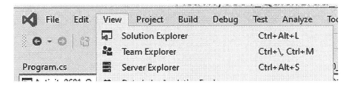

Figure 6-12. *Opening the server explorer*

In the server explorer, right-click Data Connections, and select Add Connection. When the Data Source Chooser comes up, select Microsoft SQL Server. Make sure to uncheck the option for Always use this selection in case you might have a reason to use a different approach in the future (see Figure 6-13).

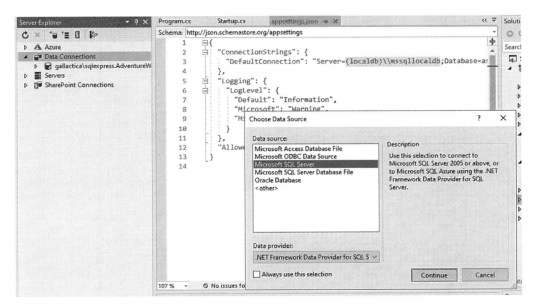

Figure 6-13. *Adding the server connection to the local db file*

255

In the Add Connection dialog, in the Server Name box, place the name of your *SQL* Server that you are using based on your appsettings connection string. For example, if you changed nothing, the server is likely (localdb)\mssqllocaldb.

Remember to take out the extra slash character when trying to connect, as there are likely two slashes in your appsettings file!

Select the database name from the drop-down. Note that if you aren't connected correctly to the server in the Server Name box, then you will not see any databases here, so you'd need to go back and input the correct server name first. Figure 6-14 shows the server and database connection for my local database file.

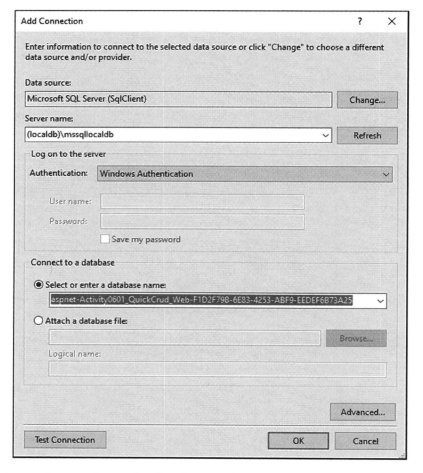

Figure 6-14. *Connecting to the database in the Server Explorer*

Use the Test Connection button to validate that you are able to connect, and then hit the OK button to set the database server connection.

Once you are connected correctly, open the server in the Data Connections portion of the Server Explorer to validate the tables are there. You can also view data in the AspNetUsers table to make sure your login user info is stored as you would expect (see Figure 6-15).

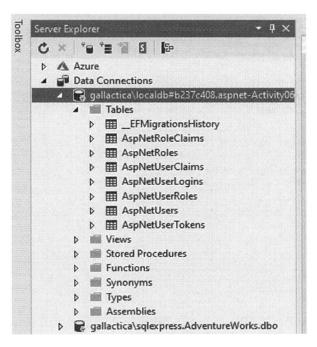

Figure 6-15. *Viewing the database in the Server Explorer*

Step 4: Create a model, then a migration

Now that we are able to work with our data and have ensured everything is set up as expected, we can create a simple model and then leverage the scaffolding to see some quick CRUD operations.

Let's create a simple Item model with a Category as per some of the previous work we've done (without the auditing, Genres, and other features of the models we've made in previous activities). Add the two files, Item and Category, to the Models folder in the web application. Bring similar code as from our previous work into play to give the Item and Categories a relationship.

An example of what the item class could look like this:

```
public class Item
{
    [Key]
    [Required]
    public int Id { get; set; }

    [StringLength(50)]
    public string Name { get; set; }

    public virtual int CategoryId { get; set; }
    public virtual Category Category { get; set; }
}
```

The Category class could look as follows:

```
public class Category
{
    [Key]
    [Required]
    public int Id { get; set; }

    [StringLength(50)]
    public string Name { get; set; }

    public virtual List<Item> Items { get; set; } = new List<Item>();
}
```

Once the two classes are created and the relationship is formed, add the two classes to the ApplicationDbContext as public DbSet properties:

```
public class ApplicationDbContext : IdentityDbContext
{
    public DbSet<Item> Items { get; set; }
    public DbSet<Category> Categories { get; set; }

    public ApplicationDbContext(DbContextOptions<ApplicationDbContext>
    options)
```

```
        : base(options)
    {
    }
}
```

Before moving on, one thing I didn't do in the previous code is make the Name as a [Required] field. In most cases, that should likely have been required. Feel free to add a [Required] annotation attribute to each Name field in each class if you so desire.

Next, build the project, and then run the command add-migration createTables_ItemsAndCategories in the PMC, which will generate the migration, which should look similar to the one shown in Figure 6-16.

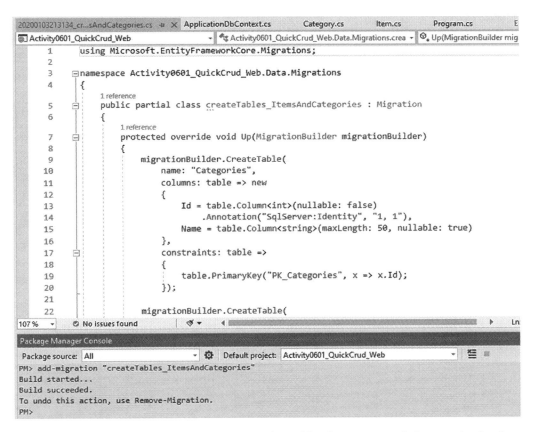

Figure 6-16. *The migration for creating the tables for Items and Categories in the web application*

Finally, run the command update-database to apply the changes, and then examine the tables in the Server Explorer to make sure they were created correctly (see Figure 6-17).

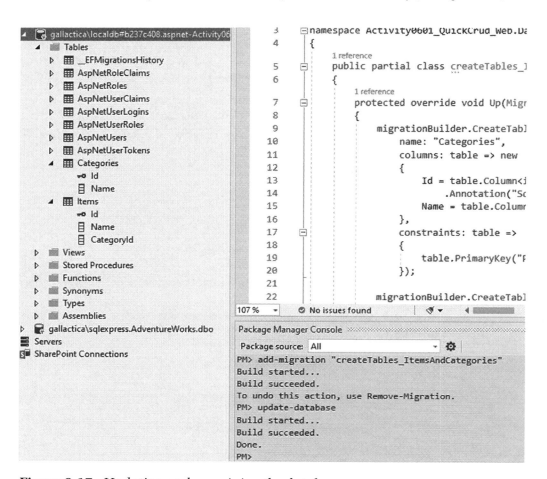

Figure 6-17. Updating and examining the database

Step 5: Scaffold the controller

In the *ASP.Net MVC web application*, we can easily scaffold our controllers once our database is set up correctly. To do this, we just perform a couple of quick actions, and this will give us the views that we need on top of the actions and routes to run a simple CRUD-enabled website. Again, this is not production-ready, but we can leverage this to see some CRUD actions without doing a lot of LINQ work ourselves.

Right-click the Controllers folder, and then select Add ➤ Controller (review Figure 6-18).

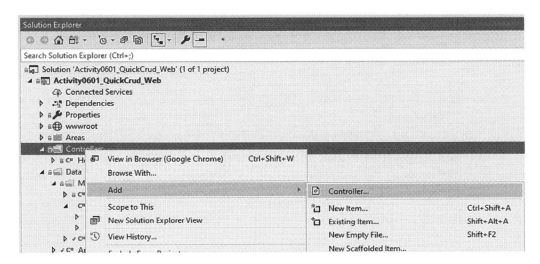

Figure 6-18. *Adding a new Controller*

In the next dialog, select MVC Controller with Views, using Entity Framework, and then select Add. The Add New Scaffolded item dialog is shown in Figure 6-19.

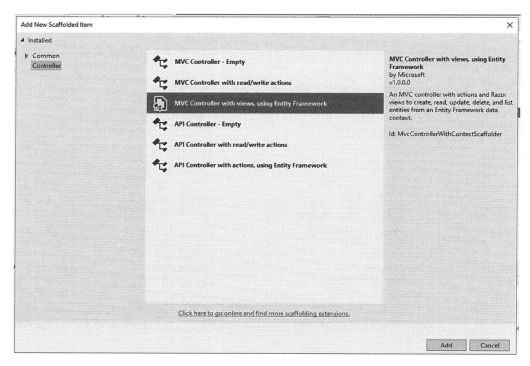

Figure 6-19. *The Add New Scaffolded Item dialog allows us to select the generation tools to use for creating the Controller and associated Views*

The way things work in the MVC .Net web application is by convention over configuration. Therefore, we want to name the file `ItemsController`, which will create views for the CRUD operations around the `Item` entity, as well as the route for `/Items/Index`. This route will be the default listing route for all items in the database. Also, the `/Index` route is implied, so just using `https://localhost:port/Items` will get you to the Items listing page.

In the `Add MVC Controller` with `views, using Entity Framework` dialog, select the `Item` model class and the `ApplicationDbContext` data context class. Leave the options checked for `Generate views`, `Reference script libraries,` and `Use a layout` page. Note the name of the controller is suggested to be `ItemsController`, as we would expect. Once this form is set correctly, hit the `Add` button to begin the process. Review Figure 6-20 for more information.

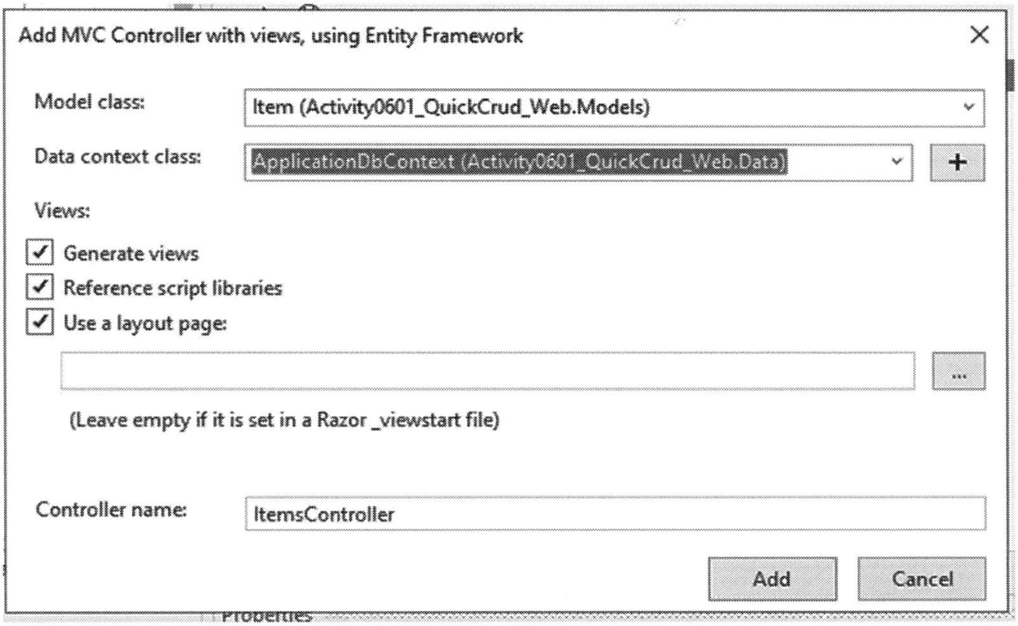

Add MVC Controller with views, using Entity Framework   ✕

Model class: Item (Activity0601_QuickCrud_Web.Models)   ⌄

Data context class: ApplicationDbContext (Activity0601_QuickCrud_Web.Data) ⌄   +

Views:

☑ Generate views
☑ Reference script libraries
☑ Use a layout page:

[   ]   ...

(Leave empty if it is set in a Razor _viewstart file)

Controller name: ItemsController

Add   Cancel

Figure 6-20. *Scaffolding the Controller and Views for the web application*

Once the `ItemsController` is generated, we can review it to see everything in action as is shown in Figure 6-21.

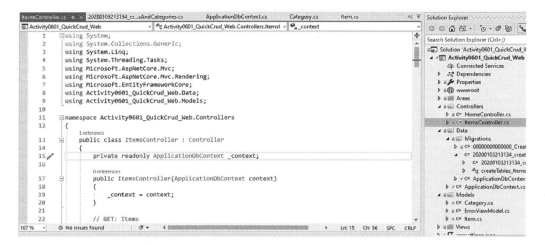

Figure 6-21. *The Items controller is generated*

Review the controller and make a quick note that the controller is receiving the injected ApplicationDbContext, which will be used to perform the CRUD operations.

Step 6: Review the controller – Read

In the next few steps, we're going to review the generated CRUD operations. We will do them in the order of Read, Create, Update, Delete, as that is the order that they will appear in the controller.

Review the default Index method, which gets all items for display. Here, we see a simple LINQ query:

```
public async Task<IActionResult> Index()
{
    var applicationDbContext = _context.Items.Include(i => i.Category);
    return View(await applicationDbContext.ToListAsync());
}
```

Note the query goes to the context (_context), gets all items, and then does an Include operation to get the categories for the items. The next statement then executes the query with the ToListAsync method and passes the results as a list to the view.

A couple of important things are happening here that we need to be aware of. The first point of note is that the Include command allows the context to get all Items and then gives the ability to load their associated Category information. This is important for displaying and choosing the associated category for an item, and this is how we will use LINQ to retrieve relationships.

The second important note here is that the query is not executed until the await operation with the ToListAsync statement. This is critical for the optimal performance of *EF*. By waiting to perform the execution, the result set can be optimized. If, for example, we wanted to order by the Name property, we should do that in the query, before calling the ToListAsync() method, which would look like this:

```
var applicationDbContext = _context.Items
                                    .OrderBy(x => x.Name)
                                    .Include(i => i.Category);
return View(await applicationDbContext.ToListAsync());
```

There is another read operation, which is used to show one individual result. In the first query, we had selected all items to a list. In the Details method, there is a parameter for the specific Id, and then it returns just that matching Item joined to the appropriate Category. This is done with the same query as earlier, but replaces ToListAsync with another LINQ statement: FirstOrDefaultAsync.

```
var item = await _context.Items
    .Include(i => i.Category)
    .FirstOrDefaultAsync(m => m.Id == id);
```

Step 7: Review the controller – Create

For the rest of the controller, we'll often see two methods working in tandem. The first method is going to retrieve some results to render to the page for viewing and taking input from the user, and the second method is the POST method that allows the Web to post back the user input for creating, editing, or deleting the Item, as defined by the user.

For the first Create method, the ApplicationDBContext Categories are returned to be placed into a SelectList, which allows the user to choose which Category to associate to the Item.

```
ViewData["CategoryId"] = new SelectList(_context.Categories, "Id", "Id");
```

The second `Create` method takes the passed in information and checks the `ModelState` to make sure it is in a valid state (i.e., lengths as expected, required fields, other `Model` constraints). Once it is valid, the data context adds the new `Item` to the database. If there is an error, the data is sent back to the web page for the user to correct any issues.

Important notes from this operation are the `Add` method against the context and the `SaveChangesAsync` method for saving the changes once the context has been modified:

```
_context.Add(item);
await _context.SaveChangesAsync();
return RedirectToAction(nameof(Index));
```

Step 8: Review the controller – Update

With items that already exist in the database, we can perform the "U" of the CRUD operation. In the controller, the name of the Update method is `Edit`. As with the `Create` method, we have an initial GET on the first `Edit` method that returns the matching result by `Id` to the page for the user to update the values and then allows the POST on a second `Edit` method to update the modified values in the database.

The initial GET finds the item to edit by `Id` and also populates the select list for `Categories` (if you are a web programmer, you likely see that this call could easily be improved by making only one call to get `Categories` and/or caching the categories):

```
var item = await _context.Items.FindAsync(id);
if (item == null)
{
    return NotFound();
}
```

The POST method allows the user to change properties and then to send those changes back for update. As with `Create`, the first thing that is checked is the state of the model. The page won't let you continue if you have missing required fields or issues with length on a field as defined in the model's *data annotations* or the *Fluent API* configuration of the model in the context. Once the state is validated, the database can perform the appropriate update.

Another nice feature in this method is that the update option automatically handles the situation where concurrency exceptions are encountered. In this case, if another user deletes the entity, the page lets you know by showing a NotFound Exception for the entity.

```
_context.Update(item);
await _context.SaveChangesAsync();
```

Step 9: Review the Controller – Delete

Our final CRUD action is the *Delete* action. Here, like the other methods in the controller, there is a GET method that allows us to get the correct item for review for delete and then a second POST method to delete the Item from the database. The first method is the same as we've seen on Edit, getting the item with information about the specifics to display to the user for confirmation of the delete operation.

The second method takes in the Id and then finds the Item in the _context again to get the object with tracking (without tracking, performing the delete won't accomplish anything). When a match is found and has been retrieved with tracking to that object, the Remove method is called to set the model state to Deleted.

```
[HttpPost, ActionName("Delete")]
[ValidateAntiForgeryToken]
public async Task<IActionResult> DeleteConfirmed(int id)
{
    var item = await _context.Items.FindAsync(id);
    _context.Items.Remove(item);
    await _context.SaveChangesAsync();
    return RedirectToAction(nameof(Index));
}
```

Step 10: Set a couple of categories, then run the application

To see all of this in action, we first need a couple of categories. We could scaffold out the categories controller and then use that to add categories. For simplicity and time, just add a couple of categories in the database directly, for example, Movies and Books. Also note that there are currently no items in the database.

Using the `Server Explorer`, select `Show Table Data`. Then manually add the two categories as shown in Figure 6-22.

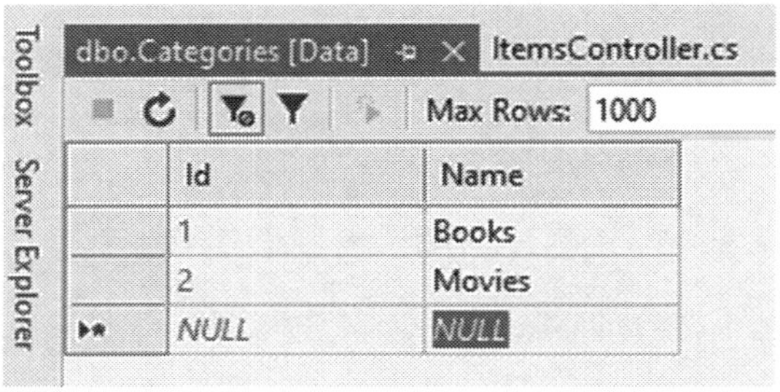

Figure 6-22. *Adding a couple of categories*

With the categories added, we can run the application to review all of this in action.

Please note, as stated a few times earlier, this is not intended to be a production-ready application. We would never want to use `Ids` as a display on the categories for selection. For instance, we would change out the `Id` to `Name` in the controller to show the actual `Name` of the `Category` for user selection. We would also add authorization and navigation to the website, among many other things, to improve the user experience of this application.

To view the items, simply type the name of the controller in the browser route:

`https://localhost:port/Items` (just add `/Items` to the `localhost:port` that is already running on your machine)

In Figure 6-23, I've added a couple of `Items` into my database using the web browser and the scaffolded `ItemsController` and views.

Figure 6-23. *Viewing the Items in the web browser*

Try to perform each CRUD operation on the various Item views. Use the Create New link to pull up the create form and the Edit, Details, and Delete to work through the rest of the CRUD operations.

Key takeaways from activity 0602

In this activity, we allowed the *.Net Web application* template to scaffold controllers around one of our ApplicationDBContext entities. By doing this, we were able to see some of the more critical LINQ operations that are needed to correctly perform CRUD operations against the database.

- Use Add to create a new entity.

- Use Update to edit the entity property values.

- Use Remove to delete the entity.

- Use Find to locate an entity.

- Use Include to join to other tables.

- Use FirstOrDefault to get a specific entity by Id or another property.

- The model state allows us to determine if there are any errors on any of the properties in the model as defined in the data annotations or Fluent API.

Chapter summary

In this chapter, we quickly discussed the idea of creating a CRUD application and how we could interact with the database for each operation. We also looked at the primary methods we'll want to be in command of to build database-enabled applications.

In our activity, we took the time to spin up a website, where we scaffolded out a controller and allowed the system to generate the main LINQ queries that we would need. This allowed us to quickly see how working with EF to create a robust solution is possible, even with a very basic understanding of LINQ.

In the next chapter, we're going to learn about how we can build code around some of the major pieces of SQL Server, including Stored Procedures, Views, and Functions.

CHAPTER 7

Stored Procedures, Views, and Functions

In this chapter, we are going to look into ways to leverage the built-in programmable features of SQL Server that allow for maximum performance and efficiency.

We've already seen that we can easily create tables in a code-first approach with Entity Framework. However, in real-world applications, we are going to need to start building out more robust database solutions. By the end of this chapter, we will have a working understanding of what it takes to leverage database objects like stored procedures, views, and functions. We'll also know how to set up our code and migrations to create and manage versions of these objects. Along the way, we'll also learn more about the *Fluent API* and how we can leverage it to further define entities and data in our solutions.

Understanding stored procedures, views, and functions

Before we dive into working with these database objects, we should make sure that we are fully aware of what they are and why we would use them. Additionally, we'll be working with datasets that don't necessarily map to a tracked database object. For that reason, we need to learn a couple of new techniques when working with our database context and the model builder.

In the course of the activities at the end of the chapter, we'll see what it takes to add a query set into the database context so that we can get the results we are expecting when working with procedures, functions, and views. First, let's take a brief moment to discuss stored procedures, functions, and views.

© Brian L. Gorman 2020
B. L. Gorman, *Practical Entity Framework*, https://doi.org/10.1007/978-1-4842-6044-9_7

Stored procedures

As developers, we can easily write code in *C#* or *VB.Net* that does repetitive operations like looping, making calculations, or mutating data. However, it is entirely possible to write code in Microsoft SQL using the *T-SQL* syntax.

Writing some code on the server has a number of advantages, with the main advantage being efficiency. When we create a stored procedure, we are essentially writing a functional unit of code that can take parameters and perform queries and data manipulation on the server. By using the server to run this prepared code, the server itself can create and store execution plans, thereby speeding up the operation in subsequent runs. An additional benefit is that using the stored procedure allows for returning the manipulated data directly, rather than returning a large set of data and then using *C#* or *VB.Net* code to further process the data in memory.

We can easily create a new procedure with the syntax `CREATE OR ALTER PROCEDURE <name>`. The easiest way to get a procedure script started is to right-click Stored Procedures under Programmability in *SSMS* and select `Stored Procedure`, which generates a script.

Great examples and use cases for stored procedures generally fall around operations such as getting large result sets and performing calculations as part of the results.

Functions

Scalar and table-valued functions are extremely versatile and can help us to easily set up a routine that can manipulate our data, even when the view selection is part of a larger query.

Like stored procedures, functions can take parameters and can be optimized by query execution plans stored on the server.

The two types of functions have distinctly different uses. For situations where a single-value result is needed, we can run the scalar function. In other situations, we might need a result set, which can be returned as an in-memory table as a table-valued function.

A good example of a scalar-valued function would be a function that manipulates data from an array into a comma-separated list as a single string, whereas a good table-valued function might be to get the items that were added in the last two weeks and then use that data to join against another table or get a limited set of data based on those results.

Views

Another scenario that happens frequently in the real world is one where we need to get some conglomerated data, which generally requires joining one or more tables. We then need to be able to perform some sort of sorting or filtering against that data, such as getting the top ten results or results where a field contains some key value.

Anytime we run into a situation where we need to denormalize our data to present a segment of data for user review or reporting and then filter that result, a view can be a very handy asset.

Where a stored procedure takes parameters and manipulates data using prepared statements, we can think of a view as a prebuilt query that gets the results as designed and allows further filtering against that data. A view is essentially like an in-memory table with denormalized data based on pre-specified table joins.

The benefit of the view is that we've abstracted the denormalization so that the filtering can happen simply, without having to also redefine the join statements. We can therefore perform a simple SELECT … WHERE query statement against the view, or we can use the view and join to other tables for even more specific results.

A very typical use of a view would be to generate data for a report, such as all items with included category name. We could then further limit that view to only return those rows that have a category name of movie.

Setting up the database to run scripts efficiently

Out of the box, EF doesn't have a super nice way to handle non-table database structures. In older versions of the .Net Framework, we were able to write files and then use those files to generate a SQL database script. Those days are gone, and that's a good thing. In code-first Entity Framework solutions, we can add a migration and then put a script in the migration directly for execution. While possible, this is not the best solution for a number of reasons.

Therefore, in order to work with non-table database objects in EF code first, we need to implement a quick solution.

The problem

To make the issues with directly scripting a stored procedure in a migration clearer, let's examine a potential migration and then an update to that procedure in a second migration.

First, here is a script that would easily generate a stored procedure to get items with genre and category information:

```
CREATE OR ALTER PROCEDURE dbo.GetItemsForListing
    @minDate DATETIME = null,
    @maxDate DATETIME = null
AS
BEGIN
    SET NOCOUNT ON;

    SELECT item.Name, item.Description, item.Notes
    , item.IsActive, item.IsDeleted, g.Name, cat.Name
    FROM dbo.Items item
    LEFT JOIN dbo.ItemGenre ig on item.Id = ig.ItemId
    LEFT JOIN dbo.Genres g on ig.GenreId = g.Id
    LEFT JOIN dbo.Categories cat on item.CategoryId = cat.Id
    WHERE (@minDate IS NULL OR item.CreatedDate >= @minDate)
    AND (@maxDate IS NULL OR item.CreatedDate <= @maxDate)
END
GO
```

This is a straightforward query, but if we put it into a migration directly, it would look like what is shown in Figure 7-1.

```
]namespace InventoryDatabaseCore.Migrations
{
    1 reference
]   public partial class CreateSproc_GetItemsForListing : Migration
    {
        8 references
        protected override void Up(MigrationBuilder migrationBuilder)
]       {
]           migrationBuilder.Sql(@"CREATE OR ALTER PROCEDURE dbo.GetItemsForListing
    @minDate DATETIME = null,
    @maxDate DATETIME = null
AS
BEGIN
    SET NOCOUNT ON;

    SELECT item.Name, item.Description, item.Notes
    , item.IsActive, item.IsDeleted, g.Name, cat.Name
    FROM dbo.Items item
    LEFT JOIN dbo.ItemGenre ig on item.Id = ig.ItemId
    LEFT JOIN dbo.Genres g on ig.GenreId = g.Id
    LEFT JOIN dbo.Categories cat on item.CategoryId = cat.Id
    WHERE (@minDate IS NULL OR item.CreatedDate >= @minDate)
    AND (@maxDate IS NULL OR item.CreatedDate <= @maxDate)
END
GO");
        }

        8 references
]       protected override void Down(MigrationBuilder migrationBuilder)
        {
]           migrationBuilder.Sql(@"IF EXISTS (SELECT * FROM    sysobjects
            WHERE  id = object_id(N'[dbo].[GetItemsForListing]')
                and OBJECTPROPERTY(id, N'IsProcedure') = 1 )
    DROP PROCEDURE dbo.GetItemsForListing
GO
");
        }
    }
}
```

Figure 7-1. *A fully scripted migration to create a stored procedure*

As you might imagine, putting the code inline inside the migration makes it somewhat tricky to do a code review on the script. Additionally, putting in the second and consecutive migrations leads to large scripts in both the Up and Down methods. For an example of how verbose the migrations could become, review Figure 7-2.

```
namespace InventoryDatabaseCore.Migrations
{
    0 references
    public partial class UpdateSproc_GetItemsForListing_RemoveGenre : Migration
    {
        8 references
        protected override void Up(MigrationBuilder migrationBuilder)
        {
            migrationBuilder.Sql(@"CREATE OR ALTER PROCEDURE dbo.GetItemsForListing
@minDate DATETIME = null,
@maxDate DATETIME = null
AS
BEGIN
    SET NOCOUNT ON;

    SELECT item.Name, item.Description, item.Notes
    , item.IsActive, item.IsDeleted, cat.Name
    FROM dbo.Items item
    LEFT JOIN dbo.Categories cat on item.CategoryId = cat.Id
    WHERE (@minDate IS NULL OR item.CreatedDate >= @minDate)
    AND (@maxDate IS NULL OR item.CreatedDate <= @maxDate)
END
GO");
        }

        8 references
        protected override void Down(MigrationBuilder migrationBuilder)
        {
            migrationBuilder.Sql(@"CREATE OR ALTER PROCEDURE dbo.GetItemsForListing
@minDate DATETIME = null,
@maxDate DATETIME = null
AS
BEGIN
    SET NOCOUNT ON;

    SELECT item.Name, item.Description, item.Notes
    , item.IsActive, item.IsDeleted, g.Name, cat.Name
    FROM dbo.Items item
    LEFT JOIN dbo.ItemGenre ig on item.Id = ig.ItemId
    LEFT JOIN dbo.Genres g on ig.GenreId = g.Id
    LEFT JOIN dbo.Categories cat on item.CategoryId = cat.Id
    WHERE (@minDate IS NULL OR item.CreatedDate >= @minDate)
    AND (@maxDate IS NULL OR item.CreatedDate <= @maxDate)
END
GO");
        }
    }
}
```

Figure 7-2. *Each migration containing an update now has multiple hard-coded stored procedure scripts in the body of the migration*

276

The complexity to perform a code review also increases, as the available choices are to compare the code in the Down method to the code in the Up method for changes or to find the previous migration for this procedure and compare the scripts as hard-coded in each migration's Up method.

As if that isn't bad enough, although we have history via this code, we don't have a well-organized history that is easy to review or even find the version for which we are looking. Once we get to version 6, for example, we would have to sort through six migrations to figure out where in the history of the code the issue we might be looking for exists.

Therefore, we need a better solution, a solution that is a nice and easy way to keep our migrations to a minimal footprint, while also giving our fellow developers an easy way to review our changes and ultimately making it easier to track code versions in a historical fashion.

The solution

As we've seen earlier, we can run a script in the migration using the migrationBuilder calling the SQL method. As with other objects in .*Net*, migrationBuilder can be extended. To make our solution, we'll be writing a simple extension that will get the script by reading a text file to a string.

After creating the extension method, all we need to do is add the text files into our project as embedded resources, and we no longer have to write our SQL scripts inline. We then reference the file directly in the migration.

In addition to removing the code from the migration file, this solution gives us the ability to easily keep and track all versions of the scripted database objects. We'll take a look at this solution in more detail in the first activity for this chapter.

Fluent API

To this point in the book, we haven't really spent a lot of time taking a look at the *Fluent API* and how we can use that in our code. When we worked with models in Chapter 4 and relationships in Chapter 5, we saw *data annotations*, and we used them to build things like required fields, string length, keys, and the various relationships between entities. We did leverage the *Fluent API* for our unique clustered index, but we didn't spend a lot of time talking about what the *Fluent API* does for us.

In addition to data annotations and direct mapping of relationships in our models, there is another tool that we can use to define entity structure and relationships. This tool is called the *Fluent API*.

The *Fluent API* can do everything you can do with data annotations, but it also allows for more specific configurations. In our activities for this chapter, we'll leverage the *Fluent API* to make sure that an entity we are creating does not generate a new table in the database or insert itself into every migration, while still being available to be used for querying objects.

In order to work with the *Fluent API*, we'll need to override another method in our database context. The method that we will override is called `OnModelCreating` which has a parameter of type `ModelBuilder`. We already set this up in Chapter 5, but if you skipped over that chapter, you might have missed this critical piece of working with the *Fluent API*.

The *Fluent API* is leveraged from this model builder with references such as

```
modelBuilder.Entity<Item>().Property(x => x.Name).IsRequired()
```

and

```
modelBuilder.Entity<Item>().HasOne(x => x.Category).WithMany(y => y.Items)
```

Even now, there are already references to the `Fluent API` in place in the projects we have been building without us even knowing about them. Take a quick look at the auto-generated file `InventoryDbContextModelSnapshot.cs` in the `InventoryDatabaseCore` project to see more *Fluent API* calls in action.

For our purposes, we'll need to dive in deeper in the override to set entities to not have a key and to act like a read-only view. We'll see this in full detail in the activities, but a sample of what we'll see looks like this:

```
modelBuilder.Entity<AllItemsPipeDelimitedString>(x =>
        {
            x.HasNoKey();
            x.ToView("AllItemsPipeDelimitedString");
        });
```

Working with the database objects

In the final part of this chapter, we will again dive into three new examples where we can learn about building out our scripting solution and working with non-table database objects.

While we are focusing on stored procedures, views, and functions, please remember that with this scripting solution using files, we'll be able to run any database script to create or modify any database objects. For example, we could easily create scripts for other objects like indexes or triggers, if desired.

Activities

Before beginning these activities, please note that these three activities build off of each other, so skipping to activity two might leave you a bit in the dark as to what happened with the stored procedures. Likewise, skipping activity two will cause you to miss the fix with an implementation for what went wrong in activity one.

Activity 0701: Working with stored procedures

In this first activity, we are going to take a first look at how we can work with stored procedures in our solution. We'll begin by looking at the inline scripting as mentioned previously. We'll then proceed to write the extension method we need to process our code as files. After getting the extension method setup, we'll conclude the activity with a final look at using the files so we can clearly see the benefits of this strategy.

Step 1: Set up

To begin, get a copy of the starter files Activity0701_StoredProcedures_Starter.zip, or continue working with your own solution that you've been building as we've moved through this book. If you are going to work with your own solution, do not use the web project in Chapter 6, but rather use the final version of your code as it existed at the end of Chapter 5. Either way, once you have your project open, make sure your database connections are correct in the `appsettings.json` file, and make sure to build and run the `update-database` command to ensure your database is current with the migrations in the project. Additionally, it is a good idea to run the program to make sure everything works before modifying it.

You may need to set the `Activity0701_WorkingWithStoredProcedures` project as the startup project to make the solution run as expected.

Step 2: Create a new migration for a simple stored procedure

After making sure your project is up to date and has all migrations applied, begin by running the following command:

`add-migration CreateSproc_GetItemsForListing.`

Provided you have no unchanged files and all models are correctly implemented in the database, this command will generate an empty migration file (see Figure 7-3).

```
1 reference
public partial class CreateSproc_GetItemsForListing : Migration
{
    8 references
    protected override void Up(MigrationBuilder migrationBuilder)
    {

    }

    8 references
    protected override void Down(MigrationBuilder migrationBuilder)
    {

    }
}
```

Figure 7-3. *An empty migration is generated when no code changes are present and the add-migration command is executed*

If for some reason your migration is not clean, you had some pending changes that needed to be applied to your local database. As long as the changes look good, you could just apply them via the update-database command and then make a new blank migration to continue with this activity.

Next, add the script to create a new stored procedure in the Up method:

```
migrationBuilder.Sql(@"CREATE OR ALTER PROCEDURE dbo.GetItemsForListing
    @minDate DATETIME = null,
    @maxDate DATETIME = null
AS
BEGIN
    SET NOCOUNT ON;

    SELECT item.Name, item.Description, item.Notes
    , item.IsActive, item.IsDeleted, g.Name, cat.Name
    FROM dbo.Items item
    LEFT JOIN dbo.ItemGenre ig on item.Id = ig.ItemId
    LEFT JOIN dbo.Genres g on ig.GenreId = g.Id
    LEFT JOIN dbo.Categories cat on item.CategoryId = cat.Id
    WHERE(@minDate IS NULL OR item.CreatedDate >= @minDate)
    AND(@maxDate IS NULL OR item.CreatedDate <= @maxDate)
END");
```

Don't run the migration yet! We have more work to do. As a personal best practice, I recommend that you make sure every migration you create is idempotent in both directions. By that, I mean you can run and rerun the Up and Down methods at will without having failures in your database. This is especially critical as you move the code to other machines.

Note that the create procedure code starts with CREATE OR ALTER, which means that even if this procedure previously existed in the database, this code would still run successfully. Do note that the CREATE OR ALTER syntax requires *SQL Server 2016* or greater, so if you are working against an older *SQL Server* version, you would need to check for existence of the procedure and then just run a straight CREATE statement when the procedure doesn't exist.

To complete the migration, we need to wire up the Downmethod. While it might be tempting to simply put the code DROP PROCEDURE <name> in the Down method, the statement is not safe for execution in all states. If the database has already deleted the procedure or it doesn't exist, this Down method execution would fail. Therefore, I recommend always checking for existence before making any DROP or ALTER statements. By safeguarding our statements, even if the object doesn't currently exist, the scripts won't fail and our migrations will continue to execute.

Add the following code to the Down(...) method of the new migration:

```
migrationBuilder.Sql("DROP PROCEDURE IF EXISTS dbo.GetItemsForListing");
```

For clarity, the entire migration is shown in Figure 7-4.

```
11 references
protected override void Up(MigrationBuilder migrationBuilder)
{
    migrationBuilder.Sql(@"CREATE OR ALTER PROCEDURE dbo.GetItemsForListing
        @minDate DATETIME = null,
        @maxDate DATETIME = null
    AS
    BEGIN
        SET NOCOUNT ON;

        SELECT item.Name, item.Description, item.Notes
        , item.IsActive, item.IsDeleted, g.Name, cat.Name
        FROM dbo.Items item
        LEFT JOIN dbo.ItemGenre ig on item.Id = ig.ItemId
        LEFT JOIN dbo.Genres g on ig.GenreId = g.Id
        LEFT JOIN dbo.Categories cat on item.CategoryId = cat.Id
        WHERE(@minDate IS NULL OR item.CreatedDate >= @minDate)
        AND(@maxDate IS NULL OR item.CreatedDate <= @maxDate)
    END");
}

11 references
protected override void Down(MigrationBuilder migrationBuilder)
{
    migrationBuilder.Sql("DROP PROCEDURE IF EXISTS dbo.GetItemsForListing");
}
```

Figure 7-4. *The migration to create the GetItemsForListing stored procedure, with an idempotent Down method to handle rollback of the database changes*

Now that the migration is complete, run the command update-database to add the stored procedure into the database (review Figure 7-5).

```
PM> add-migration CreateSproc_GetItemsForListing
Build started...
Build succeeded.
To undo this action, use Remove-Migration.
PM> update-database
Build started...
Build succeeded.
Applying migration '20200118053914_CreateSproc_GetItemsForListing'.
Done.
PM>
```

Figure 7-5. *The PMC commands run to create the migration and to update the database with our custom script*

We can validate the existence of the procedure in our database via SSMS or in the Server Explorer as shown in previous activities.

Additionally, as a developer, I often like to run the Down method just to make sure I don't have any issues. To do that now, just find the name of the previous migration and run the update-database -migration <previous_migration_name>, which will revert the database to the prior migration. The migration name can be found either in the name of the file that was just generated, or you can review the dbo.__EFMigrationsHistory table in the database to find the name. This reminds us that we can always tell which migrations have been applied by comparing the existing MigrationId values in the database table to the files in the Migrations folder in our solution.

Make sure to check the database after reverting to ensure the new procedure has indeed been dropped. Once satisfied that the migration works in both directions, rerun the update-database command to complete this step of the activity. At this point, you'll have the migration applied and the procedure will exist in your database.

Step 3: Create the MigrationBuilder extension

At this point, we could create a new migration and run an update against the stored procedure to see how that would look. However, we have already discussed this approach, and we can see what this approach would look like in Figure 7-2. Therefore, knowing that we could continue on this path, there is no need to rehash it here. However, this is an excellent time to examine a better solution.

In *EF6*, we were able to call a method on the migration called SqlResource. This method would take in the file and read it for execution. At the time of this writing, this SqlResource method does not exist in *EFCore*.

Therefore, the first thing we need to do to get to a better solution is to create a new extension that will extend the `MigrationBuilder` class. The extension method could be named anything we want, but since we're emulating behavior from *EF6*, we'll call it the same thing: `SqlResource`.

Once the method is created, we'll leverage the fact that the script is nothing more than text that needs to be run in the migration builder. We can therefore just put our code into a flat **.sql* file, add that file to our project as an embedded resource, and then use our extension method to read the file as a stream for execution.

First, add a new folder under the `Migrations` folder entitled `Scripts` as shown in Figure 7-6.

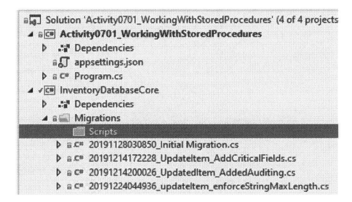

Figure 7-6. *A new folder entitled Scripts is added in the Migrations folder*

The location of this folder is going to be important, but the location of the extension inside this folder will be critical so that we don't have to worry about the path to our script files.

In the new `Scripts` folder, create a new class file called `MigrationBuilderSqlResource.cs`. We'll write our extension in this class. Also, in the `Scripts` folder, create a new subfolder called `Procedures`. In each object folder, we'll create subfolders for each object by name for better organization and maintenance. Create a subfolder called `GetItemsForListing` in the `Procedures` folder, and then create two files in the folder `GetItemsForListing.v0.sql` and `GetItemsForListing.v1.sql`. For clarity, the overall look of my project structure as described is shown in Figure 7-7.

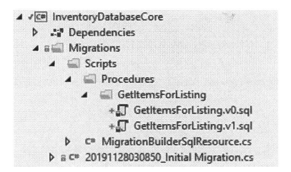

Figure 7-7. *Setting up the scripts and extensions hierarchy in the Migrations folder*

Modify the `MigrationBuilderSqlResource.cs` file with the following code, making sure to bring in any missing using statements so the code will compile:

```
public static class MigrationBuilderSqlResource
{
    public static OperationBuilder<SqlOperation> SqlResource(this
    MigrationBuilder mb, string relativeFileName)
    {
        using (var stream = Assembly.GetAssembly(typeof(MigrationBuilder
        SqlResource)).GetManifestResourceStream(relativeFileName))
        {
            using (var ms = new MemoryStream())
            {
                stream.CopyTo(ms);
                var data = ms.ToArray();
                var text = Encoding.UTF8.GetString(data, 3,
                data.Length - 3);
                return mb.Sql(text);
            }
        }
    }
}
```

For clarity, the using statements you will need to add will be as follows:

```
using Microsoft.EntityFrameworkCore.Migrations;
using Microsoft.EntityFrameworkCore.Migrations.Operations;
using Microsoft.EntityFrameworkCore.Migrations.Operations.Builders;
using System.IO;
using System.Reflection;
using System.Text;
```

Next, add the text from the create statement in the previous migration to both the v0 and the v1 version of the GetItemsForListing.v*.sql files.

Once these are in place, further modify the v1 version of the file to remove references to the Genres table from the procedure as follows:

```
CREATE OR ALTER PROCEDURE dbo.GetItemsForListing
    @minDate DATETIME = null,
    @maxDate DATETIME = null
AS
BEGIN
    SET NOCOUNT ON;

    SELECT item.Name, item.Description, item.Notes
    , item.IsActive, item.IsDeleted, cat.Name
    FROM dbo.Items item
    LEFT JOIN dbo.Categories cat on item.CategoryId = cat.Id
    WHERE(@minDate IS NULL OR item.CreatedDate >= @minDate)
    AND(@maxDate IS NULL OR item.CreatedDate <= @maxDate)
END
```

When finished, the v1 file should look like what is shown in Figure 7-8.

```
GetItemsForListing.v1.sql  ⇔ ×   GetItemsForListing.v0.sql        MigrationBuilderSqlResource.cs
▶ ▪ ■ ✓ 國 ■┃ ■┃ ■┃                                        ▼ ┃ ⁱ╕ ┃ 𝄐┃ ▼ ╚ᵒ ┃ 國┃
 1 ⊟CREATE OR ALTER PROCEDURE dbo.GetItemsForListing
 2      @minDate DATETIME = null,
 3      @maxDate DATETIME = null
 4  AS
 5 ⊟BEGIN
 6      SET NOCOUNT ON;
 7
 8 ⊟    SELECT item.Name, item.Description, item.Notes
 9      , item.IsActive, item.IsDeleted, cat.Name
10      FROM dbo.Items item
11      LEFT JOIN dbo.Categories cat on item.CategoryId = cat.Id
12      WHERE(@minDate IS NULL OR item.CreatedDate >= @minDate)
13      AND(@maxDate IS NULL OR item.CreatedDate <= @maxDate)
14  END
15
```

Figure 7-8. *The updated version of the stored procedure to get Items removes the reference to genres*

To be clear, the v0 file text is just the exact text from the Up method for creating the stored procedure as in the first migration, without the wrapping migrationBuilder. Sql(@"... code. This v0 file is our rollback option, so we want to get back to where we were at the end of the previous migration if we roll back our current migration using this file.

Before setting up a migration, it's not a bad idea to double-check that the code you will be creating is going to execute as expected. If you want, you could take the select statement from the v1 file and execute it in SSMS to validate the results no longer contain any references to the Genres table, have no duplicated entries, and work to return results as expected. You could even execute the whole script and then make a call to the stored procedure. Since the start is CREATE OR ALTER, even running the migration would just restore the same procedure code.

With both files containing the code as expected, rebuild and then add a new migration using the command:

add-migration UpdateProc_GetItemsForListing_RemoveGenre

This generates a blank migration as expected.

In the Up method, simply reference the new extension with the path to the v1 file as follows (use the namespace from the extension, followed by the path from that location to the file):

migrationBuilder.SqlResource("InventoryDatabaseCore.Migrations.Scripts. Procedures.GetItemsForListing.GetItemsForListing.v1.sql");

Add the v0 version to the Down method:

```
migrationBuilder.SqlResource("InventoryDatabaseCore.Migrations.Scripts.
Procedures.GetItemsForListing.GetItemsForListing.v0.sql");
```

For clarity, the migration is shown in Figure 7-9.

```
1 reference
public partial class UpdateProc_GetItemsForListing_RemoveGenre : Migration
{
    9 references
    protected override void Up(MigrationBuilder migrationBuilder)
    {
        migrationBuilder.SqlResource("InventoryDatabaseCore.Migrations.Scripts.Procedures.GetItemsForListing.GetItemsForListing.v1.sql");
    }

    9 references
    protected override void Down(MigrationBuilder migrationBuilder)
    {
        migrationBuilder.SqlResource("InventoryDatabaseCore.Migrations.Scripts.Procedures.GetItemsForListing.GetItemsForListing.v0.sql");
    }
}
```

Figure 7-9. *The migration file which allows for updating and rolling back the procedure change using files instead of inline SQL*

As with other files, make sure to add the using statement so that the code will compile. The using statement that needs to be added should be using InventoryDatabaseCore.Migrations.Scripts;.

Rebuild and attempt to update the database. Even if your path is correct, you should see an error for an object reference not set to an instance of an object (see Figure 7-10).

Figure 7-10. *Failure to set the script files as embedded resources or incorrect paths to the files will generate a cryptic Object Reference not set to an instance of an object error*

One thing we didn't do prior to trying to run our migration is to make sure that all scripts are added as embedded resources. Now that we've seen this error, we know we need to set the files as Embedded resource in the properties. Figure 7-11 shows how to select a file and set it as an embedded resource.

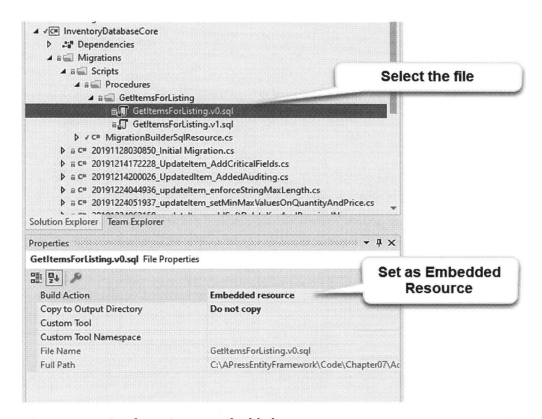

Figure 7-11. *Set the scripts as embedded resources*

Set both script files as Embedded resource and then rebuild and run the update-database command again. This time we should be able to execute the migration as expected (review Figure 7-12).

```
Object reference not set to an instance of an object.
PM> update-database
Build started...
Build succeeded.
Applying migration '20200118071523_UpdateProc_GetItemsForListing_RemoveGenre'.
Done.
PM> |
```

Figure 7-12. *The update-database command works as expected to read the file once we've embedded the files as resources*

If you continue to get an object reference error, make sure you have set your path correctly in the Up method, using the namespace for your MigrationBuilderSqlResource.cs file, followed by the folders and file names.

Don't forget to double up on the procedure name in the relative file name, since the file is in a folder with the same name as the file.

Review your procedures in the database using *SSMS* or the *Server Explorer* to validate that your stored procedure is now up to date and does not reference the genre any longer. For further practice, roll back the migration to make sure your v0 file is working as expected, and then reapply the migration. If you've followed exactly, your rollback command should be

update-database -migration CreateSproc_GetItemsForListing

Review the database again to validate the genre code is back in the stored procedure as expected on rollback, and then run the command update-database to get your database migrations up-to-date.

Step 4: Execute and use the results from the stored procedure

There are a number of ways to get our code to execute a stored procedure. We could write code against a regular ADO.Net SqlCommand object, passing in the parameters and working with the data by getting a DataReader and reading it into a list of objects. This approach is how we would have worked through executing stored procedures (or other commands) in the past and doesn't leverage Entity Framework. Even so, that approach is still a very viable solution.

However, this is a book on Entity Framework, so we should stick with that approach and see how we can get EF to execute the stored procedure and return results for us.

In the Main method of the Program.cs file in the activity 0701 project, add a new method after ListInventory called GetItemsForListing. For clarity, this change is shown in Figure 7-13.

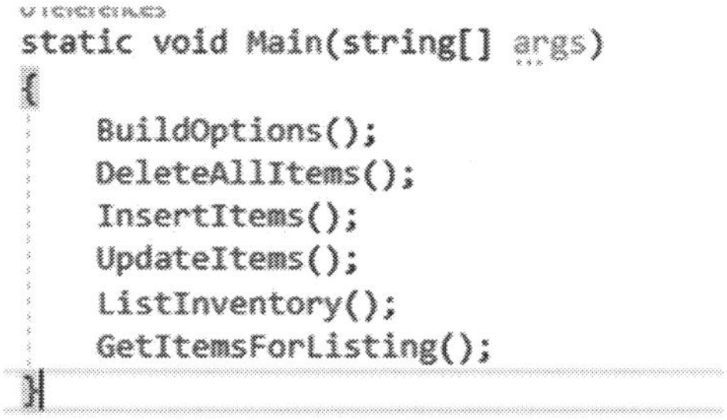

```
static void Main(string[] args)
{
    BuildOptions();
    DeleteAllItems();
    InsertItems();
    UpdateItems();
    ListInventory();
    GetItemsForListing();
}
```

Figure 7-13. *Adding the GetItemsForListing method to the Main method*

Next, write the GetItemsForListing method as follows:

```
static void GetItemsForListing()
{
    using (var db = new InventoryDbContext(_optionsBuilder.Options))
    {
        var results = db.Items.FromSqlRaw("EXECUTE dbo.
        GetItemsForListing").ToList();
        foreach (var item in results)
        {
            Console.WriteLine($"ITEM {item.Id}] {item.Name}");
        }
    }
}
```

Now run the code. We get an error about a duplicate key (review Figure 7-14).

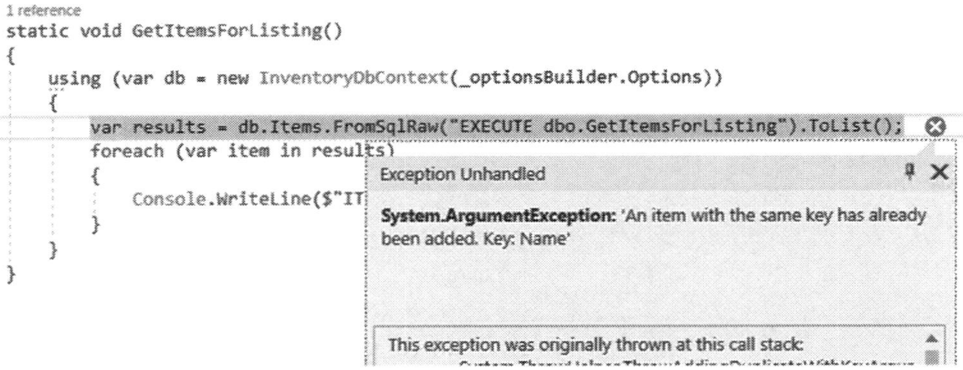

```
1 reference
static void GetItemsForListing()
{
    using (var db = new InventoryDbContext(_optionsBuilder.Options))
    {
        var results = db.Items.FromSqlRaw("EXECUTE dbo.GetItemsForListing").ToList();  ⊗
        foreach (var item in results)
        {
            Console.WriteLine($"IT
        }
    }
}
```

> Exception Unhandled   ⚏ ✕
>
> **System.ArgumentException:** 'An item with the same key has already
> been added. Key: Name'
>
> This exception was originally thrown at this call stack:

Figure 7-14. *An error for duplicate key in the result set*

The reason this happens is because in the data results, there are two columns with the name "Name." Because of this naming conflict, the collection can't be iterated correctly to display the Name property.

One fix would be a new migration, where we explicitly name the fields so there are no duplicates. Since the result has two fields that are named the same, this could be confusing. For that reason, let's fix the procedure to explicitly name the field CategoryName.

Add a new migration with the command add-migration UpdateProc_GetItemsForListing_ExplicitColumnNames, and set the Down method to reference the file from the Up method of the previous migration. Then set the Up method to reference a new v2 of the script. Remember to add the using statement for the InventoryDatabaseCore.Migrations.Scripts. For clarity, the new migration should have the following code:

```
public partial class UpdateProc_GetItemsForListing_ExplicitColumnNames :
Migration
{
    protected override void Up(MigrationBuilder migrationBuilder)
    {
        migrationBuilder.SqlResource("InventoryDatabaseCore.Migrations.
        Scripts.Procedures.GetItemsForListing.GetItemsForListing.v2.sql");
    }
```

```
protected override void Down(MigrationBuilder migrationBuilder)
{
    migrationBuilder.SqlResource("InventoryDatabaseCore.Migrations.
    Scripts.Procedures.GetItemsForListing.GetItemsForListing.v1.sql");
}
}
```

Next, create the v2 version of the script. Copy the code from v1, and update the text to explicitly select the cat.Name as CategoryName. For clarity, review the code for the v2 script as follows:

```
CREATE OR ALTER PROCEDURE dbo.GetItemsForListing
    @minDate DATETIME = null,
    @maxDate DATETIME = null
AS
BEGIN
    SET NOCOUNT ON;

    SELECT item.Name, item.Description, item.Notes
    , item.IsActive, item.IsDeleted, cat.Name as CategoryName
    FROM dbo.Items item
    LEFT JOIN dbo.Categories cat on item.CategoryId = cat.Id
    WHERE(@minDate IS NULL OR item.CreatedDate >= @minDate)
    AND(@maxDate IS NULL OR item.CreatedDate <= @maxDate)
END
```

Don't forget to set the new v2 script file as an embedded resource.

After creating the file and the migration, run the update-database command.

Once the database is updated, rerun the program to see results, which will generate yet another error (see Figure 7-15).

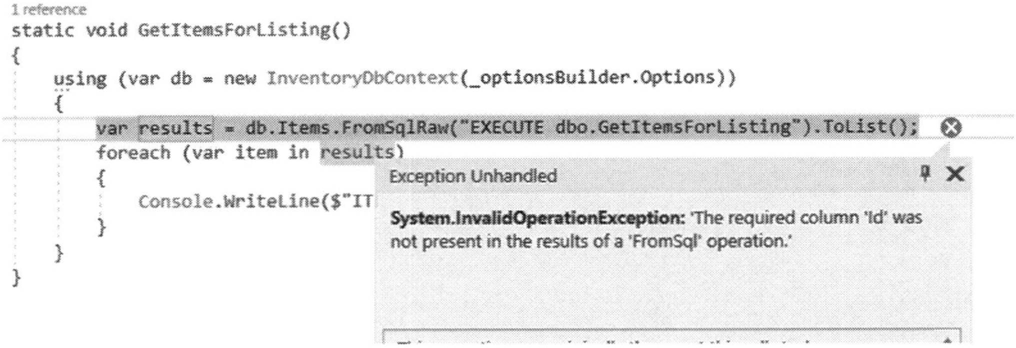

```
1 reference
static void GetItemsForListing()
{
    using (var db = new InventoryDbContext(_optionsBuilder.Options))
    {
        var results = db.Items.FromSqlRaw("EXECUTE dbo.GetItemsForListing").ToList(); ⊗
        foreach (var item in results)
        {
            Console.WriteLine($"IT
        }
    }
}
```

Exception Unhandled   ⏻ ✕

System.InvalidOperationException: 'The required column 'Id' was
not present in the results of a 'FromSql' operation.'

Figure 7-15. *The Id column we're trying to display is not returned*

Here we see that the error is due to the fact that a required field Id is not returned. This is actually a really big problem. In order to make this query work, we would have to select every single field, whether it is required or not in the Model, because we are querying against the Items table joined to the Categories table. If the field maps to the database, we must get something for that field in order for the FromSqlRaw query to return and map to an Item that has a reference to a Category.

To make matters even worse, the query would also be required to return all of the auditing fields we have built in. While this might not be a big deal in a small set of data, the overhead might quickly balloon out of control. Furthermore, we are likely trying to list lightweight information about the Items, and then when the user asks to modify or work with one of the items, we would get more useful information about the specific Item. For all of these reasons, adding in all the fields to our stored procedure would be a very bad practice and a terrible idea.

Ultimately, we need to find a better solution to this problem, either with the direct call to select just what we want or a common class that we could leverage to run the query directly with *ADO.Net* and map it back. To continue to stick with *EF*, we need to take our first look at working with the *Fluent API*.

Step 5: Use the Fluent API to map out a result set entity for the stored procedure

In order to use the *Fluent API* for mapping the results, we need a *DTO (data transfer object)* that will map the exact results we are looking for in our result set. In this case, a class that stores the fields as defined in the v2 version of our procedure GetItemsForListing.

In the InventoryModels project, add a new folder Dtos and then add a new class GetItemsForListingDto, to the class, and then add the following code to the class:

```
public class GetItemsForListingDto
{
    public string Name { get; set; } = "";
    public string Description { get; set; } = "";
    public string Notes { get; set; } = "";
    public bool IsActive { get; set; } = true;
    public bool IsDeleted { get; set; } = true;
    public string CategoryName { get; set; } = "";

}
```

For clarity on the code and the placement in the solution, review Figure 7-16.

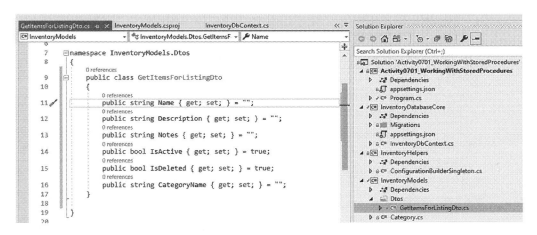

Figure 7-16. *The GetItemsForListingDto class*

After adding the class, we need to add the item to the InventoryDbContext. Prior to *EFCore 3.0*, we could have used an object called DbQuery<T> instead of DbSet<T>. With *EFCore 3.0+,* the DbQuery<T> object is obsolete. Going forward, all code should use the DbSet<T> syntax and then configure the entity to have no key and work as a read-only dataset using the *Fluent API*.

As of EFCore 3.0, the DbQuery<T> object is obsolete.

Add the following line of code after the `public DbSet<Genre> Genres` property to the `InventoryDbContext` and remember to add the correct using statement for the `InventoryModels.Dtos` namespace:

```
public DbSet<GetItemsForListingDto> ItemsForListing { get; set; }
```

With this addition, if we created a migration right now, the migration would request for us to add a new table `ItemsForListing` to the database. We don't want to do this, of course. If you want to see this in action, run the `add-migration` command with any name to see the generated code, and then run `remove-migration` to delete the migration.

Next, we need to add the following line of code to leverage the *Fluent API* in the `OnModelCreating` method to allow for the result set to be used from the context without generating a table in the database. Add the following code into the `InventoryDbContext.OnModelCreating` method after the code for the unique clustered index we created in Chapter 5:

```
modelBuilder.Entity<GetItemsForListingDto>(x =>
{
    x.HasNoKey();
    x.ToView("ItemsForListing");
});
```

Finally, we need to update the program so that we are making the correct calls using the new result set object. In the main program `GetItemsForListing` method, update the code to get the results from the new `DbSet<GetItemsForListingDto> ItemsForListing`, and change the `Console.WriteLine` to use fields we actually have (we didn't ever retrieve the `Id` for the Item). The reworked code should look as follows:

```
static void GetItemsForListing()
{
    using (var db = new InventoryDbContext(_optionsBuilder.Options))
    {
        var results = db.ItemsForListing.FromSqlRaw("EXECUTE dbo.
         GetItemsForListing").ToList();
        foreach (var item in results)
        {
```

```
            Console.WriteLine($"ITEM {item.Name} - {item.Description}");
        }
    }
}
```

For clarity, review Figure 7-17 to see the critical changes to the code.

```
1 reference
static void GetItemsForListing()
{
    using (var db = new InventoryDbContext(_optionsBuilder.Options))
    {
        var results = db.ItemsForListing.FromSqlRaw("EXECUTE dbo.GetItemsForListing").ToList();
        foreach (var item in results)
        {
            Console.WriteLine($"ITEM {item.Name} - {item.Description}");
        }
    }
}
```

Figure 7-17. *The GetItemsForListing method after reworking to use the new context set ItemsForListing, with changes emphasized*

Now when we run the program, we get results as expected, and as shown in Figure 7-18.

```
New Item: Batman Begins
New Item: Inception
New Item: Remember the Titans
New Item: Star Wars: The Empire Strikes Back
New Item: Top Gun
ITEM Top Gun - I feel the need, the need for speed
ITEM Batman Begins - You either die the hero or live long enough to see yourself become the villain
ITEM Inception - You mustn't be afraid to dream a little bigger
ITEM Star Wars: The Empire Strikes Back - He will join us or die, master
ITEM Remember the Titans - Attitude reflects leadership
C:\APressEntityFramework\Code\Chapter07\Activity0701_WorkingWithStoredProcedures_Starter\Activity0701_Work
```

Figure 7-18. *The stored procedure is executed, and we can leverage the results as expected*

Step 6: Use parameters to avoid SQL Injection attacks

Unless you are brand new to database programming you've likely heard of the term *"SQL Injection."* If you haven't heard of the term, suffice it to say that injection is one of the *OWASP* top ten security risks and has been on that list for my entire career as a developer.

A *SQL Injection* attack can happen any time we don't protect the parameters we're passing to our database. For example, if we pass a regular string where we took some user input for a search for the last name, perhaps a malicious user comes along and puts this as the value to search for

```
Gorm' ; update users set password = 'Password1'; select * from information_
schema.tables; --
```

All you were trying to get from the user was a last name to search for, but they understood you were likely running a query to search by last name, and if you don't parameterize the query, they can inject more code into your statement. In this case, the attacker is trying to update all the user passwords to 'Password1' and also get a list of all database tables returned in the query. For this reason, we want to make sure we are never using any kind of input from the user without first parameterizing it.

One last thought about *SQL Injection* that often goes overlooked is that it may happen in places you don't necessarily expect it to happen. I've seen lots of stored procedures throughout my career that build dynamic *SQL* and execute that dynamically built query directly within the procedure. In all such cases, you must be extra careful that you have not created an opportunity for the attacker to inject anything unexpected or malicious into your *SQL* statements. Even if the query is parameterized, if you are creating *SQL* statements from fields, your attacker could potentially save code into the field that will compromise your dynamic statements once concatenated.

Therefore, to make our statement more secure, let's look at parameterizing our call to the stored procedure. In the Main method for the program, add another method called `GetItemsForListingWithParams`. Then add the method with the following code (once again, you'll need another using statement: `Microsoft.Data.SqlClient`):

```
static void GetItemsForListingWithParams()
{
    var minDate = new SqlParameter("minDate", new DateTime(2020, 1, 1));
    var maxDate = new SqlParameter("maxDate", new DateTime(2021, 1, 1));

    using (var db = new InventoryDbContext(_optionsBuilder.Options))
    {
        var results = db.ItemsForListing
                        .FromSqlRaw("EXECUTE dbo.GetItemsForListing
                        @minDate, @maxDate", minDate, maxDate)
```

```
            .ToList();
    foreach (var item in results)
    {
        Console.WriteLine($"ITEM {item.Name} - {item.Description}");
    }
  }
}
```

Run the program to validate that both the call with no params and the call with params get data as expected. Feel free to test the parameters by modifying the dates on the parameters to make it so that the stored procedure will not return results.

Final thoughts

When working with stored procedures, by adding a simple extension, we can easily script out our changes and use the files in our migrations. Once that is in place, we have the ability to easily see the versions of each database object as well as could easily compare two files to see the changes for a migration.

We learned a great deal about how to work with scripted database objects in this activity, including

- How to use a DTO object to map the result set of a stored procedure or other scripted result

- How to modify the Fluent API to set an entity type to not have a key and act like a read-only view

- How to protect our code from SQL Injection attacks by parameterizing the queries

Now that we've seen how to work with scripted objects, we can move on to the next activity, where we'll learn about working with the different types of functions.

Activity 0702: Working with functions and seed data

In this activity, we are going to learn how to create and work with functions. Additionally, we'll briefly touch on the difference between scalar-valued functions and table-valued functions.

Step 1: Set up

To begin, continue where you've left off in the previous activities, or grab a copy of the starter files `Activity0702_WorkingWithFunctions_Starter.zip`. Once you've opened and built the project, make sure to run the `update-database` command to ensure your database is synced up with the current migrations. Additionally, run the program to ensure that you have all of the code working to insert, update, and read data and that the correct starter project is set.

It is critical that you have either completed activity 0701 before working on this activity or that you start with the activity 0702 starter files. The code in this activity will leverage part of the solution as built-in activity 0701 for scripting database objects in migrations.

Step 2: Script out a new scalar-valued function

The first type of function we want to build is a scalar-valued function. These functions are used to get a single value, usually as the result of a calculation. They are highly useful for one-off executions, but dangerous if you include them as a join in a query (essentially executing the function one time for every use in each row).

A good use of this would be to get a calculation that would be difficult to achieve without multiple built-in SQL commands being executed to return a single result. Another use could be to do something like get a list of the unique values of a field, alphabetized, as a comma-separated value string. Instead of a comma, I prefer to use a pipe, just in case a field value has a comma in it.

The easiest way to see what the script should be would be to right-click the Functions folder under `Programmability` and select New ➤ `Scalar-valued Function`, which will generate the script (see Figure 7-19).

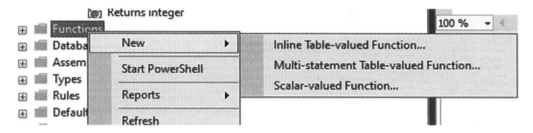

Figure 7-19. *Creating a new scalar-valued function*

Once generated, the function has a lot of overhead that can be removed, and then we note that the first part of the function requires a name and any parameters that we would want to include. The next statement is the return declaration and then the function concludes with the function body.

Let's modify the function to take the IsActive BIT as a parameter and then set the return type to VARCHAR(2500). We'll write the body to get a pipe-delimited list of the names of all active items in alphabetical order where the IsActive flag is matched.

Create a new folder named Functions under the Migrations\Scripts folder in the InventoryDatabaseCore project. In the Functions folder, add a subfolder for the function ItemNamesPipeDelimitedString, and then add a file ItemNamesPipeDelimitedString.v0.sql to the folder (see Figure 7-20 for clarification).

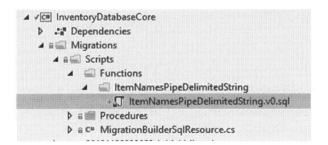

Figure 7-20. *Created the file for the new function in the Scripts hierarchy*

Don't forget to set the new ItemNamesPipeDelimitedString.v0.sql file as an embedded resource.

Add the following code to the new file to script the creation of the function:

```
CREATE OR ALTER FUNCTION [dbo].[ItemNamesPipeDelimitedString]
(@IsActive BIT)
RETURNS VARCHAR (2500)
AS
BEGIN
    RETURN (SELECT STRING_AGG (Name, '|')
            FROM Items
            WHERE IsActive = @IsActive)
END
```

Step 3: Add a new migration and update the database

Now that we have the file in place, add a new migration with the command add-migration CreateFunction_ItemNamesPipeDelimitedString.

In the migration Up method, add the line

```
migrationBuilder.SqlResource("InventoryDatabaseCore.Migrations.Scripts.
Functions.ItemNamesPipeDelimitedString.ItemNamesPipeDelimitedString.
v0.sql");
```

Then in the migration Down method, add the line

```
migrationBuilder.Sql("DROP FUNCTION IF EXISTS dbo.
ItemNamesPipeDelimitedString");
```

Run the update-database command to get the function into the database. Verify the function exists in your database by reviewing it in *SSMS* or in the *Server Explorer*.

Step 4: Get the result set from the function into a mapped entity with no defined key

In the real world, we'd likely use this function in concert with something else like a stored procedure or another result set. For illustrative purposes, we're just going to call it to validate that it works.

Before we can run this function to see it in action, just like with the stored procedure, we need to set a result that we can return that isn't tracked in the database.

302

To make sure we can easily work with this result set, we need to create an entity in our Models project that simply has the string return type that we'll be getting from our function.

In the Models project under the Dtos folder, add a new class file AllItemsPipeDelimitedStringDto.cs with one public string property called AllItems:

```
public class AllItemsPipeDelimitedStringDto
{
    public string AllItems { get; set; } = "";
}
```

Now that we have this result object which we can map our function result to; we can go ahead and modify the InventoryDbContext to add a new DbSet object to it. In the InventoryDatabaseCore project, in the InventoryDbContext, add the following line of code after the DbSet<Entity> declarations:

```
public DbSet<AllItemsPipeDelimitedStringDto> AllItemsOutput { get; set; }
```

Next, we need to update the OnModelCreating method to add the *Fluent API* mapping to set the new result set to having no key and working as a read-only database object. Add the following code into the OnModelCreating Method:

```
modelBuilder.Entity<AllItemsPipeDelimitedStringDto>(x =>
{
    x.HasNoKey();
    x.ToView("AllItemsOutput");
});
```

Step 5: Make the program changes to execute the function and get the results

In the Main method of the program file in the activity 0702 project, in the Program.cs file in the Main method, add a new method call AllActiveItemsPipeDelimitedString. In the method, add the following code:

```
static void AllActiveItemsPipeDelimitedString()
{
    using (var db = new InventoryDbContext(_optionsBuilder.Options))
```

```
{
    var isActiveParm = new SqlParameter("IsActive", 1);

    var result = db.AllItemsOutput
                    .FromSqlRaw("SELECT [dbo].
                    [ItemNamesPipeDelimitedString] (@IsActive)
                    AllItems", isActiveParm)
                    .FirstOrDefault();

    Console.WriteLine($"All active Items: {result.AllItems}");
}
}
```

Run the program to see the results. They should be similar to what is shown in Figure 7-21.

```
New Item: Batman Begins
New Item: Inception
New Item: Remember the Titans
New Item: Star Wars: The Empire Strikes Back
New Item: Top Gun
ITEM Top Gun - I feel the need, the need for speed
ITEM Batman Begins - You either die the hero or live long enough to see yourself become the villain
ITEM Inception - You mustn't be afraid to dream a little bigger
ITEM Star Wars: The Empire Strikes Back - He will join us or die, master
ITEM Remember the Titans - Attitude reflects leadership
ITEM Top Gun - I feel the need, the need for speed
ITEM Batman Begins - You either die the hero or live long enough to see yourself become the villain
ITEM Inception - You mustn't be afraid to dream a little bigger
ITEM Star Wars: The Empire Strikes Back - He will join us or die, master
ITEM Remember the Titans - Attitude reflects leadership
All active Items: Batman Begins|Inception|Remember the Titans|Star Wars: The Empire Strikes Back|Top Gun

C:\APressEntityFramework\Code\Chapter07\Activity0702_WorkingWithFunctions\Activity0702_WorkingWithFunctions\!
```

Figure 7-21. *The results of executing the function*

Step 7: Create a new table-valued function

Repeat steps 2–5 for a new function called GetItemsTotalValue. Again, we're doing a bit of a contrived example here, but we'll just get a list of items with Id, Name, Quantity, Price, and Total Value [calculated] where IsActive is true. As a reminder, the steps will be as follows:

- Script out a new table-valued function and modify it to get the data (see script).

- Add the folder for the function and create the migration using the SqlResource approach.

- Create and map a result set DTO for the function.

- Execute a method call that gets the data and outputs it to the screen.

Begin by creating a new subfolder called GetItemsTotalValue in the Functions folder. Add a new file called GetItemsTotalValue.v0.sql, and add the script for an inline table-valued function with the following code:

```
CREATE OR ALTER FUNCTION dbo.GetItemsTotalValue (
    @IsActive BIT = true
)
RETURNS TABLE
AS
RETURN
(
    SELECT Id, [Name], [Description], Quantity, PurchasePrice, Quantity *
    PurchasePrice as TotalValue
    From Items
    Where IsActive = @IsActive
)
```

As always, don't forget to make the file an embedded resource. For clarity on what this should look like, review Figure 7-22.

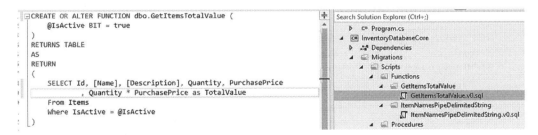

Figure 7-22. *Added the new script in the correct folder in the hierarchy and set the file as an embedded resource*

Add a new migration with the command add-migration CreateFunction_ GetItemsTotalValue. Add the v0 script to the Up method.

```
migrationBuilder.SqlResource("InventoryDatabaseCore.Migrations.Scripts.
Functions.GetItemsTotalValue.GetItemsTotalValue.v0.sql");
```

Bring the using statements in and the drop function code to the Down method:

```
migrationBuilder.Sql("DROP FUNCTION IF EXISTS dbo.GetItemsTotalValue");
```

Complete the migration by running the update-database command.

Next, add a new *DTO* in the Dtos folder in the InventoryModels project called GetItemsTotalValueDto to map results for execution. The code for the class is

```
public class GetItemsTotalValueDto
{
    public int Id { get; set; }
    public string Name { get; set; } = "";
    public string Description { get; set; } = "";
    public int Quantity { get; set; }
    public decimal? PurchasePrice { get; set; }
    public decimal? TotalValue { get; set; }
}
```

Add the new GetItemsTotalValueDto to the InventoryDbContext as a DbSet:

```
public DbSet<GetItemsTotalValueDto> GetItemsTotalValues { get; set; }
```

Configure the *Fluent API* to ensure no table is created for the new *DTO*. Add the following code to the OnModelCreating method in the InventoryDbContext, following the code we created previously for the AllItemsPipeDelimitedStringDto:

```
modelBuilder.Entity<GetItemsTotalValueDto>(x =>
        {
            x.HasNoKey();
            x.ToView("GetItemsTotalValues");
        });
```

Finally, add code to the main activity Program class, in the Main method called GetItemsTotalValues and then implement the function to run the execution of the function and display results:

```
static void GetItemsTotalValues()
{
    using (var db = new InventoryDbContext(_optionsBuilder.Options))
```

```
    {
        var isActiveParm = new SqlParameter("IsActive", 1);

        var result = db.GetItemsTotalValues
                        .FromSqlRaw("SELECT * from [dbo].
                        [GetItemsTotalValue] (@IsActive)", isActiveParm)
                        .ToList();

        foreach (var item in result)
        {
            Console.WriteLine($"New Item] {item.Id,-10}" +
                              $"|{item.Name,-50}" +
                              $"|{item.Quantity,-4}" +
                              $"|{item.TotalValue,-5}");
        }
    }
}
```

Run the program to get the results (review Figure 7-23).

```
ITEM Remember the Titans - Attitude reflects leadership
All active Items: Batman Begins|Inception|Remember the Titans|Star Wars: The Empire Strikes Back|Top Gun
New Item]        351|                                        Top Gun|   0|
New Item]        352|                                   Batman Begins|   0|
New Item]        353|                                       Inception|   0|
New Item]        354|             Star Wars: The Empire Strikes Back|   0|
New Item]        355|                            Remember the Titans|   0|

C:\APressEntityFramework\Code\Chapter07\Activity0702_WorkingWithFunctions\Activity0702_WorkingWithFunction
```

Figure 7-23. *The results from running the function*

Step 8: Seeding data with the Fluent API

Now that we can render some of the data for Categories, it's time to put some default data into the database. We'll also do some default data for Genres as well as fix up the creation of items to make our data more apparent.

When we want to have some default values that should always exist, the best place to put these is into a seed method. We can use the seed to make sure that certain data is placed into the tables if it doesn't already exist. The seed will run automatically after every call to update-database in the *PMC* locally, and when released to production, we'd make sure the migrations are triggered to ensure both migrations and seeds are applied and run.

There are a couple of approaches to working with seed data. The first way we can do this is in the *Fluent API*. Other than using the *Fluent API*, we can create seed methods that we trigger from the OnModelCreating method where we can execute some custom code.

Add the following code at the bottom of the OnModelCreating() method, following the code we recently added for the GetItemsTotalValues:

```
modelBuilder.Entity<Genre>(x => {
        x.HasData(
            new Genre() { Id = 1, CreatedDate = DateTime.Now,
            IsActive = true, IsDeleted = false, Name = "Fantasy" },
            new Genre() { Id = 2, CreatedDate = DateTime.Now,
            IsActive = true, IsDeleted = false, Name = "Sci/Fi" },
            new Genre() { Id = 3, CreatedDate = DateTime.Now,
            IsActive = true, IsDeleted = false, Name = "Horror" },
            new Genre() { Id = 4, CreatedDate = DateTime.Now,
            IsActive = true, IsDeleted = false, Name = "Comedy" },
            new Genre() { Id = 5, CreatedDate = DateTime.Now,
            IsActive = true, IsDeleted = false, Name = "Drama" }
        );
    });
```

Right now, if we want to add that data, we need to create a migration, which would script out the insert of this data into the database. For now, let's hold off on that so that we can get some categories and category colors into the database as well.

Step 9: Rolling our own custom migrator

To roll our own migration with seed data, we need a new project. We *could* stub this into the Main method of the Program file, but this would be a bad practice in the real world (as is putting in the Items, by the way). The reason this is a bad idea is that having the custom migration in the Main method of the executing program is only safe for one instance at a time. Likely, your real-world application will have more than one concurrent user.

Another benefit of creating this custom project is that we can include the execution of this project in our build pipeline, thereby making sure to run migrations on the database at the end of our deploy process before starting up the application.

Create a new console project called InventoryDataMigrator. Reference the InventoryDatabaseCore and InventoryHelpers projects, and bring in the NuGet Packages for all the *Entity Framework* and configuration files that we've been using. Note that InventoryModels will be available by the fact that it is referenced in the InventoryDatabaseCore project. An easy way to bring in all the NuGet packages is to open the project file and just modify it with the same ItemGroup entries that exist in the activity console project. Use this code (making sure to match your current version if not the same as mine):

```
<ItemGroup>
  <PackageReference Include="Microsoft.EntityFrameworkCore" Version="3.1.4" />
  <PackageReference Include="Microsoft.EntityFrameworkCore.Design"
  Version="3.1.4">
    <PrivateAssets>all</PrivateAssets>
    <IncludeAssets>runtime; build; native; contentfiles; analyzers;
    buildtransitive</IncludeAssets>
  </PackageReference>
  <PackageReference Include="Microsoft.EntityFrameworkCore.SqlServer"
  Version="3.1.4" />

  <PackageReference Include="Microsoft.Extensions.Configuration.
  FileExtensions" Version="3.1.4" />
  <PackageReference Include="Microsoft.Extensions.Configuration.Json"
  Version="3.1.4" />
</ItemGroup>
```

Then build the project to bring in the packages. Once this is completed, you could open the NuGet Package Manager and just review that everything is installed as expected.

Make sure to put a hard copy of the appsettings.json file in your directory with the program, so that you can get access to your database. Additionally, don't forget to set the file as Content with Copy to Output Directory set to Copy if newer.

Leverage the setup that is in the Program.cs file of the activity project to get direct access to the database context in the migrator project. Make sure that you add all required using statements so the code will compile. At this point, your code should look like this:

```
class Program
{
    static IConfigurationRoot _configuration;
    static DbContextOptionsBuilder<InventoryDbContext> _optionsBuilder;

    static void BuildOptions()
    {
        _configuration = ConfigurationBuilderSingleton.ConfigurationRoot;
        _optionsBuilder = new DbContextOptionsBuilder<InventoryDbConte
        xt>();
        _optionsBuilder.UseSqlServer(_configuration.GetConnectionString("In
        ventoryManager"));
    }

    static void Main(string[] args)
    {
        BuildOptions();
    }
}
```

In the Main method of your migrator project, create a new method called EnsureAndRunMigrations. In the method, add the following code to start:

```
static void EnsureAndRunMigrations()
{
    using (var db = new InventoryDbContext(_optionsBuilder.Options))
    {
        db.Database.Migrate();
    }
}
```

Having this code would be sufficient to kick off migrations automatically, but we also want to add custom seed data into our pipeline. To do that, add a new method call in the Main method called ExecuteCustomSeedData following the call to EnsureAndRunMigrations call. Then write the method with code as follows:

```
private static void ExecuteCustomSeedData()
      {
          using (var context = new InventoryDbContext(_optionsBuilder.
          Options))
          {
              var categories = new BuildCategories(context);
              categories.ExecuteSeed();
          }
      }
```

Now add a new class file into the migrator project called BuildCategories.cs as named in the preceding method. In the BuildCategories class, add a method called ExecuteSeed and a constructor that has a parameter for the InventoryDbContext. Make sure to add any missing using statements. Additionally, you'll need to add a private read-only InventoryDbContext _context; statement to create a variable to hold the value of the injected InventoryDbContext.

```
public class BuildCategories
{
    private readonly InventoryDbContext _context;

    public BuildCategories(InventoryDbContext context)
    {
        _context = context;
    }

    public void ExecuteSeed()
    {
        //_context.Categories.Add...
    }
}
```

Now add the following code into the ExecuteSeed method of the BuildCategories class:

```
if (_context.Categories.Count() == 0)
{
    _context.Categories.AddRange(
        new Category()
        {
            CreatedDate = DateTime.Now,
            IsActive = true,
            IsDeleted = false,
            Name = "Movies",
            CategoryColor = new CategoryColor() { ColorValue = "Blue" }
        },
        new Category()
        {
            CreatedDate = DateTime.Now,
            IsActive = true,
            IsDeleted = false,
            Name = "Books",
            CategoryColor = new CategoryColor() { ColorValue = "Red" }
        },
        new Category()
        {
            CreatedDate = DateTime.Now,
            IsActive = true,
            IsDeleted = false,
            Name = "Games",
            CategoryColor = new CategoryColor() { ColorValue = "Green" }
        }
    );
    _context.SaveChanges();

    var movies = _context.Categories.FirstOrDefault(x => x.Name.ToLower().
    Equals("movies"));
    var blue = _context.CategoryColors.FirstOrDefault(x => x.ColorValue.
    ToLower().Equals("blue"));
```

```
movies.CategoryColorId = blue.Id;
var books = _context.Categories.FirstOrDefault(x => x.Name.ToLower().
Equals("books"));
var red = _context.CategoryColors.FirstOrDefault(x => x.ColorValue.
ToLower().Equals("red"));
books.CategoryColorId = red.Id;
var games = _context.Categories.FirstOrDefault(x => x.Name.ToLower().
Equals("games"));
var green = _context.CategoryColors.FirstOrDefault(x => x.ColorValue.
ToLower().Equals("green"));
games.CategoryColorId = green.Id;
_context.SaveChanges();
}
```

Now, when we run the project, we'll get migrations to execute as well as running this seed. Note that the seed will only execute if there are no Categories in the database, which is by design to protect from concurrent runs creating duplicates.

In the Package Manager, add a new migration with the command add-migration Seed_Genre_Category_and_Colors. This will generate a new migration as shown in Figure 7-24.

```
1 reference
public partial class Seed_Genre_Category_and_Colors : Migration
{
    16 references
    protected override void Up(MigrationBuilder migrationBuilder)
    {
        migrationBuilder.InsertData(
            table: "Genres",
            columns: new[] { "Id", "CreatedByUserId", "CreatedDate", "IsActive", "IsDeleted", "LastModifiedDate", "LastModifiedUserId", "Name" },
            values: new object[,]
            {
                { 1, null, new DateTime(2020, 1, 21, 6, 2, 5, 469, DateTimeKind.Local).AddTicks(9090), true, false, null, null, "Fantasy" },
                { 2, null, new DateTime(2020, 1, 21, 6, 2, 5, 471, DateTimeKind.Local).AddTicks(9465), true, false, null, null, "Sci/Fi" },
                { 3, null, new DateTime(2020, 1, 21, 6, 2, 5, 471, DateTimeKind.Local).AddTicks(9551), true, false, null, null, "Horror" },
                { 4, null, new DateTime(2020, 1, 21, 6, 2, 5, 471, DateTimeKind.Local).AddTicks(9555), true, false, null, null, "Comedy" },
                { 5, null, new DateTime(2020, 1, 21, 6, 2, 5, 471, DateTimeKind.Local).AddTicks(9558), true, false, null, null, "Drama" }
            });
    }

    16 references
    protected override void Down(MigrationBuilder migrationBuilder)
    {
        migrationBuilder.DeleteData(
            table: "Genres",
            keyColumn: "Id",
            keyValue: 1);

        migrationBuilder.DeleteData(
```

Figure 7-24. *The migration is a script to seed data from the genres from the Fluent Api configuration*

313

Don't run `update-database`. Instead, we'll run the migrator project we created to both execute the migration and seed the categories and colors.

`Right-click` the `InventoryDataMigrator` project and select `Debug` ➤ `Start new instance`. This will run to completion (review Figure 7-25).

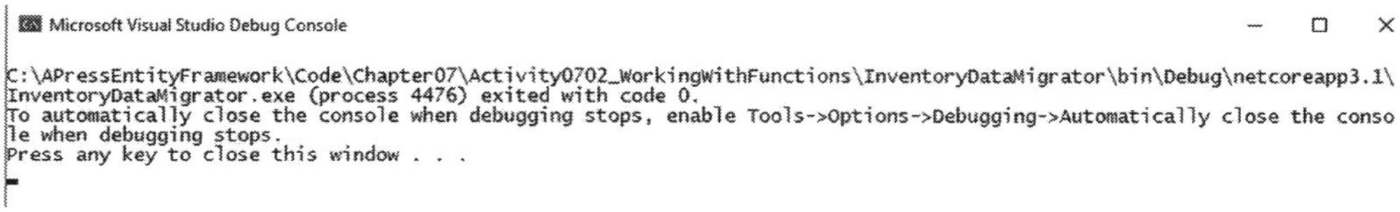

Figure 7-25. *The InventoryDataMigrator project runs to completion to execute the migrations and seed the data*

Use SSMS to check your database to ensure that your data was inserted as expected for `Genres`, `Categories`, and `CategoryColors`, with the following queries:

```
SELECT * from dbo.Genres
SELECT * from dbo.Categories
SELECT * from dbo.CategoryColors
SELECT * FROM __EFMigrationsHistory ORDER BY MigrationId DESC
```

Review your data in the database for the `Genres`, `Categories`, and `CategoryColors` tables. Also note that your migration has executed in the `__EFMigrationsHistory` table. If you run `update-database` in the *PMC* now, you should get the notification that all migrations have been run (see Figure 7-26).

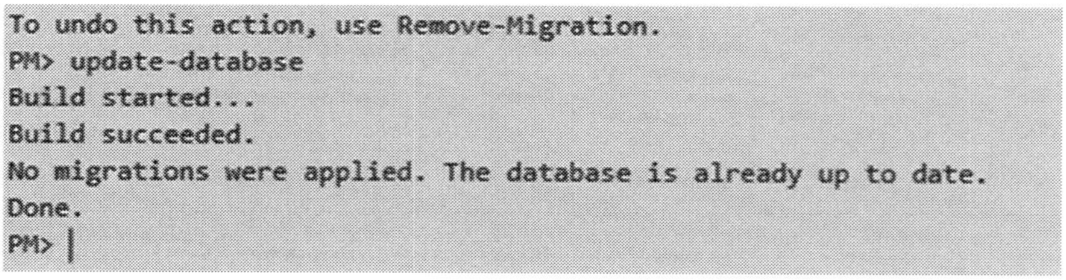

Figure 7-26. *No migrations need to be applied because our migrator project ran them for us*

Step 10: Create an Items builder

Add a new file called BuildItems.cs to your InventoryDataMigrator project, and create a private instance variable and constructor that has a parameter for the InventoryDbContext, just like we did in the BuildCategories class. Also stub out the ExecuteSeed method.

```
public class BuildItems
{
    private readonly InventoryDbContext _context;

    public BuildItems(InventoryDbContext context)
    {
        _context = context;
    }

    public void ExecuteSeed()
    {
        //...code
    }
}
```

After stubbing out the class, add a method call to build the Items in the ExecuteCustomSeedData method:

```
private static void ExecuteCustomSeedData()
{
    using (var context = new InventoryDbContext(_optionsBuilder.Options))
    {
        var categories = new BuildCategories(context);
        categories.ExecuteSeed();
        var items = new BuildItems(context);
        items.ExecuteSeed();
    }
}
```

Finally, let's add the items we want to have in our project going forward to the ExecuteSeed method in your database. Feel free to modify this any way you see fit or desire.

315

```
if (_context.Items.Count() == 0)
{
    var movie = _context.Categories.FirstOrDefault(x => x.Name.ToLower()
    == "movies");
    var book = _context.Categories.FirstOrDefault(x => x.Name.ToLower() ==
    "books");
    var game = _context.Categories.FirstOrDefault(x => x.Name.ToLower()
    == "games");

    var scifi = _context.Genres.FirstOrDefault(x => x.Name.ToLower() ==
    "sci/fi");
    var fantasy = _context.Genres.FirstOrDefault(x => x.Name.ToLower()
    == "fantasy");
    var horror = _context.Genres.FirstOrDefault(x => x.Name.ToLower() ==
    "horror");
    var comedy = _context.Genres.FirstOrDefault(x => x.Name.ToLower() ==
    "comedy");
    var drama = _context.Genres.FirstOrDefault(x => x.Name.ToLower() ==
    "drama");

    var createdDate = DateTime.Now;

    _context.Items.AddRange(
       new Item()
       {
           CategoryId = movie.Id,
           CreatedDate = createdDate,
           CurrentOrFinalPrice = 19.99m,
           IsActive = true,
           IsDeleted = false,
           IsOnSale = false,
           Name = "Top Gun",
           Description = "I feel the need, the need for speed",
           PurchasedDate = createdDate,
           PurchasePrice = 18.50m,
           Quantity = 1,
```

```
        ItemGenres = new List<ItemGenre> {
            new ItemGenre { GenreId = comedy.Id }
        }
    },
    new Item()
    {
        CategoryId = movie.Id,
        CreatedDate = createdDate,
        CurrentOrFinalPrice = 12.99m,
        IsActive = true,
        IsDeleted = false,
        IsOnSale = true,
        Name = "Batman Begins",
        Description = "Why do we fall, Bruce?",
        PurchasedDate = createdDate,
        PurchasePrice = 14.50m,
        Quantity = 4,
        ItemGenres = new List<ItemGenre> {
            new ItemGenre { GenreId = scifi.Id } ,
            new ItemGenre { GenreId = drama.Id }
        }
    },
    new Item()
    {
        CategoryId = book.Id,
        CreatedDate = createdDate,
        CurrentOrFinalPrice = 35.99m,
        IsActive = true,
        IsDeleted = false,
        IsOnSale = true,
        Name = "Practical Entity Framework",
        Description = "The book that teaches practical application
        with EF",
        PurchasedDate = createdDate,
```

```
            PurchasePrice = 44.50m,
            Quantity = 100
        },
        new Item()
        {
            CategoryId = book.Id,
            CreatedDate = createdDate,
            CurrentOrFinalPrice = 6.99m,
            IsActive = true,
            IsDeleted = false,
            IsOnSale = false,
            Name = "The Lord of the Rings",
            Description = "The fellowship of the Ring",
            PurchasedDate = createdDate,
            PurchasePrice = 12.50m,
            Quantity = 7,
            ItemGenres = new List<ItemGenre> {
                new ItemGenre { GenreId = scifi.Id },
                 new ItemGenre { GenreId = fantasy.Id }
            }
        },
        new Item()
        {
            CategoryId = game.Id,
            CreatedDate = createdDate,
            CurrentOrFinalPrice = 23.99m,
            IsActive = true,
            IsDeleted = false,
            IsOnSale = false,
            Name = "Battlefield 5",
            Description = "First person shooter",
            PurchasedDate = createdDate,
            PurchasePrice = 44.50m,
            Quantity = 17,
```

```
        ItemGenres = new List<ItemGenre> {
            new ItemGenre { GenreId = scifi.Id }
        }
    },
    new Item()
    {
        CategoryId = game.Id,
        CreatedDate = createdDate,
        CurrentOrFinalPrice = 0.00m,
        IsActive = true,
        IsDeleted = false,
        IsOnSale = false,
        Name = "World Of Tanks",
        Description = "AN MMO WW2 Tanks First-Person Shooter",
        PurchasedDate = createdDate,
        PurchasePrice = 0.00m,
        Quantity = 1
    }
);

_context.SaveChanges();
}
```

Once your code is complete, manually delete all of the items, category colors, and categories from the Items, CategoryColors, and Categories tables from your database:

```
DELETE FROM CategoryColors
DELETE FROM Categories
DELETE FROM Items
```

Next, use the Debug ➤ Start new instance to run the migrator project to execute the item builder seed.

Finally, remove the calls at the start of our activity program that delete and generate/ update items. Also delete the call to the GetItemsForListing method and delete the method or comment the method out, so that the list of Items will only print once. To finish the cleanup, delete all the unused methods for item create/update. For clarity, the Main method from my program file is shown in Figure 7-27.

```
0 references
static void Main(string[] args)
{
    BuildOptions();
    ListInventory();
    GetItemsForListingWithParams();
    AllActiveItemsPipeDelimitedString();
    GetItemsTotalValues();
}
```

Figure 7-27. *The new version of the Main method no longer needs to create items*

Run the project to see the final result, which should look similar to the results in Figure 7-28.

```
Microsoft Visual Studio Debug Console                                      —    □    ×
New Item: Batman Begins
New Item: Battlefield 5
New Item: Practical Entity Framework
New Item: The Lord of the Rings
New Item: Top Gun
ITEM Top Gun - I feel the need, the need for speed
ITEM Batman Begins - Why do we fall, Bruce?
ITEM Practical Entity Framework - The book that teaches practical application with EF
ITEM The Lord of the Rings - The fellowship of the Ring
ITEM Battlefield 5 - First person shooter
ITEM World Of Tanks - AN MMO WW2 Tanks First-Person Shooter
All active Items: Top Gun|Batman Begins|Practical Entity Framework|The Lord of the Rings|Battlefield 5|World Of Tanks
New Item] 127     |Top Gun                       |1    |18.50
New Item] 128     |Batman Begins                 |4    |58.00
New Item] 129     |Practical Entity Framework    |100  |4450.00
New Item] 130     |The Lord of the Rings         |7    |87.50
New Item] 131     |Battlefield 5                 |17   |756.50
New Item] 132     |World Of Tanks                |1    |0.00
C:\APressEntityFramework\Code\Chapter07\Activity0702_WorkingWithFunctions\Activity0702_WorkingWithFunctions\bin\Debug\ne
tcoreapp3.1\Activity0702_WorkingWithFunctions.exe (process 4524) exited with code 0.
To automatically close the console when debugging stops, enable Tools->Options->Debugging->Automatically close the conso
le when debugging stops.
Press any key to close this window . . .
```

Figure 7-28. *The final run of activity 0702 shows the data and working functions*

Final thoughts

In this activity, we created a scalar-valued function and a table-valued function using migrations in our new file-based approach.

We also continued to work with objects using the *Fluent API* for each of these result sets to ensure no new tables were added to the database.

We concluded the activity by seeding data from the *Fluent API* and by creating a custom solution of our own to run migrations and seed data.

Activity 0703: Working with views

In our final activity for this chapter, we are going to work with views in our database. Based on what we've learned in the previous activities, we can easily create a view. This should almost be muscle memory by now for us.

Step 1: Set up

To begin, continue where you've left off in the previous activities, or grab a copy of the starter files Activity0703_WorkingWithViews_Starter.zip. Once you've opened and built the project, make sure to run the update-database command to ensure your database is synced up with the current migrations (or use the Debug ➤ Start new instance on the migrator project). Additionally, run the program to ensure your program works as expected.

It is critical that you have completed activities 0701 and 0702 before working on this activity or that you start with the activity 0703 starter files. The code will leverage part of the solutions as built-in activities 0701 and 0702 for scripting database objects in migrations.

Step 2: Add the view as a script

Begin in the InventoryDatabaseCore project by creating a new folder in the Migrations/Scripts folder for Views. Add a new folder for ItemsWithGenres, and then add the script ItemsWithGenres.v0.sql. Add the following code to the script:

```
CREATE OR ALTER VIEW ItemsWithGenres AS
SELECT i.Id, i.[Name], i.[Description], i.IsActive, i.IsDeleted
       , g.Id GenreId, g.[Name] Genre, g.IsActive [GenreIsActive],
       g.IsDeleted [GenreIsDeleted]
FROM items i
LEFT JOIN ItemGenre ig on i.Id = ig.ItemId
LEFT JOIN Genres g on ig.GenreId = g.Id
```

Again, don't forget to set the new file as an embedded resource.

Step 3: Add the view DTO and set the view in the InventoryDbContext

In the InventoryModels project, add a folder for Views, then create a class file called ItemsWithGenresDto.cs, and add the properties to match the result set for the view as scripted in step 2:

```
public class ItemsWithGenresDto
{
    public int Id { get; set; }
    public string Name { get; set; } = "";
    public string Description { get; set; } = "";
    public bool IsActive { get; set; } = true;
    public bool IsDeleted { get; set; } = false;

    public int? GenreId { get; set; }
    public string Genre { get; set; } = "";
    public bool? GenreIsActive { get; set; } = true;
    public bool? GenreIsDeleted { get; set; } = false;

}
```

Next, add the public DbSet<ItemsWithGenresDto> ItemsWithGenres {get;set;} to the InventoryDbContext.

Step 4: Update the Fluent API for the view

As with the procedures and functions, update the *Fluent API* to handle the new view with no key and set the view to be a read-only view. Add the following code into the OnModelCreating method, following the call that seeds Genre data.

```
modelBuilder.Entity<ItemsWithGenresDto>(x =>
{
    x.HasNoKey();
    x.ToView("ItemsWithGenres");
});
```

Step 5: Create the migration

Make sure that you've set the InventoryDatabaseCore project as the default in the PMC, and then add the view into the database by running the command add-migration CreateView_ItemsWithGenres. Note that this might ask us to update the genre data, because we have a dynamic date/time in the create statement. Run the remove-migration command to roll back the migration.

In the InventoryDbContext, hard-code a created date for the Genre data. We're going to have to update at least once (otherwise our data will get deleted or constantly ask us to update).

```
var createdDate = new DateTime(2020, 01, 01);
modelBuilder.Entity<Genre>(x => {
    x.HasData(
        new Genre() { Id = 1, CreatedDate = createdDate, IsActive = true
                    , IsDeleted = false, Name = "Fantasy" },
        new Genre() { Id = 2, CreatedDate = createdDate, IsActive = true
                    , IsDeleted = false, Name = "Sci/Fi" },
        new Genre() { Id = 3, CreatedDate = createdDate, IsActive = true
                    , IsDeleted = false, Name = "Horror" },
        new Genre() { Id = 4, CreatedDate = createdDate, IsActive = true
                    , IsDeleted = false, Name = "Comedy" },
        new Genre() { Id = 5, CreatedDate = createdDate, IsActive = true
                    , IsDeleted = false, Name = "Drama" }
    );
});
```

Run the command add-migration update_genreCreatedDate. You should see an update with the hard-coded create date for the Genre data. Update the database with the update-database command. Now run the command add-migration CreateView_ItemsWithGenres migration again. This time it should be blank. Lesson learned – don't put dynamic data in the HasData seed method in the Fluent API!

After creating the migration, add the v0 file declaration to the Up method:

```
migrationBuilder.SqlResource("InventoryDatabaseCore.Migrations.Scripts.
Views.ItemsWithGenres.ItemsWithGenres.v0.sql");
```

And add the DROP VIEW IF EXISTS statement to the Down() method:

```
migrationBuilder.Sql("DROP VIEW IF EXISTS dbo.ItemsWithGenres");
```

Then update the database by running the update-database command or by right-clicking the migrator project and selecting Debug ➤ Start new instance.

Step 6: Make the call and get the data from the new view

In the activity's main Program class, in the Main method, add a method call to a new method named GetItemsWithGenres. Then, create the method, with the following code:

```
static void GetItemsWithGenres()
{
    using (var db = new InventoryDbContext(_optionsBuilder.Options))
    {
        var result = db.ItemsWithGenres.ToList();

        foreach (var item in result)
        {
            Console.WriteLine($"New Item] {item.Id,-10}" +
                              $"|{item.Name,-50}" +
                              $"|{item.Genre??""",-4}");
        }
    }
}
```

Finally, run the project to see the updated results. Your output should be similar to the output shown in Figure 7-29.

```
Microsoft Visual Studio Debug Console                                          —   □   ×
New Item: The Lord of the Rings
New Item: Top Gun
ITEM Top Gun - I feel the need, the need for speed
ITEM Batman Begins - Why do we fall, Bruce?
ITEM Practical Entity Framework - The book that teaches practical application with EF
ITEM The Lord of the Rings - The fellowship of the Ring
ITEM Battlefield 5 - First person shooter
ITEM World Of Tanks - AN MMO WW2 Tanks First-Person Shooter
All active Items: Top Gun|Batman Begins|Practical Entity Framework|The Lord of the Rings|Battlefield 5|World Of Tanks
New Item] 127        |Top Gun                          |1    |18.50
New Item] 128        |Batman Begins                    |4    |58.00
New Item] 129        |Practical Entity Framework       |100  |4450.00
New Item] 130        |The Lord of the Rings            |7    |87.50
New Item] 131        |Battlefield 5                    |17   |756.50
New Item] 132        |World Of Tanks                   |1    |0.00
New Item] 127        |Top Gun                          |Comedy
New Item] 128        |Batman Begins                    |Sci/Fi
New Item] 128        |Batman Begins                    |Drama
New Item] 129        |Practical Entity Framework       |
New Item] 130        |The Lord of the Rings            |Sci/Fi
New Item] 130        |The Lord of the Rings            |Fantasy
New Item] 131        |Battlefield 5                    |Sci/Fi
New Item] 132        |World Of Tanks                   |

C:\APressEntityFramework\Code\Chapter07\Activity0703_WorkingWithViews\Activity0703_WorkingWithViews\bin\Debug\netcoreapp3.1\Ac
tivity0703_WorkingWithViews.exe (process 11032) exited with code 0.
To automatically close the console when debugging stops, enable Tools->Options->Debugging->Automatically close the console whe
n debugging stops.
Press any key to close this window . . .
```

Figure 7-29. *The output from the completed activity shows the items with their genres using the data from the new view*

Final thoughts

In this final activity, we've seen how to set up a view and corrected a couple of things that needed to be fixed up.

Like stored procedures and functions, we can create a new view with simple scripts and then execute the scripts via migrations. Once the view is created, we can then add it as an object and make sure it is an entity set with no key and set it to be a read-only view using the Fluent API. Once this information is in place, it is fairly easy to get the results of the view.

Conclusion

In this chapter, we have spent a lot of time learning about how to work with database objects. We've covered how to work with functions, views, and stored procedures. We also dove into creating seed data and handling migrations from the *Fluent API* and from our own custom solution.

In the next chapter, we'll take our first deeper dive into working with LINQ to do some sorting, filtering, and paging of results.

CHAPTER 8

Sorting, Filtering, and Paging

In this chapter, we're going to build on what we've learned in the previous seven chapters. To this point, we have created a database using the code-first approach, and now are ready to start working with the data in a more robust fashion.

It's time to learn LINQ

Now that our data is modeled and we have the `InventoryDBContext` in place to get the data, we need to start learning and working with *LINQ* in our solutions. To be clear, LINQ exists outside of *Entity Framework*, with options like *LINQ to Objects*, *LINQ to XML*, and even *LINQ to ADO.Net*, so don't make the mistake of thinking that LINQ is just for working with the *Entity Framework*. For our purposes, we're going to focus on *LINQ to Entities*, which allows us to work against *EF* with LINQ queries. Before we move on, however, let's first address the elephant in the room.

LINQ is not the problem

One of the most prevalent misconceptions about working with LINQ and *EF* is that using LINQ is slow and bulky. Additionally, many developers have struggled with some of the concepts around making LINQ performant. To answer the question, yes, absolutely, LINQ is highly performant. The real problem is not LINQ per se. The real problem exists with the way LINQ is implemented by the developer. As with any programming language, if the developer doesn't set things up correctly, the language cannot do its best work.

© Brian L. Gorman 2020
B. L. Gorman, *Practical Entity Framework*, https://doi.org/10.1007/978-1-4842-6044-9_8

Use a profiler or another tool

There are some instances where we can instantly find and fix issues with our queries. In other cases, we might be receiving complaints from users about pages taking too long to load, but we didn't realize there was a performance issue. To make sure that our code is not causing problems, it's critical to have some sort of tool that helps us trace through execution and identify bottlenecks.

There are many tools available for this specific reason, with the most popular tool being the *Entity Framework Profiler*. The *Entity Framework Profiler* is a solid tool for determining execution bottlenecks and other issues with our code, but using it requires purchasing a license.

When working with web solutions, there is another alternative that I highly recommend called *Stackify Prefix*. Using the free version of prefix does require installing a program on your machine and at the time of this writing only works for web solutions. In order to work against non-web solutions, you would need to upgrade to the paid version of the program.

Another tool that a developer could use is simply to turn on the *SQL Server Profiler* to monitor calls to your database. This tool is also great for seeing what is going on with our database calls. The main drawback is that the *SQL Server Profiler* can be a bit chatty without configuration. Additionally, to get the filters set correctly so that the tool can be used well takes a lot of practice. For our purposes, we'll be using this tool in our activities for this book, but I highly encourage you to check out the other available tools as well.

Issues and solutions

In order to make sure we don't fall into some of the more common incorrect implementations, let's first examine a few statements and then examine the problems they have, as well as the way to correctly implement the code.

Issue #1: Pre-fetching results, then iterating to filter

There are a number of things that *Entity Framework* does well. One of the things that *EF* handles well is *lazy loading* results as needed. Lazy loading is essentially the art of getting the data just in time, without pulling all the data until needed.

A great example of where this takes place is when we build out queries to get data into a list. The data from the query is only pulled when the query is executed. This is why when you are debugging an application, you might have seen statements like "*Expanding the results view will enumerate the IEnumerable*" when debugging database calls.

Because of this implementation and the misconceptions around it, one of the most prevalent issues when working with *Entity Framework* is causing these executions to take place and then doing more work against the data that should have been done before the execution.

Consider the following statement:

```
var people = db.Person.ToList().OrderByDescending(x => x.LastName);
```

as compared to

```
var query = db.Person.OrderByDescending(x => x.LastName);
var result = query.Take(10);

foreach (var person in result)
```

In the first example, the call to get the results ToList will bring back all the results in the table, and then iterate those results to sort on all of the table rows, whereas in the second query, the deferred execution allows for the query to apply the transformations prior to the execution, thereby only needing to work with the limited results. As would be expected, the second query can perform much better in most situations.

Issue #2: Not disconnecting your data

We've already seen a few queries in our work to this point that fetched data for display. In those queries, we did something like DBContext.Entity.ToList, where we got a list of the objects in the database. What we maybe didn't know at the time is that each one of these entities in the result set has change tracking enabled. Change tracking allows the DBContext to track the changes that have happened, so that we can perform any updates and save changes back to the database.

If the only thing you are going to do with your data is render it for review, there is no need to track the changes. Additionally, if you are working in a stateless environment like the Web, when you are going to perform an update, you likely will retrieve the data to be updated again before massaging that data with the appropriate updates. Consider the following code again, as it could be used to get a list of Person objects and display those people on a grid for review:

```
var query = db.Person.OrderByDescending(x => x.LastName);
var result = query.Take(10);

foreach (var person in result)
```

The user would likely then select one of the Person objects to modify and then make their changes and post that data back to the controller, where the controller would then retrieve the Person by Id, update the fields, and then save the changes.

In this and similar scenarios, the first call could have been done in a disconnected fashion, as is shown here:

```
var query = db.Person.AsNoTracking().OrderByDescending(x => x.LastName);
var result = query.Take(10);

foreach (var person in result)
```

It is even possible to set your *Entity Framework* DBContext so that all of your requests are set to operate without change tracking. This can be accomplished by adding the following statement to the DBContext constructor:

```
ChangeTracker.QueryTrackingBehavior = QueryTrackingBehavior.NoTracking;
```

A final thought is that any query that uses a projection to a DTO or an anonymous class will also not be tracking an entity, since no entity exists for that DTO or anonymous class. We'll be taking a look at using DTOs and anonymous classes when we talk about LINQ with projections in the next chapter.

Issue #3: IEnumerable vs. IQueryable

Which object type should we use when creating our queries, and why? There are many to choose from. In most queries, the end result is a collection of objects, which are often rendered as a List<T>. As we saw in issue #1, it's not always ideal to get the results into a List<T>. This issue is really the same as getting items into a list too early in the process, but by understanding the differences here, we can gain a very good understanding of how to write the best code when working with *EF*.

To go deeply into the difference between IEnumerable and IQueryable, the main differences come down to when and where the code is executed. Is query execution on the server side or in-memory? What about filtering, sorting, limiting, and/or transforming that data? These questions are the most critical concerns we should have when determining performance of our query. Table 8-1 shows how each of these object types handles queries and filtering.

Table 8-1.   *IEnumerable vs. IQueryable and how they each handle queries and filtering*

	IEnumerable	**IQueryable**
Initial Query	Server side	Server side
Filtering	Client side	Server side

Looking at the table and based on our overall discussion, it should be clear by now that lazy loading with deferred execution can generally allow for our queries to be more performant, as well as limit our results to only include the objects that we need in scope.

The fact that the IEnumerable object requires pulling data at the onset means that lazy loading is off the table when using an IEnumerable object such as a List<T>. The IQueryable object, however, allows for building out your entire query, with filters, and then on execution only getting the exact data that is needed into memory.

Practical application

In the next part of the chapter, we're going to be working with LINQ to build out some real-world queries that require filtering, paging, and sorting. As we do this, we'll take a look at ways that work that aren't as efficient as possible, and then we'll fix the queries so that we have a full command of how to write the most efficient queries we need to accomplish the task at hand.

Activity 0801: Sorting, paging, and filtering

In this activity, we're going to use LINQ to build out robust and efficient queries for use in our applications.

In most applications, there is some requirement to display a grid or list of objects that contains the data for each of the objects. Additionally, the application generally provides the user an ability to sort the items and enter a text-based search for items that match and provides the ability to page through results.

As we've discussed previously, we can either get all the results at once and then filter them in memory, or we can pull only the data we need to display at the current time. Depending on what you are trying to accomplish, there are advantages and disadvantages in each approach to consider. As always, as the developer, it will be up to you to make the correct choice.

For our activity, we could take some time and build out our entire Items database with lots of records. Please feel free to do that if you'd rather continue working with our Items database. However, in the interest of time, and to help us see the ramifications of non-performant queries, the starter files will point to our previously installed instance of the AdventureWorks database. If for some reason you don't have AdventureWorks installed, you could refer back to Chapter 2, where we were working against the existing AdventureWorks database for more information.

Step 1: Get the starter files for setup

Begin by getting a copy of the starter files Activity0801_Sorting_Filtering_Paging. Open the files and build the solution out. At the start of this activity, there is nothing to run and no database migrations are outstanding. Make sure to edit the connection string in the appsettings.json file to ensure your database connection is set correctly for the *AdventureWorks* database. If, for some reason, you'd rather just create the starter pack yourself, you can easily do so. There isn't much to it. Simply implement the following instructions:

1. Create a new .Net Core Console Project.

2. Find the EF_Activity001 project folder from the end of Chapter 3, copy it to your local solution directory, and add a reference to it.

3. Find the `InventoryHelpers` project folder from any of the projects in Chapter 7, copy it to your local solution directory, and add a reference to it.

4. Add the `appsettings.json` file from `EF_Activity001` into the main activity project for the database connection string, and edit the connection string to your needs. Don't forget to make the file as content with the action "Copy if newer."

5. Install each of the NuGet packages individually through the NuGet Package Manager:

   a. `Microsoft.EntityFrameworkCore`

   b. `Microsoft.EntityFrameworkCore.Design`

   c. `Microsoft.EntityFrameworkCore.SqlServer`

   d. `Microsoft.Extensions.Configuration.FileExtensions`

   e. `Microsoft.Extensions.Configuration.Json`

   Note: Make sure your versions match across all projects; you may need to update `EF_Activity001` to a newer version.

6. Add the code that follows into the Program.cs class in the main activity project, add any missing using statements, and then run the project to validate you have no errors:

```
class Program
{
    private static IConfigurationRoot _configuration;
    private static DbContextOptionsBuilder<AdventureWorksContext>
    _optionsBuilder;

    static void Main(string[] args)
    {
        BuildOptions();
    }
}
```

```
static void BuildOptions()
{
    _configuration = ConfigurationBuilderSingleton.
    ConfigurationRoot;
    _optionsBuilder = new DbContextOptionsBuilder<Adventure
    WorksContext>();
    _optionsBuilder.UseSqlServer(_configuration.GetConnection
    String("AdventureWorks"));
}
}
```

Step 2: Comparing two queries

To begin, let's start by looking at the execution of two queries that will garner the exact same results. This will give us a chance to see the difference in how queries are applied during execution.

Create two new methods in the Main method of the program file. The first method should be called ListPeopleThenOrderAndTake. The second method should be called QueryPeopleOrderedToListAndTake.

```
static void Main(string[] args)
{
    BuildOptions();
    Console.WriteLine("List People Then Order and Take");
    ListPeopleThenOrderAndTake();
    Console.WriteLine("Query People, order, then list and take");
    QueryPeopleOrderedToListAndTake();
}
```

Both methods will get a result of ten People, ordered. In fact, we've already seen a similar query in Chapter 2, as well as mentioned in the text for this chapter.

In the ListPeopleThenOrderAndTake method, add the following code:

```
static void ListPeopleThenOrderAndTake()
{
    using (var db = new AdventureWorksContext(_optionsBuilder.Options))
    {
```

```
    var people = db.Person.ToList().OrderByDescending(x => x.LastName);
    foreach (var person in people.Take(10))
    {
        Console.WriteLine($"{person.FirstName} {person.LastName}");
    }
  }
}
```

In the QueryPeopleOrderedToListAndTake method, add the following code:

```
static void QueryPeopleOrderedToListAndTake()
{
    using (var db = new AdventureWorksContext(_optionsBuilder.Options))
    {
        var query = db.Person.OrderByDescending(x => x.LastName);
        var result = query.Take(10);

        foreach (var person in result)
        {
            Console.WriteLine($"{person.FirstName} {person.LastName}");
        }
    }
}
```

Make sure that you've added any missing using statements; then run the code to ensure that both are returning the same ten records. Your results should be similar to what is shown in Figure 8-1.

```
Microsoft Visual Studio Debug Console
List People Then Order and Take
Michael Zwilling
Michael Zwilling
Jake Zukowski
Judy Zugelder
Carla Zubaty
Patricia Zubaty
Karin Zimprich
Karin Zimprich
Kimberly Zimmerman
Jo Zimmerman
Query People, order, then list and take
Michael Zwilling
Michael Zwilling
Jake Zukowski
Judy Zugelder
Patricia Zubaty
Carla Zubaty
Karin Zimprich
Karin Zimprich
Tiffany Zimmerman
Marc Zimmerman

C:\APressEntityFramework\Code\Chapter08\Activity0801
```

Figure 8-1. *The results of running both methods*

Step 3: Perform a server analysis on the code we just wrote

As we've seen, both queries perform fairly well in these examples, and both return the exact same results. Therefore, we must ask, are these two queries equally effective and efficient when it comes to the implementations?

To find out, let's perform an analysis. In SSMS, turn on the tool to profile your server calls by going to Tools ➤ SQL Server Profiler. Enabling SQL Server Profiler is highlighted in Figure 8-2 for clarity.

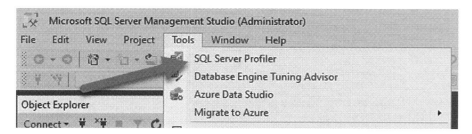

Figure 8-2. *Bring up the SQL Server Profiler with the menu item in SSMS*

After bringing up the profiler, connect to your local database, or whatever database connection you are using for the *AdventureWorks* database. Connecting to a SQLExpress database is shown in Figure 8-3. Make sure to use the correct server based on your implementation.

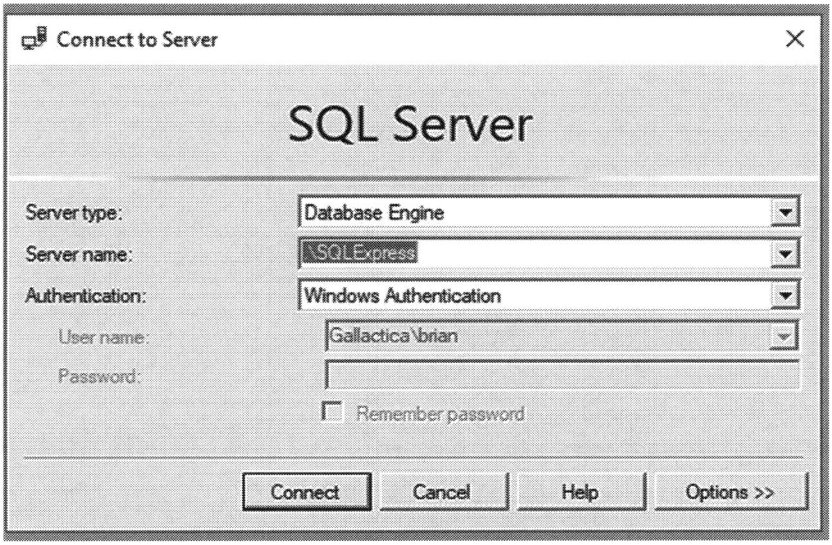

Figure 8-3. *Connect to the database*

After connecting, you could name your Trace, or just hit Run. Either way, hit Run to start the trace (see Figure 8-4).

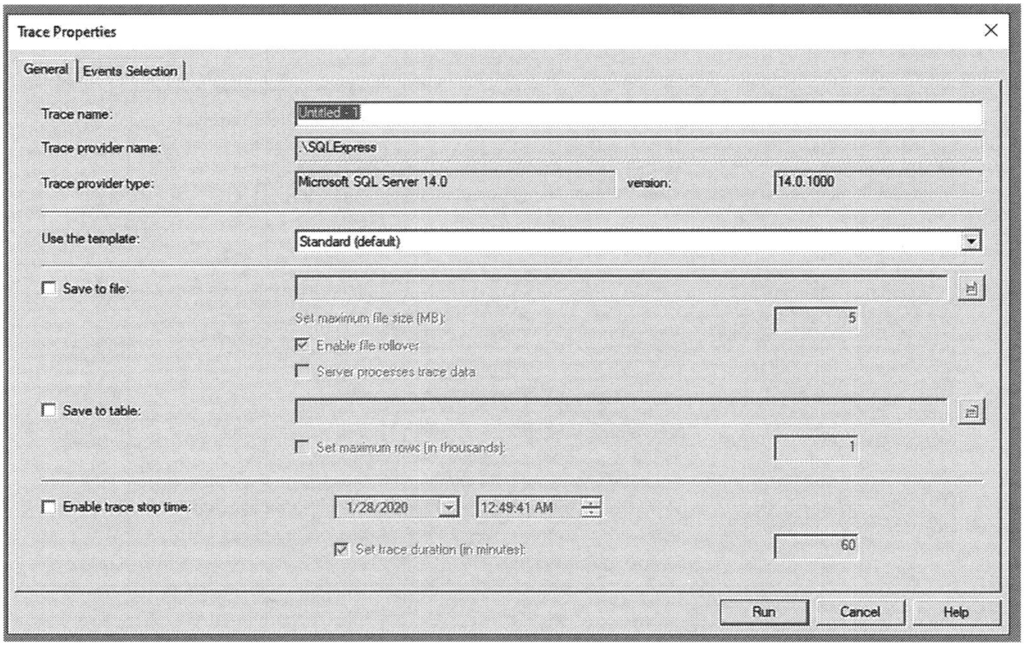

Trace Properties   ✕

General | Events Selection |

Trace name: |Untitled - 1|

Trace provider name: |\SQLExpress|

Trace provider type: |Microsoft SQL Server 14.0| version: |14.0.1000|

Use the template: |Standard (default)| ▼

☐ Save to file: | | 📁

                               Set maximum file size (MB): | 5|

                               ☑ Enable file rollover

                               ☐ Server processes trace data

☐ Save to table: | | 📁

                               ☐ Set maximum rows (in thousands): | 1|

☐ Enable trace stop time: |1/28/2020   ▼| |12:49:41 AM ⬍|

                               ☑ Set trace duration (in minutes): | 60|

                                                    Run   Cancel   Help

Figure 8-4. *Start a new trace; optionally, name it something useful if you would like*

Once the trace is running, you'll see anything that hits your database for operations against the datastore (review Figure 8-5).

Figure 8-5. *The SQL Server Profiler trace is listening for events*

At any point, you can clear the trace window by hitting the eraser button on the toolbar (as shown in Figure 8-6).

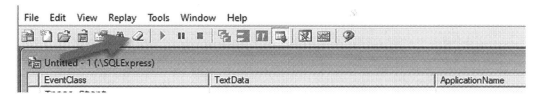

Figure 8-6. *Use the eraser button to clear the trace*

Once you have cleared out your window, go back to the code and place breakpoints on the start of each method and the end of each method. This will help us to easily track the code that is executed in each statement (see Figure 8-7).

Because SQL Server is running, you may get notifications about Locks and Audits periodically in the window. While these can be filtered out, you can always just clear the window before running your code.

```
31        static void ListPeopleThenOrderAndTake()
32        {
33            using (var db = new AdventureWorksContext(_optionsBuilder.Options))
34            {
35                var people = db.Person.ToList().OrderByDescending(x => x.LastName);
36                foreach (var person in people.Take(10))
37                {
38                    Console.WriteLine($"{person.FirstName} {person.LastName}");
39                }
40            }
41        }
42

      1 reference
43        static void QueryPeopleOrderedToListAndTake()
44        {
45            using (var db = new AdventureWorksContext(_optionsBuilder.Options))
46            {
47                var query = db.Person.OrderByDescending(x => x.LastName);
48                var result = query.Take(10);
49
50                foreach (var person in result)
51                {
52                    Console.WriteLine($"{person.FirstName} {person.LastName}");
53                }
54            }
```

Figure 8-7. *The code with breakpoints, ready for profiling*

Run the code, and make sure to clear the profiler before running the queries. Make sure to review the SQL Server Profiler often to see the queries as we build out this activity. A sample of the output is shown in Figure 8-8.

EventClass	TextData	ApplicationName	NTUserName	LoginName	CPU	Reads	Writes	Duration	
Audit Login	-- network protocol: LPC set quote...	Core Microso...	brian	Gallac...					
SQL:BatchStarting	SELECT [p].[BusinessEntityID], [p]....	Core Microso...	brian	Gallac...					
SQL:BatchCompleted	SELECT [p].[BusinessEntityID], [p]....	Core Microso...	brian	Gallac...	297	3621	0	1490	

Figure 8-8. *The first query profiled in the SQL Server Profiler*

Here, we see the first query as sent to SQL Server for getting results. If we click the query, we can see the direct query in the window below the log. Also note that it looks like the query executed twice. It did not. What we're seeing is the start and end of the batch request. The BatchCompleted entry (highlighted in the figure) contains the execution time, reads, and other information about the query. Drilling into the entry to get the query text is shown in Figure 8-9.

```
SELECT [p].[BusinessEntityID], [p].[AdditionalContactInfo], [p].[Demographics], [p].[EmailPromotion],
[p].[FirstName], [p].[LastName], [p].[MiddleName], [p].[ModifiedDate], [p].[NameStyle], [p].[PersonType],
[p].[rowguid], [p].[Suffix], [p].[Title]
FROM [Person].[Person] AS [p]
```

Figure 8-9. *The first query as executed according to the profiler*

While your numbers may be different than mine (i.e., 3821 reads and execution duration of 1490 is unique to my run), your query text should be exactly the same as mine.

Let's execute that query text in our SQL Server with a new query to the database directly to see the results for ourselves.

Right-click your AdventureWorks database entry in SSMS and select New Query to open a new query window. Copy and paste the query from the Profiler into the window. The query should be as follows:

```
SELECT [p].[BusinessEntityID], [p].[AdditionalContactInfo], [p].
[Demographics], [p].[EmailPromotion], [p].[FirstName], [p].[LastName], [p].
[MiddleName], [p].[ModifiedDate], [p].[NameStyle], [p].[PersonType], [p].
[rowguid], [p].[Suffix], [p].[Title]
FROM [Person].[Person] AS [p]
```

Run the query to see the results (as is shown in Figure 8-10).

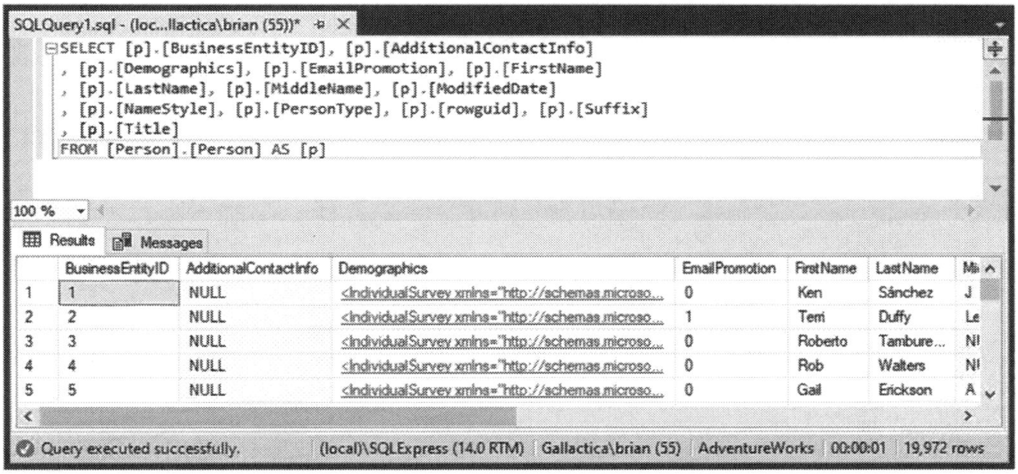

Figure 8-10. *The results of the query*

Important notes here, for my query, are that the execution took about a second and returned nearly 20,000 rows. That's pretty much to be expected when pulling all people into a list.

Clear out the profiler again and continue through the second query (review Figure 8-11).

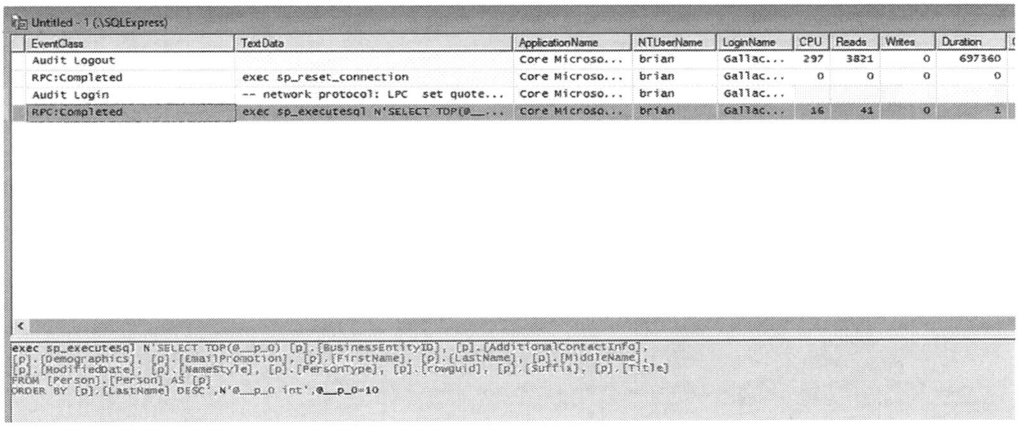

Figure 8-11. *The second method as executed and profiled in the SQL Server Profiler*

Running through the second query provides the following in the SQL Server Profiler showing that a stored procedure was executed and here we have only 41 reads with a duration of 1. Again, your execution times may vary, but your query should be

```
exec sp_executesql N'SELECT TOP(@__p_0) [p].[BusinessEntityID], [p].
[AdditionalContactInfo], [p].[Demographics], [p].[EmailPromotion], [p].
[FirstName], [p].[LastName], [p].[MiddleName], [p].[ModifiedDate], [p].
[NameStyle], [p].[PersonType], [p].[rowguid], [p].[Suffix], [p].[Title]
FROM [Person].[Person] AS [p]
ORDER BY [p].[LastName] DESC',N'@__p_0 int',@__p_0=10
```

Take that code and run it in the SSMS query window to see it perform there as well (as shown in Figure 8-12).

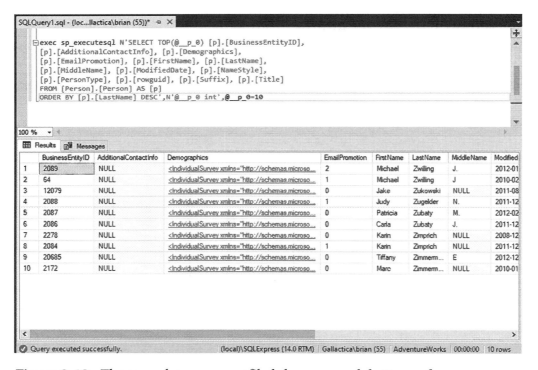

Figure 8-12. *The second query as profiled shows a much better performance, as well as only the results we wanted*

Here we can easily see that only returning the ten results we wanted is much more efficient. Additionally, the ordering was done for the result set on the server, not in memory.

Clearly, how we write our queries matters when working with *Entity Framework*. Just getting the results we want does not always mean we are using *EF* correctly.

Step 4: Filtering our results

By now we should know that pulling code into a list before doing sorting and filtering is a bad thing. For that reason, we won't be pulling into a list until the end of the query from this point on. If you want to prove it out, however, feel free to repeat a similar test run to what we have done previously.

As with most things, it will be up to you as the developer to find the correct approach to what your system needs. For this next part, we'll be filtering by partial name or by the Person Type. In your real-world applications, you will likely need to allow the user to give you input to filter results in a manner similar to this approach.

Add code in the Main method to add a statement to ask the user for a search term, and then use that term in a method called FilteredPeople:

```
Console.WriteLine("Please Enter the partial First or Last Name, or the
Person Type to search for:");
var result = Console.ReadLine();
FilteredPeople(result);
```

In the FilteredPeople(string filter) method, use the following code with a LINQ statement to correctly filter the results before pulling into a List for reviewing the results:

```
static void FilteredPeople(string filter)
    {
        using (var db = new AdventureWorksContext(_optionsBuilder.
        Options))
        {
            var searchTerm = filter.ToLower();
            var query = db.Person.Where(x => x.LastName.ToLower().
            Contains(searchTerm)
                                        || x.FirstName.ToLower().
                                        Contains(searchTerm)
```

343

```
                                                    || x.PersonType.ToLower().
                                                    Equals(searchTerm));

              foreach (var person in query)
              {
                  Console.WriteLine($"{person.FirstName} {person.
                  LastName}, {person.PersonType}");
              }
          }
      }
```

Now run the code to ensure it works, entering some text to filter, such as "Gonza" or "Mich" or "VC" (review Figure 8-13 to see sample results).

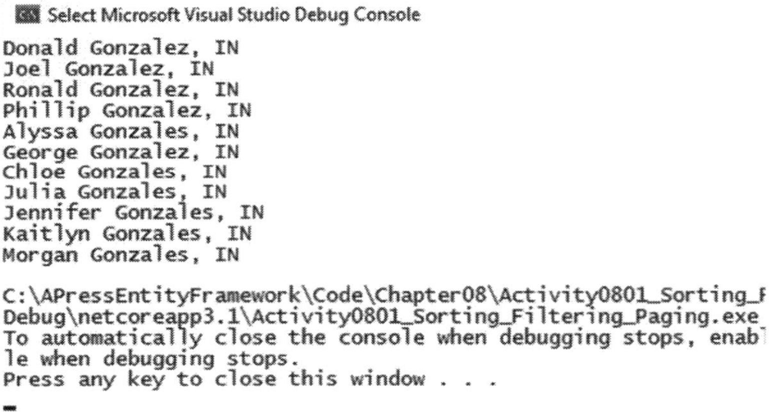

Figure 8-13. *Searching for anyone with a partial name match to Gonza*

Grabbing the query from SQL Server Profiler yields the following query that was executed on the server:

```
exec sp_executesql N'SELECT [p].[BusinessEntityID], [p].
[AdditionalContactInfo]
, [p].[Demographics], [p].[EmailPromotion], [p].[FirstName], [p].[LastName]
, [p].[MiddleName], [p].[ModifiedDate], [p].[NameStyle], [p].[PersonType]
, [p].[rowguid], [p].[Suffix], [p].[Title]
FROM [Person].[Person] AS [p]
```

344

```
WHERE (((@__searchTerm_0 = N'''')
OR (CHARINDEX(@__searchTerm_0, LOWER([p].[LastName])) > 0))
OR ((@__searchTerm_0 = N'''')
OR (CHARINDEX(@__searchTerm_0, LOWER([p].[FirstName])) > 0)))
OR (LOWER([p].[PersonType]) = @__searchTerm_0)',N'@__searchTerm_0
nvarchar(50)'
,@__searchTerm_0=N'gonza'
```

This shows that the query was filtered by lower based on the search term I sent in from the previous query. Running the code shows some 288 results. Figure 8-14 shows the query with results.

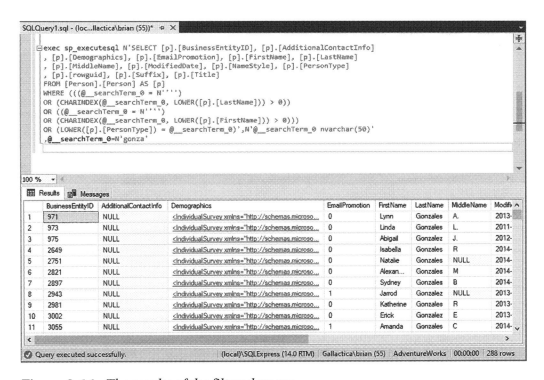

Figure 8-14.   *The results of the filtered query*

Run a couple more to see the results you would expect and validate that the query is working.

Now you might be asking about *SQL Injection* at this point. What happens if I search for O'Brien, for example, or try to run some other malicious code in my search term? Figure 8-15 gives a look at an attempt at SQL Injection.

```
Please Enter the partial First or Last Name, or the Person Type to search for:
o'bri
Tim O'Brien, VC

C:\APressEntityFramework\Code\Chapter08\Activity0801_Sorting_Filtering_Paging\Activity0
Debug\netcoreapp3.1\Activity0801_Sorting_Filtering_Paging.exe (process 5188) exited wit
To automatically close the console when debugging stops, enable Tools->Options->Debuggi
le when debugging stops.
Press any key to close this window . . .
```

Figure 8-15. *Seeing what happens if adding key characters to our filter*

This renders the following query:

```
exec sp_executesql N'SELECT [p].[BusinessEntityID], [p].
[AdditionalContactInfo], [p].[Demographics], [p].[EmailPromotion], [p].
[FirstName], [p].[LastName], [p].[MiddleName], [p].[ModifiedDate], [p].
[NameStyle], [p].[PersonType], [p].[rowguid], [p].[Suffix], [p].[Title]
FROM [Person].[Person] AS [p]
WHERE ((([@__searchTerm_0 = N'''') OR (CHARINDEX(@__searchTerm_0, LOWER([p].
[LastName])) > 0)) OR ((@__searchTerm_0 = N'''') OR (CHARINDEX(@__
searchTerm_0, LOWER([p].[FirstName])) > 0))) OR (LOWER([p].[PersonType]) =
@__searchTerm_0)',N'@__searchTerm_0 nvarchar(50)',@__searchTerm_0=N'o''bri'
```

And we can see that the search term is indeed protected from the single quote, suggesting that our LINQ query is parameterized. Even so, it's still our responsibility to make sure that this is the case.

As an additional test, we could try the old standard - passing the text "' or 1=1 --" into the search filter to see if our query returns filter results or all the results in the database. When the query does not return all the results, we can have some assurance that our query is working as expected without being open to SQL Injection.

Step 5: Paging the filtered results

Even with filtering in place, we saw that our results contained some 288 results in the previous query. While there may be some instances where you would be fine with returning all of these results (your UI control handles paging well and won't freeze up with large result sets), it is often ideal to just page the results and get only the records being rendered to the user at the time of the request.

To do this easily, we can further modify our LINQ query from step 4. Add a new method that uses the same search term for simplicity. Call the method `FilteredAndPag` `edResult([filter], [pageNumber], [pageSize])`. Write the method to take the string filter as before, this time also returning a number of records equal to page size and the results from the expected page.

To prove it out, just do a `for` loop around the call in the `Main` method to simulate paging. Add a breakpoint to the database call to see each page in action. Use a page size of 5, 10, 15, 20, or 25. For even more fun, make sure to order the results by Last Name so that they are not just filtered but also sorted and paged.

```
int pageSize = 10;
for (int pageNumber = 0; pageNumber < 10; pageNumber++)
{
    Console.WriteLine($"Page {pageNumber + 1}");
    FilteredAndPagedResult(result, pageNumber, pageSize);
}
```

When making the call, we can see paged results as expected. Please note that if you do a more extensive search, the code as written will print out page numbers with no results. If you don't like that functionality, you could move the printout of the page to the method and only show the page number if there are results to print.

```
static void FilteredAndPagedResult(string filter, int pageNumber, int
pageSize)
{
    using (var db = new AdventureWorksContext(_optionsBuilder.Options))
    {
        var searchTerm = filter.ToLower();
        var query = db.Person.Where(x => x.LastName.ToLower().
        Contains(searchTerm)
```

```
                                        || x.FirstName.ToLower().
                                        Contains(searchTerm)
                                        || x.PersonType.ToLower().
                                        Equals(searchTerm))
                            .OrderBy(x => x.LastName)
                            .Skip(pageNumber * pageSize)
                            .Take(pageSize);

        foreach (var person in query)
        {
            Console.WriteLine($"{person.FirstName} {person.LastName},
            {person.PersonType}");
        }
    }
}
```

And the result as rendered when searching for "Gonz" is shown in Figure 8-16.

```
Lucas Gonzales, IN
Page 9
Luis Gonzales, IN
Luke Gonzales, IN
Lynn Gonzales, SC
Madison Gonzales, IN
Marcus Gonzales, IN
Mariah Gonzales, IN
Marissa Gonzales, IN
Megan Gonzales, IN
Melanie Gonzales, IN
Melissa Gonzales, IN
Page 10
Miguel Gonzales, IN
Miranda Gonzales, IN
Morgan Gonzales, IN
Mya Gonzales, IN
Natalie Gonzales, IN
Nathan Gonzales, IN
Nicole Gonzales, IN
Noah Gonzales, IN
Olivia Gonzales, IN
Oscar Gonzales, IN

C:\APressEntityFramework\Code\Chapter08\Activity0801_Sorting_Filtering
```

Figure 8-16. *The result when searching with filtered and sorted and paged results*

Again, it is critical to inspect your queries in the profiler to make certain they are performing as expected. The paging method makes multiple calls, as we would anticipate, each one limited to the correct set of results. The final query looked as follows for me during execution:

```
exec sp_executesql N'SELECT [p].[BusinessEntityID], [p].
[AdditionalContactInfo], [p].[Demographics], [p].[EmailPromotion], [p].
[FirstName], [p].[LastName], [p].[MiddleName], [p].[ModifiedDate], [p].
[NameStyle], [p].[PersonType], [p].[rowguid], [p].[Suffix], [p].[Title]
FROM [Person].[Person] AS [p]
WHERE ((((@__searchTerm_0 = N'''') OR (CHARINDEX(@__searchTerm_0, LOWER([p].
[LastName])) > 0)) OR ((@__searchTerm_0 = N'''') OR (CHARINDEX(@__
searchTerm_0, LOWER([p].[FirstName])) > 0))) OR (LOWER([p].[PersonType]) =
@__searchTerm_0)
ORDER BY [p].[LastName]
OFFSET @__p_1 ROWS FETCH NEXT @__p_2 ROWS ONLY',N'@__searchTerm_0
nvarchar(50),@__p_1 int,@__p_2 int',@__searchTerm_0=N'gon',@__p_1=90,@_
_p_2=10
```

By validating this approach, we can see that *EF* is highly performant against large database tables as long as our queries are written correctly. To see how much worse the performance could have been, you could try that last method by pulling to a list first and then doing the filtering, ordering, and paging on the results.

Just imagine the performance hit you would have if you made the call for every page in this code, pulling back all nearly 20,000 records. Then, only after getting all 20,000 records on each iteration, perform another operation to further filter down to just the 10 records you need on every page this is displayed to the *UI*.

Step 6: Disconnecting the result sets

For the next part of this activity, I want to go back to one other issue we mentioned previously. For every single result we pulled back in this application, we did not need to keep tracking in place.

To make our queries as lightweight as possible, therefore, we can simply add the .AsNoTracking() statement to each query, right after the db.Person statement. Go ahead and do that now. Search for db.Person in your code, and replace with db.Person. AsNoTracking.

Run the code again to validate it works. If you continue to profile the code, you may see some performance increases in the duration column, but they are likely not extremely noticeable on the IQueryable methods.

Another thing we could do is disable the tracking completely on the entire context. Locate the AdventureWorksContext in the EF_Activity001 project, and add the following to the public constructors:

```
ChangeTracker.QueryTrackingBehavior = QueryTrackingBehavior.NoTracking;
```

Setting the entire context to avoid tracking behaviors is shown in Figure 8-17.

```
namespace EF_Activity001
{
    9 references
    public partial class AdventureWorksContext : DbContext
    {
        0 references
        public AdventureWorksContext()
        {
            ChangeTracker.QueryTrackingBehavior = QueryTrackingBehavior.NoTracking;
        }

        4 references
        public AdventureWorksContext(DbContextOptions<AdventureWorksContext> options)
            : base(options)
        {
            ChangeTracker.QueryTrackingBehavior = QueryTrackingBehavior.NoTracking;
        }
    }
```

Figure 8-17.   *Turning off tracking for the entire context*

At this point, running the project will still work, and the results should again be essentially as performant as possible.

Final thoughts

In this activity, we've seen how to use sorting, filtering, and paging to refine our results. By making certain to optimize our query formation, we've set up our *Entity Framework* instance to optimize for both performance and functionality when working against a large dataset.

Final thoughts for this chapter

This chapter gave us our first deep dive into working with LINQ, and specifically working with LINQ to Entities. We still have a lot to learn when it comes to LINQ, but with the knowledge we gained in this chapter, we now understand the impact that a few differences in how things are coded can work. The main takeaways from this chapter are

- Make sure to perform the execution of the queries at the latest possible opportunity in the codebase.

- Remember to disable change tracking when entities do not need to stay connected for tracking in the `DBContext`.

- When working with LINQ to Entities and the Entity Framework in general, make sure to use some sort of profiler to help examine the actual queries you are executing on the database.

In the next chapter, we'll continue looking at how we can use LINQ to get results from our database into disconnected DTO objects using projections and anonymous classes.

CHAPTER 9

LINQ for Queries and Projections

Data in the real world

In this chapter, we are going to learn how to use queries in complex scenarios to get the data we want. To this point, we've worked with the database in a fairly superficial manner. As this is a book on practical application of the concepts, we really need to experience working with data in real-world scenarios.

Often, when working with data, there will be a need to perform join operations across multiple tables and then use that data in some manner. There are a couple of approaches that we can employ in these scenarios.

LINQ vs. stored procedures

In the past, we would simply create views and stored procedures to make all the joins and then rely on the database server to optimize the execution plans for these scenarios.

With LINQ, we are able to command the server to perform the joins and get the data just as easily as if we had written a stored procedure. The benefits of using LINQ include the fact that we can be much more flexible, with the ability to simply change a few things here and there to get a more advanced result set. By using LINQ, we also avoid having to rewrite or modify an entire stored procedure and, along with that, avoid the necessity of going through the governance channels that are involved in pushing changes to the production database.

There are a couple of drawbacks to this approach, however. The major thing to consider is what was discussed earlier – execution plans. With stored procedures, the server itself will store a cached execution plan. This means that while you still have

353

© Brian L. Gorman 2020
B. L. Gorman, *Practical Entity Framework*, https://doi.org/10.1007/978-1-4842-6044-9_9

the pain of the first execution runtime, the second and consecutive executions of that stored procedure should be more efficient. LINQ does not allow the server to store up an execution plan, so each query must be treated like a new execution on the server. Even with optimized queries, the loss of the execution plan might be enough to consider using a stored procedure in some instances.

Complex data and the code-first approach

After getting our data from these complex join queries, either via a stored procedure or through LINQ queries, we need to be able to pass it to our controller or view layers or, at minimum, to some other layer where the data will be utilized.

When we built out our models in the code-first approach, we were able to quickly create the exact structures that we wanted to exist in our database. With data being returned from our database from a complex query, we're not going to want to have a table or other structure that is directly modeled in the code-first approach.

A couple of options exist for us, which would allow us to use that data efficiently. As with any system, you, as the developer, should consider the best approach for your system. Additionally, you'll want to make sure any architecture decisions you make are based on the standards of your organization.

The first approach you could easily take is to just keep adding models to your Models project. Another approach you could take is to modify some of the existing models to hold transformed data. Always remember that unless you create direct dependencies and/or add the model to the DBContext, in the code-first approach, a model can exist without needing to be migrated into the database. Furthermore, on existing models that you have, simply adding the data annotation [NotMapped] to any field will allow you to add fields that do not get placed into the database, even if the model is part of the database schema.

While this approach works well, and may even be the desired approach in your current system, I would advise against using this strategy. There are two downfalls to this approach that I simply prefer to avoid. They both relate to confusion and maintainability in the future.

First of all, having fields that are NotMapped in your models, just clutter them up with more fields, while also making it so, the model and the database itself are not in a one-to-one synchronized relationship. Again, it's not necessary to map fields one to one in the model to what's in the table, but it becomes more confusing in the long run, especially over time and as the models continue to change.

The second issue with this approach is that your Models project can start to experience class explosion, and, as with the first problem, now you'll have entire classes that don't map to the database, which can add yet another layer of confusion.

DTOs, view models, or domain models

Before I get hate mail, let's clear a few things up. *DTOs*, *View Models*, and *Domain Models* are not the same thing and generally should not be used in an interchangeable manner. Clearly, each has a specific purpose. For example, you can have view models that don't map to any database objects at all, with a primary purpose of just mapping information for user interaction on a screen. You might also see domain models that could be the result of data from multiple models interacting with each other for some specific behavior. DTOs, on the other hand, could just be a simple way to map fields from one data type to another. So yes, these three objects are not even close to the same thing. That being said, when I'm talking about DTOs for the rest of this chapter, a DTO could be substituted in your system with a view model or a domain model, if that's what makes sense for your system.

Decoupling your business or view logic from the database

One of the better approaches is to create DTO objects that map the data needed for the next layer of the system to a class specifically molded to meet the needs of the business or view logic. We generally would place these DTOs in some sort of stand-alone project or at least at some layer of the architecture that is separate from the database Models project.

By placing the data into specific DTOs in a separate project, we can be much more granular about the structure and application of these objects. This solves the problems created previously with having too many classes and fields in the Models project and classes, respectively. In the end, our business logic or view layer logic is then decoupled from our database logic, which is a very good thing.

Sometimes, a pre-defined object is overkill

In some cases, going to the trouble of creating a DTO object is not practical and can lead to excessive overhead in our projects. When it's our data and we want it now, but we don't want to build out yet another class to hold that modeled data, we can perform an operation known as projecting the data into an anonymous classes (or anonymous types).

Anonymous classes were introduced in C# 2.0, so they've been around for some time now. Likely you've seen some sort of application where an anonymous class was defined for quick use within a method or class body. A simple anonymous class for an Item type might look like this:

```
var item = new { Name = "ROG Strix Scar II", Brand = "Asus", Price =
2199.99 };
```

In that declaration, a new anonymous class was created and assigned to the item variable. If we wanted, we could then use that object just like any other class while it remained in scope. For example, we could write out the details of the item with calls to item.Name and item.Brand.

Putting that knowledge to use, we can easily see how it would be easy to use LINQ to get some data and then combine that with the ability to create a new anonymous type to model that data.

For example, a simple query against the Person table in the AdventureWorks joined to the Employee table, then joined to the SalesPerson table, further joined to OrderHeaders, then OrderDetails, and all the way through to Product could yield some great results which we might want to map to just have access to the fields Product.Name, SalesPerson.FirstName, OrderHeader.OrderDate, and others. That kind of interaction can easily be accomplished using LINQ and anonymous types in a query similar to this one:

```
var salesReportDetails = db.SalesPerson.Select(sp => new
{
    beid = sp.BusinessEntityId,
    sp.BusinessEntity.BusinessEntity.FirstName,
    sp.BusinessEntity.BusinessEntity.LastName,
    sp.SalesYtd,
    Territories = sp.SalesTerritoryHistory.Select(y => y.Territory.Name),
    OrderCount = sp.SalesOrderHeader.Count(),
```

```
    TotalProductsSold = sp.SalesOrderHeader.SelectMany(y =>
    y.SalesOrderDetail).Sum(z => z.OrderQty)
}).Where(srds => srds.SalesYtd > filter).AsQueryable()
        .OrderBy(srds => srds.LastName).ThenBy(srds => srds.FirstName).
        ThenByDescending(srds => srds.SalesYtd)
        .Take(20).ToList();
```

One tool to rule them all

Anytime we have fully modeled our DTO objects and perform a bunch of queries, we'd run into the same problem. At some point, we'd be manually creating an instance of some DTO object and then mapping each field, one by one to the DTO object from either a model or an anonymous type.

While this approach works, like many others, it is not the best solution. For one thing, writing line after line of code to map one object to another object that is often nearly identical in structure is tedious. This approach also can lead to errors where the programmer accidentally copies and pastes the field mappings and forgets to update one or two so that now the field has incorrect or no data in it. This is where *AutoMapper* comes in like Mighty Mouse, singing "Here I come to save the day!" Even so, even AutoMapper runs into some limburger cheese every now and then.

AutoMapper

The most successful tool available today that correctly translates objects from one type to another is AutoMapper, which is available here: `www.nuget.org/packages/automapper/`.

In addition to the ability to correctly map one type to another, AutoMapper has an even niftier ability to project data from LINQ queries directly into their types, thereby even skipping the step of getting the data into one type and then calling AutoMapper's `Map<T>` function. Don't worry if this is unclear right now; as we work through the following activities, we'll understand more about what is going on.

While it is unmistakably the best tool for the job, highly performant, and simple to use for mappings and projections, the main issue I've run into with AutoMapper is the complexity of getting set up to use the tool correctly in a project. Once you get past the initial setup (correctly) and then learn a couple of quick tricks about how the tool syntax works to automatically map identically named fields while providing ways to code for the exceptions to the rule (i.e., mapping fields that don't have the same name), the value of AutoMapper easily becomes worth the initial price point, which is free, with an ounce of pain. By the time we complete this chapter, I imagine you will think of AutoMapper as the friend that you don't really want to talk to, but have to rely on in your most critical times of need.

Chapter 9 Activities: Using LINQ, decoupled DTO classes, projections, anonymous types, and AutoMapper

In the activities for this chapter, we're going to build out a solution to use LINQ to perform some more complex queries against the *AdventureWorks* database. We'll then see the differences between different approaches to working with LINQ with projections to anonymous types while considering the performance implications of each choice we make.

After getting through the more advanced interactions with LINQ, we'll move back to our inventory project, where we'll set up AutoMapper.

We'll then finish up with a look at using AutoMapper to project our data from one type to another, making sure to spend some time working with directly and indirectly mapped fields.

Activity 0901: Working with LINQ in complex queries

For our first activity, we're going to dive a lot deeper into working with LINQ in our projects. To this point, we've seen some of the really great features of LINQ with the ability to quickly select IEnumerable or IQueryable result sets, and we've learned how to chain commands to filter, sort, and apply other transformations. However, we've not spent a lot of time working across table joins.

As we start joining tables, we'll be bringing more data into the result sets than we'll likely need to send back for use by the calling program. As we then start working with this data, not only will we need to combine the results of different tables, but we'll want to pare them down to contain only specific pieces of information.

There are a couple of ways we can pare things down, with the first being that we can just select everything and then manually transform that data in memory into some sort of DTO object for transmission. The other option is we can limit our queries to get just the right amount of information for our results and then send that information in some sort of DTO object. As we've seen before, the more we can form our queries, the better we can expect our performance to be.

Step 1: Get set up

The easiest way to get going on this project is to just grab the starter files `Activity_0901_QueriesAndProjections_Starter.zip`. After getting the files, make sure to confirm that the connection strings are pointed to your local version of the *AdventureWorks* database, and then build the project and run it. You'll be prompted to view all salespeople, and entering a "y" will show the results as seen in Figure 9-1.

```
Microsoft Visual Studio Debug Console
Would you like to view all salespeople? [y/n]
y
EF_Activity001.SalesPerson
EF_Activity001.SalesPerson
EF_Activity001.SalesPerson
EF_Activity001.SalesPerson
EF_Activity001.SalesPerson
EF_Activity001.SalesPerson
EF_Activity001.SalesPerson
EF_Activity001.SalesPerson
EF_Activity001.SalesPerson
EF_Activity001.SalesPerson
EF_Activity001.SalesPerson
EF_Activity001.SalesPerson
EF_Activity001.SalesPerson
EF_Activity001.SalesPerson
EF_Activity001.SalesPerson
EF_Activity001.SalesPerson
C:\APressEntityFramework\Code\Chapter09\Activity0901_QueriesAndProjections\Activity0901_Queri
netcoreapp3.1\Activity0901_QueriesAndProjections.exe (process 11664) exited with code 0.
To automatically close the console when debugging stops, enable Tools->Options->Debugging->Au
le when debugging stops.
Press any key to close this window . . .
```

Figure 9-1. *The initial run of the activity files is shown, with no useful output*

As we can see, that's not very useful.

Note, as an alternative to the starter pack, you could just create a new .Net Core Console application and follow these steps to get your project to the same state as the setup files:

1. Get the EF_Activity001 project folder from the end of activity 0801 and place it in the same directory as your new solution, and then reference the project in the new console application.

2. Get the InventoryHelpers project folder from the end of activity 0801 and place it in the same directory as your new solution, and then reference the project in the new console application.

3. Use the NuGet Package Manager to ensure that the new console project has a reference to each of the following NuGet packages:

    a. Microsoft.EntityFrameworkCore

    b. Microsoft.EntityFrameworkCore.Design

    c. Microsoft.EntityFrameworkCore.SqlServer

    d. Microsoft.Extensions.Configuration.FileExtensions

    e. Microsoft.Extensions.Configuration.Json

4. Copy the appsettings.json file from the EF_Activity001 project and place it in the folder with the new project. Make sure to set the file as Build Action ➤ Content, Copy to Output Directory: Copy if newer.

5. Use the code that follows to set up the Program.cs file in your new project:

```
class Program
{
    static IConfigurationRoot _configuration;
    static DbContextOptionsBuilder<AdventureWorksContext>
    _optionsBuilder;
    static void BuildOptions()
    {
```

```csharp
        _configuration = ConfigurationBuilderSingleton.
        ConfigurationRoot;
        _optionsBuilder = new DbContextOptionsBuilder<Adventure
        WorksContext>();
_optionsBuilder.UseSqlServer(_configuration.GetConnectionString
("AdventureWorks"));
    }

    static void Main(string[] args)
    {
        BuildOptions();
        Console.WriteLine("Would you like to view all salespeople?
        [y/n]");
        var input = Console.ReadLine();
        if (input.StartsWith("y", StringComparison.
        OrdinalIgnoreCase))
        {
            ShowAllSalesPeople();
        }
    }

    private static void ShowAllSalesPeople()
    {
        using (var db = new AdventureWorksContext(_optionsBuilder.
        Options))
        {
            var salesPeople = db.SalesPerson.Take(20).ToList();
            foreach (var sp in salesPeople)
            {
                Console.WriteLine(sp);
            }
        }
    }
}
```

Step 2: Start getting more useful results, and find some limitations

Find the `SalesPerson.cs` file in the `EF_Activity01` project, and add a new `ToString` override method using the following code:

```
public override string ToString()
{
    return $"BID: {BusinessEntityId} | TID: {TerritoryId} | Quota:
    {SalesQuota} | Bonus: {Bonus} | YTDSales: {SalesYtd}";
}
```

Run the project. The results are still not useful (review Figure 9-2).

```
Would you like to view all salespeople? [y/n]
y
BID: 274 | TID:    | Quota:    | Bonus: 0.0000 | YTDSales: 559697.5639
BID: 275 | TID: 2 | Quota: 300000.0000 | Bonus: 4100.0000 | YTDSales: 3763178.1787
BID: 276 | TID: 4 | Quota: 250000.0000 | Bonus: 2000.0000 | YTDSales: 4251368.5497
BID: 277 | TID: 3 | Quota: 250000.0000 | Bonus: 2500.0000 | YTDSales: 3189418.3662
BID: 278 | TID: 6 | Quota: 250000.0000 | Bonus: 500.0000 | YTDSales: 1453719.4653
BID: 279 | TID: 5 | Quota: 300000.0000 | Bonus: 6700.0000 | YTDSales: 2315185.6110
BID: 280 | TID: 1 | Quota: 250000.0000 | Bonus: 5000.0000 | YTDSales: 1352577.1325
BID: 281 | TID: 4 | Quota: 250000.0000 | Bonus: 3550.0000 | YTDSales: 2458535.6169
BID: 282 | TID: 6 | Quota: 250000.0000 | Bonus: 5000.0000 | YTDSales: 2604540.7172
BID: 283 | TID: 1 | Quota: 250000.0000 | Bonus: 3500.0000 | YTDSales: 1573012.9383
BID: 284 | TID: 1 | Quota: 300000.0000 | Bonus: 3900.0000 | YTDSales: 1576562.1966
BID: 285 | TID:    | Quota:    | Bonus: 0.0000 | YTDSales: 172524.4512
BID: 286 | TID: 9 | Quota: 250000.0000 | Bonus: 5650.0000 | YTDSales: 1421810.9242
BID: 287 | TID:    | Quota:    | Bonus: 0.0000 | YTDSales: 519905.9320
BID: 288 | TID: 8 | Quota: 250000.0000 | Bonus: 75.0000 | YTDSales: 1827066.7118
BID: 289 | TID: 10 | Quota: 250000.0000 | Bonus: 5150.0000 | YTDSales: 4116871.2277
BID: 290 | TID: 7 | Quota: 250000.0000 | Bonus: 985.0000 | YTDSales: 3121616.3202

C:\APressEntityFramework\Code\Chapter09\Activity0901_QueriesAndProjections\Activity0901_QueriesAn
netcoreapp3.1\Activity0901_QueriesAndProjections.exe (process 5556) exited with code 0.
```

Figure 9-2. *Getting salesperson results with an overridden ToString method shows more information but is still not very useful*

Before we do this correctly, I want to highlight a way that works, but is not going to be the best solution. Return to the Program.cs file and locate the ShowAllSalesPeople method. Replace the original loop with the code as follows:

```
foreach (var sp in salesPeople)
{
    var x = db.Person.FirstOrDefault(x => x.BusinessEntityId ==
    sp.BusinessEntityId);
```

```
if (x != null)
{
    Console.WriteLine($"{sp} | {x.LastName}, {x.FirstName}");
}
}
}
```

Run the code to see the output (see Figure 9-3).

```
Would you like to view all salespeople? [y/n]
y
BID: 274 | TID:    | Quota:          | Bonus: 0.0000 | YTDSales: 559697.5639 | Jiang, Stephen
BID: 275 | TID: 2  | Quota: 300000.0000 | Bonus: 4100.0000 | YTDSales: 3763178.1787 | Blythe, Michael
BID: 276 | TID: 4  | Quota: 250000.0000 | Bonus: 2000.0000 | YTDSales: 4251368.5497 | Mitchell, Linda
BID: 277 | TID: 3  | Quota: 250000.0000 | Bonus: 2500.0000 | YTDSales: 3189418.3662 | Carson, Jillian
BID: 278 | TID: 6  | Quota: 250000.0000 | Bonus: 500.0000 | YTDSales: 1453719.4653 | Vargas, Garrett
BID: 279 | TID: 5  | Quota: 300000.0000 | Bonus: 6700.0000 | YTDSales: 2315185.6110 | Reiter, Tsvi
BID: 280 | TID: 1  | Quota: 250000.0000 | Bonus: 5000.0000 | YTDSales: 1352577.1325 | Ansman-Wolfe, Pamela
BID: 281 | TID: 4  | Quota: 250000.0000 | Bonus: 3550.0000 | YTDSales: 2458535.6169 | Ito, Shu
BID: 282 | TID: 6  | Quota: 250000.0000 | Bonus: 5000.0000 | YTDSales: 2604540.7172 | Saraiva, José
BID: 283 | TID: 1  | Quota: 250000.0000 | Bonus: 3500.0000 | YTDSales: 1573012.9383 | Campbell, David
BID: 284 | TID: 1  | Quota: 300000.0000 | Bonus: 3900.0000 | YTDSales: 1576562.1966 | Mensa-Annan, Tete
BID: 285 | TID:    | Quota:          | Bonus: 0.0000 | YTDSales: 172524.4512 | Abbas, Syed
BID: 286 | TID: 9  | Quota: 250000.0000 | Bonus: 5650.0000 | YTDSales: 1421810.9242 | Tsoflias, Lynn
BID: 287 | TID:    | Quota:          | Bonus: 0.0000 | YTDSales: 519905.9320 | Alberts, Amy
BID: 288 | TID: 8  | Quota: 250000.0000 | Bonus: 75.0000 | YTDSales: 1827066.7118 | Valdez, Rachel
BID: 289 | TID: 10 | Quota: 250000.0000 | Bonus: 5150.0000 | YTDSales: 4116871.2277 | Pak, Jae
BID: 290 | TID: 7  | Quota: 250000.0000 | Bonus: 985.0000 | YTDSales: 3121616.3202 | Varkey Chudukatil, Ranjit
```

Figure 9-3. *The output with the sales person's name included*

Do you see the problem with the working solution? If not, recall our use of the SQL Profiler in Chapter 8. Go ahead and turn on the profiler and watch your queries run for the preceding code to see the issue with this solution (review Chapter 8 for information on working with the *SQL Profiler* in *SSMS*). Figure 9-4 shows the output from this query to help illuminate the problem.

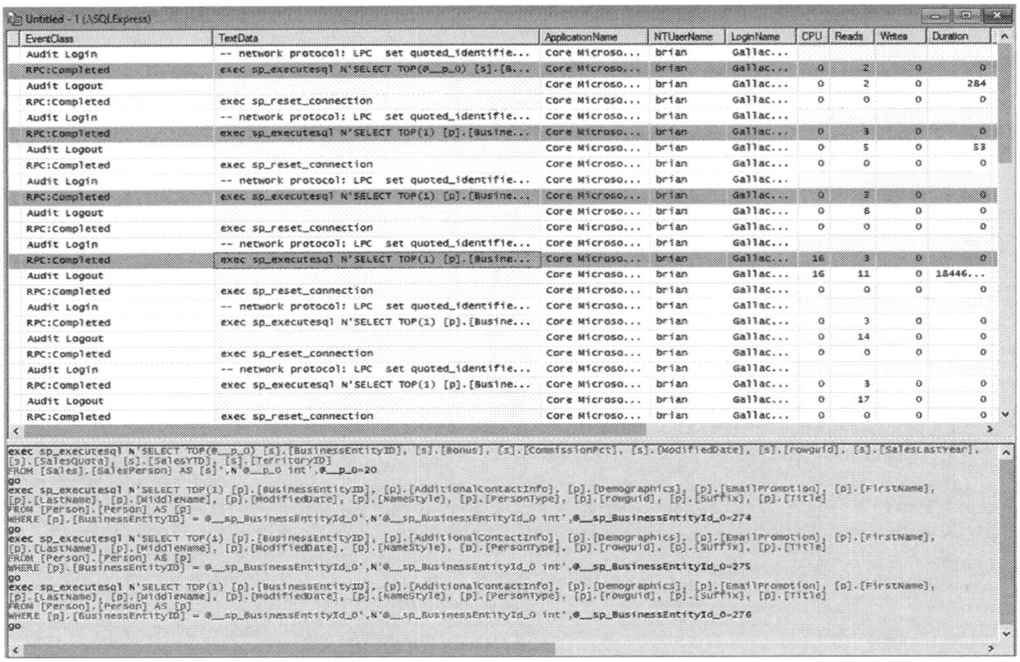

Figure 9-4. *SQL Profiler shows that our previous solution is making too many database calls*

Reviewing the output shows what is known as an *n+1 error* where for each element we are doing another query. If you reverse it, you might understand it more easily – there is one query to get all results and then one more query for every result (n queries), resulting in n + 1 total queries. Here, we limited the query to 20 results, so we had 21 total queries. We need to fix this problem.

Step 3: Use navigation properties to get results

As a code-first developer, our first approach should be to attempt to use navigation properties to get more useful information. Therefore, let's try to get the first and last name of the SalesPerson using navigation properties. Because *AdventureWorks* has a lot of stuff going on across multiple schemas, we need to be sure to double-check relations to use navigations correctly. The SalesPerson navigation for BusinessEntity will map to HumanResources.Employee, which also has a navigation for BusinessEntity to Person, where the first and last name of the person can be found. Therefore, we go from

SalesPerson to Employee to Person using the BusinessEntity property of each object. Because of this, our code will look repetitive. Review the database diagram shown in Figure 9-5.

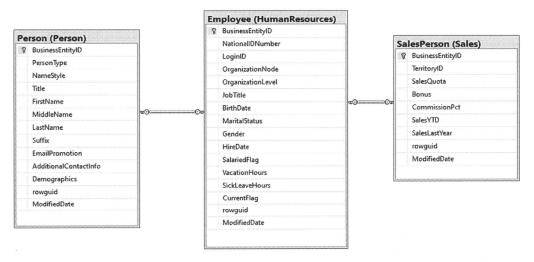

Figure 9-5. *The SalesPerson is linked to the Person table via the Employee table with three different schemas*

With this knowledge, our navigation would look like

SalesPerson.BusinessEntity.BusinessEntity.FirstName

to get to the Person.FirstName from a SalesPerson object. This is not ideal, but it works.

In the Program.cs file of the main project, in the ShowAllSalesPeople method, replace the working loop with a new loop as defined in the following code:

```
foreach (var sp in salesPeople)
{
    Console.WriteLine($"{sp} | {sp.BusinessEntity.BusinessEntity.LastName}" +
                    $", {sp.BusinessEntity.BusinessEntity.
                    FirstName}");
}
```

Run the program to see what happens (see Figure 9-6).

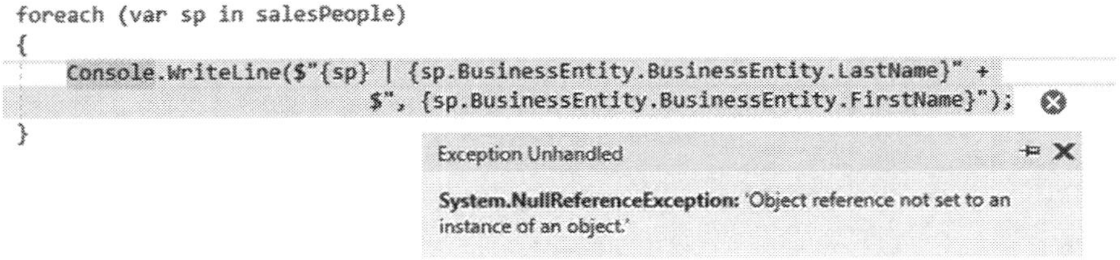

```
foreach (var sp in salesPeople)
{
    Console.WriteLine($"{sp} | {sp.BusinessEntity.BusinessEntity.LastName}" +
                      $", {sp.BusinessEntity.BusinessEntity.FirstName}");    ⊗
}
```

Exception Unhandled   ⊞ X

System.NullReferenceException: 'Object reference not set to an
instance of an object.'

Figure 9-6. *The navigation properties are not filled, so we get a null reference
exception*

As we can see, this solution is not yet working. Since we never told our LINQ query
to populate the navigations for `Employee` and `Person`, they are both null. While we might
hope that *EF* would just let us do this and populate our results, it does not automagically
happen when we've coded a direct reference to this navigation.

Fortunately, we can tell LINQ up front that we will be using these navigations. Modify
the original query to the following code:

```
var salesPeople = db.SalesPerson
                    .Include(x => x.BusinessEntity)
                    .ThenInclude(y => y.BusinessEntity)
                    .Take(20).ToList();
```

Now rerun the program to see results. The results should be the same as before (see
Figure 9-3). The difference now is that we have better performance.

Make sure to review the *SQL Profiler* to validate the improvement in our overall code
(for more information, see Figure 9-7).

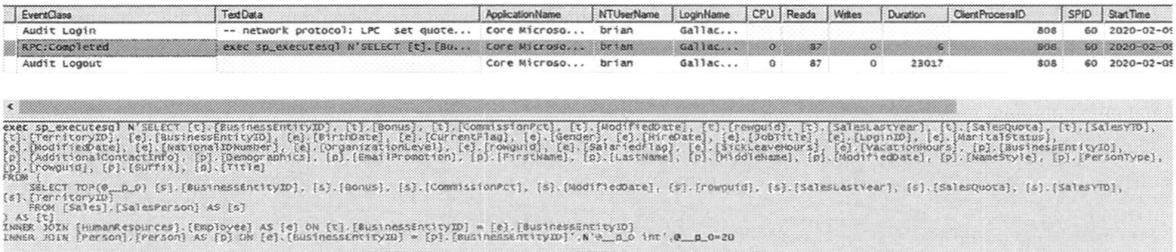

Figure 9-7. *The SQL Profiler shows that our code is now only running one query
to get all the results with related table information included*

This is looking much better. But is this the *best* solution available? Do we really need all that information? Look more closely at the query, and take note of the fact that all the fields from SalesPerson, Employee, and Person are being returned, even though we aren't using the majority of them. To get even more efficient results, we need to start using projections.

Step 4: Use projections to get more efficient queries

To start with the idea of projections, let's consider what they are, and why they are going to help us. Projections are just a way for us to use anonymous classes to model results from a query. With LINQ, we can use the Select operator and then define the projection right in our query. Before we do that, we should decide exactly what data we want to return.

For our code, let's get the salesperson's first and last name and then their quota, YTD sales, sales last year, and bonus. Let's also get the BusinessEntityId from the SalesPerson table, just in case we need that for modification or other purposes.

Add a new private static method in the Program.cs file called ShowAllSalesPeopleUsingProjection:

```
private static void ShowAllSalesPeopleUsingProjection()
{
    using (var db = new AdventureWorksContext(_optionsBuilder.Options))
    {
        //code here...
    }
}
```

In the using statement, replace the comment //code here... with the following query:

```
var salesPeople = db.SalesPerson
                .Include(x => x.BusinessEntity)
                .ThenInclude(y => y.BusinessEntity)
                .Select(x => new {
                  x.BusinessEntityId,
                  x.BusinessEntity.BusinessEntity.FirstName,
                  x.BusinessEntity.BusinessEntity.LastName,
                  x.SalesQuota,
```

```
          x.SalesYtd,
          x.SalesLastYear
      }).ToList();
```

After the query, use the following for loop to print out the information from the anonymous type:

```
foreach (var sp in salesPeople)
{
    Console.WriteLine($"BID: {sp.BusinessEntityId} | Name: {sp.LastName}" +
          $", {sp.FirstName} | Quota: {sp.SalesQuota} | " +
          $"YTD Sales: {sp.SalesYtd} | SalesLastYear {sp.
          SalesLastYear}");
}
```

In the main program, add a statement to get all the sales people using projections, and respond to the user input, calling the method when directed:

```
Console.WriteLine("Would you like to view all salespeople using
projections? [y/n]");
input = Console.ReadLine();
if (input.StartsWith("y", StringComparison.OrdinalIgnoreCase))
{
    ShowAllSalesPeopleUsingProjection();
}
```

Run the program to see the output (review Figure 9-8).

```
Would you like to view all salespeople? [y/n]
n
Would you like to view all salespeople using projections? [y/n]
y
BID: 274 | Name: Jiang, Stephen | Quota:    | YTD Sales: 559697.5639 | SalesLastYear 0.0000
BID: 275 | Name: Blythe, Michael | Quota: 300000.0000 | YTD Sales: 3763178.1787 | SalesLastYear 1750406.4785
BID: 276 | Name: Mitchell, Linda | Quota: 250000.0000 | YTD Sales: 4251368.5497 | SalesLastYear 1439156.0291
BID: 277 | Name: Carson, Jillian | Quota: 250000.0000 | YTD Sales: 3189418.3662 | SalesLastYear 1997186.2037
BID: 278 | Name: Vargas, Garrett | Quota: 250000.0000 | YTD Sales: 1453719.4653 | SalesLastYear 1620276.8966
BID: 279 | Name: Reiter, Tsvi | Quota: 300000.0000 | YTD Sales: 2315185.6110 | SalesLastYear 1849640.9418
BID: 280 | Name: Ansman-Wolfe, Pamela | Quota: 250000.0000 | YTD Sales: 1352577.1325 | SalesLastYear 1927059.1780
BID: 281 | Name: Ito, Shu | Quota: 250000.0000 | YTD Sales: 2458535.6169 | SalesLastYear 2073505.9999
BID: 282 | Name: Saraiva, José | Quota: 250000.0000 | YTD Sales: 2604540.7172 | SalesLastYear 2038234.6549
BID: 283 | Name: Campbell, David | Quota: 250000.0000 | YTD Sales: 1573012.9383 | SalesLastYear 1371635.3158
BID: 284 | Name: Mensa-Annan, Tete | Quota: 300000.0000 | YTD Sales: 1576562.1966 | SalesLastYear 0.0000
BID: 285 | Name: Abbas, Syed | Quota:    | YTD Sales: 172524.4512 | SalesLastYear 0.0000
BID: 286 | Name: Tsoflias, Lynn | Quota: 250000.0000 | YTD Sales: 1421810.9242 | SalesLastYear 2278548.9776
BID: 287 | Name: Alberts, Amy | Quota:    | YTD Sales: 519905.9320 | SalesLastYear 0.0000
BID: 288 | Name: Valdez, Rachel | Quota: 250000.0000 | YTD Sales: 1827066.7118 | SalesLastYear 1307949.7917
BID: 289 | Name: Pak, Jae | Quota: 250000.0000 | YTD Sales: 4116871.2277 | SalesLastYear 1635823.3967
BID: 290 | Name: Varkey Chudukatil, Ranjit | Quota: 250000.0000 | YTD Sales: 3121616.3202 | SalesLastYear 2396539.7601

C:\APressEntityFramework\Code\Chapter09\Activity0901_QueriesAndProjections\Activity0901_QueriesAndProjections\bin\Debug
netcoreapp3.1\Activity0901_QueriesAndProjections.exe (process 13788) exited with code 0.
```

Figure 9-8. *The output using a projection*

Once again, let's review the output in SQL Profiler to see if we're in a better place (results are shown in Figure 9-9).

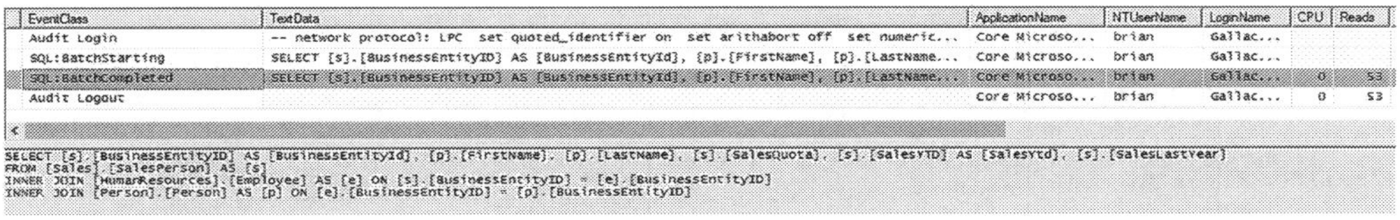

Figure 9-9. *Reviewing SQL Profiler for our latest run with the projection shows quite a substantial improvement in our query*

Now that query looks a lot more like what I would write directly against the database. No more call to the `sp_executesql` stored procedure, and only the fields we want are selected. To be sure, run the program again and execute both of the queries. You should see a substantial difference in the number of read operations between the two queries, even if there is minimal performance difference.

One last thing to see before we move on. Go back to the query and remove the line

```
.Include(x => x.BusinessEntity).ThenInclude(y => y.BusinessEntity)
```

and then run the program again. What do you think will happen (see results in Figure 9-10)?

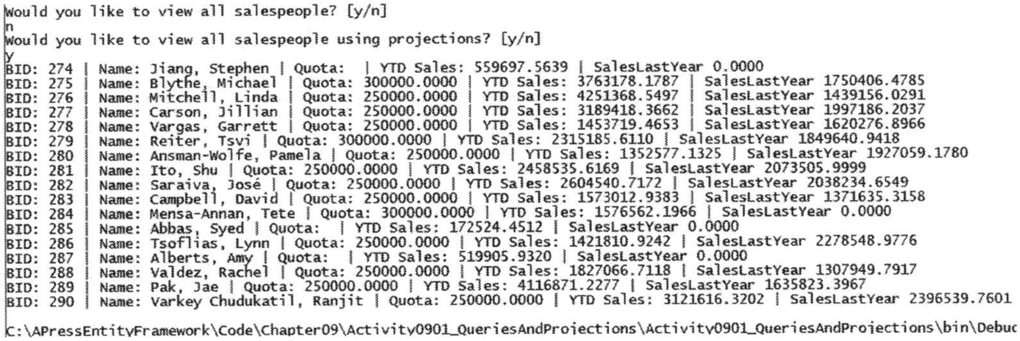

Figure 9-10. *Projections let LINQ know what to include automagically*

If you guessed that everything would still work, you were absolutely correct! By using a projection, we've not only improved the efficiency of our query that is being executed on our database, but we've also eliminated the need to manually define what will be included in relational data. Now we have a solid foundation for using LINQ with projections and we understand when to perform the various transformations. Even so, we are going to need to go just a bit deeper in the real world.

Step 5: Getting deep relational data with filters and sorting

For this final part of our activity, we are going to solve a real-world-like business problem. Imagine your solution needs to get data for a manager that reports on salesperson info (as discussed earlier), but also includes things like the territories that the salesperson is in, the number of orders, and a count of products that the sales person has sold. The manager also needs to sort by last name and then first name and needs to be able to filter the list to only those who have hit a certain sales dollar amount.

This is some heavy lifting for sure and might be worthy of views and stored procedures, depending on how much data and manipulation you truly need.

For our purposes, we're going to use LINQ to define the information we need, combined with everything else we've learned to this point.

There are things I want to focus on along the way, so rather than building this all at once, let's build from the top down and see a few things in action as we go.

Let's start with the basics of the previous ask. We need to get a lot of the same information we've already seen, but we also need a list of the territories, a count of total orders, and a count of total products. Total products will be tricky because there is a quantity in each order detail. Review Figure 9-11 to see the overall structure of the database that we need to be aware of for our results to work as expected.

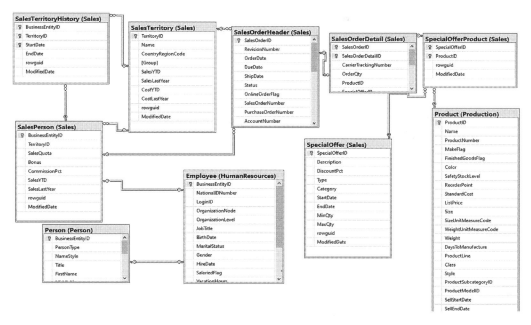

Figure 9-11. *The database diagram shows some critical relationships we'll need to consider in our query*

With this in mind, let's start by adding a method call in the `Main` method of the `Program.cs` file called `GenerateSalesReport`. As with the other methods in this program, wrap the call in an option to give the user an option to opt in or out of running the method.

```
input = string.Empty;
Console.WriteLine("Would you like to view the sales report?");
input = Console.ReadLine();
if (input.StartsWith("y", StringComparison.OrdinalIgnoreCase))
{
    GenerateSalesReport();
}
```

After creating the method call, let's start by looking at how we can use LINQ to get some more advanced data. As we build our skills, we'll hone this query down to one call and then use a projection. Start by writing the method as follows to get the territories for a salesperson:

```
private static void GenerateSalesReport()
{
    using (var db = new AdventureWorksContext(_optionsBuilder.Options))
    {
        var salesReportDetails = db.SalesPerson.Select(sp => new
        {
            beid = sp.BusinessEntityId,
            sp.BusinessEntity.BusinessEntity.FirstName,
            sp.BusinessEntity.BusinessEntity.LastName,
            Territories = sp.SalesTerritoryHistory
                            .Select(y => y.Territory.Name)
        }).Take(20).ToList();

        foreach (var srd in salesReportDetails)
        {
            Console.WriteLine($"{srd.beid}| {srd.LastName}, {srd.
            FirstName}" +
                $"| {string.Join(',', srd.Territories)}");
        }
    }
}
```

In this code, we've used a projection to get the salesperson with details and all of their territory names into an IEnumerable<string>. Since we are not going to need the entire territory object, but just the name, we can use the Select to get the Name of each Territory, and LINQ will place this into an IEnumerable<string> for us. To prevent too many results, we'll just get the top 20 results into our list.

Run the program to see the results, which should be similar to the output shown in Figure 9-12.

```
Would you like to view the sales report?
y
274| Jiang, Stephen|
275| Blythe, Michael| Northeast,Central
276| Mitchell, Linda| Southwest
277| Carson, Jillian| Central,Northeast
278| Vargas, Garrett| Canada
279| Reiter, Tsvi| Southeast
280| Ansman-Wolfe, Pamela| Northwest
281| Ito, Shu| Southwest
282| Saraiva, José| Canada,United Kingdom
283| Campbell, David| Northwest
284| Mensa-Annan, Tete| Northwest
285| Abbas, Syed|
286| Tsoflias, Lynn| Australia
287| Alberts, Amy|
288| Valdez, Rachel| Germany
289| Pak, Jae| Canada
290| Varkey Chudukatil, Ranjit| France
```

Figure 9-12. *The sales report generated with the salesperson details and their territories*

Next, let's get their order counts. To do this, we're going to need to get all the sales orders and use those results. Add the following line of code to the query after the declaration for the Territories in the projection:

```
OrderCount = sp.SalesOrderHeader.Count()
```

For clarity, your overall code with the OrderCount added should be

```
var salesReportDetails = db.SalesPerson.Select(sp => new
{
    beid = sp.BusinessEntityId,
    sp.BusinessEntity.BusinessEntity.FirstName,
    sp.BusinessEntity.BusinessEntity.LastName,
    Territories = sp.SalesTerritoryHistory
                    .Select(y => y.Territory.Name),
    OrderCount = sp.SalesOrderHeader.Count()
}).Take(20).ToList();
```

Add the order count to the overall printout by adding a line in the loop of sales report details:

```
$"| Order Count: {srd.OrderCount}"
```

This should create a foreach loop as follows:

```
foreach (var srd in salesReportDetails)
{
    Console.WriteLine($"{srd.beid}| {srd.LastName}, {srd.FirstName} |" +
        $"{string.Join(',', srd.Territories)} |" +
        $"Order Count: {srd.OrderCount}");
}
```

Run the program to see the results (review Figure 9-13).

```
Would you like to view the sales report?
y
274| Jiang, Stephen | |Order Count: 48
275| Blythe, Michael |Northeast,Central |Order Count: 450
276| Mitchell, Linda |Southwest |Order Count: 418
277| Carson, Jillian |Central,Northeast |Order Count: 473
278| Vargas, Garrett |Canada |Order Count: 234
279| Reiter, Tsvi |Southeast |Order Count: 429
280| Ansman-Wolfe, Pamela |Northwest |Order Count: 95
281| Ito, Shu |Southwest |Order Count: 242
282| Saraiva, José |Canada,United Kingdom |Order Count: 271
283| Campbell, David |Northwest |Order Count: 189
284| Mensa-Annan, Tete |Northwest |Order Count: 140
285| Abbas, Syed | |Order Count: 16
286| Tsoflias, Lynn |Australia |Order Count: 109
287| Alberts, Amy | |Order Count: 39
288| Valdez, Rachel |Germany |Order Count: 130
289| Pak, Jae |Canada |Order Count: 348
290| Varkey Chudukatil, Ranjit |France |Order Count: 175
```

Figure 9-13. *The sales report with salesperson details, territories, and the number of orders for that salesperson*

Next, we need to get the total number of products sold. This is going to be more difficult because of the setup of the tables and the fact that an order detail might have multiple products in it based on quantity. To get this right, we need to get all of the order details for each order header and then sum up the quantity of products sold across all of those order details. To make this happen, we'll leverage the power of SelectMany. The SelectMany operator will allow us to instantly grab all the order details and use them as a result set in our query. Add the following line of code to the projection in the query after the call to get the OrderCount (don't forget to add a comma after the sp.SalesHeader. Count() statement):

```
TotalProductsSold = sp.SalesOrderHeader
                        .SelectMany(y => y.SalesOrderDetail)
                        .Sum(z => z.OrderQty)
```

Next, add the total number of products sold to the printout by adding the following line of code to the end of the output string (don't forget to add a pipe delimiter after the order count in the string):

```
$"Products Sold: {srd.TotalProductsSold}");
```

Figure 9-14 shows the expected results with the Products Sold in the output. Run the program to compare your results.

```
Would you like to view the sales report?
y
274| Jiang, Stephen | |Order Count: 48 |Products Sold: 3095
275| Blythe, Michael |Northeast,Central |Order Count: 450 |Products Sold: 23058
276| Mitchell, Linda |Southwest |Order Count: 418 |Products Sold: 27229
277| Carson, Jillian |Central,Northeast |Order Count: 473 |Products Sold: 27051
278| Vargas, Garrett |Canada |Order Count: 234 |Products Sold: 11544
279| Reiter, Tsvi |Southeast |Order Count: 429 |Products Sold: 16431
280| Ansman-Wolfe, Pamela |Northwest |Order Count: 95 |Products Sold: 7360
281| Ito, Shu |Southwest |Order Count: 242 |Products Sold: 15397
282| Saraiva, José |Canada,United Kingdom |Order Count: 271 |Products Sold: 15220
283| Campbell, David |Northwest |Order Count: 189 |Products Sold: 8172
284| Mensa-Annan, Tete |Northwest |Order Count: 140 |Products Sold: 5650
285| Abbas, Syed | |Order Count: 16 |Products Sold: 825
286| Tsoflias, Lynn |Australia |Order Count: 109 |Products Sold: 4123
287| Alberts, Amy | |Order Count: 39 |Products Sold: 2012
288| Valdez, Rachel |Germany |Order Count: 130 |Products Sold: 7033
289| Pak, Jae |Canada |Order Count: 348 |Products Sold: 26231
290| Varkey Chudukatil, Ranjit |France |Order Count: 175 |Products Sold: 14085
```

Figure 9-14. *The sales report with salesperson info, territories, order counts, and total products sold*

Now that we have this basic data, we can start to further refine our results. The report wants to order by the salesperson name and then wants us to allow for filtering by total sales (which we also still need to add to our query).

Add the following code to the query after the line:

```
sp.BusinessEntity.BusinessEntity.LastName,:
sp.SalesYtd
```

Next, we need to add a filter. At the start of the method, prompt the user to enter a minimum dollar amount for SalesYtd.

Place the following code at the start of the GenerateSalesReport method before the using statement, making sure to just exit if the user enters malicious or incorrect data:

```
Console.WriteLine("What is the minimum amount of sales?");
var input = Console.ReadLine();
decimal filter = 0.0m;

if (!decimal.TryParse(input, out filter))
{
    Console.WriteLine("Bad input");
    return;
}
```

For clarity, the new code statement is shown in Figure 9-15 to make sure it is clear where to place the statement.

```
private static void GenerateSalesReport()
{
    Console.WriteLine("What is the minimum amount of sales?");
    var input = Console.ReadLine();
    decimal filter = 0.0m;

    if (!decimal.TryParse(input, out filter))
    {
        Console.WriteLine("Bad input");
        return;
    }

    using (var db = new AdventureWorksContext(_optionsBuilder.Options))
    {
        var salesReportDetails = db.SalesPerson.Select(sp => new
```

Figure 9-15. The prompt to get a filter amount from the user

In the query chain, after completing the Select with projection, and before the call to Take(20), add the following additional chained command:

```
}).Where(srds => srds.SalesYtd > filter)
    .OrderBy(srds => srds.LastName)
        .ThenBy(srds => srds.FirstName)
            .ThenByDescending(srds => srds.SalesYtd)
    .Take(20).ToList();
```

Here, we've set the filter to limit on SalesYtd based on the user input.

For clarity, the entire query is shown in Figure 9-16.

```
var salesReportDetails = db.SalesPerson.Select(sp => new
{
    beid = sp.BusinessEntityId,
    sp.BusinessEntity.BusinessEntity.FirstName,
    sp.BusinessEntity.BusinessEntity.LastName,
    sp.SalesYtd,
    Territories = sp.SalesTerritoryHistory
                        .Select(y => y.Territory.Name),
    OrderCount = sp.SalesOrderHeader.Count(),
    TotalProductsSold = sp.SalesOrderHeader
                            .SelectMany(y => y.SalesOrderDetail)
                            .Sum(z => z.OrderQty)
}).Where(srds => srds.SalesYtd > filter)
    .OrderBy(srds => srds.LastName)
        .ThenBy(srds => srds.FirstName)
            .ThenByDescending(srds => srds.SalesYtd)
    .Take(20).ToList();
```

Figure 9-16. *The entire query to get the sales report data*

Add a statement to the output to also print out the salesperson's YTD sales. You could place this statement right after the name and before the territory names.

```
$"YTD Sales: {srd.SalesYtd} |" +
```

Run the program to see the results, which should be similar to the output shown in Figure 9-17 (your results may vary based on your sales amount filter).

```
500000
287| Alberts, Amy |YTD Sales: 519905.9320 |  |Order Count: 39 |Products Sold: 2012
280| Ansman-Wolfe, Pamela |YTD Sales: 1352577.1325 |Northwest |Order Count: 95 |Products Sold: 7360
275| Blythe, Michael |YTD Sales: 3763178.1787 |Northeast,Central |Order Count: 450 |Products Sold: 23058
283| Campbell, David |YTD Sales: 1573012.9383 |Northwest |Order Count: 189 |Products Sold: 8172
277| Carson, Jillian |YTD Sales: 3189418.3662 |Central,Northeast |Order Count: 473 |Products Sold: 27051
281| Ito, Shu |YTD Sales: 2458535.6169 |Southwest |Order Count: 242 |Products Sold: 15397
274| Jiang, Stephen |YTD Sales: 559697.5639 |  |Order Count: 48 |Products Sold: 3095
284| Mensa-Annan, Tete |YTD Sales: 1576562.1966 |Northwest |Order Count: 140 |Products Sold: 5650
276| Mitchell, Linda |YTD Sales: 4251368.5497 |Southwest |Order Count: 418 |Products Sold: 27229
289| Pak, Jae |YTD Sales: 4116871.2277 |Canada |Order Count: 348 |Products Sold: 26231
279| Reiter, Tsvi |YTD Sales: 2315185.6110 |Southeast |Order Count: 429 |Products Sold: 16431
282| Saraiva, José |YTD Sales: 2604540.7172 |Canada,United Kingdom |Order Count: 271 |Products Sold: 15220
286| Tsoflias, Lynn |YTD Sales: 1421810.9242 |Australia |Order Count: 109 |Products Sold: 4123
288| Valdez, Rachel |YTD Sales: 1827066.7118 |Germany |Order Count: 130 |Products Sold: 7033
278| Vargas, Garrett |YTD Sales: 1453719.4653 |Canada |Order Count: 234 |Products Sold: 11544
290| Varkey Chudukatil, Ranjit |YTD Sales: 3121616.3202 |France |Order Count: 175 |Products Sold: 14085
```

Figure 9-17. *The current sales report after modifications for filtering and sorting*

The report is looking pretty good based on our original request. We could be content at this point, but there is one more thing to consider, projections to a DTO.

Step 6: Finish the query by projecting to a DTO instead of an anonymous class

Since we're going to be getting a listing of results, let's end by defining a *DTO* object to hold those results. This will allow us to see one last point – that we can project into a pre-defined object, not just into anonymous classes. This is highly useful in larger systems, as the ability to communicate with a pre-defined object makes it much easier to transfer data between layers.

Ordinarily I'd recommend putting DTOs in a separate project. For brevity, however, we'll just add them in a folder in the EF_Activity001 project.

Create a new method that will run along with the GenerateSalesReport called GenerateSalesReportToDTO, and make the call in the Main method in the same block as the call to GenerateSalesReport. This will double up our database calls for the sales report, but we'll get to see both in action this way. You could comment out the original if you only want the last method to run.

```
input = string.Empty;
Console.WriteLine("Would you like to view the sales report?");
input = Console.ReadLine();
if (input.StartsWith("y", StringComparison.OrdinalIgnoreCase))
{
    GenerateSalesReport();
    GenerateSalesReportToDTO();
}
```

In the GenerateSalesReportToDTO method, copy and paste the code from the GenerateSalesReport method. Extract the repeated code for prompting for a filter to a new method called GetFilterFromUser.

```
private static decimal GetFilterFromUser()
{
    Console.WriteLine("What is the minimum amount of sales?");
    var input = Console.ReadLine();
    decimal filter = 0.0m;
```

```
    if (!decimal.TryParse(input, out filter))
    {
        Console.WriteLine("Bad input");
        return 0.0m;
    }
    return filter;
}
```

Next, add a new DTO named SalesReportListingDto.cs in a new folder called DTOs in the EF_Activity01 project. Add the following code to the new DTO:

```
public class SalesReportListingDto
{
    [Required]
    public int BusinessEntityId { get; set; }
    public string FirstName { get; set; }
    public string LastName { get; set; }
    public decimal? SalesYtd { get; set; }
    public IEnumerable<string> Territories { get; set; }
    public int TotalProductsSold { get; set; }
    public int TotalOrders { get; set; }
    public string DisplayName => $"{LastName}, {FirstName}";
    public string DisplayTerritories => string.Join(",", Territories);
    public override string ToString()
    {
        return $"BID: {BusinessEntityId} |{DisplayName,25}|
        {DisplayTerritories,25}|" +
            $"{SalesYtd} | Orders: {TotalOrders} |" +
            $"Products Sold: {TotalProductsSold}";
    }
}
```

In the GenerateSalesReportToDTO method, change the query to the following code:

```
var salesReportDetails = db.SalesPerson.Select(x => new
SalesReportListingDto
{
    BusinessEntityId = x.BusinessEntityId,
    FirstName = x.BusinessEntity.BusinessEntity.FirstName,
    LastName = x.BusinessEntity.BusinessEntity.LastName,
    SalesYtd = x.SalesYtd,
    Territories = x.SalesTerritoryHistory.Select(y => y.Territory.Name),
    TotalOrders = x.SalesOrderHeader.Count(),
    TotalProductsSold = x.SalesOrderHeader
                            .SelectMany(y => y.SalesOrderDetail)
                            .Sum(z => z.OrderQty)
}).Where(srds => srds.SalesYtd > filter)
    .OrderBy(srds => srds.LastName)
        .ThenBy(srds => srds.FirstName)
            .ThenByDescending(srds => srds.SalesYtd);
```

Finally, change the foreach loop to leverage the fact that the DTO has an overridden ToString method in it:

```
foreach (var srd in salesReportDetails)
{
    Console.WriteLine(srd);
}
```

Run the program to see the final results. Make a note that I've commented out the original call so only one sales report prints. In this implementation, we've also removed the Take(20), which is fruitless since there are only 17 salespeople in the database. Finally, we removed the call to .ToList(), since putting the object into a foreach loop will implicitly call to the object for iteration, leveraging the fact that it is an IEnumerable.

The final results you get should look similar to what is shown in Figure 9-18.

```
Would you like to view the sales report?
y
What is the minimum amount of sales?
250000.0
BID: 287 |Alberts, Amy          |                        |519905.9320 | Orders: 39 |Products Sold: 2012
BID: 280 |Ansman-Wolfe, Pamela  |Northwest               |1352577.1325 | Orders: 95 |Products Sold: 7360
BID: 275 |Blythe, Michael       |Northeast,Central       |3763178.1787 | Orders: 450 |Products Sold: 23058
BID: 283 |Campbell, David       |Northwest               |1573012.9383 | Orders: 189 |Products Sold: 8172
BID: 277 |Carson, Jillian       |Central,Northeast       |3189418.3662 | Orders: 473 |Products Sold: 27051
BID: 281 |Ito, Shu              |Southwest               |2458535.6169 | Orders: 242 |Products Sold: 15397
BID: 274 |Jiang, Stephen        |                        |559697.5639 | Orders: 48 |Products Sold: 3095
BID: 284 |Mensa-Annan, Tete     |Northwest               |1576562.1966 | Orders: 140 |Products Sold: 5650
BID: 276 |Mitchell, Linda       |Southwest               |4251368.5497 | Orders: 418 |Products Sold: 27229
BID: 289 |Pak, Jae              |Canada                  |4116871.2277 | Orders: 348 |Products Sold: 26231
BID: 279 |Reiter, Tsvi          |Southeast               |2315185.6110 | Orders: 429 |Products Sold: 16431
BID: 282 |Saraiva, José         |Canada,United Kingdom   |2604540.7172 | Orders: 271 |Products Sold: 15220
BID: 286 |Tsoflias, Lynn        |Australia               |1421810.9242 | Orders: 109 |Products Sold: 4123
BID: 288 |Valdez, Rachel        |Germany                 |1827066.7118 | Orders: 130 |Products Sold: 7033
BID: 278 |Vargas, Garrett       |Canada                  |1453719.4653 | Orders: 234 |Products Sold: 11544
BID: 290 |Varkey Chudukatil, Ranjit|France               |3121616.3202 | Orders: 175 |Products Sold: 14085

C:\APressEntityFramework\Code\Chapter09\Activity0901_QueriesAndProjections\Activity0901_QueriesAndProjections\bi
```

Figure 9-18. *The final results of the sales report using the projection to the SalesReportListingDto*

Final thoughts on activity 0901

In this activity, we were able to take a much deeper dive into working with LINQ queries to join data across tables. Additionally, we saw some good and bad ways to query the data and used the SQL Profiler to prove the efficiency of our results. We finished up by looking at projections, where we learned that we can cast data to an anonymous class or a pre-defined class in the projection.

Activity 0902: Setting up AutoMapper

In this second activity for our chapter, we're going to set up *AutoMapper* in our custom inventory project. After we get set up, we'll do a quick check to see that things are in place correctly for using AutoMapper.

Step 1: Getting started

To begin this activity, either get a copy of the `Activity0902_SettingUpAutomapper_ Starter.zip` files, or just use your existing project as you left it from the end of Chapter 7, after activity 0703. As with other setups, make sure that your database connections are in place, that the project builds, that your database is up-to-date by running an update-database command, and that the project runs as expected.

Finally, you could create your own starter project by creating a new console application, bringing in and referencing the additional projects as they were at the end of activity 0703, adding the appropriate NuGet packages, and then updating the Program.cs file to match the file as of the end of activity 0703.

Step 2: Get the package

In the Package Manager Console, set the project to `Activity0902_SettingUpAutomapper` (or your main program project) and run the command `Install-Package AutoMapper`. Alternatively, both packages could be installed through the NuGet Package Manager by searching for AutoMapper (review Figure 9-19).

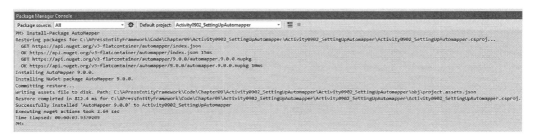

Figure 9-19. *Installing the AutoMapper package to our solution*

Next, install the dependency injection package by running the command `Install-Package AutoMapper.Extensions.Microsoft.DependencyInjection` (see Figure 9-20).

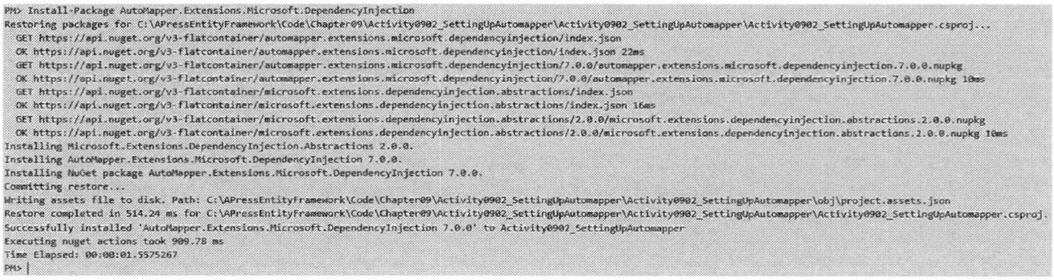

Figure 9-20. *Installing the AutoMapper.Extensions.Microsoft. DependencyInjection package*

Once these packages are installed, we're done! Just kidding.

Step 3: Create the Inventory Mapper Profile

In order for AutoMapper to work correctly, we have to let it know what types we want to map. We're going to attempt to keep this really simple. However, if you'd like to learn more about how AutoMapper is set up and how it works, review the README.md file here: *https://github.com/AutoMapper/AutoMapper*. Additionally, more information can also be found here: *http://docs.automapper.org/en/latest/*.

Let's begin by adding a new class to handle our mapping declarations. We could just do all the mapping in the main Program.cs file, but in the real world, you're going to want your mapping configuration to be separate from your program logic.

Add a new class to the main project called InventoryMapper.cs. This class needs to inherit from a base class called Profile, which requires the using statement using AutoMapper;. In theory, you can separate your various business unit mapping logic into separate classes. We don't have enough going on in our solution right now, so we'll just map everything in this new class. The nice thing about this class being an AutoMapper profile is that it's easier to put into the configuration this way for all maps in the profile.

In the constructor for the InventoryMapper class, add a method call named CreateMaps. Then stub out the CreateMaps method. In the CreateMaps method, we'll place all of our inventory mapping logic. For now, even though it will not work correctly, just add the following two lines of code (ItemDto and CategoryDto are not yet created):

```
CreateMap<Item, ItemDto>();
CreateMap<Category, CategoryDto>();
```

When that is all set up, your code should look like this:

```
public class InventoryMapper : Profile
{
    public InventoryMapper()
    {
        CreateMaps();
    }

    private void CreateMaps()
    {
        CreateMap<Item, ItemDto>();
        CreateMap<Category, CategoryDto>();
    }
}
```

As of right now, the code will not compile, so we need to create the two DTO classes that don't currently exist.

Step 4: Create the DTO objects

In the last step, we mapped the Item and Category to matching DTO classes. To make this work, in the InventoryModels project under the Dtos folder, add a new class ItemDto.cs. In the ItemDto.cs, add two string fields – Name and Description.

```
public class ItemDto
{
    public string Name { get; set; }
    public string Description { get; set; }
}
```

For clarity, the position of the new file is shown in Figure 9-21.

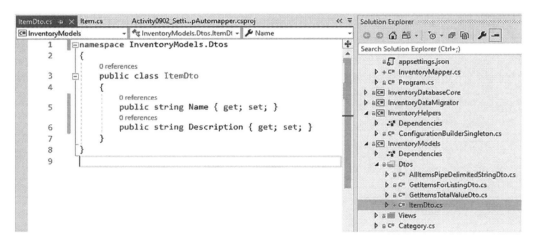

Figure 9-21.   *The ItemDto class*

Add a second class in the Dtos folder called CategoryDto.cs. Don't worry about any code in that *DTO* for now; just leave the default empty implementation (we need this so our code will compile and run).

```
public class CategoryDto
{

}
```

Save your changes, then go back to the InventoryMapper file in the main project, and add the statement using InventoryModels.Dtos; to the top of the file. This fixes the issue for the two DTO types in the mapping profile.

Step 5: Modify the main program to set up AutoMapper and configure the mappings

Back in the Main method in the Program.cs file, add a new method call to BuildMapper right after the BuildOptions method. Add the method with a blank body for now. Remember that the method must be static to work in the program (not because of AutoMapper).

In the space between the class declaration and the Main method, following the _optionsBuilder variable, add three static variables using the following code:

```
private static MapperConfiguration _mapperConfig;
private static IMapper _mapper;
private static IServiceProvider _serviceProvider;
```

Make sure to also add the using statement: using AutoMapper;.

Next, we need to set the configuration for AutoMapper, and we need to inject it using a service collection and a service provider. This will set up our ability to use AutoMapper.

In the BuildMapper method, add the following code, and then add the using statement using Microsoft.Extensions.DependencyInjection;:

```
_configuration = ConfigurationBuilderSingleton.ConfigurationRoot;
_optionsBuilder = new DbContextOptionsBuilder<InventoryDbContext>();
_optionsBuilder.UseSqlServer(_configuration.GetConnectionString("InventoryM
anager"));
```

The earlier statement sets up a service collection to allow us to use dependency injection where AutoMapper is concerned. The service collection then gets AutoMapper and we inject the service profile assembly. If we had other assemblies, we could just add them in the same call by using commas to separate the different assemblies.

After adding the service, we need to set up the mapping configuration. Add the following lines in the BuildMapper method after the three we just added previously:

```
_mapperConfig = new MapperConfiguration(cfg => {
    cfg.AddProfile<InventoryMapper>();
});
_mapperConfig.AssertConfigurationIsValid();
_mapper = _mapperConfig.CreateMapper();
```

These lines of code set up the configuration and tell AutoMapper to use the InventoryMapper profile (which currently has two type mappings and will eventually have more). Using the profile keeps this section much cleaner than manually adding all of the maps directly to the configuration as inline code.

We then make sure that our configuration is valid and conclude by instantiating our mapper using the CreateMapper call.

At this point, AutoMapper is set up correctly. If we run the program, we should not get any errors, even though we aren't implementing any concrete uses of AutoMapper yet. For clarity, the finished BuildMapper method is shown in Figure 9-22.

```
1 reference
static void BuildMapper()
{
    var services = new ServiceCollection();
    services.AddAutoMapper(typeof(InventoryMapper));
    _serviceProvider = services.BuildServiceProvider();

    _mapperConfig = new MapperConfiguration(cfg => {
        cfg.AddProfile<InventoryMapper>();
    });
    _mapperConfig.AssertConfigurationIsValid();
    _mapper = _mapperConfig.CreateMapper();
}
```

Figure 9-22. *The BuildMapper method is completed, and AutoMapper is now configured with two type mappings from the InventoryMapper profile class*

Step 6: Leverage AutoMapper

Now that we have AutoMapper in place, we can leverage it to see the power it gives us.

In the ItemDto class in the InventoryModels project Dtos folder, add an override for ToString that just prints out the Name and Description with a nice padding effect as follows:

```
public override string ToString()
{
    return $"{Name,25} | {Description}";
}
```

Back in the Program class, find the ListInventory method. In that method, add the following line of code between the database call and the printout of the results:

```
var result = _mapper.Map<List<Item>, List<ItemDto>>(items);
```

Then change the output line to

```
result.ForEach(x => Console.WriteLine($"New Item: {x}"));
```

When completed, the ListInventory code should be

```
static void ListInventory()
{
    using (var db = new InventoryDbContext(_optionsBuilder.Options))
    {
        var items = db.Items.Take(5).OrderBy(x => x.Name).ToList();
        var result = _mapper.Map<List<Item>, List<ItemDto>>(items);
        result.ForEach(x => Console.WriteLine($"New Item: {x}"));
    }
}
```

Run the program to see AutoMapper in action. If you want, put a breakpoint on the output statement to see how the result object was correctly mapped from the items list (review Figure 9-23).

```
1 reference
static void ListInventory()
{                              [0]        {Batman Begins       | Why do we fall, Bruce?}
                               [1]        {Battlefield 5       | First person shooter}
    using (var db =           [2]        {Practical Entity Framework | The book that teaches practical application with EF}
    {                          [3]        {The Lord of the Rings   | The fellowship of the Ring}
        var items =           [4]        {Top Gun              | I feel the need, the need for speed}
        var result            Raw View

        result.Fo    result   Count = 5    riteLine($"New Item: {x}"));
    }
}
```

Figure 9-23. *The result is a list of ItemDto objects, correctly mapped from the original list of items*

And the overall output looks as expected as is shown in Figure 9-24.

```
New Item: Batman Begins               | Why do we fall, Bruce?
New Item: Battlefield 5               | First person shooter
New Item: Practical Entity Framework  | The book that teaches practical application with EF
New Item: The Lord of the Rings       | The fellowship of the Ring
New Item: Top Gun                     | I feel the need, the need for speed
ITEM Top Gun - I feel the need, the need for speed
ITEM Batman Begins - Why do we fall, Bruce?
ITEM Batman Begins - Why do we fall, Bruce?
ITEM Practical Entity Framework - The book that teaches practical application with EF
ITEM The Lord of the Rings - The fellowship of the Ring
ITEM The Lord of the Rings - The fellowship of the Ring
ITEM Battlefield 5 - First person shooter
ITEM World Of Tanks - The book that teaches practical application with EF
All active Items: Batman Begins|Battlefield 5|Practical Entity Framework|The Lord of the Rings|To
New Ttem|        417|                                           Top Gun|   1|18 50
```

Figure 9-24. *The output with our new AutoMapper modifications*

Final thoughts on activity 0902

In this activity, we were able to successfully set up AutoMapper to map one object type to another. We created the mapping configuration by setting up the services in our project to hold a single instance of AutoMapper.

We also set up an InventoryMapper profile where we can easily add and work with the specific mappings for the inventory system.

Finally, when we created the configuration, we made sure to add the InventoryMapper profile when instantiating the mapper for variable use in our system.

One thing to note is that AutoMapper does great when the field names line up exactly with each other. Here, both classes, Item and ItemDto, had fields with identical names – Name and Description.

When the field names don't line up, then we need to do a bit more with AutoMapper configurations to make things work as expected. We'll see how to do that in our final activity for this chapter.

Activity 0903: Working with AutoMapper in system

In the final activity for our chapter, we're going to continue working with AutoMapper and LINQ so that we can solidify our knowledge of how to both work with LINQ in some more advanced queries and also so that we can be in a good place to fully leverage the power of AutoMapper in the future.

Step 1: Get set up

For this activity, you can either continue where you left off on the last project, or you can get a copy of the starter files `Activity0903_WorkingWithAutomapper_Starter.zip`. If you choose the starter pack, as always, make sure that your database connection string is configured correctly, then save and build the project, and run the update-database command to make sure you don't have any missing migrations. Finally, run the program to ensure that it works correctly before proceeding.

Step 2: Perform a more advanced query

In a previous activity, we created a stored procedure to get items for listing. Let's add a new call that will re-create the procedure results using LINQ and projections, now that we've seen how to do that in our previous chapter.

Add a new method `GetItemsForListingLinq`, and call the method from the `Main` method. In the `GetItemsForListingLinq` method, add the code as follows:

```
var minDateValue = new DateTime(2020, 1, 1);
var maxDateValue = new DateTime(2021, 1, 1);

using (var db = new InventoryDbContext(_optionsBuilder.Options))
{
```

```
var results = db.Items.Select(x => new
{
    x.CreatedDate,
    CategoryName = x.Category.Name,
    x.Description,
    x.IsActive,
    x.IsDeleted,
    x.Name,
    x.Notes
}).Where(x => x.CreatedDate >= minDateValue && x.CreatedDate <=
maxDateValue)
.OrderBy(y => y.CategoryName).ThenBy(z => z.Name)
.ToList();

foreach (var item in results)
{
    Console.WriteLine($"ITEM {item.CategoryName}| {item.Name}
    - {item.Description}");
}
}
```

One thing to note is that we can't project into the DTO as we did in the stored procedure because of the need to leverage the `CreatedDate` field from the Item. If we wanted to fix that, we could just add the field to the DTO. Comment out all method calls except the stored procedure and the new LINQ version of the get listings methods.

Running the program gives output similar to what is shown in Figure 9-25.

```
ITEM Top Gun - I feel the need, the need for speed
ITEM Batman Begins - Why do we fall, Bruce?
ITEM Practical Entity Framework - The book that teaches practical application with EF
ITEM The Lord of the Rings - The fellowship of the Ring
ITEM Battlefield 5 - First person shooter
ITEM World Of Tanks - AN MMO WW2 Tanks First-Person Shooter
ITEM Books| Practical Entity Framework - The book that teaches practical application with EF
ITEM Books| The Lord of the Rings - The fellowship of the Ring
ITEM Games| Battlefield 5 - First person shooter
ITEM Games| World Of Tanks - AN MMO WW2 Tanks First-Person Shooter
ITEM Movies| Batman Begins - Why do we fall, Bruce?
ITEM Movies| Top Gun - I feel the need, the need for speed

C:\APressEntityFramework\Code\Chapter09\Activity0903_WorkingWithAutomapper\Activity0903_WorkingWit
netcoreapp3.1\Activity0903_WorkingWithAutomapper.exe (process 10540) exited with code 0.
To automatically close the console when debugging stops, enable Tools->Options->Debugging->Automat
le when debugging stops.
Press any key to close this window . . .
```

Figure 9-25. *The display using the stored procedure and LINQ to get listings*

If your output doesn't match mine exactly, that may be due to you having set different genres and different items than what I have in my database. It's always a good idea to validate that your results match what is to be expected based on your data.

Imagine that in the original stored procedure, there exists a small error due to including the join to the Genres and ItemGenres tables that could have been left behind when we removed the Genre data from the stored procedure. With LINQ, we avoid making the same type of mistake. This is where LINQ can really be a powerful ally, mainly because it is more flexible than a stored procedure. To fix an issue with the original procedure, we generally have to go through governance procedures to update a stored procedure on the database server. With LINQ, we can just fix our mistake in the code and then deploy a patch.

Step 3: Update the DTO so that it maps to the correct type

In the previous run, we ended up with an anonymous type that we used for our output due to the fact that we had to leverage the CreatedDate, and the CreatedDate is not part of our DTO.

As mentioned previously in activity 0902, we can easily modify our DTO object to include the CreatedDate, and then we can project directly to that type in our query. However, this could lead to some complications in other areas of the code. Instead, let's create a new DTO that extends the original and adds the CreatedDate field.

Create a new class in the InventoryModels project in the Dtos folder called GetItemsForListingWithDateDto.cs, and then inherit from the original GetItemsForListingDto class. Add the property for the CreatedDate field. When completed, your code should look as follows:

```
public class GetItemsForListingWithDateDto : GetItemsForListingDto
{
    public DateTime CreatedDate { get; set; }
}
```

For clarity, the code and placement are shown in Figure 9-26.

391

Figure 9-26. *The new DTO is placed in the InventoryModels project, inherits from the existing DTO, and adds one additional property*

After creating the new DTO, modify the original query so that it projects directly to a new `GetItemsForListingDto`, rather than using an anonymous class:

```
var results = db.Items.Select(x => new GetItemsForListingWithDateDto
{
    CreatedDate = x.CreatedDate,
    CategoryName = x.Category.Name,
    Description = x.Description,
    IsActive = x.IsActive,
    IsDeleted = x.IsDeleted,
    Name = x.Name,
    Notes = x.Notes
}).Where(x => x.CreatedDate >= minDateValue && x.CreatedDate <=
maxDateValue)
    .OrderBy(y => y.CategoryName).ThenBy(z => z.Name).ToList();
```

And then run the program to make sure it still works, with no errors on the other method(s). Your output should be the same as before and should be similar to what is shown in Figure 9-27.

```
Select Microsoft Visual Studio Debug Console
ITEM Top Gun - I feel the need, the need for speed
ITEM Batman Begins - Why do we fall, Bruce?
ITEM Practical Entity Framework - The book that teaches practical application with EF
ITEM The Lord of the Rings - The fellowship of the Ring
ITEM Battlefield 5 - First person shooter
ITEM World Of Tanks - AN MMO WW2 Tanks First-Person Shooter
ITEM Books| Practical Entity Framework - The book that teaches practical application with EF
ITEM Books| The Lord of the Rings - The fellowship of the Ring
ITEM Games| Battlefield 5 - First person shooter
ITEM Games| World Of Tanks - AN MMO WW2 Tanks First-Person Shooter
ITEM Movies| Batman Begins - Why do we fall, Bruce?
ITEM Movies| Top Gun - I feel the need, the need for speed

C:\APressEntityFramework\Code\Chapter09\Activity0903_WorkingWithAutomapper\Activity0903_Workin
netcoreapp3.1\Activity0903_WorkingWithAutomapper.exe (process 11164) exited with code 0.
To automatically close the console when debugging stops, enable Tools->Options->Debugging->Aut
le when debugging stops.
Press any key to close this window . . .
```

Figure 9-27. *The projected query works as expected*

Step 4: Using AutoMapper to project results to a type

One of the more powerful features of AutoMapper is the ability to project directly to a type, even if the query is returning another type. When we originally set up AutoMapper in the previous activity, we saw that we were able to map an Item to an ItemDto. The ItemDto was a much pared-down version of the Item, which will often be the case with *DTOs*.

The thing we didn't leverage in that original example was the ability that AutoMapper has to just project directly to the type we want, thereby combining the query and the mapping into one statement.

If you commented out the ListInventory method, go ahead and uncomment it now so that it will execute on the next run. Additionally, you could comment out both of the GetItemsForListing... methods to clear up the output.

Add a new method called ListInventoryWithProjection to the Main method following the original ListInventory method. In the new method, place the following code:

```
using (var db = new InventoryDbContext(_optionsBuilder.Options))
{
    var items = db.Items.Take(5)
                    .OrderBy(x => x.Name)
                    .ProjectTo<ItemDto>(_mapper.ConfigurationProvider)
                    .ToList();
    items.ForEach(x => Console.WriteLine($"New Item: {x}"));
}
```

393

Notice in this code that it is nearly identical to the original method, with the exception of the call to `.ProjectTo<T>(IConfigurationProvider)`. In this instance, we were able to easily map to the `ItemDTO` from the result object at the same time that we performed the query, saving the extra step of performing the mapping. To get the code to compile, we also need to add the using statement `using AutoMapper.QueryableExtensions;`.

Step 5: Handling the times when the fields don't line up exactly

As we close up our look at AutoMapper and using projections with LINQ in our codebase, I want to cover one last point. There are going to be times in the real world where your database object and your DTO do not map property to property. Perhaps your DTO is a combination of a couple of objects, or perhaps your DTO needs to transform some of the data from the object and use that in its life cycle. Either way, a one-to-one mapping of fields in DTOs to objects is likely an unreasonable expectation.

The great news is that AutoMapper allows for us to map the fields as we see fit. Sometimes, we can tell AutoMapper to ignore the field altogether. Other times, we need to map in both directions and sometimes just in one direction.

To show how this works, we'll use a bit of a contrived example. Reviewing our data in the inventory system, we have categories, and each category has a color. Additionally, we have items that belong to one category and zero-to-many genres.

Suppose we want to get an output of our categories and their associated colors, but instead of using the table fields Name, we'll use `Category` and `ColorValue` will just be `Color`. We can set all this up with a friendly DTO and a couple of tweaks in the mapping configuration.

Begin by creating a new class called CategoryColorDto.cs in the Inventory Models project in the Dtos folder. This DTO will map to the `CategoryColor`. In the new DTO, just add the one field, `Color`, which will be a string that maps to `ColorValue`.

```
public class CategoryColorDto
{
    public string Color { get; set; }
}
```

In the `CategoryDto` class that we created earlier in the activity, add two properties as follows:

```
public string Category { get; set; }
public CategoryColorDto CategoryColor { get; set; }
```

Next, go into the `InventoryMapper` file in the main activity project to create and modify the mappings.

For the first map, when mapping `Category` to `CategoryDto`, change the code to the following:

```
CreateMap<Category, CategoryDto>()
    .ForMember(x => x.Category, opt => opt.MapFrom(y => y.Name))
    .ReverseMap()
    .ForMember(y => y.Name, opt => opt.MapFrom(x => x.Category));
```

And then add a new map for `CategoryColor` to `CategoryColorDto` as follows:

```
CreateMap<CategoryColor, CategoryColorDto>()
    .ForMember(x => x.Color, opt => opt.MapFrom(y => y.ColorValue))
    .ReverseMap()
    .ForMember(y => y.ColorValue, opt => opt.MapFrom(x => x.Color));
```

By reversing the map with the ReverseMap call and going in the other direction, it is now possible to map one of the database objects to the corresponding *DTO* and also to go from the DTO back to a database object.

If one of the classes had an extra field that didn't map to anything, we could make a statement like

```
.ForMember(x => x.AFieldNotMappable, opt => opt.Ignore())
```

Note that the use of the Ignore method tells AutoMapper to skip trying to match the particular field to any field in the target object.

Finally, let's do a quick query in the main program to see this in action.

Add a new method in the Main method of the Program class called
ListCategoriesAndColors. In the ListCategoriesAndColors method, add the following
code:

```
using (var db = new InventoryDbContext(_optionsBuilder.Options))
{
    var results = db.Categories
                    .Include(x => x.CategoryColor)
                    .ProjectTo<CategoryDto>(_mapper.ConfigurationProvider).
                    ToList();

    foreach (var c in results)
    {
        Console.WriteLine($"{c.Category} | {c.CategoryColor.Color}");
    }
}
```

Running the program lets us see the results with the new projections mapping as
expected (see Figure 9-28).

```
Microsoft Visual Studio Debug Console
New Item: Batman Begins              | Why do we fall, Bruce?
New Item: Battlefield 5              | First person shooter
New Item: Practical Entity Framework | The book that teaches practical application with EF
New Item: The Lord of the Rings      | The fellowship of the Ring
New Item: Top Gun                    | I feel the need, the need for speed
New Item: Batman Begins              | Why do we fall, Bruce?
New Item: Battlefield 5              | First person shooter
New Item: Practical Entity Framework | The book that teaches practical application with EF
New Item: The Lord of the Rings      | The fellowship of the Ring
New Item: Top Gun                    | I feel the need, the need for speed
Movies | Blue
Books | Red
Games | Green

C:\APressEntityFramework\Code\Chapter09\Activity0903_WorkingWithAutomapper\Activity0903_Worki
netcoreapp3.1\Activity0903_WorkingWithAutomapper.exe (process 12564) exited with code 0.
To automatically close the console when debugging stops, enable Tools->Options->Debugging->Au
le when debugging stops
```

*Figure 9-28. The program works with projections even when field names are not
identical*

Note that in this method, we did use the Include syntax as the original code is
grabbing categories and their colors. If we select the CategoryColor, AutoMapper will
not be able to make the projection correctly from the internal CategoryColorDto from a

CategoryColor, and we cannot use an anonymous type with ProjectTo. Using Include allows the selection of the data and then mapping is completed successfully.

If you want to see the error, change the .Include(x => x.CategoryColor) to .Select(x => x.CategoryColor) and run the program. Figure 9-29 shows the error that happens when trying to select and project.

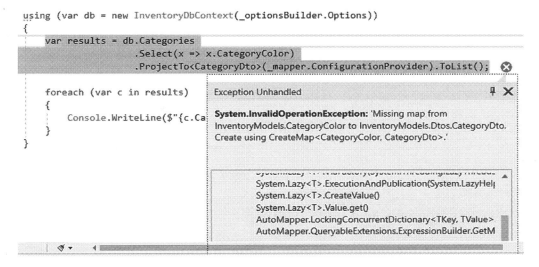

Figure 9-29. *Using Select is not possible when there is a nested mapping*

And finally, if you must use Select, you'll have to abandon AutoMapper and just manually do the projections yourself. In this case, the code would look like this:

```
var results = db.Categories
        .Select(x => new CategoryDto
        {
            Category = x.Name,
            CategoryColor = new CategoryColorDto { Color = x.CategoryColor.
            ColorValue }
        });
```

Final thoughts on activity 0903

In this final activity, we were able to see the real power of working with AutoMapper in our *EF* queries. Once we have AutoMapper set up, and learn the syntax that is necessary to create mappings, we can really start leveraging AutoMapper as a great tool to make our queries more succinct and generally just as performant as if we had written them without AutoMapper.

The added benefits of using AutoMapper include the fact that we can utilize the `.ProjectTo<T>()` call to automatically map our results from one type to another. By doing this, we don't have to make manual calls to the mapper for object conversion.

Finally, using AutoMapper allows us to easily create configurations that set our conversions in place throughout our system. This means we don't have to spend any time writing manual conversions of objects, field by field. Not having to do the manual conversion also eliminates issues where we simply forget to map a field or accidentally map to the wrong field.

Final thoughts for this chapter

This chapter gave us a deep dive into using LINQ in complex queries. We were able to see how important it is to write our queries correctly, so as to leverage the efficiency of *EF*. This also reminds us that even as we develop, we should be running some sort of analyzer tool in order to validate that our SQL queries generated by *EF* are working with maximum efficiency.

After we took our deeper look at working with LINQ, we then moved into the importance of working with AutoMapper in our systems. Without AutoMapper, we have a lot of manual work that we must do when we layer our architecture and don't just use our base models throughout the system.

Although AutoMapper has a bit of an initial learning curve for both setup and a few pieces of syntax for mapping fields, once these are taken care of, the tool becomes an invaluable piece of our systems.

As we close this chapter, we are now in a really great place with our knowledge of *EF* and working with LINQ in our systems. As we move forward, we'll be hitting some more common scenarios that you will likely encounter in your systems. We'll start by looking at data encryption in the next chapter.

CHAPTER 10

Encryption of Data

Keeping your system's data secure

You've implemented a system, and you've created the best database structure you can architect. Your system is taking off, and you have hundreds or thousands of clients and many gigabytes of customer data on your server. Things couldn't be better, right? Then you get a notification that something has gone wrong with your database. Somehow, a malicious entity has gained information about all of your customers because you were storing that information in your database in plain text. This nightmare scenario could be you, if you don't take at least some minimal measures to prevent it.

Data at rest

In today's world, it is essentially unacceptable to keep any personal customer data at rest in your system in an unencrypted fashion. By having this data in plain text, you are putting yourself and your company at risk for major lawsuits when a breech occurs. Even storing your data off premises at a *CSP* (cloud service provider) like *Microsoft Azure* or *Amazon AWS* is not going to be enough to protect you and your data.

Encryption in the past vs. encryption today

In this chapter, we are going to dive into some of the tenets of encryption using *Microsoft SQL Server*. Additionally, we'll see how encryption of data at rest can be accomplished in two different approaches by looking into a *Transparent Data Encryption (TDE)* solution and an *AlwaysEncrpyted* solution. Both solutions in our activities will use EFCore.

© Brian L. Gorman 2020
B. L. Gorman, *Practical Entity Framework*, https://doi.org/10.1007/978-1-4842-6044-9_10

Likely, when you think of encryption, the first thing you think of is passwords, so let's start by taking a look at how we can correctly protect user passwords, and then we'll move into looking at the other fields in our database tables.

Passwords

Password mismanagement is probably the most egregious error a system developer can commit. Today we have a number of options that can help with this issue. The simplest option available is to use a single-sign-on solution via a third-party provider.

SSO via social logins

Today we have many platforms available that provide tools to use their platform as a means to identify users and allow for us to easily build a single-sign-on solution (SSO). If you don't like managing users, and you are building a noncorporate business solution, there is very little reason to not just use the SSO capabilities of one or more of these platforms.

Facebook, Google, Microsoft, LinkedIn, and others all provide solutions that are easy to wire up into your applications. When doing this, you are able to let those providers do the heavy work of managing the user's passwords, and all you need to do is associate the user in your system with the authentication information that comes back from the provider, such as the validated email of a user as returned from the third-party provider.

In general, to set up these third-party solutions, you would just go to the provider of choice and create an application at their developer tools portal, which will give you the app id and token secrets that you need in order to authenticate against the third-party provider. Once the user has authenticated, the appropriate user information (such as email or other identifiers) is handed back to you for your use in your system.

ASP.Net built-in authentication

Another option you have that helps with preventing user password mismanagement comes in the form of the `IdentityDbContext`, which is part of the `AspNetCore.Identity.EntityFramework` namespace. ASP.Net with EF6 also had the same sort of structure, with an `IdentityDbContext`.

When using the `IdentityDbContext`, we are able to easily create a new solution that handles user authentication for us. At inception, the system creates all the tables necessary for users and roles, as well as identity claims. With all of this in place, we simply needed to perform a few actions to register and/or authenticate users.

When registering users with built-in identity management, the user password is automatically hashed and salted. This makes it impossible for us to get the user password back to plain text. In this scenario, if a user loses their password, they need to go through a validation process to reset the password to a new password.

Salting and hashing

If you must create your own custom database user solution, you should follow a hashing and salting pattern to make sure you hash and salt your user passwords. In case you are not familiar with why this is important, let's consider a couple of scenarios.

Please don't even consider using a plain-text password storage solution for anything past a simple demo MVP solution (and even then, using plain text should be avoided if possible).

Now that you agree that storing passwords as plain text is a terrible idea, are you thinking encryption alone is good enough? The answer, of course, is no. Encryption is a two-way process. Anything that is encrypted can be decrypted if the common encryption algorithm and key(s) are known. So, turning on `AlwaysEncrypted` on your fields only scrambles them from being plain text, but does not make it impossible to reverse the encryption (if it did, we couldn't store user information like names, social security numbers, and such in an always encrypted column).

With hashing, we use a unique algorithm to set the length of our data to a fixed length. By combining the unique password with the hash and applying the hashing algorithm during encryption, we get a value that is mathematically improbable to reverse engineer. Storing this hash in the database table allows the password to be decrypted by applying that hash to the password as entered by the user and using the same algorithm to decrypt for authentication. Therefore, we are no longer storing the password, but are storing a hash that when combined with user input can be encrypted with the hash and compared to determine that the hashed results match.

What happens, though, when two users have the same password? Without anything else, the hash value would be identical, and this could lead to a security issue. Although it would still be tough to figure it out, a malicious user who has access to your data might be able to run common passwords and determine them from the identical hash values. Additionally, if they know the hashed value of a particular password, and have proper access, they could update the stored hash for all users to the known hash value and then log in and impersonate anyone in the system, including your admin users.

In this contrived example, I have three users that have the same password, and Figure 10-1 shows what it would look like if the exact same hash was used for each of them when the password hash was generated.

PasswordHash

AQAAAEAACcQAAAAEHDZvGSCj9w7IfjdRnRVpQ4D4GS/NQOBS+NU/dDd+5hbFx0fkMvQSDPTPBB2fvW2A==

AQAAAEAACcQAAAAEHDZvGSCj9w7IfjdRnRVpQ4D4GS/NQOBS+NU/dDd+5hbFx0fkMvQSDPTPBB2fvW2A==

AQAAAEAACcQAAAAEHDZvGSCj9w7IfjdRnRVpQ4D4GS/NQOBS+NU/dDd+5hbFx0fkMvQSDPTPBB2fvW2A==

Figure 10-1. *A database with three users that have the same password generated with the same hash*

Using a salt in addition to the hash allows us to create a unique hash for each user that still maps correctly to a regenerated hash with salt and user input. The reason this works is because the salt is going to be unique for the user based on some other generation tactic, like a timestamp or a computer serial number or something else that is unique. The password is then combined with the salt and then hashed, and therefore every user, even users with the same password, generates a unique hashed password value. Figure 10-2 shows users that are registered with the same password, but the hash is generated with a salt so that the password hash is unique to all users.

PasswordHash

AQAAAEAACcQAAAAEBeame7+uQcv/XaCN3tYEOQi6KkCKS2qzOKc9mNdWDKW8txP5v8wQugXGmXU7B0T9A==

AQAAAEAACcQAAAAEE91PQdiX1vioUzaXCKFYYsdqmfaT/CW8a64ITDMm8Fg1L/15Df92ubcWOYnpuDxJA==

AQAAAEAACcQAAAAEGFZUyH5yCiqZYjneadf6/PYQKc8vBfI8pG+br8XpI46MXHsjYR+z28bC3d4fPKHIw==

Figure 10-2. *Three users with the same password have unique PasswordHash values when a salt is used*

Protecting sensitive user information

There are a couple of ways to implement encryption on data at rest using *SQL Server*. If your SQL Server version is version 2016 or greater, the easiest way to implement encryption is to use the `AlwaysEncrypted` functionality of SQL Server. If you are on a previous version of SQL Server, encryption is still straightforward, but involves a more manual interaction with the data.

Encryption basics

In order to encrypt columns in the database, we need to have two keys. The first key is the master key that protects the keys in the system. The second key is the individual key to encrypt columns.

With `AlwaysEncrypted`, creation of the encryption keys is very easily accomplished using SSMS to encrypt columns. If no master key exists, one is created. When a column is encrypted, a column encryption key can be generated or, if one already exists, can be reused.

When encrypting with the `AlwaysEncrypted` approach, two types of encryption can be used. The first is *Deterministic*, and the second is *Randomized*. The main difference here is that if you are going to be joining to the column or if you are going to use it as a condition in a query, you will want to use the deterministic type. If you are just encrypting the data and it isn't going to be critical in a join or other queries, you can just use the randomized type.

In SQL Server versions prior to 2016, or in current versions where you don't want to use `AlwaysEncrypted`, you can leverage the *Transparent Data Encryption* method *(TDE)*.

To work with TDE in any SQL Server instance, you need to generate a certificate for the server and then generate one or more keys to use when encrypting columns. To read columns, you'll need to use the encryption key as part of your transaction. Additionally, you'll use scripts for encryption of columns.

Since TDE requires more interaction, a general approach that works well is to leverage stored procedures any time data from an encrypted column is queried or transformed.

Which type to use

Each type of encryption has advantages and disadvantages. Let's consider a couple of things that are important considerations for anyone who is developing a secure system.

TDE is server-side encryption, so data is well encrypted on the server, but the decryption also happens at the server, and then the raw data is sent over the pipe to the UI. There are ways to enforce encryption on the pipe as well, but that requires more configuration. Additionally, the keys for the encryption must be managed at the database level, so they are based on the database and server where they are generated.

The nice thing about TDE is that it can be more performant since the encryption and decryption happen at the server. TDE also works on any version of SQL Server since 2008. One last thing about TDE is that since it is handled on the server, any database admin with execution rights can decrypt the data and see the actual sensitive data as stored in the table, and a compromised database likely means compromised keys.

AlwaysEncrypted is limited to being used from SQL Server 2016 and newer, so older systems or any system with a SQL Server back end that is less than the 2016 version cannot leverage AlwaysEncrypted. AlwaysEncrypted functionality is not database specific, however. The encryption takes place on the client side of the operation, and the encrypted data is passed on the pipe and directly stored in the database table. This means that transmission of the data over the pipe is done with the data already encrypted with no extra configuration needed.

This client-side encryption also means that any SQL Server admin cannot just decrypt the information using server certificates without a client library. Of course, SSMS can be easily configured to be the client library with a few tweaks on the connection, so your data is still not secure from a malicious database administrator who has the right server credentials.

As we'll see in the upcoming activities, encrypting specific columns with AlwaysEncrypted functionality is as easy as a few clicks, and this goes for tables with or without data. In contrast, encrypting the data using TDE requires us to go through an entire migration process. AlwaysEncrypted leverages client-side decryption, while TDE sends the data plain text to and from the server. TDE makes up for its longer setup time by generally performing better than AlwaysEncrypted would perform.

One final thought, which you can find more information on if you read more into the topic of encryption, is that you are going to need to implement a good key-management strategy. Consider your risk for a compromised key and how you might have a plan in place to migrate to a new key in case such an event does happen. Also consider and test what happens with keys on backup and restore in the various scenarios, as well as moving to a new database server.

Ultimately, it will be up to you to make sure that you mitigate the risk by managing your keys well, and it's also up to you to implement a risk management strategy to handle scenarios where the keys are compromised, or the server fails.

Chapter 10 Activities: Using Always Encrypted with EFCore and using TDE with EFCore

In the activities for this chapter, we are going to cover two different ways to encrypt our data at rest. We'll start by implementing `AlwaysEncrypted`, and we'll conclude with an activity that implements TDE. We'll do both solutions in *EFCore*, but you can be certain that *EF6* would be just as able to be used for these activities. In fact, it is probably more likely you would see TDE in an *EF6* (or older) implementation, mostly due to the fact that TDE has been around a lot longer.

Activity 1001: Using Always Encrypted in an EFCore solution

In this first activity, we're going to learn how to set up `AlwaysEncrypted` in our InventoryManager database solution and then work with it in our codebase.

The great news about always encrypted is that we can use it in a greenfield solution, in a legacy solution when creating new tables, or in tables that already exist, even if the encrypted columns have data.

Step 1: Get set up

To begin this activity, get a copy of the files `Activity1001_Using_AlwaysEncrypted_Starter.zip`. Open the project, double-check the connection strings, and make sure to run the update-database command to ensure your database is current at the start of the activity. Alternative to getting the starter files, you could continue with the files as they were at the end of Chapter 9, or just create a new project and follow these steps (skip these steps if you are using existing files or the starter pack):

405

1. Create a new .Net Core Console app named appropriately.

2. Get the project folders for the InventoryDatabaseCore, InventoryDataMigrator, InventoryHelpers, and InventoryModels projects. Add references to the InventoryDatabaseCore and Inventoryhelpers project in your new console application project.

3. Get the NuGet packages updated by building the solution, and then use the NuGet Package Manager to ensure your new console application project has the following NuGet packages referenced:

   a. Automapper

   b. Automapper.Extensions.Microsoft.DependencyInjection

   c. Microsoft.EntityFrameworkCore

   d. Microsoft.EntityFramewokCore.SqlServer

   e. Microsoft.EntityFrameworkCore.Design

   f. Microsoft.Extentions.Configuration.FileExtensions

   g. Microsoft.Extensions.Configuration.Json

4. Get the InventoryMapper.cs file in place in the new console application.

5. Get the appsettings.json in place in the new console application, making sure to set as Content ➤ Copy if newer.

6. Get the code from the activity 0903 Program.cs file, and place in the new Program.cs file in your new console project.

7. Build the solution, and then run update-database in the PMC to make sure everything is in place

With everything set up, run the program to see the initial results (review Figure 10-3).

If you are running code from the end of Chapter 9, some of your output may vary based on what methods you have enabled and what methods are commented out. The output in Figure 10-3 is calling all methods in the constructor.

```
New Item] 127       |Top Gun                                    |1    |18.50
New Item] 128       |Batman Begins                              |4    |58.00
New Item] 129       |Practical Entity Framework                 |100  |4450.00
New Item] 130       |The Lord of the Rings                      |7    |87.50
New Item] 131       |Battlefield 5                              |17   |756.50
New Item] 132       |World Of Tanks                             |1    |0.00
New Item] 127       |Top Gun                                    |Comedy
New Item] 128       |Batman Begins                              |Sci/Fi
New Item] 128       |Batman Begins                              |Drama
New Item] 129       |Practical Entity Framework                 |
New Item] 130       |The Lord of the Rings                      |Sci/Fi
New Item] 130       |The Lord of the Rings                      |Fantasy
New Item] 131       |Battlefield 5                              |Sci/Fi
New Item] 132       |World Of Tanks                             |
ITEM Books| Practical Entity Framework - The book that teaches practical application with EF
ITEM Books| The Lord of the Rings - The fellowship of the Ring
ITEM Games| Battlefield 5 - First person shooter
ITEM Games| World Of Tanks - AN MMO WW2 Tanks First-Person Shooter
ITEM Movies| Batman Begins - Why do we fall, Bruce?
ITEM Movies| Top Gun - I feel the need, the need for speed
Movies | Blue
Books | Red
Games | Green

C:\APressEntityFramework\Code\Chapter10\Activity1001_Using_AlwaysEncrypted\Activity1001_Using_Always
```

Figure 10-3. *The initial results yield items and categories with colors*

Now that you've ensured the code is working as expected, we can encrypt some columns. As a quick reminder, `AlwaysEncrypted` will not work if you are using a version of SQL Server prior to SQL Server 2016.

Step 2: Enable Always Encrypted

Open the inventory database in SSMS to view the tables. Expand the `Items` table to see the columns, and run a query like `SELECT TOP 1000 * FROM [InventoryManager].[dbo].[Items]`. The results of this query are shown in Figure 10-4.

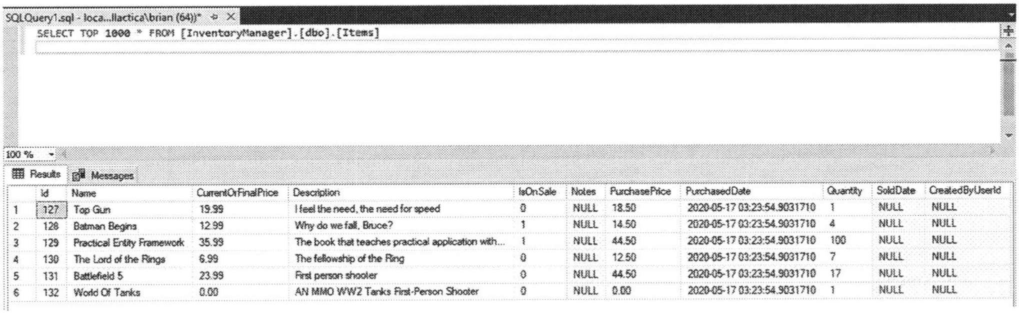

	Id	Name	CurrentOrFinalPrice	Description	IsOnSale	Notes	PurchasePrice	PurchasedDate	Quantity	SoldDate	CreatedByUserId
1	127	Top Gun	19.99	I feel the need, the need for speed	0	NULL	18.50	2020-05-17 03:23:54.9031710	1	NULL	NULL
2	128	Batman Begins	12.99	Why do we fall, Bruce?	1	NULL	14.50	2020-05-17 03:23:54.9031710	4	NULL	NULL
3	129	Practical Entity Framework	35.99	The book that teaches practical application with...	1	NULL	44.50	2020-05-17 03:23:54.9031710	100	NULL	NULL
4	130	The Lord of the Rings	6.99	The fellowship of the Ring	0	NULL	12.50	2020-05-17 03:23:54.9031710	7	NULL	NULL
5	131	Battlefield 5	23.99	First person shooter	0	NULL	44.50	2020-05-17 03:23:54.9031710	17	NULL	NULL
6	132	World Of Tanks	0.00	AN MMO WW2 Tanks First-Person Shooter	0	NULL	0.00	2020-05-17 03:23:54.9031710	1	NULL	NULL

Figure 10-4. *The Items table without AlwaysEncrypted enabled*

In the real-world applications that you are building, you will need to determine which columns you want to encrypt. For this application, let's encrypt the Name, Description, and Notes fields of the Items table.

Right-click the table and select Encrypt Columns, as shown in Figure 10-5.

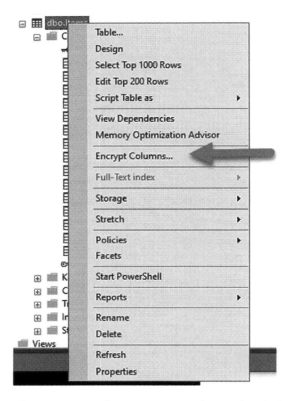

Figure 10-5. *Select the Encrypt Columns option after right-clicking the table in SSMS*

When the Always Encrypted wizard starts, select Next (review Figure 10-6).

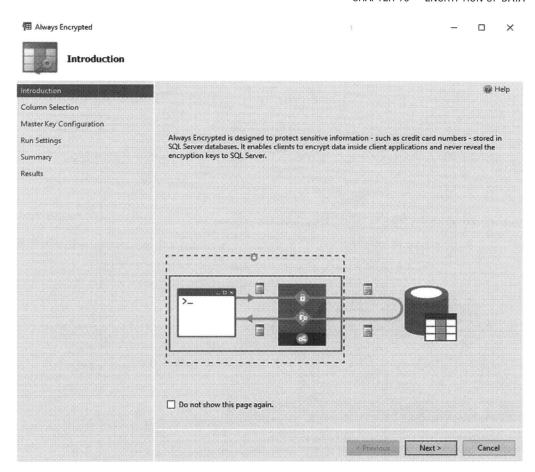

Figure 10-6. *The first step of the Always Encrypted wizard*

In the Column Selection window, select the three columns we are going to encrypt. For this encryption, assume we might limit or search on Name and Description, but not on Notes. Therefore, select the *Deterministic* option for Name and Description, and select the *Randomized* option for Notes. See Figure 10-7 for clarity on the fields to mark for processing and the selected encryption type for each of the targeted columns.

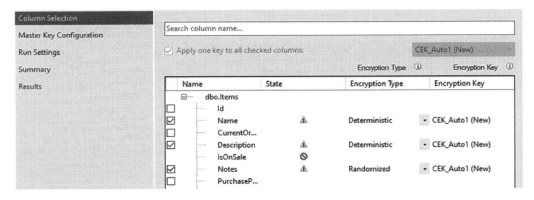

Figure 10-7. *Selecting the columns for encryption*

Select Next to continue to the Master Key Configuration step in the Always Encrypted wizard.

Leave the column master key set to auto-generated, and choose your place of storage, either in your Windows certificate store or in an *Azure Key Vault*. Leave the master key source set to the Current User for the certificate store, or log into Azure and select the key vault to store the encryption master key (see Figure 10-8).

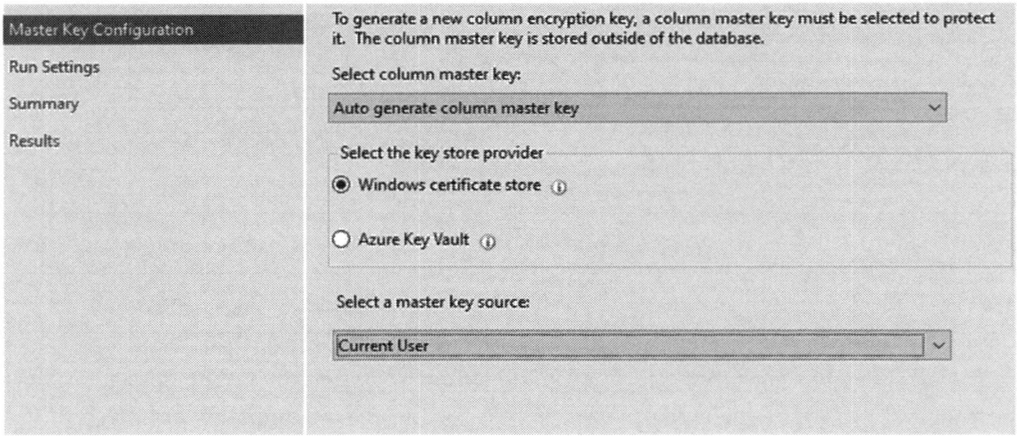

Figure 10-8. *Configure the master key settings*

Select Next to continue to the Run Settings step of the wizard. At this step, either run it now or generate a *PowerShell* script to do the encryption later. Go ahead and leave this selected as Proceed to finish now, and then hit the Next button to move to the summary step (for clarity, review Figure 10-9).

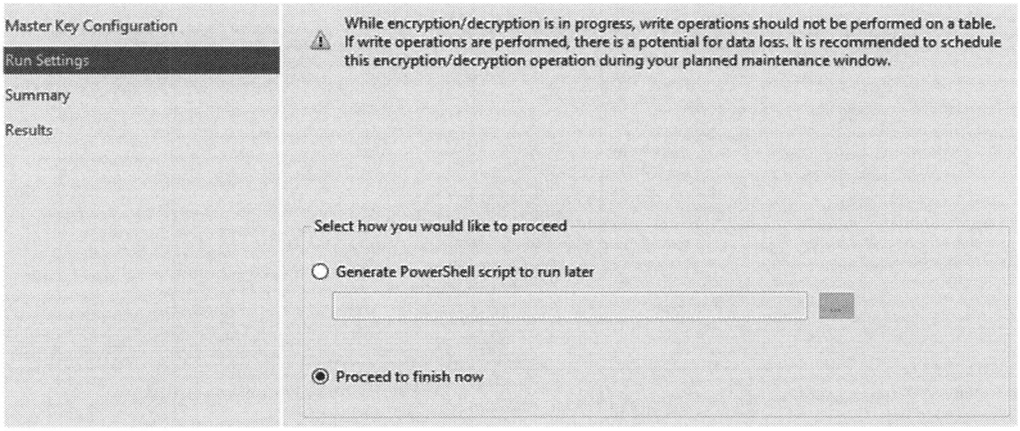

Figure 10-9. *Selecting the run settings for key generation and encryption*

Review the summary screen, where it will tell you the database you are running against and the keys that will be generated, along with the columns and encryption type on each. The summary screen is shown in Figure 10-10.

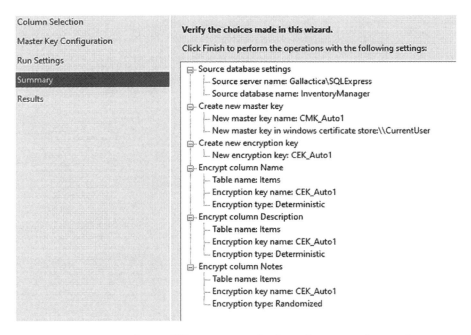

Figure 10-10. *Review what will be encrypted when the wizard completes*

Complete the wizard by hitting the Finish button, which will kick off the encryption process (see Figure 10-11).

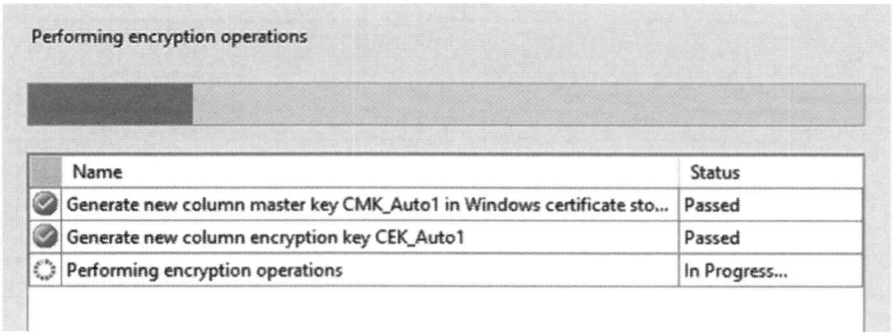

Figure 10-11. *The encryption is in process after hitting the Finish button*

The encryption process will run to completion, barring any errors (as shown in Figure 10-12).

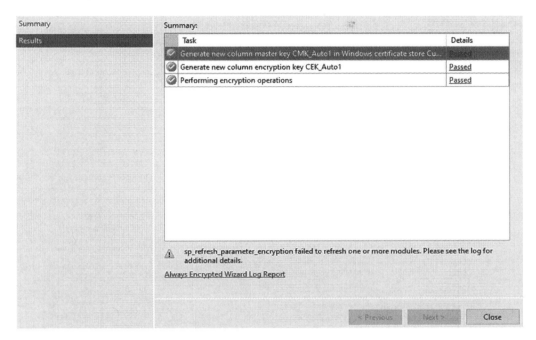

Figure 10-12. *The encryption process has completed successfully*

Step 3: Review the data

Run the same query you ran in step 2 to see the data in the Items table. The results should now include the encrypted fields as expected (see Figure 10-13).

Id	Name	Curre...	Description	IsOnSale	Notes	Purchas...
127	0x011F219796E39A3318AD5C1F065175427BF6F8DB3247608...	19.99	0x019B333868B802441A6EC339817227745BE791E5738186615C...	0	NULL	18.50
128	0x01AA0EB73A08BA9C07F22FE0158EDADF18BCFBB101D51D...	12.99	0x01F26F406E23A48B3D087378AF73B527E280CE45FE61C0B0...	1	NULL	14.50
129	0x0160853DB77B74FBA28E2E6BF796D765D8D9C688E364F80...	35.99	0x01AE6BBC8E29D3F3AA96591F8767294B104042A5D934D670...	1	NULL	44.50
130	0x0130790422CC22A92073F3A10C06FF0024EA279A3F2C0F74F...	6.99	0x019325B654EC62B822AB2085CE6CD30BA7681B38F8B9E5D5...	0	NULL	12.50
131	0x01131A9CDC0B6D8594A06632D5F220E1D6E1314B679A8E6...	23.99	0x0151B44DCC9D32EB3CA8B6DABE00FEAFA1C9C64B5D5FA8...	0	NULL	44.50
132	0x0151E326361C3097D96589EAB7636FC74A9D938E1EC96F38...	0.00	0x01E0F0CD101C11E21C4F1BBE31A6DD9BE16BAAF36E793B4...	0	NULL	0.00

Figure 10-13. *The data is encrypted, even if data was already present*

When I ran this query, I didn't have anything in the Notes column for any of the entries. It is clear, however, that the Name and Description fields that were there are now encrypted as expected. If your data is not showing as encrypted, it may be that the fields are being decrypted by SSMS based on your settings. A quick rerun of the wizard would validate the fields that are encrypted (don't reapply the wizard if you do take a look).

Step 4: Review the data in SSMS

Just to make sure our data is not corrupted, let's go ahead and double-check by configuring SSMS to be our client that will encrypt and decrypt the settings. Close your current connection to the database to ensure a new one opens.

Open a new connection dialog to your SQL Server instance on SSMS, and then select the Options << button (see Figure 10-14).

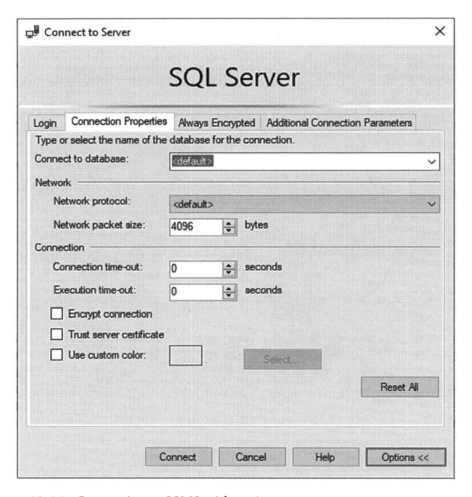

Figure 10-14. *Connecting to SSMS with options*

414

Select the Always Encrypted tab, then check the Enable Always Encrypted (column encryption) checkbox (see Figure 10-15). We are not using enclaves in our solution, but if you were, you could set the enclave information here. Also note, if you are on an older version of SSMS, you won't have the always encrypted tab.

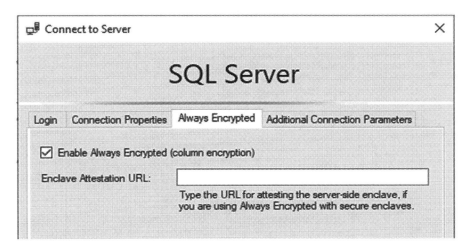

Figure 10-15. *Enabling Always Encrypted*

If you are on an older version, you will likely need to set the Additional Connection Parameters. If you are on the latest versions of SQL Server and SSMS, you will not need to. If you can't connect with just the always encrypted setting enabled, add the statement
    Column Encryption Setting=enabled
to your *Additional Connection Parameters* tab (see Figure 10-16 for clarity).

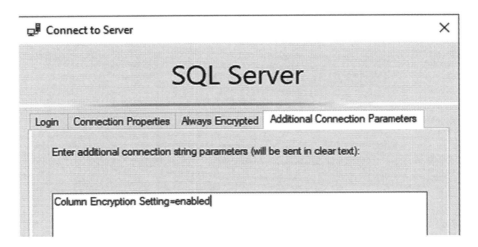

Figure 10-16. *Set the Connection Parameters, but only if on an older version of SSMS*

Once you have established a new connection with the correct settings, run the query to select the top 1000 Items. This time you'll see the data decrypted as expected.

If you added parameters in the Additional Connection Parameters tab, you may see a pop-up the first time you connect. Allow the operation to proceed as expected.

One final note here is that you may need to restart SSMS for the new settings to take effect.

Now that we've set up the always encrypted database fields, let's see what happens when we work with our application.

Step 5: Run the application

Before running the solution, we need to change one thing. We need to set our database connection string to let it know that it needs to decrypt data. To do this, add the statement Column Encryption Setting=Enabled; to the end of your current connection string in the appsettings.json file. For clarity, here is what my connection string looks like once I've added the Column Encryption Setting:

```
"ConnectionStrings": {
    "InventoryManager": "Data Source=localhost;Initial Catalog=InventoryMan
ager;Trusted_Connection=True;Column Encryption Setting=Enabled;"
}
```

Make sure to update all connection strings to use this new setting across all projects.

Return to the activity files, then **comment out all of the non-builder method calls in the Main method except for ListInventoryWithProjection**, and run the application against our encrypted database. Do you think that it will work as is? The answer is highlighted in Figure 10-17.

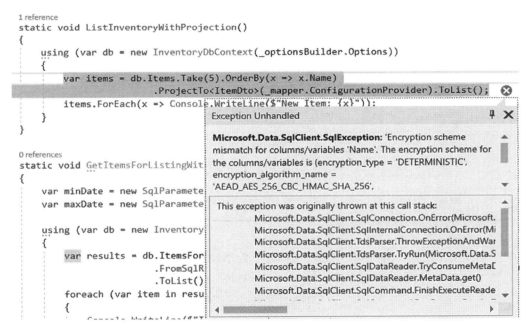

Figure 10-17. *Using Projections on encrypted data does not work*

Here, we see an exception is thrown. The reason this happens is because AlwaysEncrypted uses client-side decryption. In this case, we're trying to work against encrypted Item fields for Name and Description before decrypting them.

> If we had set up our AlwaysEncrypted solution to also include enclaves, it might
> be possible to continue using these projections, since more operations could be
> handled on the server side.

This is going to be the biggest issue with using LINQ against AlwaysEncrypted
database columns when not using enclaves. We won't be able to leverage these columns
without first decrypting the data. This is where using AlwaysEncrypted can take a big
performance hit.

In our current solution, we can still create a projection, but we can't do any ordering,
sorting, paging, or filtering until the entire result set is decrypted on the client side.

Update the query for items to use the following code:

```
var items = db.Items.OrderBy(x => x.Name).Take(5)
                .Select(x => new ItemDto {
                    Name = x.Name, Description = x.Description
                })
                .ToList();
```

If you try to run this code, you can see the ordering will not be applied in a way that
generates the results we would expect (review Figure 10-18).

```
Select Microsoft Visual Studio Debug Console
New Item: Battlefield 5            | First person shooter
New Item: Top Gun                  | I feel the need, the need for speed
New Item: The Lord of the Rings    | The fellowship of the Ring
New Item: World Of Tanks           | AN MMO WW2 Tanks First-Person Shooter
New Item: Practical Entity Framework | The book that teaches practical application with EF

C:\APressEntityFramework\Code\Chapter10\Activity1001_Using_AlwaysEncrypted\Activity1001_Using_
netcoreapp3.1\Activity1001_Using_AlwaysEncrypted.exe (process 13912) exited with code 0
```

Figure 10-18. *The output from the projection with ordering before getting to a*
decrypted list shows that the ordering is happening on encrypted data

This query result is clearly not ordered by Name, and does not get the two records that
start with "B" as part of the top five results in order.

Therefore, to this point, the only solution I've been able to come up with is to just
pull the Items using the standard query. If you think about this, it mostly makes sense,
because the data is first decrypted on the client side and then we can work with it after
decryption.

Comment out the call to the ListInventoryWithProjection method and create a new method ListInventoryWithAlwaysEncrypted. In the new method, add the following code:

```
static void ListInventoryWithAlwaysEncrypted()
{
    using (var db = new InventoryDbContext(_optionsBuilder.Options))
    {

        var theItems = db.Items.ToList().OrderBy(x => x.Name).Take(5);
        var items = _mapper.Map<List<ItemDto>>(theItems);
        items.ForEach(x => Console.WriteLine($"New Item: {x}"));
    }
}
```

This code generates the following output when run (review Figure 10-19).

```
New Item: Batman Begins             | Why do we fall, Bruce?
New Item: Battlefield 5             | First person shooter
New Item: Practical Entity Framework | The book that teaches practical application with EF
New Item: The Lord of the Rings     | The fellowship of the Ring
New Item: Top Gun                   | I feel the need, the need for speed
```

Figure 10-19. *The output is correct, but only when we first decrypt everything and then perform the ordering and take operations*

Step 6: Fix the Method to Get the Items for Listing using LINQ

Uncomment the GetItemsForListingLinq method, and run the application to reveal that this method will also fail. To make the GetItemsForListingLinq method work, we need to do a couple of things. First, we must get the Items to a list right away before performing the Select. Once that works, we could run the application, but we'll still see an error. Any thoughts on what it might be?

The projection has Category information in it. In the original projection, we can get the category information only when needed. With AlwaysEncrypted on, we first need to get the information up front, and then we can project.

So the two changes to this code are to include a call to ToList early, but also we must include the Category with an Include statement. Change the results line in the GetItemsForListingLinq method to the following code:

```
var results = db.Items.Include(x => x.Category).ToList().Select(x => new
GetItemsForListingWithDateDto
```

When executed, this query will include the category and get the data to the list, and then we can work in memory with the decrypted objects to further project them. For clarity, the new results query should look as is shown in Figure 10-20.

```
using (var db = new InventoryDbContext(_optionsBuilder.Options))
{
    var results = db.Items.Include(x => x.Category).ToList()
                     .Select(x => new GetItemsForListingWithDateDto
    {
        CreatedDate = x.CreatedDate,
        CategoryName = x.Category.Name,
        Description = x.Description,
        IsActive = x.IsActive,
        IsDeleted = x.IsDeleted,
        Name = x.Name,
        Notes = x.Notes
    }).Where(x => x.CreatedDate >= minDateValue && x.CreatedDate <= maxDateValue)
        .OrderBy(y => y.CategoryName).ThenBy(z => z.Name).ToList();

    foreach (var item in results)
    {
        Console.WriteLine($"ITEM {item.CategoryName}| {item.Name} - {item.Description}");
    }
}
```

Figure 10-20. *The updated GetItemsForListingLinq method contains the Include and ToList statements early in the LINQ query*

And running the solution gets us the results we are expecting without errors.

Step 7: Turn on other method calls

To complete the coding portion of this activity, uncomment the code for all method calls in the Main method except ListInventory, ListInventoryWithProjection, and AllActiveItemsPipeDelimitedString. Run the program to get similar results to what is shown in Figure 10-21.

```
New Item: Batman Begins          | Why do we fall, Bruce?
New Item: Battlefield 5          | First person shooter
New Item: Practical Entity Framework | The book that teaches practical application with EF
New Item: The Lord of the Rings  | The fellowship of the Ring
New Item: Top Gun                | I feel the need, the need for speed
ITEM Top Gun - I feel the need, the need for speed
ITEM Batman Begins - Why do we fall, Bruce?
ITEM Practical Entity Framework - The book that teaches practical application with EF
ITEM The Lord of the Rings - The fellowship of the Ring
ITEM Battlefield 5 - First person shooter
ITEM World Of Tanks - AN MMO WW2 Tanks First-Person Shooter
New Item] 127    |Top Gun                           |1   |18.50
New Item] 128    |Batman Begins                     |4   |58.00
New Item] 129    |Practical Entity Framework        |100 |4450.00
New Item] 130    |The Lord of the Rings             |7   |87.50
New Item] 131    |Battlefield 5                     |17  |756.50
New Item] 132    |World Of Tanks                    |1   |0.00
New Item] 127    |Top Gun                           |Comedy
New Item] 128    |Batman Begins                     |Sci/Fi
New Item] 128    |Batman Begins                     |Drama
New Item] 129    |Practical Entity Framework        |
New Item] 130    |The Lord of the Rings             |Sci/Fi
New Item] 130    |The Lord of the Rings             |Fantasy
New Item] 131    |Battlefield 5                     |Sci/Fi
New Item] 132    |World Of Tanks                    |
ITEM Books| Practical Entity Framework - The book that teaches practical application with EF
ITEM Books| The Lord of the Rings - The fellowship of the Ring
ITEM Games| Battlefield 5 - First person shooter
ITEM Games| World Of Tanks - AN MMO WW2 Tanks First-Person Shooter
ITEM Movies| Batman Begins - Why do we fall, Bruce?
ITEM Movies| Top Gun - I feel the need, the need for speed
Movies | Blue
Books | Red
Games | Green

C:\APressEntityFramework\Code\Chapter10\Activity1001_Using_AlwaysEncrypted\Activity1001_Using_A
```

Figure 10-21. *The final output with data being returned from the database, decrypted, then projected, and ordered*

You might have noted that we left a few methods out here. We'll address other issues as we do some cleanup later in the book. If you're really wanting to clean them up, the ListInventory and ListInventoryWithProjection methods would just require a call to ToList early in the chain so that ordering and taking a limited number can happen as expected. The stored procedure will not work in our current setup, so the options are to not sort or filter in the stored procedure and handle it client side or just get the data client side and handle sorting and filtering on the client.

Final thoughts on activity 1001

In this activity, we saw how easy it was to set up the AlwaysEncrypted database encryption on our InventoryManager database. Unfortunately, we also saw that once we have set up the always encrypted database columns, we must work with our queries

421

in a manner that first retrieves the results and decrypts them before performing any ordering, filtering, or paging. As we've learned in previous chapters, this is not the most efficient way to work with LINQ to generate result sets.

Activity 1002: Using transparent data encryption

While it is more likely that you will encounter the need to use TDE in an older EF6 project, it is entirely possible to implement TDE in .Net Core as well. Therefore, we'll be using our .Net Core project that connects to the AdventureWorks database to complete this activity. Regardless of the version of EF where we are implementing this solution, the real meat of this activity will happen at the database level, with keys generated, column changes (which could/will be a code-first change), and then the heavy use of stored procedures to work with the data for read and write operations after fields are encrypted.

A quick review of TDE vs. AlwaysEncrypted

As a review of what we've already covered, where `AlwaysEncrypted` worked in the client side with encryption, sending encrypted data over the wire and simply storing the encrypted values in the database, the TDE solution is going to be entirely server side on the database; with keys specific to the database, encryption handled after data is received before insert/update and before sending back to the client. All of the data being decrypted at the database means plain-text values going across the wire without additional configuration.

How TDE can be a better choice for your solutions

Where TDE will really shine is going to be in overall performance, as compared to the `AlwaysEncrypted` solution. In TDE, with the data encryption/decryption happening at the database in procedures, everything will be in an execution plan, and there won't be any issues with projecting data on the client side as the data will already be well formed before being sent back to the client – often as the exact shape of the Model or DTO that the client needs.

Step 1: Get set up

To begin, grab a copy of the `Activity1002_Using_Transparent_Data_Encryption_Starter.zip` files, extract them, double-check your connection string, and make sure that you have the *AdventureWorks* database set up. Run an `update-database` command to make sure the migrations are up to date on your machine. Additionally, it will likely be a good idea to run an add-migration to make sure you don't have any pending model/database changes. If the migration is clear, just delete it. If not, consider just running it to get your database set up. If you don't have an implementation of *AdventureWorks* up and running on your system, refer back to the opening chapters of this book for getting set up with *AdventureWorks*.

As an alternative to using the starter files, it would be possible to continue working with files as of the end of activity 0901. If you desire to build your own starter pack, please use the EF_Activity001 and InventoryHelpers projects so you will be set up to work against the AdventureWorks database with migrations.

Run the program to make sure it works as expected before proceeding. Output should be similar to what is shown in Figure 10-22.

```
Would you like to view all salespeople using projections? [y/n]
n
Would you like to view the sales report?
y
What is the minimum amount of sales?
20500
BID: 285 |                      Abbas, Syed|                      |172524.4512 | Orders: 16 |Products Sold: 825
BID: 287 |                      Alberts, Amy|                      |519905.9320 | Orders: 39 |Products Sold: 2012
BID: 280 |              Ansman-Wolfe, Pamela|             Northwest|1352577.1325 | Orders: 95 |Products Sold: 7360
BID: 275 |                   Blythe, Michael|      Northeast,Central|3763178.1787 | Orders: 450 |Products Sold: 23058
BID: 283 |                   Campbell, David|             Northwest|1573012.9383 | Orders: 189 |Products Sold: 8172
BID: 277 |                   Carson, Jillian|      Central,Northeast|3189418.3662 | Orders: 473 |Products Sold: 27051
BID: 281 |                        Ito, Shu|              Southwest|2458535.6169 | Orders: 242 |Products Sold: 15397
BID: 274 |                   Jiang, Stephen|                      |559697.5639 | Orders: 48 |Products Sold: 3095
BID: 284 |               Mensa-Annan, Tete|             Northwest|1576562.1966 | Orders: 140 |Products Sold: 5650
BID: 276 |                  Mitchell, Linda|             Southwest|4251368.5497 | Orders: 418 |Products Sold: 27229
BID: 289 |                       Pak, Jae|                Canada|4116871.2277 | Orders: 348 |Products Sold: 26231
BID: 279 |                     Reiter, Tsvi|             Southeast|2315185.6110 | Orders: 429 |Products Sold: 16431
BID: 282 |                   Saraiva, José| Canada,United Kingdom|2604540.7172 | Orders: 271 |Products Sold: 15220
BID: 286 |                   Tsoflias, Lynn|             Australia|1421810.9242 | Orders: 109 |Products Sold: 4123
BID: 288 |                   Valdez, Rachel|               Germany|1827066.7118 | Orders: 130 |Products Sold: 7033
BID: 278 |                  Vargas, Garrett|                Canada|1453719.4653 | Orders: 234 |Products Sold: 11544
BID: 290 |Varkey Chudukatil, Ranjit|                France|3121616.3202 | Orders: 175 |Products Sold: 14085

C:\APressEntityFramework\Code\Chapter10\Activity1002_Using_TransparentDataEncryption\Activity1002_Using_Transpar
ncryption\bin\Debug\netcoreapp3.1\Activity1002_Using_TransparentDataEncryption.exe (process 6596) exited with co
```

Figure 10-22. *The initial output is similar to the output from the end of activity 0901*

Step 2: Discuss the TDE migration strategy, including backup

This migration strategy will work for any database that has existing data where you need to implement TDE to protect your data at rest. Our solution is an *EFCore* implementation, and we have a lot of data. Your solution in the real world is likely similar, even if it's in an *EF6* solution.

The steps we need to consider for migration of existing data to encrypted data at rest with TDE are as follows:

- First, back up the existing data to another column to hold the data during encryption procedures for each column to be encrypted.

- Second, back up all of the data that will eventually be encrypted.

- Third, create all of the keys and certificates necessary to encrypt and decrypt data with TDE.

- Fourth, drop any constraints on the target columns.

- Fifth, change the column type for the columns to be encrypted to `varbinary(max)`. This will destroy the existing data in those columns. Constraints will no longer be possible once the column is encrypted.

- Sixth, perform a transformation operation where the backup column is encrypted and inserted into the original column.

- Seventh, delete the backup column(s) from the table. Before you do this, make sure to fully document the column type and length. This will be critical during decryption, and if you don't keep a record of it, you'll have to review backups or go through the migrations or scripts to see what they were before.

- Finally, for every operation around the table with encrypted data, create the Insert, Update, and Read procedures that will be necessary to work with plain-text data inserted to an encrypted column or encrypted data returned to a plain-text result set.

Sounds fairly straightforward, right? It's actually not too bad. We'll walk through these steps together. There is one final note to consider, however. If you are working through the chapters of this book out of order, there are other chapters that depend on the *AdventureWorks* database to be set up and not have encrypted columns. While you could likely just restore the database at any point from the original download, you may wish to make a backup of the database before performing the remaining steps in this activity to avoid conflicts with other chapters.

If you are working on an actual database for your work or personal projects, I would recommend backing everything up before starting, in the off chance that something goes awry.

If at any point you want to create a backup of your database, simply right-click the database in SSMS and select Tasks ➤ Back Up (see Figure 10-23).

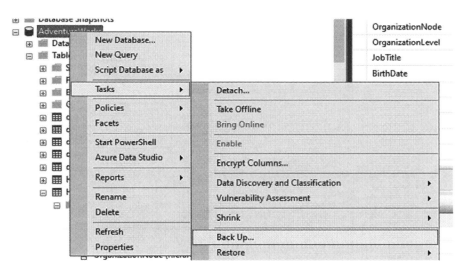

Figure 10-23. *Backing up the database*

Perform a full, copy-only backup and store the file in a convenient location for easy recovery (as shown in Figure 10-24).

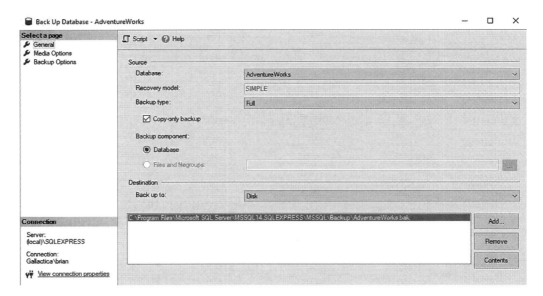

Figure 10-24. *Perform a full, copy-only backup to the default file location for backups*

Clicking OK will execute the backup (see Figure 10-25).

Figure 10-25. *The backup is completed successfully*

Step 3: Begin the migration strategy

Referring to the preceding steps, the first thing we want to do is perform a migration to add backup columns for every field we want to encrypt.

While a real-world scenario would likely have many tables and columns to encrypt or decrypt, we're going to home in on the HumanResources.Employee table in the *AdventureWorks* database. You should have no problem extrapolating what we learn from this activity to other tables and fields if you want to practice more or when you eventually are implementing your real-world solutions.

The columns we want to encrypt will be

- NationalIDNumber

- JobTitle

- BirthDate

- MaritalStatus

- Gender

- HireDate

We could do other fields and other tables, but this will be where we stop for this activity. One bummer about these fields is that there isn't a decimal field to encrypt/decrypt in this result set, but the decryption strategy will be the same as the others, just if you have a decimal field to encrypt/decrypt, don't forget to convert to the correct type and size as you decrypt.

For the first part of the strategy, let's add the backup fields to the model. We could do this by just writing a script and including it in the migration. The choice is yours on how you would like to proceed. If using a script, another thing you could consider is just selecting the whole table into a backup table and then encrypting from a select on that table. There are many solutions available for the migration.

In our example, I'm going to use full database migrations so that there is a small chance I could roll it back without too many issues. Again, you could write manual rollback scripts and just use them to protect your data.

If you have not validated that you have no pending migrations, before continuing, you should try to add a migration and make sure it is blank. If not blank, evaluate and run if there are no issues. If the migration is blank as expected, run the Remove-Migration command.

Add the following code to the bottom of the HumanResources.Employee model (the file is named Employee.cs and it's located in the EF_Activity001 project. The file has annotations for [Table("Employee", Schema = "HumanResources")]):

```
[StringLength(15)]
public string NationalIDNumberBackup { get; set; }
[StringLength(50)]
public string JobTitleBackup { get; set; }
[Column(TypeName = "date")]
public DateTime BirthDateBackup { get; set; }

[StringLength(1)]
public string MaritalStatusBackup { get; set; }

[Required]
[StringLength(1)]
public string GenderBackup { get; set; }

[Column(TypeName = "date")]
public DateTime HireDateBackup { get; set; }
```

Add a migration to update the table using the command add-migration EncryptionMigration_Step1. After the migration runs, validate that it only contains the expected fields. When the migration generates, some of the fields may be set to nullable: false and have a default value set on them. As long as the field we are backing up is also not nullable, this should not be an issue. If the field that is being backed up allows null, but the backup field does not, then override the definition in the migration to set the value to nullable: true and remove the default value. For example, in my version, BirthDate, Gender, and HireDate are all required fields. Figure 10-26 shows a sample of what the migration should look like.

```
1 reference
public partial class EncryptionMigration_Step1 : Migration
{
    1 reference
    protected override void Up(MigrationBuilder migrationBuilder)
    {
        migrationBuilder.AddColumn<DateTime>(
            name: "BirthDateBackup",
            schema: "HumanResources",
            table: "Employee",
            type: "date",
            nullable: false,
            defaultValue: new DateTime(1, 1, 1, 0, 0, 0, 0, DateTimeKind.Unspecified));

        migrationBuilder.AddColumn<string>(
            name: "GenderBackup",
            schema: "HumanResources",
            table: "Employee",
            maxLength: 1,
            nullable: false,
            defaultValue: "");

        migrationBuilder.AddColumn<DateTime>(
            name: "HireDateBackup",
            schema: "HumanResources",
            table: "Employee",
            type: "date",
            nullable: false,
            defaultValue: new DateTime(1, 1, 1, 0, 0, 0, 0, DateTimeKind.Unspecified));

        migrationBuilder.AddColumn<string>(
            name: "JobTitleBackup",
```

Figure 10-26. *The first migration is adding columns to store the original field data to ensure we don't lose data during this process*

If you were running this process against an EF6 implementation, the migration would look a bit more succinct, but would still accomplish the same goal of adding columns.

Run the update-database command to add the backup columns to the database as shown in Figure 10-27.

```
PM> update-database
Specify the '-Verbose' flag to view the SQL statements being applied to the target database.
Applying explicit migrations: [202002190627009_EncryptionMigration_Step1].
Applying explicit migration: 202002190627009_EncryptionMigration_Step1.
Running Seed method.
PM>
```

Figure 10-27. *The database is updated to have the backup columns*

Step 4: Run a script to back up the data for the target columns

Begin by adding a new migration using the command add-migration
EncryptionMigration_Step2_BackupData.

Once the migration is created, either add some inline T-SQL to back up the table data
or you could also implement a file-management solution like we've seen earlier in the
text. For this activity, and for purposes of brevity, we'll just do our scripting within the
migration files.

In the Up method of the migration, add the following code:

```
migrationBuilder.Sql(@"UPDATE [HumanResources].[Employee]
    SET [NationalIDNumberBackup] = [NationalIDNumber]
        ,[JobTitleBackup] = [JobTitle]
        ,[BirthDateBackup] = [BirthDate]
        ,[MaritalStatusBackup] = [MaritalStatus]
        ,[GenderBackup] = [Gender]
        ,[HireDateBackup] = [HireDate]"
);
```

For this migration, there is nothing to do in the down method. If we need to roll back,
we'll have to manually intervene to save our data.

Next, run the update-database command to execute the script (see Figure 10-28).

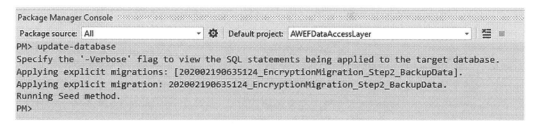

Figure 10-28. Updating the database runs the script

Finally, double-check your database table to make sure that the data migrated as expected. Use a query similar to the following to validate your data was copied correctly during the migration:

```
SELECT [NationalIDNumber],[NationalIDNumberBackup],
    [JobTitle] ,[JobTitleBackup],
    [BirthDate] ,[BirthDateBackup],
    [MaritalStatus] ,[MaritalStatusBackup],
    [Gender],[GenderBackup],
    [HireDate],[HireDateBackup]
FROM [AdventureWorks].[HumanResources].[Employee]
```

For clarity, the results should look similar to what is shown in Figure 10-29.

```
SELECT [NationalIDNumber],[NationalIDNumberBackup],
    [JobTitle] ,[JobTitleBackup],
    [BirthDate] ,[BirthDateBackup],
    [MaritalStatus] ,[MaritalStatusBackup],
    [Gender],[GenderBackup],
    [HireDate],[HireDateBackup]
FROM [AdventureWorks].[HumanResources].[Employee]
```

	NationalIDNumber	NationalIDNumberBackup	Job Title	Job Title Backup	Birth Date	Birth Date Backup
1	295847284	295847284	Chief Executive Officer	Chief Executive Officer	1969-01-...	1969-01-29
2	245797967	245797967	Vice President of Engineering	Vice President of Engineering	1971-08-...	1971-08-01
3	509647174	509647174	Engineering Manager	Engineering Manager	1974-11-...	1974-11-12
4	112457891	112457891	Senior Tool Designer	Senior Tool Designer	1974-12-...	1974-12-23
5	695256908	695256908	Design Engineer	Design Engineer	1952-09-...	1952-09-27
6	998320692	998320692	Design Engineer	Design Engineer	1959-03-...	1959-03-11

Figure 10-29. Verifying the data was backed up successfully

Step 5: Create a new script to generate the database keys

In order to make the database keys successfully, you'll need to have three things. First, you'll need a certificate. Second, you'll need to create the symmetric keys. Finally, you'll need a place to back up your keys. You'll also need a strong password that can be used for the keys. An important note is that anyone that is executing the migration to create the scripts will need to make sure to have the hard-coded file path in place for storage of local backup certificates and keys. Another consideration would be a personal *KeyVault* at *Azure*.

Make sure to validate that the physical drive contains the proper folder for storing backups of the certificates and keys generated by the migration script for creating encryption keys.

Begin by validating the folder for backup. For this activity, a suggestion could be C:\Data\DatabaseKeys. In the real world, you'll want to do something with them to keep them secure after generation. Create the folder C:\Data\DatabaseKeys or a similar folder of your choosing for storing the physical key files (review Figure 10-30).

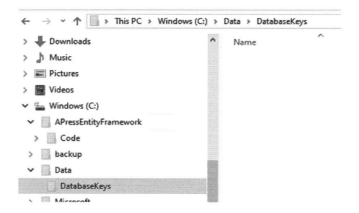

Figure 10-30. *The folder to store the database keys after generation*

Once the storage location is in place, create a new migration by running the command add-migration EncryptionMigration_Step3_CertsAndKeysGeneration.

After the migration is created, we need to add four statements for execution into the Up method, in the exact order listed as follows (you should use a better password, but make sure you can remember it):

```
migrationBuilder.Sql(@"IF NOT EXISTS (SELECT *
        FROM sys.symmetric_keys WHERE symmetric_key_id = 101)
    BEGIN
        CREATE MASTER KEY ENCRYPTION BY PASSWORD = 'Password#123'
    END");

migrationBuilder.Sql(@"CREATE CERTIFICATE AW_tdeCert
        WITH SUBJECT = 'AdventureWorks TDE Certificate'");

migrationBuilder.Sql(@"BACKUP CERTIFICATE AW_tdeCert TO
        FILE = 'C:\Data\DatabaseKeys\AW_tdeCert.crt'
    WITH PRIVATE KEY
    (
        FILE = 'C:\Data\DatabaseKeys\AW_tdeCert_PrivateKey.crt',
        ENCRYPTION BY PASSWORD = 'Password#123'
    )");

migrationBuilder.Sql(@"CREATE SYMMETRIC KEY AW_ColumnKey
                        WITH ALGORITHM = AES_256
                        ENCRYPTION BY CERTIFICATE AW_tdeCert;
                    ");
```

Once again, we won't be doing anything in the Down method for this migration.

With all of this in place, run the update-database command to execute the certificate generation (as in Figure 10-31).

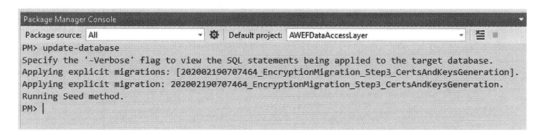

Figure 10-31. The migration is applied as expected

Now validate that the keys are generated in the database and in the file store.

To validate, open SSMS and expand the Security folder under the database, and then look at Certificates and Symmetric Keys. The keys we created should be there. You may need to refresh your database if you already had SSMS open. Provided the migration worked as expected, your database should look similar to what is shown in Figure 10-32.

Figure 10-32. *The keys are generated after the migration is applied*

Next, look at the folder on the physical drive to see that the key and cert are backed up as expected (review Figure 10-33).

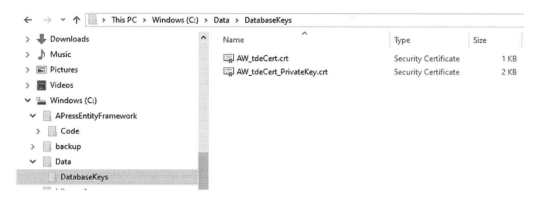

Figure 10-33. *The certificates are backed up on the physical drive as expected*

Store your keys somewhere secure.

Step 6: Drop the constraints and indexes on the target columns

Now that we're ready to encrypt data and we have our target column data backed up, we need to set the columns that we're using in our database to store the encrypted data.

First, we must drop all the constraints and indexes on the fields that will be changing. We can do that easily with a script.

If you miss one along the way, just update your script file, and then run the drop manually. Otherwise, make sure to change this script to be idempotent.

Add a new migration with the command `add-migration EncryptionMigration_Step4_DropConstraints`. In this migration, add a `SQLResource` to script the constraints for dropping. We have a bunch of check constraints to drop on each of these columns. You may want to keep a record of what they do as you may want to enforce these constraints in the procedures that insert and/or update data in the future.

In the migration's Up command, we need to add drop statements to get rid of all constraints on the fields we are encrypting. For this reason, open your HumanResources. Employee table in SSMS and review the Constraints folder. Your constraints will have a unique name, so you will not simply be able to use the same script as me for three of your statements. Review Figure 10-34 for more information.

Figure 10-34. *The constraints on the Employee table have some unique identifiers that will be unique to your database implementation*

Add the following migration builder statements to your Up method to remove the constraints and indexes on fields we will be encrypting:

```
migrationBuilder.Sql(@"ALTER TABLE[HumanResources].[Employee]
      DROP CONSTRAINT[CK_Employee_MaritalStatus]");

migrationBuilder.Sql(@"ALTER TABLE[HumanResources].[Employee]
      DROP CONSTRAINT[CK_Employee_HireDate]");

migrationBuilder.Sql(@"ALTER TABLE[HumanResources].[Employee]
      DROP CONSTRAINT[CK_Employee_Gender]");
```

```
migrationBuilder.Sql(@"ALTER TABLE[HumanResources].[Employee]
        DROP CONSTRAINT[CK_Employee_BirthDate]");

migrationBuilder.DropIndex(
        name: "AK_Employee_NationalIDNumber",
        schema: "HumanResources",
        table: "Employee");
```

Technically, we *should* put the scripts in place to recreate these indexes in the Down method. For brevity, we'll skip it this time. If you want to do this correctly, just right-click each constraint and index we are dropping, script as create to a new query window, and use that generated script in `migrationBuilder.Sql(@"code");` statements. Remember to set a new statement anytime a GO command is encountered.

Run the `update-database` command to update the database and then validate that the constraints have been dropped from the database by refreshing your database in SSMS and reviewing the existing constraints (see Figure 10-35).

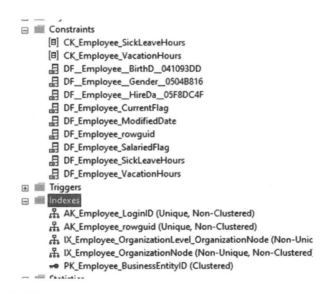

Figure 10-35. *Validating that the constraints are gone*

Step 7: Change the data type for target columns to varbinary(max) byte[ ]

For the next change, we're going to modify the data for the employees table. We need to change all fields to varbinary(max) in the database that will hold encrypted data. When we do this, the data will be lost from these target columns. Since we're going to be performing destructive changes on the table, it is critical that you have previously run the step where data was backed up to another field. If for some reason you skipped that step, go back now and back up your data.

Return to the HumanResources.Employee model, and change the DataType for all of the targeted columns we're encrypting to byte[ ] and remove any length constraints and column type mappings from the columns (keep required constraints, and remember if any fields in your solution are mapped such as NationalIdNumber => NationalIDNumber as you may wish to restore those mappings in the scripts you will use later to get the data):

```
[Required]
public byte[] NationalIdnumber { get; set; }

//other fields left alone here

[Required]
public byte[] JobTitle { get; set; }
public byte[] BirthDate { get; set; }
[Required]
public byte[] MaritalStatus { get; set; }
[Required]
public byte[] Gender { get; set; }
public byte[] HireDate { get; set; }
```

If you aren't using migrations in your solution, simply create a script at this step that alters the table to set all the target columns to be type varbinary(max).

Look into the AdventureWorksContext. Find the line of code modelBuilder.Entity<Employee>(entity =>. Under this entity, remove the mapping that demands an index for the national id number if it still exists.

```
entity.HasIndex(e => e.NationalIdnumber)
                .HasName("AK_Employee_NationalIDNumber")
                .IsUnique();
```

If you don't remove this, but it was already removed from the database, your next migration may not run correctly.

Next, add a new migration with the command add-migration Encryption_Step5_ ChangeColumnDataTypes.

If the first statement of the generated migration is still trying to drop the index AK_ Employee_NationalIDNumber, then go into SSMS and run the following statement to ensure the index does not exist:

```
DROP INDEX [AK_Employee_NationalIDNumber] ON [HumanResources].[Employee]
```

Then manually remove the statement to drop the index from your migration.

After the migration is created as expected, run the update-database command to change the data types on the table. This will also rename the NationalIDNumber column to NationalIdNumber since we removed the mapping in the model.

Also remember at this point, if your solution relies on these columns, everything that touches them will need to be modified after this operation to restore your system to working order.

At this point, we get an error for not being able to convert an nvarchar field to a binary field. The error tells us to fix it, we need to use the CONVERT function (see Figure 10-36).

```
ClientConnectionId:5eef348b-a238-4d36-8dbc-780c9d4f6cd2
Error Number:257,State:3,Class:16
Implicit conversion from data type nvarchar to varbinary(max) is not allowed. Use the CONVERT function to run this query.
PM>
```

Figure 10-36. *The migration fails to convert*

To fix this, we need to do a manual update of our migration. It's not ideal, but it does work.

In the migration, for every field that was currently `nvarchar`, we need to do a temp column and then convert that to the real column as `binary`. It will look like this:

```
migrationBuilder.AddColumn<byte[]>(
    name: "NationalIdnumberTemp",
    schema: "HumanResources",
    table: "Employee",
    nullable: true,
    comment: "Unique national identification number such as a social
             security number.");
migrationBuilder.Sql(@"UPDATE HumanResources.Employee SET
NationalIdnumberTemp = CONVERT(varbinary, NationalIdNumber)");
migrationBuilder.DropColumn("NationalIdNumber", "Employee",
"HumanResources");
migrationBuilder.RenameColumn(
    name: "NationalIdnumberTemp",
    schema: "HumanResources",
    table: "Employee",
    newName: "NationalIdnumber");
```

Where the first step is to add a temp column, then convert the existing column into the temp column. Then drop the original column, and finally, rename the temp column to the original column. Do the same for `Gender`, `MaritalStatus`, and `JobTitle`.

Marital Status:

```
migrationBuilder.AddColumn<byte[]>(
    name: "MaritalStatusTemp",
    schema: "HumanResources",
    table: "Employee",
    nullable: true,
    comment: "M = Married, S = Single");
migrationBuilder.Sql(@"UPDATE HumanResources.Employee SET MaritalStatusTemp
= CONVERT(varbinary, MaritalStatus)");
migrationBuilder.DropColumn("MaritalStatus", "Employee", "HumanResources");
migrationBuilder.RenameColumn(
    name: "MaritalStatusTemp",
    schema: "HumanResources",
```

```
    table: "Employee",
    newName: "MaritalStatus");
```

Job Title:

```
migrationBuilder.AddColumn<byte[]>(
    name: "JobTitleTemp",
    schema: "HumanResources",
    table: "Employee",
    nullable: true,
    comment: "Work title such as Buyer or Sales Representative.");
migrationBuilder.Sql(@"UPDATE HumanResources.Employee SET JobTitleTemp =
CONVERT(varbinary, JobTitle)");
migrationBuilder.DropColumn("JobTitle", "Employee", "HumanResources");
migrationBuilder.RenameColumn(
    name: "JobTitleTemp",
    schema: "HumanResources",
    table: "Employee",
    newName: "JobTitle");
```

Gender:

```
migrationBuilder.AddColumn<byte[]>(
    name: "GenderTemp",
    schema: "HumanResources",
    table: "Employee",
    nullable: true,
    comment: "M = Male, F = Female");
migrationBuilder.Sql(@"UPDATE HumanResources.Employee SET GenderTemp =
CONVERT(varbinary, Gender)");
migrationBuilder.DropColumn("Gender", "Employee", "HumanResources");
migrationBuilder.RenameColumn(
    name: "GenderTemp",
    schema: "HumanResources",
    table: "Employee",
    newName: "Gender");
```

The DateTime columns will also throw errors, as would other types, so make sure to update them to use the same swap operations as well:

HireDate:

```
migrationBuilder.AddColumn<byte[]>(
    name: "HireDateTemp",
    schema: "HumanResources",
    table: "Employee",
    nullable: true,
    comment: "Employee hired on this date.");
migrationBuilder.Sql(@"UPDATE HumanResources.Employee SET HireDateTemp =
CONVERT(varbinary, HireDate)");
migrationBuilder.DropColumn("HireDate", "Employee", "HumanResources");
migrationBuilder.RenameColumn(
    name: "HireDateTemp",
    schema: "HumanResources",
    table: "Employee",
    newName: "HireDate");
```

BirthDate:

```
migrationBuilder.AddColumn<byte[]>(
    name: "BirthDateTemp",
    schema: "HumanResources",
    table: "Employee",
    nullable: true,
    comment: "Date of birth.");
migrationBuilder.Sql(@"UPDATE HumanResources.Employee SET BirthDateTemp =
CONVERT(varbinary, BirthDate)");
migrationBuilder.DropColumn("BirthDate", "Employee", "HumanResources");
migrationBuilder.RenameColumn(
    name: "BirthDateTemp",
    schema: "HumanResources",
    table: "Employee",
    newName: "BirthDate");
```

Furthermore, it is likely the Down method won't work for us at this point, so let's comment the code out rather than spend time remapping all of the data types.

If you wanted to ensure that works, you could try to reverse the process of going from a byte[] back to the original type. This would require a similar swapping algorithm.

Run the update-database command. This should work as expected (review Figure 10-37).

```
PM> update-database
Build started...
Build succeeded.
Applying migration '20200522224104_Encryption_Step5_ChangeColumnDataTypes'.
Done.
PM>
```

Figure 10-37. *The migration updates as expected*

And validation of the columns in the database shows that we have gotten our data columns migrated to store encrypted data as shown in Figure 10-38.

Figure 10-38. *The columns are converted as expected*

One last thing at this step is to run another add-migration to make sure that we don't have any bleed from our last migration since we did alter it overall. Run the add-migration make-sure-no-bleed command. Once that comes up empty, go ahead and run the command remove-migration.

Use SSMS to validate that data columns are showing as encrypted by running the query SELECT * FROM HumanResources.Employee. Some fields should have cryptic values like 0x43006800690065006600200004500780065006300750074006900760076006500.

Further validate that the data is not yet ready by running the following script in a new query window:

```
OPEN SYMMETRIC KEY AW_ColumnKey
DECRYPTION BY CERTIFICATE AW_tdeCert;

SELECT BusinessEntityID, LoginID,
ISNULL(CONVERT(nvarchar(15), decryptbykey([NationalIDNumber])), '')
[NationalIdNumber], [NationalIDNumberBackup],
ISNULL(CONVERT(nvarchar(50), decryptbykey([JobTitle])), '') [JobTitle],
[JobTitleBackup],
ISNULL(CONVERT(DateTime, decryptbykey([BirthDate])), null) [BirthDate],
[BirthDateBackup],
ISNULL(CONVERT(nvarchar(1), decryptbykey([MaritalStatus])),'')
[MaritalStatus] ,[MaritalStatusBackup],
ISNULL(CONVERT(nvarchar(1), decryptbykey([Gender])),'')
[Gender],[GenderBackup],
ISNULL(CONVERT(datetime, decryptbykey([HireDate])), null)
HireDate,[HireDateBackup]
FROM [AdventureWorks].[HumanResources].[Employee]

CLOSE ALL SYMMETRIC KEYS
```

The script we just ran shows that we have successfully encrypted the columns, but we did lose the data. Good thing we have everything backed up. Now we just need to encrypt the data into the correct columns.

Step 8: Encrypt the backup data into the new columns

For this step, we're going to run a migration that will encrypt the varchar data and datetime data that we've stored in backup columns and put it into the varbinary columns that are now holding the encrypted data.

Create a new migration using the command add-migration EncryptionMigration_ Step6_EncryptBackupDataIntoOriginalColumns.

In the Up method of the migration, we're going to run some custom SQL to move our backup data into the destination columns. To do this, we're going to need to encrypt the data.

The important moving pieces of this process will be to first open the symmetric key to allow the encryption process to take place, as well as naming the certificate to use for decryption. In the quick check we did at the end of the last step, we used the same process. We also set the decryption to take place using a built-in function called decryptByKey. In this method, we'll do the inverse where we're encrypting, using a function called encryptByKey.

The simple commands to open and close the keys wrap the statements are OPEN SYMMETRIC KEY AW_ColumnKey

DECRYPTION BY CERTIFICATE AW_tdeCert; to open the encryption and CLOSE ALL SYMMETRIC KEYS to end the ability to use the keys for encryption and decryption.

To get our script in place, go to the Up method in the migration and add the following code:

```
migrationBuilder.Sql(@"OPEN SYMMETRIC KEY AW_ColumnKey
    DECRYPTION BY CERTIFICATE AW_tdeCert;

UPDATE [HumanResources].[Employee]
    SET [NationalIDNumber] = encryptByKey(Key_GUID('AW_ColumnKey'),
    CONVERT(varbinary(max), [NationalIDNumberBackup]))
        ,[JobTitle] = encryptByKey(Key_GUID('AW_ColumnKey'),
        CONVERT(varbinary(max), [JobTitleBackup]))
        ,[BirthDate] = encryptByKey(Key_GUID('AW_ColumnKey'),
        CONVERT(varbinary(max), [BirthDateBackup]))
        ,[MaritalStatus] = encryptByKey(Key_GUID('AW_ColumnKey'),
        CONVERT(varbinary(max), [MaritalStatusBackup]))
```

```
      ,[Gender] = encryptByKey(Key_GUID('AW_ColumnKey'),
      CONVERT(varbinary(max), [GenderBackup]))
      ,[HireDate] = encryptByKey(Key_GUID('AW_ColumnKey'),
      CONVERT(varbinary(max), [HireDateBackup]))
   CLOSE ALL SYMMETRIC KEYS; ");
```

Note that the function encryptByKey(Key_GUID('keyname'), ...) allows us to use the symmetric encryption keys. Also note that the first part of the script opens the key by certificate and the last part just closes all the keys. We will have to use similar commands in SSMS and stored procedures to get data or insert/update data.

Run the migration using the update-database command.

Now let's verify our data.

Using the same symmetric-key-open-and-close pattern that we used for the update script and in the script at the end of part 7, run to see that the data has been successfully added to our encrypted columns (review Figure 10-39).

```
OPEN SYMMETRIC KEY AW_ColumnKey
 DECRYPTION BY CERTIFICATE AW_tdeCert;

SELECT BusinessEntityID, LoginID,
 ISNULL(CONVERT(nvarchar(15), decryptbykey([NationalIDNumber])), '') [NationalIdNumber], [NationalIDNumberBackup],
 ISNULL(CONVERT(nvarchar(50), decryptbykey([JobTitle])), '') [JobTitle], [JobTitleBackup],
 ISNULL(CONVERT(DateTime, decryptbykey([BirthDate])), null) [BirthDate], [BirthDateBackup],
 ISNULL(CONVERT(nvarchar(1), decryptbykey([MaritalStatus])), '') [MaritalStatus] ,[MaritalStatusBackup],
 ISNULL(CONVERT(nvarchar(1), decryptbykey([Gender])), '') [Gender],[GenderBackup],
 ISNULL(CONVERT(datetime, decryptbykey([HireDate])), null) HireDate,[HireDateBackup]
 FROM [AdventureWorks].[HumanResources].[Employee]

 CLOSE ALL SYMMETRIC KEYS
```

BusinessEntityID	LoginID	NationalIdNumber	NationalIDNumberBackup	JobTitle	JobTitleBackup	BirthDate
1	adventure-works\ken0	295847284	295847284	Chief Executive Officer	Chief Executive Officer	1900-01-0
2	adventure-works\terri0	245797967	245797967	Vice President of Engineering	Vice President of Engineering	1900-01-0
3	adventure-works\roberto0	509647174	509647174	Engineering Manager	Engineering Manager	1900-01-0
4	adventure-works\rob0	112457891	112457891	Senior Tool Designer	Senior Tool Designer	1900-01-0
5	adventure-works\gail0	695256908	695256908	Design Engineer	Design Engineer	1900-01-0
6	adventure-works\jossef0	998320692	998320692	Design Engineer	Design Engineer	1900-01-0
7	adventure-works\dylan0	134969118	134969118	Research and Development Manager	Research and Development Manager	1900-01-0
8	adventure-works\diane1	811994146	811994146	Research and Development Engineer	Research and Development Engineer	1900-01-0
9	adventure-works\gigi0	658797903	658797903	Research and Development Engineer	Research and Development Engineer	1900-01-0
10	adventure-works\michael6	879342154	879342154	Research and Development Manager	Research and Development Manager	1900-01-0
11	adventure-works\ovidiu0	974026903	974026903	Senior Tool Designer	Senior Tool Designer	1900-01-0
12	adventure-works\thierry0	480168528	480168528	Tool Designer	Tool Designer	1900-01-0
13	adventure-works\janice0	486228782	486228782	Tool Designer	Tool Designer	1900-01-0
14	adventure-works\michael8	42487730	42487730	Senior Design Engineer	Senior Design Engineer	1900-01-0

Figure 10-39. *Viewing the decrypted data*

Step 9: Delete the backup columns

The final step that remains for the encryption migration is to just go back to the `Employee` model and delete our backup columns. To keep them in the final solution, I'm just commenting them out. You would do well to just delete them from your code.

After deleting the backup columns from the model, add a final migration using the command `add-migration EncryptionMigration_Step7_DeleteBackupColumns`.

This migration should scaffold and work as expected to remove the backup columns from the table.

Run the migration with the command to `update-database`. Then validate that the columns are removed from your table in SSMS.

As an alternative to removing the columns from your model, you could just set them all as `NotMapped` and potentially rename them to something like `FieldNameValue` and set the type. This would be one way to allow the decrypted data to be brought through the system in the default model.

Final thoughts on activity 1002

In this activity, we were able to see both what it takes to use TDE encryption in SQL server and how we could perform a migration for columns in the database that we want to encrypt at rest.

If we were to continue working with this system, we would need to write stored procedures for all of the read and write operations against the encrypted columns where we could then inject the use of the symmetric keys as we did in our sample queries in this activity.

Furthermore, we would need some sort of DTO or ViewModel that housed the actual field data to be able to send the data around in our system once it is decrypted.

While it would be interesting to complete this activity with those activities, all of the tools that you would need to do this are available in the samples we've already worked through.

Final thoughts for this chapter

Now that we've worked through this chapter, we've seen how we can work with both `AlwaysEncrypted` and TDE Encryption in our solutions. We've also seen what it takes to modify our systems so that we can work against the encrypted data.

Although the overall encryption is not necessarily using *EF* – as most is done through the server or through settings on the server and a required client library – the fact remains that once the data is encrypted, we need to be able to work with it.

In each of the activities, we were able to see some of the trickier aspects and issues that could arise in our real-world solutions as we implement or need to migrate and implement encryption at rest on our data.

In our next chapter, we're going to dive into how we can set up our solutions to test our Entity Framework and database code with unit and integration tests.

PART III

Enhancing the Data Solution

CHAPTER 11

Repository and Unit of Work Patterns

In this chapter, we are going to talk in detail about two critical patterns that exist and that should be on the radar of every database developer, whether we are using Entity Framework or not. The good news is that *EF* actually handles a lot of the *unit of work (UoW)* and *repository (repo)* work for us. The bad news is that *EF* is sometimes not exactly what we need when implementing our solutions.

To learn more about these patterns and how we can work with them, we'll start this chapter by discussing each pattern and why they are important, and then we'll finish the chapter by reworking our inventory system so that it is layered with our own simple repository for working with Items. After we layer the solution, we'll have the ability to implement a simple UoW pattern on top of working with Entity Framework.

The repository pattern

The repository pattern is one of the more popular patterns when working with databases. If you aren't using a full repository pattern, you are likely using something that is very close to the repository pattern. If not, you're likely writing a lot of redundant code around the operations to interact with your data.

The sources of information are plentiful

There are many resources that discuss the repository pattern, but almost all of them point back to Martin Fowler's definition as defined in the book *Patterns of Enterprise Application Architecture*. Microsoft has a great write-up on the repository pattern,

451

© Brian L. Gorman 2020
B. L. Gorman, *Practical Entity Framework*, https://doi.org/10.1007/978-1-4842-6044-9_11

which can be found here: `https://docs.microsoft.com/en-us/dotnet/`
`architecture/microservices/microservice-ddd-cqrs-patterns/infrastructure-`
`persistence-layer-design`.

If you want all the official definitions and more in-depth discussions of the pattern, I
recommend you take a look at those two resources.

The repository pattern abstracts the database plumbing code from the implementation

That being said, the reason we want to work with the repo pattern is to make our life
a lot easier when it comes to working with our database. The way the pattern works is
that the repository puts a layer in place that allows the programmer to write common
code operations and rely on the repository to handle the plumbing that is necessary to
connect and perform operations against the database.

Ever since *generics* and *expressions* were added to *.Net*, it's been possible to write
custom repository patterns. It would even be possible without these tools, albeit not as
convenient. However, before Entity Framework, it was commonplace to write code that
created a connection and then added a command to the connection. After adding the
command, we'd set the command type and give it text – either the name of the stored
procedure or the actual SQL command. Then we'd add parameters if necessary.

After getting that all set up, we'd fill a reader or a dataset, and then we'd have to work
with that dataset line by line and field by field in order to hydrate our objects for us in
code. And that was just for one of our operations. Click repeat on this for the next entity
or call to any read or write operation.

Entity Framework's built-in repository

Entity Framework with its implemented repository abstracted all of that out of our sight.
Instead of creating a new connection and setting up the command for every call we want
to make, we wire up *EF*, then just ask for one of the repositories to the DBSet<T> objects,
and, with ease, can Add, Update, Remove, and perform many other actions.

In the end, this is the essence of the repository pattern. We are no longer writing the
plumbing that is needed to build and execute commands. We can generally get a result
and map it or push it directly into our matching type object, without having to loop row
by row and field by field to get the data from our call into our business layer object.

Additionally, using the *EF* repository gives us the tracking changes that we need in order to easily just push an object change back into the database. As we've seen in previous chapters, there are good and bad ways to go about working with these calls, but *EF* has implemented the repository to make those basic database operations obscure.

The unit of work pattern

In addition to the repository pattern, *EF* also implements a unit of work pattern. As with the repo pattern, the roots of the UoW pattern can also be traced back to Martin Fowler's book on *Patterns of Enterprise Application Architecture*.

Using a unit of work

Inserting data, updating data, and deleting data are three manipulation operations that are common to most systems when working with the database. Every time we make a call, however, there is some overhead. Additionally, sometimes we don't want one of the calls to be committed if subsequent calls fail.

The unit of work pattern gives the ability to group these operations. Everything that needs to be done when the operations are ready is tracked and/or managed by the unit of work. When the unit is completed, all of the tracked operations are applied to get the database to match the current state of the objects in memory. Generally, if one part of the unit fails during a unit of work operation, the entire unit is rolled back.

Combining the repository and the unit of work

Now that we're somewhat aware of what both of these patterns are, let's talk about why putting them together as *EF* does is such a powerful tool.

The one-two punch

As we've seen, the repository pattern abstracts the lower-level operations for interacting with the database from the business code. With *EF*, we don't have to create connections and commands directly. We design the system by putting DBSet<T> into the context. Then we can just call against those DBSet<T> objects to add, remove, update, and otherwise manipulate the data.

While the repository portion of *EF* is working, the unit of work portion of *EF* is also in play. We encounter this in the fact that every time we start doing work with the repositories, we ultimately need to make a call to SaveChanges to get the changes to be applied and committed to the database.

Ultimately, what is going on is that *EF* serves up objects in memory to mimic the state of the database and keeps track of their previous state. When we tell *EF* it is time to save changes, *EF* can use the modified state of the object to determine what calls need to be made. The calls are then run just as if we had written the code to connect and execute commands ourselves.

A couple of drawbacks

Using *EF* is a great tool for almost all scenarios we encounter; however, the nature of how both the repo and UoW patterns are applied can lead to a few issues and drawbacks.

One major concern that a lot of developers share is general overhead. As we've seen in previous chapters, and as we understand with the UoW as we've discussed here, tracking the state of every entity in memory can lead to some performance issues. For this reason, *EF* has exposed the ability to avoid tracking the object against the database with the AsNoTracking statement.

Another concern that we'll encounter as a developer will be related to concurrency. What happens to my changes if another user applies their changes first? With *EF*, generally if an error like this happens, the operation will have to be retried, sometimes at the expense of refreshing data. This can get a bit expensive in a system where lots of transactions are taking place.

A third concern is that it can be tricky to apply partial changes, or partial changes may be applied even if the transaction fails. For example, if we're solely working with *EF* and we need to perform a number of operations, perhaps we only want to save some changes but not all of them. Calling save changes on the context will save all of the changes as performed in memory by the UoW, not just some of the changes. In the opposite direction, if some of the operations make mutating change calls to stored procedures and those procedures are executed, it may be impossible to rely on *EF* to roll those changes back, as the procedure may have already run against the database. In cases such as this, we often have to make sure that *EF* is not applying transactions on the procedure calls, or determine some way to ensure that our database is restored to the proper state even if untracked changes are applied.

Finally, not only is there risk when multiple operations may have taken place to make it so your change can't be applied; there is risk when using transactions that either you can get a dirty read, which is the case when you pull data from the database but that data is in process of being changed by another user, or you might get a situation where your operations are causing deadlocks in the system. A deadlock in this case is a situation where you start a transaction and perform a read of data from any table. As you are using a transaction, that table becomes locked for read/write operations to other users until you commit your changes.

In general, rely on EF

With everything that *EF* does provide, it is generally a good idea to rely on what *EF* is doing around these two patterns (repo and UoW). Implementing our own solutions can look like the right solution, but may introduce a lot of risk.

Always remember that *EF* is going to apply changes as a unit of work for you, so you can generally rely on it rolling back correctly on failure, as well as trust that applying changes will only be allowed when the data is clean and in the proper state to be committed.

Separation of concerns

A final topic that we need to discuss in this chapter is the idea of separation of concerns. *Separation of concerns (SoC)* is a well-known principle in computer science. The overall idea is that you want to keep minimal functionality in its own layer and area of concern, rather than tightly coupling everything together. We already do a lot of programming with SoC implicit as we build out separate classes for modeling our objects. While they may be relational, we don't often make a class that contains multiple objects in it.

For example, when we programmed our solution, we didn't put the properties for Genre in the Item class. We used a many-to-many relationship so that Genres could be their own concern and so that Items could have the ability to be separate from Genres and Categories. This is basic separation of concerns.

Logical separation of concerns

To make our solution robust, it would be ideal to not only separate the concerns across objects but also to separate concerns across layers. In this manner, we can make functional units or components that can more easily be interchanged with new components or logic as the needs arise. This makes our overall solution easier to maintain.

Another benefit of separation of concerns into layers is that we can then start correctly using dependency injection to inject the dependent components into other layers. By doing this, as long as the components are coded to a common interface, the business layer doesn't care what the database layer is doing nor how, just as long as the data is returned as expected.

Final benefits of separating our concerns

The final benefit of separating our layers into individual components that are not tightly coupled will be to facilitate ease of testing.

As the system stands as of the end of Chapter 10, it would be very difficult to unit test our solution. We could likely put some integration testing into place in the solution, but there wouldn't be a good way to just test the service layer without connecting to an actual database.

With all of this in mind, it's time to work through these concepts in our solution.

Chapter 11 Activities

To continue making our project more robust, the activities in this chapter are going to take the time to layer our solution into a more robust solution that is more loosely coupled. We will not be completely uncoupled, but we will get to a much more *SOLID* place with our code. Additionally, we'll be ready for unit testing and integration testing our solution which we'll do in the next chapter.

To kick off our activities for this chapter, we'll start with an activity to layer our solution. By the end of the first activity, our code will have a functioning database layer and a functioning business/service layer, and each layer will be coded against an interchangeable and injectable interface.

We'll finish the chapter by using our solution to implement our own custom units of work around batching on insert, update, and delete operations. To make this happen, we'll once again implement the operations to manipulate the database data in the database layer. We'll use transactions to wrap the units of work.

With all of that in mind, let's get started.

Activity 1101: Layering our solution

In this first activity, we are going to work through layering our solution. To be clear, this is less of a database activity and more of an architecture exercise. Therefore, if you are not interested in this activity, you should feel free to skip it. That being said, I do feel like this is a great exercise in understanding how we can set up layering and position the solution for full dependency injection and testing in the future.

Uncoupling this solution

As it stands right now, the solution is very tightly coupled, in that there is database code in the *UI* layer (our console). Ideally, we want to separate the layers out for a number of reasons, mostly involving *SOLID* architecture, robustness, maintenance, and testing.

Additionally, separating this solution into layers is going to give us a great ability to rework different pieces of the application in the future without having to rewrite the entire application. Operations like switching or implementing a new user interface will be easily possible, as will changing out the database if needed.

By the end of this activity, we are going to have a much more robust solution with a layered architecture that is decoupled at each layer via interfaces and segregation of work.

Step 1: Getting set up

To begin, grab a copy of the `Activity1101_LayeringOurSolution_Starter.zip` files, extract them, double-check your connection string, and make sure that you have the *InventoryManager* database setup. Run an `update-database` command to make sure the migrations are up to date on your machine for this activity. Run the starter console project to make sure the solution works out of the box. Alternatively, you could continue working with your ongoing solution that you've been building throughout the project. The activity 1101 files and projects in the solution are the same as the final version of activity 1001.

Additionally, I am working from the assumption that the database has AlwaysEncrypted enabled on the Items table as per the activities in Chapter 10. It should not matter if you do or do not have AlwaysEncrypted on; however, my decisions and code are entirely the result of refactoring based on encryption.

Running the initial solution should produce output similar to what is shown in Figure 11-1 and does depend on which method calls you have or have not enabled in the Main method.

```
Select Microsoft Visual Studio Debug Console
New Item]  127          |Top Gun                          |1       |18.50
New Item]  128          |Batman Begins                    |4       |58.00
New Item]  129          |Practical Entity Framework       |100     |4450.00
New Item]  130          |The Lord of the Rings            |7       |87.50
New Item]  131          |Battlefield 5                    |17      |756.50
New Item]  132          |World Of Tanks                   |1       |0.00
New Item]  127          |Top Gun                          |Comedy
New Item]  128          |Batman Begins                    |Sci/Fi
New Item]  128          |Batman Begins                    |Drama
New Item]  129          |Practical Entity Framework
New Item]  130          |The Lord of the Rings            |Sci/Fi
New Item]  130          |The Lord of the Rings            |Fantasy
New Item]  131          |Battlefield 5                    |Sci/Fi
New Item]  132          |World Of Tanks
ITEM Books| Practical Entity Framework - The book that teaches practical application with EF
ITEM Books| The Lord of the Rings - The fellowship of the Ring
ITEM Games| Battlefield 5 - First person shooter
ITEM Games| World Of Tanks - AN MMO WW2 Tanks First-Person Shooter
ITEM Movies| Batman Begins - Why do we fall, Bruce?
ITEM Movies| Top Gun - I feel the need, the need for speed
Movies | Blue
Books  | Red
Games  | Green

C:\APressEntityFramework\Code\Chapter11\Activity1101_LayeringOurSolution\Activity1101_LayeringOu
oreann3 1\Activity1101 LayeringOurSolution.exe (process 12196) exited with code 0
```

Figure 11-1. *Running the starter project works as expected*

Step 2: Adding the database layer project

In general, I like to work from the bottom up, so for this activity, we'll start with the database and work back to the *UI*. If you are more comfortable, you can work in the other direction or piece it together as we go. It's ultimately up to you how you want to implement your own solutions.

Create a new project in the solution by right-clicking the solution and selecting Add ➤ New Project as shown in Figure 11-2.

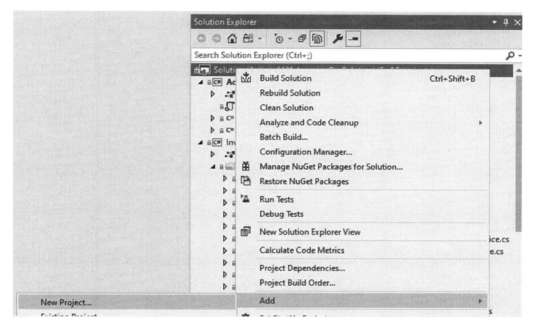

Figure 11-2. *Adding a new project to the solution*

The new project needs to be a Class Library (.Net Core). If you are having trouble finding the Class Library (.Net Core), remember to use the filters for project type (review Figure 11-3).

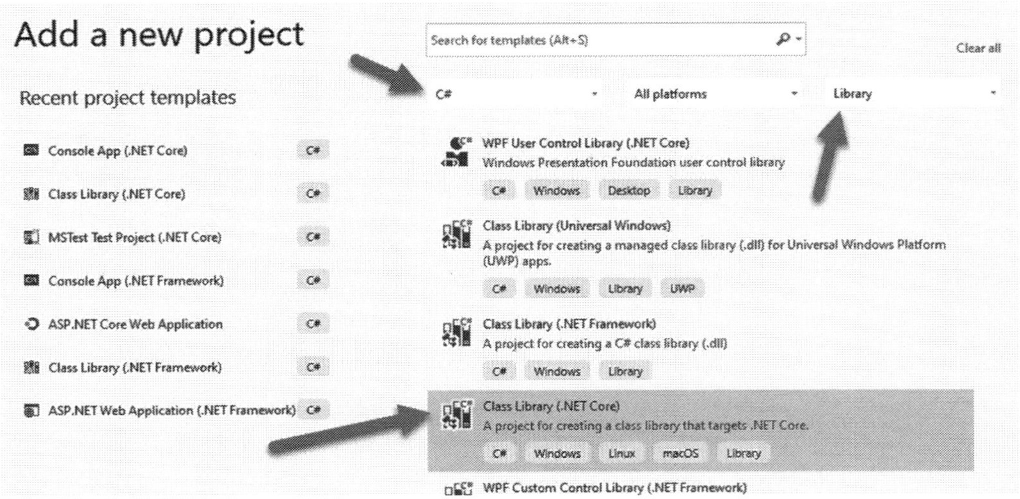

Figure 11-3. *Creating a new Class Library (.Net Core)*

Name the project InventoryDatabaseLayer when prompted, and make sure to save it in the same folder as your overall solution (it should default to this location). Your input form should be similar to what is shown in Figure 11-4.

Figure 11-4. *Naming and creating the project*

Hit the Create button to create the new project.

Rename the default `Class1.cs` file by right-clicking the file and selecting Rename. Name the file `InventoryDatabaseRepo.cs` and select Yes when prompted to rename dependent objects (see Figure 11-5).

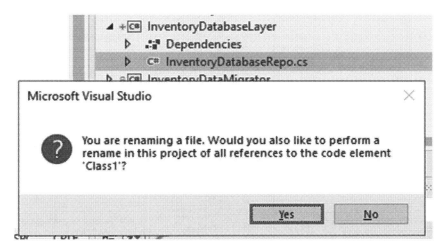

Figure 11-5. *Renaming the default file*

Add a new class file to the project called `IInventoryDatabaseRepo.cs`. This will be our layer's interface, and we'll implement the interface in the file we just renamed.

```
public interface IInventoryDatabaseRepo
{

}
```

Make sure to implement the interface on the `InventoryDatabaseRepo` class:

```
public class InventoryDatabaseRepo : IInventoryDatabaseRepo
{

}
```

Step 3: Add the business layer project

Repeat the previous steps, but create a project named `InventoryBusinessLayer`.
As with the database project, include the two files, one as an interface and one as a
class that implements the interface. Name the class `ItemsService` and the interface
`IItemsService`. For clarity, the overall structure is shown in Figure 11-6.

Figure 11-6. *The Inventory Business Layer project is stubbed out*

Step 4: Add AutoMapper to the two-layer projects

In the solution, I am going to make the mapper available in both layers. We'll ultimately
inject both the mapper and the database context into the layers. To make this happen,
we need to add references to the `AutoMapper` packages to both layers. Use the `Tools ➤`
`NuGet Package Manager ➤ Manage NuGet Packages for Solution` to add `AutoMapper`
and the `AutoMapper Extensions` to both the service and database layer projects.

Step 5: Create database operations in the database layer

To make the database layer work, first we need to reference an existing projects.

Right-click the project and select `Add ➤ Reference`. Select the
InventoryDatabaseCore project (see Figure 11-7).

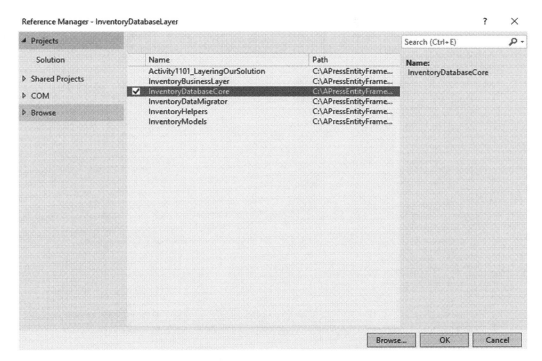

Figure 11-7. *Selecting the InventoryDatabaseCore project for reference in the database layer project*

After adding the reference, note that the InventoryModels project is referenced through the InventoryDatabaseCore project. Once you've validated references, add the following code into the IInventoryDatabaseRepo interface:

```
public interface IInventoryDatabaseRepo
{
    List<ItemDto> ListInventory();
    List<GetItemsForListingWithDateDto> GetItemsForListingLinq(DateTime
    minDateValue, DateTime maxDateValue);
    List<GetItemsForListingDto> GetItemsForListingFromProcedure(DateTime
    dateDateValue, DateTime maxDateValue);
    List<GetItemsTotalValueDto> GetItemsTotalValues(bool isActive);
    List<ItemsWithGenresDto> GetItemsWithGenres();
    List<CategoryDto> ListCategoriesAndColors();
}
```

Don't forget to add the appropriate using statements so the code will compile.

Implement the methods in the `InventoryDatabaseRepo` class by hovering on the class and selecting `Implement interface` (see Figure 11-8).

Figure 11-8. *Implementing the interface*

At the end of this operation, you'll have six methods that are throwing a new `NotImplementedException` stubbed out in your InventoryDatabaseRepo class.

Step 6: Implement the database operations

In this step, we're going to implement all six methods, one by one. Let's start with the `ListInventory` method. Note that the auto-generated methods are in alphabetical order, but the interface methods are not. I recommend making sure to keep your interface and your class methods lined up, and you can choose which one you want to reorder. I'm going to reorder the interface to make it alphabetical, even though that will not be the order of use in the program.

In the `ListInventory` method, replace the line for throwing a new `NotImplementedException` with the following code (it is expected that this code will not yet compile due to using variables that we haven't added):

```
var items = _context.Items.AsEnumerable().OrderBy(x => x.Name).ToList();
return _mapper.Map<List<ItemDto>>(items);
```

Immediately we see that the code is asking for a context and the mapper. Instead of creating them in this layer, we're going to inject them. Additionally, we've added a call that requires the using statement for LINQ.

Create a constructor for the InventoryDatabaseRepo class, and take in the two parameters. Additionally, create two private read-only parameters to store the context and mapper objects.

```
private readonly InventoryDbContext _context;
private readonly IMapper _mapper;

public InventoryDatabaseRepo(InventoryDbContext context, IMapper mapper)
{
    _context = context;
    _mapper = mapper;
}
```

Always remember to add any missing using statements when possible to ensure the code will compile.

At this point, the ListInventory method should compile and the project should build. This ListInventory method is our default method to just get all of the items ordered by name.

Next, let's update the GetItemsForListingLinq method. In this method, add the following code:

```
return _context.Items.Include(x => x.Category).AsEnumerable()
            .Select(x => new GetItemsForListingWithDateDto
{
    CreatedDate = x.CreatedDate,
    CategoryName = x.Category.Name,
    Description = x.Description,
    IsActive = x.IsActive,
    IsDeleted = x.IsDeleted,
    Name = x.Name,
    Notes = x.Notes
}).Where(x => x.CreatedDate >= minDateValue && x.CreatedDate <=
maxDateValue)
        .AsQueryable().OrderBy(y => y.CategoryName).ThenBy(z => z.Name).
        ToList();
```

This GetItemsForListingLinq method will get the Items and select them into the DTO, and then order by CategoryName and then by Name.

For the next implementation, we'll look at using the stored procedure. For the GetItemsForListingFromProcedure method, implement the following code:

```
var minDateParam = new SqlParameter("minDate", dateDateValue);
var maxDateParam = new SqlParameter("maxDate", maxDateValue);

return _context.ItemsForListing
            .FromSqlRaw("EXECUTE dbo.GetItemsForListing @minDate, @maxDate"
                          , minDateParam, maxDateParam)
            .ToList();
```

Here, we've leveraged the GetItemsForListing stored procedure with a data range.

Next, we'll leverage the function to get the Items with their total values. Add the following code to the GetItemsTotalValues Method:

```
var isActiveParm = new SqlParameter("IsActive", 1);


return _context.GetItemsTotalValues
            .FromSqlRaw("SELECT * from [dbo].[GetItemsTotalValue]
            (@IsActive)", isActiveParm)
            .ToList();
```

This is the code to leverage the table-valued function.

For the GetItemsWithGeneres method, just make a call to return everything from the view:

```
return _context.ItemsWithGenres.ToList();
```

Finally, implement the code for the ListCategoriesAndColors method. Use this code to complete the class (as highlighted in Figure 11-9):

```
return _context.Categories
                        .Include(x => x.CategoryColor)
                        .ProjectTo<CategoryDto>(_mapper.
                        ConfigurationProvider).ToList();
```

```
public List<CategoryDto> ListCategoriesAndColors()
{
    return _context.Categories
                    .Include(x => x.CategoryColor)
                    .ProjectTo<CategoryDto>(_mapper.ConfigurationProvider).ToList();
}
```

Figure 11-9. *The ListCategoriesAndColors method is implemented*

With all of this code in place, we've implemented our items database operations that we'll leverage in the program. In a real-world scenario, we'd also want to do some inserting and updating in this layer. For more practice, feel free to implement Insert, Update, and Delete methods.

Step 7: Create operations in the service layer

For our purposes, all but one of the service layer methods are going to be simple pass-throughs. The overall idea is that the service exposes operations and could further manipulate the data that is returned from the data layer.

Begin by adding a project reference to the InventoryDatabaseLayer project in the InventoryBusinessLayer project. Note that through the InventoryDatabaseLayer reference, the InventoryBusinessLayer project will have nested references to the InventoryModels project (see Figure 11-10 for clarity).

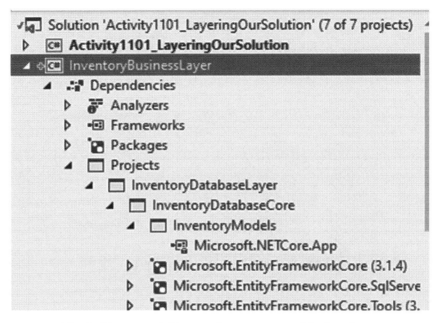

Figure 11-10. *The indirect and direct references are added to the Inventory Business Layer project*

Next, implement the following code in the IItemsService interface:

```
List<GetItemsForListingWithDateDto> GetItemsForListingLinq(DateTime
minDateValue, DateTime maxDateValue);
List<GetItemsForListingDto> GetItemsForListingFromProcedure(DateTime
minDateValue, DateTime maxDateValue);
AllItemsPipeDelimitedStringDto GetItemsPipeDelimitedString(bool isActive);
List<GetItemsTotalValueDto> GetItemsTotalValues(bool isActive);
List<ItemsWithGenresDto> GetItemsWithGenres();
List<CategoryDto> ListCategoriesAndColors();
List<ItemDto> ListInventory();
```

Note that while the interface is mostly a one-to-one implementation of the same methods from the database layer, it certainly would not need to be. Additionally, there is one more method added to get the pipe-delimited string. The scalar function for the pipe-delimited string no longer works due to AlwaysEncrypted.

468

Now that the methods are defined in the service interface, implement the methods in the service class. As before, just use the auto-defined interface implementation.

Next, we'll add a constructor to the service method using the following code:

```
private readonly IInventoryDatabaseRepo _dbRepo;

public ItemsService(InventoryDbContext dbContext, IMapper mapper)
{
    _dbRepo = new InventoryDatabaseRepo(dbContext, mapper);
}
```

Note that we're just passing the context and the mapper on, and we're going to build our business layer around the database layer.

Step 8: Implement the service layer operations

Now that we've stubbed out the methods, we need to implement them. For every method other than the pipe-delimited string method, we're just going to return a call to the database layer for the method with the same name.

In the GetItemsForListingFromProcedure method, add the following code:

```
return _dbRepo.GetItemsForListingFromProcedure(minDateValue, maxDateValue);
```

And in the GetItemsForListingLinq method, add the following:

```
return _dbRepo.GetItemsForListingLinq(minDateValue, maxDateValue);
```

In the GetItemsTotalValues method, add this line of code:

```
return _dbRepo.GetItemsTotalValues(isActive);
```

In the GetItemsWithGenres, add the following line:

```
return _dbRepo.GetItemsWithGenres();
```

In the ListCategoriesAndColors method, call through to the database layer on the same method name:

```
return _dbRepo.ListCategoriesAndColors();
```

And in the `ListInventory` method, add the following:

```
return _dbRepo.ListInventory();
```

Finally, we need to work out the solution for the `GetItemsPipeDelimitedString` method. In the original code, this was a call to a scalar function. With encryption as set up in the activities in Chapter 10, we are no longer able to get decrypted data on the server, so we'll just get the items into memory and then use a `StringBuilder` to create the pipe-delimited list.

Use the following code to generate all items as a pipe-delimited string of their names:

```
var items = ListInventory();
var sb = new StringBuilder();

foreach (var item in items)
{
    if (sb.Length > 0)
    {
        sb.Append("|");
    }
    sb.Append(item.Name);
}

var output = new AllItemsPipeDelimitedStringDto();
output.AllItems = sb.ToString();
return output;
```

Step 9: Rework the console program

In this final step, we're going to rework the console program to bring in the layers as needed and be able to make the calls to get the data. We will still inject the mapper and the database context from this program. In real-world applications, we would have the builders in place so that any *UI* layer could be used with the injection still working as expected.

Begin by deleting all the method calls other than `BuildOptions` and `BuildMapper` from the `Main` method. We'll add them back shortly.

Additionally, add a reference to the `BusinessLayer` project into the main Activity1101_ LayeringOurSolution project, and remove the direct reference to the InventoryDatabaseCore project. From now on, all data will come via the service layer project.

Once the reference is in place, create a new using statement after the `BuildMapper` call that creates and wraps an inventory database context. Inside the using statement, create a new service layer object. Right before the using statement, create two `DateTime` variables for minDate and maxDate. Set the minDate variable to the beginning of this year and the maxDate to the beginning of next year.

```
BuildOptions();
BuildMapper();

var minDate = new DateTime(2020, 1, 1);
var maxDate = new DateTime(2021, 1, 1);

using (var db = new InventoryDbContext(_optionsBuilder.Options))
{
    var svc = new ItemsService(db, _mapper);
}
```

Inside the using statement, add the following code to leverage all of the service methods that directly or indirectly leverage the database layer:

```
var svc = new ItemsService(db, _mapper);
Console.WriteLine("List Inventory");
var inventory = svc.ListInventory();
inventory.ForEach(x => Console.WriteLine($"New Item: {x}"));

Console.WriteLine("List inventory with Linq");
var items = svc.GetItemsForListingLinq(minDate, maxDate);
items.ForEach(x => Console.WriteLine($"ITEM| {x.CategoryName}|
{x.Name} - {x.Description}"));

Console.WriteLine("List Inventory from procedure");
var procItems = svc.GetItemsForListingFromProcedure(minDate, maxDate);
procItems.ForEach(x => Console.WriteLine($"ITEM| {x.Name} -
{x.Description}"));

Console.WriteLine("Item Names Pipe Delimited String");
var pipedItems = svc.GetItemsPipeDelimitedString(true);
Console.WriteLine(pipedItems.AllItems);
```

```
Console.WriteLine("Get Items Total Values");
var totalValues = svc.GetItemsTotalValues(true);
totalValues.ForEach(item => Console.WriteLine($"New Item] {item.Id,-10}" +
                    $"|{item.Name,-50}" +
                    $"|{item.Quantity,-4}" +
                    $"|{item.TotalValue,-5}"));

Console.WriteLine("Get Items With Genres");
var itemsWithGenres = svc.GetItemsWithGenres();
itemsWithGenres.ForEach(item => Console.WriteLine($"New Item] {item.Id,-10}" +
                    $"|{item.Name,-50}" +
                    $"|{item.Genre?.ToString().PadLeft(4)}"));

Console.WriteLine("List Categories And Colors");
var categoriesAndColors = svc.ListCategoriesAndColors();
categoriesAndColors.ForEach(c => Console.WriteLine($"{c.Category} |
{c.CategoryColor.Color}"));
```

Run the program to validate it works (results should be similar to what is shown in Figure 11-11).

```
Microsoft Visual Studio Debug Console
ITEM|  Top Gun - I feel the need, the need for speed
ITEM|  Batman Begins - Why do we fall, Bruce?
ITEM|  Practical Entity Framework - The book that teaches practical application with EF
ITEM|  The Lord of the Rings - The fellowship of the Ring
ITEM|  Battlefield 5 - First person shooter
ITEM|  World Of Tanks - AN MMO WW2 Tanks First-Person Shooter
Item Names Pipe Delimited String
Batman Begins|Battlefield 5|Practical Entity Framework|The Lord of the Rings|Top Gun|World Of Tanks
Get Items Total Values
New Item] 127          |Top Gun                            |1    |18.50
New Item] 128          |Batman Begins                      |4    |58.00
New Item] 129          |Practical Entity Framework         |100  |4450.00
New Item] 130          |The Lord of the Rings              |7    |87.50
New Item] 131          |Battlefield 5                      |17   |756.50
New Item] 132          |World Of Tanks                     |1    |0.00
Get Items With Genres
New Item] 127          |Top Gun                            |Comedy
New Item] 128          |Batman Begins                      |Sci/Fi
New Item] 128          |Batman Begins                      |Drama
New Item] 129          |Practical Entity Framework         |
New Item] 130          |The Lord of the Rings              |Sci/Fi
New Item] 130          |The Lord of the Rings              |Fantasy
New Item] 131          |Battlefield 5                      |Sci/Fi
New Item] 132          |World Of Tanks                     |
List Categories And Colors
Movies | Blue
Books  | Red
Games  | Green
```

Figure 11-11. *The program works as expected*

Finally, remove all the original method calls in the console app program file which have zero references, as they are no longer going to be used.

Final thoughts on activity 1101 – layering our solution

At this point, we've completed the layering portion of our activity. We implemented a database layer with a repo of actions that is modeled in an interface. We then created a service layer to expose operations to a *UI* layer. Because both layers we created implemented an interface, we can inject different implementations of these layers in the future if desired.

After creating the business and data layers, we then refactored the program to leverage the layers instead of implementing database code directly in the program.

Now that we have our code refactored to a layered approach, we can add a few more methods to complete CRUD operations and then implement a custom unit of work pattern to close out the chapter.

Activity 1102: Rolling our own UoW

In this second activity for this chapter, we are going to create our own unit of work using transactions in our *Inventory Database Manager* solution.

Transactions are easy and effective

Entity Framework itself has built-in transactions, but sometimes you want to make sure that a number of operations complete before saving the entire unit of work. Even though the individual calls to SaveChanges are transactional, when you need a group of these operations to work together and save on success, you also will want them all to roll back in the case when something fails.

As we work to further create our custom repository, we can create methods that leverage their own unit of work by wrapping the operations for each unit of work in transactions.

As a last and final statement on this matter, I will again urge you to use caution when using transactions in a highly volatile environment with high traffic volumes. Working with transactions on your own could lead to many scenarios that end in deadlock, resulting in users having long load times on different pages in the solution. Therefore, if you must use transactions, I remind you to look into the different transaction isolation levels, as well as fully test your system under load of multiple concurrent users to ensure you have not created a deadlock in your solution.

Use the using statement for transaction life cycles

When it comes to working with transactions, just like when we connect and work with the database context, we can rely on the fact that the transaction implements `IDisposable`. With that knowledge, we know that we can wrap the transaction in a using statement, making it very easy to handle the overall unit of work.

For our activity, we're going to do a couple of simple CRUD operations that will simply call the context to savechanges and rely on its underlying unit of work.

We'll then create a somewhat contrived example where we want to make sure that we can insert, update, or delete an entire group of items. If any of the operations fail in the group, then we will roll back the entire transaction. This will be our custom unit of work implementation.

Step 1: Steps

To begin, grab a copy of the `Activity1102_TransactionsAndUnitOfWork_Starter.zip` files, extract them, double-check your connection string, and make sure that you have the `InventoryManager` database set up. Run an `update-database` command to make sure the migrations are up to date on your machine. We're picking up where we left off after activity 1101, but we're going to change a number of things in order to fully implement our desired solution. Run the program to make sure it works as expected. Alternatively, continue working with your project after having completed activity 1101.

Step 2: Modify the database interface and project

For this activity, we are going to use our database layer like a full database repo as provided by Entity Framework. We are going to use our service layer to manage calls to that database layer. Additionally, we're going to create some methods that have units of work in them, where we will start a transaction and keep the transaction open until all changes have completed.

To start our development process, we are going to work from the database up to the *UI* program layer. To make our solution work as expected, first we need to fix a couple of things that we would likely have caught if we had good unit and integration tests.

First, we'll change the `ListInventory` method in the `InventoryDatabaseRepo` file in the `InventoryDatabaseLayer` project. For this method, let's return a full `Item` class instead of the `ItemDto` (the service layer will do the mapping). Let's also include the `Category` with the `Item`, and let's finish the method by making sure to only return non-deleted entities. Change the `ListInventory` method to use the following code:

```
public List<Item> ListInventory()
{
    return _context.Items.Include(x => x.Category)
                .AsEnumerable()
                .Where(x => !x.IsDeleted)
                .OrderBy(x => x.Name).ToList();
}
```

Make sure to modify the signature of the ListInventory method in the interface file IInventoryDatabaseRepo to also return a `List<Item>` instead of a `List<ItemDto>` by replacing the original code with this code: `List<Item> ListInventory();`.

Additionally, changing the signature to the full model will likely require you to update your using statements. Go ahead and make sure to do that now.

At this point, the solution will no longer build. This is expected since we've modified the interface signature and have not responded to this change elsewhere in the code. We will get this fixed later in the activity.

Next, we need to add four new method signatures for create, update, and delete operations to the IInventoryDatabaseRepo interface as follows:

```
int InsertOrUpdateItem(Item item);
void InsertOrUpdateItems(List<Item> items);
void DeleteItem(int id);
void DeleteItems(List<int> itemIds);
```

After defining the methods in the interface, we need to implement them.

In the database project, stub out the four methods by using the auto-generated method implementations. Optionally, move them to the bottom of the class and break the alphabetical listing so they are easy to find. The code can be generated, but it should be similar to the following:

```
public int InsertOrUpdateItem(Item item)
{
    throw new NotImplementedException();
}

public void InsertOrUpdateItems(List<Item> items)
{
    throw new NotImplementedException();
}

public void DeleteItem(int id)
{
    throw new NotImplementedException();
}

public void DeleteItems(List<int> itemIds)
{
    throw new NotImplementedException();
}
```

In the `InsertOrUpdateItem(Item item)` method, add code to call to update if the item id is greater than zero, or just insert if the id is not greater than zero.

```
public int InsertOrUpdateItem(Item item)
{
    if (item.Id > 0)
    {
        return UpdateItem(item);
    }
    return CreateItem(item);
}
```

476

Next, create the two methods, one for CreateItem and one for UpdateItem as private methods using the following code:

```
private int CreateItem(Item item)
{
    _context.Items.Add(item);
    _context.SaveChanges();
    var newItem = _context.Items.ToList()
                    .FirstOrDefault(x => x.Name.ToLower()
                    .Equals(item.Name.ToLower()));

    if (newItem == null) throw new Exception("Could not Create the item as
    expected");

    return newItem.Id;
}

private int UpdateItem(Item item)
{
    var dbItem = _context.Items.FirstOrDefault(x => x.Id == item.Id);
    dbItem.CategoryId = item.CategoryId;
    dbItem.CurrentOrFinalPrice = item.CurrentOrFinalPrice;
    dbItem.Description = item.Description;
    dbItem.IsActive = item.IsActive;
    dbItem.IsDeleted = item.IsDeleted;
    dbItem.IsOnSale = item.IsOnSale;
    dbItem.Name = item.Name;
    dbItem.Notes = item.Notes;
    dbItem.PurchasedDate = item.PurchasedDate;
    dbItem.PurchasePrice = item.PurchasePrice;
    dbItem.Quantity = item.Quantity;
    dbItem.SoldDate = item.SoldDate;
    _context.SaveChanges();
    return item.Id;
}
```

For the InsertOrUpdateItems(List<Item> items) method, we're going to use a transaction to batch our unit of work around all items for create or update. In this manner, if one of the operations in the batch fails, the whole transaction will be rolled back.

Implement the method with code as follows:

```
public void InsertOrUpdateItems(List<Item> items)
{
    using (var transaction = _context.Database.BeginTransaction())
    {
        try
        {
            foreach (var item in items)
            {
                var success = InsertOrUpdateItem(item) > 0;
                if (!success) throw new Exception($"Error saving the item
{item.Name}");
            }

            transaction.Commit();
        }
        catch (Exception ex)
        {
            //log it:
            Debug.WriteLine(ex.ToString());
            transaction.Rollback();
            throw ex;
        }
    }
}
```

Notice that this method uses the using statement to wrap the batch execution into a transaction. When all operations complete successfully, the transaction is committed. If any of the iterations fail to save correctly, then the exception is thrown and logged, and the entire transaction is rolled back.

The really nice thing to note is that even though we are calling to the context to save changes on each iteration, we are still able to roll the entire transaction back. This can also be useful in an insert and then update scenario, where you need to get an item inserted, then get the id of that item, and use it to update some other piece of the system.

Finally, let's follow this same pattern to implement the two Delete methods:

```csharp
public void DeleteItem(int id)
{
    var item = _context.Items.FirstOrDefault(x => x.Id == id);
    if (item == null) return;
    item.IsDeleted = true;
    _context.SaveChanges();
}

public void DeleteItems(List<int> itemIds)
{
    using (var transaction = _context.Database.BeginTransaction())
    {
        try
        {
            foreach (var itemId in itemIds)
            {
                DeleteItem(itemId);
            }

            transaction.Commit();
        }
        catch (Exception ex)
        {
            //log it:
            Debug.WriteLine(ex.ToString());
            transaction.Rollback();
            throw ex;   //make sure it is known that the transaction failed
        }
    }
}
```

This will complete our database layer for now. Next, we'll move up to the service layer. Keep in mind that as of right now, the solution is still not able to be built, but the InventoryDatabaseLayer project can be built individually if you would like to check your code for accuracy and/or errors.

Step 3: Modify the ItemsService interface and implementation in the InventoryBusinessLayer project

The service layer (InventoryBusinessLayer.ItemsService) will now need to respond to the new methods in the database layer, as well as do some mapping for Item to ItemDto to get our code back to a buildable and working state.

Begin by adding four new methods to the service layer interface as follows:

```
int InsertOrUpdateItem(CreateOrUpdateItemDto item);
void InsertOrUpdateItems(List<CreateOrUpdateItemDto> item);
void DeleteItem(int id);
void DeleteItems(List<int> itemIds);
```

We'll also need to add the CreateOrUpdateItemDto class to be able to compile this code and get it to a working state. In the InventoryModels project, under the *Dtos* folder, create a new file called CreateOrUpdateItemDto.cs, and add the following code to the file:

```
public class CreateOrUpdateItemDto
{
    public int Id { get; set; }
    public string Name { get; set; }
    public string Description { get; set; }
    public string Notes { get; set; }
    public int CategoryId { get; set; }
    public bool IsActive { get; set; }
    public bool IsDeleted { get; set; }
}
```

Implement the four methods as defined in the IItemsService interface, and optionally move them to the bottom of the ItemsService code file to make it easy to find them all.

The first thing we need to do is to be able to list the inventory and return it as an ItemDto. This will require the mapper implementation to be in the ServiceLayer.

At the top of the ItemsService class, add the line of code private read-only IMapper _mapper; after the line for creating the read-only dbRepo. Then add the instantiation _mapper = mapper; into the constructor method. Figure 11-12 highlights the instantiation of the mapper into the constructor.

```
private readonly IInventoryDatabaseRepo _dbRepo;
private readonly IMapper _mapper;

1 reference
public ItemsService(InventoryDbContext dbContext, IMapper mapper)
{
    _dbRepo = new InventoryDatabaseRepo(dbContext, mapper);
    _mapper = mapper;
}

2 references
```

Figure 11-12. *Leveraging the mapper in the service layer requires a reference to it*

In the ListInventory method, change the statement to

return _mapper.Map<List<ItemDto>>(_dbRepo.ListInventory());

This change should resolve any issues that existed with the ListInventory method.

Next, implement the code to get the data from the database layer. We are going to again be just doing mostly a pass-through at this service layer.

```
public int InsertOrUpdateItem(CreateOrUpdateItemDto item)
{
    if (item.CategoryId <= 0)
    {
        throw new ArgumentException("Please set the category id before
        insert or update");
    }
    return _dbRepo.InsertOrUpdateItem(_mapper.Map<Item>(item));
}
```

```
public void InsertOrUpdateItems(List<CreateOrUpdateItemDto> items)
{
    _dbRepo.InsertOrUpdateItems(_mapper.Map<List<Item>>(items));
}

public void DeleteItem(int id)
{
    if (id <= 0)
    {
        throw new ArgumentException("Please set a valid item id before
        deleting");
    }
    _dbRepo.DeleteItem(id);
}

public void DeleteItems(List<int> itemIds)
{
    try
    {
        _dbRepo.DeleteItems(itemIds);
    }
    catch (Exception ex)
    {
        //TODO: better logging/not squelching
        Console.WriteLine($"The transaction has failed: {ex.Message}");
    }
}
```

The interesting things to note here are that we'll make sure to have a couple of guard clauses in place to prevent issues as well as handle the cases when the transactions don't succeed. In the real world, we'd also want to implement better logging to avoid just squelching issues.

Another interesting point is that our mapper now needs to go in both directions between Item and ItemDto. Therefore, we will also need a mapping for the new CreateOrUpdateDto.

In the Main activity project, in the `InventoryMapper.cs` file, add the command `.ReverseMap()` to the map item for the mapping of `Item` to `ItemDto` to make the map go in both directions:

```
CreateMap<Item, ItemDto>().ReverseMap();
```

Then add a new mapping for `Item` to `CreateOrUpdateItemDto` as follows to the `CreateMaps` method, making sure to ignore the `Category` after reversing the mapping:

```
CreateMap<Item, CreateOrUpdateItemDto>()
    .ReverseMap()
    .ForMember(x => x.Category, opt => opt.Ignore());
```

For clarity, please review Figure 11-13.

```
1 reference
private void CreateMaps()
{
    CreateMap<Item, ItemDto>().ReverseMap();
    CreateMap<Item, CreateOrUpdateItemDto>()
        .ReverseMap()
        .ForMember(x => x.Category, opt => opt.Ignore());
    CreateMap<Category, CategoryDto>()
        .ForMember(x => x.Category, opt => opt.MapFrom(y => y.Name))
        .ReverseMap()
        .ForMember(y => y.Name, opt => opt.MapFrom(x => x.Category));
    CreateMap<CategoryColor, CategoryColorDto>()
        .ForMember(x => x.Color, opt => opt.MapFrom(y => y.ColorValue))
        .ReverseMap()
        .ForMember(y => y.ColorValue, opt => opt.MapFrom(x => x.Color));
}
```

Figure 11-13. *The updated InventoryMapper class*

Now that our layers are done, we need to add some code to run the program. At this point, the solution should build successfully. Go ahead and build the solution to verify your code is in place and ensure there are no compiler errors before proceeding.

Step 4: Build the insert logic

Start implementing the user layer by updating the Main method in the Program.cs file to allow for inserting new items.

After the call to list out the categories and colors, add the following code:

```
Console.WriteLine("Would you like to create items?");
var createItems = Console.ReadLine().StartsWith("y", StringComparison.
OrdinalIgnoreCase);
if (createItems)
{
    Console.WriteLine("Adding new Item(s)");
    CreateMultipleItems(svc);
    Console.WriteLine("Items added");

    inventory = svc.ListInventory();
    inventory.ForEach(x => Console.WriteLine($"Item: {x}"));
}
```

Next, add the CreateMultipleItems code as a private static method:

```
private static void CreateMultipleItems(IItemsService svc)
{
    Console.WriteLine("Would you like to create items as a batch?");
    bool batchCreate = Console.ReadLine().StartsWith("y", StringComparison.
    OrdinalIgnoreCase);
    var allItems = new List<CreateOrUpdateItemDto>();

    bool createAnother = true;
    while (createAnother == true)
    {
        var newItem = new CreateOrUpdateItemDto();
        Console.WriteLine("Creating a new item.");
        Console.WriteLine("Please enter the name");
        newItem.Name = Console.ReadLine();
        Console.WriteLine("Please enter the description");
        newItem.Description = Console.ReadLine();
        Console.WriteLine("Please enter the notes");
```

```
newItem.Notes = Console.ReadLine();
Console.WriteLine("Please enter the Category [B]ooks, [M]ovies,
[G]ames");
newItem.CategoryId = GetCategoryId(Console.ReadLine().Substring(0,
1).ToUpper());

if (!batchCreate)
{
    svc.InsertOrUpdateItem(newItem);
}
else
{
    allItems.Add(newItem);
}

Console.WriteLine("Would you like to create another item?");
createAnother = Console.ReadLine().StartsWith("y",
StringComparison.OrdinalIgnoreCase);

if (batchCreate && !createAnother)
{
    svc.InsertOrUpdateItems(allItems);
}
        }
    }
}
```

Make sure to add the missing using statements for System.Collections.Generic and InventoryModels.Dtos so the code would compile once we add the missing GetCategoryId method.

There are a couple of interesting things happening in this method. First, we're taking user input to validate if they want to do a one-off insert or use a batched approach on the insert. We then gather the details from the user until they are done, and each time through we either add the new item to the database and save changes or we add the new item to a list of items to add later in a batch.

Either way, when the user has completed their operations, they have either entered multiple items and saved each item entry, or they have added multiple items and then saved them all in a batch of operations within a transaction.

Also notice that in this method is a call to a common method called GetCategoryId to get the Category so that we can assign the correct category id to the item as we add it. Let's add that common GetCategoryId method next as another private static method that returns an integer.

```
private static int GetCategoryId(string input)
{
    switch (input)
    {
        case "B":
            return _categories.FirstOrDefault(x => x.Category.ToLower().
            Equals("books"))?.Id ?? -1;
        case "M":
            return _categories.FirstOrDefault(x => x.Category.ToLower().
            Equals("movies"))?.Id ?? -1;
        case "G":
            return _categories.FirstOrDefault(x => x.Category.ToLower().
            Equals("games"))?.Id ?? -1;
        default:
            return -1;
    }
}
```

As you may have noticed, we now have to have a reference for all of the categories in the system. At the top of the method, with the other class-level variable declarations, add this line:

```
private static List<CategoryDto> _categories;
```

Then set the categories in the Main method for use in our insert and update logic. Right above the place in the Main method where we just added the create items logic, add the line of code to set the static categories variable to the result of the call to ListCategoriesAndColors:

```
_categories = categoriesAndColors;
```

For clarity, the new code is shown in place in Figure 11-14.

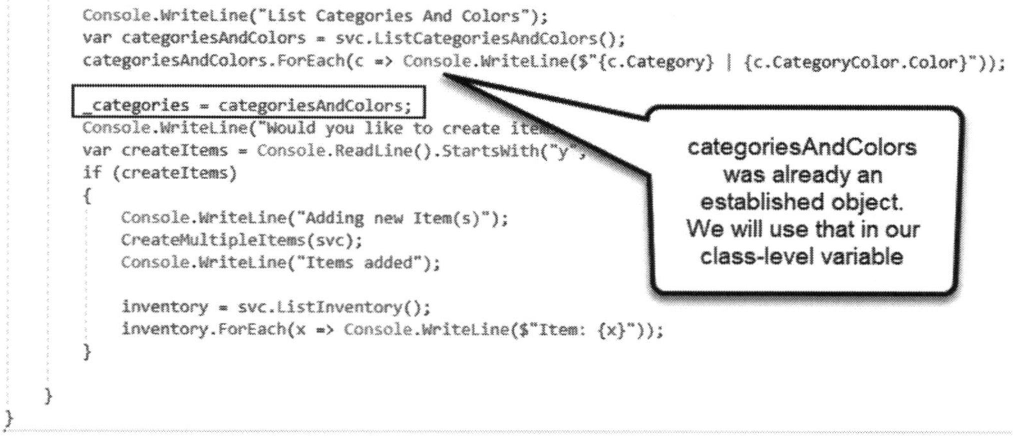

```
    Console.WriteLine("List Categories And Colors");
    var categoriesAndColors = svc.ListCategoriesAndColors();
    categoriesAndColors.ForEach(c => Console.WriteLine($"{c.Category} | {c.CategoryColor.Color}"));

    _categories = categoriesAndColors;
    Console.WriteLine("Would you like to create item
    var createItems = Console.ReadLine().StartsWith("y",
    if (createItems)
    {
        Console.WriteLine("Adding new Item(s)");
        CreateMultipleItems(svc);
        Console.WriteLine("Items added");

        inventory = svc.ListInventory();
        inventory.ForEach(x => Console.WriteLine($"Item: {x}"));
    }

}
}
```

> categoriesAndColors
> was already an
> established object.
> We will use that in our
> class-level variable

Figure 11-14. *Setting the categories*

Update any missing references, including System.Linq, and then note that we also
still need to add the Id property to the CategoryDto object. Back in the InventoryModels
project in the CategoryDto object, add the Id property as follows:

```
public int Id { get; set; }
```

We can now run the program and add some items. On the first run, add a single item.
You don't have to copy me, of course, but a sample run might look like what is shown in
Figure 11-15.

```
Would you like to create items?
y
Adding new Item(s)
Would you like to create items as a batch?
n
Creating a new item.
Please enter the name
Harry Potter and the Sorcerer's Stone
Please enter the description
The first of 8 Harry Potter movies
Please enter the notes
Was originally titled "Harry Potter and the Philosopher's Stone"
Please enter the Category [B]ooks, [M]ovies, [G]ames
M
Would you like to create another item?
n
Items added
Item: Batman Begins              | Why do we fall, Bruce?
Item: Battlefield 5              | First person shooter
Item: Harry Potter and the Sorcerer's Stone | The first of 8 Harry Potter movies
Item: Practical Entity Framework | The book that teaches practical application with EF
Item: The Lord of the Rings      | The fellowship of the Ring
Item: Top Gun                    | I feel the need, the need for speed
Item: World Of Tanks             | AN MMO WW2 Tanks First-Person Shooter

C:\APressEntityFramework\Code\Chapter11\Activity1102_TransactionsAndUnitOfWork\Activity110:
n\Debug\netcoreapp3.1\Activity1102_TransactionsAndUnitOfWork.exe (process 9640) exited witl
To automatically close the console when debugging stops, enable Tools->Options->Debugging->:
```

Figure 11-15. *Adding a new movie to the inventory database*

After the first item is added, run the program again and add items as a batch. Feel free to put a debugger break in the database layer to see the operations in action as you are running them.

By the end of the exercise, try to have three or four disposable items to play with for the remaining parts of this activity (see Figure 11-16 for sample output after the operation is completed).

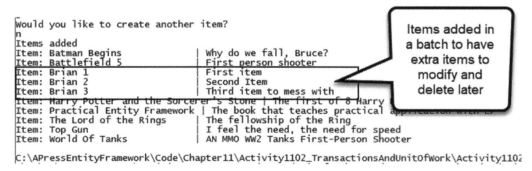

Figure 11-16. *Adding items as a batch, ending up with three new items total*

Step 5: Build the update logic

Now that the code is in place to insert the Items, we need to be able to update the Items. To do this, we need to add the logic to prompt the user for input as we did in the Insert method. Add the following code in the Main program after the insert logic calls (following the end of the if (createItems) block):

```
Console.WriteLine("Would you like to update items?");
var updateItems = Console.ReadLine().StartsWith("y", StringComparison.
OrdinalIgnoreCase);
if (updateItems)
{
    Console.WriteLine("Updating Item(s)");
    UpdateMultipleItems(svc);
    Console.WriteLine("Items updated");

    inventory = svc.ListInventory();
    inventory.ForEach(x => Console.WriteLine($"Item: {x}"));
}
```

Then add the UpdateMultipleItems method after the GetCategoryId method using the following code:

```
public static void UpdateMultipleItems(IItemsService svc)
{
    Console.WriteLine("Would you like to update items as a batch?");
    bool batchUpdate = Console.ReadLine().StartsWith("y", StringComparison.
OrdinalIgnoreCase);
    var allItems = new List<CreateOrUpdateItemDto>();

    bool updateAnother = true;
    while (updateAnother == true)
    {
        Console.WriteLine("Items");
        Console.WriteLine("Enter the ID number to update");
        Console.WriteLine("*******************************");
        var items = svc.ListInventory();
        items.ForEach(x => Console.WriteLine($"ID: {x.Id} | {x.Name}"));
```

```
Console.WriteLine("*******************************");
int id = 0;
if (int.TryParse(Console.ReadLine(), out id))
{
    var itemMatch = items.FirstOrDefault(x => x.Id == id);
    if (itemMatch != null)
    {
        var updItem = _mapper.Map<CreateOrUpdateItemDto>(_mapper.
        Map<Item>(itemMatch));
        Console.WriteLine("Enter the new name [leave blank to keep
        existing]");
        var newName = Console.ReadLine();
        updItem.Name = !string.IsNullOrWhiteSpace(newName) ?
        newName : updItem.Name;
        Console.WriteLine("Enter the new desc [leave blank to keep
        existing]");
        var newDesc = Console.ReadLine();
        updItem.Description = !string.IsNullOrWhiteSpace(newDesc) ?
        newDesc : updItem.Description;
        Console.WriteLine("Enter the new notes [leave blank to keep
        existing]");
        var newNotes = Console.ReadLine();
        updItem.Notes = !string.IsNullOrWhiteSpace(newNotes) ?
        newNotes : updItem.Notes;
        Console.WriteLine("Toggle Item Active Status? [y/n]");
        var toggleActive = Console.ReadLine().Substring(0, 1).
        Equals("y", StringComparison.OrdinalIgnoreCase);
        if (toggleActive)
        {
            updItem.IsActive = !updItem.IsActive;
        }

        Console.WriteLine("Enter the category - [B]ooks, [M]ovies,
        [G]ames, or [N]o Change");
        var userChoice = Console.ReadLine().Substring(0, 1).
        ToUpper();
```

490

```
            updItem.CategoryId = userChoice.Equals("N",
            StringComparison.OrdinalIgnoreCase) ? itemMatch.CategoryId
                                : GetCategoryId(userChoice);

            if (!batchUpdate)
            {
                svc.InsertOrUpdateItem(updItem);
            }
            else
            {
                allItems.Add(updItem);
            }
        }
    }

    Console.WriteLine("Would you like to update another?");
    updateAnother = Console.ReadLine().StartsWith("y",
    StringComparison.OrdinalIgnoreCase);
    if (batchUpdate && !updateAnother)
    {
        svc.InsertOrUpdateItems(allItems);
    }
    }
}
```

Note that this method gives the user a chance to perform a single update and save or to batch the updates into one transaction.

We also need to add the Id to the ItemDto. In the InventoryModels projects in the Dtos folder, locate the ItemDto.cs file and add the Id property to it using this line of code: public int Id { get; set; }. Then add an additional property for CategoryId as public int CategoryId { get; set; }.

For clarity, review Figure 11-17 to see the completed implementation of the
ItemDto class:

```
namespace InventoryModels.Dtos
{
    4 references
    public class ItemDto
    {
        2 references
        public int Id { get; set; }
        3 references
        public string Name { get; set; }
        1 reference
        public string Description { get; set; }
        1 reference
        public int CategoryId { get; set; }

        0 references
        public override string ToString()
        {
            return $"{Name,-25} | {Description}";
        }
    }
}
```

Figure 11-17. *The ItemDto class after updating to contain the two new properties*

Run the program and update with the single update and then run again and update
as a batch. Feel free to put a breakpoint in the business or database layer to see the code
in action. Figure 11-18 shows what it might look like to add an item.

```
Enter the ID number to update
*******************************
ID: 128 | Batman Begins
ID: 131 | Battlefield 5
ID: 134 | Brian 1
ID: 135 | Brian 2
ID: 136 | Brian 3
ID: 133 | Harry Potter and the Sorcerer's Stone
ID: 129 | Practical Entity Framework
ID: 130 | The Lord of the Rings
ID: 127 | Top Gun
ID: 132 | World Of Tanks
*******************************
135
Enter the new name [leave blank to keep existing]
Brian 2 Updated
Enter the new desc [leave blank to keep existing]
Updated as a single record
Enter the new notes [leave blank to keep existing]

Toggle Item Active Status? [y/n]
n
Enter the category - [B]ooks, [M]ovies, [G]ames, or [N]o Change
N
Would you like to update another?
n
Items updated
Item: Batman Begins                       | Why do we fall, Bruce?
Item: Battlefield 5                       | First person shooter
Item: Brian 1                             | First item
Item: Brian 2 Updated                     | Updated as a single record
Item: Brian 3                             | Third item to mess with
Item: Harry Potter and the Sorcerer's Stone | The first of 8 Harry Potter movies
Item: Practical Entity Framework | The book that teaches practical application with EF
Item: The Lord of the Rings               | The fellowship of the Ring
Item: Top Gun                             | I feel the need, the need for speed
Item: World Of Tanks                      | AN MMO WW2 Tanks First-Person Shooter
```

Figure 11-18. *Updating a single item*

The last part of the program needs to be able to delete the items.

Step 6: Build the delete logic

For this final part of the program, we'll follow the same logic we've followed earlier to delete either one item at a time or a batch of items.

Update the Main method to include logic for deleting Items, and also add a statement that lets the user know the program is done executing. Following the if (updateItems) block of code we just added in the previous step, add the following code to complete the Main method:

```
Console.WriteLine("Would you like to delete items?");
var deleteItems = Console.ReadLine().StartsWith("y", StringComparison.
OrdinalIgnoreCase);
```

```
    if (deleteItems)
    {
        Console.WriteLine("Deleting Item(s)");
        DeleteMultipleItems(svc);
        Console.WriteLine("Items Deleted");

        inventory = svc.ListInventory();
        inventory.ForEach(x => Console.WriteLine($"Item: {x}"));
    }
}
Console.WriteLine("Program Complete");
```

After implementing this logic in the Main method, add the code to delete multiple items in a method called DeleteMultipleItems(IItemsService svc). As you can see, the method should have an injectable ItemsService object.

```
public static void DeleteMultipleItems(IItemsService svc)
{
    Console.WriteLine("Would you like to delete items as a batch?");
    bool batchDelete = Console.ReadLine().StartsWith("y", StringComparison.
    OrdinalIgnoreCase);
    var allItems = new List<int>();

    bool deleteAnother = true;
    while (deleteAnother == true)
    {
        Console.WriteLine("Items");
        Console.WriteLine("Enter the ID number to delete");
        Console.WriteLine("*****************************");
        var items = svc.ListInventory();
        items.ForEach(x => Console.WriteLine($"ID: {x.Id} | {x.Name}"));
        Console.WriteLine("*****************************");
        if (batchDelete && allItems.Any())
        {
            Console.WriteLine("Items scheduled for delete");
            allItems.ForEach(x => Console.Write($"{x},"));
            Console.WriteLine();
            Console.WriteLine("*****************************");
        }
```

```csharp
int id = 0;

if (int.TryParse(Console.ReadLine(), out id))
{
    var itemMatch = items.FirstOrDefault(x => x.Id == id);
    if (itemMatch != null)
    {
        if (batchDelete)
        {
            if (!allItems.Contains(itemMatch.Id))
            {
                allItems.Add(itemMatch.Id);
            }
        }
        else
        {
            Console.WriteLine($"Are you sure you want to delete the
            item {itemMatch.Id}-{itemMatch.Name}");
            if (Console.ReadLine().StartsWith("y",
            StringComparison.OrdinalIgnoreCase))
            {
                svc.DeleteItem(itemMatch.Id);
                Console.WriteLine("Item Deleted");
            }
        }
    }
}

Console.WriteLine("Would you like to delete another item?");
deleteAnother = Console.ReadLine().StartsWith("y",
StringComparison.OrdinalIgnoreCase);

if (batchDelete && !deleteAnother)
{
    Console.WriteLine("Are you sure you want to delete the
    following items: ");
    allItems.ForEach(x => Console.Write($"{x},"));
```

495

```
                Console.WriteLine();
                if (Console.ReadLine().StartsWith("y", StringComparison.
                OrdinalIgnoreCase))
                {
                    svc.DeleteItems(allItems);
                    Console.WriteLine("Items Deleted");
                }
            }
        }
}
```

Run the program to see it all in action. Make sure to test the ability to delete a single item and a batch of items. Figure 11-19 shows a sample run where I deleted one entry:

```
Would you like to delete items?
y
Deleting Item(s)
Would you like to delete items as a batch?
n
Items
Enter the ID number to delete
********************************
ID: 128 | Batman Begins
ID: 131 | Battlefield 5
ID: 134 | Brian 1
ID: 135 | Brian 2 Updated
ID: 136 | Brian 3
ID: 133 | Harry Potter and the Sorcerer's Stone
ID: 129 | Practical Entity Framework
ID: 130 | The Lord of the Rings
ID: 127 | Top Gun
ID: 132 | World Of Tanks
********************************
136
Are you sure you want to delete the item 136-Brian 3
y
Item Deleted
Would you like to delete another item?
n
Items Deleted
Item: Batman Begins                      | Why do we fall, Bruce?
Item: Battlefield 5                      | First person shooter
Item: Brian 1                            | First item
Item: Brian 2 Updated                    | Updated as a single record
Item: Harry Potter and the Sorcerer's Stone | The first of 8 Harry Potter movies
Item: Practical Entity Framework | The book that teaches practical application with EF
Item: The Lord of the Rings      | The fellowship of the Ring
Item: Top Gun                    | I feel the need, the need for speed
Item: World Of Tanks             | AN MMO WW2 Tanks First-Person Shooter
Program Complete
```

Figure 11-19. *Deleting an Item from the inventory database*

Step 7: Update the transaction scope

The program is completed, but we'd be missing out if we didn't pay attention to one last detail. That detail is transaction scope.

Right now, we have a couple of batch methods that just use transactions in a using statement. When working with transactions, we'll need to make sure to put our code into scope instead of just running a plain transaction. By doing this, we can ensure control over the transaction's isolation level. If we don't set the isolation level, in a busy application, we'll likely run into issues with deadlocks and/or concurrency conflicts.

Return to the InventoryDatabaseLayer project and find the method for InsertOrUpdateItems in the InventoryDatabaseRepo.cs file. Change the InsertOrUpdateItems method to use a scope instead of a raw transaction by changing the using statement with the following code:

```
using (var scope = new TransactionScope(TransactionScopeOption.Required
        , new TransactionOptions
            { IsolationLevel = IsolationLevel.ReadUncommitted }))
{
    try
    { //leave the rest of the code as is.
```

After updating the code, change the calls for transaction.Commit() to scope. Complete() and just remove the call for transaction.Rollback().

For clarity, review Figure 11-20, which shows the updated code in its entirety.

```
public void InsertOrUpdateItems(List<Item> items)
{
    using (var scope = new TransactionScope(TransactionScopeOption.Required
                , new TransactionOptions
                    { IsolationLevel = IsolationLevel.ReadUncommitted }))
    {
        try
        {
            foreach (var item in items)
            {
                var success = InsertOrUpdateItem(item) > 0;
                if (!success) throw new Exception($"Error saving the item {item.Name}");
            }

            scope.Complete();
        }
        catch (Exception ex)
        {
            //log it:
            Debug.WriteLine(ex.ToString());
            throw ex;
        }
    }
}
```

Figure 11-20. *Using a scope to set isolation level on a transaction to avoid deadlocks*

To finish up, also change the delete method's transaction to use a similar transaction scope, and then run the program to make sure it still works as expected. Review Figure 11-21 for clarity.

```
public void DeleteItems(List<int> itemIds)
{
    using (var scope = new TransactionScope(TransactionScopeOption.Required
                , new TransactionOptions
                { IsolationLevel = IsolationLevel.ReadUncommitted }))
    {
        try
        {
            foreach (var itemId in itemIds)
            {
                DeleteItem(itemId);
            }

            scope.Complete();
        }
        catch (Exception ex)
        {
            //log it:
            Debug.WriteLine(ex.ToString());
            throw ex;  //make sure it is known that the transaction failed
        }
    }
}
```

Figure 11-21. *Using the TransactionScope in the DeleteItems method*

Final thoughts on activity 1102

In activity 1102, we were able to build out our own repository and then implement a couple of units of work in the solution. As we've discussed, *EF* itself has built-in repository and unit of work patterns, and, in most cases, we should just leverage the built-in features of *EF*.

However, even with the abilities of *EF*, there are times when we want to take more control of the logic and, along with that, how and what is applied to the database. In these cases, using our own versions of the repository and unit of work patterns on top of what EF offers can generally work to meet our needs.

Final thoughts for this chapter

This chapter gave us a chance to really build out our solution to make it very robust. Additionally, we had a chance in this chapter to discuss the two major patterns in any database *object-relational mapper (ORM)*.

The first pattern – the *repository pattern* – allows us to work with any entity using the same default signatures for each operation. *EF* has a great repository pattern built in, where we can generally leverage the context and start adding, deleting, updating, and listing data with just a few simple calls and not a lot of work on our part.

The second pattern we discussed was the *unit of work pattern*. In the *UoW* pattern, we want to make sure that our solution is robust across an entire business process. While *EF* has a built-in unit of work, waiting to save changes may not always be the most performant solution and/or may lead to a lot of frustration if operations are consistently rejected or don't work as expected due to small or unforeseen errors.

To overcome any limitations we encounter, we saw how to easily create our own repositories for managing the business and data relationship. We also learned how to use transactions to allow the completion of our own custom units of work to save changes or roll back the changes if any part of the transaction fails.

Now that our solution is layered for separation of concerns, robust with our database and operations that we've built out, and we have the knowledge we need, we could consider releasing this code to production. However, shipping the code as is right now would be extremely risky, because we haven't set up unit and integration tests. In the next chapter, we'll add unit and integration tests so that we can modify our code in the future without fear, as well as have confidence that the system is ready to ship.

CHAPTER 12

Unit Testing, Integration Testing, and Mocking

Testing your code is a must-have, not a nice-to-have

Your system has thousands of lines of code. There is at least one user interface (UI) that connects to your business layer, and your system has multiple user interfaces, from Web to device to desktop to scanners to monitors, and more. And now it's time to change some code. Perhaps that code has been around for a while. Chances are, you didn't write the code. The system certainly has some extremely risky scenarios where broken code can mean loss of revenue (even millions), or, in an even more high-risk scenario, lives might hang in the balance.

The code needs to be changed

The directive to make some modifications to the code has been passed to you. As a result, you will be changing code deep in the core components of one of the pillars of the system, and you need to ensure that all the other pieces of the system remain functional after these changes.

Also, as if this task wasn't already sufficiently risky, there aren't any resources available to help you perform a full regression test on the other business layer components or the UI for each of the supported devices. Like it or not, this is bound to happen to you and maybe already has at some point in your career.

© Brian L. Gorman 2020
B. L. Gorman, *Practical Entity Framework*, https://doi.org/10.1007/978-1-4842-6044-9_12

The database is the lifeblood of the application

Even though the UI often defines how the users see and interact with the data, the database is the place where the roots of the system live. Without the database, without the business layer transformations, and without the robustness of your overall domain design, the UI would just be a form on a page that pretends to do something for the user.

Testing saves your sanity and protects the system

In the previous scenario, having a full suite of automated tests that can be run would be the ideal place to be. Our book will not go into automated UI testing solutions like Selenium or Cypress.IO, but as the back-end developer or full-stack developer responsible for the business and database layers of the application, we do need some solutions.

There are many different layers of testing that could be used, however; so how much testing is enough testing, and how does each type work? Furthermore, what does it mean to mock and what are the various reasons for using each type of testing.

Two different approaches leading to the ability to test changes

In this chapter, we are going to take some time to examine two ways in which we can test the database portion of our code. While taking these various approaches to testing, we'll see what the differences are between unit tests and integration tests.

Unit testing

The first approach to testing our code is likely one you've heard of before – unit testing. Unit testing is the ability to run tests against the codebase that are simple, repeatable, and are not dependent on other portions of the system – i.e., single units under test. Furthermore, unit tests do not require a connection to any database or other data storage mechanisms. In some instances, files might be used in unit tests, but only as an aid to test the system under test.

There are many different approaches to writing unit tests. Most developers agree on two basic patterns for writing tests, which really come down to one overall testing strategy. We will use both approaches in conjunction with each other in our unit tests.

The first approach is a simple red-green-refactor approach, where you write the test and ensure the test fails if the code is bad, then you write the code to pass the test, and then you refactor your tests to eliminate any duplicated code.

The second approach is using the arrange-act-assert approach. In this approach, for each unit test you write, start by arranging the data for the test, then perform the single act that needs to be tested, and finish the test with assertions to validate the data is in place as expected.

For more information on unit testing, including the AAA pattern and how to write unit tests in Visual Studio, please review this link from Microsoft: `https://docs.microsoft.com/en-us/visualstudio/test/unit-test-basics?view=vs-2019`.

Libraries utilized

While performing our unit tests, we'll also need to mock data. To accomplish mocking, we'll be using one of the more popular mocking libraries: *Moq*. For our unit testing, we'll also use the *Shouldly* library.

Integration testing

The second form of testing we'll be looking at is integration testing. For integration testing, we will be leveraging the .Net in-memory database instance to generate an in-memory version of our database, and then we'll write our integration tests against that database.

The nice thing about this implementation will be that it will be lightweight and portable to any development environment. Additionally, the use of the in-memory database means that we never have to be concerned with data being out of sync in our integration tests based on other users or some test database state. With integration testing, we also have no fear that we might screw up a shared test database or even a local development database, since we'll not be connecting to the actual databases.

One drawback to using in-memory database solutions might be that they are not fully functioning, or they might just not be robust enough. Therefore, if your solution has a lot of stored procedures integrated into the solution, or a number of database-heavy operations using functions, you should consider just pointing your integration tests at a database hosted in a local test database specifically for testing on your development machine.

Of course, the other solution to not having access to functions and procedures is just to mock the results of your stored procedures, but that sort of defeats the purpose of an integration test.

Chapter 12 Activities: Unit and Integration Testing

For our learning in this chapter, we're going to cover two different types of unit tests in two different activities and apply them to our homegrown inventory system solution.

Each activity will cover aspects of unit testing as we build our solutions. While this simple work will not make us testing experts, it should provide us with the foundation to become a testing expert through trial and error in the future.

The first activity we'll do is going to implement some simple unit tests against the business layer in our system. While we will keep these activities simple, this unit testing solution will show us how we can mock some data and work with it in our unit tests to ensure the system is functioning correctly at the business layer without being coupled to the database layer or connected to an actual database.

The second activity we will do will show us what it takes to set up our integration testing and will also show us how to ensure that our database is working as expected with the code we are writing.

By having the fully functioning data-integration tests, we can see the operation of our system from start to finish with real data, not just fabricated expected data.

By implementing each of these solutions, we'll see the differences in the two approaches. We'll also learn why both have their place in our system. Additionally, seeing all of this in action will set us up to have the peace of mind that we desire in the future when it's time to modify the system.

Activity 1201: Unit testing with mocking

In this first activity, we'll set up our solution and then set the unit tests in place that will help us to determine that our code is functioning correctly at the business layer level as expected.

Mocking for our tests

As we set up these unit tests, we'll see how the data can be mocked and used in the unit tests to show the solution working as expected in both good- and bad-data scenarios.

Step 1: Get set up

To begin, grab a copy of the `Activity1201_UnitTestingWithMocking_Starter.zip` files, and get them going on your machine. As before, make sure to set connections and run database migrations to ensure your code and database are up to date and that there are no issues. Run the program to make sure it works. You should see the regular output from our program as per the output at the end of Chapter 11. Alternatively, you could continue working with your own existing code that you've been building through the book around the inventory system. As a reminder, as of the end of Chapter 11, we have the ability to do basic CRUD actions against our database (review Figure 12-1 for sample output).

```
New Item] 127        |Top Gun                                    |Comedy
New Item] 128        |Batman Begins                              |Sci/Fi
New Item] 128        |Batman Begins                              |Drama
New Item] 129        |Practical Entity Framework                 |
New Item] 130        |The Lord of the Rings                      |Sci/Fi
New Item] 130        |The Lord of the Rings                      |Fantasy
New Item] 131        |Battlefield 5                              |Sci/Fi
New Item] 132        |World Of Tanks                             |
New Item] 133        |Harry Potter and the Sorcerer's Stone      |
New Item] 134        |Brian 1                                    |
New Item] 135        |Brian 2 Updated                            |
New Item] 136        |Brian 3                                    |
List Categories And Colors
Movies | Blue
Books | Red
Games | Green
Would you like to create items?
n
Would you like to update items?
n
Would you like to delete items?
n
Program Complete

C:\APressEntityFramework\Code\Chapter12\Activity1201_UnitTestingWithMocking\Activit:
```

Figure 12-1. *The project runs as expected*

Step 2: Add the unit testing project to the solution

Right-click the Solution and select Add ➤ New Project (as shown in Figure 12-2).

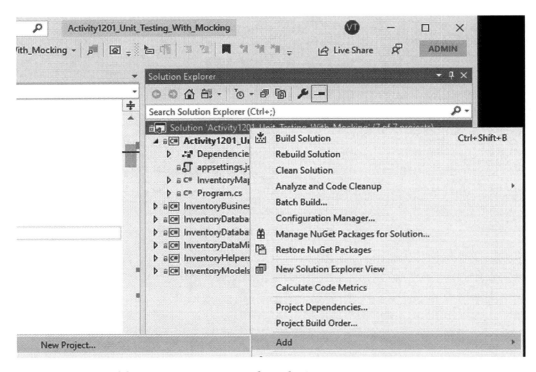

Figure 12-2. *Adding a new project to the solution*

Use the filter to select a Test project, and then select the MSTest Test Project for
.Net Core (review Figure 12-3).

Figure 12-3. *Creating a new MSTest Project*

Name the project InventoryManagerUnitTests and then create it (see Figure 12-4).

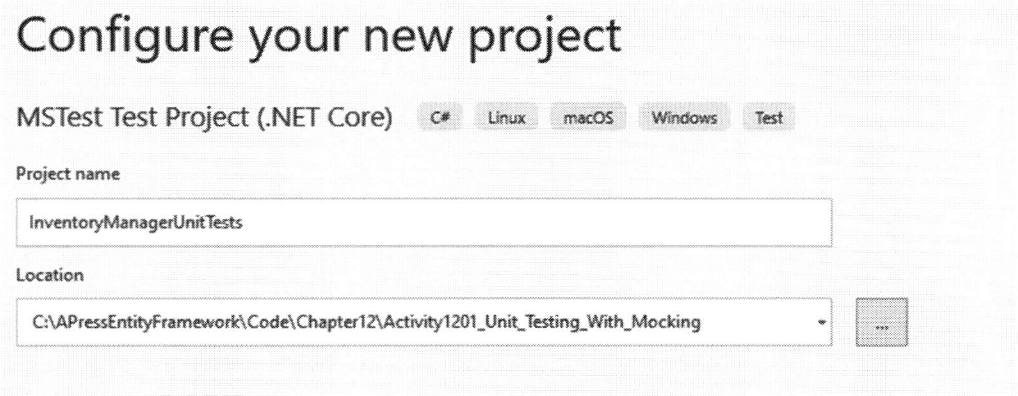

Configure your new project

MSTest Test Project (.NET Core)   C#   Linux   macOS   Windows   Test

Project name

InventoryManagerUnitTests

Location

C:\APressEntityFramework\Code\Chapter12\Activity1201_Unit_Testing_With_Mocking   ▾   ...

Figure 12-4. *Create the InventoryManagerUnitTests project*

Next, update the NuGet packages for the testing framework. Open the NuGet Package Manager and select the Updates tab. There will likely be four new package updates that you should get for the testing project. Check the box to select all packages, and then hit the Update button to get everything up to date. Figure 12-5 shows an overview of taking care of these updates for clarity.

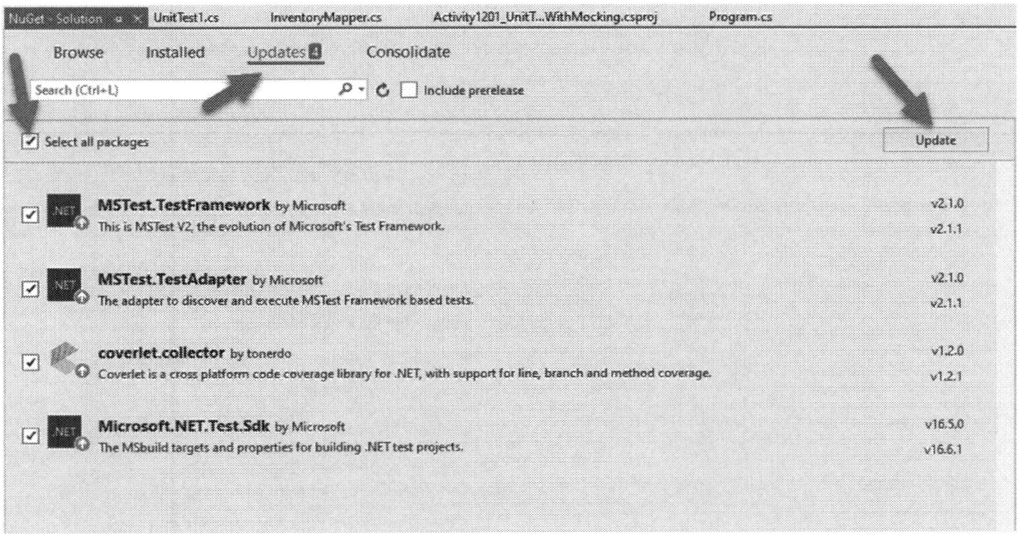

NuGet - Solution ⊟ ×   UnitTest1.cs   InventoryMapper.cs   Activity1201_UnitT...WithMocking.csproj   Program.cs

Browse   Installed   **Updates 4**   Consolidate

Search (Ctrl+L)   🔎 ▾   ↻   ☐ Include prerelease

☑ Select all packages   Update

☑ **MSTest.TestFramework** by Microsoft   v2.1.0
This is MSTest V2, the evolution of Microsoft's Test Framework.   v2.1.1

☑ **MSTest.TestAdapter** by Microsoft   v2.1.0
The adapter to discover and execute MSTest Framework based tests.   v2.1.1

☑ **coverlet.collector** by tonerdo   v1.2.0
Coverlet is a cross platform code coverage library for .NET, with support for line, branch and method coverage.   v1.2.1

☑ **Microsoft.NET.Test.Sdk** by Microsoft   v16.5.0
The MSbuild targets and properties for building .NET test projects.   v16.6.1

Figure 12-5. *Updating the NuGet packages in our new Testing project*

After updating the packages, rename `UnitTest1.cs` to `InventoryManagerUnitTests.cs`. Select `Yes` when it asks you to rename other references (review Figure 12-6).

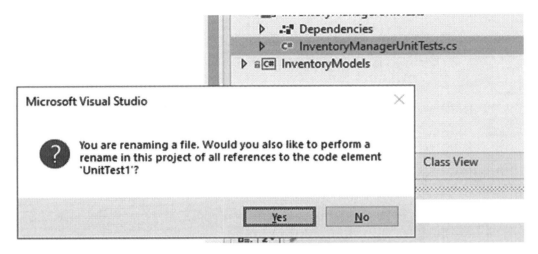

Figure 12-6. *Renaming the default class*

Step 3: Write the first unit test

We're going to need to bring in a bunch of references and libraries to make everything work, so let's start with creating a reference to the service project.

Right-click the unit testing project and select `Add Reference`. Then choose the service layer project (InventoryBusinessLayer) as a reference (as shown in Figure 12-7).

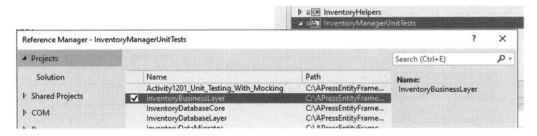

Figure 12-7. *Adding the Business Layer project to the unit tests*

Remember that the ultimate goal for these unit tests is just to test the service layer and not to test the actual database code. We'll get to the database code in the next activity for integration tests.

508

Also, please remember that this solution is simple, so the mocking may seem redundant and somewhat tedious for not a lot of gain. It is my hope that you will see the value and then take what you learn here and apply it to your more advanced real-world scenarios.

Using the code that follows, add a private instance of the IItemsService to the class and follow that with a method that will run before every test using the [TestInitialize] attribute:

```
private IItemsService _serviceLayer;

[TestInitialize]
public void testBeforeTestRuns()
{
    _serviceLayer = new ItemsService();
}
```

Add the using statement for the InventoryBusinessLayer project so that the IItemsService object will be defined.

We'll note that the ItemsService won't work as constructed here and come back to fix that in a moment. We need a context in order for the ItemsService to work.

Next, rename the default test to TestGetItems() and then place code in the method as follows (or simply just replace the TestMethod1 with this code):

```
[TestMethod]
public void TestGetItems()
{
    var result = _serviceLayer.ListInventory();
    Assert.IsNotNull(result);
    Assert.IsTrue(result.Count > 0);
}
```

Step 4: Add Moq to the test project

Next, we need to add the *Moq* library to our unit testing project. Temporarily comment out the broken service layer line of code so that the projects will build as expected. Then use the NuGet Package Manager to Manage NuGet Packages for the Solution.

Browse for *Moq* and then add it to the InventoryManagerUnitTests project using the Install button (see Figure 12-8 for clarity).

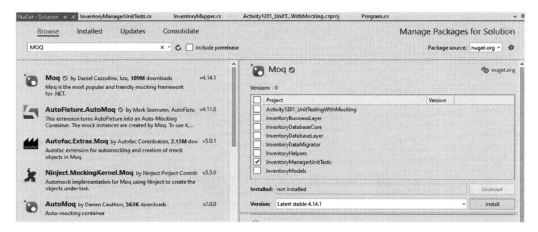

Figure 12-8. *Adding Moq to the project*

After adding Moq, the next thing we need to do is create a mock of our service layer so that we can understand how this works.

The first step when authoring any unit tests is identifying what exactly is your system under test. Our system under test will be the service layer project. Before we do that, however, let's just see a simple instance of Moq in action to get a feeling for how using Moq works.

Under the private IItemsService _serviceLayer line of code, add a new line of code: private Mock<IItemsService> _mockServiceLayer;. In the TestInitialize method, instantiate a new version of this object with the line of code: _mockServiceLayer = new Mock<IItemsService>();. Additionally, add the using statement for Moq to make sure that the Mock object is defined. For clarity, the expected code to this point is shown in Figure 12-9.

```
[TestClass]
0 references
public class InventoryManagerUnitTests
{
    private IItemsService _serviceLayer;
    private Mock<IItemsService> _mockServiceLayer;

    [TestInitialize]
    0 references
    public void testBeforeTestRuns()
    {
        //_serviceLayer = new ItemsService();
        _mockServiceLayer = new Mock<IItemsService>();
    }

    [TestMethod]
    ◈ | 0 references
    public void TestGetItems()
    {
        var result = _serviceLayer.ListInventory();
        Assert.IsNotNull(result);
        Assert.IsTrue(result.Count > 0);
    }

}
```

Figure 12-9. *Initializing a mocked version of the service layer and the current code in our unit test to this point*

Next, in the GetItems test, change the method to reference the mock service layer object and call to ListInventory with the following code:

```
var result = _mockServiceLayer.Object.ListInventory();
```

With that in place, we are ready to run our test. Use the key chord *ctrl+r and* then *ctrl+t* to run the test. When running, we get an error, as shown in Figure 12-10.

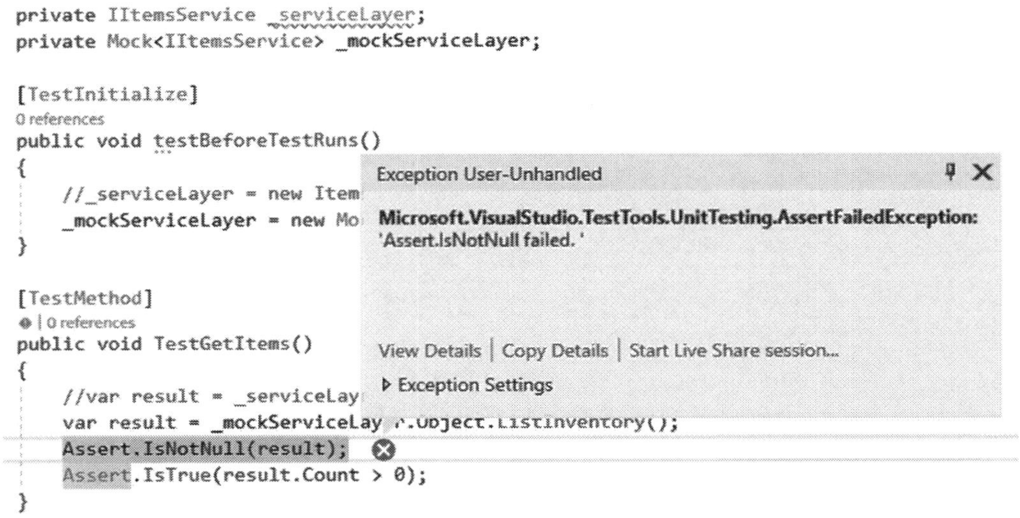

```
private IItemsService _serviceLayer;
private Mock<IItemsService> _mockServiceLayer;

[TestInitialize]
0 references
public void testBeforeTestRuns()
{
    //_serviceLayer = new Item
    _mockServiceLayer = new Mo
}

[TestMethod]
* | 0 references
public void TestGetItems()
{
    //var result = _serviceLay
    var result = _mockServiceLay r.Object.ListInventory();
    Assert.IsNotNull(result);  ⊗
    Assert.IsTrue(result.Count > 0);
}
```

Exception User-Unhandled   ⊓ ✕

Microsoft.VisualStudio.TestTools.UnitTesting.AssertFailedException: 'Assert.IsNotNull failed. '

View Details | Copy Details | Start Live Share session...

▷ Exception Settings

Figure 12-10. *The first test is failing for being null when expected values should exist*

The reason this result is null is because we need to actually set up our test to return results. Moq works by injecting values into the mocked object for you to use when you are testing. Simply calling the method is not sufficient to mock your result. You actually need to define it and what its value will be when called.

In the initialize method, add a new list of ItemDto, using whatever you want for the text of each item:

```
var items = new List<ItemDto>() {
    new ItemDto() { Id = 1, Name="Star Wars IV: A New Hope"
                        , Description = "Luke's Friends", CategoryId = 2  },
    new ItemDto() { Id = 2, Name="Star Wars V: The Empire Strikes Back"
                        , Description = "Luke's Dad", CategoryId = 2  },
    new ItemDto() { Id = 3, Name="Star Wars VI: The Return of the Jedi"
                        , Description = "Luke's Sister", CategoryId = 2}
};
```

Next, set up the mock service layer to return that list when the method for listing inventory is found. Make sure to also add the using statement for InventoryModels.

Dtos so the code will compile. After the line of code that creates the new Mock<IItemsService>, add the following line of code:

```
_mockServiceLayer.Setup(m => m.ListInventory()).Returns(items);
```

Now run the unit test as before. It should be no surprise that the test is now passing. Here is the bad news. This test is absolutely useless. Figure 12-11 shows what the passing test looks like in the Test Explorer. If you can't currently see the Test Explorer, you can open it from the View ➤ Test Explorer menu item or via the key-chord combination of ctrl+E, T.

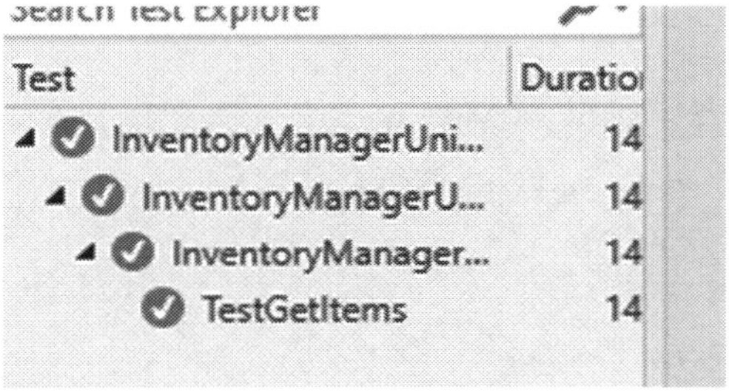

Figure 12-11. *The test passes and results are shown in the Test Explorer window*

The reason this test is useless is because we told the test exactly how to pass. Nothing was really tested. Now, I don't know about you, but I surely don't want to write code for the sake of code and green checkmarks.

Don't fret, however, because there was value in this part of the activity. That value was seeing how Moq works.

- First, you create an instance of the thing you don't really want to instantiate that you need.

- Then you tell the thing what to return when its methods are called.

- Finally, you can use that to enhance your unit testing for your system under test without coupling to other dependencies.

Now we are armed with the knowledge to make sure we actually do some good testing.

We want our system under test to be the service layer. In order to make it work, we need a *mapper* and we need a *mocked database layer instance*. However, the one thing we do not want in our unit test is an actual database context, so we need to be able to create a mock on the database layer.

Step 5: Mocking the injectable types, then testing the service layer

Comment out or remove the code for mocking the items service. We no longer need it. I'll leave it in my final solution for reference purposes only.

At this point, you should have the private class variable for the _serviceLayer, the instantiation that doesn't work in the initialization method (uncomment it now if you didn't already), and set the TestGetItems back to using the service layer we actually want to test. The current code for your class should now be as follows:

```
private IItemsService _serviceLayer;

[TestInitialize]
public void testBeforeTestRuns()
{
    _serviceLayer = new ItemsService();
    var items = new List<ItemDto>() {
        new ItemDto() { Id = 1, Name="Star Wars IV: A New Hope"
                                , Description = "Luke's Friends",
                                CategoryId = 2  },
        new ItemDto() { Id = 2, Name="Star Wars V: The Empire Strikes Back"
                                , Description = "Luke's Dad", CategoryId = 2  },
        new ItemDto() { Id = 3, Name="Star Wars VI: The Return of the Jedi"
                                , Description = "Luke's Sister", CategoryId = 2}
    };
}

[TestMethod]
public void TestGetItems()
{
```

```
    var result = _serviceLayer.ListInventory();
    Assert.IsNotNull(result);
    Assert.IsTrue(result.Count > 0);
}
```

Currently, the line for serviceLayer = new ItemsService() will not work. We'll fix this soon.

To make this work, we need to set up the AutoMapper mappings. We'll use the same code we've used for the Program project. We also need to add the references to AutoMapper into our test project.

Start by bringing in AutoMapper using the NuGet Package Manager. I assume that is an operation you are in command of by now. If not, refer to the previous example, only this time use the Installed tab, and then select the two AutoMapper projects and install them both to the InventoryManagerUnitTests project (see Figure 12-12).

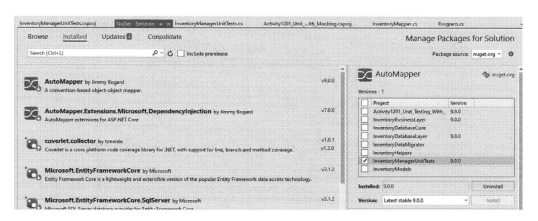

Figure 12-12. *Adding AutoMapper to the test project*

Add a new class InventoryMapper.cs to the project, and then copy and paste the code from the program's InventoryMapper.cs file to this test project file. For our simple project, it is not worth building a new library to keep from sharing just a few lines of code (review Figure 12-13 for clarity – remember that this is the exact same code from InventoryMapper in the main activity project).

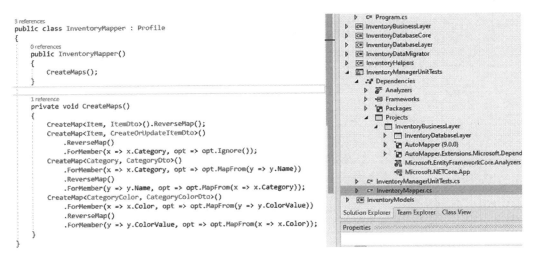

```
3 references
public class InventoryMapper : Profile
{
    0 references
    public InventoryMapper()
    {
        CreateMaps();
    }

    1 reference
    private void CreateMaps()
    {
        CreateMap<Item, ItemDto>().ReverseMap();
        CreateMap<Item, CreateOrUpdateItemDto>()
            .ReverseMap()
            .ForMember(x => x.Category, opt => opt.Ignore());
        CreateMap<Category, CategoryDto>()
            .ForMember(x => x.Category, opt => opt.MapFrom(y => y.Name))
            .ReverseMap()
            .ForMember(y => y.Name, opt => opt.MapFrom(x => x.Category));
        CreateMap<CategoryColor, CategoryColorDto>()
            .ForMember(x => x.Color, opt => opt.MapFrom(y => y.ColorValue))
            .ReverseMap()
            .ForMember(y => y.ColorValue, opt => opt.MapFrom(x => x.Color));
    }
}
```

Figure 12-13. *The InventoryMapper class in the testing project using the exact same code as in the main Activity project, copied and pasted for simplicity*

Next, we'll use the `ClassInitialize` *attribute* to make sure the mapper is set up when the test harness is instantiated. The `ClassInitialize` method needs a `TestContext`.

Add the class-level variables following the declaration of the `_serviceLayer` so that the mapper will work as expected:

```
private static MapperConfiguration _mapperConfig;
private static IMapper _mapper;
private static IServiceProvider _serviceProvider;
public TestContext TestContext { get; set; }
```

Add the code from the *Program's* `BuildMapper` method and the new *Initializer* method in the InventoryManagerUnitTests file as follows:

```
[ClassInitialize]
public static void BeforeAllTests(TestContext testContext)
{
    var services = new ServiceCollection();
    services.AddAutoMapper(typeof(InventoryMapper));
```

```
_serviceProvider = services.BuildServiceProvider();

_mapperConfig = new MapperConfiguration(cfg =>
{
    cfg.AddProfile<InventoryMapper>();
});
_mapperConfig.AssertConfigurationIsValid();
_mapper = _mapperConfig.CreateMapper();
}
```

Next, we need to get our database layer mocked. To do this, we need to create another variable to hold the IInventoryDatabaseRepo mock. Add the call to create a mocked database layer project as follows: private Mock<IInventoryDatabaseRepo> _mockInventoryDatabaseRepo;. And then use the TestInitialize method to set up the mocking object as the first line in the testBeforeTestRuns method: _mockInventoryDatabaseRepo= new Mock<IInventoryDatabaseRepo>();.

Also add a method to set up the inventory database repo mock layer and stub it out. Name the method SetupDbRepoMock. Add a line after the creation of the _mockInventoryDatabaseRepo to call the SetupDbRepoMock method. We'll fill the SetupDbRepoMock method in after a while. Make sure to bring in any missing using statements.

For clarity, the current code for the testBeforeTestRuns and SetupDbRepoMock methods is shown in Figure 12-14.

```
[TestInitialize]
0 references
public void testBeforeTestRuns()
{
    _mockInventoryDatabaseRepo = new Mock<IInventoryDatabaseRepo>();
    SetupDbRepoMock();
    _serviceLayer = new ItemsService();
    var items = new List<ItemDto>() {
        new ItemDto() { Id = 1, Name="Star Wars IV: A New Hope"
                               , Description = "Luke's Friends", CategoryId = 2  },
        new ItemDto() { Id = 2, Name="Star Wars V: The Empire Strikes Back"
                               , Description = "Luke's Dad", CategoryId = 2  },
        new ItemDto() { Id = 3, Name="Star Wars VI: The Return of the Jedi"
                               , Description = "Luke's Sister", CategoryId = 2}
    };
}


1 reference
private void SetupDbRepoMock()
{

}
```

Figure 12-14. *The mocking of the InventoryDatabaseRepo is now able to be compiled, but we still can't create a new service layer*

Now that we have a mocked DBRepoLayer, let's create a constructor on the service layer that takes an injectable repo layer object. In this way, we don't care about the context specifically. Additionally, we'll need to pass the mapper in so that mapping can happen in the service layer as expected. In the ItemsService.cs file in the InventoryBusinessLayer project, add the following explicit constructor code:

```
public ItemsService(IInventoryDatabaseRepo dbRepo, IMapper mapper)
{
    _dbRepo = dbRepo;
    _mapper = mapper;
}
```

For clarity, review Figure 12-15 to see the two explicit constructors as they should now exist in your ItemsService class.

```
public class ItemsService : IItemsService
{
    private readonly IInventoryDatabaseRepo _dbRepo;
    private readonly IMapper _mapper;

    2 references
    public ItemsService(InventoryDbContext dbContext, IMapper mapper)
    {
        _dbRepo = new InventoryDatabaseRepo(dbContext, mapper);
        _mapper = mapper;
    }

    1 reference
    public ItemsService(IInventoryDatabaseRepo dbRepo, IMapper mapper)
    {
        _dbRepo = dbRepo;
        _mapper = mapper;
    }
}
```

Figure 12-15. *Creating a new constructor on the ServiceLayer to allow an injectable repo*

As you might imagine, the second constructor is a better way to code so that we can decouple the data layer from the service layer. To clean up, therefore, we should remove the original constructor and rework our UI code to make sure it is only passing in composite versions of the interface, rather than a tightly coupled database layer. Unit testing is already pointing out simple ways to improve the code. Go ahead and remove the original constructor now.

Then make sure to instantiate and then inject the repo into the service layer in the main Program.cs file (you can run it to validate that nothing is broken by doing this). Reference the following code and make the update back in the original Main method for the main activity project:

```
using (var db = new InventoryDbContext(_optionsBuilder.Options))
{
    //decouple the database from the service layer using the
    //dbRepo interface
    var dbRepo = new InventoryDatabaseRepo(db, _mapper);
    var svc = new ItemsService(dbRepo, _mapper);
    Console.WriteLine("List Inventory");
```

For clarity, review Figure 12-16.

```
using (var db = new InventoryDbContext(_optionsBuilder.Options))
{
    //decouple the database from the service layer using the
    //dbRepo interface
    var dbRepo = new InventoryDatabaseRepo(db, _mapper);
    var svc = new ItemsService(dbRepo, _mapper);

    Console.WriteLine("List Inventory");
```

Figure 12-16. *The Items Service is built with a prebuilt Database Repo layer for further decoupling of the layers*

Return to the unit testing project. Fix the creation of the service layer to use the mocked database repository layer and the AutoMapper object by modifying the line of code setting the _serviceLayer = new ItemsService(...) to the following:

```
_serviceLayer = new ItemsService(_mockInventoryDatabaseRepo.Object, _
mapper);
```

Run the unit test. It should fail since we haven't told the _
mockInventoryDatabaseRepo object how to respond to calls yet (see Figure 12-17).

```
[TestMethod]
♦ | 0 references
public void TestGetItems()
{
    //var result = _mockServiceLayer.Object.ListInventory();
    var result = _serviceLayer.ListInventory();
    Assert.IsNotNull(result);
    Assert.IsTrue(result.Count > 0);  ⊗
}
```

Exception User-Unhandled   ⋕ ✕

Microsoft.VisualStudio.TestTools.UnitTesting.AssertFailedException:
'Assert.IsTrue failed. '

View Details | Copy Details | Start Live Share session...
▷ Exception Settings

Figure 12-17. *The service and repo layers work, but no data is returned*

Depending on your settings, you may not see this pop up. If you do not see it, you can easily review the test results in the Test Explorer to see that the Assert.IsTrue failed message is thrown as expected.

Even though the data worked, our test failed because the result count was zero. This is to be expected since we haven't set any data. Let's add that data in to see the magic start to happen.

Step 6: Setting up the database layer repo data

To fully test the solution, we need Items, Categories, CategoryColors, Genres, and the ability to get all of that from our mock database repository layer object.

Let's start with basic Items, giving them Categories with Colors.

Ordinarily, you would write your test and then refactor. To save time, remember that we're going to want access to this data for testing at some point. Create your lists of Items, Categories, and Category colors outside of the method.

At the top of the InventoryManagerUnitTests class, add the following class-level variables:

```
private List<Item> _allItems;
private List<CategoryColor> _allColors;
private List<Category> _allCategories;
private const string COLOR_BLUE = "Blue";
private const string COLOR_RED = "Red";
private const string COLOR_GREEN = "Green";
private const string CAT1_NAME = "CAT1 Books";
private const string CAT2_NAME = "CAT2 Movies";
private const string CAT3_NAME = "CAT3 Music";
private const string ITEM1_NAME = "Item 1 Name";
private const string ITEM2_NAME = "Item 2 Name";
private const string ITEM3_NAME = "Item 3 Name";
private const string ITEM1_DESC = "Item 1 DESC";
private const string ITEM2_DESC = "Item 2 DESC";
private const string ITEM3_DESC = "Item 3 DESC";
private const string ITEM1_NOTES = "Item 1 Notes Good";
```

```
private const string ITEM2_NOTES = "Item 2 Notes Fair";
private const string ITEM3_NOTES = "Item 3 Notes Poor";
```

Then modify the SetupDbRepoMock method to contain the following code:

```
_allColors = new List<CategoryColor>() {
    new CategoryColor(){ Id = 1, ColorValue = COLOR_BLUE },
    new CategoryColor() { Id = 2, ColorValue = COLOR_RED },
    new CategoryColor() { Id = 3, ColorValue = COLOR_GREEN}
};
var color1 = _allColors.Single(x => x.Id == 1);
var color2 = _allColors.Single(x => x.Id == 2);
var color3 = _allColors.Single(x => x.Id == 3);

_allCategories = new List<Category>() {
    new Category() {Id = 1, CategoryColorId = 1, CategoryColor = color1
                , IsDeleted = false, IsActive = true, Name = CAT1_NAME },
    new Category() {Id = 2, CategoryColorId = 2, CategoryColor = color2
                , IsDeleted = false, IsActive = true, Name = CAT2_NAME },
    new Category() {Id = 3, CategoryColorId = 3, CategoryColor = color3
                , IsDeleted = false, IsActive = true, Name = CAT3_NAME
    }
};
var category1 = _allCategories.Single(x => x.Id == 1);
var category2 = _allCategories.Single(x => x.Id == 2);
var category3 = _allCategories.Single(x => x.Id == 3);

_allItems = new List<Item>() {
    new Item() { Id = 1, CategoryId = 1, Category= category1, IsDeleted =
    false
                , IsActive = true, Name = ITEM1_NAME, Description =
                ITEM1_DESC
                , Notes = ITEM1_NOTES },
    new Item() { Id = 2, CategoryId = 2, Category= category2, IsDeleted =
    false
                , IsActive = true, Name = ITEM2_NAME, Description =
                ITEM2_DESC
                , Notes = ITEM2_NOTES },
```

```
new Item() { Id = 3, CategoryId = 3, Category= category3, IsDeleted =
false
                , IsActive = true, Name = ITEM3_NAME, Description =
                ITEM3_DESC
                , Notes = ITEM3_NOTES }
};

_mockInventoryDatabaseRepo.Setup(x => x.ListInventory()).Returns(_
allItems);
```

Now that we have our mocking in place, let's try running the test again. Your results should be similar to what is shown in Figure 12-18.

Figure 12-18. *This time our test works*

Step 7: Make the test more robust using Shouldly

To finish up this first test activity, let's test for actual values. One way we can do this is to use normal, built-in *Microsoft* testing.

Next, we should get *Shouldly* in place. To do this, add the appropriate *NuGet* package for Shouldly using methods already discussed in this chapter (see Figure 12-19).

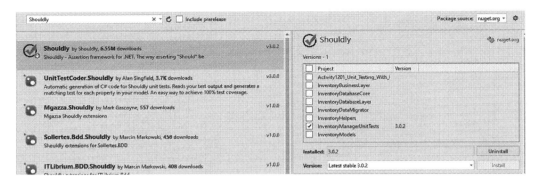

Figure 12-19. *Add Shouldly to the test project*

With Shouldly in place, return to the test we have written.

Leave the original tests as is, but add the following lines of code and then add the missing using statements for Shouldly as needed:

```
result.ShouldNotBeNull();
result.Count.ShouldBeGreaterThan(0);
result.Count.ShouldBe(3);
result.First().Name.ShouldBe(ITEM1_NAME);
result.First().CategoryId.ShouldBe(1);
```

Here, we see that *Shouldly* just gives a much nicer way to test than using *Assert* all the time.

Run the test in debugger to see the code work as expected and pass each *Shouldly* test. For clarity, the final version of the TestGetItems method is shown in Figure 12-20.

```
[TestMethod]
● | 0 references
public void TestGetItems()
{
    //var result = _mockServiceLayer.Object.ListInventory();
    var result = _serviceLayer.ListInventory();
    Assert.IsNotNull(result);
    Assert.IsTrue(result.Count > 0);

    result.ShouldNotBeNull();
    result.Count.ShouldBeGreaterThan(0);
    result.Count.ShouldBe(3);
    result.First().Name.ShouldBe(ITEM1_NAME);
    result.First().CategoryId.ShouldBe(1);
}
```
≤ 1ms elapsed

Figure 12-20. *All Shouldly Tests are passing*

Final thoughts on activity 1201 – unit testing with mocking

We have clearly not implemented every test that we need at this point for the service layer to be fully tested; however, I will leave the rest of that to you for your practice.

By taking a look at mocking in this activity, we have seen that we can inject objects into our system under test so that we can easily determine if that step of the process is working as expected without having to couple that layer to an implementation.

Mocking in our unit tests is extremely useful to us as we can see that the service layer, although small in this project, is performing as expected provided it is given the correct data.

If we were to go deeper, we would need to add, update, and remove items in our testing by manipulating the data returned by the mocking objects. That may be a bit of overkill, however. If you can count on your data mapping correctly and getting items correctly and passing the correct information to the database, the manipulation of the underlying data is really made up until you test it in an integration test.

In the next activity, we'll see what it takes to get going for testing our solution with an integration test against an actual database implementation.

Activity 1202: Integration testing with the .Net in-memory database

In this second activity for Chapter 12, we'll set up our solution and then set the integration tests in place that will help us to determine that our code is functioning properly at the database level as expected.

Using an in-memory database solution

As we set up these integration tests, we'll see how we can leverage an in-memory database solution to perform actual data operations, thereby validating that the database is functioning properly as expected.

Step 1: Get set up

To begin, grab a copy of the `Activity1202_InMemoryIntegrationTesting_Starter.zip` files, and get them going on your machine. As before, make sure to set connections and run database migrations to ensure your code and database are up to date and that there are no issues. Run the program to make sure it works. You should see the regular output from our program. Alternatively, you could just continue with the files from activity 1201 and proceed with this activity.

Step 2: Add a new XUnit test project

In this activity, we'll be building out our integration tests. To further our study, we'll be using *XUnit* instead of the default *Microsoft Test* suite. I think you'll agree this is worth the move when you see it in action.

To start, add a new *XUnit* testing project to the solution (refer to Figure 12-21).

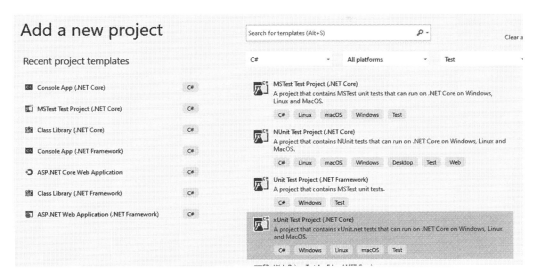

Figure 12-21. Adding a new XUnit Test Project to the solution

Name the test `InventoryManagerIntegrationTests` and create the project. This will bring up the default test that uses the `[Fact]` `Attribute`. A fact is a test that runs one time and takes no parameters.

XUnit also has a second type of test, the `[Theory]`. The theory test uses inline data to set conditions and uses parameters to allow a single test to be run multiple times.

In order to do anything, we're going to need to get access to the database. To do this, in the `InventoryManagerIntegrationTests` project, add a reference to the `InventoryDatabaseLayer` project (see Figure 12-22).

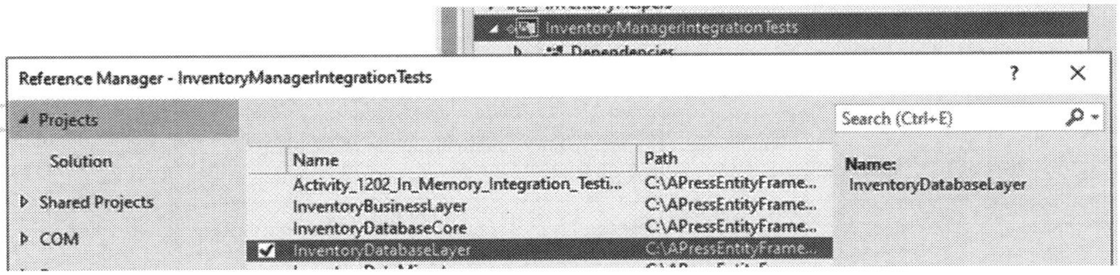

Figure 12-22. Adding a reference to the InventoryDatabaseLayer project

After adding the reference to the project, let's set up the things we need in order to make this test work as an integration test.

The default file and class name that was generated during project creation is UnitTest1. Let's change that to the same name as the project, InventoryManagerIntegrationTests. When prompted, select Yes for renaming the other references.

Let's add a constructor that sets up our data. In the constructor, call a method SetupOptions and then stub out the method as a private void method.

```
public class InventoryManagerIntegrationTests
{
    public InventoryManagerIntegrationTests()
    {
        SetupOptions();
    }
    private void SetupOptions()
    {

    }
    [Fact]
    public void Test1()
    {

    }
}
```

Our project is also going to need references to *EntityFramework, AutoMapper,* and *Shouldly.* Add the following references from the *NuGet Package Manager:*

```
Automapper
Automapper.Extensions.Microsoft.DependencyInjection
Microsoft.EntityFrameworkCore
Microsoft.EntityFrameworkCore.SqlServer
Microsoft.EntityFrameworkCore.Tools
Microsoft.Net.Test.SdkShouldly
xunit
xunit.runner.visualstudio
coverlet.collector
```

Additionally, we need a new package called Microsoft.EntityFrameworkCore. InMemory (as shown in Figure 12-23).

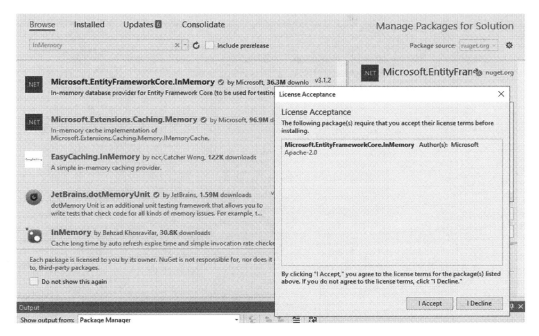

Figure 12-23. *Add the EntityFramework packages to the integration testing project, including the EntityFrameworkCore.InMemory package*

Additionally, make sure to run the updates for all packages so that you have the latest version of all of the packages, but be careful you do not update to the .Net 5 version of things (we're working in .Net Core 3.1.x).

In the SetupOptions method, we'll create our database. Add a class-level variable to store the options at the top of the class file as DbContextOptions<InventoryDbContext> _options;

Then add the code to instantiate the in-memory database in the setup method:

```
private void SetupOptions()
{
    _options = new DbContextOptionsBuilder<InventoryDbContext>()
                .UseInMemoryDatabase(databaseName: "InventoryManagerTest")
                .Options;
}
```

For clarity, the code for the SetupOptions method is shown in Figure 12-24.

```
1 reference
private void SetupOptions()
{
    _options = new DbContextOptionsBuilder<InventoryDbContext>()
                    .UseInMemoryDatabase(databaseName: "InventoryManagerTest")
                    .Options;
}
```

Figure 12-24. *The SetupOptions method creates the in-memory database for us to use*

Next, we need to set up the mapper, just as we've done in the previous activity. Create a file called InventoryMapper.cs in the project and copy the code from the InventoryMapper class from the main activity project or from the InventoryManagerUnitTests project.

Once the Inventory mapper is in place, add three class-level variables to the InventoryManagerIntegrationTests class, right after the declaration of the DbContextOptions:

```
private static MapperConfiguration _mapperConfig;
private static IMapper _mapper;
private static IServiceProvider _serviceProvider;
```

Next, set up the mapping configuration and mapper by adding the following code in the SetupOptions method following the initialization of the _options variable:

```
var services = new ServiceCollection();
services.AddAutoMapper(typeof(InventoryMapper));
_serviceProvider = services.BuildServiceProvider();

_mapperConfig = new MapperConfiguration(cfg =>
{
    cfg.AddProfile<InventoryMapper>();
});
_mapperConfig.AssertConfigurationIsValid();
_mapper = _mapperConfig.CreateMapper();
```

Make sure to add any using statements that are needed to ensure the code will compile.

Finally, add a class-level variable to be used for creating a new version of the InventoryDatabaseRepo object in tests:

```
private IInventoryDatabaseRepo _dbRepo;
```

For clarity, the current code from the InventoryManagerIntegrationTests project is shown in Figure 12-25.

```
1 reference
public class InventoryManagerIntegrationTests
{
    DbContextOptions<InventoryDbContext> _options;
    private static MapperConfiguration _mapperConfig;
    private static IMapper _mapper;
    private static IServiceProvider _serviceProvider;
    private IInventoryDatabaseRepo _dbRepo;

    0 references
    public InventoryManagerIntegrationTests()
    {
        SetupOptions();
    }

    1 reference
    private void SetupOptions()
    {
        _options = new DbContextOptionsBuilder<InventoryDbContext>()
                        .UseInMemoryDatabase(databaseName: "InventoryManagerTest")
                        .Options;
        var services = new ServiceCollection();
        services.AddAutoMapper(typeof(InventoryMapper));
        _serviceProvider = services.BuildServiceProvider();

        _mapperConfig = new MapperConfiguration(cfg =>
        {
            cfg.AddProfile<InventoryMapper>();
        });
        _mapperConfig.AssertConfigurationIsValid();
        _mapper = _mapperConfig.CreateMapper();
    }


    [Fact]
    ● | 0 references
    public void Test1()
    {

    }
}
```

Figure 12-25. *The class is set up with options and the mapper objects to inject into the database layer for operational integration testing*

Finally, bring all the constants in from the InventoryManagerUnitTests project. We will reuse these to build actual data in this project. Add them to the top of the InventoryManagerIntegrationTests class.

```
private const string COLOR_BLUE = "Blue";
private const string COLOR_RED = "Red";
private const string COLOR_GREEN = "Green";
private const string CAT1_NAME = "CAT1 Books";
private const string CAT2_NAME = "CAT2 Movies";
private const string CAT3_NAME = "CAT3 Music";
private const string ITEM1_NAME = "Item 1 Name";
private const string ITEM2_NAME = "Item 2 Name";
private const string ITEM3_NAME = "Item 3 Name";
private const string ITEM1_DESC = "Item 1 DESC";
private const string ITEM2_DESC = "Item 2 DESC";
private const string ITEM3_DESC = "Item 3 DESC";
private const string ITEM1_NOTES = "Item 1 Notes Good";
private const string ITEM2_NOTES = "Item 2 Notes Fair";
private const string ITEM3_NOTES = "Item 3 Notes Poor";
```

Now that we have most of the framework in place, let's set the default data.

Step 3: Setting the default data for our integration tests

Change the default Test1 test method name to TestListInventory. In the method, add a using statement and instantiate the context. Then use the context and the mapper to instantiate a dbRepo. Additionally, add a method call before the using statement to call to BuildDefaults. Stub out the BuildDefaults method. All of this can be accomplished with the following code:

```
[Fact]
public void TestListInventory()
{
    //arrange
    BuildDefaults();

    using (var context = new InventoryDbContext(_options))
    {
```

```
        //act
        //assert
    }
}

private void BuildDefaults()
{

}
```

In the BuildDefaults method, add code to create the three Colors, Categories, and Items. Additionally, add code to prevent creation if the database already exists with the default items.

```
using (var context = new InventoryDbContext(_options))
{
    //skip creation if items already exist:
    var item1Detail = context.Items.SingleOrDefault(x => x.Name.
    Equals(ITEM1_NAME));
    var item2Detail = context.Items.SingleOrDefault(x => x.Name.
    Equals(ITEM2_NAME));
    var item3Detail = context.Items.SingleOrDefault(x => x.Name.
    Equals(ITEM3_NAME));
    if (item1Detail != null && item2Detail != null && item3Detail != null)
    return;

    var color1 = new CategoryColor() { ColorValue = COLOR_BLUE };
    var color2 = new CategoryColor() { ColorValue = COLOR_RED };
    var color3 = new CategoryColor() { ColorValue = COLOR_GREEN };

    var cat1 = new Category() {  CategoryColor = color1, IsActive = true,
    IsDeleted = false
                                    , Name = CAT1_NAME };
    var cat2 = new Category() {  CategoryColor = color2, IsActive = true,
    IsDeleted = false
                                    , Name = CAT2_NAME };
    var cat3 = new Category() {  CategoryColor = color3, IsActive = true,
    IsDeleted = false
                                    , Name = CAT3_NAME };
```

```
    context.Categories.Add(cat1);
    context.Categories.Add(cat2);
    context.Categories.Add(cat3);
    context.SaveChanges();

    var category1 = context.Categories.Single(x => x.Name.Equals(CAT1_NAME));
    var category2 = context.Categories.Single(x => x.Name.Equals(CAT2_NAME));
    var category3 = context.Categories.Single(x => x.Name.Equals(CAT3_NAME));

    var item1 = new Item() { Name = ITEM1_NAME, Description = ITEM1_DESC,
    Notes = ITEM1_NOTES
                            , IsActive = true, IsDeleted = false,
                            CategoryId = category1.Id };
    context.Items.Add(item1);
    var item2 = new Item() { Name = ITEM2_NAME, Description = ITEM2_DESC,
    Notes = ITEM2_NOTES
                            , IsActive = true, IsDeleted = false,
                            CategoryId = category2.Id };
    context.Items.Add(item2);
    var item3 = new Item() { Name = ITEM3_NAME, Description = ITEM3_DESC,
    Notes = ITEM3_NOTES
                            , IsActive = true, IsDeleted = false,
                            CategoryId = category3.Id };
    context.Items.Add(item3);
    context.SaveChanges();
}
```

Now we're ready to create and run our first integration test.

Step 4: Writing the integration test

In the TestListInventory test, inside the context using block, create a new
DatabaseRepo object and then get the inventory items. Add the following code in the
"act" portion of the test:

```
_dbRepo = new InventoryDatabaseRepo(context, _mapper);
var items = _dbRepo.ListInventory();
```

Assert that the inventory items are as expected from the database by adding the following code in the "assert" portion of the TestListInventory method (don't forget to bring in the using statement for Shouldly):

```
items.ShouldNotBeNull();
items.Count.ShouldBe(3);
var first = items.First();
first.Name.ShouldBe(ITEM1_NAME);
first.Description.ShouldBe(ITEM1_DESC);
first.Notes.ShouldBe(ITEM1_NOTES);
first.Category.Name.ShouldBe(CAT1_NAME);
```

Run the test and debug to see it in action. The test should pass as expected (as shown in Figure 12-26).

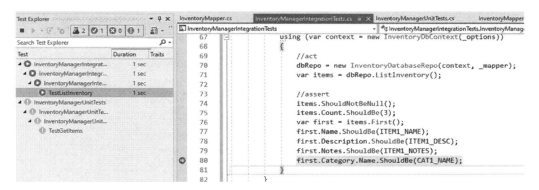

Figure 12-26. *The integration test for listing the inventory works as expected*

At this point, we have everything in place to finish writing our integration tests. In each remaining scenario, we'd just need to map out the data and make sure it exists in the database as expected.

Step 5: Using a theory to create multiple runs of the same test with parameters

With *XUnit*, we can create a theory that will let us run a test multiple times. Consider the listing of the items as we ran before. With three items, the last part of the code could list each one individually. However, what if we could write the code once and test all the items?

For this test, let's test all the categories and colors, but test them with only one test.

Add the following test method as a theory with three inline-data setups, one for each category:

```
[Theory]
[InlineData(CAT1_NAME, COLOR_BLUE)]
[InlineData(CAT2_NAME, COLOR_RED)]
[InlineData(CAT3_NAME, COLOR_GREEN)]
public void TestCategoryColors(string name, string color)
{
    //arrange
    BuildDefaults();

    using (var context = new InventoryDbContext(_options))
    {
        //act
        _dbRepo = new InventoryDatabaseRepo(context, _mapper);
        var catcolors = _dbRepo.ListCategoriesAndColors();

        catcolors.ShouldNotBeNull();
        catcolors.Count.ShouldBe(3);

        var item = catcolors.FirstOrDefault(x => x.Category.Equals(name));
        item.ShouldNotBeNull();
        item.CategoryColor.Color.ShouldBe(color);
    }
}
```

Let's move BuildDefaults from all test methods and place the call in the InventoryManagerIntegrationTests constructor. We have code in place to guard against creating the data if it already exists.

Run the TestListInventory method to make sure that it did not break with this refactoring.

Then run the TestCategoryColors tests. They should all pass at this point.

Final thoughts on activity 1202

In this second activity, we created the ability to run integration tests in memory using the *EFCore* built-in, in-memory database.

Running integration tests gives us the ability to test actual data from the database. After setting up the database, we were able to add our items, categories, and colors to the database by working directly with the context.

With data in place, we are able to test any of the available inventory methods that are performed with *LINQ* against the DBContext.

At the end of this activity, we've only tested two of the methods. If you would like more practice, spend some time testing the insert, update, and delete methods.

One last thought is to remember that with the in-memory version of the database, we don't have access to stored procedures, so they will need to be tested outside of your integration tests to make sure they work as expected.

Final thoughts for this chapter

In this chapter, we covered two of the ways that we can write tests against our database and solution code. The first testing strategy is to write unit tests. The second testing strategy is to use integration tests.

Unit tests

Unit tests are great for testing the layered code outside of the actual database implementation. We saw this in action when we mocked the database layer and told it what to return so that we could test the functionality of our service layer.

Integration tests

Integration tests are critical when you want to test the overall functionality of an actual database with your code. Integration tests provide assurance that we can rely on our database layer and DBContext to function as expected.

Shouldly and XUnit

In addition to the two types of tests, we also saw the differences between *MSTest* and *XUnit* Tests. We also pulled the *Shouldly* library in so that we could easily test our code using a more user-friendly syntax.

Dependencies and injection to decouple layers

In order to test a system, dependencies must be injectable. We spent a lot of time in the last two chapters working to decouple the system and code to an interface so that we could get to this point.

With our system layered out and tested with both unit and integration tests, we can start to feel much more confident in our architecture, as well as have more peace of mind during maintenance operations.

In the next chapter, we are going to look at what it takes to work with *Entity Framework* and a lightweight *ORM* called *Dapper*. Using these two solutions together can be extremely powerful and efficient.

CHAPTER 13

Alternatives to Entity Framework: Dapper

In a book about Entity Framework, it might surprise you to find a chapter that is not about Entity Framework. However, there are times when Entity Framework might not be the best choice for you. Additionally, it would be an error to not mention that there are alternatives available, especially when many professionals agree that it would be nice to know about and use alternatives in various scenarios.

In this chapter, we're going to briefly walk away from *EF* to discuss other options for working against our database as a way to enhance our toolkit. Don't worry, we're not going to walk far enough that *EF* is out of sight.

Lightweight ORMs

Sometimes a fully functional ORM is overkill. The overhead that comes with fully tracked entities and lazy loading might hurt your application's performance.

Perhaps all you are doing is just fetching data to show to a screen, without any possibility of updating that data.

Perhaps you don't want to keep everything relational at all times or track the data changes because you will just send the updated entity and re-fetch the entity anyway.

Perhaps you have thousands of lines of data, and you want to be able to skip working with LINQ and just write raw SQL queries to gain performance for searches.

Perhaps you have an extremely complex query that is difficult to formulate in LINQ and, even if you do get it to work, is just not the way you would have written that SQL statement. Maybe you just need to do a massive amount of processing in a CRON job and don't want to wire up the entire ORM.

In any event, there are many reasons that using a lightweight ORM can help you with some of these situations and should be considered.

© Brian L. Gorman 2020
B. L. Gorman, *Practical Entity Framework*, https://doi.org/10.1007/978-1-4842-6044-9_13

Entity Framework is likely sufficient, if you use it correctly

Before we go diving into *Dapper* (or another lightweight ORM), it would be prudent of us to remember that a lot of the gain we get from an ORM can also be accomplished with *EF*.

For example, if we remember back a few chapters ago, we covered how to pull queries with the `AsNoTracking` extension. When we add that extension into our queries, we can disconnect the data from the database, at least for purposes of tracking.

Additionally, if we have massive table joins or other operations that might not perform well in LINQ, we can consider using views and stored procedures.

Therefore, before we go all in on leveraging a lightweight ORM, we should make sure that we have paid due diligence to examining the features in *EF*.

Benefits of using a lightweight ORM

Even with everything that *EF* can do, a lightweight ORM can generally offer some benefits over *EF*. These benefits are usually related to simplicity, maintenance, and/or performance.

The first performance gain that a lightweight ORM can offer is that you get direct access to writing the SQL queries you will use, whereas *EF* generally relies on you to set up a LINQ query which then translates that into SQL for execution. With an ORM, you are generally writing the direct SQL you want to call. We know that we can profile the LINQ-generated SQL, but sometimes doing multiple table joins with LINQ can get a bit muddy.

Another way that you can benefit from using a lightweight ORM could be with execution plans. Remember from our previous chapters how LINQ does not cache an execution plan? As it turns out, some lightweight ORMs can actually cache your call for you. This means that the second and consecutive calls made in the ORM can potentially benefit from this caching. For example, Dapper uses a `ConcurrentDictionary` to store queries with parameter information (see the documentation at `https://github.com/StackExchange/Dapper#limitations-and-caveats`).

Drawbacks with Dapper

As with any solution, there are good and bad things that must be considered. Working with Dapper can be extremely effective in the right situation, but in the wrong situation, you may find yourself wanting a different approach.

Flat data

When working with Dapper, you do get the control you want when working with SQL, but the end result is generally a flat set of data. Where EF offers navigation properties, Dapper does not. So, this means that any data you need to include from joined tables needs to be manually hydrated.

Therefore, if you are just pulling data for a view or flat data from a single table, Dapper is an excellent choice. When needing to do things with joined data, such as our Items with CategoryName and our Categories with CategoryColors, it becomes a bit more costly. Even with the cost, Dapper is still highly performant, as we'll see in our upcoming activity.

Learning curve

Most of us are probably very comfortable with LINQ by now and have a generally useful understanding of getting the data exactly as we need it. Hopefully the previous chapters where we discussed efficiency of queries have also grown our skillset in this area.

With Dapper, we have yet another tool to learn. While this is not a bad thing, it becomes more to add to the maintenance plan for the system, as well as another thing that developers will need to know to work with the solution.

If the developer is not very familiar with T-SQL, this can also add to the learning curve.

In the end, we'll be using Dapper with *SlapperAutomapper* to help when working with data. Therefore, the approach we are taking in this solution means developers would need to not only know *EF* but also Dapper, SlapperAutomapper, and T-SQL.

Implementing a hybrid solution

Since you will want to keep your *EF* Implementation around the CRUD operations for creating, updating, and deleting, but may want to get some enhanced performance on read operations, implementing a hybrid solution can be an excellent architectural choice.

A couple of drawbacks to a hybrid solution are that your dev team now needs to know all of the tools in the stack, not just *EF* and LINQ or Dapper, SlapperAutomapper, and T-SQL, but all of them combined. Additionally, implementing a hybrid solution might lead to messy code where some developers query with LINQ and *EF* and others query with Dapper and SlapperAutomapper. As such, you'll want to be clear about your policy around when, where, and how to use each piece when developing a hybrid approach. A lot of that confusion can be cleared up just by discussing the reasons, benefits, and drawbacks of each of the implemented ORMs.

To complete this chapter, we're going to implement Dapper and SlapperAutomapper in our solution for use as a hybrid option for querying our data. We aren't going to learn everything about Dapper and SlapperAutomapper, so if you want to dive deeper after reading this chapter and working the activity, make sure to check out the official documentation. The documentation will also give you more information about how and when Dapper might be the right choice for your solutions.

You can find the official documentation here:

`https://github.com/StackExchange/Dapper`

Additional information about SlapperAutomapper can be found here:

`https://github.com/SlapperAutoMapper/Slapper.AutoMapper`

Activity 1301: Implementing a hybrid solution with Dapper

As we've discussed in this chapter, using a lightweight *ORM* can provide benefits for our solutions, especially related to performance. For that reason, in this activity, we are going to implement a hybrid solution with *Dapper* with *SlapperAutomapper* and *EFCore*.

Providing a read-only data layer alternative

In order to make our solution work well and be architected for success, we'll provide implementations for our data layer at the read and write level. In this way, we can inject a new read object that implements Dapper while still keeping the fully functioning version of our *EF* implementation in place.

Step 1: Steps

To begin, grab a copy of the `Activity1301_DapperAndEFCoreHybrid_Starter.zip` files, extract them, double-check your connection string, and make sure that you have the *InventoryManager* database set up. Run an `update-database` command to make sure the migrations are up to date on your machine. Once that is completed, run the application to make sure it is working as expected. Alternatively, you could continue with the InventoryManager project you have been working with on your own machine. Additionally, you could run any unit and integration tests to validate that they are also working as expected. Once the project runs, your output should be similar to what is shown in Figure 13-1.

```
Microsoft Visual Studio Debug Console
New Item] 127        |Top Gun                                    |Comedy
New Item] 128        |Batman Begins                              |Sci/Fi
New Item] 128        |Batman Begins                              |Drama
New Item] 129        |Practical Entity Framework
New Item] 130        |The Lord of the Rings                      |Sci/Fi
New Item] 130        |The Lord of the Rings                      |Fantasy
New Item] 131        |Battlefield 5                              |Sci/Fi
New Item] 132        |World Of Tanks                             |
New Item] 133        |Harry Potter and the Sorcerer's Stone      |
New Item] 134        |Brian 1                                    |
New Item] 135        |Brian 2 Updated                            |
New Item] 136        |Brian 3                                    |
List Categories And Colors
Movies | Blue
Books | Red
Games | Green
Would you like to create items?
n
Would you like to update items?
n
Would you like to delete items?
n
Program Complete

C:\APressEntityFramework\Code\Chapter13\Activity1301_DapperAndEFCoreHybrid\Activity1301_DapperAndEF
netcoreapp3.1\Activity1301_DapperAndEFCoreHybrid.exe (process 11208) exited with code 0.
To automatically close the console when debugging stops, enable Tools->Options->Debugging->Automati
le when debugging stops
```

Figure 13-1. *The starter project is up and running as expected*

Step 2: Implement the Dapper and SlapperAutomapper libraries

In order to work efficiently with Dapper, we're going to need to implement both the Dapper and SlapperAutomapper libraries.

Open the `Manage NuGet Packages` for Solution dialog, and select the `Browse` tab. Enter `Dapper` to search for the `Dapper` library.

Once you locate the `Dapper` library, select it and add it to the `InventoryDatabaseLayer` project (see Figure 13-2).

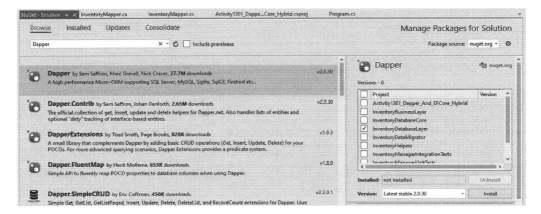

Figure 13-2. *Using NuGet Package Manager to get Dapper into the InventoryDatabaseLayer project*

At the time of this writing, the `Slapper.Automapper` package `v.2.0.0.9` is in beta, but we need that to work with the *.Net Core framework*. It is currently not listed in the Packages when browsing in the `Package Manager Console`.

If we look on *NuGet.Org*, we can find the package, as is shown in Figure 13-3.

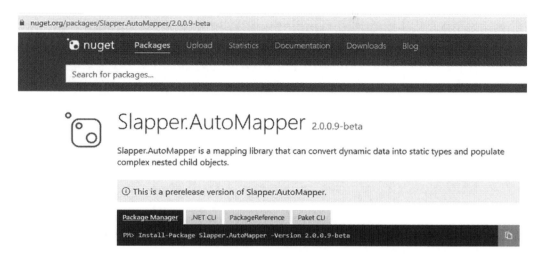

Figure 13-3. *Finding Slapper.Automapper v2.0.0.9 -beta on NuGet.Org*

Perhaps by the time you are reading this, it will be an official package. Until then, the best way to get it is to select the `InventoryDatabaseLayer` project in the `PackageManagerConsole` and then run the command as listed on the *NuGet.Org* page.

Open the *PMC*, then select the `InventoryDatabaseLayer` Project, and then run the command:

```
Install-Package Slapper.AutoMapper -Version 2.0.0.9-beta
```

Review Figure 13-4 for clarity.

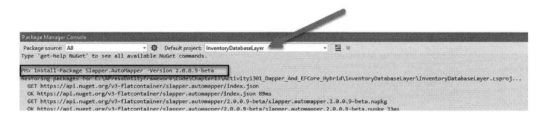

Figure 13-4. *Running the command in the PMC against the InventoryDatabaseLayer project to get the beta version of Slapper.Automapper installed*

Once everything is installed, you can validate that it was installed by building the project and reviewing the packages in the *NuGet Package Manager (as seen in Figure 13-5)*.

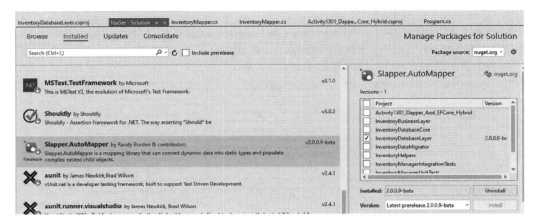

Figure 13-5. *Reviewing the NuGet Package Manager to see that the correct libraries are installed*

Additionally, reviewing the `InventoryDatabaseLayer.csproj` file reveals the correctly referenced packages. Figure 13-6 shows a possible version of your InventoryDatabaseLayer.csproj file and clarifies that all of the expected packages are listed as package references.

```
InventoryDatabaseLayer.csproj  ⊗ ✕   NuGet - Solution      InventoryMapper.cs      InventoryMapper.cs      Activity1301_Dappe...Core_Hybrid.csproj
 1 ⊟<Project Sdk="Microsoft.NET.Sdk">
 2
 3 ⊟   <PropertyGroup>
 4         <TargetFramework>netcoreapp3.1</TargetFramework>
 5     </PropertyGroup>
 6
 7 ⊟   <ItemGroup>
 8         <PackageReference Include="AutoMapper" Version="9.0.0" />
 9         <PackageReference Include="AutoMapper.Extensions.Microsoft.DependencyInjection" Version="7.0.0" />
10         <PackageReference Include="Dapper" Version="2.0.30" />
11         <PackageReference Include="Slapper.AutoMapper" Version="2.0.0-beta" />
12     </ItemGroup>
13
14 ⊟   <ItemGroup>
15         <ProjectReference Include="..\InventoryDatabaseCore\InventoryDatabaseCore.csproj" />
16         <ProjectReference Include="..\InventoryModels\InventoryModels.csproj" />
17     </ItemGroup>
18
19 </Project>
20
```

Figure 13-6. *Reviewing the InventoryDatabaseLayer.csproj file to see the referenced packages*

If you haven't already, make sure everything builds as expected with no errors.

Step 3: Create the new interfaces and implementations in the InventoryDatabaseLayer project

In order to create a new repository to leverage Dapper, we're going to refactor our database and business layer interfaces. One of the principles of SOLID design is *interface segregation*. To make our solution a bit more robust, we should isolate read and write into their own implementations. We're going to do that now.

In the InventoryDatabaseLayer project, in the IInventoryDatabaseRepo class, add two new empty interfaces, IInventoryDatabaseRepoReadOnly and IInventoryDatabaseRepoWriteOnly, using the following code:

```
public interface IInventoryDatabaseRepoReadOnly
{

}

public interface IInventoryDatabaseRepoWriteOnly
{

}
```

Next, move the methods associated with read operations into the IInventoryDatabaseRepoReadOnly interface. Cut and paste the following methods from the IInventoryDatabaseRepo into the IInventoryDatabaseRepoReadOnly interface:

```
List<Item> ListInventory();
List<GetItemsForListingWithDateDto> GetItemsForListingLinq(DateTime
minDateValue, DateTime maxDateValue);
List<GetItemsForListingDto> GetItemsForListingFromProcedure(DateTime
dateDateValue, DateTime maxDateValue);
List<GetItemsTotalValueDto> GetItemsTotalValues(bool isActive);
List<ItemsWithGenresDto> GetItemsWithGenres();
List<CategoryDto> ListCategoriesAndColors();
```

And then move the methods associated with writing by cutting and pasting the following methods from the IInventoryDatabaseRepo into the IInventoryDatabaseRepoWriteOnly interface:

```
int InsertOrUpdateItem(Item item);
void InsertOrUpdateItems(List<Item> items);
void DeleteItem(int id);
void DeleteItems(List<int> itemIds);
```

Finally, implement both interfaces in the full-version IInventoryDatabaseRepo interface, by simply adding the implements operator and the two interface names to the IInventoryDatabaseRepo declaration:

```
public interface IInventoryDatabaseRepo : IInventoryDatabaseRepoReadOnly,
IInventoryDatabaseRepoWriteOnly
{

}
```

Make sure to run all the build the solution and run unit tests now to ensure that nothing that was currently implemented was broken by this refactoring.

For clarity, the overall code for this repo after refactoring is shown in Figure 13-7.

```
1 reference
public interface IInventoryDatabaseRepoReadOnly
{
    4 references | ⊘ 1/1 passing
    List<Item> ListInventory();
    2 references
    List<GetItemsForListingWithDateDto> GetItemsForListingLinq(DateTime minDateValue, DateTime maxDateValue);
    2 references
    List<GetItemsForListingDto> GetItemsForListingFromProcedure(DateTime dateDateValue, DateTime maxDateValue);
    2 references
    List<GetItemsTotalValueDto> GetItemsTotalValues(bool isActive);
    2 references
    List<ItemsWithGenresDto> GetItemsWithGenres();
    3 references
    List<CategoryDto> ListCategoriesAndColors();
}


1 reference
public interface IInventoryDatabaseRepoWriteOnly
{
    3 references
    int InsertOrUpdateItem(Item item);
    2 references
    void InsertOrUpdateItems(List<Item> items);
    3 references
    void DeleteItem(int id);
    2 references
    void DeleteItems(List<int> itemIds);
}


6 references
public interface IInventoryDatabaseRepo
                    : IInventoryDatabaseRepoReadOnly, IInventoryDatabaseRepoWriteOnly
{

}
```

Figure 13-7. *The IInventoryDatabaseRepo interface hierarchy contains the ability to segregate read and write operations by interface if desired*

Step 4: Create the new interfaces and implementations in the InventoryBusinessLayer project

Next, we need to do the same type of refactoring in the InventoryBusinessLayer project for the IItemsService interface, which will create a similar separation of concerns for reading and writing to and from the data layer.

As in step 3, begin by creating two new interfaces, then cut and paste the appropriate methods to each interface for implementation, and finally set the default interface to implement both read and write interfaces. The refactored code should look as follows:

```
public interface IItemsServiceReadOnly
{
    List<GetItemsForListingWithDateDto> GetItemsForListingLinq(DateTime
    minDateValue, DateTime maxDateValue);
    List<GetItemsForListingDto> GetItemsForListingFromProcedure(DateTime
    minDateValue, DateTime maxDateValue);
    AllItemsPipeDelimitedStringDto GetItemsPipeDelimitedString(bool
    isActive);
    List<GetItemsTotalValueDto> GetItemsTotalValues(bool isActive);
    List<ItemsWithGenresDto> GetItemsWithGenres();
    List<CategoryDto> ListCategoriesAndColors();
    List<ItemDto> ListInventory();
}

public interface IItemsServiceWriteOnly
{
    int InsertOrUpdateItem(CreateOrUpdateItemDto item);
    void InsertOrUpdateItems(List<CreateOrUpdateItemDto> item);
    void DeleteItem(int id);
    void DeleteItems(List<int> itemIds);
}

public interface IItemsService : IItemsServiceReadOnly,
IItemsServiceWriteOnly
{
}
```

For clarity, the refactored code is also shown in Figure 13-8.

```
1 reference
public interface IItemsServiceReadOnly
{
    2 references
    List<GetItemsForListingWithDateDto> GetItemsForListingLinq(DateTime minDateValue, DateTime maxDateValue);
    2 references
    List<GetItemsForListingDto> GetItemsForListingFromProcedure(DateTime minDateValue, DateTime maxDateValue);
    2 references
    AllItemsPipeDelimitedStringDto GetItemsPipeDelimitedString(bool isActive);
    2 references
    List<GetItemsTotalValueDto> GetItemsTotalValues(bool isActive);
    2 references
    List<ItemsWithGenresDto> GetItemsWithGenres();
    2 references
    List<CategoryDto> ListCategoriesAndColors();
    9 references
    List<ItemDto> ListInventory();
}

1 reference
public interface IItemsServiceWriteOnly
{
    3 references
    int InsertOrUpdateItem(CreateOrUpdateItemDto item);
    3 references
    void InsertOrUpdateItems(List<CreateOrUpdateItemDto> item);
    2 references
    void DeleteItem(int id);
    2 references
    void DeleteItems(List<int> itemIds);
}

5 references
public interface IItemsService : IItemsServiceReadOnly, IItemsServiceWriteOnly
{
}
```

Figure 13-8. *The refactored IItemsService hierarchy*

Once again, it is a good idea to run the unit tests to make sure that nothing is broken by this refactoring.

Step 5: Get SQLite in the integration testing project

We're going to be implementing a Dapper repo soon, but before we do that, we're going to need to have the ability to work with an actual database connection for Dapper. Therefore, we need to use SQLite for our in-memory solution. Perhaps in the future, the EFCore In-Memory solution will work as expected. Perhaps I just haven't set it up correctly, but when I try to use it, I continually get an error about not being able to establish a connection. SQLite fills the gaps nicely for us for use in our integration testing. Additionally, even Microsoft has issued warnings against relying on the operation of the EFCore In-Memory database, so SQLite is a great choice for testing our Dapper operations.

Return to the *NuGet Package Manager* for the solution, and browse to find
`Microsoft.Data.Sqlite.Core`, and install it to the `InventoryManagerIntegrationTests`
project. Along with that search, you should see three other packages that we want.
They are `Microsoft.Data.Sqlite.Core`, `Microsoft.EntityFrameworkCore.Sqlite`,
and `Microsoft.EntityFrameworkCore.Sqlite.Core`. The version number should
match your EFCore version. Figure 13-9 shows a closer look at installation of the four
packages. Figure 13-9 was taken when version 3.1.4 was the latest version of EFCore. You
should continue to use the most recent version, and your version should match your
implementation of EFCore (i.e., 3.1.x).

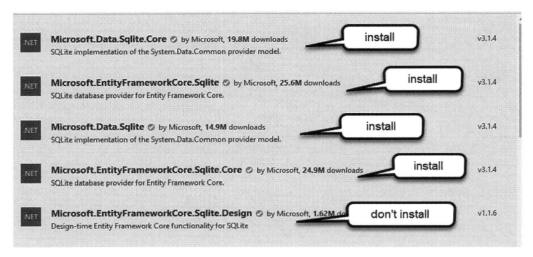

Figure 13-9. *Installing the four packages to get SQLite into our testing project*

Now that we have SQLite in the testing project, let's add the methods we'll need in
order to create an instance of SQLite to run during testing.

In the `InventoryManagerIntegrationTests`, add a method to `SetupSqlite` in the class,
add three private class-level variables at the top of the class, and call the setup method
from the constructor. Use the following code as a guide (and don't forget to add any
missing using statements):

```
//DAPPER Testing
private const string sqlLiteConnectionString = "DataSource=:memory:";
private SqliteConnection _connection;
private InventoryDbContext _context;
```

```
public InventoryManagerIntegrationTests()
{
    SetupOptions();
    BuildDefaults();
    SetupSqlite();
}

private void SetupSqlite()
{

}
```

Next, implement the method to set up the tests for running SQLite. Additionally, we'll make a call to a method that we'll write next to seed the data.

```
private void SetupSqlite()
{
    _connection = new SqliteConnection(sqlLiteConnectionString);
    _connection.Open();
    var options = new DbContextOptionsBuilder<InventoryDbContext>()
            .UseSqlite(_connection)
            .Options;
    _context = new InventoryDbContext(options);
    _context.Database.EnsureCreated();
    BuildSqliteData();
}
```

Always remember to bring in any missing using statements if you haven't already.

After creating the instance, we need to seed some data for testing.

While there is likely a way we could refactor the setup to work with both our EFCore In-Memory solution and SQLite, to just get this test project working with data, let's create a new method and implement the setup specifically for SQLite.

Use the following code to implement the BuildSqliteData method for seeing our test data:

```
private void BuildSqliteData()
{
    //skip creation if items already exist:
    var item1Detail = _context.Items.SingleOrDefault(x => x.Name.
    Equals(ITEM1_NAME));
    var item2Detail = _context.Items.SingleOrDefault(x => x.Name.
    Equals(ITEM2_NAME));
    var item3Detail = _context.Items.SingleOrDefault(x => x.Name.
    Equals(ITEM3_NAME));
    if (item1Detail != null && item2Detail != null && item3Detail != null)
    return;

    var color1 = new CategoryColor() { ColorValue = COLOR_BLUE };
    var color2 = new CategoryColor() { ColorValue = COLOR_RED };
    var color3 = new CategoryColor() { ColorValue = COLOR_GREEN };

    var cat1 = new Category()
    {
        CategoryColor = color1,
        IsActive = true,
        IsDeleted = false,
        Name = CAT1_NAME
    };
    var cat2 = new Category()
    {
        CategoryColor = color2,
        IsActive = true,
        IsDeleted = false,
        Name = CAT2_NAME
    };
    var cat3 = new Category()
    {
        CategoryColor = color3,
        IsActive = true,
```

```
    IsDeleted = false,
    Name = CAT3_NAME
};
_context.Categories.Add(cat1);
_context.Categories.Add(cat2);
_context.Categories.Add(cat3);
_context.SaveChanges();

//with sql lite, need to build out the id for the category.
categorycolorid for mappings
var catColor1 = _context.CategoryColors.Single(x => x.ColorValue.
Equals(COLOR_BLUE));
var catColor2 = _context.CategoryColors.Single(x => x.ColorValue.
Equals(COLOR_RED));
var catColor3 = _context.CategoryColors.Single(x => x.ColorValue.
Equals(COLOR_GREEN));
var category1 = _context.Categories.Single(x => x.Name.Equals(CAT1_NAME));
var category2 = _context.Categories.Single(x => x.Name.Equals(CAT2_NAME));
var category3 = _context.Categories.Single(x => x.Name.Equals(CAT3_NAME));

category1.CategoryColorId = catColor1.Id;
category2.CategoryColorId = catColor2.Id;
category3.CategoryColorId = catColor3.Id;
_context.SaveChanges();

var item1 = new Item()
{
    Name = ITEM1_NAME,
    Description = ITEM1_DESC,
    Notes = ITEM1_NOTES,
    IsActive = true,
    IsDeleted = false,
    CategoryId = category1.Id
};
```

```
        _context.Items.Add(item1);
        var item2 = new Item()
        {
            Name = ITEM2_NAME,
            Description = ITEM2_DESC,
            Notes = ITEM2_NOTES,
            IsActive = true,
            IsDeleted = false,
            CategoryId = category2.Id
        };
        _context.Items.Add(item2);
        var item3 = new Item()
        {
            Name = ITEM3_NAME,
            Description = ITEM3_DESC,
            Notes = ITEM3_NOTES,
            IsActive = true,
            IsDeleted = false,
            CategoryId = category3.Id
        };
        _context.Items.Add(item3);
        _context.SaveChanges();
}
```

The first part of the BuildSqliteData method is going to be exactly the same as the setup for our original testing. The second part of the method requires that we ensure the category color id is set for each category, which we did not have to do in the original testing.

With *SQLite* setup, run the tests to make sure nothing is broken to this point, even though we aren't leveraging the *SQLite* instance yet.

Step 6: Add the Dapper Layer, and test it

Now we are ready to build our read-only Dapper repo. To do this, we can follow standard TDD procedures. First, implement two tests in the IntegrationTests project.

```
[Fact]
public void TestDapperListInventory()
{
}

[Theory]
[InlineData(CAT1_NAME, COLOR_BLUE)]
[InlineData(CAT2_NAME, COLOR_RED)]
[InlineData(CAT3_NAME, COLOR_GREEN)]
public void TestDapperCategoryColors(string name, string color)
{
}
```

With those tests in place, add the following code to the top of each test method:

```
var repo = new InventoryDatabaseDapperRepo(_context.Database.
GetDbConnection(), _mapper);
```

To make this compile, we need to create the implementation of InventoryDatabaseDapperRepo. Note that we are passing in a database connection and our previously built mapper object, in case we need to use it eventually.

In the InventoryDatabaseLayer project, add a new class file called InventoryDatabaseDapperRepo.cs. Add the constructor and class-level variables to the class as shown in the following, and make sure to implement the IInventoryDatabaseRepoReadOnly interface, and bring in any missing using statements:

```
public class InventoryDatabaseDapperRepo : IInventoryDatabaseRepoReadOnly
{
    private readonly IDbConnection _connection;
    private readonly IMapper _mapper;

    public InventoryDatabaseDapperRepo(IDbConnection connection, IMapper
    mapper)
    {
        _connection = connection;
        _mapper = mapper;

        if (_connection.State == ConnectionState.Closed)
        {
```

```
            _connection.Open();
        }
    }
```

For clarity, the initial work for creating the Dapper repo is shown in Figure 13-10. Note that currently the code will not compile because the interface is not yet implemented correctly.

```
using AutoMapper;
using System.Data;

namespace InventoryDatabaseLayer
{
    3 references
    public class InventoryDatabaseDapperRepo : IInventoryDatabaseRepoReadOnly
    {
        private readonly IDbConnection _connection;
        private readonly IMapper _mapper;

        2 references | ⬥ 0/4 passing
        public InventoryDatabaseDapperRepo(IDbConnection connection, IMapper mapper)
        {
            _connection = connection;
            _mapper = mapper;

            if (_connection.State == ConnectionState.Closed)
            {
                _connection.Open();
            }
        }
    }
}
```

Figure 13-10. *Setting up the Dapper Repo instance*

Next, use the built-in generation tools to implement the interface with the default exception implementations. When completed, the following code should have been added into your class, and the solution should be buildable:

```
public List<GetItemsForListingDto> GetItemsForListingFromProcedure(DateTime
dateDateValue, DateTime maxDateValue)
{
    throw new NotImplementedException();
}
```

```
public List<GetItemsForListingWithDateDto> GetItemsForListingLinq(DateTime
minDateValue, DateTime maxDateValue)
{
    throw new NotImplementedException();
}

public List<GetItemsTotalValueDto> GetItemsTotalValues(bool isActive)
{
    throw new NotImplementedException();
}

public List<ItemsWithGenresDto> GetItemsWithGenres()
{
    throw new NotImplementedException();
}

public List<CategoryDto> ListCategoriesAndColors()
{
    throw new NotImplementedException();
}

public List<Item> ListInventory()
{
    throw new NotImplementedException();
}
```

Return to the InventoryManagerIntegrationTests project and add code to the TestDapperListInventory test as follows:

```
var repo = new InventoryDatabaseDapperRepo(_context.Database.
GetDbConnection(), _mapper);
var result = repo.ListInventory();

result.ShouldNotBeNull();
result.Count.ShouldBe(3);
var one = result.Single(x => x.Name == ITEM1_NAME);
one.ShouldNotBeNull();
one.Name.ShouldBe(ITEM1_NAME);
one.Description.ShouldBe(ITEM1_DESC);
```

```
one.Notes.ShouldBe(ITEM1_NOTES);
one.Category.Name.ShouldBe(CAT1_NAME);

var two = result.Single(x => x.Name == ITEM2_NAME);
two.ShouldNotBeNull();
two.Name.ShouldBe(ITEM2_NAME);
two.Description.ShouldBe(ITEM2_DESC);
two.Notes.ShouldBe(ITEM2_NOTES);
two.Category.Name.ShouldBe(CAT2_NAME);

var three = result.Single(x => x.Name == ITEM3_NAME);
three.ShouldNotBeNull();
three.Name.ShouldBe(ITEM3_NAME);
three.Description.ShouldBe(ITEM3_DESC);
three.Notes.ShouldBe(ITEM3_NOTES);
three.Category.Name.ShouldBe(CAT3_NAME);
```

Ordinarily, we'd run the test to see that it is currently broken, fix the test, then move on, and then run it to see that it is working (i.e., red-green-refactor). For brevity, add the following code to the TestDapperCategoryColors test:

```
var catcolors = repo.ListCategoriesAndColors();
catcolors.ShouldNotBeNull();
catcolors.Count.ShouldBe(3);

var item = catcolors.SingleOrDefault(x => x.Category.Equals(name));
item.ShouldNotBeNull();
item.CategoryColor.Color.ShouldBe(color);
```

Run the tests; all Dapper tests should fail as expected. Figure 13-11 shows the expected output in the Test Explorer window.

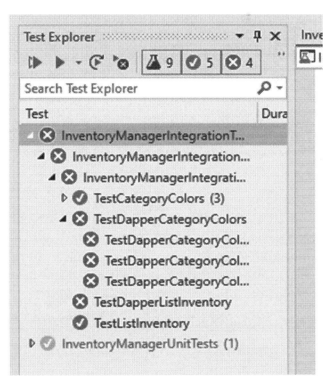

Figure 13-11. *The Dapper Repo tests fail as expected*

Go back to the Dapper repo, and add the following code into the ListInventory method:

```
var sql = $"SELECT i.Id, i.Name, i.Description, i.Notes, i.IsDeleted,
i.CategoryId " +
            ", c.Name as CategoryName" +
            " FROM Items i INNER JOIN Categories c on i.CategoryId = c.Id" +
            " WHERE i.IsDeleted = @isDeleted";
var result = _connection.Query<dynamic>(sql, new { isDeleted = 0 });
Slapper.AutoMapper.Configuration.AddIdentifiers(typeof(Item), new
List<string> { "Id" });
Slapper.AutoMapper.Configuration.AddIdentifiers(typeof(Category), new
List<string> { "CategoryId" });
```

```
var output = (Slapper.AutoMapper.MapDynamic<Item>(result) as
IEnumerable<Item>).OrderBy(x => x.Name).ToList();

//have to hydrate the relationship:
foreach (var item in output)
{
    item.Category = _connection.Query<Category>("SELECT * FROM Categories
    where ID = " + item.CategoryId).First();
}
return output;
```

Also add the using statements for Dapper and Linq so the code will compile.

There are a few things we need to notice about this code.

First of all, we wrote a direct T-SQL statement in code. This is one of the powers of Dapper. You can directly implement the T-SQL code you want and execute it.

A second point of interest is that we used the simple call

```
var result = _connection.Query<dynamic>(sql, new { isDeleted = 0 });
```

to make a query that returned a dynamic result since we are joining data and flattening it. If we were directly calling to just get Item without Category info, we could have used the Item type instead of dynamic type.

The third interesting piece of code is using the Slapper.Automapper library to define the relationships and then casting the data back into our C# class objects:

```
Slapper.AutoMapper.Configuration.AddIdentifiers(typeof(Item), new
List<string> { "Id" });

Slapper.AutoMapper.Configuration.AddIdentifiers(typeof(Category),
new List<string> { "CategoryId" });

        var output = (Slapper.AutoMapper.MapDynamic<Item>(result) as
        IEnumerable<Item>).OrderBy(x => x.Name).ToList();
```

Also note that we first pulled the data and then mapped it, then ordered it, and sent it to a list.

Finally, since the data is flat, and our code needs to show the Category name, we need to hydrate that data with a loop. This is obviously a bit of a code smell. Ideally, we would use Dapper to only get the flat data, not needing to worry about relationships.

```
//have to hydrate the relationship:
foreach (var item in output)
{
    item.Category = _connection.Query<Category>("SELECT * FROM Categories
    where ID = " + item.CategoryId).First();
}
return output;
```

Run the tests to make sure the inventory test works as expected with our updated code.

To complete our testing, add the following code to the ListCategoriesAndColors method in the Dapper repo:

```
public List<CategoryDto> ListCategoriesAndColors()
{
    var sql = "SELECT c.Id, c.Name, cc.Id as CategoryColorId, cc.ColorValue " +
                "FROM Categories c " +
                "INNER JOIN CategoryColors cc " +
                    "ON c.CategoryColorId = cc.Id";
    var result = _connection.Query<dynamic>(sql);

    Slapper.AutoMapper.Configuration.AddIdentifiers(typeof(Category), new
    List<string> { "Id" });

    Slapper.AutoMapper.Configuration.AddIdentifiers(typeof(CategoryColor),
    new List<string> { "CategoryColorId" });

    /*
     map
    */
    var output = (Slapper.AutoMapper.MapDynamic<Category>(result) as
    IEnumerable<Category>).ToList();
    foreach (var category in output)
    {
        category.CategoryColor = _connection.Query<CategoryColor>
        ("SELECT * FROM CategoryColors where ID = "
```

```
                                              + category.CategoryColorId).First();
    }

    return _mapper.Map<List<CategoryDto>>(output);
}
```

Once again, run the tests to see that all of them are now passing as expected (see Figure 13-12).

Figure 13-12. *All tests that are written are passing*

Step 7: Implement the Readonly Items service

Our database layer is complete, but we need to write the service layer in order to expose the Dapper database layer.

In the InventoryBusinessLayer project, add a new file called ItemsServiceReadOnly.cs. Implement the IItemsServiceReadOnly interface, and generate the interface implementations so the code will compile. When completed, the ItemsServiceReadOnly class should look like this:

```
public class ItemsServiceReadOnly : IItemsServiceReadOnly
{
    public List<GetItemsForListingDto> GetItemsForListingFromProcedure(Date
    Time minDateValue, DateTime maxDateValue)
    {
        throw new NotImplementedException();
    }

    public List<GetItemsForListingWithDateDto>
    GetItemsForListingLinq(DateTime minDateValue, DateTime maxDateValue)
    {
        throw new NotImplementedException();
    }

    public AllItemsPipeDelimitedStringDto GetItemsPipeDelimitedString(bool
    isActive)
    {
        throw new NotImplementedException();
    }

    public List<GetItemsTotalValueDto> GetItemsTotalValues(bool isActive)
    {
        throw new NotImplementedException();
    }

    public List<ItemsWithGenresDto> GetItemsWithGenres()
    {
        throw new NotImplementedException();
    }

    public List<CategoryDto> ListCategoriesAndColors()
    {
        throw new NotImplementedException();
    }
```

```
    public List<ItemDto> ListInventory()
    {
        throw new NotImplementedException();
    }
}
```

Create two class-level variables and a constructor for the ItemsServiceReadOnly class with the following code (don't forget to add the missing using statements):

```
private readonly InventoryDatabaseDapperRepo _dbRepo;
private readonly IMapper _mapper;

public ItemsServiceReadOnly(InventoryDatabaseDapperRepo dbRepo, IMapper mapper)
{
    _dbRepo = dbRepo;
    _mapper = mapper;
}
```

We've only implemented a couple of the methods in the actual repo, but we could still do all the simple pass-through methods in this class. For purposes of brevity, we'll only do the two we have tested and are going to use in this activity. Feel free to implement the rest for practice if you desire.

Both implemented methods are going to just pass through the call to the database layer. In the ListInventory method, add the following code:

```
return _mapper.Map<List<ItemDto>>(_dbRepo.ListInventory());
```

Then, in the ListCategoriesAndColors method, add this code:

```
return _dbRepo.ListCategoriesAndColors();
```

For clarity, the implementations are illustrated in Figure 13-13.

```
4 references
public List<CategoryDto> ListCategoriesAndColors()
{
    return _dbRepo.ListCategoriesAndColors();
}

8 references | ⊘ 1/1 passing
public List<ItemDto> ListInventory()
{
    return _mapper.Map<List<ItemDto>>(_dbRepo.ListInventory());
}
}
```

Figure 13-13. *Implementing the two pass-through methods from the new read-only service to the Dapper database repo*

Step 8: Work with the Dapper implementation in code

Now that the solution is working as expected in test, and we have the read-only service in place to call to the Dapper repo, let's implement the two methods in the Main program of the main activity project to see it play out with a real database.

In the Main method of the Program.cs file, comment out or remove all the code except the two calls to the original database repo for ListInventory (lines 41–43) and ListCategoriesAndColors (lines 69–72). For simplicity, I've removed the code so you can see exactly what I'm asking you to do (the final solution files will still contain all original code).

```
static void Main(string[] args)
{
    BuildOptions();
    BuildMapper();

    var minDate = new DateTime(2020, 1, 1);
    var maxDate = new DateTime(2021, 1, 1);

    using (var db = new InventoryDbContext(_optionsBuilder.Options))
    {
        var dbRepo = new InventoryDatabaseRepo(db, _mapper);
        var svc = new ItemsService(dbRepo, _mapper);
```

```
        Console.WriteLine("List Inventory");
        var inventory = svc.ListInventory();
        inventory.ForEach(x => Console.WriteLine($"New Item: {x}"));
        /*** commmented code here ***/
        Console.WriteLine("List Categories And Colors");
        var categoriesAndColors = svc.ListCategoriesAndColors();
        categoriesAndColors.ForEach(c => Console.WriteLine($"{c.Category} |
        {c.CategoryColor.Color}"));
        /*** commented code here ***/
    }
    Console.WriteLine("Program Complete");
}
```

Run the program to make sure you have only the two methods being called (review Figure 13-14).

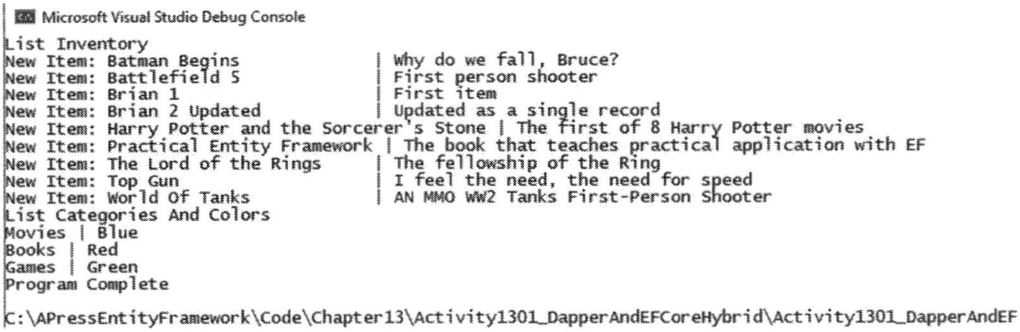

Figure 13-14. *Current code that is executing only runs the List Inventory and List Categories and Colors methods*

With the program limited, it will be easier to see our Dapper database layer working. At the end of the using block for the InventoryDbContext, add the following code:

```
//Read only dapper
var dbDapperRepo = new InventoryDatabaseDapperRepo(db.Database.
GetDbConnection(), _mapper);
var svc2 = new ItemsServiceReadOnly(dbDapperRepo, _mapper);

Console.WriteLine("List Inventory from Dapper");
var dapperInventory = svc2.ListInventory();
```

```
dapperInventory.ForEach(x => Console.WriteLine($"New Item: {x}"));

Console.WriteLine("List Categories And Colors From Dapper");
var dapperCategoriesAndColors = svc2.ListCategoriesAndColors();
dapperCategoriesAndColors.ForEach(c => Console.WriteLine($"{c.Category} |
{c.CategoryColor.Color}"));
```

With this code, there are a couple of things to note. The main thing to note is that we create a new version of the Dapper repository using the context that is already in scope to ultimately get to the database connection string. We could have loaded it via the appsettings.json file and just created a new connection. However, since we have everything in place already for the existing context, this is an easier approach.

In addition to the database connection, we also pass the instantiated AutoMapper object through to the read-only methods.

Once the repo is set up, we then create a version of the service by injecting our repo and the instantiated AutoMapper object.

With the service in place, we just need to make the calls and print the results as is done in the original calls for the full service.

Once all of this is in place, we've seen how to leverage both *EF* and Dapper in the same solution, and we could easily apply what we've learned here to make our own solutions more robust.

Run the program to see the Dapper repo versions working in the Main method. Figure 13-15 shows the final results.

```
List Categories And Colors
Movies | Blue
Books | Red
Games | Green
List Inventory from Dapper
New Item: Batman Begins                 | Why do we fall, Bruce?
New Item: Battlefield 5                 | First person shooter
New Item: Brian 1                       | First item
New Item: Brian 2 Updated               | Updated as a single record
New Item: Harry Potter and the Sorcerer's Stone | The first of 8 Harry Potter movies
New Item: Practical Entity Framework    | The book that teaches practical application with EF
New Item: The Lord of the Rings         | The fellowship of the Ring
New Item: Top Gun                       | I feel the need, the need for speed
New Item: World Of Tanks                | AN MMO WW2 Tanks First-Person Shooter
List Categories And Colors From Dapper
Movies | Blue
Books | Red
Games | Green
Program Complete

C:\APressEntityFramework\Code\Chapter13\Activity1301_DapperAndEFCoreHybrid\Activity1301_DapperAndEF(
```

Figure 13-15. *The Dapper repository is leveraged through the service layer via the Main method*

Final thoughts on activity 1301

In this activity, we implemented a hybrid solution that combined *EF* and Dapper. By using the Dapper lightweight ORM, we can achieve some performance gains and write SQL directly for some of our complex queries. Adding the Slapper.Automapper tool to enhance Dapper allows us to easily integrate with C# types after retrieving results from Dapper.

Final thoughts for this chapter

In this chapter, we've walked through using a lightweight ORM to supplement our database activities. We started by talking about the various benefits and drawbacks that we might encounter when using both *EF* as the only database solution and when implementing a lightweight ORM to provide some performance enhancements.

Dapper with Slapper.Automapper

For our solution, as we implemented the Dapper library with the Slapper.Automapper library, we saw that Dapper is a powerful tool that allows for quick and efficient access to the database. One of the main benefits outside of performance is also the ability to write and use our own T-SQL commands directly against the database from code.

Cached queries and direct access

We also discussed the benefit of caching the queries that are executed as implemented with Dapper. The performance benefits of a direct access to the database along with these cached queries can really pay off in large systems.

Multiple table joins, flat, and relational data

Using Dapper is not necessarily something that should be done in every project, however. Certainly, there are situations where using *EF* is a better choice. In cases where we are doing multiple table joins and need more than just flat data, Dapper falls a bit short. This is by design. The concession here is that getting data with Dapper is going to be more efficient, but part of that efficiency means that relational data is not preserved. Adding Slapper.Automapper gives the ability to quickly map the data as returned from Dapper into the expected output data types.

Interface segregation and inversion of control

Finally, we saw the benefits in this solution of having our layered architecture with decoupled constructors. By coding to the interface implementations, we can easily inject either type of service or repository as needed going forward.

While we didn't end up implementing every individual method, this solution gave us a great chance to see the use of a third-party, lightweight *ORM* in our solution.

We are positioned well for success

At this point, we've covered almost all of the main aspects of a solution that is implementing *Entity Framework* and working with MS SQL to create robust solutions. While there are a few methods that are incomplete, we have the tools we need to work with *EF* in a professional setting. There are just a few more things that are important to know as we continue to grow as *EF* developers.

In our final chapter, we'll finish the book by focusing on the changes that *EFCore* has brought us, asynchronous operations, and where we are going to go from here with *EF* into the future.

PART IV

Recipes for Success

CHAPTER 14

Asynchronous Data Operations and Multiple Database Contexts

In this chapter, we'll cover two final critical concepts, as we discuss asynchronous operations and using multiple database contexts in our solutions.

At the end of this chapter, we'll have seen how we can implement the database layer while leveraging the power of multiple cores in our computers. We'll also have taken a look at how it is possible to use more than one database context in our solutions.

Asynchronous operations

The first concept we need to talk about is working with asynchronous operations. To this point, we've done everything with all methods being synchronous. However, in most practical applications, we'll be leveraging the power of asynchronous programming.

Multithreaded programming

As our computer architectures changed from being processor speed oriented as the metric of superiority to processor speed plus core count oriented, multithreaded programming became much more popular and much more important in our day-to-day work.

The main problem with multithreaded programming is that it is difficult. There are many issues to consider before diving into multithreaded programming. Race conditions lead to your asynchronous code executing processes or methods out of order. Thread pools run out of available threads and can still cause pieces of your program to become unresponsive. In a worst-case scenario, threads get locked in an infinite loop and your entire application becomes unresponsive.

B. L. Gorman, *Practical Entity Framework*, https://doi.org/10.1007/978-1-4842-6044-9_14

Because of the overall difficulty of asynchronous programming, the original rate of adoption was not that high. In fact, the main use prior to the `TaskParallelLibrary` (TPL) being introduced for most developers was likely just to keep desktop forms from appearing to be locked while processes ran in the background after pressing a button. I even wrote a blog post in 2009 on how to use events, delegates, and threads to avoid running into that specific problem.

Because of the difficulty of multithreaded programming, and the various technical problems associated with it, the .Net Framework was expanded to make our lives a whole lot better.

Async, await, and the TaskParallelLibrary

In the .Net world, async and await keywords first showed up in the *.Net 3.0 Framework*, but didn't become widely adopted and useable until the `TaskParallelLibrary` (*TPL*) was introduced in .Net 4.

The TPL gave all of us the ability to specify the Task operations with return types that we have come to rely on in our asynchronous code. With the TPL, we can also rely on the fact that issues with concurrency are handled correctly. For example, using the await operator or requesting to get the result of a parallel operation gives us the assurance that our code will not continue to execute until the threaded operation has completed.

Responsive solutions for the end user

To put this more into perspective, think of websites from the early 2000s through about 2010. Perhaps you've even heard the term *Web 2.0*. Prior to *Web 2.0* and other initiatives that happened at the end of the 2000s into the 2010s, websites were mostly one user doing one thing for themselves, or essential duties that they would perform, or were just simple, static files. *Web 2.0* really grasped the idea that there should be multiple users interacting in the same systems and that each user should see information in real time.

With *Web 2.0*, it was more common to expect your changes to be immediately reflected to other users of the same system. This led to new approaches to web services and a movement into REST APIs, as well as things like the `AjaxControlToolkit` and `SignalR`, to provide an ability to abstract programmers from having to work directly with `websockets`. In the end, real-time dashboards as part of partial pages were able to immediately display results to the end user. Where a single-threaded approach would need to load all of the page data and then render it, and also get all of the page data from the server to re-render even the smallest changes, *Web 2.0* essentially moved us to having multithreaded web pages with various portions responding to different threads and no longer having to reload the whole page to see a simple change on one metric.

All of this brings us to the place where we want to land for our database as well. If you create a dashboard that requires ten different pieces of information from the database, you don't want the database calls to stop the page from working, and you don't want the page to wait to respond until all ten different calls have completed.

By placing our database calls into asynchronous operations, our web solutions can also remain asynchronous, and the overall responsiveness of the site appears to be much better, even if there are still calls that bottleneck the process.

Asynchronous database operations

With the TPL and the ability to define a return type that is based on a threaded operation, we can leverage our processor architecture. Using `async` and `await` with our operations obfuscates the need to do the heavy lifting of multithreading ourselves, and we can get to a much more responsive solution with less concern about the underlying issues involved with multithreading.

Programming the database operations to also happen in an asynchronous manner thereby gives us the full power to leverage the TPL and the `async` and `await` keywords.

In other words, by using asynchronous database operations, we'll get to keep programming as if we are working with commands in a synchronous manner, while leveraging the power of our multiple-core processors and the underlying multithreading that is available to us. Utilizing asynchronous database operations ultimately helps us to keep our applications responsive while querying the database in the most efficient manner possible.

Basic asynchronous syntax

Without going into a lot of detail here, setting our methods to use asynchronous operations is very straightforward. We will cover all of this in detail in our first activity later in this chapter.

To sum up what it takes to implement asynchronous operations, the main changes will require us to

- Rework all methods to be `async Task` operations

- Change all database calls to happen with the built-in async abilities of *EF*

- Refactor any queries that don't work as written in an asynchronous pattern

- Use the async/await pattern throughout the application

- Show how to execute an async operation from a synchronous context

Multiple database contexts

In most applications, a single database context can handle your needs. However, while it is not necessary and should ultimately be used with caution, there will be times when using multiple contexts can be beneficial.

Single sign on (SSO)

The most common reason I can conceive that you would want to have multiple database contexts would be in a company where you have a suite of applications and you want to provide custom sign-on capabilities to users (outside of Azure AD or an on-premises Active Directory).

In this solution, rather than require your users register for all of your applications, you can have an SSO solution where once a user is registered with one of your applications, the same user and password combination can be used for all of them.

It's certainly true that you could replicate the data in the tables for user management across all of your applications with a background process. However, if all applications connect to and use the same database for identity, you can do much less work and have much less of a chance for error.

Business units

Another solution that might lend itself to multiple contexts would be a situation where you want to separate units within your corporation into their own database solutions while providing a single application to interact with the data.

For example, consider a large banking corporation that has units of work around accounting practices, customer management, financial investment operations, marketing, insurance, lending, and collections.

In this corporation, certain employees would likely need access to pieces of information in all units, such as a customer account with balance and perhaps payment and balance history in combination with mortgage and credit card information. Other business unites might only need access to one or two of the pieces of information. For example, marketing employees might only need access to customer name and address information. Furthermore, some information might be entirely confidential, and, due to regulations, knowing that information could lead to a potential violation of federal law (such as a fairness in lending act), so it may be critical to keep a clear separation of concerns to provide boundaries that cannot be circumvented.

When a case such as this exists, you'll likely need to expose certain shared data across line-of-business applications, or you may need to have directly created contexts to leverage only the parts of each system that should be accessible. Again, the choice here is which is better for your company – from background jobs to sync your data on some time interval to direct immediate access to the most valid dataset that you can provide, the choices and implementations will be your responsibility as the developer.

Multiple contexts require a bit more work

If our solution is going to use multiple contexts, there are a few things we'll need to be aware of.

The first thing to be certain to address is the injection of the context and the creation of the context at startup. Most applications will inject their context at startup, but you'll be required to also include any additional contexts. Using the additional contexts also generally requires a shared library that can leverage the shared contexts.

The second critical piece of information that is important when working with multiple contexts is the knowledge of the commands to run in the package manager console. With a single context, a simple `add-migration` or `update-database` command can be run at will. Once you have introduced a second context into the solution, the PMC will need you to explicitly specify which context to use when running these commands.

Finally, using multiple contexts requires that everyone is on the same page as to the standards and approaches used in unit testing and interface segregation. While you could get by without this, it will be nice to know that any library developed around a context is fully unit and integration tested. Additionally, if there are security concerns, the ability to get just a read-only version of the context without much work should be readily available.

Putting it into practice

We've now done a good deal of talking about asynchronous operations and the database, as well as using multiple contexts.

For the remainder of the chapter, we'll work through these scenarios to see what it takes to get set up, as well as learn about how to work with commands and code when making asynchronous calls or trying to add or update the database from the code-first approach to database development.

Activity 1401: Asynchronous database operations

In our first activity, we are going to rework our inventory database library to use asynchronous operations.

Leveraging async and await

The main purpose of this activity is to give us the ability to implement calls that rely on the *async/await* pattern. By doing this, we should be able to free up our applications to continue processing as well as optimize the performance of our own database operations to leverage the power of multithreading without all the heavy lifting.

As mentioned previously, there will be a few things we have to refactor, and the changes will ripple up all the way to our program. This also means we'll have to refactor our tests. In the end, this solution will be much more like what we'll encounter in any real-world application going forward.

Step 1: Steps

To begin, grab a copy of the `Activity1401_AsynchronousDatabaseOperations_Starter.` `zip` files, extract them, build the project, double-check your connection string, and make sure that you have the *InventoryManager* database set up. Run an `update-database` command to make sure the migrations are up to date on your machine. Additionally, you could run an `add-migration` command to ensure that you don't have any pending changes. Assuming there are none, you could then just run the `remove-migration` command to clean up the empty migration. If you have pending changes, consider just updating the database to match the current solution using the `update-database` command.

Alternatively, you could just continue using your InventoryManager solution that you've been building through the previous chapters in this book, with your code in the same state as it was at the end of Chapter 13.

Step 2: Begin at the database level

To make the changes work, we're going to have to touch most of the layers in some way or another, including the tests. We'll start by reworking all of the database calls and move up the layers from there. Along the way, we'll see how to make calls with async/await, as well as see the ability to run from a synchronous method when we get to the program.

Starting in the `InventoryDatabaseLayer`, open the `IInventoryDatabaseRepo` interface. In the interface, change all of the methods to be asynchronous by wrapping each return type with `Task<T>`. When the method is void, simply change the method to be a `Task`. Make sure to add the using statement `using System.Threading.Tasks;`. When the code is updated, it should look as follows:

```
public interface IInventoryDatabaseRepoReadOnly
{
    Task<List<GetItemsForListingDto>> GetItemsForListingFromProcedure
    (DateTime dateDateValue, DateTime maxDateValue);
    Task<List<GetItemsForListingWithDateDto>> GetItemsForListingLinq
    (DateTime minDateValue, DateTime maxDateValue);
    Task<List<GetItemsTotalValueDto>> GetItemsTotalValues(bool isActive);
    Task<List<ItemsWithGenresDto>> GetItemsWithGenres();
    Task<List<CategoryDto>> ListCategoriesAndColors();
    Task<List<Item>> ListInventory();
}
```

```
public interface IInventorDatabaseRepoWriteOnly
{
    Task<int> InsertOrUpdateItem(Item item);
    Task InsertOrUpdateItems(List<Item> items);
    Task DeleteItem(int id);
    Task DeleteItems(List<int> itemIds);
}

public interface IInventoryDatabaseRepo : IInventoryDatabaseRepoReadOnly,
IInventorDatabaseRepoWriteOnly
{
}
```

Build the project. There will be a number of errors, as should be expected (review Figure 14-1).

Figure 14-1. *Reworking the interface causes a number of expected build errors*

We can use the errors to work out the problems going forward as a road map. We already know that we changed the interface that is implemented by two classes. The next step is to rework the two implementations. **Do not** select "*implement interface,*" or you'll get a number of duplicated methods. Instead, let's fix the methods and the code that goes with them.

In the InventoryDatabaseRepo, begin by fixing the method signatures to match the methods in the interface. This is done by once again wrapping the return types with Task<T> or setting the return type to Task when the method is void. Additionally, each method needs to be declared as an async method. For example, the public List<GetItemsForListingDto> GetItemsForListingFromProcedure(...) method becomes public async Task<List<GetItemsForListingDto>> GetItemsForListingFromProcedure(...).

Make sure to add the using statement for System.Threading.Tasks.

After fixing all the signatures, a number of errors will be created. We'll now walk through each method and fix the internal code.

Make note that some methods don't have an error, but only have a green squiggly line under the method name. Hovering on the name of the method reveals the issue (see Figure 14-2).

Figure 14-2. *Methods that are asynchronous expect to await within the method*

While you can have an async method that does not have an await operation in it and still have valid execution, the warning here is to remind you that you made an asynchronous method without an await operation. We want to await the database call. To do this, we need to make a couple of changes.

Begin by adding the keyword await between return and _context. ItemsForListing.... This change will highlight the operation with a red-squiggly underline. The error created is that the List<GetItemsForListingDto> does not contain a definition for *awaiter*. To fix this, we need to change .ToList() to .ToListAsync():

```
public async Task<List<GetItemsForListingDto>> GetItemsForListingFromProced
ure(DateTime dateDateValue, DateTime maxDateValue)
{
    var minDateParam = new SqlParameter("minDate", dateDateValue);
    var maxDateParam = new SqlParameter("maxDate", maxDateValue);

    return await _context.ItemsForListing
                    .FromSqlRaw("EXECUTE dbo.GetItemsForListing
                     @minDate, @maxDate", minDateParam, maxDateParam)
                    .ToListAsync();
}
```

Next, let's fix the GetItemsForListingLinq method. This fix will be more involved. Because of the way this query is built and because of the database encryption we have implemented, we have to get the list back sooner than would be ideal. Making this method asynchronous will force us to rework the ordering a bit as well.

Begin by creating a new variable called result and set it to await the call to get the items with the included category and select into the GetItemsForListingWithDateDto using the where limitations, but then direct the results ToListAsync() at this point.

```
var result = await _context.Items.Include(x => x.Category)
            .Select(x => new GetItemsForListingWithDateDto
                {
                    CreatedDate = x.CreatedDate,
                    CategoryName = x.Category.Name,
                    Description = x.Description,
                    IsActive = x.IsActive,
                    IsDeleted = x.IsDeleted,
                    Name = x.Name,
                    Notes = x.Notes
                })
            .Where(x => x.CreatedDate >= minDateValue && x.CreatedDate
            <= maxDateValue)
            .ToListAsync();
```

Then use the return statement to return that list with ordering as expected:

```
return result.OrderBy(y => y.CategoryName).ThenBy(z => z.Name).ToList();
```

This change will allow us to get the list in an asynchronous manner and then we have to do the ordering. The IOrderedEnumerable will not work asynchronously as the code is written, so, while not ideal, at least we got the limited results with the query. If we wanted, we could get the query as an AsyncEnumerable, which would allow for async enumeration of the results, but here we'll just fetch the results with the await operation and then order the resulting list in memory.

For clarity, the completed GetItemsForListingLinq method is illustrated in Figure 14-3.

```
public async Task<List<GetItemsForListingWithDateDto>> GetItemsForListingLinq(DateTime minDateValue, DateTime maxDateValue)
{
    var result = await _context.Items.Include(x => x.Category)
                    .Select(x => new GetItemsForListingWithDateDto
                    {
                        CreatedDate = x.CreatedDate,
                        CategoryName = x.Category.Name,
                        Description = x.Description,
                        IsActive = x.IsActive,
                        IsDeleted = x.IsDeleted,
                        Name = x.Name,
                        Notes = x.Notes
                    })
                    .Where(x => x.CreatedDate >= minDateValue && x.CreatedDate <= maxDateValue)
                    .ToListAsync();

    return result.OrderBy(y => y.CategoryName).ThenBy(z => z.Name).ToList();
}
```

Figure 14-3. *The reworked GetItemsForListingLinq method is now asynchronous*

Now let's move on to the GetItemsTotalValues method. This method is another simple fix where we just need to make the method async Task<T>, then add the await operator to the database call, and complete by changing the ToList call to ToListAsync. Since we're here, also fix the parameter declaration to use the passed in parameter instead of the hard-coded value of 1. The reworked method should be as follows:

```
public async Task<List<GetItemsTotalValueDto>> GetItemsTotalValues
(bool isActive)
{
    var isActiveParm = new SqlParameter("IsActive", isActive);

    return await _context.GetItemsTotalValues
                    .FromSqlRaw("SELECT * from [dbo].[GetItemsTotalValue]
                    (@IsActive)", isActiveParm)
                    .ToListAsync();
```

}Continuing down the code, the ListCategoriesAndColors method is another simple fix - making the method async Task<T> and then adding the await operator and changing ToList to ToListAsync. The method GetItemsWithGenres is similar. The two completed methods should look as follows:

```
public async Task<List<CategoryDto>> ListCategoriesAndColors()
{
    return await _context.Categories
                    .Include(x => x.CategoryColor)
```

```
.ProjectTo<CategoryDto>(_mapper.ConfigurationProvider).ToListAsync();
}

public async Task<List<ItemsWithGenresDto>> GetItemsWithGenres()
{
    return await _context.ItemsWithGenres.ToListAsync();
}
```

The ListInventory() method is next, and it will require a few changes. For this method, we'll again start by getting results with await and ToListAsync and then change to include the OrderBy. To see the error we would get without proper refactoring, just add await and change the return of ToList to ToListAsync. We'll see the error is regarding the fact that the IOrderedEnumerable does not allow a ToListAsync call (review Figure 14-4).

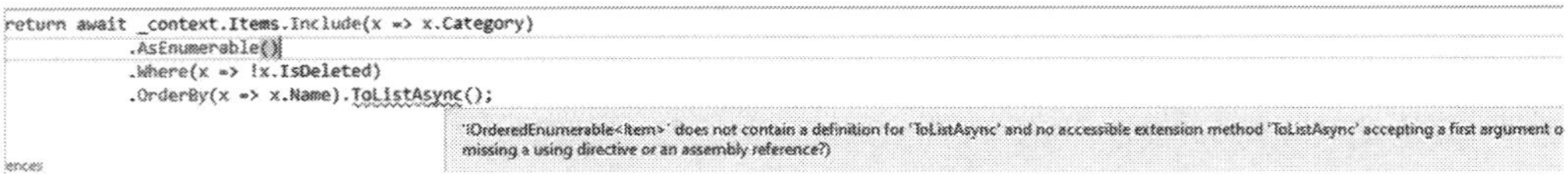

```
return await _context.Items.Include(x => x.Category)
        .AsEnumerable()
        .Where(x => !x.IsDeleted)
        .OrderBy(x => x.Name).ToListAsync();
```

'IOrderedEnumerable<Item>' does not contain a definition for 'ToListAsync' and no accessible extension method 'ToListAsync' accepting a first argument o
missing a using directive or an assembly reference?)

Figure 14-4. *The IOrderedEnumerable does not allow a ToListAsync() operation*

Refactor the code for the ListInventory method as follows:

```
public async Task<List<Item>> ListInventory()
{
    var result = await _context.Items.Include(x => x.Category)
                .Where(x => !x.IsDeleted).ToListAsync();
    return result.AsEnumerable().OrderBy(x => x.Name).ToList();
}
```

In the InsertOrUpdateItem method, add await statements before each call to Update or Create an item:

```
public async Task<int> InsertOrUpdateItem(Item item)
{
    if (item.Id > 0)
    {
```

```
    return await UpdateItem(item);
  }
  return await CreateItem(item);
}
```

In the `InsertOrUpdateItems` method, change the method to async Task and then simply add an await statement before the call to `InsertOrUpdateItems`:

```
var success = await InsertOrUpdateItem(item) > 0;
```

For the `CreateItem` method, we get to see our first save. Here, we'll add await operations to the first two lines. Additionally, we'll change the Add method to AddAsync and the SaveChanges method to SaveChangesAsync.

```
private async Task<int> CreateItem(Item item)
{
    await _context.Items.AddAsync(item);
    await _context.SaveChangesAsync();
    var newItem = _context.Items.ToList()
                    .FirstOrDefault(x => x.Name.ToLower()
                    .Equals(item.Name.ToLower()));

    if (newItem == null) throw new Exception("Could not Create the item as
    expected");

    return newItem.Id;
}
```

For the get of the new item, we need to just make the call to get the items, but this time limit to single or default async:

```
private async Task<int> CreateItem(Item item)
{
    await _context.Items.AddAsync(item);
    await _context.SaveChangesAsync();
    var newItem = await _context.Items.SingleOrDefaultAsync(x => x.Name.ToLower()
                    .Equals(item.Name.ToLower()));

    if (newItem == null) throw new Exception("Could not Create the item as
    expected");
```

587

```
    return newItem.Id;
}
```

For the UpdateItem method, we need to make a couple of similar changes. Add await to the call to get Items, and also change the FirstOrDefault call to SingleOrDefaultAsync.

Using FirstOrDefaultAsync would also work here, but we should never get more than one result on a unique Id, so it would be more accurate to use SingleO rDefault/SingleOrDefaultAsync for this call.

```
var dbItem = await _context.Items.SingleOrDefaultAsync(x => x.Id == item.Id);
```

Additionally, add the await operator and change SaveChanges to SaveChangesAsync right before returning the item id:

```
await _context.SaveChangesAsync();
```

When complete, the UpdateItem should look as follows:

```
private async Task<int> UpdateItem(Item item)
{
    var dbItem = await _context.Items.SingleOrDefaultAsync(x => x.Id == item.Id);
    dbItem.CategoryId = item.CategoryId;
    dbItem.CurrentOrFinalPrice = item.CurrentOrFinalPrice;
    dbItem.Description = item.Description;
    dbItem.IsActive = item.IsActive;
    dbItem.IsDeleted = item.IsDeleted;
    dbItem.IsOnSale = item.IsOnSale;
    dbItem.Name = item.Name;
    dbItem.Notes = item.Notes;
    dbItem.PurchasedDate = item.PurchasedDate;
    dbItem.PurchasePrice = item.PurchasePrice;
    dbItem.Quantity = item.Quantity;
    dbItem.SoldDate = item.SoldDate;
    await _context.SaveChangesAsync();
    return item.Id;
}
```

For the DeleteItem method, add the await and change the call to
SingleOrDefaultAsync for the query to get the matching item. Also add the await and
change the SaveChanges call to SaveChangesAsync.

```
public async Task DeleteItem(int id)
{
    var item = await _context.Items.SingleOrDefaultAsync(x => x.Id == id);
    if (item == null) return;
    item.IsDeleted = true;
    await _context.SaveChangesAsync();
}
```

Finally, change the DeleteItems method to await the call to DeleteItem method:

```
try
{
    foreach (var itemId in itemIds)
    {
        await DeleteItem(itemId);
    }

    scope.Complete();
}
```

To complete this portion of the activity, we need to also refactor the Dapper
implementation.

To do this, once again change all the method signatures on each method to
match the asynchronous changes as defined in the interface. Most of these methods
are unimplemented, so we can just leave them. They will have a green squiggly line
indicating that they do not implement an await operator, but that will not break the
compiler or the program execution, even if the method had other synchronous code in it.

For clarity, I've collapsed all of the methods and am including a screenshot (see
Figure 14-5) so that you can see what the method signatures should look like in the
InventoryDatabaseDapperRepo class.

```
public class InventoryDatabaseDapperRepo : IInventoryDatabaseRepoReadOnly
{
    private readonly IDbConnection _connection;
    private readonly IMapper _mapper;

    3 references | ⊘ 4/4 passing
    public InventoryDatabaseDapperRepo(IDbConnection connection, IMapper mapper)[...]

    3 references
    public async Task<List<GetItemsForListingDto>> GetItemsForListingFromProcedure(DateTime da

    3 references
    public async Task<List<GetItemsForListingWithDateDto>> GetItemsForListingLing(DateTime min

    3 references
    public async Task<List<GetItemsTotalValueDto>> GetItemsTotalValues(bool isActive)[...]

    3 references
    public async Task<List<ItemsWithGenresDto>> GetItemsWithGenres()[...]

    6 references | ⊘ 6/6 passing
    public async Task<List<CategoryDto>> ListCategoriesAndColors()[...]

    7 references | ⊘ 2/2 passing
    public async Task<List<Item>> ListInventory()[...]
}
```

Figure 14-5. *The InventoryDatabaseDapperRepo class with methods changed to implement asynchronous operations. For brevity, method bodies are not shown in the image but do exist in the code*

To complete the code changes in the InventoryDatabaseDapperRepo, we need to fix the two methods that are implemented. Beginning with ListCategoriesAndColors, change the code for the first var result = _connection.Query... to var result = await _connection.QueryAsync<dynamic>(sql);.

Then change the code in the foreach method call to get the first match with an asynchronous call:

category.CategoryColor = await _connection.QueryFirstAsync<CategoryColor> ("SELECT * FROM CategoryColors where ID = "+ category.CategoryColorId);

After completing these changes, the entire method should look like the following code:

```
public async Task<List<CategoryDto>> ListCategoriesAndColors()
{
    var sql = "SELECT c.Id, c.Name, cc.Id as CategoryColorId, cc.ColorValue " +
                "FROM Categories c " + "INNER JOIN CategoryColors cc " +
                "ON c.CategoryColorId = cc.Id";
    var result = await _connection.QueryAsync<dynamic>(sql);
    Slapper.AutoMapper.Configuration.AddIdentifiers(typeof(Category),
    new List<string> { "Id" });
    Slapper.AutoMapper.Configuration.AddIdentifiers(typeof(CategoryColor),
    new List<string> { "CategoryColorId" });

    /*
     map
    */
    var output = (Slapper.AutoMapper.MapDynamic<Category>(result) as
    IEnumerable<Category>).ToList();
    foreach (var category in output)
    {
        category.CategoryColor = await _connection
                    .QueryFirstAsync<CategoryColor>("SELECT * FROM
                    CategoryColors where ID = "
                                        + category.CategoryColorId);
    }

    return _mapper.Map<List<CategoryDto>>(output);
}
```

Complete similar changes to the two _connection.Query calls in the ListInventory method. The code should look as follows when you complete the refactor:

```
public async Task<List<Item>> ListInventory()
{
    var sql = $"SELECT i.Id, i.Name, i.Description, i.Notes, i.IsDeleted,
    i.CategoryId " + ", c.Name as CategoryName" +
                " FROM Items i INNER JOIN Categories c on i.CategoryId = c.Id" +
                " WHERE i.IsDeleted = @isDeleted";
```

```
var result = await _connection.QueryAsync<dynamic>(sql, new { isDeleted = 0 });
Slapper.AutoMapper.Configuration.AddIdentifiers(typeof(Item), new
List<string> { "Id" });
Slapper.AutoMapper.Configuration.AddIdentifiers(typeof(Category), new
List<string> { "CategoryId" });

var output = (Slapper.AutoMapper.MapDynamic<Item>(result) as
IEnumerable<Item>).OrderBy(x => x.Name).ToList();

//have to hydrate the relationship:
foreach (var item in output)
{
    item.Category = await _connection
                .QueryFirstAsync<Category>("SELECT * FROM Categories
                where ID = "+ item.CategoryId);
}
    return output;
}
```

This will complete our refactor operations on the InventoryDatabaseLayer project. Build the project to get the next set of errors (see Figure 14-6).

Figure 14-6. *Errors in the BusinessLayer and in the integration tests now exist*

Step 3: Update the integration tests to use asynchronous database operations

Now that our database layer is fully updated, we need to begin the next layer of fixes by first fixing the integration tests and making sure they still work as expected.

Open the InventoryManagerIntegrationTests class file in the IntegrationManagerTests project.

Begin by changing the four methods that have Fact or Theory attributes to be asynchronous. This is easily accomplished by simply changing the keyword void to be async Task. Yes, it is really that easy (see Figure 14-7 for reference).

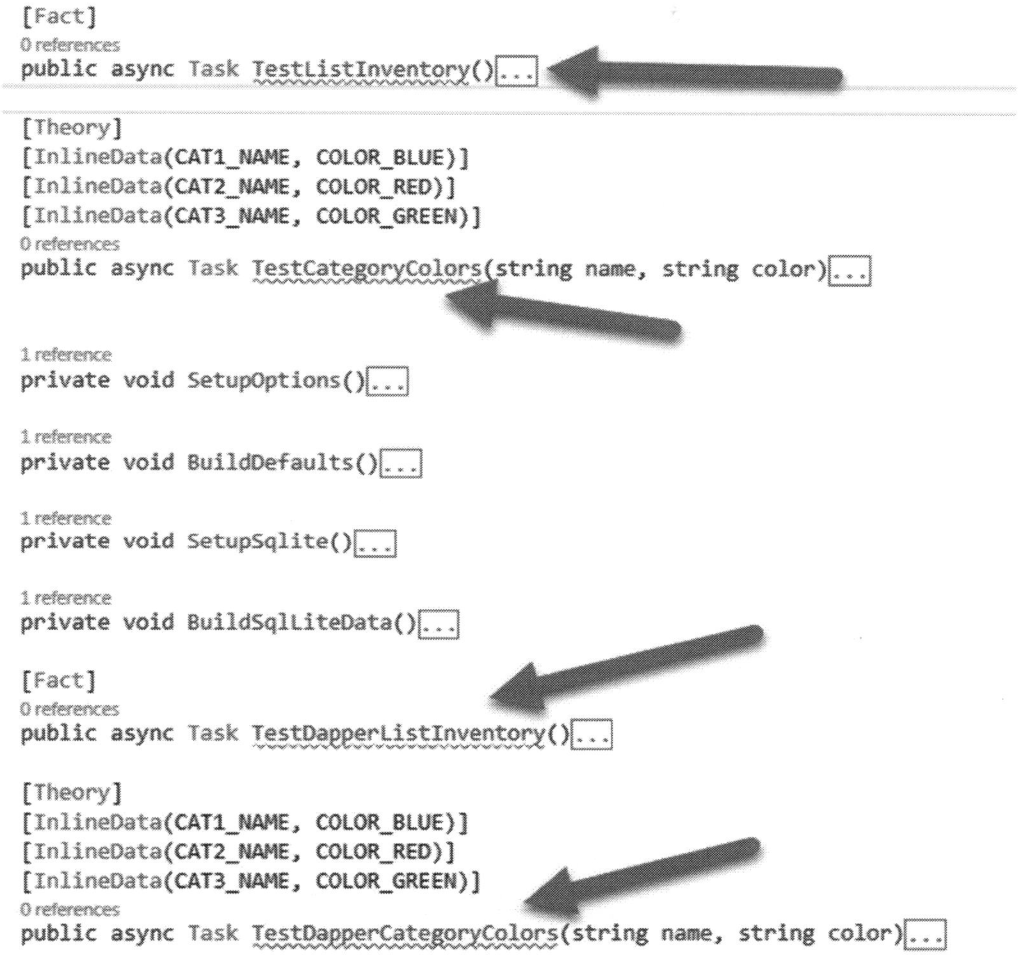

```
[Fact]
0 references
public async Task TestListInventory()...  ⬅
```

```
[Theory]
[InlineData(CAT1_NAME, COLOR_BLUE)]
[InlineData(CAT2_NAME, COLOR_RED)]
[InlineData(CAT3_NAME, COLOR_GREEN)]
0 references
public async Task TestCategoryColors(string name, string color)...
```

```
1 reference
private void SetupOptions()...
```

```
1 reference
private void BuildDefaults()...
```

```
1 reference
private void SetupSqlite()...
```

```
1 reference
private void BuildSqlLiteData()...
```

```
[Fact]
0 references
public async Task TestDapperListInventory()...
```

```
[Theory]
[InlineData(CAT1_NAME, COLOR_BLUE)]
[InlineData(CAT2_NAME, COLOR_RED)]
[InlineData(CAT3_NAME, COLOR_GREEN)]
0 references
public async Task TestDapperCategoryColors(string name, string color)...
```

Figure 14-7. *The four test methods are changed to become asynchronous tests*

Make sure to add the using statement for System.Threading.Tasks so that the code will compile.

In the each of the four methods identified in Figure 14-7, simply find any calls to the _dbRepo objects and add the await operator to allow for the methods to operate asynchronously. For example, in TestListInventory, change var items = _dbRepo. ListInventory(); to var items = await _dbRepo.ListInventory();

There should be four calls to `await` added to the test project when this is completed:
In TestListInventory

```
var items = await _dbRepo.ListInventory();
```

In TestCategoryColors

```
var catcolors = await _dbRepo.ListCategoriesAndColors();
```

In TestDapperListInventory()

```
var result = await repo.ListInventory();
```

In TestDapperCategoryColors

```
var catcolors = await repo.ListCategoriesAndColors();
```

Rebuild the project. There are still errors for the `InventoryBusinessLayer` that need to be fixed. However, we can run the integration tests. Run them now to validate that our asynchronous code is working as expected (see Figure 14-8 for sample test output).

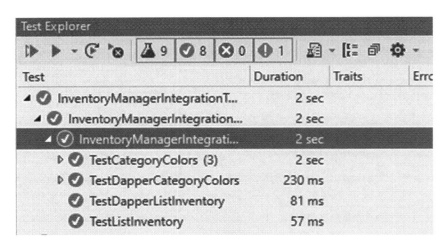

Figure 14-8. *The integration tests should all be passing at this point*

Step 4: Update the business layer

The next step in refactoring our code is to refactor the business layer. This will be a fairly easy and quick operation, now that the deeper database layer is already refactored and validated to be working via the integration tests.

As with the interface for the database layer, refactor all method signatures in the IItemsService file to be configured for asynchronous operations. Don't forget to also add the using statement for System.Threading.Tasks. When completed, the code for the interfaces in the IItemsService.cs file should be as follows:

```
public interface IItemsServiceReadOnly
{
    Task<List<GetItemsForListingWithDateDto>>
    GetItemsForListingLinq(DateTime minDateValue, DateTime maxDateValue);
    Task<List<GetItemsForListingDto>> GetItemsForListingFromProcedure(DateT
    ime minDateValue, DateTime maxDateValue);
    Task<AllItemsPipeDelimitedStringDto> GetItemsPipeDelimitedString(bool
    isActive);
    Task<List<GetItemsTotalValueDto>> GetItemsTotalValues(bool isActive);
    Task<List<ItemsWithGenresDto>> GetItemsWithGenres();
    Task<List<CategoryDto>> ListCategoriesAndColors();
    Task<List<ItemDto>> ListInventory();
}

public interface IItemsServiceWriteOnly
{
    Task<int> InsertOrUpdateItem(CreateOrUpdateItemDto item);
    Task InsertOrUpdateItems(List<CreateOrUpdateItemDto> item);
    Task DeleteItem(int id);
    Task DeleteItems(List<int> itemIds);
}

public interface IItemsService : IItemsServiceReadOnly,
IItemsServiceWriteOnly
{
}
```

In the ItemsService implementation, make sure to modify all method signatures to be *asynchronous*, and then simply add the await keyword before any call to the repo object. As always, don't forget to add the necessary using statements into the file. For example, the GetItemsForListingFromProcedure looks as follows after being refactored:

```
public async Task<List<GetItemsForListingDto>> GetItemsForListingFromProced
ure(DateTime minDateValue, DateTime maxDateValue)
        {
            return await _dbRepo.GetItemsForListingFromProcedure(minDateValue,
            maxDateValue);
        }
```

The only other change that needs to be made that will be different from all the other methods is any call to the ListInventory method and a major change in the ListInventory method. In that method, since we're mapping, first get the result, and then map as follows:

```
public async Task<List<ItemDto>> ListInventory()
{
    var result = await _dbRepo.ListInventory();
    return _mapper.Map<List<ItemDto>>(result);
}
```

Make sure to also update any calls in other methods to the ListInventory method to include an await operator, i.e., var items = await ListInventory(); such as in the GetItemsPipeDelimitedString method.

Each of the following code snippets will highlight the changes to the ItemsService class as it should be at completion:

```
//GetItemsForListingFromProcedure
public async Task<List<GetItemsForListingDto>> GetItemsForListingFromProced
ure(DateTime minDateValue, DateTime maxDateValue)
{
    return await _dbRepo.GetItemsForListingFromProcedure(minDateValue,
    maxDateValue);
}
```

```
//GetItemsForListingLinq:
public async Task<List<GetItemsForListingWithDateDto>>
GetItemsForListingLinq(DateTime minDateValue, DateTime maxDateValue)
{
    return await _dbRepo.GetItemsForListingLinq(minDateValue, maxDateValue);
}
```

GetItemsPipeDelimitedString:

```
public async Task<AllItemsPipeDelimitedStringDto> GetItemsPipeDelimited
String(bool isActive)
{
    var items = await ListInventory();
    var sb = new StringBuilder();

    foreach (var item in items)
    {
        if (sb.Length > 0)
        {
            sb.Append("|");
        }
        sb.Append(item.Name);
    }

    var output = new AllItemsPipeDelimitedStringDto();
    output.AllItems = sb.ToString();
    return output;
}
//GetItemsPipeDelimitedString
public async Task<AllItemsPipeDelimitedStringDto> GetItemsPipeDelimited
String(bool isActive)
{
    var items = await ListInventory();
    var sb = new StringBuilder();

    foreach (var item in items)
    {
        if (sb.Length > 0)
        {
```

```
            sb.Append("|");
        }
        sb.Append(item.Name);
    }

    var output = new AllItemsPipeDelimitedStringDto();
    output.AllItems = sb.ToString();
    return output;
}
//GetItemsTotalValues:
public async Task<List<GetItemsTotalValueDto>> GetItemsTotalValues(bool isActive)
{
    return await _dbRepo.GetItemsTotalValues(isActive);
}
//GetItemsWithGenres:
public async Task<List<ItemsWithGenresDto>> GetItemsWithGenres()
{
    return await _dbRepo.GetItemsWithGenres();
}

//ListCategoriesAndColors
public async Task<List<CategoryDto>> ListCategoriesAndColors()
{
    return await _dbRepo.ListCategoriesAndColors();
}
//ListInventory
public async Task<List<ItemDto>> ListInventory()
{
    var result = await _dbRepo.ListInventory();
    return _mapper.Map<List<ItemDto>>(result);
}

//InsertOrUpdateItem
public async Task<int> InsertOrUpdateItem(CreateOrUpdateItemDto item)
{
    if (item.CategoryId <= 0)
    {
```

```
        throw new ArgumentException("Please set the category id before
        insert or update");
    }
    return await _dbRepo.InsertOrUpdateItem(_mapper.Map<Item>(item));
}

//InsertOrUpdateItems
public async Task InsertOrUpdateItems(List<CreateOrUpdateItemDto> items)
{
    await _dbRepo.InsertOrUpdateItems(_mapper.Map<List<Item>>(items));
}

//DeleteItem and DeleteItems:
public async Task DeleteItem(int id)
{
    if (id <= 0) throw new ArgumentException("Please set a valid item id
    before deleting");
    await _dbRepo.DeleteItem(id);
}

public async Task DeleteItems(List<int> itemIds)
{
    try
    {
        await _dbRepo.DeleteItems(itemIds);
    }
    catch (Exception ex)
    {
        Console.WriteLine($"The transaction has failed: {ex.Message}");
    }
}
```

Now that our ItemsService is updated, we also need to update the ItemsServiceReadOnly
to use asynchronous operations.

Once again, update all of the method signatures to be asynchronous in nature and add the using statement for System.Threading.Tasks. As most of these methods are not implemented, we only need to update the ones that are; in this case, ListCategories AndColors and ListInventory. As with the previous operations, we'll need to return the ListInventory into a variable and then map it, but these two implementations are very easy. The code for the two methods that need to be altered is as follows:

```
public async Task<List<CategoryDto>> ListCategoriesAndColors()
{
    return await _dbRepo.ListCategoriesAndColors();
}

public async Task<List<ItemDto>> ListInventory()
{
    var items = await _dbRepo.ListInventory();
    return _mapper.Map<List<ItemDto>>(items);
}
```

The remaining methods aren't implemented, so just make sure they have the correct signatures as shown in Figure 14-9.

```
3 references
public async Task<List<GetItemsForListingDto>> GetItemsForListingFromProcedure(DateTime minDateValue, DateTime maxDateValue)
{
    throw new NotImplementedException();
}

3 references
public async Task<List<GetItemsForListingWithDateDto>> GetItemsForListingLinq(DateTime minDateValue, DateTime maxDateValue)
{
    throw new NotImplementedException();
}

3 references
public async Task<AllItemsPipeDelimitedStringDto> GetItemsPipeDelimitedString(bool isActive)
{
    throw new NotImplementedException();
}

3 references
public async Task<List<GetItemsTotalValueDto>> GetItemsTotalValues(bool isActive)
{
    throw new NotImplementedException();
}

3 references
public async Task<List<ItemsWithGenresDto>> GetItemsWithGenres()
{
    throw new NotImplementedException();
}
```

Figure 14-9. *The remaining methods just need the updated signatures for asynchronous operations*

This completes our refactoring of the business layer. Rebuild the project to see the next set of errors, which will be in the InventoryManagerUnitTests and the overall program itself.

Step 5: Update the unit tests

Now that the business layer is in place, we need to update the unit tests. Open the InventoryManagerUnitTests file in the InventoryManagerUnitTests project.

There won't be a lot to change in this project since we just have the one test. For the setup however, we need to do something a bit different. Since we are going to be mocking an asynchronous return, we need to get the _allItems object as the result of a Task. To do this, we can simply use the call Task.FromResult(_allItems).

In the SetupDbRepoMock, change the _mockInventoryDatabaseRepo.Setup(...) call to be:

```
_mockInventoryDatabaseRepo.Setup(x => x.ListInventory())
                    .Returns(Task.FromResult(_allItems));
```

Next, change the TestGetItems method to be async Task, and await the _serviceLayer.ListInventory call:

```
[TestMethod]
public async Task TestGetItems()
{
    //var result = _mockServiceLayer.Object.ListInventory();
    var result = await _serviceLayer.ListInventory();
    Assert.IsNotNull(result);
    Assert.IsTrue(result.Count > 0);
    result.ShouldNotBeNull();
    result.Count.ShouldBeGreaterThan(0);
    result.Count.ShouldBe(3);
    result.First().Name.ShouldBe(ITEM1_NAME);
    result.First().CategoryId.ShouldBe(1);
}
```

This completes our refactor for the unit tests. Build the project and see the next set of errors which should all relate to the program itself. Run the unit tests to make sure that it passes as expected. Figure 14-10 shows the output of the unit tests running successfully.

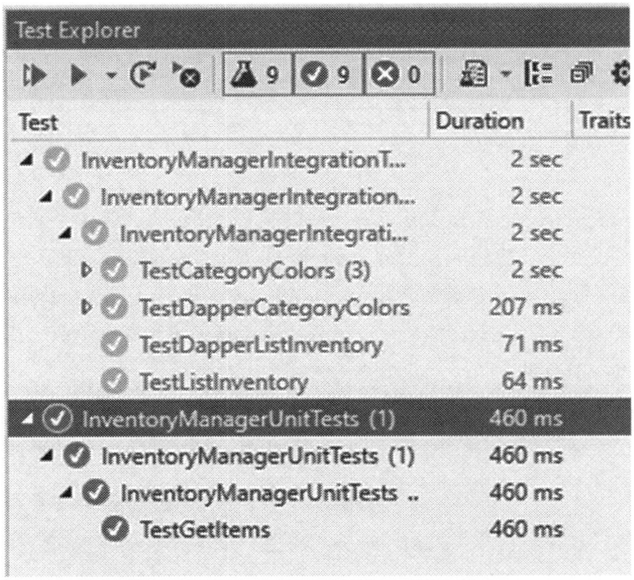

Figure 14-10. *The Unit tests are now passing as expected*

All that remains is to fix the main program.

Step 6: Update the Program

To complete the system and allow it to work, we need to update the Program. In this part of the activity, we have all the code turned on and just need to get the calls to work with the new asynchronous code.

One thing that will happen is that there are a number of calls to ListInventory. For this reason, the first thing we should do is create a helper method to get the Inventory List. This will also give us a chance to see how to run an asynchronous piece of code from within a synchronous context.

Add the following code to the Program class after the Main method and before the CreateMultipleItems method:

```
private static List<ItemDto> GetInventoryList(IItemsService svc)
{
    return Task.Run(() => svc.ListInventory()).Result;
}
```

Make sure to also add the using statement for.

In this code, we see the call to Task.Run(() => ...).Result; That line of code allows us to tell the system to run a command and then use a lambda to inject the asynchronous code to run. Since our method is not asynchronous, we cannot await the result. Therefore, we add the call to .Result at the end of the statement, which tells the system to wait until a result is returned.

Now that we have our common code for getting inventory, let's fix the rest of the code.

To begin, replace any calls in the code to svc.ListInventory with the new method call to GetInventoryList(svc). There should be six places to replace and the one result that we just created with our new method. For example, the line var inventory = svc. ListInventory(); becomes var inventory = GetInventoryList(svc);.

Using the find and replace tool of ctrl + H, enter the svc.ListInventory() search term and replace all but the new method with GetInventoryList(svc).

After completion, run another find operation to validate you have six method calls to GetInventoryList(svc) as illustrated in Figure 14-11.

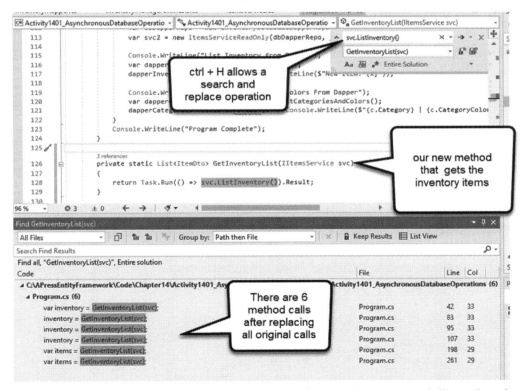

Figure 14-11. *A simple find can help validate that we have successfully replaced all six calls to get the items*

Rebuild the solution to see further errors. Each issue revolves around the fact that the method went from being synchronous to asynchronous. To fix the rest of the calls, look for a call to the business layer and then initiate the call using the Task.Run syntax learned previously.

For example:

```
var items = svc.GetItemsForListingLinq(minDate, maxDate);
```

becomes

```
var items = Task.Run(() => svc.GetItemsForListingLinq(minDate, maxDate)).
Result;
```

Make sure to just leave the Dapper service call to get inventory as is and wrap with a Task.Run operation, as the interface type is not interchangeable as written:

```
var dapperInventory = Task.Run(() => svc2.ListInventory()).Result;
```

When this is completed, the code for the Main method with all code uncommented should be as follows (note, for a complete version of the code, see the Activity1401_ AsynchronousDatabaseOperations_Final.zip files):

```
static void Main(string[] args)
{
    BuildOptions();
    BuildMapper();

    var minDate = new DateTime(2020, 1, 1);
    var maxDate = new DateTime(2021, 1, 1);

    using (var db = new InventoryDbContext(_optionsBuilder.Options))
    {
        //decouple the database from the service layer using the
        //dbRepo interface
        var dbRepo = new InventoryDatabaseRepo(db, _mapper);
        var svc = new ItemsService(dbRepo, _mapper);
        Console.WriteLine("List Inventory");
        var inventory = GetInventoryList(svc);
        inventory.ForEach(x => Console.WriteLine($"New Item: {x}"));
```

```
Console.WriteLine("List inventory with Linq");
var items = Task.Run(() => svc.GetItemsForListingLinq(minDate,
maxDate)).Result;
items.ForEach(x => Console.WriteLine($"ITEM| {x.CategoryName}|
{x.Name} - {x.Description}"));

Console.WriteLine("List Inventory from procedure");
var procItems = Task.Run(() => svc.GetItemsForListingFromProcedure(
minDate, maxDate)).Result;
procItems.ForEach(x => Console.WriteLine($"ITEM| {x.Name} -
{x.Description}"));

Console.WriteLine("Item Names Pipe Delimited String");
var pipedItems = Task.Run(() => svc.GetItemsPipeDelimitedString
(true)).Result;
Console.WriteLine(pipedItems.AllItems);

Console.WriteLine("Get Items Total Values");
var totalValues = Task.Run(() => svc.GetItemsTotalValues(true)).
Result;
totalValues.ForEach(item => Console.WriteLine($"New Item] {item.
Id,-10}" + $"|{item.Name,-50}" + $"|{item.Quantity,-4}" + $"|{item.
TotalValue,-5}"));

Console.WriteLine("Get Items With Genres");
var itemsWithGenres = Task.Run(() => svc.GetItemsWithGenres()).
Result;
itemsWithGenres.ForEach(item => Console.WriteLine($"New Item]
{item.Id,-10}" + $"|{item.Name,-50}" + $"|{item.Genre?.ToString().
PadLeft(4)}"));

Console.WriteLine("List Categories And Colors");
var categoriesAndColors = Task.Run(() => svc.ListCategoriesAndColors()).
Result;
categoriesAndColors.ForEach(c => Console.WriteLine($"{c.Category} |
{c.CategoryColor.Color}"));
```

```
        _categories = categoriesAndColors;
        Console.WriteLine("Would you like to create items?");
        var createItems = Console.ReadLine().StartsWith("y", StringComparison.
        OrdinalIgnoreCase);
        if (createItems)
        {
            Console.WriteLine("Adding new Item(s)");
            CreateMultipleItems(svc);
            Console.WriteLine("Items added");

            inventory = GetInventoryList(svc);
            inventory.ForEach(x => Console.WriteLine($"Item: {x}"));
        }

        Console.WriteLine("Would you like to update items?");
        var updateItems = Console.ReadLine().StartsWith("y", StringComparison.
        OrdinalIgnoreCase);
        if (updateItems)
        {
            Console.WriteLine("Updating Item(s)");
            UpdateMultipleItems(svc);
            Console.WriteLine("Items updated");

            inventory = GetInventoryList(svc);
            inventory.ForEach(x => Console.WriteLine($"Item: {x}"));
        }

        Console.WriteLine("Would you like to delete items?");
        var deleteItems = Console.ReadLine().StartsWith("y", StringComparison.
        OrdinalIgnoreCase);
        if (deleteItems)
        {
            Console.WriteLine("Deleting Item(s)");
            DeleteMultipleItems(svc);
            Console.WriteLine("Items Deleted");
```

```
        inventory = GetInventoryList(svc);
        inventory.ForEach(x => Console.WriteLine($"Item: {x}"));
    }

    //Read only dapper
    var dbDapperRepo = new InventoryDatabaseDapperRepo(db.Database.
    GetDbConnection(), _mapper);
    var svc2 = new ItemsServiceReadOnly(dbDapperRepo, _mapper);

    Console.WriteLine("List Inventory from Dapper");
    var dapperInventory = Task.Run(() => svc2.ListInventory()).Result;
    dapperInventory.ForEach(x => Console.WriteLine($"New Item: {x}"));

    Console.WriteLine("List Categories And Colors From Dapper");
    var dapperCategoriesAndColors = Task.Run(() => svc2.
    ListCategoriesAndColors()).Result;
    dapperCategoriesAndColors.ForEach(c => Console.WriteLine($"{c.
    Category} | {c.CategoryColor.Color}"));
    }
    Console.WriteLine("Program Complete");
}
```

We also need to update the create and update methods. In each method, look for any calls to the service layer (svc.), and replace them with a Task.Run operation. After rework, the CreateMultipleItems method looks like what follows:

```
private static void CreateMultipleItems(IItemsService svc)
{
    Console.WriteLine("Would you like to create items as a batch?");
    bool batchCreate = Console.ReadLine().StartsWith("y", StringComparison.
    OrdinalIgnoreCase);
    var allItems = new List<CreateOrUpdateItemDto>();

    bool createAnother = true;
    while (createAnother == true)
    {
        var newItem = new CreateOrUpdateItemDto();
        Console.WriteLine("Creating a new item.");
```

```
Console.WriteLine("Please enter the name");
newItem.Name = Console.ReadLine();
Console.WriteLine("Please enter the description");
newItem.Description = Console.ReadLine();
Console.WriteLine("Please enter the notes");
newItem.Notes = Console.ReadLine();
Console.WriteLine("Please enter the Category [B]ooks, [M]ovies,
[G]ames");
newItem.CategoryId = GetCategoryId(Console.ReadLine().Substring
(0, 1).ToUpper());

if (!batchCreate)
{
    Task.Run(() => svc.InsertOrUpdateItem(newItem));
}
else
{
    allItems.Add(newItem);
}

Console.WriteLine("Would you like to create another item?");
createAnother = Console.ReadLine().StartsWith("y", StringComparison.
OrdinalIgnoreCase);

if (batchCreate && !createAnother)
{
    Task.Run(() => svc.InsertOrUpdateItems(allItems));
}
    }
}
```

In the update multiple items method, set the svc call for two lines of code to use
the Task.Run(...) operation. First, find and set svc.InsertOrUpdateItem(updItem) to
Task.Run(() => svc.InsertOrUpdateItem(updItem));. Then find and set the
svc.InsertOrUpdateItems(allItems) method to Task.Run(() => svc.InsertOr
UpdateItems(allItems));.

Note that a void method does not need to await the result. For clarity and brevity, review Figure 14-12 to see these two lines of code that need to be altered in the UpdateMultipleItems method.

```
225          Console.WriteLine("Enter the category - [B]ooks, [M]ovies, [G]ames, or [N]o Change");
226          var userChoice = Console.ReadLine().Substring(0, 1).ToUpper();
227          updItem.CategoryId = userChoice.Equals("N", StringComparison.OrdinalIgnoreCase) ? itemMatch.CategoryId
228                                       : GetCategoryId(userChoice);
229
230          if (!batchUpdate)
231          {
232              Task.Run(() => svc.InsertOrUpdateItem(updItem));
233          }
234          else
235          {
236              allItems.Add(updItem);
237          }
238      }
239  }
240
241  Console.WriteLine("Would you like to update another?");
242  updateAnother = Console.ReadLine().StartsWith("y", StringComparison.OrdinalIgnoreCase);
243  if (batchUpdate && !updateAnother)
244  {
245      Task.Run(() => svc.InsertOrUpdateItems(allItems));
246  }
247      }
248  }
```

Figure 14-12. *The Update Multiple Items method is reworked*

Finally, fix up the `DeleteMultipleItems` by also fixing the two calls to the service layer in the code:

```
svc.DeleteItem(itemMatch.Id);
```

This becomes

```
Task.Run(() => svc.DeleteItem(itemMatch.Id));
```

Also

```
svc.DeleteItems(allItems);
```

becomes

```
Task.Run(() => svc.DeleteItems(allItems));
```

Use a find and replace operation to implement the code changes from the previous discussion. When completed, your code should look similar to what is shown in Figure 14-13.

```
286            else
287            {
288                Console.WriteLine($"Are you sure you want to delete the item {itemMatch.Id}-{itemMatch.Name}");
289                if (Console.ReadLine().StartsWith("y", StringComparison.OrdinalIgnoreCase))
290                {
291                    Task.Run(() => svc.DeleteItem(itemMatch.Id));
292                    Console.WriteLine("Item Deleted");
293                }
294            }
295        }
296    }

297
298    Console.WriteLine("Would you like to delete another item?");
299    deleteAnother = Console.ReadLine().StartsWith("y", StringComparison.OrdinalIgnoreCase);
300
301    if (batchDelete && !deleteAnother)
302    {
303        Console.WriteLine("Are you sure you want to delete the following items: ");
304        allItems.ForEach(x => Console.Write($"{x},"));
305        Console.WriteLine();
306        if (Console.ReadLine().StartsWith("y", StringComparison.OrdinalIgnoreCase))
307        {
308            Task.Run(() => svc.DeleteItems(allItems));
309            Console.WriteLine("Items Deleted");
310        }
311    }
312    }
313 }
```

Figure 14-13. *The Delete Multiple Items method is refactored*

Build and run the program. Everything should work as expected now that we have fixed up the code. Figure 14-14 shows the program in action with asynchronous operations.

Remember, if you are having problems getting the program to run, don't hesitate to just leverage the code in the final version of the files to see the completed version of these reworked method calls.

```
Microsoft Visual Studio Debug Console
n
Would you like to update items?
n
Would you like to delete items?
n
List Inventory from Dapper
New Item: Batman Begins                  | Why do we fall, Bruce?
New Item: Battlefield 5                  | First person shooter
New Item: Brian 1                        | Brian 1 Updated
New Item: Brian 2 Updated                | Test 2
New Item: Brian 7                        | Test 7
New Item: Brian 8                        | Test 8
New Item: Practical Entity Framework | The book that teaches practical application with
New Item: test 1                         | asdfa
New Item: test2                          | asdfasdf
New Item: The Lord of the Rings          | The fellowship of the Ring
New Item: Top Gun                        | I feel the need, the need for speed
New Item: World Of Tanks                 | AN MMO WW2 Tanks First-Person Shooter
List Categories And Colors From Dapper
Movies | Blue
Books | Red
Games | Green
Program Complete

C:\APressEntityFramework\Code\Chapter14\Activity1401_AsynchronousOperations\Activity1401
g\netcoreapp3.1\Activity1401_AsynchronousOperations.exe (process 9220) exited with code
To automatically close the console when debugging stops, enable Tools->Options->Debuggin
le when debugging stops.
Press any key to close this window . . .
```

Figure 14-14. *The Program in action, now completely reworked for asynchronous database operations*

This concludes the activity on asynchronous database operations.

Final thoughts on activity 1401

In this first activity for our chapter, we were able to work through getting the database operations into an asynchronous pattern. We started by changing out the lower-level database layer calls to leverage the context with async and await calls.

After working through each layer, we saw how easy it was to refactor the solution for asynchronous operations. In the end, our program remained as a synchronous method, and therefore we used the Task.Run(() => somecode).Result call to get the results of an asynchronous operation from a synchronous context.

In the next activity, we'll see what it takes to work with multiple contexts and how having the power to work with asynchronous commands can really help a solution be more responsive.

Activity 1402: Multiple database contexts

In our second activity, we are going to leverage a shared database context for single-sign-on solutions to manage user identities. To simplify this operation, we'll create a new web solution and integrate the inventory context into the solution.

The identity context

To handle the authentication and authorization in a .Net web application, the system allows for the solution to quickly generate all necessary role and user information in the `IdentityContext`.

If we were going to create a suite of applications, the ideal approach would be to generate out this identity context and place it in its own library which could then be easily leveraged in the console application and other solutions.

For purposes of brevity, I will leave that to you if you desire to do so.

Step 1: Get the files we created in Chapter 6

We created a new web application all the way back in Chapter 6. To complete this activity, we'll be starting where we left off in that activity. In the event you didn't complete those activities, you can just get the `Activity1402_Multiple_Database_Contexts_Starter.zip` files and extract them to use on your local development machine.

You may need to update the connection string in the `appSettings.json` file, as the default connection for the web app is just going to leverage the `localdb`. This simulates a situation where you have an application that connects to two different databases on two different servers.

Once up and running, make sure you can register users and log in to validate the fact that we have a prebuilt identity schema in place for managing user authentication and authorization.

Additionally, you'll need to put a few categories into the category table. This will not be the same as our inventory system, so feel free to enter anything you want.

Since I'm creating the starter pack and activity 0601 was not a long activity, I'm just running with new files. You could do the same if you so desired.

Finally, in the event you wanted to just set a few categories and ensure your users, please use the following script on your localdb or other connections after you have the website up and running and you have registered a user:

```
--validate your username
SELECT * from AspNetUsers

--if you can't login, run this with your username
UPDATE AspNetUsers
SET EmailConfirmed = 1
WHERE Id = (
    SELECT [Id]
    FROM [dbo].[AspNetUsers]
    WHERE UserName = 'brian@brian.com' --put your username here
)

--if you want to quickly add categories:
/*WARNING: running more than once will create duplicates */
INSERT INTO Categories ([Name])
VALUES ('Books')
INSERT INTO Categories ([Name])
VALUES ('Movies')
INSERT INTO Categories ([Name])
VALUES ('Games')
select * from categories
```

A copy of this script is also available in the Resources folder in the starter pack files.

Step 2: Bring the inventory libraries into the project

Once you've validated that the project works as expected, bring the libraries for
the InventoryDbContext into the solution (copy the project folders from your
activity 1401; the starter pack has them in the folder, they are just not referenced).
For this minimal implementation, we don't need the InventoryHelpers or the
InventoryDatabaseMigrator project. They are available in the starter pack if you do
want to add them at a later point. Add the projects by right-clicking the solution and
selecting "Add Existing Project" and then selecting the project file for each of the projects
listed here (at minimum):

InventoryBusinessLayer
InventoryDatabaseCore
InventoryDatabaseLayer

```
InventoryManagerIntegrationTests
InventoryManagerUnitTests
InventoryModels
```

For clarity, review Figure 14-15 to see the projects in the solution.

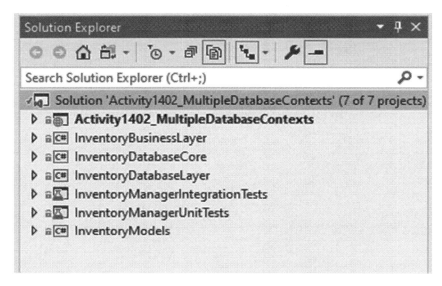

Figure 14-15. *Importing existing projects*

Once the projects are in place, add a reference to the InventoryBusinessLayer in the main project. All other references will be added via the dependency chain in the projects (see Figure 14-16 for clarity).

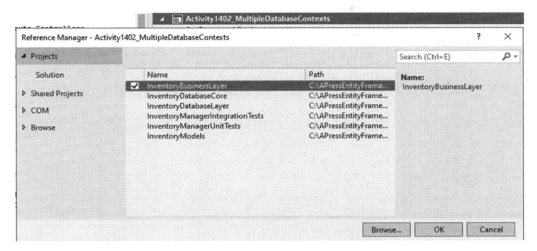

Figure 14-16. *Adding references to the InventoryBusinessLayer project*

Grab the connection string for the InventoryManagerDb out of the
InventoryDatabaseCore appsettings.json file, and put the connection string into the
web project's appsettings.json file, which should be something like this:

```
{
  "ConnectionStrings": {
    "DefaultConnection": "Server=(localdb)\\mssqllocaldb;Database=aspnet-
    Activity1402_MultipleDatabaseContexts-B0C284AA-03F8-4103-86A4-
    D55D9116B10F;Trusted_Connection=True;MultipleActiveResultSets=true",
    "InventoryManager": "Data Source=localhost;Initial Catalog=InventoryMan
    ager;Trusted_Connection=True;Column Encryption Setting=Enabled;",
  },
  "Logging": {
    ...
  },
  ...
}
```

The important thing to note is to not forget that you may need to update that
connection string to point to the correct local database instance, whether it's in
SQLExpress or SQLDeveloper edition.

Build the solution and run it. There shouldn't be any issues. If for some reason you get an issue, you may just need to make sure all of your NuGet packages are updated to the latest versions.

Step 3: Add the context to the injection for the web application

With the InventoryManager libraries ready to go, it's time to inject the context into the project so that we can use it in our web solution.

Locate the Startup.cs file in the web application. Notice the ConfigureServices method. This is where the context injection will be added. Note that there is already a statement to add the DBContext for the ApplicationDbContext – the default context that contains identity.

We need to add another AddDbContext statement, and we need to leverage the connection string that we copied in the previous step.

Copy the lines for services.AddDbContext<....."DefaultConnection")));

Paste them immediately after the first three original lines, and change the context to the InventoryDbContext and the connection string to match whatever you named your connection string in the appsettings.json file for the web project (i.e., InventoryManager). The new version of the method should be as follows:

```
public void ConfigureServices(IServiceCollection services)
{
    services.AddDbContext<ApplicationDbContext>(options =>
        options.UseSqlServer(
            Configuration.GetConnectionString("DefaultConnection")));
    services.AddDbContext<InventoryDbContext>(options =>
        options.UseSqlServer(
            Configuration.GetConnectionString("InventoryManager")));
    services.AddDefaultIdentity<IdentityUser>(options => options.SignIn.
    RequireConfirmedAccount = true)
        .AddEntityFrameworkStores<ApplicationDbContext>();
    services.AddControllersWithViews();
    services.AddRazorPages();
}
```

For clarity, the code from the ConfigureServices method is shown in Figure 14-17.

```
public void ConfigureServices(IServiceCollection services)
{
    services.AddDbContext<ApplicationDbContext>(options =>
        options.UseSqlServer(
            Configuration.GetConnectionString("DefaultConnection")));
    services.AddDbContext<InventoryDbContext>(options =>
        options.UseSqlServer(
            Configuration.GetConnectionString("InventoryManager")));
    services.AddDefaultIdentity<IdentityUser>(options => options.SignIn.RequireConfirmedAccount = true)
        .AddEntityFrameworkStores<ApplicationDbContext>();
    services.AddControllersWithViews();
    services.AddRazorPages();
}
```

Figure 14-17. *Injecting the InventoryDBContext into the solution*

Note that there is no reason we must use a different database. As long as the two contexts do not conflict with one another, you can put them both into the same database.

Run the solution to make sure there are no issues. Everything should still work as before.

Step 4: Generate Inventory controllers and views for Items

Now that we've brought our InventoryDBContext into the solution, let's generate some CRUD operations around the Inventory items in the web solution.

Right-click the Controllers folder and select Add ➤ Controller (see Figure 14-18).

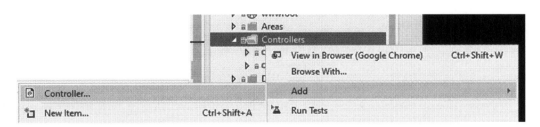

Figure 14-18. *Adding a new controller*

Select MVC Controller with views, using Entity Framework, and then hit Add (review Figure 14-19).

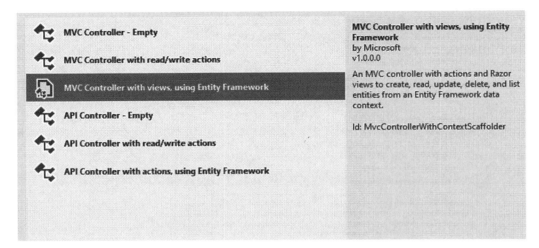

Figure 14-19. *Use the views and Entity Framework*

Next, change the context to the InventoryDbContext and select the Item model from InventoryModels. Note that the controller will be Items1Controller. Change that default name to InventoryItemsController. Figure 14-20 shows what the form should look like before hitting "Add" to scaffold the views.

Add MVC Controller with views, using Entity Framework	✕
Model class:	Item (InventoryModels) ⌄
Data context class:	InventoryDbContext (InventoryDatabaseCore) ⌄ ＋
Views:	
☑ Generate views	
☑ Reference script libraries	
☑ Use a layout page:	
	⋯
(Leave empty if it is set in a Razor _viewstart file)	
Controller name:	InventoryItemsController
	Add Cancel

Figure 14-20. *Setting up the scaffolding operation for Inventory Items*

Add the controller and let the scaffolded views be created by default.

Our inventory context is leveraged, but not our service and database layer that we've tested. By default, the solution is putting direction operations against the DBContext into the controller.

Let's run it to validate that things are working the way we would expect. Run the project and navigate to https://localhost:<yourport>/InventoryItems.

You should see whatever was in your inventory listed in the table (output should be similar to Figure 14-21).

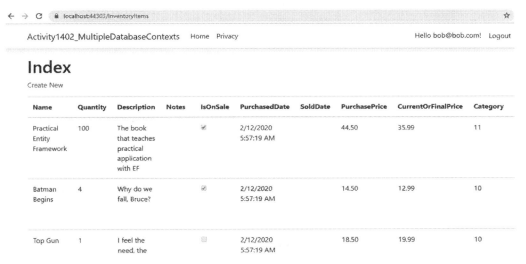

Figure 14-21. *The inventory Items context is wired up as expected*

Make sure you can also view, create, edit, and delete items.

This is not a book on web development. Therefore, we aren't going to spend any time making the web page nicer at this point. Clearly, this page is not production-ready.

A couple of final thoughts. We directly leveraged the context and injected it. To make this solution work more like a production system, it would be a good idea to set up AutoMapper and instantiate it at the services level (like we did for the context, similar to how we set everything up in the console app). Then, in the `InventoryItems Controller`, instantiate an `ItemsService` object, and only use that object to get data.

After refactoring to set the `ItemsService` in the controller, also refactor the views to use the DTO objects instead of the full-blown models.

Finally, you'd want to make sure that your drop-down list shows the `CategoryName`, not the Id so that the user could know which category they are selecting.

The amount of work it would take to do this is outside of the scope of this activity, but is a worthy endeavor to continue your learning.

Step 5: Add a new model to the web application context, add the migration, and update the database

With everything in place, let's see what it takes to add a new model and migration to our solution. To make sure that we just do this easily, let's add a new model to the web application's `ApplicationDbContext`. As this is a contrived example, let's just add a class file to create a `Model` for `States` in the activity 1402 ➤ `Models` folder. In the `State` class, have an Id, a `Name`, and an `Abbreviation`.

```
public class State
{
    public int Id { get; set; }
    public string Name { get; set; }
    public string Abbreviation { get; set; }
}
```

With the new `State` model added to the solution, add the `State` model to the `ApplicationDBContext` so it can be leveraged in code. Add the line `public DbSet<State> States { get; set; }` to the `ApplicationDbContext`. You can add the code anywhere in the class, but I generally stack my properties and then do the constructors and then other methods. For this instance, I put the `States DbSet` property after the `Categories` property and before the `Constructor`.

Now try to add the migration using our expected `add-migration` command in the PMC (make sure that the drop-down for the default project is pointing to the main activity project that contains the ApplicationDbContext file):

`add-migration CreatedStatesTable`

Even though the contexts are in different projects, EF still needs us to explicitly name the context to run the migration against. The error we get in this situation is shown in Figure 14-22.

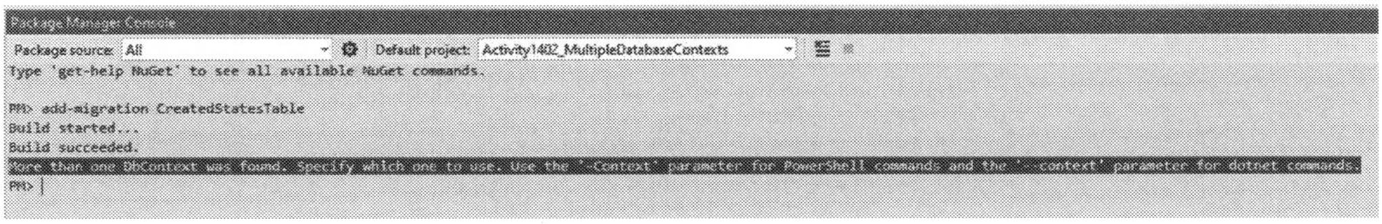

Figure 14-22. *Can't add a migration when there are multiple contexts*

Trying to run the migration in this situation generates an error due to having multiple contexts in the solution. To remedy that, the suggestion is to use the `-Context` flag. In *EF6*, we leveraged the `-ConfigurationTypeName` flag.

One other important note here. When using multiple database contexts, you should make sure they are in different namespaces, and then when you reference them, use the fully qualified name, including the namespace. This will ensure the correct migrations are associated with the correct contexts.

Add the `-Context` flag with the namespace and context name to the `add-migration` command:

`add-migration CreatedStatesTable -Context Activity1402_`
`MultipleDatabaseContexts.Data.ApplicationDbContext`

When the command add-migration <name> -Context <NameSpace>.<ClassName> is used, the migration generates as expected.

Now we just need to run `update-database`, right? You probably guessed by now that just running `update-database` will have the same problem as `add-migration`. Instead, run the command `update-database -Context Activity1402_MultipleDatabaseContexts.Data.ApplicationDbContext`.

If we wanted, we could generate the controller and views for the State model to see that it works as expected in the database. Additionally, we could go on to add more entities to the `InventoryManager` system. In that case, the database for the `InventoryManager` would reflect the migrations.

When running the update-database command, it is not as important to fully qualify with the namespace, because the program is not generating anything but is executing. In the preceding command, we could have simply run the command `update-database -context ApplicationDbContext`.

In the rare instance that you are using multiple contexts against the same database, just remember that you can't have conflicts in naming between the two contexts. Once one of them has a model that is leveraged, named States, for example, the other one would not be able to add it since they both exist in the same database. However, when multiple databases are used in conjunction with contexts, then the model names do not need to be unique and can be reused, such as Item was reused in both of our contexts for this activity.

Final thoughts on activity 1402

In this second activity for our chapter, we were able to see what it would take to leverage multiple database contexts in the same solution.

The main takeaway is that it is possible, and this opens the door for sharing data across solutions, such as sharing the user identity management portion of a suite of solutions within one database context that can be shared.

Additionally, using multiple contexts opens the door to both sharing the same database and having separate implementations, perhaps even across vendors. There is nothing stopping us from having one context connecting to SQL Server and another to Oracle.

The real difference in the way we have to work when using multiple contexts is that we have to remember to explicitly name the context in the PMC as we run commands. The command in .Net Core is simple: -Context. The command in *EF6* was a bit less intuitive and was named -ConfigurationTypeName.

In general, working with multiple contexts should be discouraged, but it is not impossible. There is added complexity that comes into play with multiple contexts. However, there are definite benefits in clear boundaries between things like users and application data, as well as potential segregation of business units.

Final thoughts for this chapter

In this chapter, we've covered a couple of very critical aspects of working with Entity Framework in our applications.

Perhaps we should have talked about asynchronous operations earlier in the book, perhaps not. Even so, using asynchronous operations will likely be the normal solution that you encounter in your day-to-day work. The benefits of leveraging multithreading without having to wire up and manage the underlying code are extremely useful.

Having our database operations working in an async/await pattern allows us to write our solutions in a more responsive manner. By using async and await, we can still write our code in a synchronous manner and not have to worry about concurrency or race conditions.

We also talked about another common issue when we discussed using multiple contexts. In most cases, as mentioned previously, I would recommend staying away from multiple contexts. That being said, it is still entirely possible for us to use this approach and beneficial in certain situations.

In our second activity for the chapter, we were able to leverage multiple contexts to prove that an application can use both an identity context that is shared among solutions and other database contexts as well. By having all of this in place, we can make a suite of applications that can easily share data. We can also segregate certain parts of our exposed surface so that users only get the access they need to specific pieces of data.

In the next and final chapter of our book, we'll discuss the changes that are coming with .Net 5 and likely are in place by the time you are reading this book. As *EF* has continued to evolve, our lives have gotten substantially better. The latest version of the .Net Framework/.Net Core architecture is a recombination of each platform into one platform to rule them all - .Net 5.

CHAPTER 15

.Net 5 and Entity Framework

In this chapter, we're going to have a brief discussion about the latest version of the .Net ecosystem: .Net 5. This new (at the time of this book writing and publication) version is slated for release in the last quarter of 2020. As such, we need to be ready to adapt to any changes that this framework will bring us.

One framework to rule them all

One thing of note is that with the .Net 5 release, there will be no more .Net Framework, and there will be no more .Net Core. Everything will be housed in the same place, and all of the moving pieces should work together from this point on. As a .Net developer, we should be able to have a similar development experience to what we are used to, even after .Net 5 is released.

A combination of the best parts of everything

According to the official blog posts and statements about .Net 5 from Microsoft's Richard Lander, the goals of .Net 5 will be to "improve .Net in a few key ways" (such as):

- *Produce a single .NET runtime and framework that can be used everywhere and that has uniform behaviors and developer experiences*

- *Expand the capabilities of .NET by taking the best of .NET Core, .Net Framework, Xamarin and Mono.*

© Brian L. Gorman 2020
B. L. Gorman, *Practical Entity Framework*, https://doi.org/10.1007/978-1-4842-6044-9_15

- *Build that product out of a single code-base that developers (Microsoft and the community) can work on and expand together and that improves all scenarios.*

—Lander, 2019

As you can imagine, this is a great thing for all of us. As Microsoft continues to expand into the future, we will be able to run our projects on any machine architecture or in containers, and we will be able to also develop from any machine. Additionally, it won't matter what we are building; our development experience will be the same. In the blog post, Richard goes on to mention

This new project and direction are a game-changer for .NET. With .NET 5, your code and project files will look and feel the same, no matter which type of app you're building. You'll have access to the same runtime, API and language capabilities with each app. This includes new performance improvements

—Lander, 2019

(references from `https://devblogs.microsoft.com/dotnet/introducing-net-5/`)

EF6, EFCore, and .NET 5

With the direction of .NET 5 being the wave of the future, we need to know what that will do to our current EF6 and EFCore applications. The really good news for us is that we should be able to keep working with our solutions.

.Net Core 3.0+ gave us the ability to use an EF6 implementation. The .Net Framework also runs EF6. .NET 5 is bringing all of this together, so both EFCore and EF6 should work as expected in .NET 5.

EFCore5

As .NET 5 is coming out, the next version of Entity framework is also being released. The next version of EF is currently referred to as EFCore5. This is going to confuse a lot of people, since it would seem that EF5 has already been released prior to EF6.

Core is going away, right?

Even more confusion with this vNext name for EF might be caused since the Core moniker is slated to go away with the .NET 5 release in November.

All of this to really just say that we might see a name change of this product, or we might not. Either way, what we can rely on is that the vNext EF – EFCore5 - is out and ready to be used and will work in the .NET 5 release that happens at the end of 2020. The good news is that it also works on the latest release of EFCore. That means that even if you don't upgrade your current production apps out of the .Net Core 3.1 release, you will likely still be able to use EFCore5.

Changes with EFCore5

I really want to talk about some of the new and useful things we can do with the vNext release – EFCore5. Likely, the things I'm talking about here won't be the only things that you'll get with the new version, but this is what I know about as of the time of this book being published. Additional information can be found here: `https://docs.microsoft.com/en-us/ef/core/what-is-new/ef-core-5.0/plan`. What follows is a summary of a few of the new features I think you'll be glad to be aware of.

Many-to-many navigation properties

`https://github.com/dotnet/efcore/issues/19003`

To be honest, I can see why this was so heavily requested to be added to the new version. In a nutshell, when working with many-to-many relationships in the past, we would create the navigation properties, and then to load the data we need to use along with appropriate includes to bring the data into our query results.

Consider our relationship between Items and Genres, which takes place through the `ItemGenre` table. If we are writing a query to get our Genre info included when we are getting Items, we have to do something like this:

```
var items = _context.Items
                .Include(x => x.ItemGenres)
                .ThenInclude(y => y.Genre)
                .ToList();
```

With the new EFCore5 MTM navigation properties, the query will be reduced to the following:

```
_context.Items.Where(i => i.ItemGenres
                         .Select(g => g.Name)).ToList();
```

Not having to directly include the join in the query will make it quite a bit more concise and will seem more readable.

Table-per-type (TPT) inheritance mapping

Table per type is a pattern that, when implemented, works exactly how it sounds. With TPT, as you build out an object hierarchy with inheritance, each new type gets its own table. Contrast this with TPH – table per hierarchy – where the entire set of objects are stored in one table.

So here is the interesting thing. TPT is already able to be implemented in EFCore 3.1. However, there are a few hoops to jump through and you end up with one table (much like TPH) that has all types in it with a simple differentiator field. As you might imagine, this can quickly become non-performant in a high-volume database. First you have to select by differentiator, and then filter the results further to get the subset of the specific type that you need for your operation. Sure, you can put indexes on things, but it still means your table grows exponentially as more types are added.

With EFCore5, we'll get true TPT capabilities. Unfortunately, as per the documentation on the plan, this may come with some breaking changes that would require rework from an existing solution moving into EFCore5.

Filtered include

Another feature that will surely help our day-to-day operations is the ability to filter an include statement. As of now, if you try to add a filter on an include, you get an exception and the query won't execute.

The filtered include will provide the ability to select only the subset of joined table rows that match based on the filter.

Rationalize ToTable, ToQuery, ToView, FromSql

In the operation of EF, there are different things that can happen, whether a query is executed, a migration generates a table definition change, and views exist with or without keys. All of this working together has led to a place where you really need to know the specific way it works for each operation.

It seems that the EFCore5 release will be working to try to make these operations standard for each To or From call so that the developer won't have to know some of the internal nuances of the build or update pipeline to get the results they need.

For example, a situation might exist where specific operations like Create, Update, and Read need to happen against a physical table, but perhaps the Read comes from a procedure result or a view. In those cases, the goal would be to correctly get objects created in the migration so that the system will work as planned.

Another goal of this work is to get the mappings to other objects working in a new way that should be easier for developers, for example, trying to get the mapping to stored procedures for your Create, Update, and Delete operations, or allowing the ability to execute raw SQL for defining objects from a query.

Migrations and deployment experience

For code-first developers, this area has consistently been one where the experience is not always ideal. If you've worked in EF6, you know that even the date of the migration is important. Each migration needs to run in order according to the date on the migration. This leads to a lot of migration conflicts where one developer beats another developer to production, and the second developer must set their database correctly by rolling back their migration, delete their migration, get the new code, update the database, and then finish by re-creating their original migration with the new timestamp and model snapshot.

This problem is especially painful when a migration conflict happens on the production database. As such, both development and deployment have been troubled by migration conflicts. This experience is vastly improved in EFCore and will continue to be improved in EFCore5.

With EFCore5, one goal will be to create a better team experience, presumably by mitigating even more of these migration conflicts and even being smart enough to handle situations that would cause a conflict.

Another major change will be that the ability to run migrations across all platforms should exist. As a result of being able to run migrations on any platform in EFCore5, the overall experience should be especially improved for Linux and Mac users.

EFCore platforms experience

As mentioned at the start of the chapter, an overarching goal of .NET 5 will be the ability to have a similar experience on all types of projects, from Xamarin to Blazor to ASP.Net web applications.

As such, another goal of the EFCore5 release will be an improved experience working with EF for all of the major platforms, not just ASP.Net.

Performance

As EF has iterated through the years, each version has added performance improvements. EFCore definitely has improved performance over EF6 on just about every metric.

I would expect that EFCore5 will continue to improve on the performance of all operations. Additionally, the documentation points out that there is a plan for a new batching API to allow multiple statements to be batched for increased performance.

Final thoughts for this chapter

In this chapter, we talked about the future of .Net with the upcoming release of .NET 5. We also discussed the fact that EFCore5 is already available and can be used within EFCore 3.1.

Likely, by the time you are reading this book, .NET 5 will be out of preview and EFCore5 will be fully implemented.

Even in the new version, things we've covered in this book will remain incredibly relevant. While there may be improvements to things like View creation and interaction or mapped stored procedures for CRUD operations, the same concepts around migrations, models, and general development of code-first databases will remain.

We concluded this chapter, and ultimately this book, with a look at the new features that will be available in EFCore5. A couple of the key features are

- Table-per-type (TPT) implementation

- Many-to-many navigation properties

- Filtered include statements

- An improved migration and deployment experience

- An overall uniform and improved experience for all development efforts regardless of platform

There will definitely be more features than we've talked about here implemented in EFCore5, so make sure to review the documentation to know exactly what is available to utilize in your solutions.

Conclusion

I hope you have enjoyed reading and working through this book as much as I've enjoyed creating it for you. Alas, the end is nigh.

Our time together doesn't have to be over, however. Please don't hesitate to connect with me on LinkedIn or Twitter. I would love to hear your story and get your thoughts on how this book has helped you in your day-to-day work.

I wish you all the best in your development endeavors. May you have peace, joy, and abundance in your life.

APPENDIX A

Troubleshooting

There are a number of activities in this book, and, while I've tried to keep them consistent, I am certain there may be times where things are a bit difficult. Therefore, I wanted to put together a quick reference to help in case something goes wrong during your application of the activities from the book.

Migrations

As you are likely aware, troubleshooting migrations can be very painful if things don't work as expected. From cryptic error messages to things that really should work not working, a lot of hair can get pulled out.

If you start working with your own solution, but then switch to one of the starter packs, you could run into some issues with conflicts, simply because my dates are clearly going to be different than yours. Keep this in mind as you build out your activities and solutions.

The overall goal would be that you would work on your own files the entire way through the book and only reference mine as a reference. However, you may wish to skip around or just have a fresh start at some point, so it is more than likely you will need or want to leverage one of the prefabricated project files.

Objects exist/objects don't exist

One of the major issues you may run into is that the initial migrations are not idempotent. Therefore, if your database already has an Items table, and you pick up my starter pack and point at your database, you'll likely get an error that the "update-database" command cannot be applied because the Items table already exists.

633

© Brian L. Gorman 2020
B. L. Gorman, *Practical Entity Framework*, https://doi.org/10.1007/978-1-4842-6044-9

In this case, you could easily do one of the recommended actions, such as comment out the code in my migration, manually insert a record into the EFMigrations table to attempt to make EF think the migration has already executed and been applied, or, in a worst-case scenario, you could just point to a new database that is clean to avoid these conflicts. Our data solutions are minimal and there are tools to quickly get you reset if you start with a fresh database.

If you try to run a migration and an object is missing, you might be able to simply add the object and try again. Another thought here could be to find the activity where the object was created and use that to build out the object and then come back to where you were in your current project.

Comment out code

One solution that we use in this text is to create a migration and then just comment out the code. This is not a recommended solution, but it works in a jam. For example, if you already created the Items table, then I have a migration that also wants to do the same thing; just comment mine out and let it execute with no effect on the schema or data in your database. Use this sparingly, but know that it can be done.

Manual insert to the database

If an object is missing, you could insert it manually with a script. This might be handy for a missing function or view or procedure.Another thing to note here is that you can attempt to make EF think that a migration has executed by simply performing an insert into the __EFMigrationsHistory table. Simply insert the migration id and product version, and the next time you run update-database, EF should skip your conflicting migration.

Additionally, if something goes horribly wrong and a migration is idempotent, you could potentially force a reset by deleting a MigrationId from the table to make EF think it still needs to run that migration.

Change DB connection

Probably one of the easiest things you could do if things are off kilter is just to change the name of the database in the connection string or point to a different server where the database doesn't exist. In this way, no conflicts could possibly exist. Also, no data exists.

After about Chapter 7 or 8, there are seed methods and a migration project. In the event you are in the latter part of the book and you need to just point to a new database, set the db connection to the new database and then run the migrator project by right-clicking and selecting Debug ➤ Start New Instance. This will ensure the database and then apply the migrations, as well as run a quick seed as seen in the text.

Feel free to use multiple databases, as well as multiple db servers. Just remember that your connection string holds all the power here. For example, the first time I went through this material, all my database work was on SQLExpress. The second time I used SQLDeveloper (localhost). There is nothing preventing you from switching servers.

Starter packs

Every activity except the first has an accompanying starter pack. If something isn't working or you just want to jump around, leverage the starter packs.

General starter pack creation

Rather than keep working with the same files, I chose to do a unique project for each activity. As you might imagine, this added a bit of work. In general, if you want to roll your own starter packs, you could follow a similar process. Here are the steps I took on generally every new project:

1. Create a new .Net Core Console application.

2. Copy and paste the existing project folders for all of the class libraries that are needed for the activity.

3. Add each class library to the solution, and build the project to restore NuGet packages.

4. Get the list of NuGet packages from the previous solution (the last completed activity) from the project file, and copy/paste that into the new activity .csproj file. This is much faster than doing them one by one in NuGet Package Manager.

5. Copy/paste the appsettings.json file from dbcore into the new activity project, add it as content, or copy if newer.

6. Set project references on the new activity to appropriate class libraries.

7. Build and run.

8. Copy/paste the code from the program file of the previous activity into the program file of the new activity (be careful – just get the methods, not the class or the namespace). Then add all the missing using statements, and run the project.

9. In some instances, I may do an update-database earlier, but I generally do it here to make sure there are no pending migrations.

10. Finally, if in doubt, add a new migration called test to ensure that there are no pending changes. This is only important if the activity is going to be adding new migrations.

What you should do every time

When you get a starter pack, make sure that you do the same thing at the start, every time.

First, build the project. Once it builds, set the connection string to point to the correct database. Then run an update-database to make sure there are no pending migrations. If the activity has migrations in it, then run an add-migration command to make sure that you don't have any untracked pending changes that could get in the way. If you do, consider just updating the database if the changes are not going to hurt anything. If no pending operations exist and you get a blank migration, just run the remove-migration command.

Finally, after all of that, make sure that the main activity project is set as the startup project and then run the project to see that it is working as expected.

Final packs

Final packs are exactly what they sound like. This is the finished version of the code as it was on my machine after the activity was completed.

Review your solution

In general, the final pack should be used as a "check your answer" solution only. If something is unclear from the text, the final pack will likely have the answer. Things like "where does this code go?" or "how did he do that?" or "I'm completely lost" can often be quickly resolved just by comparing what you have to what is in the final pack.

Use a diff tool like GitHub, VSCode, or WinMerge

A neat trick you can do (as long as your files are named the same as mine) is that you could just use a tool to do a diff on files. For example, I'll often use the built-in capability to compare files in VSCode. In rare instances when things are really off track, I might check in my code and push to GitHub, then create a branch and drop the final pack code in, and push to GitHub and create a pull request. This gives me a great tool to easily see the differences in files. Finally, other tools like WinMerge or Perforce or even GitKraken might be enough to help you see the differences in your code from the final pack.

Index